THE WRITINGS OF
MEDIEVAL WOMEN

THE WRITINGS OF MEDIEVAL WOMEN

An Anthology
Second Edition

translations and introductions by

Marcelle Thiébaux

GARLAND PUBLISHING, Inc.
New York & London / 1994

The hardcover edition of this book is published in the
Garland Library of Medieval Literature series,
Volume 100B.

Library of Congress Cataloging-in-Publication Data

The Writings of medieval women : an anthology / translations with introductions by Marcelle Thiébaux. —
3rd ed.
    p.   cm. — (Garland library of medieval
literature : vol. 100. Series B)
    Includes bibliographical references and index.
    ISBN 0–8153–0409–9. — ISBN 0–8153–1392–6
(pbk.)
    1. Literature, Medieval.   2. European literature—
Women authors.   I. Thiébaux, Marcelle.   II. Series:
Garland library of medieval literature : v. 100.
PN667.W75   1994
808.8'99287'0902—dc20   93–36822
                                                CIP

Cover design by Patricia Hefner.
Engraving of French writer Christine de Pizan from
Les Arts au Moyen Age by Paul Lacroix (Paris, 1877)
based on a 15th-century manuscript miniature.

Printed on acid-free, 250-year-life paper
Manufactured in the United States of America

To the Memory of My Parents
Anna Kirczow Thiébaux (1902–1988)
Martial Leon Thiébaux (1903–1988)

Baudonivia writing the *Life of Saint Radegund*. Reprinted by permission of Comité d'Animation de la Bibliothèque Municipale de Poitiers.

CONTENTS

Acknowledgments

Since the publication of the first edition of *The Writings of Medieval Women* in 1987, I'm indebted to many friends, colleagues, and fellow-medievalists, who helped in various ways while I prepared this expanded anthology. In addition to those I thanked at the time, I acknowledge my valued friends in the Hagiography Group of New York, guided by Jo Ann McNamara. In our sessions I had the chance to air earlier versions of several of the chapters included here and gain the benefit of the group's insights. My editors at Garland have been patiently meticulous. Particular gratitude goes to my husband, Cameron R. Bloch, for his constant encouragement, good counsels and proficiency in the mysteries of computers. Once again, I thank the St. John's University community. The Library's holdings have offered me rich resources, enhanced by the assistance I received from Eileen Kennedy and Roberta Pessah through interlibrary loans. My students' responses to materials I've tried out in the classroom have always been constructive. The English Department and the Administration of St. John's University are most generous in their continued support by granting me time for research.

Marcelle Thiébaux
St. John's University, New York

Introduction

There were always women throughout the Middle Ages who could read and write. Women liked to own and keep books, to borrow them, touch and copy them, give them to friends. Medieval women wrote books, as well as letters, poems, romances and plays. They dedicated their writings to patrons and ruling abbesses. Women wrote for their families and their lovers. They wrote for an audience. It is no longer surprising that there were many literate women in the Middle Ages. Scholars today continue to uncover and rediscover more of their writing, and to bring them forth in new editions to entertain and edify. Compositions of medieval women, some dictated and some inscribed in their own hand, have survived over twelve centuries.

The period surveyed in this anthology extends from the eve of Christianity's triumph, in the third century, to the new age of expansion in the fifteenth century, an age marked by the advent of printing presses, the European discovery of the Caribbean islands, which Columbus called the Indies, the relentless stripping of medieval altars by Church reformists, and perhaps a diminution of female autonomy.[1] The volume opens with the third century and the words of Perpetua, recorded in her African prison cell as she awaits execution. The anthology's last chapter, comprising new material in this edition from English literature, closes with letters that tell of the romantic and housewifely cares of Margery Brews Paston, letters which she sends from one or another of her houses in northern England.

During the medieval centuries, women's names appear in the documents of educated men, their kinsmen and mentors. These were women whose reading and writing ability earned notice. From the crabbed eloquence of a medieval Latin sentence, a feminine name—a Toulousan, a Burgundian, a Gothic, or a Frankish woman—will shine like a tiny point of light in a thicket. The isolated name offers a tantalizing hint of a story and a life. When her daughter died, Bassula, a fourth-century woman in southern France, carried on an animated literary friendship with her eminent son-in-law, Sulpicius Severus (known for his Life of Saint Martin of Tours). Bassula shared Sulpicius's love of letters and helped him as a muse and guiding spirit. Theudelinda was able to write her name, and she received letters from Pope Gregory, who also sent her a sumptuously ornamented Gospel lectionary for Adaloald, her little son. Adelperga, daughter of an eighth-century Lombard king, grasped with ease the golden rhetoric of the philosophers and the jeweled sayings of the poets.

In the ninth century, Irmingard, wife of Boso of Provence, read the Scriptures with her tutor. In 867 Judith (her maternal grandparents were Louis the Pious and Judith, his much-slandered queen) inherited from her father, Count Eberhard of Friuli, his copy of a book on Lombard law. Did she need to consult it in order to run the Italian estates she may have inherited as well? Together with her sisters Engeldrud and Heiliwich, Judith was also bequeathed liturgical volumes—a gospel book, a lectionary, missal and commentary, and antiphonary with ivory covers. Heiliwich got a book of saints' lives; Judith got a treatise by Alcuin on the vices and virtues.

Women liked to go to the library. Their names appear in the borrowers' lists at libraries in Cologne and Weissenburg. We can picture Richardis, wife of Emperor Charles the Fat, taking out books from the Saint Gall library, a treasurehouse that held a goodly array of classical authors. Lady Liutgart borrowed a psalter from the Weissenburg library, and so did a lady described as Gerold's widow, while "Irm.," the wife of one Reinbold, borrowed a psalter and a gradual (a book containing the choral parts of the mass). Often borrowers wanted to make their own copies. Occasionally they forgot to return books, and tucked them away for years in their personal collections.

Among other women readers is the tenth-century Mathilda, sister to Burchard of Worms; she protested she couldn't be an abbess because the only book she knew was the psalter. Hedwig, whose uncle was the Emperor Otto the Great, spent her widowhood reading the Latin poets. Beatrice of Burgundy, the second wife of Frederick Barbarossa, studied poetry and composed an epitaph for herself in eight verses of Latin. Almode, countess of Toulouse, inscribed two words with her own hand in a deed of confirmation for an abbey in 1066. Books play a role in emotional scenes. The English Queen Matilda buries her face in the book she is reading when she learns of her son's death. The nun Elisabeth fretfully flings away her psalter.

Laywomen and noblewomen whose identities have not survived commissioned for their own benefit explanatory books on, say, the Bible. Other literary patrons are named. A Countess of Hoda had annotations on the psalms composed for her in the ninth century by the two monks Richer and Ratelm. Gisela and Rotrud, Charlemagne's sister and daughter respectively, asked Alcuin to write a commentary for them on the Gospels of St. John.

Paintings and illuminations show women at their books. A queen is pictured reading beside her window, or receiving a commissioned volume from an author. The woman reader may be the Virgin Mary, surprised at her book of devotions by the Angel Gabriel. The Virgin reads as midwives prepare her for childbirth; she reads in bed while Joseph tends the baby; she reads while riding on the back of a donkey during the flight into Egypt. Depictions of the Virgin's mother, Saint Anne, show her in her maternal role, teaching her little daughter her letters.

Medieval women were teachers. Liutberga of Halberstadt taught their psalmody to girls in what seems a forerunner of a public school. Cunegonde, wife of the last Saxon Emperor, Henry II, always had her nose in a book, and later gave lessons to her niece Uta, who would become an abbess. Mothers and grandmothers were apt to be the chief sources of learning for their offspring. The "redoubtable old lady" Ansfledis is described by her grandson Hugh (Charles Martel's half brother and a future abbot of St. Wandrille) as one who "fostered in Hugh both a love of sacred learning and spiritual devotion and who urged him toward a clerical career."[2]

Medieval mothers, like Dhuoda writing in Latin, and Christine de Pizan in the vernacular, composed lengthy letters of guidance for their children. In the early Middle Ages—before the twelfth century—literacy meant a knowledge of Latin. There is ample evidence that queens and noblewomen could write Latin well enough for literary composition and for the addressing of letters, private and public. A literate woman would always find the need and opportunity to write letters without having to apologize for presuming to authorship. Women's letters were purposeful, their audiences immediate and pressing—a son, nephew, beloved, a sister in God, a powerful ruler to be placated. Maintaining ties, telling of friendship, love, or parental concern could be especially urgent during these turbulent days, with the movement of migrating peoples, of continual travel from estate to estate, of princes holding court in different residences, of parlays and councils, of exiles, pilgrimages and crusades, raids and military campaigns. Women were apt to be less mobile than men; the separations between men and women or between women bound by kinship or common interest impelled the flow of letters.

Of all the forms available to women writers, none has been so necessary and so congenial over the centuries as the letter. Since this observation was made in the first edition of this anthology in 1987, much valuable research has appeared on women's letter-writing activity.[3] It would be tempting to say that the writing of letters was for women a most "normal" form of authorship. In the fourteenth century, Chaucer describes how both Troilus and Criseyde individually write letters. Troilus labors over his, blotting it with many a tear, and struggling to get the rhetoric right—of course, he's in love. But Criseyde, who declares she's never written a letter in her life, sits down to compose her missive with little ado.

This does not mean that a medieval women might not have to wrestle with the art of a complicated letter. Dhuoda, writing a letter that stretches to a treatise to her hostage son William, coins a word "agonizatio" for her literary efforts. Any letter, however private and familiar, always afforded the writer opportunites for rhetorical flourishes in a context that could be stuffed with learning—culled perhaps from available guidebooks on how to quote Scripture in an edifying fashion. Not all familiar letters were so ambitious as Dhuoda's; many exist chiefly as expressions of concern for an absent relative. Brunhilde in the sixth century, Herchenefreda in the seventh, are anxious mothers writing to or on behalf of children. Letters could console a lonely woman. A letter from a loved one, as Radegund says, painted the writer's portrait.

Many of the translated works in the present volume are letters. The Mideast travelogue of the energetic Egeria is actually an ongoing letter to the women in her community. One of the treasures she promises to bring back with her is—another letter! This is a document of the sort termed a "fictional epistle" (though genuine to her), purporting to be a correspondence between Jesus and a contemporary king. There is the anonymous sixth-century woman's letter to another woman she admires. Caesaria writes a heartening letter to Radegund, laying down some convent rules. Radegund addresses autobiographical poems to her male relatives in the style of those famed fictional letters of classical antiquity, the *Heroides* of Ovid. Elisabeth of Schönau, the twelfth-century German mystic, writes to Hildegard of Bingen, explaining the sources of her visions. Queen Margaret of Anjou writes obsessively of her need to hunt in the royal parks. At times when autobiographies and journals are rare, letters provide intimate glimpses of their subjects.

Letters can turn into treatises; books take on epistolary form. Once a letter-writer got started, she or he might feel it worth extending the document to make a volume for a circle of readers, while apologizing—not too sincerely—for a lack of *brevitas*. Dhuoda instructs her son to share with his brother her letter, which is really a compendium of counsels on feudal conduct, and assumes there will be further readers. As the writing of letters reached a peak of popularity in the twelfth century, even the lyrics of the troubadours—men's and women's—echo the new epistolary note, with their salutations, special pleading, farewell closings (*envois* and *tornadas*) and directions to a messenger.[4]

Often women's writing, epistolary and otherwise, is politically motivated. Amalasuintha, fending off the hostile Goths at her court, sends rhetorical letters of necessity to the Emperor Justinian and the Roman Senate, seeking to salvage the remnants of her rule. She hopes her letters to the Empress Theodora may forge a bond that can transcend the meeting of friends in actuality. Hroswitha's historical epics establish the power and sanctity of Ottonian queens. The female troubadour Gormonda defends Rome in her debate poem, and unleashes vitriolic charges against the heretics. Hildegard sends epistolary diatribes and encouragements to prelates and monarchs in an effort to call them to right action. Matilda of England, suave and fluent, attempts to settle the impasse between two masculine powers— her royal husband and her spiritual father, the Archbishop of Canterbury.

There were monastic women who wrote with a different idea of power, those who formulated hagiographical portraits, often to promote a cult and to create "models of womanly power, womanly achievement, and womanly voices."[5] So Baudonivia commemorates the saintly Radegund in an early example of the genre of Christian hagiography.

Other consecrated women recounted experiences that are intensely private, written—their authors say—under extreme pressure to glorify God and teach the faithful. These mystical writers convey their ecstasy: Hildegard of Bingen, Elisabeth of Schönau, Beatrijs of Nazareth, Mechthild of Magdeburg, Julian of Norwich. And what marvelous productions issue forth— visions, prophecies and cosmologies, revelry over God's humanity, erotic lyrics patterned on Minnesang and the troubadours! Writers on heavenly love understood well the necessary stages of meekness, pleading, total surrender and rapture.

Although often metaphorically expressed, women's awareness of sexual realities was scarcely muffled or naïve. Shortly before her death Radegund confided to a few close friends that she had been visited by a divine and amorous young man in her chamber. Eight centuries later, Margery Kempe invoked the imagery of the marriage bed in her yearning for oneness with the Lord. Hrotswitha dealt straightforwardly with an attempted homosexual seduction in a saint's life, and with voyeurism and autoerotic behavior, comically portrayed, in a play. These works are translated in the present volume. Marie de France is candid about men's and women's sexuality. In her medical books, Hildegard wrote with frankness about the female body and menstruation: "When the torrent of greedy desire invaded Eve, all her veins opened into a river of blood. Hence every woman has tempests of blood within her." Hildegard had views on semen and the sexual organs, and on carnal pleasure: "A man . . . is like a stag thirsting for the fountain, he races swiftly to the woman and she to him—she like a threshing floor pounded by his many strokes and brought to heat when the grains are threshed inside her."[6]

In another mode Hildegard communicates her ecstatic visions of celestial virgins, transparent with light and treading on air. Elisabeth of Schönau spins from a fevered imagination a whole troop of saintly women including her own particular friend and protector Saint Verena, one of the 11,000 virgins whom Saint Ursula led from Britain to Rome to Cologne. Elisabeth's visions achieved such notoriety as to attract pictorial artists who created cycles of the Ursula legend and perpetuated the virgins' images.

Women also wrote to entertain, to please and to extol. Some were professionals, attached to royal courts and writing for patrons and on commission. The Byzantine Empress Eudocia in the fifth century fulfilled a role of court author when she celebrated her husband's military feats (though her bizarre saint's life presented in this anthology seems to resonate on a more personal note). Hrotswitha takes on the burden of epic historian. Both Hrotswitha and Anna Comnena, women belonging to imperial circles, have left us epics that praise a strong, dynastic male figure to whom each woman was closely connected. One in the west, one in the east, one in Latin, one in Greek, they sing respectively of the deeds of Otto of Saxony and Alexius of Constantinople. But each woman uses the epic genre to frame her applause of heroic and appealing women. Marie de France, a Frenchwoman in England, and Christine de Pizan, an Italian-born woman in France, entertained their princely betters with romantic narratives and lyrics about sexual love, whether carefree, pathetic or tragic. Christine, in addition, produced works of encyclopedic instruction that were in high demand.

It would be difficult to judge how much of the vast fund of anonymous medieval writing must have been authored by women. The Old English book of *Judith*, magnifying a chaste avenging warrior, suggests female authorship. We may speculate that a woman's imagination could have created a work like *Aucassin and Nicolette*—with its fanciful country where men bear the babies and women go to war. Anonymous troubadour poems, clearly reflecting the voices of women, have been included in this anthology, as well as the only love poems surviving from Old English: *The Wife's Lament* and *Wulf and Eadwacer*.

The writings of medieval women contribute generously to our understanding of women's lives and history, to their centuries, and to all of medieval literature. Many of the selections offered here are translated into English for the first time. The following Select Bibliography serves as a general introduction to medieval women's studies. Suggestions for specific further reading accompany each chapter.

Marcelle Thiébaux
1987, 1994

NOTES

1. Eamon Duffy, *The Stripping of the Altars: Traditional Religion in England, 1400–1580.* (New Haven: Yale UP, 1992).

Joan Kelly-Gadol suggests that medieval women enjoyed an independence that was lost after the fifteenth century. Renaissance advances did not help women. Instead, the period meant "a new subordination of women to the interests of husbands and male-dominated kin groups." See "Did Women Have a Renaissance?" *Becoming Visible: Women in European History,* ed. Renate Bridenthal and Claudia Koonz (Boston: Houghton Mifflin, 1977), p. 161.

2. Information about women readers, writers, teachers and book owners comes from Rosamond McKitterick, *Carolingians and Written Word* (Cambridge: Cambridge UP, 1989); Nora K. Chadwick, *Poetry and Letters in Early Christian Gaul* (London: Bowes and Bowes, 1955); James Westfall Thompson, *The Literacy of the Laity in the Middle Ages* (Berkeley: U of California P, 1939); Kathleen Ashley and Pamela Sheingorn, eds., *Interpreting Cultural Symbols: Saint Anne in Late Medieval Society* (Athens: U of Georgia P, 1990); and Susan Groag Bell, "Medieval Women Book Owners: Arbiters of Lay Piety and Ambassadors of Culture," *Signs: Journal of Women in Culture and Society* (Summer 1982): 742–768, repr. in *Women and Power in the Middle Ages,* ed. Mary Erler and Maryanne Kowaleski, pp. 149–187 (Athens: U of Georgia P, 1988).

By examining wills, library catalogues, household inventories, and dedications to patrons, Susan Groag Bell has identified women who acquired and collected books, tabulating 242 women book-owners from the ninth to the fifteenth centuries.

3. For instance, Catherine Moriarty, ed. *The Voice of the Middle Ages in Personal Letters, 1100–1500.* (Oxford: Lennard, 1989), which includes letters by women; Albrecht Classen, "Female Epistolary Literature from Antiquity to the Present: An Introduction," *Studia Neophilologica* 60 (1988): 3–13; Elizabeth C. Goldsmith, *Writing the Female Voice: Essays on Epistolary Literature* (Boston: Northeastern UP, 1989); Patrick Sims-Williams, "Letter-Writing," pp. 211–242 of *Religion and Literature in Western England: 600–800* (Cambridge: Cambridge UP, 1990); Karen Cherewatuk and Ulrike Wiethaus, eds. *Dear Sister: Medieval Women and the Epistolary Genre* (Philadelphia: U of Pennsylvania P, 1993).

4. Raymond Gay-Crosier observes this in *Religious Elements in the Secular Lyrics of the Troubadours* (Chapel Hill: U of North Carolina P, 1971), p. 31.

On medieval letter-writing, see Giles Constable, *Letters and Letter-Collections* (Turnhout: Brepols, 1976); Emil J. Polak, "Dictamen," *Dictionary of the Middle Ages* (New York: Charles Scribner, 1984); Martin Camargo, *Ars Dictaminis, Ars Dictandi* (Turnhout: Brepols, 1991); Emil J. Polak, *Medieval and Renaissance Letter Treatises and Form Letters* (Leiden: E.J. Brill, 1992).

5. Jo Ann McNamara, "Introduction" to *Sainted Women of the Dark Ages*, ed. and trans. by Jo Ann McNamara and John E. Halborg, with E. Gordon Whatley (Durham: Duke UP, 1992), p. 15.

6. Barbara Newman, *Sister of Wisdom: St. Hildegard's Theology of the Feminine*. Berkeley: U of California P, pp. 117, 130.

Select Bibliography

Emilie Amt, ed. *Women's Lives in Medieval Europe: A Sourcebook.* New York and London: Routledge, 1993.

Bonnie S. Anderson and Judith P. Zinsser. *A History of Their Own: Women in Europe from Prehistory to the Present.* Vol I. New York: Harper, 1988.

Kathleen Ashley and Pamela Sheingorn, eds. *Interpreting Cultural Symbols: Saint Anne in Late Medieval Society.* Athens and London: U of Georgia P, 1990.

Clarissa W. Atkinson, *The Oldest Vocation: Christian Motherhood in the Middle Ages.* Ithaca: Cornell UP, 1991.

Derek Baker, ed. *Medieval Women.* Oxford: Basil Blackwell, 1978.

Frances Beer. *Women and Mystical Experience in the Middle Ages.* Rochester, NY: Boydell and Brewer, 1992.

Judith M. Bennett. *Women in the Medieval English Countryside: Gender and Household in Brigstock Before the Plague.* New York: Oxford UP, 1987.

—— and others, eds. *Sisters and Workers in the Middle Ages.* Chicago: U of Chicago P, 1989.

Constance Berman. *The Worlds of Medieval Women: Creativity, Influence, Imagination.* Morgantown: West Virginia P, 1985.

Alcuin Blamires, ed., with Karen Pratt and C.W. Marx. *Woman Defamed and Woman Defended: An Anthology of Medieval Texts.* Oxford: Clarendon P, 1992.

Renate Blumenfeld-Kosinski. *Not of Woman Born: Representations of Caesarean Birth in Medieval and Renaissance Culture.* Ithaca: Cornell UP, 1990

Renate Bridenthal, Claudia Koonz, and Susan Stuard, eds. *Becoming Visible: Women in European History.* 2nd ed. Boston: Houghton Mifflin, 1987.

Peter Brown. *The Body and Society: Men, Women and Sexual Renunciation in Early Christianity*. New York: Columbia UP, 1988.

Vern Bullough and James Brundage, eds. *Sexual Practices and the Medieval Church*. Buffalo, New York: Prometheus Books, 1982.

E. Jane Burns. *Bodytalk: When Women Speak in Old French Literature*. Philadelphia: U of Pennsylvania P, 1993.

Caroline Walker Bynum. *Holy Feast and Holy Fast: The Religious Significance of Food to Medieval Women*. Berkeley: U of California P, 1987.

———. *Jesus as Mother: Studies in the Spirituality of the High Middle Ages*. Berkeley: U of California P, 1982.

Karen Cherewatuk and Ulrike Wiethaus. *Dear Sister: Medieval Women and the Epistolary Genre*. Philadelphia: U of Pennsylvania P, 1993.

Graciela S. Daichman. *Wayward Nuns in Medieval Literature*. Syracuse: Syracuse UP, 1986.

Sheila Delaney, trans. with introduction. *A Legend of Holy Women: A Translation of Osbern Bokenham's* Legends of Holy Women. Notre Dame, Ind.: Notre Dame UP, 1993.

Peter Dronke. *Women Writers of the Middle Ages*. Cambridge: Cambridge UP, 1984.

Georges Duby, ed. *A History of Private Life*. Vol II: *Revelations of the Medieval World*. Trans. Arthur Goldhammer. Cambridge, MA: The Belknap P of Harvard UP, 1988.

Lina Eckenstein. *Women Under Monasticism: Chapters on Saint-Lore and Convent Life Between A.D. 500 and A.D. 1500*. New York: Russell and Russell, 1896. Repr. New York, 1963.

Sharon K. Elkins. *Holy Women of Twelfth-Century England*. Chapel Hill: U of North Carolina P, 1988.

Edith Ennen, ed. *The Medieval Woman*. Trans. Edmund Jephcott. Oxford and Cambridge: Basil Blackwell, 1989.

Mary Erler, and Maryanne Kowaleski, ed. *Women and Power in the Middle Ages*. Athens: U of Georgia P, 1988.

Christine Fell, with Cecily Clark and Elizabeth Williams. *Women in Anglo-Saxon England and the Impact of 1066*. Bloomington, Indiana, 1984.

Joan M. Ferrante. *Women as Image in Medieval Literature from the Twelfth Century to Dante*. New York: Columbia UP, 1975.

————. "The Education of Women in the Middle Ages in Theory, Fact, and Fantasy." In P.A. Labalme, ed., *Beyond Their Sex: Learned Women of the European Past.* New York: New York UP, 1980.

Gloria Fiero and others. *Three Medieval Views of Women: La Contenance des fames, Le Bien des fames, Le Blasme des Fames.* New Haven: Yale UP, 1989.

Mary Jeremy Finnegan. *The Women of Helfta: Scholars and Mystics.* Athens: U of Georgia P, 1991.

Sheila Fisher and Janet E. Halley, eds. *Seeking the Woman in Late Medieval and Renaissance Writings: Essays in Feminist Contextual Criticism.* Knoxville: U of Tennessee P, 1989.

Frances Gies and Joseph Gies. *Women in the Middle Ages.* New York, 1978.

Penny Schine Gold. *The Lady and the Virgin: Image, Attitude, and Experience in Twelfth Century France.* Chicago: U of Chicago P, 1985.

Elizabeth Goldsmith. *Writing the Female Voice: Essays on Epistolary Literature.* Boston: Northeastern UP, 1989.

Kathryn Gravdal. *Ravishing Maidens: Writing Rape in Medieval French Literature and Law.* Philadelphia: U of Pennsylvania P, 1991.

Sibylle Harksen. *Women in the Middle Ages.* Trans. by Marianne Herzfeld. New York: A. Schram, 1975.

Marta Harley, trans. *A Revelation of Purgatory by an Unknown Fifteenth-Century Woman Visionary.* Lewiston, N.Y.: Edwin Mellen, 1985.

David Herlihy. *Opera Muliebria: Women and Work in Medieval Europe.* Philadelphia: Temple UP, 1990.

Julia Bolton Holloway, Constance S. Wright and Joan Bechtold, eds. *Equally in God's Image: Women in the Middle Ages.* New York: Peter Lang, 1990.

Danielle Jacquart and Claude Thomasset. *Sexuality and Medicine in the Middle Ages.* Trans. by Matthew Adamson. Princeton: Princeton UP, 1988.

Judith Jesch. *Women in the Viking Age.* Rochester, NY: Boydell and Brewer, 1991.

Penelope D. Johnson. *Equal in Monastic Profession: Religious Women in Medieval France.* Chicago: U of Chicago P, 1991.

Barbara Kanner, ed. *The Women of England: From Anglo-Saxon Times to the Present.* Hamden, Conn.: Archon Books, 1979.

Alice Kemp-Welch. *Of Six Medieval Women.* First published 1913. Repr. Williamstown, MA: Corner House Publishers, 1972.

Julius Kirshner and Suzanne F. Wemple, eds. *Women of the Medieval World. Essays in Honor of John H. Mundy*. New York: Basil Black-well, 1985.

Christiane Klapisch-Zuber, ed. *A History of Women in the West: Silences of the Middle Ages*. Cambridge, MA: Belknap P of Harvard UP, 1992.

Margaret Wade Labarge. *The Small Sound of a Trumpet: Women in Me-dieval Life*. Boston: Beacon Press, 1986.

Jean Laporte. *The Role of Women in Early Christianity*. Lewiston, N.Y.: Edwin Mellen, 1982.

Gerda Lerner. *The Creation of Feminist Consciousness from the Middle Ages to Eighteen-Seventy*. New York: Oxford UP, 1993.

Linda Lomperis and Sarah Stanbury, eds. *Feminist Approaches to the Body in Medieval Literature*. Philadelphia: U of Pennsylvania P, 1993.

Angela M. Lucas. *Women in the Middle Ages: Religion, Marriage, and Let-ters*. New York: St. Martin's, 1983.

Jo Ann McNamara. "Sexual Equality and the Cult of Virginity in Early Christian Thought." *Feminist Studies* 3 (1976), pp. 145–158.

——— and John E. Halborg, with E. Gordon Whatley, eds. and trans. *Sainted Women of the Dark Ages*. Durham and London: Duke UP, 1992.

Carol M. Meale, ed. *Women and Literature in Britain: 1150–1500*. New York: Cambridge UP, 1993.

John Giles Milhaven. *Hadewijch and Her Sisters: Other Ways of Loving and Knowing*. Albany: State University of NY P, 1993.

Bella Millet and Jocelyn Wogan-Browne, eds. *Medieval Prose for Women: Selections from the Katherine Group and Ancrene Wisse*. Oxford: Clarendon P, 1990.

Louise Mirrer, ed. *Upon My Husband's Death: Widows in the Literature and Histories of Medieval Europe*. Ann Arbor: U of Michigan P, 1992.

Craig A. Monson, ed. *The Crannied Wall: Women, Religion, and the Arts in Early Modern Europe*. Ann Arbor: U of Michigan P, 1992.

Rosemarie Thee Morewedge, ed. *The Role of Women in the Middle Ages*. Albany: State University of New York P, 1975.

Catherine Moriarty, ed. *The Voice of the Middle Ages in Personal Letters, 1100–1500*. Oxford: Lennard, 1989.

Katherine Morris. *Sorceress or Witch? The Image of Gender in Medieval Ice-land and Northern Europe*. Lanham, Maryland: UP of America, 1991.

John A. Nichols and Lillian Thomas Shank, eds. *Medieval Religious Women*. Kalamazoo: Cistercian Publications, 1984.

Nancy F. Partner, ed. "Studying Medieval Women: Sex, Gender, Feminism." *Speculum: A Journal of Medieval Studies* (April 1993; special issue).

Pierre J. Payer. *The Bridling of Desire: Views of Sex in the Later Middle Ages*. Toronto: U of Toronto P, 1993.

Régine Pernoud. *La femme au temps des cathédrales*. Paris: Stock, 1980.

Elizabeth Alvilda Petroff, ed. *Medieval Women's Visionary Literature*. New York: Oxford UP, 1986.

Eileen Power. *Medieval Women*. M.M. Postan, ed. Cambridge: Cambridge UP, 1975.

Douglas Radcliff-Umstead, ed. *The Roles and Images of Women in the Middle Ages and Renaissance*. Pittsburgh: U of Pittsburgh Publications on the Middle Ages and Renaissance, 1975.

Mary Beth Rose, ed. *Women in the Middle Ages and the Renaissance: Literary and Historical Perspectives*. Syracuse: Syracuse UP, 1986.

Joel T. Rosenthal, ed. *Medieval Women and the Sources of Medieval History*. Athens: U of Georgia P, 1990.

Beryl Rowland, ed. and trans. *Medieval Woman's Guide to Health. The First English Gynecological Handbook*. Kent, Ohio: Kent State UP, 1981.

Eva Martin Sartori and Dorothy Wynne Zimmerman, eds. *French Women Writers: A Biobibliographical Sourcebook*. New York: Greenwood P, 1991.

David M. Scholer, ed. *Women in Early Christianity*. New York: Garland, 1993.

Shulamith Shahar. *The Fourth Estate: A History of Women in the Middle Ages*. Trans. Chaya Galai. London and New York, 1983.

————. *Childhood in the Middle Ages*. London and New York: Routledge, 1990.

Pauline Stafford. *Queens, Concubines, and Dowagers: The King's Wife in the Early Middle Ages*. Athens: U of Georgia P, 1983.

Susan Mosher Stuard, ed. *Women in Medieval Society*. Philadelphia: U of Pennsylvania P, 1976.

————. *Women in Medieval History and Historiography*. Philadelphia: U of Pennsylvania P, 1987.

Sally Thompson. *Women Religious: The Founding of English Nunneries after the Norman Conquest.* New York: Oxford UP, 1991.

Mary Ellen Waithe, ed. Introduction by Joan Gibson. *A History of Women Philosophers: Medieval, Renaissance and Enlightenment Women Philosophers, A.D. 500–1600.* Boston: Kluwer Academic P, 1989.

Suzanne Fonay Wemple. *Women in Frankish Society: Marriage and the Cloister, 500–900.* Philadelphia: U of Pennsylvania P, 1981.

Ulrike Wiethaus, ed. *Maps of Flesh and Light.* Syracuse: Syracuse UP, 1993.

Katharina Wilson, ed. *Medieval Women Writers.* Athens: U of Georgia P, 1984.

The Writings of
Medieval Women

CHAPTER 1

Prisoner, Dreamer, Martyr

Perpetua of Carthage (d. March 7, 203)

Early in the third century, when persecutions against Christians were raging like a virus in the North African city of Carthage, a young woman named Vibia Perpetua was arrested with four friends.

At twenty-two she was their leader and guiding spirit, rallying them in their last crisis and urging them to "stand fast in the faith." Daughter of an upper-class provincial family, Perpetua was a young mother still nursing her son, but she willingly embraced the suffering revealed in the diary she wrote from her prison cell. With her was Felicity, a slave, and three young men. Another friend voluntarily joined them later. When arrested, the young people were Christian catechumens, beginners still taking instruction. The fact that they had themselves baptized in prison worsened the case against them, showing them to be more intransigeant than ever. After a trial they were sentenced to confront the beasts in the arena, part of a birthday celebration for the Emperor Geta. One died in the jail. The others were slain in the arena.

Martyrdom meant bearing witness, and belonged to the program of Christianity from the beginning. On the day of his Ascension Christ is said to have announced to the apostles their task: "You are to be my witnesses in Jerusalem and throughout Judaea, in Samaria, yes, and to the ends of the earth."[1] The apostles had simply to give witness to what they had heard and seen and to keep on witnessing, unshaken and unswerving, even if they were dragged before kings and governors. "They will lay hands on you and persecute you. They will deliver you to synagogues and prisons . . . and all on account of my name. This will result in your being witnesses to them . . . They will put some of you to death."[2] Inasmuch as Christ bore witness with the testimony of blood that he had come as the Messiah, the witness who put her life or his life on the line for Christ was a martyr in the strict sense.

Understandably, then, the martyrs who died for the faith earned reverence. The blood of the martyrs was the seed of the Church, wrote the Christian theologian Tertullian, a contemporary of Perpetua's who was born at Carthage. The followers of dead martyrs showed this reverence by gathering and cherishing the bodily remains, "dearer than precious jewels and finer than gold,"[3] often at great risk since burial was forbidden to criminals whom the state executed for breaking the law. Declaring oneself to be a Christian wasn't the crime. It was refusing to worship the Emperor and honor the religion of the Roman state: offering sacrifice, pouring and tasting libations to the Punic/Roman divinities. Jupiter Optimus Maximus and Juno Caelestis, the bearded Baal-Saturn with his sickle and solar disk, Bacchus, Demeter, and Kore were among those with shrines and altar mounds in pleasant courtyards and terraces, under porticoes, or beside sheltered pools. The town of Thuburbo—where Perpetua and her friends were arrested, some thirty kilometers southwest of Carthage—boasted an imposing temple of Baalat and one of Mercury in the forum. Mingled with the worship of the Roman gods were ominous rites of infant sacrifice, inherited from Phoenician cults of Baal and Moloch, whom African Romans inscribed as MLK. Of the priestly sacrifice of children, Tertullian reports, "To this day that holy crime persists in secret."

The gravity of the crime of not worshiping all the deities was evident. Christians imperiled the well-being of the state by flouting the fury of the gods, who were known to visit famines, earthquakes, and other disasters on those who ignored their cults.

The martyrs were the first heroes of Christianity, mere mortals, really, but gifted with heroic strength at their final moment of need. Even though it was possible for Christians to fake it—to go through the motions of the sacrifices, pay a deputy, or buy false certificates of participation—astoundingly large numbers chose torture and death. Their eagerness to die explained why the Roman state had eventually to concede the impossibility of conquering Christianity by fire and sword. The "sword" was the metaphor of the notorious gladiator shows.

Until Christianity became a threat, gladiator spectacles were public events, military funeral games staged by wealthy patricians to venerate their dead. Prominent citizens, too, might be forced to subsidize beast shows as a kind of status tax. The African arena (the word meant "sand," which in practical terms was sifted over the blood after each combat) could be decorated with props and scenery to simulate wilderness settings into which animal cages were lowered with pulleys. Gladiators engaged in combat with each other or with wild animals. Starved animals were set at each other's throats. Condemned victims were loosed in the arena unarmed, or given rudimentary weapons like bows and arrows or firebrands to defend themselves. Attendants and slaves officially employed in the sports sometimes dressed as gods—Mercury, Pluto, Charon. The sight led Tertullian to describe the arena as "the temple of all the demons." Victims who were condemned criminals or war captives were paraded around, often forced to wear the garb of Roman priests and priestesses before being stripped and driven to the wild beasts. Leopards, lions, bulls, bears, elephants, antelopes, even crocodiles were likely to show up as their adversaries. After human victims were sufficiently mauled, they were delivered the *coup de grace*, the *jugulum*, or the slitting of their throats by gladiators whose job that was.[4]

Not only were the arena sports wildly popular as theatrical entertainment, but citizens also wanted mementos, costly decorative artifacts, in their homes. A mosaic found in a villa near Leptis Magna, North Africa, portrays a scene from the death games. A roped bull tussles with a chained bear, a nude man challenges a horse with a hooked baton, a soldier goads another nude man with a whip to confront a charging lion. The second nude man shows resistance.[5] Another mosaic from a house in Smirat shows gladiators impaling bleeding leopards on their lances while a patron runs forward from the sidelines with the prize money. An even more gruesome depiction survives from the house known as the Domus Sollertiana at the city of Thysdrus near the African east coast. The artist renders a panther clambering up on a bound prisoner, both hind claws fixed into one staggering knee, front paws gripping his shoulder and breast while the animal eats the man's eyes and face. Blood spouts graphically.[6]

Gladiators, *venatores*, and *bestiarii* (swordsmen, huntsmen, and animal fighters) were professional athletes employed in the games. Unlike the stripped victims, they were sufficiently armed. They were "stars" in the public eye, their performances compensated with bags of denars and gold coins. Usually of humble birth, the athletes achieved their gaudy celebrity by the strength of body and brawn. Their allegedly glamorous lives were violent and usually short. Popularly viewed as heroes endowed with sexual as well as athletic prowess, gladiators were thought appealing to women. The Latin *gladius*, or sword, also colloquially meant penis, and gladiators were apt to be represented pictorially as phallic combatants.[7]

Beasts and gladiators figure in the story of Perpetua. Her male companions are mangled finally by a leopard. Drenched in their own blood, they hear the mobs roaring with ironic wit, "Well washed! Well washed!" (*salvum lotum*). This was a customary greeting of good health exchanged by friends after a bath and could be found inscribed in a bathing pool or grotto.

There are ancient amphitheaters dotting North Africa, including one at Thuburbo and a 27,000–seat amphitheater at Thysdrus. These offer rich excavation sites whose ruins can be seen today. The gladiator mosaics described previously date from the early third century, the period of Perpetua's death.

It is important to note that Perpetua's journal and the surrounding testimony are not legend but constitute a document that survives in numerous Latin manuscripts, some abridged, with one Greek version, the last found in Jerusalem. Before the journal begins, an eyewitness's introduction bearing the marks of a sermon is written in a far more scholarly and convoluted style than the lucid, unadorned words of Perpetua. This introduction, with allusions to the preservation of texts, gives an oral reminder of the martyrdom to those who already know it at first hand, and it introduces the holy event to those who now learn of it through hearing (*nunc cognoscitis per auditum*).

The opening states the document's fourfold purpose: to verify the acts of God and to honor God, to teach men and women and to comfort them. The introduction raises the question of the greater authority of *older* history over recent and contemporary. But these contemporary prophecies and visions will, in their turn, attain the respectability of the old, as the preacher points out. Today's news will become great history. So the preacher exhorts the hearers to venerate the new, especially as the new becomes identified with the world's "last days."

As distinct from the preacher's overarching, didactic view of slow-gathering historic time, Perpetua's journal measures the painful day-to-day passage of time intimately experienced by a condemned woman who waits for her execution. The word "days" drums like a refrain. Perpetua's account of prison life sounds quite convincing. There are also mysterious notes and omissions. Where is her husband? Why is her father the only member of her family who, she says, does not rejoice at her plight? These questions may one day find answers.

Perpetua's memory was kept green and thriving. Saint Augustine of Carthage wrote sermons in honor of his compatriots, Perpetua and Felicity, and their names are in the Roman calendar of saints. Mosaics of the two, garbed as slave and mistress, survive in Ravenna. During the great period of church building in the fourth century, a Byzantine church known as the Damous-el-Karita (the House of Charity) was consecrated at Carthage. This was the largest church in North Africa. A short walk from the church led to a wide cemetery where one could read the inscription indicating the tomb of the martyred Perpetua. One such inscription stated that it was in the Great Basilica that the bodies of the holy martyrs Perpetua and Felicity were buried: *Basilicam Majorum ubi corpora sanctarum martyrum Perpetuae atque Felicitatis sepulta sunt.*[8]

By the mid-ninth century the legend appears in abbreviated form in the *Old English Martyrology* for March 7. The author may have found the story in the Sermons of St. Augustine:

> On the seventh day of the month is the commemoration of the holy women St. Perpetua and St. Felicity, whose bodies rest in the large town of Carthage in Africa. Perpetua dreamt when she was in her girlhood that she

had the appearance of a man and that she had a sword in her hand and that she fought with it valiantly. All this was afterwards fulfilled at her martyrdom, when she overcame the devil and the heathen persecutors with manly determination [*werlice gepohte*]. Then there was Felicity, a Christian woman, and she was with child as she was sent to prison for Christ's sake. When therefore the persecutors were about to dismiss her, she wept and prayed to God to rid her of the child, and then she brought it forth on the same night in the seventh month of her pregnancy, and she suffered martyrdom for Christ's sake.[9]

The record of Perpetua's martyrdom consists of four parts: Sections 1–2 give the introduction and eyewitness report, perhaps by Tertullian or one of his circle; Sections 3–10 are Perpetua's own words, her personal narrative of the period in prison before her death and the journal's central document; Sections 11–13 move to the narrative of a fellow prisoner, Saturus, who relates his own vision and gives testimony to Perpetua; Sections 14–21 round off the journal with an eyewitness's conclusion and account of Perpetua's death and those of her comrades.

Introductory Sermon by an Eyewitness

1. From ancient times, examples of the faith have been committed to writing in order to verify God's grace and provide guidance for human-kind. The aim of recalling the past through the written word has also been to honor God and reassure humanity. Why then should we not record more recent events for these purposes? For some day such events will also become ancient. Future ages will need them, even though in their own time they seemed less important because ancient history claims the greater respect.

People who think that there is a single Holy Spirit for all times and periods ought to reflect that more current events should be considered more important. An overflowing grace has been promised for these last days of the world. The Lord said, *"In the last days I will pour out of my spirit upon all flesh; and their* sons and their daughters shall prophesy and on my servants and handmaids I will pour out of my spirit, and the young men shall see visions and the old men shall dream dreams."[10]

In the same way that we responded to those prophecies, so too should we recognize and worship the new prophecies and new visions that were promised. All the other virtues of the Holy Spirit we believe have been bestowed upon the Church so that the Church might dispense such gifts to everyone, as the Lord distributes to all people.[11] This is why we think it necessary to set these things down and make them known through this text for the glory of God, so that no one whose faith is feeble or hopeless may think that divine grace was available only to the ancients, whether they earned it by martyrdom or visions. For God always accomplishes what he promises, both as testimony to nonbelievers and blessing to the faithful.

And so my brothers and little ones, *what we have heard and touched with our hands we proclaim also to you, so that those of you*[12] who were there among them may keep in mind the glory of the Lord and those who learn of it now through hearing may be in the company of the holy martyrs, and through them be with the Lord Jesus Christ, to whom is due glory and honor for ever and ever. Amen.

Eyewitness's Introduction to the Journal

2. Several young catechumens were arrested: Revocatus and Felicity, both slaves who served together, then Saturninus and Secundulus. With them was Vibia Perpetua.[13] She came of a good family; she was well brought up and a respectably married woman. She had a father and mother and two brothers, one of whom was also a catechumen. At her breast she nursed an infant son and was herself about twenty-two years old. What follows here narrates the whole sequence of her ordeal as she wrote it in her own hand, with her own thoughts about it left untouched.

The Prison Journal and the Dreams of Perpetua

3. We were still with the escorting officers when my father, because of his affection for me, wanted to talk me out of all this and overturn my resolve.

"Father," I said, "as an example, do you see a vessel lying here, a pitcher or whatever it is?" And he said, "Yes, I see it." I said, "Could that be called by any other name than what it is?" And he said, "No, it couldn't be called by any other name than what it is." "Well, then, neither can I call myself anything other than what I am, a Christian."

This *word* drove my father to a fury, and he fell upon me as if he would tear out my eyes. But he simply raged and then he left, defeated along with his diabolical reasoning. For a few days I didn't have my father around and I gave thanks to God, for I felt restored by his staying away. In the space of these few days we were baptized and the Holy Spirit counseled me not to ask for anything from that water but bodily endurance.

A few days later we were taken to prison. I was badly frightened because I had never before been in such darkness. What a terrible day!—the suffocating heat because of the crowding, and the guards manhandling us. And worst of all, I was torn with anxiety because of my baby.

Then Tertius and Pomponius, those holy deacons who were attending to us, bribed someone so that we were allowed to transfer for a few hours to a better prison cell where we felt cooler. Once out of the dungeon, we were free to look after our needs. I nursed my baby, who was already faint with hunger. My anxiety caused me to speak to my mother about him. I consoled my brother and I entrusted the baby to them. I was exhausted for I saw how exhausted they were because of me. For many days I suffered such worries as these. Then I worked things out so I could have my baby stay with me in the prison. I right away grew stronger, relieved as I was of my worry and anxiety for the baby. All at once my prison seemed like a palace to me. I preferred being there to anywhere else!

4. My brother then said to me, "My lady sister, you have already earned such great honor that surely you may ask for a vision to learn whether you must suffer or be granted a

reprieve." And I knew that I could speak with the Lord, whose great blessings I had already experienced, so I promised him faithfully: "I'll tell you tomorrow."

I then asked, and this was shown to me.

The First Vision

I saw a ladder of bronze that rose to extravagant length, as high as heaven,[14] and so narrow that only one person at a time could climb it. Attached to its sides was every kind of iron instrument—swords, lances, hooks, knives, and javelins. If you climbed recklessly or without paying attention, you would be butchered and your flesh would stick to the iron implements.

At the foot of the ladder skulked a snake of monstrous size that menaced those who tried to climb and made them fearful of ascending.

But Saturus went up first. (It was he who after matters had progressed gave himself up voluntarily when we were arrested, since he worried about us. He had greatly heartened us, but at the time of our arrest, he was not present). When he reached the top of the ladder, he turned around and said to me, "Perpetua! I'm waiting for you, but be careful that the snake doesn't sting you." I said, "It won't harm me, in the name of Jesus Christ!" The snake, as if fearing me, stretched its head out from under that ladder. I used its head as the ladder's first rung, stepped on it and climbed up. And I saw an immense space of a garden. There in its midst was a white-haired man, tall in a shepherd's cloak, and he was milking sheep. Standing around him were many thousands of people clothed in garments of shining white.

The man lifted his head and gazed at me, saying, "You are welcome, child."[15] He called me to him and gave me a mouthful of what seemed to be the cheese he was milking. I received it in my cupped hands and I ate it, while all those who were standing around said, "Amen." At the sound of the word I awoke and still tasted something sweet, not knowing what it could be. I spoke immediately to my brother, and we both knew that there would be suffering to come. We realized we could have no more hope of this world.

5. A few days later, a rumor circulated that we would have
a hearing. Also, my father came down from the city. He was
consumed with fatigue, and approached with the intent of
dissuading me. "Daughter," he said, "have pity on my white
hairs. Have pity on your father if I am worthy of having you call
me your father, if I have with these hands brought you up to
reach this flower of your life, if I have cherished you over all
your brothers! Do not abandon me to be shamed by men. Have
regard for your brothers, look upon your mother and your aunts,
look upon your son who will be unable to live after your death.
Put aside this haughty spirit of yours or you will ruin us all.
None of us will ever be able to speak freely if anything happens
to you!"

My father said these things out of love for me. He kissed
my hands and threw himself at my feet. Weeping, he no longer
called me "daughter" but "Lady." I was in anguish for my
father's plight, for he alone of all my family would not rejoice to
see my situation. I consoled him, saying, "All will be resolved at
the prisoners' scaffold as God wills. For you must know that we
are not in command of ourselves but in God's control." And he
went from me, overwhelmed with grief.

6. Another day, as we were eating our late morning meal,
we were abruptly hurried off for a hearing. We came to the
forum and the rumor spread quickly around the neighborhood
and an enormous crowd gathered. We mounted the prisoners'
scaffold. The others were interrogated, and they confessed.
When it came to me, my father showed up with my son and
dragged me from the step crying, "Perform the sacrifice—have
pity on your infant!" As for the governor Hilarianus, who had
received the sword of judicial power as successor to the late
justice Minucius Timinianus,[16] he too urged, "Spare your father's
white hair, spare the infancy of your boy! Perform the rite for the
safety of the emperors!"

I replied, "I will not do it." "Are you a Christian?"
Hilarianus asked. And I replied, "I am a Christian." And when
my father stood firm and tried to force me to change, Hilarianus
ordered him turned out and had him struck with a stick. I felt
pity for my father, as if I myself had been struck, and so I
grieved for his wretched old age.

Then Hilarianus sentenced us all, and we were condemned to the beasts. In high spirits we went back to our prison cell. I was still nursing my infant, who was used to taking the breast, so I quickly sent the deacon Pomponius to my father's house to ask for the infant. But my father would not hand him over. And then as God willed, the baby no longer desired the breast, and my breasts were not inflamed either. So I did not suffer any vexation over the baby or any soreness in my breasts.

The Second Vision

7. A few days later, while all of us were at prayer, suddenly in the midst of a prayer I uttered the name Dinocrates. I was astounded, for he had not come to my mind until then, and I was filled with sorrow when I remembered his fate. Then I realized that I might be permitted to pray for him and that I was obligated to do so, and I began to pray very intently and to lament greatly for him before the Lord. That same night I received a vision which was this: I saw Dinocrates walking from a place of darkness where there were a large number of people. He appeared very hot and thirsty, his clothes were soiled, and his face pale. The ulcer on his face was just as it had been when he died.

Dinocrates had been my brother in the flesh, but at the age of seven had died very miserably of a cancerous disease of the face. The manner of his death had sickened everyone.

For him I now prayed, but between the two of us was a very great void so that neither of us could approach the other. Dinocrates stood beside a pool full of water. The edge was so high that it rose above him and he had to stretch as if to drink the water. And I grieved for him. Although the pool was full, he was unable to drink because the edge was so high above him.

I awoke, and realized that my brother was suffering, but I was sure that I would be able to help him in his affliction. I prayed for him each day until we were transferred to the fortress prison. For it had been arranged that we were to fight in the military games held on the emperor Geta's birthday. I prayed for my brother day and night, groaning and shedding tears that my prayer might be granted.

The Third Vision

8. On the day that they kept us chained, I experienced this vision: I saw the same place I had seen before, but now Dinocrates was clean and nicely dressed and refreshed. I saw a scar where the ulcer had been. The edge of the pool I had seen the last time had lowered to the child's navel. On the edge was a golden drinking vessel filled with water that flowed from it ceaselessly. Dinocrates walked over and began to drink from it and the vessel never emptied. When he had drunk his fill he joyously ran to play in the way children do. I awoke, recognizing that he had been released from his affliction.

9. After a few days, an officer named Pudens, the warden of the prison, began to notice us with respect for he observed that there was some great power in us. He began to admit other people to our cell so that we might bring relief to one another. As the day of the combat games drew near, my father came, and he was haggard and worn down. He started to tear his beard and scattered the hairs on the ground. He prostrated himself before me and cursed the years of his life, speaking the kinds of words that would move every living creature. And I sorrowed for his unhappy old age.

The Fourth Vision

10. The day before we were to fight, I had a vision of the deacon Pomponius coming to the prison gates and knocking very energetically. I went to open the gates for him. He wore a flowing white robe and richly braided sandals. He said, "Perpetua, we are waiting for you. Come." He took my hand and we began to walk over rugged and tortuous paths. At last we arrived out of breath at the amphitheater, and he guided me to the middle of the arena. "Don't be afraid," he said. "I will be here with you, and I will strive by your side." Then he went away.

I looked out over a vast crowd, who regarded me with astonishment. Since I knew I was condemned to the beasts, I wondered that they didn't loose the beasts against me. Then coming toward me was an Egyptian of loathsome appearance.

He had his adjutants, and had come to engage me in combat. Handsome young men were by my side, my own adjutants and supporters.

My clothing was stripped off, and I became a man. My assistants began to rub me with oil as they customarily do for an athletic contest. On the other side the Egyptian was rolling in the sand.

Then a man of towering size came out, so huge that he dominated the summit of the amphitheater. He wore an unbelted tunic of purple with two stripes running across the middle of his chest. He had elaborately decorated sandals of gold and silver. He carried a baton like that of an athletic trainer, and a green branch heavy with golden apples.

He made a bid for silence, and said, "If this Egyptian is victorious over her, he shall kill her with the sword. But if she wins, she shall receive this branch." Then he drew away.

We approached each other and began to lash out with our fists. My adversary kept trying to seize my feet but I kept on kicking him in the face with my heels. I felt myself rising up in the air and I pummeled him as if I were no longer touching the ground. When I saw there was a slight delay, I interlaced the fingers of my two hands and grasped his head. He fell face down on the ground and I placed my heel on his head. The people began to shout, and my adjutants chanted hymns of victory. I went over to the trainer and received the branch. He kissed me, saying, "Daughter, peace be with you." Victorious, I walked to the Portal of the Living.[17]

I awoke then, knowing that I would have to fight not against beasts but against the Devil, and that I would win.

This is what I have written up to the night before the contest. If any wish to write of the outcome of the battle, let them do it.

[The visions of Perpetua's fellow martyr, Saturus, occupy Section 11–13. Section 14 reports the death of Secundulus in prison. The anonymous narrator provides the conclusion of the gladiatorial combats, first introducing Perpetua's servant, Felicity.]

Eyewitness Report

15. The grace of God touched Felicity, too, as it will be shown. When arrested she was pregnant and was now in her eighth month. The day of the spectacle was approaching, and she became greatly disquieted that the ordeal might be deferred because of her pregnancy, since it is against the law for pregnant women to be put to death. If deferred, she would have to pour forth her blood afterwards, along with common criminals. Her fellow martyrs were heavy-hearted at the thought of having to leave behind so good a companion to make her journey alone on the same highway to hope. Two days before the contest, they prayed together to the Lord in their grief. Soon after their prayers, Felicity felt the onset of her labor pains. Because of the natural difficulty of an eighth-month delivery, she suffered a great deal of pain in giving birth.

One of the prison guards said to her, "If you are suffering so much now, what will you do when you are thrown to the beasts? You didn't think of *them* when you were unwilling to perform the sacrifice."

Felicity answered, "I am suffering alone now, but later there will be Another in me who will endure the pain for me as I am enduring now for him." She gave birth to a girl, whom one of her sisters brought up as her own daughter.

16. [After apologizing for his inadequacy, the eyewitness continues with another example of Perpetua's persistence and mettle.]

Once, when the guard was abusing the prisoners even more harshly than usual (because some rather untrustworthy men had warned that we might break out of jail by using certain kinds of incantations or magic), Perpetua said right to his face, "Why don't you let us even refresh ourselves? We're the most famous of the accused. We're Caesar's! We're supposed to fight on his birthday. Wouldn't they congratulate you if you brought us out looking fit on that occasion?"

The guard bristled and grew red-faced. Then he ordered the prisoners to be handled more humanely, and said that Perpetua's brothers and some other people should be permitted to visit her and take a meal together. And by now the warden in charge of the jail was one of the faithful.

17. The day before the games, they were eating their last dinner, which is usually called the "free banquet," though they didn't call it that but made it instead an *agape* [the love feast of the early Christians]. They spoke firmly to the people, warning them about God's justice, and attested to the joy they would have in their suffering. They laughed at people who came running to see them out of curiosity. Saturus said, "Won't tomorrow be enough for you? Why are you willing to look at what you detest? Today we're friends, tomorrow we'll be enemies. Study our faces closely so that you'll know who we are on that day." Then the people went away stunned, and many of them became believers.

18. The day of the martyrs' victory was filled with light. In high spirits, their faces composed, they proceeded from the prison to the amphitheater as if they were marching to heaven. If they trembled at all, it was with joy rather than fear.

Perpetua followed with tranquil footsteps like the wife of Christ and beloved of God. Her face was radiant, her shining gaze thwarted the common stares of all the people. Felicity was with them, rejoicing that she had safely given birth so that now she might battle against the beasts. She had advanced from the midwife to the gladiators' nets, washed first in the blood of childbirth and ready to meet a new baptism of blood.

They were conducted to the gates, and the men were compelled to don the robes of the priests of Saturn while the women were to be gowned as priestesses of Ceres. But Perpetua high-mindedly protested against this to the end. "We came here willingly so that our liberty would not be defiled. We agreed we would give up our lives as long as we would do nothing of the sort. We made a pact with you about this."

Even the unjust recognize the just. The tribune conceded. The martyrs were led in without special costumes. Perpetua chanted psalms as if she had already placed her heel on the Egyptian's head. The others, when they came within view of Hilarianus, made gestures and threw back their heads, saying: "You condemn us, and God will condemn you!"

The crowds flew into a fury and demanded that the martyrs be flogged by a row of gladiatorial huntsmen. The Christians greeted this with joy for they were following in the Passion of the Lord.

[In Section 19 Saturus and Revocatus wrestle a leopard, a bear, and a wild boar.]

20. But for the young women, the Devil had furnished a rather savage heifer. This was not usual, but the creature was chosen to match their female sex. They were stripped, tangled in the nets and brought forward. The populace was horrified to see that one was a delicate young girl and the other a young woman who had just given birth, her breasts still leaking with milk. So the women were called back and clothed in unbelted tunics.

First Perpetua was tossed by the heifer, and she fell on her back. When she sat up, she pulled down the tunic to cover her thighs, since it was torn along the side. She was more aware of her modesty than her injury. She found her hair clasp, which had fallen out, and pinned back her disheveled hair for she thought it was not becoming to a martyr to suffer with her hair in disarray. She did not want to appear to be in mourning at her moment of glory.

She got up and saw that Felicity had been crushed down and went over to her. She reached out her hands and helped her up. As they stood there, the crowd's avidity seemed to be blunted, and so the two women were called back to the Sanavivarian Portal.

The catechumen Rusticus took care of Perpetua there. She appeared to be waking from a profound slumber, for the spirit had filled her and ravished her. She began to look around her, and everyone was astounded to hear her ask, "When are we going to be taken back to that heifer or whatever it was?" And when she heard that this had already happened, she didn't at first believe it until she saw the signs of her struggle on her body and tunic. Then she called to her brother and said to him and to the catechumen, "*You must stand fast in the faith,*[18] and love one another and do not be shattered by our passion."

21. Perpetua, however had yet to savor more pain. She was pierced to the bone and she screamed aloud. Then she took the

shaking right hand of the gladiator, who was just a raw recruit, and directed it to the cutting of her own throat.

NOTES

1. Acts 1.8.

2. Luke 2.12.

3. The Martyrdom of St. Polycarp (second century), *The Acts of the Christian Martyrs*, introduction, texts, and translations by Herbert Musurillo (Oxford: Clarendon P, 1972), pp. 16–17.

4. Keith Hopkins, *Death and Renewal: Sociological Studies in Roman History* (Cambridge UP, 1983), pp. 1–30.

5. *The Oxford Illustrated History of Christianity*, ed. John McManners (New York: Oxford UP, 1990), p. 44, plate.

6. David Soren, Aicha ben Abed ben Khader, Hedi Slim, *Carthage: Uncovering the Mysteries and the Splendors of Ancient Tunisia* (New York: Simon and Schuster, 1990), pp. 206–209, with plates. The authors are curators and directors of archaeological excavations in Tunisia.

7. Hopkins, *Death and Renewal*, p. 20.

8. Soren and others, *Carthage*, p. 259. Musurillo's edition (p. 109) cites Ernest Diehl, *Inscriptiones Latinae Christianae Veteres* (Berlin: Weidmann, 1961), nos. 2040–41. The inscription is cited in Paul Monceaux, *Histoire littéraire de l'Afrique chrétienne*, I, 73 note.

9. *Early English Text Society* 116 (1900), ed. George Herzfeld, p. 35.

10. Acts 2.17–18, paraphrasing the prophet Joel 2.28.

11. Compare I Cor. 7.17.

12. I. John 1.3.

13. These five Christians are arrested together. Saturus, the sixth of the group, will join the prisoners of his own free will. It is Saturus who appears in Perpetua's vision.

14. Jacob's dream (Gen. 28.12) reveals "a ladder set up on the earth, and the top of it reached to heaven."

15. Although the journal is in Latin, the venerable shepherd addresses the dreamer with the Greek *téknon* (child).

16. Tertullian names Hilarianus as the governor of Africa.

17. Porta Sanavivaria, the gate through which the winners exited.

18. I. Cor. 16.13.

FURTHER READING

Jacqueline Amat. *Songes et visions: L'au-delà dans la littérature latine tardive*, pp. 68–76. Paris: Etudes Augustiniennes, 1985.

Peter Brown. *The Body and Society: Men, Women, and Sexual Renunciation in Early Christianity*. New York: Columbia UP, 1988.

Keith Hopkins. "Murderous Games." In *Death and Renewal*, pp. 1–30. Cambridge: Cambridge UP, 1983.

C. Mertens. "Les premiers martyrs et leurs rêves," *Revue d'histoire ecclésiastique* 81 (1986): 5–46.

Paul Monceaux. "La 'Passion' de Sainte Perpétué." In *Histoire littéraire de l'Afrique Chrétienne depuis les origines jusqu' à l'Invasion Arabe*, pp. 70–96. Paris, 1901.

Perpetua. Peter Dronke. "Perpetua." In *Women Writers of the Middle Ages*, pp. 1–16. Translation and commentary. Cambridge: Cambridge UP, 1984.

———. Herbert Musurillo, ed. *"Passio Sanctarum Perpetuae et Felicitatis."* In *The Acts of the Christian Martyrs*, pp. 106–131. Introduction, texts, and translations. Oxford: Clarendon P, 1972.

———. C.J.M.J. van Beek, ed. *Passio Sanctarum Perpetuae et Felicitatis*. Nijmegen, 1936.

———. Patricia Wilson Kastner, G. Ronald Kastner, and others. "The Martyrdom of Perpetua." In *A Lost Tradition: Women Writers of the Early Church*, pp. 1–32. Introduction and translation. Lanham, Maryland: UP of America, 1981.

W.H. Shewring. *The Passion of Saints Perpetua and Felicity*, London: Sheed and Ward, 1931.

David Soren, Aicha ben Abed ben Khader, and Hedi Slim. *Carthage: Uncovering the Mysteries and the Splendors of Ancient Tunisia*. New York: Simon and Schuster, 1990.

Marie-Louise von Franz. *The Passion of Perpetua.* Jungian Classics Series, 2. Irving, Texas: Spring Publications, 1980.

CHAPTER 2

A Pilgrim to the Holy Land

Egeria of Spain (381–384)

The last groans of Christian martyrs had scarcely died away, the last recorded execution in Palestine carried out in 310, when the great age of pilgrimage and relic hunting began. Late in the fourth century, an energetic woman of rank and leisure traveled from northwest Spain to Asia Minor, Palestine, and Egypt. She left a record of her three-year journey in a simple Latin that is striking for its spontaneity and colloquial directness. At the same time it conveys a commonsense piety and an abundance of information about the sacred topography. Her travel book, in the form of a letter to her monastic sisters, shows her responsive to the idea that the sacred was localized in geographical space.

With the Edict of Milan in 313, the Christians had won a reprieve from persecution; with the Council of Nicaea in 325, their faith became the official religion of the Roman Empire. The victorious emperor Constantine launched a church-building program and urged Christians to visit Palestine's holy places.

A few earlier travelers had shown interest in walking on the sacred ground where events of the Bible had been enacted. Melito of Sardis in the second century wrote his brother that he wished to see "where it all happened and the truth was proclaimed."[1] Origen, the Egyptian-born theologian and author of an ambitious gloss on the Song of Songs, visited Bethlehem among other places in 230. He made the journey in part to elude his enemies, but he also had an exegetical aim: to see the locales he intended to write about. The anonymous Bordeaux Pilgrim (333 A.D.) left a first-hand account that predates Egeria's, including a roster of sites and distances between stopping places.

Constantine wished to eradicate paganism and to connect his building agenda to his own espousal of the Christian faith. In May 330, he laid the foundation stones of the "New Rome," his city of Constantinople, over ancient Byzantium. In Palestine, he ordered holy caves converted to holy churches. Now with his announced mission, the age saw the building, restoration, and ornamenting of tombs, shrines and churches, monasteries, and hospices for the sick, all drawing pilgrims in large numbers. The places that stirred interest were the caves and houses of Old Testament personages (and a few of the New), the tombs of the martyrs, and sites connected with Christ's ministry.

Egeria's itinerary takes her across vineyards, orchards, cultivated fields and valleys, fountains, fruitful gardens, ruins, tombs, and palaces, as she lists the monuments of Scripture. Roman roads had fixed the routes, which the pilgrims occasionally leave for side excursions trekking across sandy wastes on muleback or following the shoreline where the saddled animals walked through the sea. At times the party needs the armed escort of Roman soldiers. Often they trudge. Mount Sinai, declares Egeria, would have been impossible on saddled beasts, and so the pilgrims scale the mountain on foot, hiking straight upward, not taking an easier spiraling ascent. By the sixth century more then 3,000 stone steps, two stone gates, and a great many pilgrimage "stations" would be established at Sinai, with pilgrims climbing from St. Catherine's monastery (originally St. Mary's) at the foot of the holy mountain to its peak. Egeria's arduous climb to Sinai marked the beginning of a long tradition, that of the ascent of Mount Sinai's "ladder to God," which evolved as a figure of typology in literature, art, and architecture in the later Middle Ages and Renaissance.[2]

In Jerusalem, a city bustling with new construction and teeming with people, Egeria visits buildings in their pristine freshness, resplendent with cloisters, fountains, and colonnades. The place is crowded to the jostling point with the faithful, for whom hostels and inns provide refreshment and shelter. Although Jerome, who had moved to Bethlehem in 385, maintained that holy Jerusalem had its share of the usual thieves, murderers, poisoners, idolaters, and adulterers like any other metropolis, the city seemed, in the eyes of Eusebius, to be the "new Jerusalem," the jeweled heavenly citadel of the Apocalypse.

Paula and her daughter Eustochium, two of Jerome's closest friends, write from the convent Paula has founded in Bethlehem to the widowed Marcella in Rome, urging her to join them. The women also find Jerusalem a little worldly for their tastes—too many churches, too many foreigners. They prefer the rustic tranquility and quieter music of "Christ's village," where even the plowman sings hymns and alleluias, and the farmer chants David's psalms while he trims his vines with a curved knife. In the confusion of the big city, they observe, the babel of psalm singers betokens as many choirs as there are nations. But the city's atmosphere, gala with the joyful noise of hymns, inspires Bishop Asterius of Amasea, a contemporary of Egeria's, to exclaim that "without the martyrs our life would have no festivals!"[3]

Women were conspicuous in this busy time and place, pursuing their own good works in the holy cities. Olympias of Constantinople, descended from a powerful court magnate, became a deaconess of piously ascetic habits who used her wealth to support the church there. She dispensed alms to the poor and, with her letter-writing, encouraged the newly designated bishop of Constantinople, John Chrysostom. Many travelers flocking to the graves of the saints and to the Holy Land were women. Some are hardly more than names about whom a few details are known: devout Bassa, superior of a monastery, or lady Flavia, founder of a church of the martyr Julian on the Mount of Olives. Others are very well documented.

Perhaps the most renowned of the early visitors was Helena, Emperor Constantine's elderly mother, whom he had sent to Jerusalem in 325 or 326 to supervise his building program. Helena's finding the wood of the True Cross, the *lignum crucis*, was a report that began circulating not long after her death in 329, upon her return to Constantinople. There are at least half a dozen observers testifying to the event, and their accounts emanate from Gelasius, who was then the Bishop of Caesarea. Egeria reports (chap. 25.9) that under Helena's supervision, the Church of the Holy Sepulchre in Jerusalem was built by Constantine, and decorated with gold, mosaic, and precious marble. Oddly, however, she does not mention Helena's role, and Eusebius remains silent about the alleged discovery as well.

But Bishop Ambrose of Milan wrote in 395 a full account of Helena's "finding," in which he praised her lowly origins as an innkeeper (*stabularia*) and pleasing to God. The finding legend would become permanently fixed in the Christian imagination throughout the entire Middle Ages. The eighth-century Old English poem *Elene* portrays her as a militant questing voyager and challenger of the Jews.

While Helena's visit was religious in effect, her arrival as the Augusta, moving in state throughout her son's vast dominions, took on the style and purposes of an imperial procession. Lavishly attended, she visited provinces beyond the Holy Land, bestowing gifts, hearing petitions, and freeing unfortunates. She became the paradigm, and set the tone for other women of rank and prestige who would move from shrine to shrine, their aims more purely pilgrim-like, but women who would wield unmistakable influence through the grandeur of their humility.[4]

Paula and Eustochium were pilgrims from the west. Of Paula Jerome wrote: "She prostrated herself before the Cross and worshiped as though she could see the Lord hanging there. Entering the Sepulchre of the Resurrection, she kissed the Stone which the angel had removed from its mouth. And with faithful lips she touched the place where the Lord's body had lain, as a thirsty man drinks welcome water." The pilgrim's emotional and bodily involvement is illustrated by another woman, Megetia, who at a shrine at Uzalis beat so hard on the protective grille that it gave way. Pushing inside, she laid her head on the relics and wept on them.[5]

Other wellborn women journeying from the west were Silvia (related to a praetorian prefect), Poemenia (member of the imperial family), the elder Melania (a noble matron who was Olympias's mentor), and her granddaughter Melania. Poemenia founded her Church of the Ascension on the Mount of Olives. Nearby on the same site, Melania the elder built her monastery between 377 and 400, offering hospitality to fifty virgins. Like Egeria, this Melania was of Spanish origin. Inasmuch as the

Emperor Theodosius (the Great) was from their homeland, born in the province of Segovia, it is very likely that the women had friends in the imperial court, whether the emperor himself, or his numerous Spanish attendants.[6]

Egeria's journey begins with her celebrating Easter in Constantinople in 381, an occasion that must have been sacral and social as well as momentous, for the Second Ecumenical Council was held there from May to July, 381, in confirmation of Catholic Christianity. Although it may seem odd that the author mentions neither Theodosius nor other luminaries of the imperial court, it should be noted that she does not identify her monastic hosts either. There is a marked absence of names and living personalities in the *Itinerarium*.

Nor does she pay heed to current events, to the raging of the barbarians at every frontier. "Above all, it must be recognized," wrote the anonymous author of *De rebus bellicis (On Warlike Matters)*, on conditions around 366–75, "that wild nations are pressing upon the Roman Empire and howling round about it everywhere, and treacherous barbarians are assailing every frontier."

Paula's and Jerome's friend, Marcella, would be mercilessly battered by soldiers ransacking her house in Rome. Jerome wrote: "I cannot enumerate without horror all the calamities of our age. For the last twenty years and more, Roman blood has been shed daily between Constantinople and the Julian Alps, Scythia, Thrace, Macedonia, Dardania, Dacia, Thessaly, Achaea, Epirus, Dalmatia, and both Pannonias have lain prey to Goths, Sarmatians, Quadi, Alans, Huns, Vandals, and Marcomans who have ravaged, destroyed and pillaged them." The Sueves, Alans, and Vandals would soon invade Egeria's homeland.

In 381, a few months before the Council of Constantinople, the career of the old Visigothic chieftain, Athanaric, a long-term enemy of the Romans, culminated dramatically. Deserted by his own people, Athanaric managed to reach Constantinople where he surrendered himself to the Romans. Two weeks later he died. Theodosius, by way of displaying Rome's power and desire for peace, gave him a solemn state funeral. Visigothic soldiers were even then banqueting and rioting in Theodosius's imperial court, with Theodosius using extreme stratagems to split their strength when he could—heaping feasts and favors on some, inviting them to his tent, urging rivalries to smoulder, and inciting deadly brawls.

Egeria fails to observe any of this. Her attention remains single-mindedly riveted on her subject of the Christian journey.

Who was Egeria? Since the discovery in 1884 of the unique and incomplete manuscript of her journey, investigations have brought details of her identity to light. In about 650, the Spanish hermit monk Valerius of Vierzo wrote a letter to his brothers, holding up Egeria as a model of pious vigor. Although she was a representative of "feeble womanhood," her example, he said, ought to reduce them all to blushes of shame considering their own robust strength. He was praising the "nun," the *sanctimonialis Aetheria* who centuries earlier had written about her strenuous pilgrimage to the East. Valerius identified her home as Vierzo, like his own, far to the northwest of Spain: "from the farthest shore of the ocean on the west" (*extremo occidui maris Oceani litore exorta*).[7]

Valerius was an observer of Christian Latin culture in Spain under the Visigothic kings of Toledo. Although churches had existed in Spain as early as the 250s, and Catholicism had begun to take hold, a sturdy paganism was still well rooted in the rustic mentality. Theodosius himself might outlaw pagan customs in his Codes of 380, and command the destruction of pagan temples, but the magical cults died hard. Divinations and propitiatory rites were held in houses, at crossroads, and by fountains and rivers, sacred groves, and stones. When rustic altars attracted too much attention, the rites went underground and would thrive there quietly for centuries to come.[8]

At the same time, a form of Christian monastic living was developing. Egeria belonged, it seems, to a house of consecrated women in Galicia, a community of which there were many kinds and orders, not necessarily cloistered and still able to move about freely. She may have been a deaconess, for she greets the deaconess Marthana at Thecla's shrine as a dear friend. She addresses her book to ladies (*dominae*) in her own country, and one in particular as "Your Grace" (*affectio vestra*). Although she has been identified at different times as Silvania, Silvia, Echeria, or Aetheria, scholarly opinion generally agrees on calling her Egeria.[9]

Egeria is thought to have made her trip between 381 and 384. Her itinerary[10] probably began with the celebration of Easter in Constantinople in 381. From there she traveled southward to Jerusalem, then descended further south to Egypt where she visited the monks at Thebes, a trip that took her from 381 to 383. Returning to Galilee and *Jerusalem* in 383, when she may have made her notes on the liturgy, she then journeyed south again to reach *Mount Sinai* by January 384. Going back again to the Galilee region she took several side excursions before leaving Jerusalem to journey north to Antioch. From Antioch she moved northeast to *Edessa*, arriving there in April 384. A month later, in May 384, she traveled west along the coast to visit the shrine of *St. Thecla at Isauria* in the province of Seleucia. Upon her final arrival in Constantinople, in June or July of 384, she writes to her sisters that she is off to St. John's in Ephesus.

In contrast to these zigzagging peregrinations, the book of the *Itinerarium* is organized according to its own logic. There are two main divisions. The first, wide-ranging part of the work, moves from Sinai and Egypt, tracing the steps of the Israelites in Exodus, moving northward through Palestine, Syria, and Mesopotamia before heading back toward Constantinople. The second part focuses on the sites, buildings, and liturgy of one city, Jerusalem.

The extant manuscript of the first part begins in the middle of a sentence. These opening paragraphs are given below in the first selection. The traveler's literary response to the Holy Land's breathtaking topography has been called stylistically bland. As she notes several times, the land appears "immense and very smooth." Egeria's plain, unpretentious sentences flow as smoothly into one another as do the pale features of her land-scape as she perceives it. Her voice runs on. Clauses are more often linked paratactically by "and" rather than by subordin-ating conjunctions which would express more complex relationships of thought.

It would seem that the interaction between this topo-graphy and this viewer does not demand the psychological and syntactical complexity that a more romantic or egotistical

traveler might experience and strive to express. What is called
for is *sermo humilis*, the plain speech that St. Augustine took note
of and through whose limpid purity marvels can shine. Here the
Israelites died for their greed, here they worshiped the Golden
Calf, here Moses heard God speak from the Burning Bush, still
budding. What verbal variety is needed? The eloquent panorama
extends placidly through space and endures through time,
astounding less for its diversity than for the ageless events it
contains.

Egeria examines the spot where Lot's wife became a pillar
of salt. She doesn't pretend it's still there, having sunk
apparently into the Dead Sea. She passes the Red Sea at Clysma.
As she moves north, her stops include the graves of Job and
Moses, the pool of John the Baptist near Salem, and Abraham's
house at Carrae. Her visits to King Abgar's palace at Edessa in
the province of Osrhoene, and to Thecla's shrine at Seleucia in
Isauria—both from this first part of the *Itinerarium*—are the
sources of the next two translated passages.

The Abgar Epistles were a Christian document of popular
renown. Although Pope Gelasius eventually declared them
apocryphal in 494, they continued to be rewritten with the piling
on of fresh miracles. In his *History of the Church* Eusebius recorded the texts of Abgar's and Jesus' letters, which he found in
Edessa. Abgar invites Jesus to the palace in Edessa, hoping to be
cured of an illness. He has heard of the Savior's healing the sick
and raising the dead without the use of herbs or potions—simply
with *words*.

Jesus replies in a letter that he is unable to accept the royal
invitation, since he has to fulfill his mission. He promises to send
a disciple:

> Happy are you who believed in me without having seen
> me! For it is written of me that those who have seen me
> will not believe in me, and that those who have not seen
> me will believe and live. As to your request that I should
> come to you, I must complete all that I was sent to do here,
> and on completing it must at once be taken up to the One
> who sent me. When I have been taken up I will send you
> one of my disciples to cure your disorder and bring life to
> you and those with you. And your fortress shall be
> blessed, and no enemy shall rule over it forever.[11]

Legend had it that Jesus entrusted his letter and a portrait of himself to the messenger Ananias. After the Ascension of Jesus, the Apostle Thomas sent Thaddeus, one of the seventy designated disciples, to Edessa.

This letter, resembling the Gospel of John,[12] was welcomed as genuine in England and Ireland in the eighth century. A lection, the liturgical reading for a particular day, contains a copy of Jesus' letter to Abgar. The rubric indicates that "no one who carries it will be harmed by his enemies or their spells [*carmina*], by the snares of the Devil, by hail or thunder, at home or in the city, by sea or land, by day or night." The lection casts light on Alcuin's protest against those who carry gospel sayings written on parchment worn around their necks instead of in their hearts.[13]

Egeria preserves a lively account of her visit to the palace, where she learns how Jesus' epistle miraculously foiled the city's enemies, the Persians, only twenty years earlier. She secures copies of the letters from the bishop of Edessa; their authenticity interests her, and she is convinced that she has received the most complete version.

Soon after leaving Edessa, Egeria heads for the shrine of St. Thecla, whose tomb was believed to be at Meriamlik, just outside Seleucia, in the Roman province of Isauria. This Isaurian sanctuary was the saint's most important; hordes of pilgrims frequented it. Thecla had a strong following, as the many versions of her legend show in Greek, Latin, Syriac, Armenian, Slavonic, and Arabic. Her fifth-century *Life* by Basil of Seleucia was based on the Acts of Paul and Thecla, current in the second century.

Thecla's legend tells of a highborn virgin of Iconium in Asia Minor, who has overheard St. Paul preaching in a neighbor's house. Smitten—at the apostle's words—with a fervor for virginity and asceticism, Thecla refuses to wed the man to whom she is betrothed. When Paul is arrested for hindering the young from lawful marriage, Thecla visits him in prison and sits at his feet, enthralled by his doctrine. Paul is beaten and driven from the city, while the girl is ordered to be burned alive. Numerous adventures and escapes follow some involving wild beasts, with Thecla's continually seeking out

Paul. A noteworthy feature of the life is Thecla's cutting her hair and wearing male clothing. Thecla spends her final years as an anchoress dwelling in caves near Seleucia, and baptizes herself on the last day of her life. Her feast is September 23 or 24.[14]

Despite, or maybe because of, the legend's sprucing up with the frank stuff of romance, the cult of Thecla persisted. Tertullian, Athanasius, Jerome, and Ambrose regarded her as an actual person. Claudian Claudianus, the fourth-century Christian poet (author of the well-known *Rape of Proserpine*) mocks the Romans in a satiric verse for relying on the saints to fend off the barbarians: "May the hand of St. Thecla grant success to the Roman forces!" Venantius Fortunatus honors her in his poem *Ad virgines* (book viii.4). In eighth-century England girls are named Thecla, while in the ninth century she appears in the *Old English Martyrology* along with Euphemia of Chalcedon, both saints of Asia Minor. By the eleventh century she is one of the virgins charmingly revered in a lyric by Sigibert of Gembloux. "Here Is the Holy Throng of Virgins" pictures an endless stream of girls who wander in a field to pick flowers, red roses for the Passion with the lilies and violets of love:

> *Hinc virginalis sancta frequentia,*
> *Gertrudis, Agnes, Prisca, Cecilia,*
> *Lucia, Petronilla, Tecla*
> *Agatha, Barbara, Juliana*

The reading of the The Acts of Thecla in Egeria's presence would have regaled the faithful. As Thecla's cult grew, the emperor Zeno had her basilica magnificently rebuilt a century after Egeria's visit. Basil's *Life* describes the majestic ceremonies at that time, as well as the eagerness of the mobs in spite of the heat, dust, and elbowing confusion.

In sum, this first part of the *Itinerarium* charts the journey to Sinai and the route of Exodus (chaps. 1–9); the visits to Mount Nebo where Moses died (chaps. 10–12), Job's tomb (chaps. 13–16), the tomb of St. Thomas the Apostle and the Palace of Abgar in Edessa, and Abraham's house in Haran (chaps. 17–21); the meeting with Marthana at the tomb of St. Thecla in Isauria, and the journey on to the Basilica of St. Euphemia in Chalcedon (chaps. 22–23).

After her wider travels, the second division of Egeria's *Itinerarium* concentrates on the daily liturgy and the liturgical year, together with buildings and sites in and around Jerusalem. Its topics are the divine office and the Sunday liturgy (chap. 24 and beginning chap. 25); the Epiphany (end of chap. 25); the Feast of the Presentation (chap. 26); Lent and its customs (chaps. 27–28); Holy Week, concluding with the Easter Vigil (chaps. 29–38); Easter (chaps. 39–41); the Feast of the fortieth day after Easter (chap. 42); Pentecost and the time that follows (chap. 43–44); the preparation of catechumens for Baptism (chaps. 45–47); and the feast of the Dedication of the Basilica of the Holy Sepulchre (chaps. 48–49).

This division forms a smaller, more intense pilgrimage. Egeria tells of the Churches of the Nativity at Bethlehem, and of Lazarus at Bethany. On the Mount of Olives she describes the holy site of the Ascension, called *Imbomon* ("on the hillock"), where a church would soon be built, as well as the church called *Eleona*, erected over the grotto where Christ taught the apostles after his Ascension. Inside Jerusalem she visits the Church of Sion, on which site the Last Supper was shared in an upper room. She elaborately describes the sanctuaries of the Holy Sepulchre on Golgotha.

From the Jerusalem portion of the diary is translated Egeria's glowing depiction of the Easter Vigils. She is the first to document the veneration of the Cross (the *adoratio crucis*), an Eastern ceremony conducted in Jerusalem and already well developed at this date, although it was not adopted in Rome until the seventh century. Her testimony is extremely valuable, for it proves that the Cross had been believed found, whether by Helena or by a nameless noblewoman and a bishop. Since Egeria mentions that several bishops participated in the ceremony, it is very likely that Gelasius, the Bishop of Caesarea who originated the account of the Finding of the Cross, was present.

The Adoration of the Cross formed the basis of a liturgical custom that eventually entered the drama of the medieval church. In the ninth century, Amalarius, Bishop of Metz, managed to incorporate the adoration rite into the mass, although he encountered some initial resistance to this novelty. In England in about 970, St. Ethelwold of Winchester compiled the *Regularis Concordia* ("Monastic Agreement") for the use of English monks and nuns. The text includes stage directions telling two deacons to hold the veiled cross and sing: "Behold the wood of the Cross" (*Ecce lignum crucis*).[15] The ritual, perceived as a dramatic gesture, opened the way to the fully fledged Easter play.

Egeria's description is an important one for its visualization and tactile enactment—lips to Cross—of a devotion that, combined with liturgy, would bestow a symbolic form to the earliest religious theater. Her report contains some earthy realism, besides, about the faithful who may be tempted to nip off souvenir bites of the sacred wood. Contributing to the spectacle, as Egeria recounts it, are the flares of the candlelight processional as the noisily groaning faithful make their way through the city, commemorating the agony, arrest, scourging, and crucifixion of Jesus.

Egeria explains how on Holy Thursday the people have held vigil from midnight to cockcrow on the hill of the Ascension on the Mount of Olives. They then move on to an elegant church, built on the site where Jesus prayed after he had parted from his disciples and just before his betrayal. The people will remain in church for prayer, hymns, and gospel readings. The Good Friday ceremony leading to the veneration of the Cross is the subject of the fifth passage below.

Page numbers refer to the text of the *Itinerarium Egeriae* edited by Franceschini and Weber.

1. "These Were Shown According to the Scriptures"

... These were shown according to the Scriptures. As we walked, meanwhile, we arrived at a certain place where the mountains through which we journeyed opened out into an immense valley, wide, very smooth, and especially lovely, and across the valley appeared Sinai, the holy mountain of God. Now this place where the mountains opened out is joined to that place where the Memorials of Greed are situated.[16] As soon as we arrived in that place, those holy guides who accompanied us gave us advice and said, "It is the custom for those who come here to offer up a prayer from the location where the mountain of God first comes into view," and consequently we did so. From that place to the mountain of God it was about four miles in all to traverse the valley, which, as I said, is immense.

Now the valley itself is very vast, lying below the edge of the mountain of God, which, as far as we could gauge with our eyes or as they themselves said, is almost sixteen miles long, and they described it as four miles wide. This was the same valley we had to cross in order to climb the mountain. It was in this same immense and extremely smooth valley that the children of Israel lingered while the sainted Moses ascended the mountain of the Lord and remained there forty days and forty nights. This, too, is the valley where the calf was made, and the location is pointed out to this day, for a great stone was fixed there, and it stands on the very site. And furthermore, this is that same valley at whose head is the place where the sainted Moses grazed the flocks of his father-in-law and where God spoke to him once again from the burning bush. (*Itinerarium*, chaps. 1–2, pp. 37–38)

2. From the Summit of Mount Sinai to Mount Horeb

Really, on the summit of Mount Sinai itself there is nothing but the church and the cave where the sainted Moses was. No one lives there. A reading from the whole Book of Moses was held in that very place, the offering was made in the correct way, and we received communion.

As we were about to leave the Church, the priests gave us blessed gifts,[17] that is, fruits that grow on the mountain. Now this sacred Mount Sinai is completely rockbound, so that no shrubs will grow. But down at the foot of these mountains—either this one which is in the middle, or those around it—there is a small patch of earth where the holy monks diligently set their little trees and orchards and beds of cultivation. Close to these they build their cells. Although it looks as if they have picked fruits from the mountain earth, they have actually raised them by the labor of their own hands.

After we received communion then, and the holy men had given us the blessed gifts, and we had come out the church door,

I started to ask them to show us each of the places. Right away those holy men agreed to show us every one. They pointed out that cave where the sainted man Moses was[18] when he climbed the mountain of God a second time to receive once again the tablets, after he had broken the first ones on account of the people's sins. They said besides they would also show us whatever we wanted to see, places they knew about themselves.

This I want you to know, cherished lady sisters, about the place where we were standing—that is, with the mountains all around us as we stood beside the church. We were gazing from the summit of the central mountain peak at the mountains below, which earlier had seemed nearly impossible for us to climb. I don't really think that I have ever seen any higher, except for the middle peak which is even higher. Now as we stood on that middle peak, those below us looked to be no more than little hills.

From there we could see Egypt and Palestine, the Red Sea, and the Parthenian Sea[19]—the part that flows to Alexandria—as well as the infinite boundaries of the Saracens.[20] All of this we saw spread below us.[21] I could scarcely believe it! Those holy men pointed out each sight to us.

We had been so desirous of seeing this that we had climbed eagerly. And now we began our descent from the summit of God's mountain, so that we might climb another mountain that is joined to it. This is called Horeb, and it is the place where the holy prophet Elijah fled from the sight of King Ahab, and the place where God said to him, "Why are you here, Elijah?" as it is written in the Books of the Kingdoms.[22] (*Itinerarium*, Chapters 3 and 4, pp. 40–41)

3. King Abgar's Letters

The holy bishop of the city[23] was a truly religious man, both monk and confessor.[24] He cordially welcomed me, and said to me, "I see, daughter, that because of your piety you have imposed upon yourself the great hardship of traveling to these places from the far ends of the earth. So if you wish, we shall show you the places the Christians rejoice to see." Giving thanks first to God, I begged him to be good enough to do what he had promised.

He led me first to the palace of King Abgar[25] where he showed me a huge statue of the king. Everyone said it was a very good likeness, fashioned of a marble as lustrous as pearl. It was evident, when one confronted those features face to face, that Abgar had been a wise and distinguished man. The holy bishop told me, "That is King Abgar, who, even before he saw the Lord, believed in him as the true son of God." Next to the statue was another one made of similar marble, which he said was a statue of Magnus, the king's son. The expression of the features had also something pleasing about it.

Next we entered an inner part of the palace, where we saw pools full of fish. I have never encountered fish of such great size, so hallowed, and so delicious.[26] There is no other source of water inside the city, except for this one that flows from the palace. It is like an immense silver river. The holy bishop then told me about this water:

"King Abgar wrote to the Lord, and some time afterward the Lord wrote back to Abgar, sending the letter by his courier Ananias, just as it is written in this same letter. Time went by. Then the Persians swooped down and encircled the city. Abgar immediately took the Lord's epistle to the city gate, together with his entire army, and he prayed before the people. He said, 'Lord Jesus, you promised us that no enemy should invade this city, but now the Persians are attacking us.' When he had said this, he held the open letter high in his upraised hands. Suddenly thick darkness fell outside the city, clouding the eyes of the Persians, who were packed around the city at a distance of three miles. They were quickly disoriented by the darkness, and could hardly set up their camp, let alone encircle the entire city at that distance of three miles.

"The Persians were so disorganized that they could find no way of gaining entrance to the city to launch their attack, so they posted guards around the locked city and held it under siege for several months. Eventually, when they saw there was no way of their getting to the city, they thought of forcing the inhabitants to die of thirst.

"Now, daughter, in those days, that little hill you see above the city furnished the city's water. Realizing this, the Persians diverted the water course away from the city and made it flow in a different direction, toward their own camp. Suddenly, on the very day and hour that the Persians diverted the flow of water, this fountain you see here in this spot gushed forth by God's command. From that day to this it has continued, by the grace of God. But at that very moment, the stream the Persians had diverted dried up, so that those who were besieging the city could not drink from it even for one day. It is that way now, for no drop of moisture has ever been seen flowing from it to this day.

"And so by the will of God who had promised it, they were forced to return at once to their home in Persia. Since then, whenever an enemy has wanted to attack the city, the letter has been brought out and read before the gate. Immediately, according to God's wish, all the enemy has been driven out."

The holy bishop informed me that these springs had gushed forth where formerly there had been a field within the city. The field lay below Abgar's palace. "It had been built, as you can see, on higher ground, for so it was customary to build palaces in those days. But after the fountains gushed forth here, Abgar built the palace for his son Magnus, whose statue you see beside his father's, so that the fountains might be enclosed within the palace walls."

It was particularly pleasing to me that I received these same letters from Abgar to the Lord and the Lord to Abgar, which the holy bishop read to us there. For although I have copies of them at home, I was quite pleased to accept these from him, in case the ones at home are lacking something. Certainly, the copy I was given here seems to have more in it. You will read them yourselves, ladies of my heart, when I return to our country, if Jesus our God wills it. (*Itinerarium*, chap. 19, pp. 60–62)

4. The Shrine of St. Thecla

St. Thecla's shrine is a three-day journey from Tarsus.[27] We were extremely happy to go there, especially since it was so close. I left Tarsus, still in the province of Cilicia, and arrived at a city called Pompeiopolis,[28] which is on the sea. From there I crossed the border into Isauria, where I stayed at the city of Corycus.[29] On the third day I reached a city called Seleucia of Isauria.[30] As soon as I arrived I visited the bishop, a very holy man who had been a monk. I also saw a most beautiful church in that city.

St. Thecla's is just outside the city on a flat hilltop about fifteen hundred paces away, and as I needed a place to sleep, I chose to go on and stay there. Near the holy church there is nothing but countless numbers of individual monastic cells for men and women both. And there I came upon a very dear friend of mine, a holy deaconess named Marthana.[31] Everyone in the East attests to her way of life. I knew her in Jerusalem when she had come up on pilgrimage for the purpose of prayer. Now she was supervising the cells of apotactites[32] or virgins. When she saw me, her pleasure and mine were so great that I am unable to describe it.

But let me get back to my subject. There are a great many monastic cells all about that same hill. In the middle a huge wall surrounds the church, which contains the shrine. The shrine itself is extremely beautiful. The reason for the wall's having been built is to protect the church against the Isaurians. They are a bad sort who often turn to banditry and must be prevented from trying anything against the monastery that is established there.

In the name of God, I arrived at the shrine, where they conducted both prayer and a reading of all the Acts of St. Thecla. I gave boundless thanks to Christ our God, that he deigned to fulfill my desires so completely, unworthy and undeserving though I am.

And so I remained two days, visiting the monks and the apotactites, both the men and women who were there. After prayer and communion, I turned back to Tarsus to resume my journey. I made my quarters there for three days; then in God's name I set out from there to continue my route. Then on the very day I set out, I arrived at a resting place called Mansocrene, at the foot of Mount Taurus.[33] There I put up for the night.

The next day we went up Mount Taurus. We resumed a route that was familiar to us, since on our way out we had already crossed through each province, namely Cappadocia, Galatia, and Bithynia. I reached Chalcedon, where there is a shrine much talked about, that of St. Euphemia.[34] I had long known about it, and I stopped there.

On the following day I crossed the sea and arrived at Constantinople. I thanked Christ our God, who deigned to grant me such grace, despite my lack of worth and merit. For he deigned to grant me not only the will to go on this journey, but also the ability to ramble everywhere I wished and, finally, to return to Constantinople. When I got there, I never ceased giving thanks in all the churches, the shrine of the apostles, and those many martyrs' shrines to Jesus our God, who so deigned to grant me his mercy.

Ladies, light of mine, once I have sent this letter to Your Grace from this place where I am now, it is my plan to go up, in Christ's name, to Ephesus in Asia. I want to pray at the shrine of the blessed apostle John.[35]

If indeed after this I am still alive and able to learn about other places, I shall either tell you about them myself when I am with you—God willing—or I shall report them to Your Grace. Certainly, if anything else occurs to my mind, I shall write about it. I beg you, ladies, light of my eyes, to deign to remember me, whether in this bodily life, or beyond the body hereafter.[36] (*Itinerarium*, chaps. 22–23, pp. 65–67)

5. Good Friday in Jerusalem and the Adoration of the Cross

Then all the people, even the smallest children, go down to Gethsemane[37] on foot, together with the bishop. They sing hymns. There is such a great crowd of people, and they are so worn out with their nightlong vigil and weakened from each day's fasting, that they descend the steep hill to Gethsemane very slowly. They sing hymns as they go. More than two hundred church candles light their way.[38]

When everyone has arrived in Gethsemane, the proper prayer is read first, then the hymn is sung. The gospel passage is read recounting Jesus' arrest. During the reading there is such howling and roaring among the people, along with weeping, that it is likely that the people's groans can be heard at the far end of the city. And now they walk, singing hymns, and they arrive at the gate at an hour when they can recognize one another. From there they go through the middle of the city together. Old and young, rich and poor, all appear there on this special day when no one leaves the vigil before morning. In this manner the bishop is escorted from Gethsemane to the gate, and from the gate through the entire city to the Cross.

When they have arrived before the Cross, the day is already beginning to grow light. There, finally, they read the whole gospel account of how the Lord was led before Pilate and all that was written that Pilate said to the Lord and to the Jews.

After this the bishop speaks to the people, comforting them, since they have suffered such exertions through the night and will continue to do so during this day. He urges them not to be weary but to hope in God, since their exertions will be richly rewarded. Comforting them as much as he can, he tells them, "Go, for now, each of you to your homes, and sit down a while. Then at the second hour of the day [8 o'clock] be back here so that until the sixth hour [noon] you will be able to see the sacred wood of the Cross, trusting that it will assure future salvation for each of us. From that hour of noon on, when we must gather here again before the Cross, we must conduct readings and prayers until nightfall."

The sun has still not yet risen when the people are dismissed from the Cross. Those who are stalwart go on to pray at Sion, at the pillar where the Lord was scourged.[39] Then people go back home to rest for a little while, but before long everyone is back. A bishop's throne is set up on Golgotha, behind the Cross which now stands there.[40] The bishop is seated on his throne and a linen-covered table is placed before him. Deacons stand around the table. The silver coffer, ornamented with gold, is brought which contains the sacred wood of the true Cross. The coffer is opened and the wood of the Cross is displayed on the table together with the superscription.[41]

While the Cross is on the table, the bishop, remaining seated, holds down the ends of the holy wood with his hands.[42] The deacons also guard it as they stand around him. They all now guard it this way for it is customary for the people to approach the table one by one, both the faithful and the catechumens. They bow to the table, kiss the sacred wood, and then move along. I don't know when it was, but someone is said to have bitten off a piece of the sacred wood and stolen it. For this reason it is guarded now by the deacons who surround it, so that no one will dare to do this again.

Now all the people pass before it one by one, bowing and touching it first with the forehead, then with the eyes. Then they kiss it before they move on. No one, however, reaches out a hand to touch it. (*Itinerarium*, chaps. 36–37, pp. 79–81)

NOTES

1. Eusebius, Bishop of Caesarea (260–340 A.D.) in Palestine, mentions this. G.A. Williamson, trans., *The History of the Church from Christ to Constantine* (New York: Penguin, 1967), book 4, chap. 26, p. 189.

2. John G. Demaray, *Dante and the Book of the Cosmos* (Philadelphia: The American Philosophical Society, 1987), traces the artistic transformation of physical pilgrimage into sacred geography, mapping, and typology. On Sinai, see pp. 26–28.

3. E.D. Hunt, *Holy Land Pilgrimage in the Later Roman Empire: A.D. 312–460* (Oxford: Clarendon P, 1982), pp. 8 and 23 (on Eusebius and Asterius). "The Letter of Paula and Eustochium" is translated in *The Palestine Pilgrim's Text Society* (London, 1889), I: 9–16; D. Ruiz Bueno, ed., *Cartas de San Jerónimo*, 2 vols. (Madrid, 1962), I: 318–334 (Letter 46); and *PL* 22.325–1197.

4. Kenneth G. Holum, "Hadrian and St. Helena: Imperial Travel and the Origins of Christian Holy Land Pilgrimage," in *The Blessings of Pilgrimage*, ed. Robert Osterhout (U of Illinois P, 1990), pp. 66–81. And see Jan Willem Drijvers, *Helena Augusta*, trans. Brill, (Leiden, 1992); Stephan Borgehammar, *How the Holy Cross Was Found: From Event to*

Medieval Event, Bibliotheca theologiae practicae 47 (Stockholm: Almquist & Wiksell, 1991).

5. Jerome's Letter 108 to Eustochium is cited in John Wilkinson, *Egeria's Travels*, p. 20. Letters of Jerome, notably this one, along with his commentaries and lists of recommended reading proved popular. One such document appears among the belongings of a seventh century English abbess. Patrick Sims-Williams, *Religion and Literature in Western England, 600–800* (Cambridge: Cambridge UP, 1990), p. 196 and note.

On Megetia, see Peter Brown, *The Cult of the Saints* (Chicago: U of Chicago P, 1981), p. 88, from the "Miracles of Stephen," *Patrologia Latina* 41.847.

6. E. D. Hunt remarks, "It is hard to deny some connexion with Theodosius and his predominantly Spanish entourage . . . Egeria's own arrival in the capital is concurrent with this drift of the emperor's supporters from his western homeland." *Holy Land and Pilgrimage*, pp. 164–65.

7. Vierzo (or Bierzo) was the Roman town of Bergidum in the province of Leon, near Galicia. The letter is translated in John Wilkinson, *Egeria's Travels*, pp. 174–178.

8. Joyce N. Hillgarth, "Popular Religion in Visigothic Spain," in *Visigothic Spain: New Approaches*, ed. Edward James (Oxford: Clarendon P, 1980), pp. 3–60.

9. Her name is discussed by Gringas, *Egeria: Diary*, pp. 2–7, and Wilkinson, *Egeria's Travels*, pp. 235–236.

10. Locations in italics pertain to the translations below, which are presented, however, in the order in which they appear in the *Itinerarium*.

11. Eusebius, *History of the Church*, p. 67, and Wilkinson, *Egeria's Travels*, pp. 151–152.

12. John 20.29: "Blessed are they that have not seen and yet have believed."

13. Patrick Sims-Williams, *Religion and Literature*, p. 295 and note.

14. For the Acts of Paul and Thecla, see M.R. James, *The Apocryphal New Testament* (Oxford UP, 1953), pp. 272–281; also, *Vita Theclae*, in *Vie et Miracles de Sainte Thècle*, ed. G. Dagron, Subsidia Hagiographica 62 (Brussels: Société des Bollandistes, 1978).

Peter Brown analyzes the appeal of Thecla's legend in *The Body and Society: Men, Women, and Sexual Renunciation in Early Christianity* (Columbia UP, 1988), especially pp. 156–59, 328–329, and her portrayal as the Socratic chairperson in the *Symposium* of Methodius (third century), p. 184. John Anson's "The Female Transvestite in Early Monasticism," *Viator* 5 (1974): 1–32, treats the cross-dressing theme.

15.   O.B. Hardison, "The Lenten Agon," essay 3 in *Christian Rite and Christian Drama in the Middle Ages* (Baltimore: The Johns Hopkins Press, 1965), notably pp. 128–134, 192–198 and passim.

16.   The burial place (*sepulchra concupiscentiae* of the Vulgate) of the Israelites whom God struck with a plague for devouring the flesh of quails (Numbers 11.32–34). Tomblike structures littered the valley, according to Peter the Deacon, the twelfth-century librarian of Monte Cassino.

17.   The *eulogia*, or "blessed gift," sometimes meant the mass wafer, or any sanctified offering or token of friendship. In the pilgrimage context, *eulogia* specifically meant a holy souvenir. Very often it was a small decorated vial or ampoule (*ampulla*) containing sacred earth, oil, or water. But the blessing might be simply verbal or, in the case of Egeria, the fruit of the monks' labor. See Cynthia Hahn, "Loca Sancta Souvenirs: Sealing the Pilgrim's Experience," in *The Blessings of Pilgrimage*, ed. Robert Osterhout (Chicago: U of Illinois P, 1990), pp. 85–96.

18.   Exodus 33.22.

19.   The eastern Mediterranean.

20.   Egeria's is one of the early uses of the word *Saraceni*, from the Arabic *sharquiyin*, "easterners," to indicate the peoples of a region of Arabia (John Wilkinson, *Egeria's Travels*, p. 215). Jerome uses the word and so does the historian Ammianus Marcellinus.

21.   Guides informed the pilgrims that the blue haze visible from the peak was actually the water, though modern visitors say that it cannot be seen.

22.   I Kings 19.9. Egeria uses titles for books of the Bible that correspond to the old Latin translation from the Greek Old Testament. "The Books of the Kingdoms" referred to both Samuel and Kings. Jerome was still translating the Vulgate (for which he would use the Hebrew), and would not finish it until 404 (Wilkinson, pp. 6, 215).

23.   Egeria's party of pilgrims has arrived in the city of Edessa (mod. Urfa), which meant a twenty-five-day journey from Jerusalem. But no Christian coming to the Holy Land, she writes, failed to visit this city. Rich in sculptures and mosaics, Edessa was the stronghold of Syriac-speaking Christendom, and the location of the first Christian edifice. Egeria's party had already visited the city's most treasured relic, the remains of St. Thomas the Apostle, buried outside the walls. On Edessa, see J.B. Segal, *Edessa: "The Blessed City"* (Oxford: Clarendon P,

1970); Cyril Mango, *Byzantium: The Empire of the New Rome* (London: Weidenfeld and Nicolson, 1980).

24. A confessor was a Christian who had heroically acknowledged and suffered for the faith without having attained martyrdom. Of the three "confessor" bishops Egeria admires in Mesopotamia, two at least—Eulogius of Edessa and Protogenes of Carrhae—had resisted the Arians and had endured exile to Egypt under the emperor Valens. E.D. Hunt, *Holy Land Pilgrimage*, p. 165.

25. Abgar V, called Ukkama (the Black), signifying that he was blind or dark-skinned, was one of a Mesopotamian dynasty of kings that had lasted 375 years in Edessa. A contemporary of Jesus, Abgar reigned between 4 B.C. and 50 A.D. But the story of his correspondence with Jesus sprang up in about the middle of the third century, under Abgar IX, who was the first Christian king of Osrhoene.

26. The famed fish pools of Edessa, surviving to this day, and the springs that fed them, were the subject of ancient lore and practice. The sacred wells of healing waters surrounded by statuary were the scene of rites honoring the Syrian mother goddess Atargatis (the Greek Hera). Mermaid effigies can be seen today in the museum at Urfa.

27. Tarsus, capital of the province of Cilicia, was St. Paul's birthplace (Acts 21.39).

28. This ancient seacoast city of Soloi, destroyed in 91 B.C. and the refuge of pirates, was rebuilt in 63 B.C. by Pompey. Its ruins and long row of Corinthian columns can still be seen not far from the beach of Viransehir in Turkey.

29. The modern Turkish city of Korgos. Cicero, when governor of Cilicia, lived here between 52 and 50 B.C.

30. Founded in the third century B.C., and so called to distinguish it from several other cities of the same name. The modern Silifke is about three miles north of the old city.

31. Deaconesses in the third and fourth centuries were charged with charity, hospitality, the care of the poor and sick, and the supervision of ecclesiastical widows and virgins. Eastern deaconesses fulfilled clerical functions, administering the sacraments to women in particular. In the absence of clergy they would have read the sacred texts and attended to the lamps and oil of the altar. Like deacons, they were expected to assist bishops. Marthana, the only living person named in Egeria's book, was praised by Basil in his *Life of St. Thecla*.

32. The name for ascetic sects in the third and fourth centuries in Cilicia, Pamphylia and Phrygia, referring to men and women who aspired to special purity by practicing rigorous fasts and other

penances. Egeria seems to use the term synonymously with "virgins" as those given to renunciation, though elsewhere she uses the Greek *parthenae* for virgins. Egeria's abundant scattering of Greek vocabulary has been noted by Väänänen (*Journal-Epître*, p.135). "The reading of the lessons in church had to be done in Greek," writes Egeria (chap. 47, 3–4).

33. Mansocrene or Mopsucrene was a usual stopping place between Tarsus and the Cilician Gateway (mod. Gulek Pass) through the Taurus slopes. The latter is mountain range along the southern coast of Turkey.

34. Chalcedon, the modern Turkish city of Kadiköy, was colonized in the seventh century B.C. and faced Byzantium on the Bosphorus. The cult of the Bithynian martyr Euphemia (d. 307) was founded in Egeria's time. Her feast (September 16) enjoyed high popularity, in both East and West. Bishop Asterius of Amasea (ca. 400) mentioned tablets or paintings depicting stages of her martyrdom: before the judge, tormented by having her teeth drawn with hammer and auger, sentenced to the pyre. The Council of Chalcedon in 451 attributed its success to her protection. The relics were later translated from her church in Chalcedon to St. Sophia in Constantinople. The sixth-century poet Venantius Fortunatus singled her out in his poem on virgins. Euphemia and Thecla both appear in the *Old English Martyrology*.

35. The tomb of John the Apostle was the chief pilgrim attraction of Ephesus, rich in history, and Egeria is the first to mention it. As late as 416, as St. Augustine reports, John was supposed not to be dead but asleep, awaiting Christ's Second Coming. Revered since the second century, the tomb was in Egeria's day the construction site of an important church, completed in 420.

Ephesus owed some of its ancient fame to its cult of Artemis, an issue that had occasioned the great theater riot that St. Paul notes in Acts 19.21–41. The partly restored temple of the goddess was still used when Egeria was in Ephesus. Now a major Christian center, the capital of the proconsular province of Asia and the wealthiest city of Roman Asia Minor, Ephesus was a seaport strategically placed for travel and trade. In 431 it would be the site of the Third Ecumenical Council.

36. This section, occurring midway through the *Itinerarium*, imparts a sense of closure with its expressions of thanksgiving and farewell. The broader "itinerary" ends, for Egeria proceeds next to her descriptions of Jerusalem.

37. The garden to which Jesus went with the disciples after the Last Supper, immediately before his betrayal and arrest. He withdrew a

stone's throw from them to pray that the cup might be taken away from him (Luke 22.41; Matthew 26.36–42).

38. Candles provided light as well as commemorating Jesus' arrest by a band of men with lanterns and torches (John 18.3).

39. In 404 St. Jerome wrote that the pillar where Pilate scourged Jesus was still stained with blood and now supported the church at Sion.

40. Golgotha, Aramaic for "skull," from the shape of the hill, was later called Calvary and lay outside the ancient city of Jerusalem. The Cross standing here in Egeria's account is not the "true" Cross, which will be displayed later.

41. The derisory rebuke "Jesus of Nazareth, The King of the Jews" (John 19.19) is variously worded in Matthew 27.37, Mark 15.26, and Luke 23.38.

42. This is the same cross before which Eustochium knelt, overcome with emotion, like the faithful who file by here one by one. It is clear that only a fragment of it was seen by Egeria, a piece having been sent to Constantinople, from which city Radegund later received her slender relics (see below, chapter 5). Other fragments may have similarly been in circulation.

FURTHER READING

Peter Brown. "'Daughters of Jerusalem': The Ascetic Life of Women in the Fourth Century." Chap. 13 in *The Body and Society: Men, Women, and Sexual Renunciation in Early Christianity*. New York: Columbia UP, 1988.

Mary B. Campbell. *The Witness and the Other World: Exotic European Travel Writing, 400–1600*. Ithaca and London: Cornell UP, 1988.

Paul Devos. "La 'Servante de Dieu' Poemenia." *Analecta Bollandiana* 87 (1969): 189–212.

Egeria. George E. Gingras, trans. *Egeria: Diary of a Pilgrimage*. Ancient Christian Writers. New York: Newman Press, 1970.

———. E. Franceschini and R. Weber. *Itinerarium Egeriae*. Corpus Christianorum, Series Latina, vol. 175. Turnhout and Paris: Brepols, 1965.

————. P. Maraval. *Journal de Voyage (Itinéraire).* Introduction, texte critique, traduction, notes, index et cartes. Sources chrétiennes 296 (Paris, 1982).

————. John Wilkinson. *Egeria's Travels to the Holy Land.* Warminster: Aris and Phillips, 1981.

F.C. Gardiner. *The Pilgrimage of Desire.* Leiden: Brill, 1971.

E.D. Hunt. *Holy Land Pilgrimage in the Later Roman Empire* A.D. *312–460.* Oxford: Oxford UP, 1982.

Jo Ann McNamara. "Cornelia's Daughters: Paula and Eustochium." *Women's Studies* 11 (1984): 9–27.

————. *A New Song: Celibate Women in the First Three Christian Centuries.* New York: Haworth P, 1983.

————. "Muffled Voices: The Lives of Consecrated Women in the Fourth Century." In *Medieval Religious Women,* vol. I, *Distant Echoes,* ed. John A. Nichols and Lilian Thomas Shank. Cistercian Publications, 1984.

Francis X. Murphy. "Melania the Elder: A Biographical Note." *Traditio* 5 (1947): 59–77.

Robert Osterhout, ed. *The Blessings of Pilgrimage.* Chicago: U of Illinois P, 1990.

Barbara Sargent–Baur, ed. *Journeys toward God: Pilgrimage and Crusade.* Kalamazoo: Medieval Institute Publications, Western Michigan U, 1992.

J.B. Segal. *Edessa, "The Blessed City."* Oxford: Clarendon P, 1970.

Veikko Väänänen. *Le Journal-Epître d'Egérie.* Etude linguistique. Helsinki: Suomalainen Tiedeakatemia, 1987.

CHAPTER 3

Calumniated Empress and Poet

Eudocia of Constantinople (ca. 400 - October 20, 460)

The parade of wealthy pilgrims to the Holy Land did not slacken. A generation after Egeria had come and gone, prestigious women continued to flock to Palestine to honor their chosen saints and to build *martyria*, churches, and monasteries. A pilgrimage might, however, have an ulterior purpose. In the case of Eudocia, her final pilgrimage was really a deportation.

Born Athenaïs, she took the name Eudocia upon her conversion and marriage to Emperor Theodosius II, the grandson of Theodosius the Great. About her new name she said, paraphrasing Psalm 51.18, when she was building churches in the Holy Land: "It was of me that the prophet David spoke when he said 'In thy good pleasure [*eudokia*] O Lord, the walls of Jerusalem shall be built!'"[1] In the course of her marriage, Eudocia became so embroiled in Byzantine intrigue, ecclesiastical politics, charges of adultery, and even a murder that she was compelled to leave the imperial court stripped of her retinue of officials. But she did take her august rank and fortune with her. In Jerusalem she embraced a career of church building and literature.

Eudocia was a woman whose literary background and authorial self-awareness were extremely unusual. Daughter of Leontius, a prominent Greek sophist and teacher of rhetoric, Athenaïs/Eudocia received her outstanding rhetorical and literary training in pagan Athens, perhaps in Alexandria as well. Her teachers were noted Egyptian grammarians: Hyperechius of Alexandria and Orion of Thebes, who also taught the Neoplatonic philosopher Proclus.[2] To give his daughter a poet's training meant Leontius was fairly well-to-do. Eudocia's birthplace was either Athens or Antioch. In a public reading she gave to the citizens of Antioch in later years she announced she was of that city's "proud line and blood."[3]

The romantic story of her marriage to the rather pliable and maybe homosexual Theodosius is compiled from Byzantine chronicles. On the whole their veracity is accepted, but some of the details admittedly sound fanciful. Orphaned early, and cut off from her father's fortune with only 100 gold coins, Athenaïs took refuge with one of her two aunts in Constantinople. When her brothers, Valerius and Gesius, refused to share their legacy with her, Athenaïs sought justice at the Byzantine court. There she met the Emperor's older sister, the very devout and strong-willed Pulcheria, who had been reigning jointly with Theodosius since 408 when he was seven (he was proclaimed Augustus as an infant of nine months) and she was fifteen.

Pulcheria was said to be delighted and favorably impressed with the "Greek maid" Athenaïs, who was close to her own age. She admired her splendid education and her white-skinned, blond-haired beauty. As soon as she checked with the aunts that the young Athenian was a virgin, Pulcheria introduced her as a bride for her brother. Up until now, Theodosius had principally enjoyed the company of monks and eunuchs and occupied himself with copying manuscripts. The next year, Athenaïs converted to Christianity, assuming in baptism the name Aelia Eudocia, and on June 7, 421, she married the emperor. The bride and the groom were both twenty years old. Merciful to her brothers, to whom she declared she owed her good fortune, Eudocia obtained lucrative posts for them.

Before the advent of Athenaïs/Eudocia, Pulcheria was a forceful personage at court with access to the imperial treasury, which she poured into the building of churches and helping to further the imperial patronage of monasteries. She would earn the name of "the new Helena." If Helena found the Cross, it was said, Pulcheria kept it safe. She was also the guiding political and spiritual advisor of her brother, the emperor. Theodosius, Pulcheria, and their sisters Marina, Flaccilla, and Arcadia had been left as orphans by the Emperor Arcadius and the Empress Eudoxia (that mother whom John Chrysostom had scathingly called a "Herodias"). The young siblings were in the charge of Atticus, patriarch of Constantinople.

Under Atticus's tutelage, and Pulcheria's influence, a convent routine became instituted in the imperial palace that maintained a daily schedule of extravagant piety. Atticus dedicated his treatise *On Faith and Virginity* to Pulcheria and her sisters. The princesses were pledged to celibacy, study, and prayer. Pulcheria made her virgin vow publicly at the age of fourteen, together with the dedication of a sumptuous altar. The move was astute, for it put her out of reach of the marriage recruitment schemes and preserved her freedom to follow her political and pious interests. Early in life she showed natural gifts of decisiveness and leadership, when her brother, the child emperor, was in her care. In 414 Pulcheria named herself Augusta.

Atticus's treatise touched on an issue that would in the future become explosive. This was the affirmation of the Virgin Mary as the divine *theotokos*, "mother of God." The implications of this teaching were that Christ indeed partook of two natures after the Incarnation: those of true God and true man. His human nature was, then, consubstantial with that of men and women, making redemption possible through him. And since he was also divine, his mother could be called *theotokos*. Pulcheria and her sisters received notification, in the form of a Christmas sermon, that in embracing virginity they might emulate Mary. The metaphor is boldly and bodily female: "And you also, women, you who have been renewed in Christ, who have . . . partaken of blessing in the most holy Mary, you may also receive Him in the womb of faith, the one who is born today of the Virgin. For even the blessed Virgin Mary opened herself up."[4]

The elevation and sanctification of Mary was then beneficial to all women; their sex need not be held unworthy after the fall of Eve. For a woman of Pulcheria's stamp, embracing the cult of Mary and identifying with her virgin strength, collecting her relics (her veil, girdle, and portrait),[5] and building three Marian churches gave Pulcheria a spectacular authority. She and her sisters, the virgin princesses, practiced the ascetic life in the palace and in their imperial suburban residences to which Pulcheria could retreat when necessary. In this way Pulcheria maintained an aura of sacrality and command—of *basileía*—imperial queenship suffused with divinity.

Why should the devout, virginal, and ambitious Pulcheria have welcomed the charming pagan Athenaïs as an ideal consort for her brother? There is disagreement about this matchmaking. Perhaps the marriage was devised not by Pulcheria but by those men at court who disliked Pulcheria's power, who feared and resented her, and who saw their own advancement blocked by her claims. These were men to whom the ancient religion was congenial, men friendly to the sophist Leontius. By furthering Hellenic culture, they could counteract Pulcheria's Christian prerogatives with an Augusta—namely, Eudocia—they could control. At the same time as Eudocia's elevation, her brothers were given positions as provincial prefect and Master of Offices. With this network of power, Pulcheria's enemies could set about undermining her.

On the other hand, why should Pulcheria not have taken the initiative in dictating her brother's choice of a wife? Eudocia was respectable but not socially important, just a professor's daughter. Pulcheria may have thought she could wield some mastery in the matter.[6]

All the same, it is true that in later years the two Augustas, Pulcheria and Eudocia, would find themselves at unsisterly odds in the competition for dominance.

While Pulcheria perfected her authority as an imperial virgin dedicated to Mary, publicly fostering the city's sacral growth, Eudocia fulfilled a literary role at court. In this she received encouragement. When her husband won a victory over the Persians in 421–422, Eudocia wrote a poem in hexameters celebrating the heroic feat. She is also credited with having worked with a team of philosophers to organize the life of the academy at Constantinople, promoting the support of professors and grammarians, sophists and Latin orators, and advancing the study of letters. The literary circle around Theodosius's court was one of the most prestigious in the late Roman world. The question is whether Eudocia's Christianity was a convenient veneer and her sympathies were really with educated pagans, for "the poets were almost all pagans." [7]

After the wedding of her daughter, Licinia Eudoxia, in Constantinople on October 29, 437, Eudocia made her first journey (presumably, an official pilgrimage of thanksgiving) to the Holy Land, visiting the holy places in the spring of 438. Her periods of residence in the Holy Land coincided with those of other women pilgrims from the west, such as the younger Melania.

As she traveled in state, Eudocia made lavish donations to churches along the way, and notably to the building activity at Antioch, where a bronze statue was erected in her honor. This was the occasion when she greeted the flattered citizens in a reference to their shared Greek ancestry, and read her adaptations of Homeric verses, which were enthusiastically received.

On this first pilgrimage, Eudocia also became a kind of "new Helena," and the subject of two works of art. A lyric verse and a picture represent the regal empress in her gem-encrusted gilded carriage, escorted by her imperial guard. Prostrating herself at Christ's empty tomb in the Church of the Resurrection, Eudocia awed an anonymous poet, who left these lines: "Like a servant girl she kneels before His tomb, / She before whom all men bend the knee." When she returned to Constantinople, an artist rendered the scene in mosaic or paint.[8]

Eventually when the power struggle developed within the palace between the two Augustas, Eudocia and Pulcheria, one issue that led to ecclesiastical rivalries would be the doctrinal question of the Virgin Mary as *theotokos*. Each Augusta sided with a different viewpoint and protected different men. Pulcheria espoused the orthodox belief in God's dual but fused nature, human and divine. This meant his mother Mary was rightly called the *theotokos*. Since "the Word was made flesh" in the virgin's womb, no division could exist between the divine and the human in the One Person. The heterodox Monophysites, whose proponents had originated in Egypt among the Copts, refused to subscribe to the divine nature of both Mary and Christ. This, unfortunately, was the view that Eudocia continued actively to support.

Eudocia's downfall came in the wake of palace rivalry for power, but its reasons are complicated. Theodosius, Pulcheria, and Eudocia fell out among themselves. Pulcheria moved away to one of her suburban residences. The doctrinal issue of Mary *theotokos* widened the rift and erupted into a dangerous personal dispute that drew in the bishops of the Church, notably the zealous ascetic and misogynistic bishop of Constantinople, Nestorius.

Nestorius was a strict hardliner. The people disliked him. He banned the city's "circus, theater, mimes, games and dancers." He barred women from evening psalms and prayer and from wakes, objecting to the "promiscuity" their presence would cause. With Pulcheria, the affront was deadly: he accused her of taking lovers, of bearing Satan—not Christ—in her womb, and he refused to receive Pulcheria and her women after Sunday communion. He removed her portrait from the church altar and her gown, which had served as an altar covering for the communion table.

Five days after he was ordained, Nestorius rushed to prohibit Pulcheria from taking communion with her brother in the presence of priests in the Holy of Holies of the Great Church, as was her custom: "She asked: 'Why, have I not given birth to God?' He replied: 'You? You have given birth to Satan!' And then Nestorius drove the empress from the sanctuary."[9]

Nestorius's most serious move was to denounce the doctrine of the *theotokos*, objecting that since Mary in his view was only a human being, she could not have given birth to God. The eventual fate of Nestorius, masterminded by Pulcheria, was to be accused of heresy. His works were burned, while he was deposed and exiled to the remotest part of the Great Oasis of the Egyptian desert. From time to time he wrote a fulminating letter from that dry hot place. According to the populace, The Virgin Mary deposed Nestorius. He had challenged her right to the title *theotokos*, and the popular cry was "Many years to the Augusta!" and "God will guard the protectress of the faith! You persecuted all heretics! You persecuted Nestorius . . . !"[10]

But Pulcheria had other enemies. A palace eunuch named Chrysaphius lost no time in ingeniously stirring jealousy between the two Augustas. It was also Chrysaphius who tried to push for getting Pulcheria consecrated as a deaconess, a move that would have dislodged her from the palace. He turned his weapons against Eudocia as well. What undid Eudocia completely was Chrysaphius's accusing her of adultery with Paulinus, the Master of Offices who had been her husband's friend from boyhood. The charge implied that Eudocia intended to promote her paramour to emperor and order her husband's assassination.

The legend is supplied by a sometimes capricious chronicler, John Malalas, about a sizable Phrygian apple that Theodosius gave his wife. Eudocia was then denounced for giving the apple to the handsome young Paulinus for Epiphany, since it was the custom to trade gifts on January 6. She swore that she ate it. But Theodosius was swayed, and in 440 had Paulinus executed, removing him to Cappadocia first to avoid scandal. And what about little Arcadius, Eudocia's five-year-old son? Fortunately, he died before the problem of his legitimacy could be raised.

Then followed the execution of two clergymen who had been in attendance on Eudocia in Jerusalem and were considered her confidants in Constantinople. The slaying was done by Theodosius's henchman, the *comes domesticorum* Saturninus, on Theodosius's orders. In reprisal, Eudocia's outraged response was to murder Saturninus herself.[11]

Quickly despoiled of her imperial entourage, Eudocia did not depart until a year later. Perhaps unseemly haste would have caused tongues to wag even more maliciously. Her second pilgrimage removed her definitively from the imperial court for the last eighteen years of her life.

In the Holy Land, she continued in her role as Augusta, retaining her imperial *basileía*, dispensing justice from her palace in Bethlehem. She extended protection to the Jews who wanted to pray at the ruins of Solomon's temple, though the incident escalated into deadly riots and the governor had to be called in from Caesarea. She expanded her program of good works, emulating her predecessors, those other munificent pilgrims with immense fortunes. She helped rebuild the city, its walls, its churches and hostels, and its monasteries and homes for the sick. She replaced a cross atop Poemenia's church, when fire destroyed it. She is rumored to have provided gold pieces for the monks of the Anastasis—the Church at the Holy Sepulchre—and quantities of oil for lighting it. Her fame spread. Amalasuntha's secretary, Cassiodorus, composing a commentary in the next century on Psalm 50, called Eudocia *religiosissima feminarum* (the most religious of women).

Instead of adopting an ascetic life like some of the women pilgrims (e.g., Olympias, Pulcheria, and Melania the younger), instead of hobnobbing with deaconesses and virgins, Eudocia kept a high imperial estate and made her friends among male clerics with poetic leanings.

Because she had been miraculously cured by St. Stephen,[12] whose relics she had brought to Constantinople after her first pilgrimage, Eudocia devoted herself to his cult and built a splendid basilica on the site of his martyrdom. Called then "St. Stephen's Gate," it is today the Damascus Gate. The shrine turned out to be a haven for lepers, and so was not heavily frequented by other pilgrims. Eudocia built her own tomb in its immediate neighborhood.

On July 28, 450, Theodosius died from a fall from his horse while hunting. Pulcheria succeeded as Augusta, and one of her first actions was to execute the troublesome eunuch Chrysaphius. She took as her consort the dignified former tribune Marcian, a Roman of Illyrian or Thracian background. At a distance in Jerusalem, Eudocia continued to war against her sister-in-law, giving support to the crowds of monks who rioted against Marcian's religious policies.[13] Pulcheria died three years after her brother, in July 453. Having lived her whole life in Constantinople, she had earned the real adoration of the people with her charitable and pious works, and her enhancement of the image of female *basileía*, divine female dominion. Her husband deposited her body in a sarcophagus carved of imperial porphyry, in the mausoleum of Constantine near the tomb of Theodosius the Great, her grandfather.

Seven years later Eudocia died on October 20, 460. On her deathbed she denied she had been guilty of adultery. She was buried not far from Stephen, her cherished martyr. When, seventeen years afterwards, Eudocia's granddaughter escaped to Jerusalem in flight from her husband, Hunneric the Vandal, she honored the holy places and her grandmother's tomb. She, too, eventually died in the Holy Land.

Classically trained and devoutly Christian, Eudocia poured her Athenian eloquence into Christian poetry. It was a performance that anticipates Milton by twelve centuries: to write of the Devil, the Fall, and the redemption in classical meters. In all, six works are attributed to her: (1) the Homeric hexameters celebrating her husband Theodosius's triumph over the Persians, (2) verse paraphrases of the Octateuch, the Bible's first eight books, (3) verse renderings of the prophecies of Daniel and Zachariah, (4) a Homeric address to the people of Antioch, (5) the *Homerocentones*, Homeric centos on the life of Christ, and (6) the lives of martyrs Sts. Cyprian of Antioch and Justina, composed in three books of hexameters.

A cento was a literary patchwork quilt. Lines of pagan classics were snipped intact from their context, reassembled, and "stitched" together to form a poem of perfect Christian orthodoxy. The *Homerocentones* were short poems that recast stories from the Old and New Testaments by lifting lines from classics like the *Iliad* and the *Odyssey*. One example is the startling glimpse the angel Gabriel has of Mary during the Annunciation, spinning in her chamber like a Phaeacian queen: "Sitting by the fireside with her attendant women / turning sea-purple yarn on a distaff" (*Odyssey* 6.523–53).[14]

Eudocia's most ambitious work, of which 801 lines remain, was her *Life of St. Cyprian of Antioch*—not to be confused with the more illustrious Cyprian bishop of Carthage. Although the author's aim is to present Cyprian's holiness in the long run, Eudocia displays a keen interest in showing his involvement in the pagan lore of magic. It is suggested that this background, so intimately known, formed a part of her own immediate experience as a fifth-century Greek. Since Cyprian would become bishop of Antioch, and inasmuch as Eudocia was a resident there, she would have had a strong motivation to versify Cyprian's life on the basis of existing prose accounts.

Cyprian's life traces the evil arts, the worship of the Devil, and the conversion, confession, and martyrdom of the former magus. That is the alleged purpose, but the author devotes engrossing care to delineating his career as a magus. Cyprian is intent on pimping for a friend and corrupting a beautiful young Christian woman named Justa. The tale invokes the virtuous example of Thecla (whose shrine Egeria visited, as we saw in chapter 2) when Cyprian summons his demons on behalf of the depraved youth, Aglaides, who lusts for the godly Galilean girl. Book I (322 lines), whose beginning is lost, tells the story largely from Justa's viewpoint. The narrator Eudocia understands Justa's passions and her frenzy when she tears and pounds at Aglaides, perhaps recalling the charges of adultery and murder that were laid against her back home. Justa feels temptation, her body quivers when she thinks for a moment that she might yield to her sexuality. Her prayers have a wild incantatory glory, and sound like thundering addresses to the gods in the Homeric mode.

After his repentance and conversion, Cyprian advances from deacon to priest. Sixteen years later he becomes a bishop. He welcomes Justa, renames her Justina, and makes her a deaconess in charge of a community of virgins.

Cyprian is the first-person narrator of Book II (479 lines), which lacks its ending but unfolds in fascinating detail the story of his education as a magician and his encounter with the Devil. It opens with Cyprian telling a crowd about his entire life, reviewing his misguided past as a magus, and recounting how he was thwarted in his efforts to use magic against Justa. The sections on Cyprian's education afford insight into the fourth-century pagan practices that Christianity was attempting to root out but that in areas of the dying empire would prove tough and resistant for many centuries. Eudocia's father-in-law, Theodosius I, had outlawed paganism, and monks went around looting pagan temples in the east. Yet paganism died very hard.

Eudocia depicts a restless Cyprian ranging from Greece to Ethiopia to Chaldea to Antioch, deepening his learning of the occult world—of astronomy, astrology, and alchemy. The unleashing of evil spirits emerges as allegory: Falsehood, Lust, Fraud, Hatred, Hypocrisy, and Vanity populate the world. Cyprian's Faustian quest for the world's learning culminates with the declaration that he has seen the Devil himself. Because Cyprian has poured libations and made sacrifices to the Devil and embraced his lore, the Devil offers to make Cyprian ruler of the world as a reward for his labors. The Devil in all his seductive pre-Christian splendor is depicted as a gorgeous shape with gold flowers, with glittering eyes, and crowned with a wreath of woven hair and jewels that floods the earth with brightness.

Cyprian describes the arts he employed to procure Justa for Aglaides. Under the Devil's influence, Aglaides is transformed into a winged creature, like a bird, about to fall to his death if Justa, "Christ's handmaid," had not pitied him. Becoming disenchanted with of all this world's learning, reviling the demons, and grappling with Satan, Cyprian relinquishes his occult powers and prepares to embrace Christ. Book II breaks off as Cyprian recognizes his sins and hears the shouts from the crowd. Book III recounts the martyrdom under Diocletian and Maximius of the deaconess Justina and Bishop Cyprian. The book has not survived, though its content has been summarized by Photius.[15]

Justa's triumph over Cyprian's demons drives him to repent, so that he converts to Christianity. Her grappling with the demons bent on undermining her chastity parallels the bitter struggles of virgins like St. Juliana against diabolical forces. It is worth noting that Justa effects her own cure through prayer, and succeeds in exorcising the final demon by her own efforts.

From what we know of her eventful life, the characters all seem to reflect Eudocia's personal trials. Eudocia was first elevated, then spurned by Theodosius, who turned on her. The tale of Cyprian and Justina reverses this: Cyprian first abuses Justa, then elevates her, and changes her name. Justa and Cyprian reflect different phases of Eudocia's life, the Christian and the pagan. Justa's prayers, especially her acknowledgement of sin, have a special poignance and relevance to Eudocia's own past, harried as she was by conspiracies and allegations, and bearing the taint of crime. The story surfaces briefly in England in the ninth-century *Old English Martyrology* under September 26, recounting how the sorcerer tried to turn the virgin's mind to heathendom and unclean intimacy (*to haeðendome ond to unclaenum haemede*). But his arts slipped away like wax melting before the fire.

The division of Eudocia's first two books reveals a remarkable psychic split, with the author plainly exploring in each one her two sides. In the first (in which Cyprian is the vile seducer and dealer in forbidden arts), Justa exemplifies Eudocia's newborn self as a Christian, but in the second, narrated from the first-person viewpoint, there is an almost nostalgic recollection

of the saint's pagan childhood that clearly arises from the
memories of the pagan Greek girl Athenaïs. In the following
translations, "Justa" is taken from Book I of Eudocia's Life of St.
Cyprian, while "Cyprian" is taken from Book II.

1. Justa

Justa roughly drove away all the young men, for she had
pledged herself to Christ alone as her lover and her lord.

Aglaides collected a crowd before the church. He wanted
to seize the noble young girl by force, but when they approached
her she cried aloud to heaven. The mob took up weapons and
forced her from her house. At once Justa called on a guardian
angel against Aglaides and his henchmen. But Aglaides, burning
with love for her and struck by her beauty, and not understanding what was happening, took the young woman in his
arms. Quickly she crossed herself with Christ's formidable sign,
and at once the insolent man was thrown to the ground where he
lay on his back.

Justa tore at his body with her hands, she scratched his
cheeks and his beautiful hair. She shredded his fine clothing and
rewarded him with her contempt, following the example of
Thecla. Then she entered the house of God.

Furious, Aglaides hunted down the advice of a blasphemous sorcerer named Cyprian, a man of vile actions. Aglaides
promised to pay him two talents of shining gold and silver if he
could procure the virgin by force, since she would not give in to
his desires. But neither Aglaides nor Cyprian understood the
great power of Christ.

The magician felt sorry for the wretched Aglaides. With an
incantation he summoned forth an evil demon, who materialized
at once and asked, "Why do you call? Tell me!" Cyprian
answered, "My hot longing for a Galilean Christian girl has
conquered my heart. I have to know whether you are potent
enough to lure her to my bed because I desire her exceedingly."
The stupid demon nodded in obedience, and promised he would
fulfill this demand. Cyprian then spoke to his servitor: "Recount
your accomplishments to me, so that I can rely on you."

The demon replied, "Once I was foremost among the Angels, but I deserted the Almighty Lord of the seven spheres of heaven. You know what I've done, but I will tell you all the same: My wickedly quarrelsome temper drove me to topple the foundation of the pure heavens, and I hurled down a troop of heaven's dwellers to earth. I deluded Eve, the mother of all humankind, and I stripped Adam of the joys of Paradise. I myself guided the hand of Cain against his brother, and drenched the earth with blood. Thorns and thistles grew, and the fruits of human labor were spoiled because of me. I called forth spectacles loathsome to God, I committed hoaxes and swindles. I lured human beings to worship flimsy idols and to offer up the sacrificial parts of shaggy bulls. I goaded the Hebrews ruthlessly to stretch the powerful Word of God, his Eternal Son, upon the Cross.

"I have blasted cities, I have broken down walls of fire, I have gleefully ravaged many beds with unrest. Since I have mastered all these things and innumerable others, how could I fail to the bring about the ruin of this haughty young girl?"

Cyprian was overjoyed when the accursed demon said, "Take this herb. Scatter it around that proper young woman's room.[16] I myself will get close to her and put our Father the Devil's own desires in her breast. In her dreams she'll be induced to surrender to you."

That evening at nine o'clock, Justa was engaged in singing hymns to the beneficent God. Suddenly her innermost being trembled violently, for she recognized the assault of the brazen demon who was kindling a fire in her heart, urging her to violate her own belief. Quickly she turned her mind to God and prayed to him, making the sign of the cross over all the furnishings of her room. Eloquently she spoke:

> "Ruler of all things, progenitor of that pure child Jesus Christ—you who have bound the hideous viper that possessed the throne of gloomy Tartarus;[17] you who have saved the human race from his broken shackles; you who, stretching forth your hand from the heavens adorned with burning stars, have secured the earth and the waters in the midst of chaos; you who have given fiery torches to Titan's horses,[18] and yoked the silver moon to night; you shaped a mortal man in your image and commanded him

sweetly to enjoy the garden of Paradise until you drove
him from the garden, rich with trees, when he was
deceived by the ruse of the wretched serpent in the
wooded earth; you who compassionately desired our
souls' salvation and rescued us through the wounds of
your son on the Cross, so conquering all pain in Christ's
name—for whose sake the peopled earth is shining, the
heavens grow vast, the earth's caverns remain firmly
fixed, the waters stream forth, and all things acknowledge
you alone as the ruling king—be with me, and protect
your maidservant through your powerful wisdom, so that
the evil mocker will not overcome me!

"For—beloved Creator—I wish to remain, with your aid,
an unsullied virgin. I have cherished you lovingly,
glorious Jesus and my dearly praised Lord, for you have
kindled in me the fire of love and dwell in my heart. Do
not, I beseech you, let your maidservant be subdued by
the hand of the adversary, the Demon, or let him break
your law, Blessed One. But according to your promise,
take away the wanton, foul-tongued blasphemer!"

After she prayed this way, she crossed herself with the seal
of God and in Christ's name she drove away the monstrous
demon, who was quickly chased from the room.

Completely abashed, the demon returned to Cyprian, the
sorcerer, who asked, "Where is the girl I asked you to bring to
me as quickly as possible?" His emissary replied, "I am
confounded! Do not question me! I beheld a terrible sign."

The sorcerer smiled. Now that he understood how hard
the task was, he summoned forth another spiteful demon called
Belial,[19] who said, "Let me know your heinous command. Your
Father sent me to assist you in your trouble."

Now the magus was delighted, and said, "Demon, I have
your assignment: here is a potion to give to that saintly girl. I'll
follow you, and I think she'll be swayed right away." The demon
departed.

At midnight, the most holy virgin devoutly sent up a
prayer to the Lord:

"In the deep of night, I spring from my bed, O Mighty
Creator, to cry aloud of the sins I have committed against

your goodness, your justice and truth. O gracious bestower of mercy—you who rule the air and guide the heavens; you whom the earth fears; you who have the might to crush the enemy; you who accepted the sacrifice of the patriarch Abraham as if it were a mighty hecatomb;[20] you who cast down Baal[21] and the deadly serpent; you who taught holiness to the Persian tribes by means of the holy Daniel; you who through your beloved child Christ have commanded that all be well; you who have illuminated the earth with light; you who have guided the dead to the light, according to their destiny—I pray to you, Lord. Grant that we may not be lured into sinfulness. Protect me, Lord. Let my body stay unharmed forever, allow me a life of virginity so that I may behold my wedding with Christ, our Bridegroom. Let me keep my ancient covenants, for yours is the power and the glory and the reverence. Amen."

As soon as she had prayed this way, the demon ran off, his eyes lowered because of her strength. He appeared in the presence of the magus, shamefaced. Cyprian asked, "Demon, where is the girl I asked you to bring me?" He answered, "She conquered me with a potent sign! When I looked at it, I was reduced to a quivering, shuddering mass."

At once Cyprian summoned up another, more vigorous and loftier demon of the black-eyed tribe, saying, "If you too are worthless, go away, weakling!" The demon boldly retorted, "I will bring the girl to you immediately. Prepare yourself!" "Give me a sign," said Cyprian, "that you're going to win." The demon answered, "I'll goad her body to desperation with fevers, and after six days I will make her dizzy and on that night I'll bring her to you."

The stupid demon first turned himself into the likeness of another virgin girl, dressed in the same way as Justa. He went to her and sat on her bed and spoke with guile. "Like you who take joy in your exquisite virginity, I have come from the place of Dawn. The Lord Christ sent me so that he might make me more perfect. But darling, tell me, what reward do you reap from this exquisite virginity. And what is the price you pay? I can certainly see that you're like a corpse, a dessicated body, a tree trunk dried of sap!"

The virtuous girl replied, "A reward is of no value here and now, since a higher reward will wait for me." The blasphemous demon said, "And Eve—was she a virgin in the garden of Paradise with Adam? When they joined in bed, she became a mother of children, Adam's first-born. All humanity came from her, and Eve learned great wisdom."

Justa began to listen to the demon. She was on the threshold, nearly ready to walk out of the doors of heaven, and the vile demon rejoiced that he had managed to lead the child of God into temptation. She recognized the hateful enemy's ruse, and immediately she turned to prayer. She made the sign of the cross over her whole body. She cried out and chased the wretched, ignominious creature from her house. When she had recovered some of her self-control, she said, "I know this grace that comes from the everlasting God! I have escaped a fiery sickness." She prayed, "Christ, place your gift of power in my body. Let me fear you, Glorious One! Pity me in your goodness, as I give thanks for your name."

[The sign of the cross once again baffles the demon. Cyprian has to admit he is foiled; the Cross is more puissant than his books of magic. He carries these to the house of a priest, who, on Cyprian's orders burns them. Cyprian becomes a Christian. He defeats and converts the armies of demons. At last he bestows upon Justa, now Justina, the office of deaconess in charge of a flock of girls, all handmaids to God.]

2. Cyprian

I am the one who was born Cyprian. When I was a child my parents bestowed me as a gift to Apollo.[22] In boyhood I gained a knowledge of the secret rites of the Neduporian serpent.[23] Then, approaching my seventh year, I was offered again to the Mithraic Phaëthon.[24] I was living in the high city of the nobly born Athenians, and became an inhabitant when it pleased the parents who bore me. In my tenth year, I kindled a torch to Zeus and put on Kore's white robes of sorrow.[25] Since I was dedicated as a temple attendant, I performed the snake sacrifices in the lofty city of Athena. I ascended into the groves of Olympus. There, ignorant people say, are the shrines of the shadowy blessed. I listened there to the murmuring sound of their words. I saw grasses, trees, all things wonderful to my eyes, though dangerous demons preside over them. I saw the seasons succeeding in order, and the windstorms; I looked upon different days which malignant spirits create by false appearances.

I witnessed the reckless lascivious dancing, the chorus of Melpomene, muse of song, and of others who strove greedily together. I saw some of them rejoicing, some crouching or being mocked. I saw clearly the ranking hosts of the gods and the spirits, since I lingered there forty days, and another eight. Then from powerful kingdoms throughout the land, spirits were dispatched that caused all the nations to perpetrate their worst, their most atrocious acts.

When the sun sank, I ate the fronds of tender plants. At fifteen I was a devotee of all the spirits and gods, I knew the seven ranks of priests and the deeds of the treacherous demons.

[Cyprian continues to outline the lore of demons that populate the land, air, and depths of the sea. His journeys to Phrygia in Turkey, Sparta, and the land of the Scythians, north of the Black Sea, introduce him to the art of reading omens, entrails, and the flights of birds. He travels to Egypt and Ethiopia. He learns about superhuman powers that reside in underworld beings, how sorcerers invoke horrible spirits; he learns of the stars and their laws, how sorcerers watch the dark western sky and the squalling winds that oppose them, and how they observe the origins of Erebus, the place of underworld darkness on the way to Hades. He encounters demons. At last he meets the Devil himself in all his radiance and power.]

Once the Devil knew my life and what I had done, he promised me I should rule the world, since I had striven hard for him. He admitted me to the gloomy troop of his cursed spirits. As I was going from him, he spoke to me.

"You prosper, Cyprian, in your heart." He rose up from his throne and led me forth. All his cohorts stared in wonder, and his chiefs of long standing escorted me in honor.

His face and form were in the image of gold flowers. Radiance glanced from the flame of his eyes, and on his head was a coronet of intricately woven hair, adorned with splendid jewels that filled the whole place with light.[26] His cloak was embellished in the same fashion. He held his shield over certain cities fixed in serried ranks in a curve of the globe. The earth shook when he walked. He hurled the lightning bolt like a divinity of Olympus, dazzling in his marvels, beneficent to mortals who worship him as a god.

NOTES

1. This is reported by the fifth-century author John Malalas (b. 490), *The Chronicle of John Malalas*, trans. Elizabeth Jeffreys, Michael Jeffreys, and Roger Scott, with Brian Croke and others (Melbourne: Australian Association for Byzantine Studies, 1986), p. 195.

2. Alan Cameron, "Wandering Poets: A Literary Movement," in *Literature and Society in the Early Byzantine World* (London: Variorum Reprints, 1985), p. 482.

3. Kenneth G. Holum, *Theodosian Empresses: Women and Imperial Dominion in Late Antiquity* (Berkeley and Los Angeles: U of California P, 1982), offers a fascinating, well-documented study of the women surrounding the emperor: mother, sister, wife. See especially chap. 4, "Aelia Eudocia Augusta," pp. 112–146. Among the early sources for Eudocia are, e.g., Olympiodorus of Thebes, John Malalas's *Chronicle*, Evagrius, Ammianus Marcellinus, and the seventh-century "Paschal Chronicle."

4. Atticus's Christmas sermon is cited in Holum, *Theodosian Empresses*, p. 139.

5. Eudocia is supposed to have sent the portrait of Mary, said to be painted from the living model by St. Luke. She found it in Jerusalem and sent it to Constantinople to be placed, with the rest of the Virgin's relics, at the shrine at Blachernai. (Judith Herrin, *The Formation of Christendom*, Princeton UP, 1987, p. 309.) Holum doubts the rumor, since Eudocia and Pulcheria weren't getting along. A copy of this portrait was to turn up in the 14th century in the convent of Unterlinden where it wrought miracles.

6. The two views are, respectively, those of Holum, *Theodosian Empresses*, who argues for the male conspiracy, and Alan Cameron in "Empress and Poet," in *Literature and Society*, p. 277, who thinks it unlikely.

7. Alan Cameron, "Wandering Poets," p. 508, and "Empress and Poet," p. 179, in *Literature and Society*. Did she have a "natural sympathy for highly educated pagans" and "paganizing litterateurs"? What kind of literary patronage did she wield at Constantinople and then Jerusalem, where the literary preoccupations of the day were church history and hagiography?

8. Holum, *Theodosian Empresses*, p. 187.

9. Holum, *Theodosian Empresses*, p. 153.

10. For Nestorius's clash with Pulcheria, see Holum, *Theodosian Empresses*, pp. 149, 153, 215.

11. This was the testimony of Ammianus Marcellinus and Priscus of Panium, cited in Alan Cameron ("Empress and Poet," in *Literature and Society*, p. 260), who adds, "A strange affair of which one would like to know more."

12. The killing of Stephen in Jerusalem ca. 35 A.D. is recorded in the *Acts of the Apostles*, chaps. 5–6. Called the protomartyr, the first martyr for Christ, he was driven from the city and stoned for blasphemy when he announced to the Jewish council, "Behold, I see the heavens opened and the Son of Man standing at the right hand of God!"

13. John Meyendorff, *Imperial Unity and Christian Divisions* (Crestwood, N.Y.: St. Vladimir's Seminary P, 1987), p. 188.

14. Cited in Holum, *Theodosian Empresses*, p. 219.

15. Photius, the ninth-century Patriarch of Constantinople, compiled a *Bibliotheca* of valuable extracts and abridgements of classical works, many of the originals being subsequently lost.

16. On the medieval use of erotic powders and potions, see Richard Kieckhefer, "Erotic Magic in Medieval Europe," in *Sex in the Middle Ages*, ed. Joyce E. Salisbury (New York: Garland, 1991), pp. 30–55.

17. In the *Iliad* Tartarus is the deepest abyss below Hades, and a place of punishment for rebels against Zeus. But Latin Christian writers of the later Middle Ages also use Tartarus as a synonym for Hell. The binding of Satan belongs to Christian lore, from the apocryphal Gospel of Nicodemus, which tells how Christ harrowed Hell after the Crucifixion, and chained Satan.

18. Titan belonged to an older, pre-Olympian generation of gods and is mentioned in Hesiod's *Theogony*. Greek poets often used Titan for Hyperion, the sun.

19. From the Hebrew word "worthlessness," "without value," Belial in the Old Testament is the Devil or one of the demons; St. Paul (as in II Cor. 6.15) refers to Satan by this name.

20. In Homer, a hecatomb meant a sacrifice of a hundred oxen or cattle, or the sacrifice or slaughter of victims in large number.

21. Hebrew for "lord," Baal indicated any of the Canaanite and Phoenician lesser deities.

22. Apollo, one of the most potent divinities, was associated with prophecy and healing, philosophy, law, music, and poetry. In his radiant ("Phoebus") aspect he became identified with Helios, god of the sun. Depicted as youthful in beauty and vigor, Apollo had his main shrine at Delphi.

23. These rites are unidentified. The first element of the word, *nedus*, refers to the belly, womb, bowels, or other body cavities.

24. A fusion of Mithras, a god appearing in Sanskrit and Old Persian and known to Greek writers as a deity of light, with Phaëthon, one of the shining horses of Dawn in Homer. Phaëthon was sometimes also the light-bringing son of Helios, who drove the sun's horses.

25. Kore, the virgin mother goddess, also known as Demeter, was carried off to Hades as Persephone (or Proserpine). Her mysteries were also celebrated in honor of her status as the mother goddess. Her return is part of the Eleusinian mysteries. Pluto's rape of Kore/Persephone is the central subject of the Homeric hymn to Demeter. Persephone and her mother Demeter were sometimes two persons: Demeter founded rites to mourn her daughter when Pluto ravished her to the underworld as his bride.

26. "Satan himself is transformed into an angel of light," Paul admonished (II Cor. 11.14).

FURTHER READING

Alan Cameron. *Literature and Society in the Early Byzantine World.* London: Variorum Reprints, 1985.

Hippolyte Delehaye. "Cyprien d'Antioch et Cyprien de Carthage." *Analecta Bollandiana* 39 (1921): 314–32.

Charles Diehl. "Athenaïs." Chapter 2 in *Byzantine Empresses*. Trans. Harold Bell and Theresa de Kerpely. New York: Knopf, 1963.

Eudocia. Helen Homeyer, ed. *Dichterinnen des Altertums and des frühen Mittlelalters*, pp. 113–131. Paderborn, 1979.

————. Arthur Ludwich, ed. *Eudociae Augustae Claudiani: Carminum Graecorum Reliquiae*. Teubner: Leipzig, 1887.

————. *Patrologia Graeca* 85, cols. 631–864.

————. Patricia Wilson-Kastner and others. "Eudokia." In *A Lost Tradition: Women Writers of the Early Church*, pp. 135–171. Introduction and translation. Lanham: Md.: UP of America, 1981.

F. Gregorovius. *Athenaïs: Geschichte einer byzantinischen Kaiserin*. Leipzig, 1892.

Kenneth G. Holum. *Theodosian Empresses: Women and Imperial Dominion in Late Antiquity*. Berkeley and Los Angeles: U of California P, 1982.

E.D. Hunt. "Eudocia." In *Holy Land Pilgrimage in the Later Roman Empire*, pp. 221–248. Oxford: Clarendon P, 1982.

Helen A. Mahler. *Empress of Byzantium*. Trans. with the assistance of Leona Nevler. New York: Coward McCann, 1952.

Ada B. Teetgen. *The Life and Times of the Empress Pulcheria*. London: Swan Sonnenschein, 1907.

Ioanna Tsatsou. *Empress Athanaïs-Eudocia: A Fifth-Century Byzantine Humanist*. Brookline, Mass.: Holy Cross Orthodox Press, 1977.

Auguste Friedrich von Pauly. "Eudokia." In *Realencyclopädie der classischen Altertumswissenschaft*. Revisions and Supplements, Hans Gartner and Albert Wunsch, eds. Munich: Druckenmuller, 1980.

CHAPTER 4

An Ill-Fated Gothic Queen

Amalasuintha of Italy (*ca.* 494 – April 30, 535)

The life and death of Queen Amalasuintha of Italy form a chapter in one of those murderous family dramas of the Dark Ages that might have been commemorated in a brooding saga and carried from court to court by bards and scops. Indeed, the fierceness of a Gothic forebear of hers, Ermanaric, had become part of just such a tradition.

An enlightened, conscientious queen whose main court was at Ravenna, Amalasuintha held sway in Italy after August 30, 526, until she was assassinated. She was about thirty-two when her father, Theodoric the Great, died of dysentery, though the rumors about his demise ran rampant, including one piece of pious hearsay that Pope John had ordered him thrown alive, barefoot and trussed, into the crater of a volcano. To this day his ten-sided porphyry mausoleum in Ravenna stands empty.

Scion of the Amal clan, which claimed divine descent from Gaut, the Scandinavian war god, Theodoric the Ostrogoth invaded Italy and laid siege to Ravenna. He defeated Odovacar, who himself had chased out the last Roman emperor. Theodoric had the status of a Roman commander-in-chief (*magister utriusque militiae*) to whom the emperor in Constantinople had ceded the government of Italy. He was head of his "Roman" army, which was by now manned by Goths, like his bodyguards, since he had expelled the Romans.

In 493 or 494 Theodoric married Audefleda. She was a sister of the Frankish King and warlord Clovis, founder of the Merovingian royal house. Amalasuintha's birth from the union of Theodoric and Audefleda secured the friendship of the two powerful rulers. Amal names ran in the family: Theodoric's well-

71

educated sister Amalaberga married into the house of Thuringia, where she became the aunt of Radegund of Poitiers, whose story is told in the next chapter. Theodoric had an older sister, Amalafrida, and two daughters by another marriage. As his own chosen successor and a husband for his daughter Amalasuintha, Theodoric selected Eutharic, a young Amal and the son of the boy-king Veteric. That part of the clan had been living in Spain among the Visigoths after they fled from the Huns in about 450. Amalasuintha and Eutharic were wedded in 515.

The barbarian Eutharic found acceptance with the Emperor Justinian in Constantinople. But Eutharic died before he could take on royal powers. Amalasuintha's own regency of nine years came to a crisis when her adolescent son died, and she ended by being treacherously slain—in her bath, if Gregory of Tours is to be believed—on the small island where she had been held prisoner by her elderly cousin, Theodahad.

Amalasuintha's career can be viewed against two principal historic events: first, the half-century of Gothic control in Italy lasting from 494 to 552 and, second, the ultimately triumphant efforts of Justinian to oust the Goths, reconquer Italy and bring it temporarily back under the imperial Roman administration. The whole period is marked by unrest in the Italian kingdom, where bloodthirsty rivalries escalated at the Romano-Gothic court.

The new queen, like her father, retained an admiration for Roman culture, learning, and law and for the Hellenism in which she was schooled. Her father had asked his Roman secretary Cassiodorus to provide him a list of works in philosophy so he might model himself on the philosopher-king of Plato's *Republic*. Amalasuintha, too, was supposed to have been adept in Attic eloquence. She tried to keep order and dispense justice according to lawful principles, seeing to it, for instance, that the Gothic soldiers' salaries and bonuses were paid out of tax revenues and not from wrested Roman properties. One of her significant acts was to restore to the children of Boethius—and of Symmachus, his father-in-law—the estates that Theodoric had confiscated when he had put these two to death.

Theodoric's insistence in the summer of 524 on the imprisonment, torture, and execution for treason of the Neoplatonist Boethius—who wrote that most popular of medieval books, *The*

Consolation of Philosophy, while waiting to die—resulted from a snarl of accusations and counter-accusations. The death sentence of Boethius, eventually beatified as St. Severinus Boethius, fixed the image of Theodoric as persecutor of Romans and Catholics. It sullied his generally humane record and reputation for further-ing *civilitas:* order, peaceability, and civilized harmony between Goths and Romans. After the executions, the guilty Theodoric imagined he saw the grimace and mad eyes of the dead Symmachus in a large fish served at his banquet table. Amalasuintha's effort to right her father's wrongs would, like her efforts to protect Romans maltreated by greedy Goths, prove her undoing.

Of her three male biographers—Gregory of Tours, the Byz-antine historian Procopius of Caesarea,[1] and her own secretary Cassiodorus—the latter two praise her fair-mindedness, strength of will, intellect and learning, wisdom, vigor and "masculinity." Cassiodorus affirms that she spoke Greek and Latin as well as her native Gothic tongue. A Roman in the service of the Goths, Cassiodorus had directly succeeded Boethius as Master of Offices (*magister officiorum*), a post of high responsibility. Administration of the government continued under the Gothic magnates, but the provident civil servant Cassiodorus, now about forty-three years old, labored to pave the way for Amalasuintha's legitimacy as queen of the Gothic army. Theodoric had defined the Goths as a race delighting in war. For five years after the death of Amalasuintha's son, the army had no leader, and a royal prerogative was therefore forfeited. Cassiodorus strove to upgrade Amalasuintha's status with the composition of his *Origo Gothica* ("The Origin of the Goths"), based on a gathering of oral legends.[2]

Cassiodorus had started this compilation even while Amalasuintha's son was still alive. The point was to reshape Amalasuintha's genealogy tactfully, pruning it down to just ten ancestors. He allowed the Gautic/Scandinavian war-god myth to fade into the Nordic shadows, and lopped off altogether that embarrassing grandsire, the pagan barbarian Ermanaric, dead since 375.

Ermanaric, the Ostrogothic emperor named in nearly every leading Germanic heroic chant and saga (including

Beowulf, Widsith, Deor, the Volsungassaga, The Thidrekssaga, and
the *Poetic Edda*) was that same tyrant (or sadly misadvised king,
depending on who told the story) Jörmunrek, who had
murdered his nephews to get their gold and condemned to an
atrocious death a woman named Swanhild/Sunilda. Either she
was his wife accused of adultery with his own son, or she had to
pay for a treasonous act of her unnamed husband's—the tale
varies—but Swanhild was ordered torn apart and trampled by
horses. Her brothers Sörli and Hamthir, or Sarus and Ammius
(he is the Hama who in *Beowulf* stole Ermanaric's neck ring),
avenged the act. They dealt Ermanaric a savage wound, and he
died a suicide in the face of Hunnic invaders, declaiming like an
Old Testament patriarch. As the *Volsungassaga* tells it, the
accused wife Swanhild was tied to the town gate, and the horses
were driven to gallop over her, but when she opened her eyes
wide, the horses drew back. The executioners had to cover her
face so she might be expeditiously killed.[3]

Cassiodorus might prudently rearrange the family lineage
to remove Ermanaric as a direct progenitor of Amalasuintha's,
but the legend was too notorious to suppress. We should keep in
mind that this knowledge about her background would have
strongly informed Amalasuintha's mentality and sense of who
she was. Yet, despite her capabilities and determination, she was
surrounded by Gothic magnates and warriors who couldn't
stomach a female ruler. She never had a chance for survival, let
alone sovereignty.

To compound her unpopularity, Amalasuintha also tried
to introduce the garb and ceremonies of the Byzantine court into
the Gothic kingship and to impose the Catholic (that is,
Athanasian) beliefs on her resistant Germanic courtiers, who
were firmly Arian. Part of her Catholic agenda was to foster the
building of churches, the cult of martyrs, and the cult of the
Virgin Mary. The royal treasury and royal taxes financed the
building of the church of Santa Maria Maggiore during
Amalasuintha's regency. Accompanying the reverence of the
Virgin was the heady controversial notion of Mary as *theotokos*,
divine mother of god, the belief that had rocked the Byzantines
in Eudocia's day, as we saw in chapter 3.

At time of her father's death, Amalasuintha was a widow with two children: a girl named Matasuintha and a boy of ten years. As Theodoric's grandson, the child Athalaric would have been the new king, but Amalasuintha served as regent for her son. She wanted to mold Athalaric on the pattern of a Roman ruler, and engaged tutors to oversee his education. Her plan was thwarted by the Goths' conviction that literary pursuit was unmanly. Enforced study drove a youth to cower before his teachers—old men at that. Did Amalasuintha want to cause the death of the boy and then find another husband for herself? The noble advisers prescribed riding, hunting, and skill at weaponry practiced with young comrades. They summoned evidence that Theodoric had looked unfavorably on the enfeebling effects of book learning. It was even said that the illiterate Theodoric needed a stencil to trace his signature, though the panegyrics of the learned Ennodius, bishop of Pavia, who made Theodoric out to be a well-educated royal, would seem to conflict with such a report.

Amalasuintha finally yielded. Athalaric was allowed to take after his kingly grandfather by wearing his long hair unparted, tumbling on his forehead and down over his ears. By handing him to the Goths, she gave the boy over to a life that proved his ruin (said Procopius): drunken routs, women, and other excesses led to his wasting illness. Not yet twenty, Athalaric died on October 2, 534. This left Amalasuintha at the head of the state.

But the Goths were wary of serving a woman. When she uncovered a plot against her, Amalasuintha ordered the deaths of three ringleaders. Seeing danger, she attempted to build support both at home and abroad. Already during Athalaric's illness she had turned to her married cousin Theodahad. His mother had been Theodoric's sister Amalafrida; his father Thrasamund, a king of the Vandals. After Amalasuintha lost her son, she superscribed herself *Amalasuintha regina* when she asked for approval from the emperor Justinian to name Theodahad co-ruler (*consors regni*) with her.

Theodahad was an older man with a taste for Roman letters and Platonic philosophy, and not at all a soldier. He had formerly shown a rapacious inclination to enrich himself in

Tuscany by grabbing his Roman neighbors' estates and affecting the style of a provincial "king of Tuscany" in a way that made him equally unpopular with Goths and Romans. As it unluckily happened, Theodahad was one of the Goths whom Amalasuintha had brought to justice earlier, charging him with avarice for his illegal appropriation of Theodoric's inheritance, the *patrimonium regis*. Amalasuintha's father had specifically exhorted the Goths not to pillage Roman lands. Now she forced herself to gloss over her kinsman's crimes in a letter to the Roman Senate, drawing attention to a supposedly regenerate and deeply bookish Theodahad. He himself was well aware of his divine descent from the war god Gaut, and he recognized that he was the only available Amal male. Now raised to the status of king and co-ruler, Theodahad also wrote obsequiously in November 534 for recognition from Constantinople.

At the same time, Amalasuintha started discreet negotiations with Constantinople, letters accompanied by verbal explanations carried on the persons of trusted envoys, in case the arrangement with Theodahad fell through. She had kept up friendly relations with Justinian. Should she have to flee, she now made preparations—with loaded ships holding 40,000 pounds of gold—to place herself under his protection. If need be, she would hand over the kingdom of Italy in addition. A well-appointed house was waiting for her at Durazzo, Albania, where she might rest before going on to Constantinople. Justinian, it seems, eagerly encouraged these dealings with Amalasuintha. But Theodahad, for whom the matter of the Tuscan estates still rankled, had also made overtures to Justinian and offered to sell him large chunks of the Italian kingdom in exchange for the chance of retiring in honorable comfort to the Byzantine court.

Justinian must have dealt a double game, negotiating with Amalasuintha and Theodahad both, playing one against the other until the time was ripe.

Theodahad moved swiftly, cultivating the disaffected Goths at court. Within seven months of her son's death he took Amalasuintha into custody and held her captive at Martana, an island on the Tuscan lake of Bolsena near Orvieto. Theodahad assured Justinian that he was treating her well there, considering her high-handedness in the matter of his Tuscan estates. Then

Theodahad allowed her to be slain by his retainers *(satellites)*, relatives of those same three Goths she had ordered killed as traitors. Procopius suggests that the Empress Theodora, Justinian's jealous spouse, felt threatened by the Gothic queen's beauty and dynamism, and did not want her at Constantinople. Through a conspiracy with Petrus Patricius, imperial envoy to Italy, the empress was also said to have urged the murder.

Gregory of Tours tells a different story about Amalasuintha that calls her virtue and ability into question. Although its veracity is generally doubted, it does echo the violent tenor of events at the court of Ravenna in its last throes.

As a girl, ignoring her mother's wish that she marry a king's son, the willful young Amalasuintha—writes Gregory—took as a lover a man named Traguilla from among her own slaves. With Traguilla she eloped to a nearby city where she hoped to be free. Her mother begged her angrily not to dishonor her queenly blood any longer, but to return and wed a man of a rank equal to hers. When Amalasuintha refused, her mother dispatched a band of soldiers to arrest her. The soldiers seized the lovers, slew Traguilla, and beat Amalasuintha before returning her forcibly to her mother. The young woman found an opportunity to avenge herself when mother and daughter came together to worship at the altar (both of them members of the Arian sect, according to this tale) and share the communion chalice. Amalasuintha poisoned her mother's cup, which as royals they were to have shared separately from the common people. The Italians, outraged, sent for Theodahad to be their ruler. He too was offended by her crimes. He ordered a heated steam bath prepared for her, and had her locked in the bath with one of her maids. Scalded, Amalasuintha fell to the stone floor and died.

Despite the malicious pro-Theodahad tone of Gregory's tale, perhaps elements of it should not be utterly discounted. Considering the vicious world of intrigue in which she found herself during the final years of Theodoric's rule and its aftermath, there is no reason why a spirited, ambitious woman like Amalasuintha should not have acted as forcefully as the men and women around her and have assumed stratagems that were both politic and imperious once she was in the seat of power, for however disastrously brief a time.

After Amalasuintha's death, Theodahad's wife Gudeliva sent two letters to Theodora in Constantinople in suave confirmation of her new title as "Queen of Italy." But fawning letters could not save the situation. Amalasuintha's murder gave Justinian cause for war, and he demanded the Goths' unconditional surrender. Theodahad found himself marching against the imperial army. Eventually, the Goths grew dissatisfied with this elderly intriguer Theodahad and had him slain. The command came from his successor, the new king Vitigis.

Vitigis, who had been young Athalaric's sword bearer (*comes spatharius*), came of people who were not aristocratic, but they were members of the old Gothic military *confrerie*. A seasoned warrior, Vitigis tried to consolidate his hold on the throne by taking Amalasuintha's eighteen-year-old daughter Matasuintha as a second wife, after getting rid of his first. Matasuintha's loyalty to the Goths was suspect, especially after a major fire torched a granary in Ravenna. Vitigis eventually suffered defeat. In the embattled years that followed, Justinian drove the Goths from Italy, completing the reconquest by 554. Amalasuintha's daughter, meanwhile, was granted a Roman marriage in Constantinople to a new husband, Germanus (Justinian's nephew), in keeping with her royal status. And so that luxurious and civilized haven of Constantinople, so ardently yearned for by both Amalasuintha and Theodahad, was finally attained by Amalasuintha's daughter.

Four letters by Amalasuintha lie preserved among the *Variae* of Cassiodorus. Written in the sycophantic and circuitous style of political necessity, they chart her efforts to secure the cooperation of Theodahad, the approval of the Senate, and the protection of the emperor. She wrote the first of these in 534, soon after the death of her son, the adolescent king Athalaric. In it she informs Justinian that she has offered a share of the rule of Italy to her kinsman Theodahad, and looks to Justinian for his sanction. In the second letter, Amalasuintha addresses the Roman Senate, praising Theodahad for his good qualities, including a passion for literature, and smoothing over in polished terms his past avaricious misdeeds. The third letter thanks

Justinian for a gift of statues, while the fourth addresses the Empress Theodora with amicable reverence, showing concern for her health, seemingly during a pregnancy.[4]

Letters in the child Athalaric's name are probably Amalasuintha's compositions as well.

1. Queen Amalasuintha to the Emperor Justinian

Until now, most merciful prince, we have put off the disclosure of the death of our son, of glorious memory, so as not to wound the heart of a loving friend with a sorrowful message. But now, with the help of God—who always turns harsh mischance into good fortune—we have chosen to bring to your attention matters over which you may be able to rejoice with us, and share our exultation. It is always pleasing to acknowledge the gifts of Divine Providence to those who love us.

We have brought to the scepter one who is closely connected to us by brotherly kinship, a man who may uphold the royal rank together with us by the strength of his counsel, so that he may be resplendently clothed in the purple glory of his ancestors. In this way the solace of a prudent man may lift up our spirits.

Join together now your propitious prayers. For just as we eagerly hope that all things will turn out favorably in the empire of Your Beneficence, so we will be the living proof of the kindness that you bestow upon us.

And so we add the service of a most friendly ambassador to the message that has been sent, and that we trust that you, with your inborn clemency, will look upon as the fulfillment of a vow. By this means, we hope that the peaceful relations that you maintain toward us—and that you continue to uphold for my sake especially—may be extended for the protection of my people.

For although the concord of princes is always an adornment, yours wholly ennobles me, since whoever harmoniously shares in your glory is made more fully sublime.

But since everything cannot be adequately settled in the brief space of a letter, we have, in sending our respectful greetings to you, entrusted to our envoys certain appropriate matters to be made known to you verbally. Please be willing to accept these in the accustomed manner of Your Serenity.

It is agreed, then, that I may without any doubt count on you, since we are doing those things that we recognize that you have expected us to do, concerning those people you have recommended, in fulfillment of your wishes.

2. Queen Amalasuintha to the Senate of the City of Rome

After mourning for the death of our son, of blessed memory, our concern for the people's common good has conquered a dutiful mother's heart, so that it dwells not upon the cause of her own grief but upon your prosperity. We have searched into the kind of help we might obtain to strengthen the kingdom's administration. But that Father of purity and unique mercy, who was to deprive us of a son in his young manhood, has kept alive for us the affection of a brother ripe in years.

We have chosen by God's grace the blessed Theodahad as the consort of our reign, so that we, who have until now borne in solitary deliberation the burden of the commonwealth may now carry out the achievement of all things by united counsels.

We shall be seen to be two persons in mutually working out the administration of the State, but one person in purpose. The stars of heaven themselves are controlled by the aid they give to one another and—having been made partners by their shared labor—guide the world with their lights. Heavenly power has assigned to men two hands, companionate ears, and twin eyes, so that the function that was to be fulfilled by the allied pair might be more efficiently carried out.

Rejoice, Fathers of the Senate, and commend to the heavenly powers what we have accomplished. We have desired to do nothing blameworthy, we who have—in conjunction with each other's counsel—commanded all things to be put in order. We of course preserve with liberality the kingdom's tradition, since one who is demonstrated to have a partner in her exercise of power is rightly seen to be compassionate.

With God's help, therefore, we have unbarred the imperial residence to an illustrious man of our family, who, descended from the race of the Amals, has a royal worthiness in his actions. He is patient in adversity, restrained in his prosperity, and possesses what is the most difficult kind of control: a self-control of long standing. His literary erudition adds to these good qualities, and excellently adorns an already praiseworthy nature. For it is through books that the prudent man discovers how he may become wiser. There the warrior finds how he may become staunch in his greatness of soul; there the prince learns in what manner he may control diverse peoples under an equal rule. No fortune in the world can exist that the glorious knowledge of literature does not enhance.

Welcome, too, that greater thing that the prayers of the commonwealth have gained. Your prince is even learned in ecclesiastical letters. By these we are reminded of whatever pertains to the well-being of humanity: to adjudicate correctly, to know the good, to revere the divine, and to be mindful of the Judgment to come. Indeed it is necessary—for one who believes that he will have to plead his case on account of his own actions—to follow in the footsteps of justice.[5] And so, I may observe that while reading sharpens the intelligence, divine reading continually works to perfect a dutiful person.

Let us come to that most generous sobriety of his private life, which has amassed such an abundance of gifts, such a wealth of feasts, that in the light of his former activity he will be seen to require nothing further in conducting the realm.[6] He is prompt in hospitality and most dutiful in compassion, so that although he has spent much, his worth has kept increasing through heaven's reward.

The whole world ought to hope for such a man as the one we are seen to have chosen, who—managing his own belongings reasonably—does not crave the belongings of other people. For the necessity of committing excesses is removed from princes who are accustomed to being moderate in their own expenses. The view that enjoins moderation is, of course, being praised, since too much of even what is considered to be a good thing is not acceptable.

Rejoice, then, Fathers of the Senate, and render thanks to the Heavenly Grace on our behalf, since I have ordained such a prince with me who will perform the good deeds that flow from our justice, and make his own good deeds manifest through his own sense of duty. For the virtue of his ancestors will admonish this man, and Theodoric as his uncle will effectually inspire him.

3. Queen Amalasuintha to Justinian Augustus

The kindness of Your Piety delights us so much in permitting us freely to ask for whatever we may desire from among your share of belongings in order to enhance our glory. For the heavenly powers have assigned such treasures to you that you richly abound in their gifts, and you grant with a benevolent spirit things that are necessary to those who hope for them.

And so, reverently saluting Your Clemency, I have directed the bearer of these letters to the favor of Your Excellency. In this way you may command, with God's grace, that the marble statues and other necessary items that we previously ordered Calogenitus to secure for us shall reach us by means of the present bearer. We therefore may acknowledge ourselves to be esteemed by Your Revered Piety.

You cause our prayers to be fulfilled; we are adorned with your glory. For it is known that you surpass whatever praises we can address to you.

It is fitting that, with your help, the Roman world of yours should also shine brilliantly—that world that Your Serenity's love embellishes.

4. Queen Amalasuintha to Theodora Augusta

Since it is characteristic of our way of life to seek those things that are considered to pertain to the glory of pious princes, it is appropriate to venerate you in written words—you who all agree are continually enhanced in your virtues.

Harmony exists not only between those who are in each others' presence; indeed, those joined together in the charity of the spirit have an even greater respect for each other.

For this reason, rendering to the Augusta the affection of a reverent greeting, I hope that when our legates return—those whom we have sent to the most clement and glorious prince—you will make us rejoice in your safety. Your propitious circumstances are as welcome to us as our own. It is essential to make your safety our heartfelt concern. It is well known that we hope for this unceasingly.

NOTES

1. Procopius was secretary to Belisarius, Justinian's general.

2. This work is known to us in Jordanes's abridged version under the title *Getica*, finished about 551.

3. Ursula Dronke, *The Poetic Edda: The Heroic Poems* (Oxford: Clarendon P, 1969), I:192ff. and 217ff., fully details the Ermanaric legends.

4. Procopius's *History* preserves two other letters of Amalasuintha over the Byzantine use of the Sicilian port of Lilybaeum (in modern times, Marsala): one to Belisarius and one to Justinian. Belisarius wanted to occupy the ports as a vantage point in his war against the Vandals. It is thought that these letters, too, contained implicit negotiations with Justinian in preparation for Amalasuintha's possible flight from Italy.

5. Perhaps a significant, though veiled, allusion to the past insolence of Theodahad. While this line can be taken to mean the Last Judgment, it is also a reminder that Theodahad in fact had once been prosecuted for unlawful seizure of properties. He indeed refers, in his companion speech before the Senate, to the fact that Amalasuintha had caused him plead his case publicly, prior to naming him her co-regent.

6. Amalasuintha suggests, not so subtly, that since Theodahad has already enriched himself, he probably won't see the need to continue his grasping ways.

FURTHER READING

Amalasuintha. *Monumenta Germaniae Historica: Auctorum Antiquissimorum.* Vol. 12. Cassiodorus, *Variae,* Book X, pp. 296, 298–299, 303, 304. Berlin, 1894.

―――. Procopius of Caesarea. *History of the Wars.* H.B. Dewing, trans. Vol. II, pp. 252–255; vol. III, pp. 12–43. London and New York: Loeb Library, 1914–1928.

S.J.B. Barnish, trans. with notes and introduction. *Cassiodorus: Variae.* Liverpool: Liverpool UP, 1992.

Norman H. Baynes. "Justinian and Amalasuintha." *English Historical Review* 40 (1925), 71–73.

Thomas S. Burns. *A History of the Ostrogoths.* Bloomington: U of Indiana P, 1984.

Eleanor Shipley Duckett. "The Gothic Rule in Italy: Cassiodorus, Secretary of Theodoric the Great." In *The Gateway to the Middle Ages,* pp. 58–100. New York: Macmillan, 1938.

Herwig Wolfram. *History of the Goths.* Translated by Thomas J. Dunlap. Berkeley: U of California P, 1988.

CHAPTER 5

Three Consecrated Women
of Merovingian Gaul

Radegund of Poitiers (520–August 13, 587)
Caesaria of Arles (*fl. ca.* 550)
Baudonivia of Poitiers (*fl. ca.* 605–610)

What we know of Radegund, royal founder of one of the earliest religious houses for women in Gaul, can be gathered from her epistolary poems and from three other principal sources in her own time. Gregory of Tours[1] provides information about her in several of his books. Venantius Fortunatus[2] wrote her biography and, in his profession of court poet, honored her with graceful lyrics addressed to her queenliness. He often mentions her hospitality gratefully and thanks her for gifts of food, including a homemade cheese in which her prioress, Agnes, left a delicate thumbprint. On another occasion he sends a verse tucked among fragrant herbs in a salad basket together with purple violets, royal in hue and scent. Added to Gregory's and Fortunatus's reminiscences is the biography by Baudonivia, a nun in Radegund's convent, who received an assignment from her abbess Dedimia to write the saint's life some twenty years after her death.

Radegund was born at Erfurt in the kingdom of Thuringia in about 520 during the reign of the eastern emperor Justinian. Berthar, her father, had shared Thuringia with his brothers Hermenefrid and Baderic. Radegund and her younger brother were brought up in the household of her aunt Amalaberga and uncle Hermenefrid after he had killed her father and Baderic. Radegund remembers with tearful affection her cousin and childhood playmate Hamalafred in *The Fall of Thuringia* and the *Letter to Artachis*.

The assault on Thuringia in 531 was the deed of two of Clovis's sons: Theodoric I, king of the Austrasian Franks, and his half-brother Clothar I (511–561), king of Neustria in northwestern France. After the brutal sack of Thuringia, Clothar won Radegund and her brother by lot or combat as his share of the spoils. He took them to his royal estate at Athiès on the Somme River. While waiting for her to grow old enough to marry, Clothar had Radegund educated. "She was nurtured," wrote Fortunatus, "on all that was taught by Gregory and Basil, strong Athanasius and gentle Hilary, Ambrose, Jerome, Augustine, Sedulius, Orosius, Caesarius."

In 540 the wedding of Clothar and Radegund was solemnized at Soissons, Clothar's capital city. Through her marriage, Radegund became related to the recently deceased Amalasuintha, since Clothar and Amalasuintha were cousins. As the son of the first Christian king of the Franks, Clothar was nominally a Christian. His father was Clovis. His mother, Clothilda, who was the daughter of the Burgundian king Chilperic, had founded a nunnery at Chelles near Paris and another small house at Tours. Clothar converted Radegund to Christianity, but he himself had gained a reputation for cruelty and sensuality. When he married Radegund he had other spouses and concubines; it seems that she was the fifth of his seven wives.

Clothar's political motive for marrying Radegund was to legitimize his claim to Thuringia. To Radegund the marriage was repugnant. As a wife she provoked the king's annoyance for her many pieties and mortifications. According to Venantius Fortunatus, he accused her of being more nun than queen when she avoided the conjugal bed to keep nocturnal vigils. She also arrived late at the dining table, where she was expected to preside. Radegund may have for some time wanted to evade Clothar, but when in her absence from the court he had her younger brother murdered, she felt she could no longer live with him. Allowing Clothar to think she would return, Radegund fled to Noyon, where she persuaded Bishop Médard to consecrate her as a deaconess. Despite his unwillingness to thwart Clothar, who had sent soldiers to threaten him physically, Médard acquiesced after Radegund placed her jewels and richly ornamented robes on the altar and demanded consecration.

From Noyon Radegund traveled to Tours as a pilgrim to St. Martin's tomb there. She then went to live at the villa Clothar had given her at Saix, where she extended food, baths and treatment to the sick and needy. Perhaps it was St. Hilary's shrine that drew her to Poitiers. There she was able to elude her husband, who had traveled to Tours with Bishop Germanus of Paris to try to get her back. Germanus instead dissuaded Clothar from this hope. Now in old age, Clothar was induced to donate the buildings for Radegund's monastery of Notre Dame of Poitiers, where she founded her community of women. After Clothar's death, she acknowledged his generosity.

The letter she addresssed "to the holy fathers in Christ and to the Lord Bishops" is included by Gregory of Tours in his *History of the Franks*. Not wanting the burden of administrative tasks and desiring to be free for her devotions, she transferred her authority to Agnes, with their permission, and solicited their protection:

> I asked myself, with all the ardor of which I am capable, how I could best forward the cause of other women, and how, if our Lord so willed, my own personal desires might be of advantage to my sisters. Here in the town of Poitiers I founded a convent for nuns. Clothar, my lord and King of glorious memory, instituted this and was its bene-factor. . . . I accepted the Rule in accordance with which Saint Caesaria had lived. . . . I appointed as Mother Super-ior the Lady Agnes, who became like a sister to me, and whom I have loved and brought up as if she were my daughter from her childhood onwards. . . . If the Mother Superior, Agnes, my sister in God, or her community should ever seek your help in time of trouble, because they have been molested by their enemies, I pray that they may be able to rely upon the God-given solace of your sympathy and the pastoral care that in your loving kindness you give to them.[3]

In 552 Bishop Germanus consecrated the buildings and profess-ed the nuns.

Eager to have a rule of monastic living for her women, since she was unable to count on guidance from Maroveus,

Bishop of Poitiers, Radegund turned for help to the abbess Caesaria of the monastery of St. Jean in Arles. This was the younger Caesaria; the elder woman of that name had been the sister of Bishop Caesarius.

After 567, the year the Cross came to Poitiers, Radegund sent to Arles, or she may have traveled there personally, to obtain a copy of the first monastic Rule designed for women. Caesarius, Bishop of Arles, who had jurisdiction over the southern Burgundian churches, had composed the Rule for his sister's house, the earliest female monastery in Gaul. Its church had been dedicated on August 26, 513.

Caesarius's Rule for women contained forty-one articles, a recapitulation in nineteen articles, and a prologue. The nuns were to be completely enclosed. Male visitors were out of the question, except for the clergy. Meals with visitors were also proscribed, as were the acceptance of clothing from outsiders and the exchanges of gifts and letters. Only the sick could eat meat. The women slept in dormitories, although Radegund was privileged to have her own cell. Clothing had to be plain in color, or else of milk-white wool, spun and woven on the premises. The Rule tolerated neither black nor bright colors. There was to be no silver or ornamentation. Tapestries and lavish bed coverings, pictures, decorations, and individual armoires were likewise proscribed.

Housekeeping chores were done in common, with exemptions from kitchen and laundry duty on the part of the abbess—although as Fortunatus lovingly observed, Radegund chose to scrub pots and vegetables as a special mortification. There were offices for particular tasks: the *praeposita*, or deputy abbess, the *formaria* in charge of novices; the cellarer; the gatekeeper; and the sicknurse. The women were not supposed to embroider or make elaborate woven coverlets. The only permissible needlework was the embroidering of handkerchiefs and towels which the abbess ordered. However, there is evidence that the women did spinning, for Radegund left her spindle behind.

The important work was literary. The women had to be able to read and write. They read or listened to the divine service, they copied manuscripts, and they devoted two hours each day to books. Caesaria's letter speaks out with welcoming warmth, while maintaining a rather uncompromising tone about convent behavior. These are new sisters; they can benefit from her affectionate harangue. She has a realistic awareness of the necessary adjustments ladies of rank will have to make to the enclosed and disciplined life. She knows about the wealth Radegund has at her disposal, and even anticipates the presence of poor or disinherited women among the convent's number. She mentions items in the Rule that Radegund would receive, stressing the business of reading and writing. Her array of biblical allusions gives solid backing to this aspect of the Rule and demonstrates the priority Caesaria herself gave to study. Although the Rule was strict about diet, Caesaria advises Radegund against fasting to extremes lest her health suffer.

On the matter of male visitors Caesaria speaks severely—has she heard rumors of the friendship between Fortunatus and Radegund? She exhorts the women to avoid male protectors and to conduct themselves like men, as she holds up masculine examples of strength and worth: men listen to their rulers' commands, men fight in battle to save their bodies from injury. She sees the women as combatants. Let them emulate men, but only in the spiritual sense.

The Rule provided for strict enclosure and scholarship, and evidently, Radegund's women were readers and writers. The bookish activity that went on—as well as the flurry of poems exchanged among Venantius Fortunatus, Agnes, and Radegund—created an unusual literary ambience and made Radegund's monastery a center of Christian and humanist letters. Fortunatus, for his part, acknowledged Radegund's lyrics, giving evidence of her as a poet: "You send me splendid songs on little tablets; to their dead wax you restore the honey! You prepare great feasts on holy days, but I'm more eager for your messages than your banquets. The verses you send are full of pleasing words, and with these words you bind our hearts!"[4]

Literary practitioners in the midst of such comforts of monastic life as baths and backgammon, Radegund's women had a refuge in a period of bitter, bloody political turmoil. Clothar's sons (Sigibert, Chilperic, Guntram, and Charibert) wrangled among themselves. Several of their wives were murdered. During this period of court intrigues, violence, and wars, Radegund felt the need of divine protection to recover the stability of the realm. She began to collect relics. With the help of her stepson Sigibert, with whom she enjoyed a friendly relationship, she was able to secure fragments of the Holy Cross from Constantinople. She also had blood relatives there to whom she could appeal, for it was to Constantinople that the survivors of the Thuringian war had fled. Her epistolary epic, *The Fall of Thuringia*, may have accompanied her request for a fragment of the Cross. Together with other relics, the Cross arrived in Tours between 566 and 573. Fortunatus glossed over the arrival of the relics in his *Life of Radegund*, but he celebrated the occasion with his famous hymn to the Cross:

> The banners of the King advance,
> The mystery of the Cross shines forth.
> Here the Creator of our flesh
> suspended was in His own flesh,
> upon a criminal gibbet.[5]

The monastery of the Virgin Mary was renamed Sainte Croix.

Because of her energetic piety, political and ecclesiastical connections, and the special status of her convent, Radegund probably represented a threat to her local prelate, Bishop Maroveus of Poitiers. The arrival of the relics stirred his resentment, and he left for his country house, refusing to provide the suitable ceremonies for receiving them. Radegund then turned to her friends Sigibert and Bishop Euphronius of Tours, who conducted the procession with psalms, censers, and candlelight. Nor could Maroveus be counted on to bury Radegund when the time came at last. She died on August 13, 587, and was buried three days later. "I myself was present at her funeral," wrote Gregory of Tours, who both performed the funeral ceremony and wrote her eulogy:

> The blessed Radegund, whom I mentioned at the beginning of my book about martyrs, migrated from this world after completing the labors of her life. After receiving the news of her death, I went to the convent of Poitiers that she had founded. I found her lying on a bier; her holy face was so bright that it surpassed the beauty of lilies and roses. Standing around the bier was a large

crowd of nuns, about two hundred of them, who had converted because of Radegund's preaching and adopted the holy life. According to the status of this world not only were they [descended] from senators but some were [descended] from the royal family; now they blossomed according to the rule of their piety. They stood there weeping and saying: Holy mother, to whom will you leave us orphans? To whom do you entrust us who have been abandoned? We have left our parents, our possessions, and our homeland, and we have followed you.

Gregory continues with his function in Maroveus's place:

"Since I was requested by them, I blessed the altar in her cell. But when we began to move the holy body and to escort it with the chanting of psalms, then some possessed people shouted, acknowledged this saint of God, and said that she was tormenting them. As we passed beneath the wall, a crowd of virgins began to cry and weep from the windows of the towers and from the tops of the fortifications of the walls, with the result that in the midst of the sobbing and rejoicing of the psalms no one could keep themselves from weeping. The clerics too, whose duty was the chanting of psalms could scarcely recite the antiphon because of their sobbing and weeping. Then we came to the tomb. The foresight of the abbess had prepared a wooden casket in which she placed Radegund's body, packed in spices. The container for this entombment was therefore larger [than usual]; the casket was formed by removing one side from each of two tombs and then joining them together."

The abbess and nuns went to the places where Radegund was accustomed to read and pray, weeping over her empty cell, her kneeling mat, her book, and "the spindles on which she used to weave during her long fasts."[6]

Radegund's biographers, Fortunatus and Baudonivia, praise her piety and learning: she deprived herself of sleep at night to read the Scriptures; she labored as a motherly teacher of her convent flock. As a healer and miracle worker among the sick and poor, she employed her physician, Reovalis. A tireless ascetic, she imposed mortifications on herself, harsh fasts, and vigils. In times of extreme stress she chastened her body with burning irons and chains.

The numerous miracles attributed to Radegund—her ability to feed, clothe, and care for her flock as well as the needy who came to her doors—are not just marvels of inventiveness, but are rooted in economic realities during a time of upheaval and scarcity. Radegund's high-ranking connections, the royal wealth and the land she had been able to secure for her monastery, as well as her bounty of relics had made Sainte Croix a center of stability and near-opulence, serving to attract other well-born women with fortunes to the community.

Radegund's two biographers, while complementary, are different. Fortunatus stresses her meek saintliness and rigorous asceticism, and as his lyrics show, a courtly reverence for the *lady*. Baudonivia draws attention to her subject's status as a queen of authority, who wielded political influence in the struggle between the monastery and the king. Baudonivia points out her strength as protector, her severity as an educator, and an august capacity to inspire awe, even fear.

Fortunatus dwells on Radegund's mortifications, her bathing the sores of the sick with her own hands, her kissing lepers, drudging in the kitchen, subsisting on a meatless regimen of lentils and vegetables. She prostrates herself in vigils, she gorges on her own tears. Fortunatus downplays her privileged status and her ties to the Merovingian and the Frankish kingdoms, in other words, that efficient aspect of her royalty that enabled her to bypass Maroveus and refuse to defer to him. Fortunatus hurries over the founding of the monastery, diplomatically choosing not to draw attention to Clothar's loss of his queen and his capitulation. Obviously not wanting to dwell on her clash with the authorities, he skips over Radegund's determined collecting of relics. He is chary of heaping up miracles, "lest too many arouse scorn." Wonders like the rescue at sea (described below) are not found in his biography.

Baudonivia probably wrote between 605 and 610, since Queen Brunhild (d. 614) still reigned. Baudonivia says that as a child she knew Radegund, but also relies on accounts of people who remembered her well. She borrows from Fortunatus's *Life of St. Hilary* and other hagiographical sources. Among her additions to Fortunatus are the complicated maneuvers by which Radegund built up her monastic house, paralleled by her stalwart demolition of a pagan temple. The miracle of the burning throne to punish a bold servant shows the queen's wrath from beyond the grave. Baudonivia supplies the queen's vision of the beautiful, somewhat seductive young man who visits her in her room before her death, an anticipation of the saint's celestial nuptials.

The protest of ineptitude for her task is a set piece that Baudonivia words in an ornate style, reflecting the monastery's taste for classical letters and rhetorical study. The polite protest is a mark of erudition: she shows herself well acquainted with learned sources. In her account of how Radegund secured the relic of the Cross, Baudonivia compares her with Helena in language that reveals familiarity with an early text of the *Inventio Crucis* ("The Finding of the Cross").[7] If Fortunatus, not wanting to offend Maroveus, avoided describing the brouhaha over the arrival of the Cross, Baudonivia fearlessly brings up the Jews' opposition to Helena—a motif found in some of the eastern sources—when recounting the hostility of local persons jealous of Radegund's success.

Baudonivia makes another pair of important typological references that are not in Fortunatus: Radegund's dream of the man-shaped ship (chap. 3) and Radegund's calming of the waters during a tempest at sea (chap. 17). In both chapters, Baudonivia shows that she is familiar with scriptural glosses by Augustine and other patristic writers. The dream of the man-shaped boat and the miracle of the rescued ship signify Noah's ark as the Church, and the Flood that prefigures Christian deliverance and salvation. Augustine saw the ark as a symbol of the City of God throughout this world's pilgrimage. It is the Church which is saved. The ark's measurements "symbolize the human body, in the reality of which Christ was to come, and did come, to mankind."[8]

Radegund's role, then, in building her arklike monastery (in the chapter immediately following her destruction of the temple) stocked with potent relics, was that of founder, teacher, and reliable intercessor when it came to saving her faithful from the perils of worldly and pagan tempests. The miracle of the sinking ship in chapter 17 completes the ship-dream allusion in chapter 3—an echo of God's appearance to Noah. Travelers along the world's perilous journey are delivered when they throw themselves on Radegund's mercy and seek her wisdom as the new Noah. Her servants' reward is the advent of the dove of the Holy Spirit and the stilling of the waters. The dove's return to the ark signifies (as it did with patristic writers Tertullian, Ambrose, Jerome, and Chrysostom) the new Creation and the new Christian order. The three feathers are the persons of the trinity.[9] Where the courtly Fortunatus composes a lyrical and loving encomium, Baudonivia creates a conscious hagiographical construct, typologically defining Radegund both as a "new Helena" and a "new Noah."

The typology of Noah figures, incidentally, chime harmoniously with Radegund's own allusions to the sea and shipwreck in *The Fall of Thuringia*, in which she rhetorically vows to sail, row, or swim to reach her dear Hamalafred (as earlier, she had imagined swimming in a lake of tears). If the Anglo-Saxon fondness for describing sea voyages and ships tossed on stormy waves (e.g., *The Seafarer, Elene, and Andreas*) is any indication of a similar Germanic commonplace, then here is Radegund borrowing from her Frankish traditions.

Radegund's two poems, *The Fall of Thuringia* and the *Letter to Artachis*, reveal other literary affinities, as she relives her childhood and mourns for her lost family. The work gives a strikingly detailed memoir of the little girl's passionate devotion to her older cousin, Hamalafred. Since the sack of their family's home and city, he has taken refuge with their relatives in Constantinople. The letter also grieves for her brother, slain by her husband Clothar. Radegund feels responsible, since she had begged the boy to stay with her when he had wanted to leave to join Hamalafred. Her calling her brother "a downy-bearded boy" need not be read literally, since a silky beard was conventional for young masculine beauty.[10]

Both poems contain a *planctus*, a lament for the dead. *The Fall of Thuringia* richly fuses several genres. It is a letter, in which Radegund directs that timeless epistolary complaint to Hamalafred "Why don't you write more often?" It is an autobiography, as well as an Old English elegy bespeaking the loneliness and exile heard in early Germanic poetry. Radegund as the poem's barbarian woman ("barbara," line 31) who voices her isolation, who addresses absent loved ones by name, and who pours her tears for the suffering of kinsmen and subtly upbraids the enemy forms a link to the barbarian women whose lyric utterances will be treated in chapter 7 *(The Wife's Lament and Wulf and Eadwacer)*. The risk and bleakness of a wintry sea voyage belong to the tradition of Old English elegies like the *Wanderer* and the *Seafarer*, while the decay of a great hall and the deaths of companions recall the Old English poem *The Ruin*. These are the kinds of songs Radegund might have heard in her uncle's house in Thuringia.

As a work showing classical conventions, *The Fall of Thuringia* is a miniature epic comparing the barbarian city with Troy. It also borrows its persona from Ovid's *Heroides*, letters of the bereft daughters of heroes (Andromache, for instance), who, instead of hymning victories, give voice to the obverse, the heart-broken side of war's experience, that is, the woman's. Radegund adapts a wealth of conventions to herself, transcending convention, however, in the vivid, yearning accents of a consecrated woman separated from those whom she loves in the world beyond the cloister.

1. The Fall of Thuringia

The harsh nature of war! The malevolent fate of all things! How proud kingdoms fall, suddenly in ruins! Blissful housetops that held up for long ages now lie torched, consumed beneath a huge devastation. (lines 1–4)

This hall that once flourished in imperial splendor is covered no longer with vaulted arches but with wretched cinders. A pall of pale ashes buries the steep shining roof that long ago gleamed with red-gold metal. Its potentate has been sent into captivity, subject to an enemy lord. Its former glory has fallen into lowliness. The attendant crowd of striving retainers, all of whom served together, lies filthy in the dust of death. Their life is over. The brilliant throng, the circle of court dignitaries, lies unsepulchered, deprived of the honors due to the dead. (lines 5–14)

My beloved father's sister lies stretched on the ground, her milk-white body outshining the flame-spewing, red-gold glow of her hair. Ah, the foully unburied corpses have covered the field, and so the whole nation lies in one tomb.

No longer may Troy be the only city to lament her ruin. The land of Thuringia has endured an equal massacre. From this place the married woman bound in chains was dragged by her mangled hair, not able to bid a sad farewell to the gods of her hearth. The captive was not allowed to imprint kisses on his doorpost, or turn his eyes once more to the places he would never see again. The wife walked barefoot through her husband's blood, and the tender sister stepped over her fallen brother. The child, torn from his mother's embrace, still hung on her lips, and there was no one to accord them a flood of mourning tears. It was not enough that harsh fate deprived her of her child's life. The mother, all her breath gone, had also lost her son's affectionate weeping. (lines 15–30)

But I, a barbarian woman, cannot weep enough, even though in all my wretchedness I were to swim in a lake of tears. Each person had an individual lament. I alone pour forth laments for all, since the public grief is a private grief for me. Fortune took care of those men whom the enemy forces cut down. But I endure as a sole survivor in order to mourn for them all. I am forced to weep not only for dear ones slain; I weep as well for those whom kindly, life has preserved. Often I press my eyes shut, my face wet with tears. My sighs lie quelled, but my cares are not silent! (lines 31–40)

Eagerly I look to see whether a breeze will carry some greeting. Yet not a single shadow from among all my kinsmen comes to me. Unfriendly fate has torn from my embrace the one whose look used to console me with tender love. (lines 41–44)

Since you are so far from me, doesn't my grief torment you? Has bitter misfortune taken away sweet affection? At least remember, Hamalafred, how from your earliest years of youth I used to be your Radegund, and how much you loved me when you were a sweet baby and the son of my father's brother, beloved cousin. You alone were for me what my dead father, what my mother, what my sister or brother could be considered.

Grasped by your loving hands, ah, and hanging on your sweet lips when I was a little girl, I used to be caressed by your gentle words. There was scarcely an interval of time when an hour would not bring you back. Now ages fly by and I receive no words from you. Once, my savage griefs would churn within a beating breast, as if I thought I could summon you, my cousin, back at any time, from any place.

If your father, or your mother, or some cares of the realm detained you, then—even when you hastened back—you already seemed to me to be too slow! Fate was a warning sign that I should soon be deprived of you, my dear. Cruel love does not know how to wait a long time. I used to be tormented with anxiety if one and the same house did not shelter us: if you were going out of doors, I would believe that you had gone far, far away.

Now the East hides you too in the shadows, as the West hides me. The waves of the Ocean keep me here as the Red Sea detains you. The whole globe is thrown between the two of us who love each other. A world separates those whom no lands had parted before. All that earth holds forces loving ones asunder. If earth possessed more regions, your journey from me would be even more distant! (lines 45–70)

Be more fortunate, however, there where the good wishes of your family are keeping you, more fortunate than the land of Thuringia allowed you to be! (lines 71–72)

Here, on the contrary, I am tormented, burdened by strong griefs. Why are you unwilling to send me any sign of yourself? If only a letter would arrive to paint the features of him I long for but do not see! Or if only a picture would bring me the man detained in faraway places! You restore your forebears to life by your own excellence, you revive your kinsmen by your good name. It is as if the rose color of your father's beauty plays in your own cheek. Be assured, cousin, if you would send me a message, you wouldn't be altogether absent from me. If you sent speaking pages, they would be like a brother to me.

All people have a share of good things; I have only the solace of weeping. Oh, the outrage, that the more I love the less I receive! If other people, bound by the law of affection, pursue their servants, why, I ask, am I passed over by those to whom I am joined by the blood of kinship? (lines 73–84)

Often, in order to recover a household slave, a master will force a passage over the Alps congealed with ice and snow. He bursts into a gloomy cave hewed out of the rocks—no frost or snow hinder him in his burning desire. A lover, he runs barefoot, needing no guide. He seizes his prey despite the enemy's opposition. He braves hostile weapons and his own wounds in order to capture what he desires—nor does his love spare itself! (lines 85–92)

But I, in suspense at every moment on your account, enjoy scarcely a moment of time with a free and tranquil mind. If a breeze rustles, I want to know the places that detain you. If clouds are hovering, I seek your whereabouts. Do the warlike trumpets of Persia or Byzantium claim you? Are you a ruler of rich Alexandria? Do you live in the neighborhood of the citadel of Jerusalem, where Christ was born of his virgin mother? Not a single letter with your writing discloses this, and ah, my sorrow grows heavier and takes on greater force. Therefore, if neither lands nor seas will send me a message from you, at least let a bird of good omen bring me news! (lines 93–104)

If the monastery's sacred cloister did not hold me, I would come unannounced to wherever you are dwelling. Swiftly, over the wave-smashing tempests, I would set sail and would navigate happily through seas driven by wintry winds. Hanging above the waves, and stronger than the driven waves, I would control them. What the sailor fears would not terrify her who loves you. If the waves should break up my vessel with angry storms, I would seek you out, carried over the sea by an oarsman on a plank. And if by some mischance I were prevented from grasping the wood, I would come to you weary, swimming with my hands. When I should see you again, I would deny all the dangers of the voyage. You, sweet cousin, would soon ease the woes of my shipwreck. Or, if my final fate should rob me of my querulous life, at least your hands would raise my sandy burial mound. I would pass before your sweet eyes as a sightless corpse. And you, at least, would be moved to perform my funeral rites—you who begrudge the living woman your tears!

You who now refuse your words would grant me a song of funeral lament! (lines 105–122)

Why, cousin, do I avoid mentioning my brother, and why do I put off my weeping? Why do you keep silent about his death—O the deep sorrow!—about how guiltless he was when he fell by vile treacheries, and how, having misplaced his trust, he was snatched from the earth? Unhappy me, I begin my weeping afresh when I remember his death, and suffer again while I speak of these grievous things.

He hastens away, eager to see your face, but his love is not fulfilled as long as my love stands in his way. To avoid inflicting harsh wounds on me, he stabs himself! Because he feared hurting me, he now becomes the reason for my grief. A tender downy-bearded boy, he is slain. I, his sister, being absent, did not see his terrible death. Not only did I lose him, but I did not close his dear eyes, nor did I throw myself upon him, nor did I speak words of farewell. I did not warm his cold breast with my scalding tears, nor did I receive kisses from his dear dying lips. I failed to cling tearfully to his neck in a wretched embrace. I failed, gasping, to cherish his unhappy body to my breast. Life was denied him—why could not his dying breath as a brother be caught from his lips and be given to his sister? The little gifts I fashioned for him while he was alive I would have sent as an offering for his bier. Is it not at least permitted that my love should deck his dead body? Wicked me—believe me, I am answerable, brother, for your safety! All I was to him was the cause of his death, and I did not provide him a sepulcher! (lines 123–146)

I who left my homeland once have twice been captured, for when my brother lay cut down, I suffered the enemy again. This sorrow has returned so that I may weep for father and mother, uncle and kindred at their tomb. After my brother's death there is no day free of tears, for he has taken my joy with him to the dwelling of the shades. (lines 147–152)

Was it for this that my sweet kinsmen—wretched woman that I am—achieved the highest honors, for this their royal blood and birth descended in an unbroken line? I wish that my lips did not need to describe the evils I myself have suffered, or that, troubled as I am, I did not need to be consoled by you. At least, fair cousin, I ask that your letter may hasten now, so that your kind utterance may soothe my heavy grief. (lines 153–158)

I am also solicitous about your sisters, for I cherish them with the heartfelt love of a blood relation. I am not permitted to embrace their persons, those kinswomen I love, or even as a sister eagerly kiss each of their eyes. If, as I hope, they are yet alive, I ask that you give them my greetings, and that you bear back kisses in answer to my yearning. I beg that you remember me to the kings of the Franks, who cherish me with the affection due a mother.

Breathe life-giving breezes for many long years to come! And may my own safety flourish through your good offices. Christ grant my prayers: let this page reach loving ones! And may a letter painted with sweet messages come to me in return, so that this woman—whom lingering hopes have long tormented—may be refreshed by a swift rush of attendant prayers! (lines 159–172)

2. *Letter to Artachis*

My homeland was ravaged by fire, and my family's high houses fell in the destruction that the land of Thuringia suffered by the enemy sword.

If after this I should speak—a wretched woman driven by the war's unlucky strife—what sorrows shall I, a captive woman, be drawn to first? What is left for me to mourn? Is it this nation crushed by death? or my sweet family, ruined by diverse misfortunes? (lines 1–6)

My father was cut down first, and my uncle followed: both their deaths struck me a grievous blow. One honored brother remained, but a heinous destiny causes the sandy earth to heap heavily on his tomb—and on me. All of them are dead. Ah, the tearing inward pain of her who mourns! (lines 7–11)

You, Hamalafred, were the only one left and now you lie lifeless! Do I, Radegund, ask for this after so long a time? Has your letter come to me, unhappy woman, to say this? Have I long awaited such a gift from one who loves me? Do you send me these reinforcements as your soldierly service? Do you send me these silken skeins[11] as my daily spinning portion, so that I as a sister may be consoled as I spin? Is this the way your care comforts my sorrow? Should your first and last message bring such things? Have we not hastened with our gushing tears, wishing for something different? (lines 12–21)

This galling sweetness should not have been offered to reward my hopes. Full of anguish I have racked my heart with violent feeling. Is so great a fever of spirit to be cooled by these tears? I was not entitled to see him alive or to be present at his tomb. Now I bear both these losses in addition to your funeral rites. (lines 22–26)

Dear foster child Artachis, why do I mention these things, adding your own weeping to mine? I ought instead to have offered a kinswoman's solace, but grief for the dead forces me to say bitter words. He was close to me—not bound by distant ties, but as a cousin, child of my father's brother. My father was Berthar, his was Hermenefred: we were the children of brothers, and now we are worlds apart. (lines 27–34)

You, at least, dear nephew Artachis, take the place of that gentle cousin, and be mine in affection as he once was. I beg you to send frequent inquiries to my monastery, for news of me. Let this house continue to be your defense before God, so that our constant devotion may reward you—together with your dear mother—with a worthy throne among the stars. Now may the Lord grant you blessed ones abundant safety for the present, and glory in the world to come. (lines 35–42)

3. *Caesaria to Radegund and Richild*

To the sainted ladies Radegund and Richild,[12] from the humble Caesaria:

I was filled with spiritual joy beyond measure when your letter arrived, and I have reread it. For I recognized that you have chosen to hold to the decision by which you are preparing—with God's grace—for life everlasting. You do this so that you may gain eternal riches and exultation with the saints—which are without end. May "our lord God, who raised up those who were cast down, released those who were in chains, and gave sight to the blind" (Psalms 145.7, 8) himself guide you along the right path. May he himself teach you how to do his will, and may he grant you to walk in his ways, guard his teachings, and meditate on his law. Just as the Psalmist has said: "And he will meditate on his law both day and night" (Psalms 1.2). And again, "The teaching of the Lord illuminating their eyes, the law of the Lord transforming the souls of those without blame" (Psalms 18.9, 8).

You must pay attention when divine lessons are read, as carefully as men of the world give heed when royal commands are read. Let the whole mind, thought, and contemplation dwell on the Lord's precepts. Fear them with anxious care. "Cursed be they who avoid your commands" (Psalms 118.21). And whoever does not keep any one of God's commandments even the least, "shall be called the least in the kingdom of heaven" (Matthew 5.19). Carry this out: "The meditation of my heart is always in your sight. In my heart I have hidden your words so that I may not sin against you" (Psalms 18.15; 118.11).

And because God has deigned to choose you, ladies most beloved to me, in hereditary succession to him, render thanks to him, bless him in every season. Abstain from all vice, from all sin, because "who sins is a slave to sin" (John 8.34). Love and fear the Lord, because "the eyes of the Lord are on those who fear him, and his ears turn to their prayers" (Psalms 32.18). Let a pure heart be in you, a pacific heart. Be mild and humble, patient and obedient. Heed the Lord when he says: Upon whom shall I rest if not on the humble and the peaceful? "He has put down the mighty from their seat and exalted the humble" (Luke 1.52). Granted that you desire to be holy and good and praiseworthy, living under the Rule, but there is no teaching greater or better or more precious or more splendid than the reading of the Evangelists. Observe this, hold to this: what our lord and master Christ has taught us in his words and fulfills by his examples— he who has performed so many miracles in the world that they may not be counted, and endured so many evils from his tormentors with a patience that can scarcely be believed. It is patience that commends us to God.

Hear the Apostle: "If any wish to live a godly life in Christ, let them patiently endure persecution" (II Timothy 3.12). Just as God is pleased at your endeavor in taking vows, so does the Devil grieve over it. He has thousands and thousands of devices for doing harm, and "he desires to take God's food for himself" (Psalms 103.21). For this reason, pray ceaselessly that God may act against him. "Act manfully and let your heart be comforted" (Psalms 30.25). Heed the scripture that says, "My son, go to the service of God, stand in righteousness and awe, and strengthen your soul against temptation" (Sirach 2.1).

If you had been men, you would be going out, strongly and manfully, to fight your enemies so that your body might not be injured. Fight the Devil just as strongly and manfully, so that he cannot slay your souls with his counsels and exceedingly evil strategems. Cry continually to God, "God, incline to my aid! Be my help! Do not abandon me and I will be safe!"

When you recite the Psalms, be attentive and diligent to what it says there and what it teaches you. Sing the Psalms wisely: just as the Lord remains on the cross for you; since he stayed on the cross, you too stay—as if crucified—with the work of God! Do not do otherwise! Do not dare to speak or do anything! Be peacemakers in all things, because his dwelling place [the Church] has been built in peace. "Blessed are the peacemakers, since they shall be called the children of God" (Matthew 5.9). "Let not the sun go down on your wrath" (Ephesians 4.26). "Great peace have they who love thy name, Lord, and it is not an offense to them" (Psalms 118.165). For the virginity of the flesh means nothing where wrath of heart dwells. And elsewhere Scripture says: God has commanded you to be peaceful and harmonious "together in his house" (Psalms 67.7).

I greet you with the humility and love that I owe, more than it can possibly be said, even though I am very insignificant and undiscerning. I pray God that he may deign to rule, protect, and preserve you, and that he who deigned to give you your novitiate may also deign to bring it to perfection. For it is not the one who begins but the one "who perseveres to the end that will be saved" (Matthew 24.13). Just as our humility rejoices and delights in God, concerning your undertaking, so God and his angels are happy about your profession of vows and your achievement of perfection. You have assets, I also know, since you have inherited resources in abundance.

Give as much as you can to the poor. "Store up treasures for yourself in heaven" (Matthew 6.20) so that this scripture may be fulfilled in you: "He distributed, he gave to the poor. His righteousness endures forever" (Psalms 111.9). Just as it is written: as water quenches fire so do alms wipe out all sin (cf. Tobit 4.11). Let your hope be in God, because it is written, "Cursed be the man that trusts in man" (Jeremiah 17.5).

Let there be no woman from among those entering who does not study letters. Let them be bound to know all the Psalms by memory. And as I have already said, be zealous to fulfill in all things what you read in the Evangelists. I have sent a copy of the Rule which our lord and bishop Caesarius of holy and blessed memory has made for us. See well to yourselves how you safeguard it!

Let your sisterhood be firm under my authority, because if you live according to it, you will take your place among the wise virgins and the Lord will lead you into his kingdom. You will perceive that "neither has the eye seen nor the ear heard, nor has it entered into the heart of man what the Lord has prepared for those who love him" (I Corinthians 2.9) in the land of the living where the saints rejoice in glory. There you will say, rejoicing and exulting in the Lord: "For he that is mighty has done great things for us, and holy is his name" (Luke 1.49). And "he has raised up his people in exaltation and his chosen ones in happiness" (Psalms 104.43). May God, who reigns forever, see to it that your stainless women arrive there. Amen.

It has come to me that you are fasting to excess. Do all things reasonably if you care for me and are at all times able. For if you begin to fall sick because of that excess, afterwards those things will be necessary for you that God did not intend. You will require and need to consume dainty foods out of the proper season, and you will not be able to rule over those blessed women. Heed what the Lord says in the gospel: "Not that which enters the mouth defiles a man" (Matthew 15.11). And the Apostle: "Let your service be reasonable" (Romans 12.1). Do everything, lady, in such a way—according to what you possess in the Rule you requested—that God may be blessed and praised by your good profession of vows. May you be a model for the faithful. "For whosoever shall do and teach, the same shall be called great in the kingdom of heaven" (Matthew 5.19).

Praise, therefore, and rejoice in the Lord, revered sisters in Christ, and give thanks continually that he has deigned to call you from this world's darkened way of life to the gate of tranquillity and religious rule. Be continually mindful of where you have been and to what reward you have come. Faithfully you have given up the world's darkness, and you have undertaken blissfully to see the light of Christ. You have disdained the firebrand of lust, and have attained to the cool refreshment of chastity. And because life's combat to the death is not wanting in you, be as careful about the future as you have been safeguarded from the past; for indeed all manner of sin and crime quickly returns to us if they are not fought against each day. Heed the apostle Peter when he says, "Be sober and watchful because your adversary the Devil circles around like a roaring lion seeking whom he may devour" (I Peter 5.8).

As long as we are living in this body let us fight against the Devil, day and night, with Christ the Lord as our assistant and commander. There are some undiscerning women who suppose that it is enough for them to change their clothing. For indeed, to put aside worldly dress and to assume religious garb—we can do this in the moment of an hour. We must truly work continually to uphold the practices of good persons, as long as we live, with Christ as our help. Let every soul who desires to preserve the religious Rule so strive to avoid gluttony, sexual desire, and drunkenness, that she cannot be weakened by excessive abstinence or provoked to luxury by an abundance of delicacies.

Continually read or listen to the divine lessons, because these are the ornaments of the soul. Out of them, hang precious pearls from your ears; out of them, derive your rings and bracelets. As long as you constantly perform good works, you will be adorned with these jewels. Let the woman who truly longs to safeguard the religious Rule in a stainless heart not go out in public, or else let it be made difficult. This way she may walk unstained in God's sight.

By all means, rely on male protection as infrequently as you can if you wish to guard your chastity. Nor let it be said by anyone, "My own conscience is good enough for me. Let anyone say what they like about me!" That kind of defense is wretched and fully odious to God. Look to it—you are secure in your own scruples; can you see into the scruples of the person you are speaking to? Know this most certainly, that a woman who doesn't avoid the protection of men will destroy either herself or another. Against the other vices it is useful for us to struggle employing every virtue, but you will not be able to combat lust unless you flee from living communally with men!

If you are of noble birth, be more humble in your religious life, rather than delighting in your worldly rank. "If anyone shall leave everything and follow me, he shall receive an hundred-fold and life everlasting" (Matthew 19.29). If any poor woman embraces holy living, let her give thanks to God, who will grant salvation to the poor and who will free those women from the world's shackles. "The rich will lack life's necessities and will suffer hunger, while those who seek God shall not want for all good things" (Psalms 33.11). Love one another if you wish God to dwell in your hearts, for it is written, "Who hates a brother or a sister is in darkness, and walks in darkness and doesn't know where he goes because the shadows blind his eyes" (I John 2.11).

There are perhaps women who have left their inherited fortunes to their families and are from that point forth disinherited. Let them heed the Lord when he said, "Sell all you own and give alms, for behold, all the world will be yours" (Luke 12.33). "He has distributed, he has given to the poor, and his righteousness endures forever" (Psalms 111.9).

Run the race faithfully, so that you may blissfully arrive and stand delighting and exulting in the sight of the Lord our God, who has deigned to choose you among the sheep of his flock; and in his kingdom just as in his earthly ministry, he who reigns forever will be ready to bestow thrones in heaven. Amen.

4. *The Life of St. Radegund by Baudonivia of Poitiers*

To the holy ladies adorned with the grace of worthiness, to the abbess Dedimia, and all the glorious congregation of the Lady Radegund, from Baudonivia, the most humble of all.

This task you have assigned me of writing the life of the Lady St. Radegund is like attempting to touch heaven with a fingertip. It is our duty to say the best possible things of her. But it is a task that ought to be given to those who have within them the fount of eloquence. For when such a thing is enjoined upon those eloquent persons, they are able to expound with fluency and refreshing song. On the contrary, those limited in their ideas and lacking the articulate flow can neither provide refreshment for others nor relieve their own dryness. Such persons would never attempt to write of their own accord and, if asked to write, are exceedingly fearful.

I recognize myself to be this kind of person, humble of spirit and possessing few expressive ideas. It is as important for the unlearned to keep silent as it is for the learned to speak out. Those who are well-taught can discourse eloquently upon a modest theme, whereas those lacking in education cannot produce even a modest discourse upon a great theme. For this reason, there are some who eagerly seek out an undertaking, while others shun and fear it.

Although I myself am the most humble of all the humble, yet it was she, the Lady Radegund, who reared me from childhood as her own menial household attendant and servant. And so I am able to discourse briefly, not fully, but at least incorporating some part of the immeasurable benefits I received from her illustrious example. To this end, as long as I continue publicly to commend her glorious life to the ears of her flock, I am ready to obey your most benevolent will, with an eloquence that is as devoted as it is unworthy.

Full of devotion, though lacking in erudition, I beg you for your prayers.

Let us not repeat those things that the apostolic man, the bishop Fortunatus, wrote in his Life of the blessed lady, but supply those things that he despite his comprehensiveness passed over. He enunciated it just so in his book when he said, "Let brevity suffice in the matter of the saint's virtues. Neither let an overly long account prove tedious, nor let the tale be too briefly told. Rather let the sense of the whole emerge from a few details."

Therefore, I have been inspired by the same divine Power that the blessed Radegund was so zealous to placate in this world, and with whom may she reign in the next. With simple rather than polished words do we strive to tackle the deeds she performed, and to embrace in brief space the great part of her miracles.

The Prologue ends.

Chapter 1. The Family and High Rank of Radegund and King Clothar

The first book of the life of the blessed Radegund contains an account of her royal origin and rank. There is no one who is unaware of what her conduct was when she was converted by her king and earthly consort, the lofty King Clothar. A noble sprig, she sprang from a royal race; what she inherited from her lineage she further ornamented with her faith. The noble queen, married to an earthly prince, was herself more heavenly than earthly. In that same short time of her marriage, while a bride and in the guise of a wife, she conducted herself so as to serve Christ with greater devotion. It grew clear among the laity that she acted as if she desired them to imitate her example. For while she was living in the world, even before her conversion, she was being formed by the religion of her soul as a model of the religious life. She was in no way shackled with the clogs of this world, but had girded herself with the obedience of a servant of God. She was diligent in the redemption of captives, lavish in spending for the needy, and whatever she gave to the poor she believed was for her own benefit.

Chapter 2. The Temple Built by the Franks

Although Radegund had been living until now with the king in a worldly manner, her mind was intent on Christ. I speak with God as my witness, for it is to God that the heart confesses even though the mouth is silent. From him the heart hides nothing even though the tongue does not speak. We tell what we have heard and give an eyewitness account of what we have seen.

When Radegund was invited to dine with the matron Ansifrida, she set out on the journey accompanied by a solemn procession of retainers. Traveling the length and breadth of the countryside, she came upon a place between a stretch of country and a path approaching a temple which the Franks had built. The temple was nearly a milestone's distance from the blessed queen's route. When she heard that the Franks had constructed a temple there, she ordered it to be burned down by her servants, for she judged it wicked to scorn the heavenly God and to venerate the Devil's devices.

When the Franks heard about this, they rushed to the place in a mob, attempting to defend the temple with swords and cudgels and bellowing like devils. The holy queen remained persistent and unmoved, for she bore Christ in her heart. She did not bestir her horse but sat mounted all the while until the temple had been burned to the ground. As she prayed, the people made peace among themselves. Once this was over, all of them marveled at the queen's strength and self-possession, and they blessed God.[13]

Chapter 3. The Vision She Saw of a Ship in the Form of a Man

Later, through the working of divine influence, she left the earthly king, since her vows demanded it while she was living on the country estate at Saix which the king had given her. In the first year of her conversion, she had a vision of a ship in the form of a man, with men seated on all his limbs. She herself was seated on his knee. The man said to her, "Now you are sitting on my knee, but in time you shall have your place to sit in my heart." The grace she was to enjoy was shown her.

She reported this vision quite secretly to her faithful followers, calling them as witnesses, since no one would know these things unless they were present. How discreet she was in conversation, how pious in every deed! In prosperity, in adversity, in joy, in sorrow, she was always even-tempered. She neither lost heart in adversity, nor grew proud in prosperity.

Chapter 4. How the King Wanted to Have Her Back Again—Lord John the Recluse

While she was living at that same country estate, word came that the king wanted her back. He was grieving over the loss he suffered as a result of having permitted such a queen to leave his side. Unless he could get her back, he scarcely wanted to go on living. When the blessed lady heard this, she was so extremely terrified that she gave herself over to even greater mortifications. She fitted a garment of harsh goat's hair to her tender body, she made it known that she would undergo additional torments of fasting, and she lay awake in nocturnal vigils. She threw herself wholly into her prayers. She scorned the throne of the country, she vanquished the blandishments of her spouse, she shut out the love of the world, and she chose to make an exile of herself lest she wander away from Christ. With her she still had her decorated felt cloak encrusted with gold and fashioned with gems and pearls. It was worth a thousand coins of gold. She ordered a nun named Fridovigia who was closest to her among her faithful followers, to send it to a reverend man, John, a recluse in Chinon castle. She asked him to pray for her so that she would not have to return to the world again, and asked him to send her a coarse garment of goat hair so that she might sully her body with it. He sent her the rough cloth, from which she made both undergarments and outergarments for herself. She also asked him to keep her informed if there were any cause for fear. For if the king insisted on having her back, she would rather end her life than have to return to be joined again to this earthly king, she who had already wedded the king of heaven. This man of God then spent the night in wakefulness and prayers, inspired as he was by the heavenly power. The next day he notified her that although this might be the king's will, it was not to be permitted by God. The king would be punished by God before he could take her back in marriage.

Chapter 5. How the Sainted Queen Built a Monastery in the City of Poitiers by the Order of the King Clothar—Spurning the World, She Entered Joyfully

After this pronouncement, the same Lady Radegund, her mind intent upon Christ, and inspired and aided by God, built herself a monastery at Poitiers by the order of the most high king Clothar. The apostolic man, Bishop Pientius, and the lord Astrapius quickly ordered this building to be placed under her authority. The holy queen joyfully entered this monastery, casting off the world's false allurements. There she gathered the ornaments of perfection and joined a great congregation of young girls to Christ, the immortal Bridegroom. Agnes was elected abbess, and it was agreed that Radegund would give her all of her personal goods, and she handed over her own abdicated authority. By her own jurisdiction she retained nothing for herself so that she might run unshackled, a light-armed footsoldier, in the footsteps of Christ. The more she disburdened herself in the world, the more she furnished for herself in heaven. Soon her holy profession of vows began to burn with the practice of humility, the fruitfulness of charity, the light of chastity, and the luxuriance of fasting. So completely did she surrender herself to the love of the heavenly Bridegroom that by embracing God in her pure heart she was able to feel Christ dwelling within her.

Chapter 6. How King Clothar went to Tours so That He Might Reach Poitiers and Get Back His Queen

But that malicious enemy of human happiness, whose will she loathed doing as long as she was in the world, did not cease to pursue her. She learned from messengers about the very thing she feared—namely, the arrival of the most high king together with his son, the eminent Sigibert of Tours.[14]

Chapter 7. How the Lady Radegund Sent
a Letter to the Bishop Lord Germanus—
How the King Sent the Bishop to St. Radegund
to ask Her Forgiveness, and How He Did This

When she realized this, the blessed Lady Radegund had a solemn letter composed in the presence of a sacred witness, and sent it to the apostolic man Germanus, bishop of the city of Paris,[15] who was with the king at the time. She had the letter sent secretly by her agent Proculus, with a gift and an official seal. When this man, who was filled with God, read it, he threw himself weeping at the king's feet before the tomb of St. Martin, in the presence of a sacred witness. He begged the king to abide by the message of the letter and not to go to the city of Poitiers. In sorrow, the king repented fully, understanding that this was the blessed queen's petition. He reconsidered the advice of his evil counselors. He judged himself unworthy, realizing that for a long time he had not deserved such a queen.

On the threshold of St. Martin's he prostrated himself at the feet of the apostolic man Germanus, and asked him to seek Queen Radegund's mercy on his behalf. He begged that she might forgive him for having sinned against her because of his evil counselors. As a result, divine vengeance punished those who were present—in the same way that Arius, when he disputed the Catholic faith, sent his household members off to their deaths. So it was with those who had acted against the queen. Then the king, fearing God's judgment—since the queen had been more obedient to God's will than to the king's when she had lived with him—asked Germanus to go quickly to her.

So the apostolic man, on arriving in Poitiers, went to the monastery. In the oratory dedicated to the name of the Lady Mary, he threw himself at the feet of the holy queen, begging her mercy on the king's behalf. Filled with joy that she had been snatched from the jaws of the world, she generously forgave him and prepared herself for the service of God. Wherever she went she was now unencumbered and free to follow Christ, whom she loved, and she hastened after him with a devout spirit. Deeply intent upon such things, therefore, she kept additional vigils and made herself the jailer of her own body to keep awake at night. And although she was merciful to others, she made herself her own judge; devoted to others, she was harsh in her own abstemiousness; generous to all, she was stingy with herself. For her it was not enough to be drenched in fasting unless she could conquer her own body.

Chapter 9. Her Vigils, Prayers, and Reading— Her Good Example and Her Privations

She didn't impose a chore unless she had performed it first herself. Whenever a servant of God called on her, she carefully asked him in what way he served the Lord. If she found out anything new from him that she had not done, she would at once impose the task upon herself. She would then instruct her congregation verbally about what she had already demonstrated by her example.

When the singing of psalms in her presence came to a close, she would conduct her reading. She never stopped, day or night, even while she was taking some scanty refreshment for her body. After the reading of the lesson she would say, with loving solicitude for our souls: "If you fail to understand what the reading is about, why don't you carefully search for it in the mirror of your souls?" Venturing to ask the question this way may have shown a slight lack of reverence. Yet with devout concern and motherly affection she would never give up preaching about what the lesson contained for the soul's salvation. Like the bee that chooses among different kinds of flowers to make its honey, she ardently gathered flowerets of the spirit from those who came to see her. From these blooms she ripened the fruit of good works both in herself and her followers.

Even during the night or whenever she appeared to seize an hour's nap, she always had someone read the lesson to her. If the reader felt herself growing sleepy and thought that Radegund was resting a little, she might stop reading. But Radegund's mind was absorbed in Christ, as if she were saying, "I sleep but my heart is wakeful" (Song of Songs 5.2). She would ask, "Why are you speechless? Read, don't stop!" When it was time to rise up again in the middle of the night, she was immediately ready, even if she had finished a complete cycle of services earlier and had not gotten any sleep until then. Rejoicing, she would rise up from her bed in the service of the Lord. She might have said with candor, "In the middle of night I will rise up and give thanks to you, Lord" (Psalms 119.62). Often she appeared to be asleep, and yet she chanted from the psalms while she slumbered. Really, she could have said, "The meditation of my heart is constantly in your sight" (Psalms 19.14).

Who could ever emulate the burning charity with which she loved all people! Within her glowed so many virtues: modesty with seemliness, wisdom with simplicity, sternness with mercy, erudition with humility. Hers, all told, was a life without spot, a life beyond reproach, a life in every way perfect unto itself.

Chapter 12. Her Servant Vinoperga, Who Dared to Sit on Her Throne

In addition to her miracles in praise of Christ, she performed others that frightened her followers. Vinoperga was one of her servants who through reckless presumption dared to sit on the blessed queen's cushioned chair after she had died. When she did this, the girl was struck a blow by God's judgment and burned so fiercely that everyone saw smoke pouring from her body and rising upward.

The girl cried out in the presence of all the people, confessing that she had sinned. She was on fire because she had sat in the blessed queen's chair. For three days and three nights together she suffered the heat, and screaming aloud, she cried, "Lady Radegund, I have sinned. I have done wrong. Please cool my limbs that are burnt with harsh torment. Be generously merciful; you who are renowned for your good works, you who are compassionate to all, be compassionate to me!"

Seeing her in such anguish, all the people prayed for her just as if Radegund were present, saying that whenever she was called on in good faith she was there. "Benevolent lady, spare her so that she may not be abandoned to such miserable torment!" The most blessed lady yielded to the prayers of all of them, and curbed the raging flame. She sent the girl home uninjured. And so the girl's punishment made everyone wary and respectful.

Chapter 14. The Relic of the Lord Mammas Which Lady Radegund Desired

From the time she entered the monastery, the East bore witness, and the North, South, and West proclaimed how great a number of holy relics she collected with the most faithful prayers. From every quarter she sought out those precious jewels which are hoarded in heaven and which Paradise possesses, and this devout woman succeeded in obtaining them for herself by means of gifts and prayers. Through these means, in continual meditation, she gave herself over to the chanting of psalms and hymns.

Word came to her at length about the lord Mammas,[16] the martyr whose sainted limbs reposed at Jerusalem. When she heard about this, she drank the news in avidly and thirstily. Like a person afflicted with hydropsy, who—however much she drinks from a fountain—grows increasingly thirsty, Radegund burned with the need to be drenched with God's dew. She sent the venerable priest Reovalis,[17] who was then still a layman and who to this day survives her in body, to the patriarch of Jerusalem to beg for a relic of St. Mammas. The man of God benevolently undertook to fulfill this request. He made Radegund's prayers known to his people in order to discover God's will.

On the third day, after he had celebrated the mass, he went with all the people to the blessed martyr's tomb. In a loud voice full of solemnity he publicly declared in this manner, saying, "I beg you, confessor and martyr of Christ, if the blessed Radegund is a true handmaid of Christ, let your power be revealed among the people. Allow her faithful soul to receive some relic of yours that she desires."

When the prayer was ended and all the people responded "Amen," he went into the holy sepulchre, continually announcing the blessed lady's faith. He touched the saint's members to ascertain which of these the most blessed saint would authorize to be granted to fulfill the Lady Radegund's request. He touched each finger of the right hand; when he came to the little finger, it detached itself at the pleasant touch of his hand so that it might satisfy the blessed queen's desire and fulfill her wish. The apostolic man sent the finger to the blessed Radegund with due ceremony. From Jerusalem to Poitiers the praise of God resounded continually in her honor.

Can you imagine with what fervent spirit, with what faithful devotion Radegund, awaiting the prize of such a relic, gave herself over to fasting? But while the blessed queen was rejoicing with complete enthusiasm at receiving this heavenly gift, she—together with her entire community—busied herself for a whole week in keeping vigils with the singing of Psalms, and in fasting, blessing God that she had deserved to receive such a gift. So God does not refuse his faithful who ask for a thing.

Often Radegund would gently say, as if it were an oblique manner of speaking that no one would understand, "Whoever has the care of souls must greatly fear the praise of all." But despite this, however much she wished to avoid it, the Bestower of Virtue was increasingly bent on revealing to everyone that she was faithful to him. And so, whenever there was a sick person, afflicted with any illness whatever, that person would call upon her and be restored to health.

Chapter 16. How She Sent to the Emperor for a Relic of the Wood of the Holy Cross

Now that she had gathered together relics of the saints, she would have wished for God himself to come down from his throne of majesty to dwell among us, if only that were possible. Even though she was unable to see him with her bodily eye, her spiritual understanding eagerly contemplated him with zealous prayers. But the Lord "will not deny good things to those who walk in innocence" (Psalms 83.13) and seek him out with their whole heart, soul, and mind. Such were the achievements of this sainted woman that divine benevolence showed itself favorable to her and sent her an inspiration. Both day and night the thought reposed in her heart that she might do as the blessed Helena had done.[18] Inspired with wisdom, full of the fear of God, and renowned for her good works, Helena had made a diligent search for the beneficent wood on which the world's Treasure had been suspended and weighed[19] in order to save us from the Devil's might. When the Cross arrived and was raised up, Helena ascertained that it was the same divine Cross on which God had been stretched in death.[20] She clapped her two hands together, and falling to the ground on bended knee, she adored God saying, "In truth you are Christ, the son of God, who came into the world and redeemed your own captives whom you created!"

What Helena accomplished in the East, blessed Radegund brought about in Gaul. Since she wanted in no way to act without consultation as long as she was living in the world, she sent a letter to the most excellent lord King Sigibert, under whose sovereignty the country was ruled. She asked his permission, for the sake of the whole country's well-being and the stability of his realm, to try to obtain the wood of God's Cross from the Emperor Justin.[21] The king very graciously gave his approval to the holy queen's request.

Full of devotion and kindled with ardent longing, Radegund did not send any gifts to the emperor, since she needed such moneys to serve God's poor. Instead she occupied herself with prayer in the company of the saints, whose relics she called on continually, and she dispatched messengers to the emperor. She obtained what she prayed for: the holy wood of God's Cross, ornamented with gold and jewels,[22] in addition to the many saints' relics that had been preserved in the East. Now they would reside together in one place, and she gloried very much in this.

In reply to the sainted woman's request, the emperor also sent his ambassadors with an evangeliary encrusted with gold and gems. Upon the arrival in the city of Poitiers of the wood on which the world's salvation had hung, together with the company of the saints and the Bishop,[23] the Enemy of mankind was working through his satellites, so that they rejected the world's Treasure. They were unwilling to receive it in the city, despite all the tribulations the blessed Radegund had undergone. Each one refused it for different reasons, as if joining ranks with the Jews. But it is not our place to discuss this. They would see— God knows his own people!

With blazing spirit and beating heart, Radegund sent a message to the most blessed king that the town was unwilling to receive its salvation. While her messengers were on their way back from the lord king, she entrusted for safekeeping the Cross of God and the relics of the saints to the male monastery she had founded at Tours. This was done amidst the singing of psalms.

Because of jealousy, the sacred Cross suffered no less than God himself, who, for the sake of his faithful followers, is continually being called and recalled before rulers and judges. He has endured all kinds of contempt so that his creatures shall not perish.

How much torment Radegund imposed upon herself through fasts, vigils, and the copious shedding of tears! Her entire congregation wept and lamented throughout these days until God looked down on the abjectness of his handmaid and put it into the king's heart that he must bring judgment and justice to the populace. So the devout king dispatched his loyal man, the distinguished Count Justin, to the city of Tours. There the apostolic man of God, the Bishop Lord Euphronius, was told to place the Cross of God and the saintly relics in Lady Radegund's monastery in high honor.

The blessed lady reveled joyously, and all the members of her house with her, once this advantageous gift from heaven had been bestowed upon her congregation. She gathered them together to celebrate the service of God, for she sensed in her mind that after she departed from them, they would have very little. And although she might secure relief for them once she exulted with the King of Heaven, this noble nurturer, this beneficent guide would never under any circumstances abandon her flock.[24] To her monastery she left this heavenly gift—the world's ransom from among Christ's relics—which she had sought in a faraway country for the honor of the house and the salvation of the people.

There, with the help of God's goodness and the power of heaven assisting, the eyes of the blind received light, the ears of the deaf were opened, the tongues of the mute regained their function, the lame walked, and demons were put to flight. What else is there to say? Each person, handicapped with whatever infirmity, came out of faith and regained health through the virtue of the Cross. Who can say how great a gift this sainted lady had brought to the city? Whoever lives by faith God blesses in his name. The most excellent lord king and the most serene lady Queen Brunhild (whom Radegund loved with deep affection), together with their holy priests and bishops, praised her monastery before divine witness.

Chapter 17. How Her Emissaries, Whom She Sent to the Emperor to Thank Him, Met with Danger at Sea

After she had received this divine gift, the sainted woman dispatched the priest we spoke of and other emissaries to the Emperor. As a token of thanks, she sent him a plain vestment. On their return journey, the sea grew wild and they endured many dangerous tempests and hurricanes the like of which they said they had never seen before. For forty days and forty nights on the open sea their ship was imperiled by dangers. In despair for their lives, looking death in the eyes, they made peace among themselves, for the sea threatened to engulf them. Seeing themselves at such terrible risk, they lifted their voices to heaven and cried out: "Lady Radegund, come to the aid of your servants so that we do not perish by drowning while we still serve you! Free us from death's danger, for the waves are now about to swallow us alive. You have always taken pity on those of your faithful ones who called to you. Have mercy on us! Come to the aid of your people, do not leave us to die!"

With the sound of their voices, a dove rose up from the waves and flew around the ship three times. As it flew the third time, the blessed queen's servant Banisaius reached out her hand in the name of the Trinity—whom the blessed woman always loved in her heart—and drew three feathers from its tail. She dipped them into the ocean, and the storm grew calm. The people called on the name of the blessed Radegund, and the dove appeared, restoring her servants to life from the gates of death. An immense peace settled upon the deep waters, and Radegund's people cried with loud voices, "You came, good Lady full of devotion, to free your captives from drowning in the flood!" By calling upon her, not only her own followers but also all people are saved through the goodness of their Lady Radegund. Her folk that she liberated from death brought the feathers here, arranged them, and worshipfully gave them to this holy place.

Chapter 20. The Year Before Her Death She Saw in a Vision the Place Prepared for Her

The year before she died she saw in a vision the place that was prepared for her. There came to her a very beautiful and richly dressed man who seemed youthful in age. As he addressed her he touched her sweetly and spoke caressing words to her, but she, zealous about her virtue, sought to repulse his blandishments. He said to her, "Why then are you inflamed with desire for me, and why do you seek me with tears, petition me with groans, beg me with lavish prayers? Why have you suffered so many torments for my sake, for me, who am always with you? You, precious jewel, you know that you are the foremost jewel in the diadem on my head."

There is no doubt that he himself visited her, and that she surrendered herself to him with total devotion, even while she was still alive in body, and that he showed her the glory that she was to enjoy. But this vision she very secretly confided to two quite faithful followers, adjuring them not to reveal it to anyone as long as she was still alive.

NOTES

1. Born in France and classically trained, Gregory of Tours (538–594) wrote his *History of the Franks,* in which there is a great deal about Radegund. He came to Tours in search of a cure at St. Martin's tomb. Eventually, he became St. Gregory, Bishop of Tours. Often at odds with the Merovingian kings, he tended to excuse those who—like Clovis, Clothar, and Guntram—protected the church.

2. The fluent Italian poet and rhetorician Fortunatus (530–609) resided at various courts, including that of Brunhild and Sigibert—Radegund's future stepson—for whom he wrote a wedding song. Fortunatus traveled in leisurely style via the Upper Danube and the Rhine to Cologne, Mainz, Metz, Verdun, Reims, and Paris before reaching Tours, which he visited to be cured of an eye ailment. At this stage of his life he enjoyed the friendship of Gregory and Radegund. He became a priest, then Radegund's chaplain, and eventually bishop of Poitiers. His works include occasional pieces, verse epistles, saints' lives, and hymns, notably the one to the Cross that Radegund brought to Poitiers.

3. Letter in Gregory of Tours, *History of the Franks,* 9.42, trans. Lewis Thorpe (New York: Viking Penguin), p. 535.

4. In brevibus tabulis mihi carmina magna dedisti/quae vacuis ceris reddere mella potes;/ multiplices epulas per gaudia festa ministras,/sed mihi plus avido sunt tua verba cibus:/versiculos mittis placido sermone refectos,/in quorum dictis pectora nostra ligas. *MGH: Auctores antiquissimorum,* p. 290, Song 31.

5. Vexilla regis prodeunt
   Fulget crucis mysterium
   Quo carne carnis conditor
   Suspensus est patibulo.

6. Gregory of Tours, *Glory of the Confessors,* trans. with introduction by Raymond Van Dam. (Liverpool: Liverpool UP, 1988), pp. 105–106, 108. On the merit of tears, see below p. 516, note 5.

7. E. Gordon Whatley, "The Earliest Literary Quotations from the *Inventio S. Crucis*: A Note on Baudonivia's *Vita S. Radegundis,*" forthcoming in *Analecta Bollandiana.*

8. *The City of God,* 15.26., Augustine develops the ark's similarity to the body: "And the door which it was given in its side surely represents the wound made when the side of the crucified was pierced with the spear. This, as we know, is the way of entrance for those who

come to him, because from that wound flowed the sacraments with which believers are initiated." Henry Bettenson, trans. (New York: Penguin Classics, 1984), p. 643.

And see Richard Unger, "Noah in Early Christian Art and Thought," chapter 3 in *The Art of Medieval Technology: Images of Noah the Shipbuilder* (New Brunswick, N.J.: Rutgers UP, 1991), especially pp. 32–36.

9. Fortunatus also records a miracle at sea (chapter 31), where the fisherman Florius is saved by calling on Radegund. The account lacks the features of Noah, the fully laden boat, and the circling dove, nor does it include Radegund's ship dream.

10. James A. Schultz, "Medieval Adolescence: the Claims of History and the Silence of German Narrative," *Speculum* (July, 1991): 529. Beardlessness or a newly growing beard "describes an ideal of youthful male beauty that is often invoked for those who have long since attained the status of adults, socially and sexually."

11. Radegund's *serica vellera*, skeins of Chinese silk, create a double image. They hint at the stuff spun by a woman who sings at her spinning and laments the absence of her love. The woman's spinning song is the "chanson de toile," or cloth-making song. But for Radegund the skeins also suggest the silk paper, or paper with the silky surface of the letter she receives. Papyrus from Egypt, waxed wooden tablets, and the recently introduced vellum were more usual writing materials in Radegund's day. Paper of Chinese silk probably works poetically here to suggest the distant East, where Artachis lives.

12. Since no Richild has been identified, see the information in Jo Ann McNamara, *Sainted Women*, p. 114n., that "Richild may have been the original Germanic name of Agnes."

13. Frankish paganism was thriving in Radegund's time and remained active into the next century in the dioceses of Rouen, Beauvais, Amiens, Noyon, and Cambrai. Among the *genii* the people were forbidden to invoke in their forest temple-shrines, such as the one that Radegund destroys, were the Sun and Moon, Neptune, Diana, Orcus, and Minerva. J. M. Wallace-Hadrill, *The Frankish Church* (Oxford: Clarendon P, 1983), pp. 18, 44, 56ff, 83ff.

14. Clothar's youngest son Sigibert was king of Austrasia, the ancient Frankish lands on both sides of the Rhine. Brunhild was his queen. Radegund enjoyed a cordial relationship with Sigibert, who helped her to bring the True Cross to Poitiers.

15. Germanus became bishop of Paris in 556, where he founded a monastery. He was buried in the monastery church, later known as Saint-Germain-des-Près.

16. Both St. Basil and St. Gregory of Nazianzus wrote about this eastern saint, a shepherd youth who died under Aurelian in 274 but whose remains were buried at Caesarea. Perhaps some relics were translated to Jerusalem.

17. Reovalis was a physician of Poitiers who had also studied medicine in Constantinople. Later he became a priest. His name comes up again in Gregory of Tours (*History of the Franks*, X, 10.15) because he had removed the testicles of a boy who was Radegund's servant, a medical procedure he learned in Constantinople.

18. On Helena, see above, chapter 2, p. 25.

19. The image of the Cross as a pair of scales weighing in its balances Christ, the treasure and ransom of humanity, occurs in Venantius Fortunatus's *Hymn to the Cross*.

20. Doubt that the cross might not be Christ's but one of the thieves' was dispelled, according to earlier Eastern accounts, when the sick were healed by touching the wood.

21. This was Justin II, Byzantine emperor of Constantinople, with whom Sigibert was seeking an alliance at the time. Sigibert included Radegund's petition with his own negotiations.

22. Justin had five fragments of the wood set in a cross shape within a plaque of blue enamel, decorated with a leafy scroll design. The plaque measured five centimeters in width and six centimeters in length. See Martin Conway, "St. Radegund's Reliquary at Poitiers," *The Antiquaries Journal* 3 (January 1923): 1–12.

23. Maroveus, bishop of Poitiers, refused to be present and galloped off to his country estate, according to Gregory of Tours.

24. One implication of this statement is that the strife between Sigibert and his brothers would threaten the monastery's stability.

FURTHER READING

René Aigrain. *Sainte Radegonde*. Rev. ed. Paris, 1952.

Baudonivia, "Vita Sanctae Radegundis," Liber II, pp. 377–395.

F. Brittain. *Saint Radegund: Patroness of Jesus College, Cambridge.* Cambridge: Bowes and Bowes, 1925.

Caesaria. Letter. In *PL. Supplementum*, Vol. 4.1404–1408 (Paris, 1967); and *MGH: Epistolae* Vol. 3, pp. 450–453 (Berlin, 1892).

Martin Conway. "St. Radegund's Reliquary at Poitiers." *The Antiquaries Journal* 3 (January 1923): 1–12.

Études mérovingiennes: Actes des Journées de Poitiers, 1–3 mai 1952. Paris, 1953.

Venantius Fortunatus. "Vita Sanctae Radegundis," Liber I, pp. 358–377. In *Monumenta Germaniae Historica: Scriptores Rerum Merovingicarum.* vol. 2. Hanover, 1888.

Mary C. McCarthy, trans. *The Rule for Nuns.* Washington, D.C.: Catholic UP, 1960.

Jo Ann McNamara, John Halborg, Gordon Whatley, eds. and trans. "Clothild, Queen of the Franks," pp. 38–50; "Radegund, Queen of the Franks and Abbess of Poitiers," pp. 60–105, with trans. of "The Thuringian War." Baudonivia, trans. of "The Life of Radegund," pp. 86–105; "Caesaria II, Abbess of Saint Jean of Arles," pp. 112–118, with trans. of Caesaria's Letter. In *Sainted Women of the Dark Ages.* Duke UP, 1992.

———. "A Legacy of Miracles: Hagiography and Nunneries in Merovingian Gaul." In *Women of the Medieval World: Essays in Honor of John H. Mundy.* Julius Kirshner and Suzanne F. Wemple, eds. New York, 1985.

Radegund. "De Excidio Thuringiae," and "Ad Artachis." In Venantius Fortunatus, *Monumenta Germaniae Historica: Auctorum Antiquissimorum.* Vol. 4, pt. 1. Berlin, 1991.

———. "The Fall of Thuringia." In *Sources and Analogues of Old English Poetry. The Major Latin Texts in Translation*, pp. 137–140. Trans. Michael Allen and Daniel G. Calder. Totowa, N.J.: Rowman and Littlefield, 1976.

Société des Antiquaires de l'Ouest. *Histoire de l'Abbaye de Sainte-Croix de Poitiers: Quatorze Siècles de Vie Monastique.* Poitiers, 1986.

CHAPTER 6

"Words Flowing Like Gold Fringes"

An Anonymous Letter-Writer of the Sixth Century
Eucheria of Marseilles (sixth century)

Late Roman culture was preoccupied with literary style—the poetic allusion and the topos, the epithet, the well-aimed metaphor, the *mot juste*. Two flamboyant works by sixth-century women, one steeped in classical cleverness, the other in the play of scriptural learning, show each woman taking tremendous pleasure in flaunting her language. The Christian letter-writer makes a pretense at modesty, but she is enjoying herself just as much as the pagan—if Eucheria is a pagan. Christian authors occasionally protested that they favored simpler locutions than those of the classically trained grammarians and rhetors, preferring what they called *sermo humilis*, or humble style. But the letter-writer, though addressing another pious woman of apparently loftier rank and education, finds that simplicity doesn't interest her. She cultivates the prodigal image with as lavish a hand as the epigrammatist Eucheria.

Latin schools of rhetoric in southern France were responsible for keeping up a thriving verbal activity without interruption. Gaul was known for its contests in oratory and for its professorships of rhetoric at Poitiers, Narbonne, Toulouse, and Bordeaux. Professors like Ausonius doubled as poets. Public speaker Symmachus called himself a graduate of the Garonne. "Gaulish eloquence" attracted the notice of people fond of letters, like St. Jerome. The arts of speaking and writing never ceased to be a habit, and the ongoing attention to grammar, rhetoric, and the craft of composition would account for the literary blossoming of the vernacular among the troubadours and the *trobairitz* that surfaced so brilliantly in the twelfth century.

An anonymous "letter to a friend" from one Christian woman to another is bound in the same manuscript as a fragment of Baudonivia's "prologue" to her *Life of Radegund*. This leads one to conjecture that a nun of Radegund's convent, with its literary tastes, might have written it. Affectionate friendship and the respect for erudition inspire the writer. Like Baudonivia she rhetorically protests her unworthiness. Her uses of Scripture are imaginative, in fact, wildly so, and she usually feels the need to explain them. Exuberant metaphors abound. The throat is a candleholder whose wick goes dry; the speaker's lack of eloquent "oil" invites comparison with the plea of the foolish virgins to the wise. The heart is a hinged book in which biblical knowledge is locked. Scholarship is a brilliantly colored robe, or a spindle made by Jesus, the carpenter's son, for spinning history in bright wools.

Many of these figures reflect feminine concerns, as do the letter-writer's copious allusions to concubinage, wifehood, fertility, conception, pregnancy, childbirth, and maternity to express the life of the mind and spirit. Feminine adornment and handiwork come spontaneously to the letter-writer's mind. Words are spun. Learning forms a headdress, its gold fringes flowing like words along both sides of the face. Eucheria, too, opens with a metaphor of incongruous weaving and needlework: gold threads twisted with horsehair, fine purple floss embroidered on coarse wool.

Eucheria was married to the grammarian Dynamius of Marseilles, a Frankish aristocrat. This Dynamius may or may not have been the governor of Provence of the same name, who collected rents for Pope Gregory and whose plotting against the bishop led to his losing his post, as Gregory of Tours tells in the *History of the Franks*. Marseilles was known for its Greek and Roman schools and its long tradition of letters. A patrician group of poets clustered around Dynamius. Very little of their work has survived. Extant, however, is an agreeably malicious epigram, attributed by Venantius Fortunatus to Eucheria, who he tells us was Dynamius's wife. Fortunatus had personally met Dynamius, with whom he also exchanged lyrics and letters.

Eucheria's epigram against a lowborn suitor bears the traits for which her husband's literary circle was known: refinement, complexity, and the ornate use of metaphor. A match with the oafish suitor, says the poem, would be comparable to a series of grotesque incongruities in both art and nature, which Eucheria develops in an outrageous array of *impossibilia*, conditions that violate the natural order. A bracketed last line, appearing in only one of the five manuscripts, may have been added by a later hand.

1. Anonymous Letter to a Friend

If you were not judging my silence as an offense to you—you who are of so lofty a lineage—I would have thought that the prophet's epigram applied to me when he declared, "If you have something to say, speak at once; if not, let your hand cover your mouth" (Sirach 5.12). For what could I respond, where could I venture to find the words to utter, when you embrace the entire substance of all the writings of the Bible in your letter so that you have left me nothing to say![1]

Until now, the treasure chest of the Testament has remained hidden from me, that is, the bookbinding clasps of your heart, in which a library of all the books is gathered. It certainly deserves to be gilded both inside and outside by princely gold, because it is such a faithful guardian of the words that God's finger has written.

That spouse in the mystery of Christ who satisfied the thirsting servant of Abraham with the liquid in her water jar, which she lowered down from her shoulder, has merited the testimony of the prophets (Genesis 24).[2]

Yet you, no less than she, deserve to be given honorary monuments and to be consecrated by the testimonials of witnesses. You have satisfied us—the servants of Abraham (because all who sin are his servants)—with the water jar of your heart. You have satisfied us, that is, from the treasure of an earthenware vessel.[3] I have surely drunk from this letter you have written, and have given water to my camels. That is, I have acknowledged all my vices, because I have discovered nothing of those good things that you judge to be within me. But it is perfectly clear that you have counterbalanced my unworthiness and ignorance by your good work. Whatever care your daily labor has heaped upon you, you have put this care totally in the service of vindicating me. I ought to be whatever you feel me to be, because all things are possible for the believer. But since it does not come close to me to desire it, it is impossible for me to be completely perfect.

Now in you, truly, both the desire to be perfect and the achievement of perfection exist, and both bear fruit. I have recognized the worth of what the prophet has said: "Behold a virgin shall conceive in her womb and bear a son" (Isaiah 7.14). You can freely say: "We have conceived in our womb the spirit of salvation that you, Lord, have wrought on earth, and we have given birth!" You breed the word of God, you are in labor with his sayings, and thus you give birth to the knowledge of God for our sake in such a way that you are always replete and pregnant.

Let people who doubt understand the manner in which a virgin might conceive and how she could give birth. Let them read your writings, for here is the immaculate fertility of virginal fruit. Obviously, your case is the same as Sara's. There were seven husbands dead—that is, the spirits of the world. But when the angel led Sara to the bridal chamber and she espoused Christ, the enemy lay dead.[4] As for me, unworthy as I am, I must beg my father to let me weep for my virgin garlands before I can fulfill the vow of my father's lips, because I have not shown before now any visible fruit of my virginity. My father slew the Moabites and the Ammonites, that is, he has annihilated in me the tribe of insobriety and fornication.[5] But what good is that to me if I do not have the word of God in my womb, that is to say, in my heart? And I know that virginity without learning walks in the shadow and knows not the light. The name of virginity only, which does not possess the substance, cannot in any way cross the threshold of the Bridegroom's canopy.

I carry a candelabrum, which is my throat; but I am empty because of the dryness of my wick—that is, the lightness of hollow words—since the rich oil of learning does not touch it. In this respect I know I am unworthy; at least let me implore you,

you who have an abundance of oil, to explain to me from whom I ought to acquire it.

But now I shall sometimes say what Job said to the Lord: "What can I utter when I hear such words, and what shall I respond, since I am nothing? Having spoken once, I will add nothing" (Job 40.4). I have recognized that I am earth and ashes, because I see such achievement in others. Because of this I myself feel that there is nothing in me. But it appears that the angel—the spirit, that is—speaks in you as in the example of the blessed Mary, because you are so learned in speaking.

I have guarded, I have surely guarded what the sanctuary of your heart has conceived and the fruit of your belly has brought forth (and I address you not as sister but as one who should be called Lady). You carry around and display as a sacred object "your son in Egypt" (Hosea 11.1; Matthew 2.15), that is, you offer the fruit of your teaching to us who are living in the world's darkness. I shall say without hesitation that you are one of the four prophesying virgins whom the writer of the Acts of the Apostles has described (Acts 21.8). You are without a doubt she of whom the singers of the holy Psalms have sung. You are arrayed in a garment of many colors, bearing fringes of gold (Psalm 45.13–14). For how may I interpret the gold fringes if not as the beautiful and faithful sense of your words, which flow and hang down from the two sides of your face? In them is a beautiful, brilliant-hued diversity, because out of the law, the prophets, and the evangelists, you have dyed the wording of your letter with the various colors of their testimonies.

It is clearly evident that you do not eat your bread in idleness, because your husband—he who used to be called the carpenter's son (Matthew 13.55)—has fashioned for you a spindle of the wood of learning. With it you spin, out of the splendid wool of history, threads of the spirit's words.

I confess to you, revered sister, I did not understand the prophet's words when he said, "Wheat is sweet to young men, and wine is sweet to maidens" (Zachariah 9.17) until I perceived it from the power of your words. For it is you who have the sweet wine, out of the fruits of Christ, that is, who is the true vine. You are fruitful with the joy of spiritual learning, which quickens the innermost part of your vitals with the juice of its sweetness and power. You surely rival that Shunammite virgin who was found to minister to and care for the body of King David (I Kings 1.1–4). For performing this service you have already won the reward of receiving his keys, with which you open what no one can lock and you lock what no one opens (Isaiah 22.22; Revelations 3.7). There is in you the son of Bathsheba, that is, Wisdom, which is ardently adored, so that a false brother neither lusts for you nor touches you.[6]

What your Holiness writes should surely be revered by me, since I had hidden the linen cloth that covered my loins in a hollow of the rock above the river Euphrates (Jeremiah 13.1–7). I know this: that beside the wordly precipice, the hardness of my heart, the husks of my virtue are rotten, and now, stripped of wisdom's covering, I do not recognize myself despoiled of the "old man."[7]

But because the lack of my heart's skill and the sorrow of motherly anguish have hindered my speech, and the sadness of my heart scarcely allows this little thing to be spoken, I beg that you will frequently sprinkle the dry roots of my understanding with a basketful of fertilizing dung—that is, the fecundity of your words (Luke 13.8)—so that when you come to visit me in your customary manner, you will find in me some of the fruit of your good work.

2. Eucheria of Marseilles: Satirical Verses Against a Wooer

I would twine together golden threads, glittering like metal, and heaps of bristling horsehair. I am thinking of matching a Chinese silken coverlet and the gem-encrusted weavings of Sparta to a goat hide. Let noble purple be stitched to a coarse and loathsome wool.

Let the gleaming jewel be fixed in a heavy, leaden setting. Let the pearl, its lustre now entrapped, shine dully when enclosed in steel. And in the same way let the emerald be locked in the bronze of Gaul. Let the amethyst now be paired with flint, the jasper with crags and boulders. Let even the moon now choose the chaos of Hell!

We shall also now command the lily to be joined to stinging nettles, and let the crimson rose be choked by deadly hemlock.

Now at the same time do we wish the great seething ocean to scorn its delicacies and instead prefer coarse fish. Let the rock-dwelling toad love the gilded serpent. Similarly let the trout seek out the snail for herself. Let the lofty lioness be joined with the foul fox, the ape take the keen-sighted lynx. Let the doe be joined to the donkey, the tiger to the wild ass. Marry the fleet gazelle to the plodding ox.

Let foul stinkweed now spoil the rosy nectar, let honeyed mead be mixed with bitter fruit. Let us mingle crystalline water with bodily filth, the refreshing fountain with the privy's excrement!

Let the winged swallow sport with the deadly vulture, the nightingale sing with the hateful horned owl. Let the sullen night owl stay with the clear-eyed partridge. Let the pretty dove lie down with the crow.

Let these monstrous couplings overturn for themselves the decrees of the dark fates—and let a churlish farmhand hanker for Eucheria!

[The stag, the boar, the snake will not escape—by flight, tooth, or poisoned fang—your stings, Maiorianus!]

NOTES

1. In a roundabout way, the author says, "If you weren't asking me to write, noble lady, I wouldn't dare, since I have nothing left to say after you have said it all so eloquently."

2. Like many virtuous wives of the prophets in the Old Testament, Rebecca at the well prefigures the Church and so is a bride "in the mystery of Christ."

3. The addressee is merely human, not a *figura ecclesiae* like Rebecca.

4. Tobit 3.7–17. Tobit's son Tobias marries Sara, seven of whose betrothed lovers have been successively carried off by an evil spirit, Asmodeus. At length an angel drives Asmodeus away and binds him in Egypt.

5. The writer compares herself to Jephtha's daughter (Judges 11.26ff.), whom her father vowed to sacrifice once he had defeated his enemies.

6. Bathsheba's son by David was Solomon. The "false brother" may refer to one of David's older sons laying claim to the throne.

7. After being told by the Lord to bury his linen girdle in the hole of a rock by the Euphrates, the prophet dug it up days later to find it ruined. The Lord then told him he would destroy the pride of Judah and Jerusalem in the same way. The sense is that the writer has buried her own pride and will not consider the stripping away of her old self to be a loss.

FURTHER READING

Anonymous Letter-Writer. *Monumenta Germaniae Historica: Epistolae.* Vol. 3, pp. 716–718. Berlin, 1892.

———. C.P. Caspari, ed. *Briefe, Abhandlungen und Predigten aus den zwei letzten Jahrhunderten des Kirchlichen Altertums und dem Anfang des Mittelalters*, pp. 178–182, 398–404. Christiania, 1890.

Nora K. Chadwick. *Poetry and Letters in Early Christian Gaul.* London: Bowes and Bowes, 1955.

Eucheria. Helene Homeyer, ed. and trans. *Dichterinnen des Altertums und des frühen Mittelalters*, pp. 185–187. Paderborn: Ferdinand Schöningh, 1979.

———. M. Cabaret-Dupaty, ed. and trans. *Poetae Minores*, pp. 408–416. Paris, 1842.

M.L.W. Laistner. *Thought and Letters in Western Europe A.D. 500–900.* Rev. ed. Ithaca: Cornell UP, 1957.

Auguste Friedrich von Pauly. "Eucheria." In *Realencyclopädie der classischen Altertumswissenschaft*. Revisions and Supplements, Hans Gartner and Albert Wunsch, eds. Munich: Druckenmuller, 1980.

Pierre Riché, *Education et culture dans l'occident barbare: vi–viii siècles*. 3rd ed. rev. Paris: Editions du Seuil, 1962.

CHAPTER 7

Barbarian Women, Holy Women

The Wife's Lament
Wulf and Eadwacer
Leoba of England and Germany (fl. ca. 732)

Two women's love songs appear in *The Exeter Book*. This tenth-century manuscript book contains the fullest diversity of Old English poetry written before the Normans invaded England. Though the hand that inscribed them held the pen a thousand years ago, the poems tell of an even older time, in the accents of pagan sagas sung or recited and kept alive for centuries in the popular memory.[1] They reflect a period on the continent of barbarian life without Christianity. While the Old English elegies have affinities to Latin Christianity, with its mistrust of wavering fortune and its meditations on the instability of worldly happiness and on the body's decay, no syllable of earthly hope or heavenly salvation offers comfort in these love poems. Their melancholy fatalism links them rather to women's laments in Germanic song. We are reminded of Gudrun's terrible weeping over Sigurd's body in the *Volsungassaga*, or her grief (in the Norse poem translated as "Guðrun's Goading") for her daughter Svanhildr, trampled by horses.[2]

Despite the archaic origins of the women's lyrics, they express emotions as freshly compelling as if they had been uttered today, in a culture or a city where women's lives might be anything but free. Against a stark setting of masculine rivalry and vendetta, the women's solitary voices in both *The Wife's Lament* and *Wulf and Eadwacer* mourn their separation from a cherished lover or husband. The women's own independence is gone.[3]

135

The northern peoples whom the Romans called barbarians had gained the attention (as early as the fourth century B.C.), of Greek writers, one of whom took heed of the tribe known as "Teutones." In later ages Goths, Vandals, Sueves, Batavians, Burgundians, and other Germanic ethnic groups were known to be migrating, in wagon hordes with their women and children, beyond the outer limits of the Roman Empire. The historian Tacitus in the first century A.D. gathered reports from Roman traders and military men to compose a short book in which he detailed the customs of the rugged Germanic tribes for the benefit of his own pleasure-loving Roman compatriots.

Tacitus praised the chastity and monogamy of German women, and the strength of the marriage bond. Men revered their women for their gifts of prophecy, he stated. Men offered the wedding gift of the dowry to the marriage, while women brought the men their weapons. Men listened to what women had to say, and did not scorn their advice. Women didn't exchange secret letters with their male friends and didn't feast with them in compromising situations. Adultery met with swift punishment: the woman would be stripped and her head shorn before she was driven from the house.[4]

Tacitus's true purpose was to show the Romans that the hardy Germans were a constant threat. But he misunderstood the custom of trading gifts. The dowry was really a purchase price, while the weapon symbolized the bride's father or guardian transferring to the husband the power of life and death over the woman.[5] Tacitus clearly admired the Germans. Yet, certain realities can't be ignored. Barbarian marriages were usually the result of capture or purchase, the wife being little more than chattel. "A king must pay for his queen with wealth, with goblets and bracelets," declares the Old English maxim. The barbarian woman Radegund was fought over and won as a war prize during the sack of her home in Thuringia. The English-woman Balthild was captured and sold into slavery before she attracted royal notice and became a queen. Barbarian and Merovingian kings kept wives and concubines both. After marriage, Burgundians, Visigoths, and Lombards required that an arrested adulterer pay the woman's wergild, the value set on her life, but the laws also allowed a husband to kill his wife and her companion if he caught them in the act of love.

Kings in Anglo-Saxon England seem not to have luxuriated in concubinage as the Merovingians did, so far as the records show, nor did they forcibly drive their queens into cloistered retirement. Churchmen would take notice of such abuses: the Venerable Bede singles out King Eadbald of Kent, rebuking him for acts of fornication that were worse than things the heathens did. Queens did wield influence, and several helped to convert their royal lords to Christianity. But a lady might be expected to wear ornaments so chafing that one queen believed her neck tumor, of which she would soon die, was the result. There's no evidence of killing or physical injury for adultery, but dissatisfied husbands could send their wives back and claim the refund of their bride-price. An adulterer would have to pay the woman's wergild *and* provide an additional bride-price so that the wronged husband could buy another wife. Female infanticide was in all likelihood a practice.[6]

Old English literature—written after the settlement of the Angles, Saxons and Jutes in England and after the advent of Christianity—exhibits realities about women's roles in barbarian society. Women are marginal in the greatest of extant Old English poems, *Beowulf.* The hero needs no woman to love or marry, or to inspire his actions. A woman in this world might be offered in wedlock as a "peace weaver" (*freoðuwebbe*) to smoothe over a dispute. Such is the role of the offstage Freawaru, whom Beowulf mentions in passing. She is king Hrothgar's daughter. The family hopes that her betrothal and marriage will help to compose a ruinous blood feud. Hrothgar's wife, Wealhtheow, actually makes a gracious entrance. Adorned with gold jewelry she appears in the hall to pass the wine cup at a significant moment, *after* the declaration of a verbal truce between two hot-tempered men caught up in a duel of epic bragging. The women have importance but only in the context of masculine action. In *Beowulf* ties of truest affection thrive between male comrades of the war band, or between kinsmen, like Beowulf and his uncle Hrothgar.

Heroic women figure in Old English poems built on Christian themes: *Elene*, the mother of Constantine and discoverer of the true Cross; *Juliana*, saint and martyr who wrestles with the demon; and *Judith*, the Jewish heroine who slays Holofernes and saves her people. None of these were English, of course. Strong, virtuous queens, princesses, abbesses, and holy women receive favorable notice in Bede's *History of the English Church and People* (written in Latin in 731, Englished in about 880), the *Old English Martyrology* (850 A.D.) and Aelfric's (d. 1020) *Lives of the Saints*. However, the two lyrics discussed in this chapter are unique in being the only surviving love poems in Old English, and the only poems attributed to female voices. They share the same themes as *Exeter Book* elegies featuring a male persona: loneliness, exile, forced separation over water, regret for lost felicity "as if it never had been" (words that appear in *The Wife's Lament* and *The Wanderer*), and a crowning statement of resigned wisdom.

Much is mysterious in *The Wife's Lament*, as the wealth of critical interpretation proves.[7] Is the woman of noble or queenly rank, and does her story refer to a well-known feud, perhaps as part of a larger work? The singer's lord has crossed the sea. During his absence his relatives plot against him, banishing him and condemning his wife to be immured in a solitary wilderness. Alone in this cave or hut of earth, she sings of her unhappiness and her love.

Six stages in the poem's structure trace a significant unfolding from beginning to end: (1) a prologue (lines 1–5); (2) the singer's summary of her lord's departure, her search for him, and his clan's heartless treatment of both (lines 6–14); (3) a more penetrating disclosure of the couple's relationship, his unruly nature, their mutual affinity, and her own intense feelings of love and loss (lines 15–26); (4) the singer's account of her present incarceration (lines 27–41); (5) a "gnomic" or wisdom-fraught generalization on the sufferings of the young (lines 42–47a); (6) an imagined picture of her lover in his loneliness (lines 47b-53).

Part 3 raises a problem about the number of characters in the lyric. Having followed her lord, the poet says that she found a man she deeply loved. Does this means she found *in her lord* a spouse she could revel with, a man whose kinsmen have for their own reasons cruelly banished him while holding her prisoner? Or did she find another man with whom she entered into adultery, for which crime her lord's kinsmen have now punished her and her illicit lover? Line 18 reads: *Ða ic me ful gemaecne monnan funde* ("Then I found myself a most hus-bandly man").[8] Although adultery has been proposed as a possible plot element, it makes more sense to read the beloved and husband as the same man. Part 2 already referred to the feud that divided the woman from her lord, whom she came to love deeply and sexually despite his tormented character.

What is immediately striking is the intimacy of the poetic utterance, conveyed through the flurry of first-person pronouns in all inflected forms: thirty-two in this fifty-three-line lyric: *ic, me,* and *min,* plus the five dual pronouns for "we two" and "both of us" or "both of ours." Cognates of the word "longing" appear throughout: lines 14, 29, 41, and 53, the poem's last line. The understated directness of the language is noteworthy, with the characteristic Old English *litotes,* the device in line 4 that makes an assertion by denying its negative. Much of the lyric force derives from this bare intensity, heightened by "I," "me," "mine," repeated with feverish frequency.

In parts 1 through 3 the elegy rocks to and fro in time and space: the woman recalling her unhappiness as a growing girl, her griefs past and present, the feuding far and near, her restless journeying and that of the man she loves, their sexual joy and its reversal, expressed as a "backward whorling" ("*Eft is þæt onhworfen,*" line 23), like the "wharving" of eddying waters, to use the derivative word.

But in part 4 the poem stabilizes with a visual richness as the woman describes her forest dungeon, a lodging or a cave of earth ragged with sharp thorns. The fixity of the location finds expression in the language of quasi-architectural forms: *eorðthscraefe, eorþsele, burgtunas* (the only place in which this compound word appears), and *wic,* from *vicus,* a former Roman administrative unit, sometimes at a remove from camp. Their ambiguity puzzles. Does the woman live in a cave, a series of connected caves, or a shack or a stockade? Perhaps she resides in a grave-barrow like St. Guthlac, or a mound like the "green chapel" in *Sir Gawain and the Green Knight* centuries later, or an abode like that of the woman in the nursery rhyme "who lived in a hill." Perhaps it's just a hovel fenced with stakes and half-buried in the ground.

A study illuminating this portion of *The Wife's Lament* has shown that because early "Old English lacks the vocabulary of geometric forms," the language will resort to the world of nature for its architectural terms. In the elegy, eorðscraefe can mean "cave, barrow, denehole (underground storage pit)"; *scraef* may mean a sunken hut or warehouse common in Ango-Saxon England, but it is also metaphorical for hell. A *beorg* can be a mound, hill, mountain, or barrow as well as a palisaded enclosure, while *wic* is an enclosed settlement, farm, or work area distanced from the main village. But as buildings, they have all been "homologized to natural structures."[9] Here in the lyric, the poet conveys the sense of an alienated, humanly structured, but abandoned habitation beyond the pale, delivered over to climbing briars and half smothered in earth, with overtones of the grave or an entrance to the underworld—household arrangements that, penetrated with sorrow, create a travesty of domesticity.

In this passage the singer gives free vent to her sexual yearning, contrasting her bereaved state with that of happy lovers elsewhere who find pleasure in each other's arms. Her limited mobility permits her only to walk under her tree and throughout her dwelling, but she is free to rove in imagination.

This climax of physical and emotional anguish, which both displaces her former ecstasy and laments its loss, gives way in part 5 to a passage of calm, of "philosophical" consolation. The author may be thinking of King Alfred's *Boece*, his translation of Boethius's *Consolation of Philosopy*. Everywhere, the singer acknowledges, the young are compelled to endure terrible heartache. Young men suffer despair, as her lover must be suffering. Part 6, the poem's closing, shows her rising above her own sorrow to commiserate tenderly and eloquently with her lover's plight. The details of her prison find parallels in his: her walls, surrounded by hedges and hills and overgrown with brambles, are balanced by her lover's northerly prison, encrusted with rime. He dwells under a storm-beaten cliff as she abides under an oak. Her joyless stronghold ("*wic wynna leas*," line 32) finds its answering echo in what he must be remembering of their shared happier house ("wynlicran wic," line 52).

The Wife's Lament, having opened with the singer absorbed in her own anguish, moves beyond self-pity in defined stages to a sorrowing contemplation of her beloved's ordeal. Significantly, as she surmounts her grief and thinks of his, the first-person pronouns slacken; there are only two in the last dozen lines, and these are linked to the man himself as possessives—my friend, my lover (lines 47, 50). And yet there is no hope in sight of any reunion or genuine consolation; the two sit forever apart.

More cryptic than *The Wife's Lament* is the story, whatever it may be, that lies embedded in the briefer *Wulf and Eadwacer*.[10] According to the simplest and most traditional reading, the singer and her lover Wulf, to whom she has borne a son, live on separate islands. It is her vindictive husband, Eadwacer, who keeps them apart and whom the singer addresses in line 16. The embraces of Eadwacer afford her a hateful pleasure. Now Wulf is in danger. The woman's own fierce clan, perhaps in league with her husband, are stalking Wulf and will regard his capture with satisfaction. The names "Wulf" and "Eadwacer" (the word indicates a "watcher of wealth," a spy, a guardian, with a hint of the watchdog), together with "whelp" for the child, metaphorically highlight the hunted and predatory roles of the characters. The clan's pursuit of Wulf to take, consume, or devour (*apecgan*) reinforces the notion of the chase for helpless animal prey.

Although *The Wife's Lament* addresses only the hearers or reader, *Wulf and Eadwacer* speaks to the lover and the husband as well, after directing lines 1–12 to the audience. Or, it is possible that, with the exception of those passionate utterances to Wulf himself, the poem's opening is an outcry to the husband, named only in line 16.

But to whom and about whom does the singer address the enigmatic "Ungelic is us" ("With us it isn't like that")? To the audience, to Wulf, or to Eadwacer? Does the sentence mean "Eadwacer and I are not like that" (ironically, We're in no danger, we're perfectly secure together, though I don't love him)? or "Wulf and I are not like that" (I would protect him if I could, I would never let him be savagely hunted down)? Since the line occurs twice as a refrain, it would be possible to apply the words first to Wulf and secondly to Eadwacer. Perhaps in the poetic recital of the elegy, a performer determined and controlled the interpretation.

Unlike *The Wife's Lament*, which opens on a personal note, *Wulf and Eadwacer* (lines 1–6) recounts the lovers' terrible plight, punctuated twice by the baffling "With us it isn't like that." The poem's central passage then dwells on the woman herself, her love and heartache, and her sexual ambivalence toward her "watchdog" husband. Though some readers would take the ambivalence to mean the lover, I find it difficult to link the word *laþ* ("loathsome") to Wulf. In the poem's last section, lines 11–13 address Wulf, with the echo of food (*mete*) paralleling Wulf's hunted status, while lines 14–16 taunt Eadwacer with the child's having eluded him.

The closing lines of bitter resignation display the woman's incapacity to keep her lover and herself together, despite her song. In the orbit of the song, however, they are paradoxically both held in terrible balance—symbolically united by their child—but forever lost to each other. *Wulf and Eadwacer*, like *The Wife's Lament*, distinguishes between the two modes: love that is suffered, and love's transmutation into song or storytelling. Old English *giedd* in both lyrics reappears as Chaucer's *yeddynges*, the ballads the friar sings for prizes to the accompaniment of the rote. By the fifteenth century a *yedding* is glossed as a romance. In the same period in which the songs of barbarian women were being remembered, written down, and enjoyed, English women in monasteries were devoting their emotional energies to Christ and his works. This might mean toiling in alien climates among ungrateful and malevolent heathen who were unwilling to give up their spells and poisonous charms, their bloody sacrifices of animals and slaves. Christian shrines of ancient date lay in ruins in Germany and in Frisia (that is, Holland). Holy churches must be rebuilt, the pagans reconverted, the gospel taught. The old divinities Thor and Woden must be driven out. Despite the hazards, the English Church continued to send missionaries to the continent.

One of the young women eager to go was Leoba. She was born Thrutgeba to an aged aristocratic couple, Dynne and Aebbe, in around 700 in Wessex, renamed Leobgytha, and nicknamed Leoba, "beloved." As a girl she became a novice under the abbess Tetta of Wimbourne (meaning "winestream" because its waters were so fresh and sweet), herself sister of a king of Wessex. At the request of the missionary Boniface and after an exchange of letters, Tetta agreed to release Leoba to assist him in his tasks in Germany and to supervise thirty nuns. The women installed themselves at the first monastery of Bischofsheim in Franconia in the diocese of Mainz, and became a force in the German mission.

St. Leoba's *Vita* was written probably in 836 by the monk Rudolf of Fulda, the monastery in Hesse where she lived at the end of her life. Rudolf describes Leoba as well-educated, a mighty reader. Her study included the Old and New Testaments, the writings of the church fathers, council decrees, and ecclesiastical law memorized in verse. Moreover, she was kindly, affable, and beautiful in her person. Nothing ruffled her composure. She grew very friendly with the lady Hildegard, who was Charlemagne's first wife and who often invited her to visit, liking to secure Leoba's advice on various matters. After Leoba died in 780 in a nunnery at Schönersheim near Mainz, she was buried close to Boniface at Fulda.

For the biography to which he was assigned, Rudolf relied on the notes of an older monk, who himself had interviewed Leoba's four sister-nuns Agatha, Thecla, Nana, and Eolaba. This is as close to a first-hand acquaintance with Leoba as we can get. From these sources Rudolf picked up curious reminiscences so atypical of hagiographic narrative that they probably happened. Going back to Mother Tetta's day is the mild scandal of nuns childishly stomping on and cursing over the grave of a recently dead senior sister who had disciplined them severely. So vehement were their young feet that the earth level over the corpse sank six inches. Naturally, the junior sisters were roundly scolded and set to prostrating penances. Another anecdote survives of a nun who after a long search finally located the missing church-door keys in the mouth of a dead fox outside the chapel. There is no reason to suppose that Leoba was not involved in either of these incidents. Also in Rudolf's report is a particularly intriguing dream of an endless purple thread that twines out of Leoba's mouth, as if from her bowels, and which Leoba keeps balling up in her hand.

More conventional occurrences, but not without interest, are Leoba's provoking the confession of a poor cripple who had drowned her illegitimate infant in a stream after poisoning the water and, on another occasion, curing a woman afflicted with foul-smelling hemorrhoids by feeding her milk with her own personal spoon.[11]

In *The Life of Saint Leoba* Rudolf tries to tell nearly as much about Boniface, missionary saint and martyr, as he does about Leoba, and in some ways he contrives to make the biography a dual one, though Boniface had other biographers. Boniface, who was twenty-five years older than Leoba, emerges as a most appealing, conscientious, and hard-pressed man. To help him fulfill his mission, both men and women had gathered around him. Letters flew back and forth. "Anglo-Saxons played a full part in continuing the ancient literary tradition of letter-writing and letter collecting. . . . There are purely practical communications. . . . There are also numerous letters of friendship, congratulation, exhortation, encouragement, or condolence."[12] Letters survive in Boniface's voluminous correspondence from five religious women: Aelffled, Eadburga, Eangyth, Bugga, and Leoba. A continuing theme is the love of books, pointing to a fervently shared interest of the eighth-century missionaries.

Born in England around 675 (at or near Crediton), he was christened Wynfrith, but after his first visit to Rome in 719 renamed himself Boniface. He was first a boy, then a monk at Exeter, and later a monk at Nursling near Southhampton. Devoting this time to study and writing, Boniface composed a Biblical commentary and put together the first Latin grammar written in England, convinced that a strong sense of grammar enabled one to read Scripture with attention to the fine points.

Boniface first left England when he was about forty-one, but was forced to return because the Frisian kings and people showed hostility. Two years later he departed again, this time for good. His missions took him to Hesse, Bavaria, Westphalia, Thuringia, and Würtemburg. The story is told of his hewing down a mighty oak tree, sacred to Thor, and from its timbers building a wooden oratory. On the second of his three trips to

Rome he was made a bishop of the see at Mainz. Enduring both pagan rancor and the jealousy of clerical peers, always over-worked, and tormented that he wasn't doing enough, Boniface refers often to his restless journeying; the word *peregrinatio* recurs in his writing. He met his death when, venturing into a deserted region of Frisia "in the sea marshes beyond the Zuider Zee," he was set upon by a band of piratical robbers and killed on June 5, 754. He refused to let his comrades come to his aid, and attained martyrdom. A violently cut manuscript book with which he defended himself became a cherished relic and treasure. It is still at the Landsbibliothek of Fulda in Hesse.[13]

This, then, was the man of flesh and bone that Leoba followed in devotion. The notes of emotional intensity that characterized Christian letters of spiritual friendship became something of a convention, but the affection between Leoba and Boniface is evident. Leoba's one surviving letter invokes the teacher-pupil bond, with the somewhat seductive undercurrent that this relationship can carry and that her *Vita* serves to bring forth. The letter dwells on the verbal and stylistic, speaking of rusticity and amateur effort and the beginner's laboring over the rules of prosody. Its requests are roundabout. The sweetly eager student sends a little gift of a poem and asks for orisons, not just for her parents but against the secret poisonous sins that assail her. She pleads with her master not to forget her and to correct her paper, asking furthermore for a model letter from him to guarantee that this busy man will write back! And lest the letter appear too affectionate, she conjures the kindly maternal figure of her teacher prioress Eadburga standing like a chaperone in the letter's closing lines.

Leoba's letter and life bear features in common with *The Wife's Lament* and *Wulf and Eadwacer*. She would respond to a dear kinsman's summons to live out her life in a harsh, inhospitable country, in a form of foreign exile over the water. Surrounding him are men who threaten to hunt him down, and they do. He wanders, she is fixed in a place where she must discharge duties. Leoba's letter, dated about 732, centers on themes of love and kinship. Moreover, the letter calls attention to itself as a documentary surrogate for physical closeness. In Leoba's letter, words and the struggle to achieve correct writing function as pleading gestures of desire—prayers for parents and herself, a yearning for attention, and the gift of her lyric effort to a beloved man. (So too would text serve as an extension of the body when Boniface's last injured book received its share of the cuts and blows that fell on him). The English elegies also revert at the last to the text of the song as an artifact more enduring than the fragile bond of bodily intimacy. The difference, to be sure, is the burning Christian hope that buoys Leoba's girlish effusions and contrasts strikingly with the barbarian women's desolate laments.

Rudolf's *Life of St. Leoba* is intent on showing that Boniface returned her love. Boniface begs Leoba not to give up. He "exhorted her not to abandon the country of her adoption and not to grow weary of the life she had undertaken." At the leave taking that is to be their last parting as he goes unknowingly to his death, Boniface again "pleaded with her not to leave her adopted land" and gave her his cowl, the hood of his cloak, an item sometimes taken as the insignia of the monk's very calling. So irreproachable a gift was this, one without any suspicion of sentimentality about it, that the saint's biographer records it with reverence. Perhaps it seemed to Rudolf like the passing on of a sacred mantle and trust. And yet it is a token *full* of sentiment: the gift of a personal garment that had intimately been a covering for his hair and head, for his mind and thought. Boniface furthermore commended Leoba to the senior monks of the monastery "to care for her with reverence and respect and reaffirming his wish that after his death her bones should be placed next to his in the tomb."

Despite his last uttered desire concerning Leoba's body, the nervous monks were too fearful in later years to open the martyr's tomb. When Leoba died they instead "placed her on the north side of the altar which the martyr St. Boniface himself had erected." Rudolf, her biographer, must sense the violation of the separation. He introduces a vision to show that in the popular imagination these two formed a pair, for a nameless "man from Spain," afflicted with a twitching disease, rose up cured after "he had had an ecstasy in which he saw a venerable old man, vested in a bishop's stole, accompanied by a young woman in a nun's habit, who had taken him by the hand." The romantic Rudolf

Christian hope vr.
barbarian laments

makes another, closing reference to their inseparability: "These two, though they do not share a tomb, yet lie in one place." Despite the divided tombs, the *Life* contains the two saints. Like the vision of the "man from Spain," Rudolf's text enfolds Boniface in crucial aspects of love and mission with Leoba.

1. The Wife's Lament

I tell this story about me, in my sorrow,
I sing the fate of my voyaging self. I may say that
whatever hardship I lived through since I grew up—
new griefs and old—in those days it was not worse than now.
Always I grieve in the pain of my torment. (lines 1–5)

First my lord went away from his people
over the tossing waves. I felt cold care in the dark before dawn,
wondering where my lord of the lands might be.
Then I left on a journey to seek and serve him—
a friendless wanderer in my terrible need.
That man's kinsmen began to plot
with secret scheming to split us both apart,
so that we two—widely asunder in the world—
lived most wretchedly. And longing smote me. (lines 6–14)

My lord called to me to take up my hard dwelling here.
I had few loved ones in this country,
few devoted friends. For this my mind mourns.
Then I found myself a most husbandly man,
but a man with hard luck, brooding in his heart;
he hid his moods, his murderous thoughts,
yet seemed blithe in his bearing. Very often we boasted that
none but death alone would drive us apart—
not anything else! All that is whorled backward, changed;
now it's as if it never had been,
the loving friendship the both of us had. Far and near I must
suffer the feud of my dearly loved man. (lines 15–26)

They forced me to live in a grove of the wood
under an oak tree in an earth hovel.
Old is this den of earth. I am stabbed with longing.

The valleys are dark, the hills rise high,
bitterly sharp is my garrison overgrown with brambles,
a joyless stronghold. Here very often what seizes me fiercely
is the want of my husband! There are friends on earth,
lovers living who lie clasped in their bed,
while I walk alone in the hours before daybreak
under the oak tree, throughout this earth cave
where I must remain the summerlong day,
where I can weep the sorrows
of my many hardships, because I never can
find sweet rest for that heart's grief of mine—
not for all of that longing laid on me in this life. (lines 27–41)

Always must the young be troubled in mood,
with thoughts harsh in their hearts, yet at the same time
seem blithe in bearing despite a care-burdened breast
and a swarm of sorrows. The young man must rely on himself
for all he gets of the world's joy. He must be a far-flung outlaw
in a distant country. (lines 42–47a)

                                    So my loved friend sits
under a stone cliff crusted with frost in the storm—
my lover dreary in spirit. Water flows all around him
in his bleak dwelling. That friend of mine suffers
great sorrow of heart. Too often he remembers
a more blissful house. Unhappy is anyone
who must longingly wait for a lover. (lines 47b-53)

2. Wulf and Eadwacer

For my clan he would be like a gift of booty—
they will waste him if he crosses their path.
With us it isn't like that. (lines 1–3)

Wulf is on one island, I on another—
his island is made fast, girded by fens.
Fierce men are on that island.
They will waste him if he crosses their path.
With us it isn't like that. (lines 4–8)

I yearned for Wulf in his harried wandering.
When the weather poured rain I sat here in tears.
When the brash fighter folded me in the branches of his arms,
I felt pleasure, yes, but I felt loathing too. (lines 9–12)

Wulf, my Wulf, to think about you
made me faint with sickness, for you seldom came.
It was my mood of mourning, not want of food.
Do you hear, Eadwacer? Wulf carries our forlorn
whelp to the wood.
Men can easily wrench apart what has never been wedded—
our story together. (lines 13–19)

3. Leoba

To the most reverend lord Boniface, noble in worth, dearly beloved in Christ and close to me in kinship, Leobgytha—the lowest servant of those who bear the gentle yoke of Christ—sends her greeting for his continuing health.

I beg you in your kindness to keep in memory the long friendship that you shared with Dynne, my father, in our west country. Eight years have run their course since he has departed from the light of day, and so I plead with you not to refuse to offer your prayers to God for his soul. No less do I ask you also to remember my mother Aebbe, who, as you are well aware, is related to you by ties of blood. She is still alive and much burdened by illness. I am the only daughter of both my parents. Undeserving as I am, I should be very privileged if I might welcome you as my brother, for no man of our family gives me so much trustworthiness and hope as I find in you.

I am sending you a very small gift, not because it is worthy of your favor, but so that you will remember me only a little and not hand me over to the blankness of oblivion just because you are far away, and so we shall be closely entwined with the cords of true affection forever.

Dearest brother, I beg you even more earnestly that with the leathern shield of your prayers you will protect me against the poison darts of my secret enemy. And another favor I ask you, and that is to deign to correct the countrified diction of this letter of mine and that you won't fail in your generosity to send me a model I can follow in just a few words of your own, for I am filled with breathless longing to hear from you.

These little verses written below I struggled to compose according to the rules of poetic versification. It isn't because I'm bold enough to think I have any talent but because I'm eager to practice my meager rudiments of graceful composition, and I hope to have your help. I learned the art from my schoolmistress Eadburga, who continues to persevere ceaselessly in her holy reading of Scripture.

Farewell, live longer, be happier, and pray for me!

> May the all-powerful Judge, who alone created all,
> Who pours forth light in the realm of the father
> Where it steadfastly gleams so Christ's glory may reign,
> Keep you unharmed forever in his eternal law.

NOTES

1. *The Exeter Book*, written in 970–990, contains alliterative verse, devotional pieces, a vivacious riddle collection (the plough, the cuckoo, and so on), and the bawdy riddles on the human body. Eight other elegies (e.g., *The Ruin*, *The Wanderer*, and *The Seafarer*) are in the collection. Bishop Leofric presented the book to Exeter Cathedral in 1050 when he moved the see from Crediton.

2. Daniel G. Calder and Robert E. Bjork, eds., *Sources and Analogues of Old English Poetry II* (D.S. Brewer, 1983), pp. 23–30; Ursula Dronke, *The Poetic Edda*, I, pp. 145–157.

3. Peter Dronke discusses the universality of women's songs and *cantigas de amigo* in *Medieval Latin and the Rise of the European Love Lyric* (Oxford UP, 1968), I, pp. 259ff and *passim*, and *The Medieval Lyric* (London, 1968), pp. 88–108. The latter translates *Wulf and Eadwacer* with commentary, pp. 91f.

4. Cornelius Tacitus, *Dialogus, Agricola, Germania*, trans. by Maurice Hutton and William Peterson, (Cambridge, Mass.: Loeb, rev. repr. 1970), pp. 117–216, chaps. 8, 17–19.

5. See Ronald Martin, *Tacitus* (Berkeley and Los Angeles: U of California P, 1981), p. 52.

6. Rosalind Hill, "Marriage in Seventh-Century England," in *Saints, Scholars, and Heroes: Studies in Medieval Culture in Honour of Charles W. Jones,* Margot H. King and Wesley M. Stevens, eds., 2 vols. (Collegeville, Minn., 1979), I: *The Anglo-Saxon Heritage,* pp. 67–73.

7. Recent and instructive are Marilynn Desmond, "The Voice of Exile: Feminist Literary History and the Anonymous Anglo-Saxon Elegy," *Critical Inquiry* 16 (1990): 572–90; Patricia Belanoff, "Women's Songs, Women's Language: 'Wulf and Eadwacer' and 'The Wife's Lament,'" in *New Readings on Women in Old English Literature,* Helen Damico and Alexandra Hennessey Olsen, eds. (Bloomington: Indiana UP, 1990), pp. 193–203; and Jane Chance, *Woman as Hero in Old English Literature* (Syracuse UP, 1986). All three document earlier criticism, including the quirky and eccentric. Jerome Mandel summarizes varying views on the poem's formal division, in *Alternate Readings in Old English Literature* (New York: Peter Lang, 1987), pp. 149ff. Other studies connect *The Wife's Lament* to the *The Husband's Message.*

8. In addition to the singer's explicitly voiced desire, the poem's language includes words of veiled sexual meaning, e.g., *gemaecne* (line 18) and *gerestan* (line 40). See Julie Coleman, "Sexual Euphemism in Old English," *Neuphilologische Mitteilungen* 93 (1992): 93–98.

9. Earl Anderson, "The Uncarpentered World of Old English Poetry," *Anglo-Saxon England* 20 (1991): 65–80.

10. Dolores Warwick Frese proposes a mother's lament for her son: "'Wulf and Eadwacer': The Adulterous Woman Reconsidered," pp. 273–291 in Damico and Olsen, cited above, note 7. Anne Klinck subjects the language to sensitive scrutiny in "Animal Imagery in 'Wulf and Eadwacer' and the Possibilities of Interpretation," *Papers on Language and Literature* 23 (1987): 3–13. Alain Renoir is still cited, "Wulf and Eadwacer: A Noninterpretation," in *Franciplegius,* ed. J.B. Bessinger, Jr. and Robert F. Creed (New York, 1965), pp. 147–163, for its analysis of the poem and its varying interpretations.

11. *Life of Saint Leoba,* in *The Anglo-Saxon Missionaries in Germany,* ed. and trans. C.H. Talbot (New York: Sheed and Ward, 1954), pp. 208, 209, 212, 216–17, 220–21.

12. Patrick Sims-Williams, *Religion and Literature in Western England, 600–800* (Cambridge: Cambridge UP, 1990), p. 211.

13. J.M. Wallace-Hadrill, *The Frankish Church* (Oxford: Clarendon, 1983), pp. 150–161. Of Boniface's book, Wallace-Hadrill writes (p. 159), "To look at it is to be a little shaken."

FURTHER READING

R.W. Chambers, Max Förster, Robin Flower, ed. *The Exeter Book of Old English Poetry*. London: P. Lund, Humphries and Co., 1933.

Jane Chance. *Woman as Hero in Old English Literature*. Syracuse: Syracuse UP, 1986.

Patrick W. Conner. *Anglo-Saxon Exeter: A Tenth-Century Cultural History*. Rochester, N.Y.: Boydell and Brewer, 1993.

Helen Damico and Alexandra Hennessey Olsen, eds. *New Readings on Women in Old English Literature*. Bloomington: Indiana UP, 1990.

Christine E. Fell, with Cecily Clark and Elizabeth Williams. *Women in Anglo-Saxon England, and the Impact of 1066*. London: British Museum Publications, 1984.

Nicholas Howe. *Migration and Mythmaking in Anglo-Saxon England*. New Haven: Yale UP, 1989.

George Philip Krapp and Elliott Van Kirk Dobbie, eds. *The Anglo-Saxon Poetic Records*. 6 vols. New York: Columbia UP, 1931–53. Vol. 3.

R.F. Leslie, ed. *Three Old English Elegies: The Wife's Lament, The Husband's Message, The Ruin*. Manchester: Manchester UP, 1961.

Michael Lapidge and Helmut Gneuss, eds. *Learning and Literature in Anglo-Saxon England: Studies Presented to Peter Clemoes*. Cambridge: Cambridge UP, 1985.

Leoba. Letter No. 29. M. Tangl and P. H. Kolb, eds. and trans., revised by Reinhold Rau. *Bonifatii Epistulae/Briefe des Bonifatius*, pp. 102–105. Darmstadt: Wissenschaftliche Buchgesellschaft, 1968.

Bernard James Muir. *The Exeter Book: A Bibliography*. Exeter: U of Exeter P, 1992.

Patrick Sims-Williams. "Letter-Writing." In *Religion and Literature in Western England: 600–800*, pp. 211–242. Cambridge: Cambridge UP, 1990.

————. "An Unpublished Seventh- or Eighth-Century Anglo-Latin letter in Boulogne-sur-Mer MS 74 (82)." *Medium Aevum* 48 (1979): 1–22.

C.H. Talbot, ed. and trans. "The Life of Saint Leoba by Rudolf, Monk of Fulda." In *The Anglo-Saxon Missionaries in Germany*, pp. 204–226, New York: Sheed and Ward, 1954.

CHAPTER 8

A Mother to a Young Warrior

Dhuoda of Uzès (*fl. ca.* 843)

A Carolingian woman named Dhuoda, living in Uzès, a town in southern France near Nîmes in Septimania, has left us a remarkable document in the form of a letter to her son William. Dhuoda shows herself to have been extremely well read in Scripture, in the fathers of the Church, and in Christian poets like Prudentius and Venantius Fortunatus. She was acquainted with the grammarian Donatus and displayed a fervor for the kind of etymology and numerology that she would have found in the writings of Isidore of Seville. Her "handbook," the *Liber Manualis*, is not only a guide to moral, spiritual, and feudal conduct; it is more touchingly an autobiographical work. In addition to providing details about her own life, she describes her anxiety and love for her children, particularly sixteen-year-old William, then being held hostage through his father's wishes at the court of Charles the Bald, a monarch just two years older than William.

In those tempestuous days when the Carolingian empire was breaking up, Charles—half-brother to Charlemagne's older grandsons, Lothar, Pepin, and Louis "the German"—fought bitterly to retain his hold on the crown. His mother, the empress Judith, had been accused of witchcraft and adultery, common enough slanders leveled against women considered political threats. In fact, one of her alleged lovers was Dhuoda's husband, Bernard of Septimania.[1] Whether or not this was so, Bernard, an energetic defender of the Spanish border, comes through as an embattled and cordially hated warrior in Charles's retinue. He had a way of shifting his allegiances, but after the crucial battle of Fontenay-en-Puisaye on June 22, 841, he quickly reconfirmed his homage to young Charles. To make this convincing, he sent his own son William, then nearly fifteen, as a hostage. He ordered William to swear allegiance to the seventeen-year-old Charles.

By this means Bernard hoped to ingratiate himself with his new overlord and to get back certain honors and lands of which he had been stripped. When as the governor of Septimania he had been accused of disloyalty with empress Judith, second wife of Louis the Pious, he had in 832 been deprived of this title. Bernard had already been punished through his sister Gerberga, a nun in a convent of Chalon-sur-Saône: Lothar accused her of sorcery, had her thrust into a wine cask and thrown into the Saône to drown.

It is against these barbarous realities of her time that Dhuoda's learned treatise has to be seen. When she exhorts her son to revere his superiors and his father, we sense a piety motivated by fear, self-preservation, and maternal concern as much as by a love of books—Bernard's treatment of his wife would certainly have intensified her wish to placate him. Married to Bernard at the imperial palace of Louis at Aix-en-Chapelle in June 824, Dhuoda was whisked away to the little southern town, where she was compelled to live out her days. Bernard visited her infrequently but enough to father two sons, William (b. November 29, 826) and Bernard (b. March 22, 841). Bernard took both sons from her—William when he was fourteen, and the infant Bernard before he was baptized. Parted from her children, and an outsider to the events at court, Dhuoda must have sought comfort in writing this treatise, speaking of herself in more than simply conventional commonplaces.

She mentions her marriage, the birth of her children, a woman who is her companion, and her anxiety that her illness will prevent her from writing another such book for her younger son. She tells how she has had to borrow money in order to pay for the defense of the Spanish march. It is noteworthy that Dhuoda continually emphasizes to this child of hers, caught up in the violence of the masculine world, her motherly role and authority. Intriguingly, she weaves her own name and William's in the Latin text, thus conspicuously inscribing her presence.

Dhuoda composed the *Handbook* so that William might carry and hold it in his hand. The book is in Latin, but this is not so strange for a wellborn member of the military aristocracy in the ninth century. The young Charles the Bald, William's and his father's overlord, had an excellent education and was fluent in the *lingua romana*, in Old High German and Latin. His library was filled with chiefly liturgical and biblical books that reflected more than just his personal taste. Carolingian patrons aimed "for the promotion of their royal power as Christian kings and for the consolidation of the Christian faith by disseminating the key texts on which that faith was based."[2]

Dhuoda's book deals entirely with young William's spirituality: the importance of loving God, the mystery of the Trinity, collecting and reading books, the beatitudes, arming oneself with the seven gifts of the holy spirit (wisdom, understanding, the spirit of counsel, fortitude, knowledge, godliness, the spirit of the fear of the lord), an elaborate system of number symbolism, and the value of filial respect and prayer. In view of the brutal realities of the time, these subjects may seem wondrously irrelevant for a man involved in the kind of exploits William had to face: "When you put your shoes on in the morning, prepare yourself with the gospel of peace" (Ephesians 6.15), or "Keep the canonical hours, seven times a day" (Psalms 118.164).

Dhuoda was undoubtedly mindful of churchmen like Alcuin, who had addressed similar advice to Charlemagne. She may have been assuming the role of "evangelizing woman," as women of virtue and authority were counseled to do, in order to reroute their men from vice—especially adulteries, fornications, and incest and particularly on long journeys and campaigns.[3]

Dhuoda's warnings about the fealty William owes to his lord Charles are also strongly worded. "Never let the idea of disloyalty against your lord be born or thrive in your heart. Of those who do act this way, harsh and shameful things are said. But I do not think that will be the case with you or your comrades at arms." In fact, Dhuoda—wittingly or unwittingly— makes a veiled reference to the deadly wrangling that went on among the three sons of the emperor Louis the Pious, as well as the sons' effort to rise up against their father, to put him and their stepmother out of the way, and get rid of their half-brother by accusing his mother of adultery with William's father.

By exhorting William to revere his father and by reinforc-
ing filial piety, *and* by urging him to revere the family of his
overlord, King Charles, she may well have put William into a
state of mental conflict.

William's father Bernard was in continuous difficulties at
court: accused of adultery with the wife of the emperor and
accused of conniving, treason, disloyalty, and shifting his allegiance. Seized as he tried to join Pepin, one of the rival brothers, in
an ambush to kill his former overlord Charles, he ended by being
publicly executed by beheading for accusations of treason.
Young William—loyal to his father and true to his mother's
advice—would try to avenge his father and would also be
executed, thereby earning an early death at age twenty-four.

We should recall what the state of the language was when
Dhuoda wrote (she began her book on November 30, 841, and
finished it on February 2, 843). In the military camps of the North
a pact was being hammered out by Charlemagne's grandsons in
speech plain enough for soldiers to grasp: this *lingua romana*
marked the first French document; the pact was called the Oaths
of Strasbourg (February 14, 842). And yet to her soldier son,
Dhuoda writes in the language of the Fathers, reflecting the allu-
sive style and the wordplay of her models. The text is spun out
of Scripture, much of it from the Psalms, as well as Genesis, Job,
the Wisdom books, the New Testament (notably Paul), the
Fathers of the Church (Jerome, Gregory, Augustine, Alcuin), and
the Christian poets. She calls her method "contextus," woven
together from many sources.

Dhuoda also schools William in the noble, military, and
Christian virtues of justice and courage; the protection of widows and orphans; charity to the poor; reverence for the Church
and its priesthood; respect for feudal authority; and instruction
in the vices and virtues. Perhaps more striking is her repeated
insistence on the importance of the reading habit and on the
energy it entails. One wonders if William had time to read as
much as she advised, and yet the exhortation "Lege!" is everywhere in the book in various forms. Initially Dhuoda points to
the physical connection between author and reader. She elabo-
rates upon the tangibility of the book as a thing to be grasped in
the hand, as a preliminary to reading, repeating Augustine's

definition of an enchiridion, a little guidebook "that can be clasped in the hand." When she writes that her Rule issues from her, the mother, and takes its shape in the son, her language concretizes the bond between author and reader, making it as physical as giving birth.

Indeed, Dhuoda gives the laborious effort of her authorship a word of her own invention: *agonizatio* (I.1.13; I.3.20), based on *agon*, which she uses elsewhere to refer to her husband's military combat. She exhorts her reader-son to reciprocate her authorial struggle by striving with equal effort to read and understand. Throughout the treatise, Dhuoda writes of the reading act. She uses *legere* (to read), *volvere* (to turn over, or unroll, even though the book was by now a block of leaves—a *codex libelli*), and *perscrutare* (search through, investigate, literally, to sift down to the rags and shreds), and offers advice on how to read an acrostic or to study paragraph headings to learn what follows. Reading also offers diversion, she points out, like a game of backgammon. Dhuoda's imagery about reading is particularly delightful: "Taste this book like a nourishing brew of honey"; "Read as doves do who sip the pure clear water, while being on the lookout for rapacious hawks."

Dhuoda's reference to her book as a mirror in which William may read his salvation *and* perceive his mother's image is surely astonishing. To the patristic reading of the text as a mirror of the firmament and of God's truth, Dhuoda adds her own variation. Dhuoda herself passes into the book's mirror surface as an image of piety and authority. Hers is the image that gazes back at the reader. The child will find the mother in the text. Her acrostically entwining her name with his simply reaffirms this point, by braiding even more intimately the mother/child, author/reader connections. The opening acrostic spells: *Dhuoda dilecto filio UUilhelmo salutem lege*, or "Dhuoda greets her dear son William. Read!" In the epitaph the acrostic spells: *Dhuodane*, "by (or about) Dhuoda."

1. Dhuoda's Handbook—The Text Begins

This little book has been arranged in three parts. Read all of them and you will better be able to understand the whole. I wish the three parts to be labeled in a comparable way so that they will follow the most useful sequence: the Rule of Conduct; the Form it assumes; and the Handbook. The Rule of Conduct comes from me; the Form it assumes is within you; the Handbook is as much from me as it is for you, composed by me, and established within you.

Now the "hand" in "Handbook," or *Manualis*, can be understood in many senses: sometimes it means God's power; sometimes the Son's power, and sometimes it means the Son himself. The power of God is as the Apostle says: "Humble yourself beneath the power of God's hand" (I Peter 5.6). The power of the Son is as Daniel says: "His power is an eternal power" (Daniel 7.14). When it means the Son himself, it is as the Psalmist says: "Send your hand from on high," or in other words, "Send your Son from heaven's heights" (Psalms 143.7).

All these and similar passages can be understood as Divine Activity and Power. For "hand" signifies the work completed, as the Scripture says: "The Lord's hand was laid upon me" (Ezekiel 3.22), that is to say, the redemption that has led believers to perfection. Also, "For the Lord's hand was comforting me" (Ezekiel 3.14). And again, "For his hand is with him" (Luke 1.66).

The "-alis" part of *Manualis* has many meanings. I will however explain only three of them here, according to the sayings of the Fathers. In the sense of something "winged," it means *scope*, which is "aim"; *consummation*, which is "achievement"; and *old age*, which is "ending."[4]

Or, indeed, *ales*—"wings"—signifies the herald and messenger of dawn, telling the story of the end of night and singing the light of the morning hours. What other meaning, then, could this term *Manualis* have but the end of ignorance, and the messenger that foresees the dawn of the future!

It may be said, "The night has gone before, the day is hastening" (Romans 13.12), that is, Christ, who himself has plainly said, "If I am the day and you are the hours, follow me" (John 8.12; 9.4–5; 11.9), and so forth.

Furthermore, from the beginning of this little book to the end, both in form and meaning, both in the meters and moving feet of its poetic melody and the loosened limbs of its prose, everywhere, in every part, know this: all of it has been written for the well-being of your soul and your body. What I desire is that when this work has been directed from my hand, you will willingly grasp it in your own hand, and holding it, turning it over, and reading it and studying it, you will fulfill its teachings in most worthwhile actions. For let it be said that this little book in the form of a handbook consists of words from me, and their actualization in you. As a certain one has said: "I have planted the seed, Apollo watered it, and God has made it grow" (I Corinthians 3.6).

What more can I say here, my son, except that on the basis of the good qualities you already have in you, I—with zeal for this underdaking—"have fought the good fight, and keeping the faith, I have finished the blessed race" (II Timothy 4.7). In whom do these things have value if not in that One who has said, "It is finished" (John 19.30). For whatever I have composed in this handbook, beginning with this chapter, whether it follows the Hebrew language, Greek letters, or the Latin tongue, I have completed to the end this work, which is called God.

2. In the Name of the Holy Trinity—Here Begins the Book, Dhuoda's Handbook, Which She Sent to Her Son William

I have observed that most women in this world take joy in their children. But, O my son William, I see myself, Dhuoda, living separated and far away from you. For this reason I am uneasy, as it were, and eager to be useful to you, and so I address this little book to you, which has been transcribed for me in my own name. It is for you to read as a kind of model. I rejoice that, although I am absent in body, this little book will be present. Once you have read it, it will lead your spirit back to those things that you ought to do, for my sake.

Epigram of the following work:

D ivine Lord, creator of the supreme light, author of the sky and stars, king of eternal things, Holy One,

H aving begun this work, I pray that you will, with your mercy, bring it to completion. Although I am ignorant, I strive for intelligence.

U nderstanding how to please you, and how to travel through present and future time—these things will depend on your help.

O ne and threefold, you lavish riches on your people throughout the ages.

D eserving ones will each have the heavenly rewards you allot to your servants.

A mple thanks I offer on bended knee to you, the Creator, to the extent of my ability.

D eign, I beg, to send me aid, raising me up to the skies at your right hand.

I have faith that your people will find eternal repose in that kingdom.

L imed in earth's mud though I am, a fragile exile, dragged to the very pit—

E qual to me in the lot she endures is a faithful woman friend, who also trusts in your forgiveness for her sins.

C enter of the universe, who sustains the circling orb of the heavens, you enclose the sea and the dry land in the palm of your hand.

T o you I commend William, my son. Allow him always to thrive and prosper.

O n the course he pursues, at all hours and moments, let him love you above everything else.

F ar upward to heaven's heights may he ascend with happy headlong footsteps together with your children.

I n you may his vigilant mind find guidance. May he live blessed forever.

L et him not become wrathful if he should be hurt; let him not stray far from you.

I n joy may he pursue a happy course, so that, shining with virtue, he will ascend above.

O f your will let him be mindful. You, who give without pomp, bestow intelligence upon him.

U nderstanding in faith and love, and the ability to praise you with redoubled gratitude—Holy One grant him these.

U nto him let your bounteous grace be given, with peace and safety of body and mind.

I n this world may he and his offspring flourish, possessing these good things here in such a way that he shall not lack the blessings of Heaven.

L et him read this volume and turn to it again at appropriate times, heeding the sayings of the saints and obeying them in his thoughts.

H elp him to reflect, with the intelligence he receives from you, how, when, and to whom he should offer his support.

E ndlessly, for your sake, may he pursue the four virtues, so that, keeping to them, he may accomplish anything.

L et him be generous, wise, dutiful, and brave, never straying from self-control.

M other am I to him. He will never have anyone like me, unworthy as I am.

O n him have mercy, I resolutely pray to you at every moment and hour.

S orrows and cares assail me while I strive on his behalf with my frail efforts.

A nd to you—Giver of all good things—I entrust him with gratitude.

L ands are in turmoil, kingdoms torn apart by discord. You alone remain immutable.

U pon your divine will all things depend, whether or not good people seek the proper solutions.

T o you belong the royalty, the power, the fullness of the earth extending through the world.

E verything serves you alone, you who reign forever. Have mercy on my children.

M y two sons, who were brought into the world—I pray that
they may live and always love you.

L etters at the beginning of each verse will spell the meaning.
Reader, diligently examine these to know the formula.
E ventually you will be able to understand—with swift pace—
what I have written.
G rant to me, mother of two male children, that you will pray to
the life-giving Creator to
E levate the father of these children to heaven and unite me to
them in his Kingdom.

Begin your reading with the letter **D**. With **M** all is ended. The
verses are finished. With Christ's help I will embark on the work
I have begun for my children.

3. Here Begins the Prologue

Many things are clear to many people, and yet these things
are not clear to me. Those who are like me have darkened minds
and are lacking in understanding. If I speak less, I am more. But
he "who opens the mouths of the mute and makes the tongues of
infants eloquent" (Wisdom 10.21) is always present. I Dhuoda,
although I am weak in understanding, living unworthily among
women who are unworthy, I am your mother nonetheless. It is to
you that the words of my manual are now addressed.

Just as the game of backgammon, among other pleasurable
pursuits, is generally agreed to be an apt pastime for young
people, and just as some women are accustomed to peer at their
own faces in the mirror—so that they may cleanse away the
spots of dirt and show themselves radiant and, in a worldly way,
give pleasure to their husbands—just in this way, I would like
you, in spite of the pressures of your worldly occupations, to
give your devoted attention—for my sake—to the reading of this
little book which I have addressed to you, giving it that same
degree of attention and zeal that others give to looking in the
mirror or to a game of backgammon.

Even though you own an increasing number of books, may it please you to read my little work often. May you with the help of Almighty God be enabled to understand it for your benefit. In this book, you will find in succinct form all that you want to know. You will also find in it a mirror, in which you may contemplate the health of your soul. In so doing you can please not only the world but the God who formed you from the dust of the earth. This will be necessary from every point of view, my son William, in order for you to lead a useful life in the world and be pleasing to God in all things.

My great concerns about you, O my son William, are to send you salutary words. Among these words, my vigilant heart yearns ardently to tell you—with God's help—about your birth. So in this little book, written for you as a result of my desire, these things will follow as planned.

4. Preface

In the eleventh year of the reign of our departed lord Louis, who ruled in splendor by the will of Christ,[5] I was given in lawful marriage on June 29, 824, to my lord Bernard, your father. In the thirteenth year of that reign, with God's help as I believe, your birth issued forth into the world from me, O most dearly desired first-born son.

In the course of the worsening turmoil of this wretched world, in the midst of much agitation and discord in the realm, the Emperor did not escape the common path of mortality. In fact, his life ended before he had completed the twenty-eighth year of his reign. And in the year following his death, on March 22, 841, your brother was born, the second child after you to issue from my womb—through God's mercy—in the town of Uzès. He was still a baby and had not yet received the grace of baptism when your lord and father to both of you had him taken to Aquitaine by Elefantus, the bishop of that city, and others of his followers.

But now I have remained a long time in this town—by my lord's command—deprived of your presence. While I rejoice in his campaigns, I have undertaken, because of my longing for the both of you, to have this little book copied out and sent to you, insofar as my meager cleverness permits. . . .

I have learned that your father Bernard has entrusted you to the hands of our lord King Charlemagne. I urge you to acquit yourself of your duties with a perfect goodwill. . . .

5. Seeking God: The Whelps and Puppies of Holy Church

We must seek God, you and I, my son. In his will we endure, we live, move, and exist. As for me, unworthy as I am and flimsy as a shadow, I seek him as well as I am able, and I ceaselessly ask his help to the extent of my knowledge and understanding. For this is needful in every way.

Now it sometimes happens that a troublesome little puppy among the other whelps under its master's table can seize and devour the crumbs that fall (Mark 7.28; Matthew 15.27). He who has the power to elicit speech from the mouths of dumb animals (Numbers 22.28) can, according to his mercy of old, open the mouth of my spirit (Luke 24.45) and grant me understanding. He who prepares a table in the wilderness for his faithful followers, giving them in time of need a sufficient measure of wheat, can fulfill even my will—that of a handmaid—according to his desire. So I can jump under his table, that is to say, on the lower level of the Holy Church, and gaze from afar at the little whelps—those who are ministering to the sacred altars. Then from among the crumbs of spiritual wisdom I shall be able to gather for myself and for you, O William my beautiful son, some beautiful and luminous words that are worthy and appropriate. For I know that "his mercy has never failed" (Lamentations 3.22).

6. A Reminder: Books and Mirrors

Now I give you a reminder, O my beautiful and lovable son. In the midst of your mundane concerns of this world, do not be slothful in gathering many scrolls of books. There you should learn from your masters, the most holy learned men, something greater and better than what I have written here about God the Creator. Pray to God, cherish and love him. If you do so, he will be your guardian, your guide, your companion, and your fatherland—"the way, the truth, and the life" (John 14.6). He will grant you in abundance the world's prosperity, and he will convert all your enemies to peace. . . .

What more shall I say? Dhuoda is always here to exhort you, my son, but in anticipation of the day when I shall no longer be with you, you shall have here as a memento of me this little book of moral counsels. And you can gaze upon me as on an image in a mirror, and see me reading with my bodily and spiritual eyes and praying to God concerning those obligations you are to render me. You can fully discover them here. My son, you will have learned doctors who will teach you many more examples, more eminent and of greater usefulness, but they are not of equal status with me, nor do they have a heart more ardent than I, your mother, have for you, O my firstborn son.

These words that I address to you—read them, understand them, and put them to practice. And when your little brother, whose name I do not even know as yet, has received the grace of baptism in Christ, do not be slow to win his affection, to encourage him and love him, to rouse him to go from good to better. When he shall have reached the age of speaking and reading, show him this little volume, this handbook that I have written and in which I have inscribed your name. Watch over his reading, for he is your flesh and your brother. I, Dhuoda, your mother, send reminders to both of you as if you were already—in the midst of the mundane cares of this world—about to "Lift up your heart! Look to him who reigns in the heavens!"

May the almighty, of whom—despite my unworthiness—I speak so often, render you—together with your father Bernard, my lord and seigneur—happy and cheerful in the present world! May he give you prosperity in all things. And once the course of this life is ended, may he see to it that you joyously enter the heavenly sky with the saints! Amen.

7. The Tree of Mercy

It has, in short, been written, "In whatever place the tree
has fallen, there he will be" (Ecclesiastes 11.3). By the tree is
meant each man. Whether he is good or bad, by his fruit shall he
actually be known (Matthew 7.17–20). A beautiful and noble tree
produces noble leaves and brings forth suitable fruit. This is
indicated by a great man and very faithful man. The cultivated
man deserves to be filled with the Holy Spirit and to burgeon
with leaves and fruit. He is distinguished by his sweet fragrance.
For his leaves are his words, his fruit is his judgment, or indeed,
his leaves are his intellect, his fruit his good deeds. The good tree
flourishes, but the wicked tree will be delivered to the flames. It
is written, "Every tree that does not bear good fruit shall be cut
down and thrown into the fire" (Matthew 3.10; 7.19).

The true tree, together with the vine that is in concord with
it, is our Lord Christ. That is, the Lord Jesus, from whom all
chosen trees arise and vine-shoots burgeon, has deigned to
choose the worthy branches that will bring forth beautiful fruit.
He himself says, "I am the true vine and you are the vine-
shoots." And again, "I have chosen you from the world so that
you may go and bear fruit and that your fruit shall remain. Who
remains with me and I in him will bear much fruit" (John 15.5,
16), and so forth.

It is to such a tree, therefore, that I urge you to graft
yourself, my son, so that you may cleave to him without fail,
and—since fruit means good deeds—you will be able to bring
forth much fruit. Those who behold him and have sure trust in
him are compared to this saintly tree, which is transplanted
beside the flowing water (Psalms 1.3). Those trees that have
deeply and profoundly fixed their roots in the moisture will not
grow dry in the summer season (Jeremiah 17.8). Their leaves will
always be green and abundant, and they will never fail to
produce fruit.

Why this, my son? Because, as the Apostle says, "rooted
and grounded in charity" (Ephesians 3.17), with the coming of
the Holy Spirit's grace, they will never fail in any season to
weigh their fruit for those who are nearby.

And so that you may know which trees are worthy of yielding their fruits in abundance, hear the Apostle when he says, "The fruits of the spirit are charity, joy, peace, forbearance, kindness, gentleness, patience, chastity, self-control, modesty, sobriety, vigilance, and wisdom" (Galatians 5.22–23),[6] and other virtues like these. Since those who practice such virtues will deserve to attain quite readily to the kingdom of God, graft those fruits in your mind and body, my son, and bring them forth and meditate upon them continually. In this way, with the fruit and perseverance of good works, you will deserve on the day of tribulation and adversity to be sheltered and supported by the True Tree.

8. The Epitaph for My Tomb, Which I Ask You to Inscribe

When I have finished my days, be sure that you have my name inscribed among the dead. What I wish, and ask you most emphatically to do—as if it were the present—is to have the following inscription permanently carved on the stone that marks the tomb in which my body will be buried. In this way the passersby who see this epitaph may worthily pray to God for me, unworthy woman that I am.

And for those who will some day read this Handbook that you are reading, let them also meditate on what follows, and pray to God to forgive me, as if I were already enclosed in the tomb.

Read here, Reader, the little verses of this epitaph[7]:

+ D + M +

D huoda's body, formed of earth, lies buried in this tomb. Infinite King, receive her.

H er frail and utter filth, formed of earth, has been enclosed in the depths of this tomb. Benevolent King, grant her mercy.

U lcerous and wet is her body. There is nothing more left for her but the grave's deep shadows. O King, absolve her from her faults!

O travelers of whatever age and sex who come and go this way, I
beg you to utter these words: "Great holy God, unbind her
chains!"

D riven down into the cave with her horrible wounds, hedged
round with bitter gall, she has reached the end of her filthy life.
O King, pardon her sins!

A nd lest the dark serpent seize her soul, utter this prayer:
"Merciful God, help her!"

N o traveler shall pass this way without having read this. I
adjure all that they pray, saying, "Grant her repose, Cherishing
God."

E ternal light shall be bestowed upon her in the company of the
saints. Command this, Benign God, that the Amen[8] shall
receive her after her funeral rites.

NOTES

1. Godson and kinsman to Charlemagne, Bernard was the son of
Count William of Toulouse, later known as St. Guilhem du Désert when
he established the monastery in Gellone to which he retired. He also
earned literary fame as Guillaume d'Orange of the epics.

2. Rosamond McKitterick, "Ottonian Intellectual Culture in the
Tenth Century and the Role of Theophanu," *Early Medieval Europe* 2
(1993): 57. McKitterick has written on the library of Charles the Bald in
English Historical Review 95 (1980): 28–47 and in her chapter in *Charles the
Bald: Court and Kingdom*, ed. M.T. Gibson and Janet Nelson (1990).
The names of learned men were associated with this court,
including Usuard of Paris who in 875 wrote his great Martyrology just
for Charles. He is that same Usuard who would journey to Spain in
search of relics (see chapter 9). Usuard's work contains one of the
earliest allusions to the holy virgins Martha and Saula and a few others,
who would eventually connect to Ursula and the 11,000 virgins (see
chapter 15).

3. The evangelizing role of ninth-century women has been noted
by Janet Nelson. Women didn't need to warn men against pagan
dangers, but were to reinforce the faith of practicing and possibly erring

Christians. Jonas of Orléans in *De Institutioni Laici* urged them to do this, signaling the special role of noble matrons in the pastoral ministry. Also "women of authority" (*maxime potentes feminae*) were urged to use their positions to prevent adulteries, fornications, and incest (Council of Meaux-Paris of 845 [Nelson, p. 477]), and to exhort Christians to prayer. Women were in this way seen as the custodians and guarantors of male morality. Janet L. Nelson, "Les Femmes et l'évangelisation au IXe siècle," *Revue du nord* 68 (1986): 471–485.

4. Dhuoda's imaginative etymologies are not always clear. Can she be thinking of the Germanic *alt* (old) when she finds "old age" as a meaning for "-alis"?

5. Louis the Pious, reigning with Charlemagne from 813, actually became emperor in 814. Louis died on June 20, 840.

6. Dhuoda has added a few qualities to the list.

7. These letters stand for *Dis manibus* (in God's hands), as seen on other funerary monuments.

8. Christ is called the Amen in Revelations 3.14.

FURTHER READING

Y. Bessmertny. "Le monde vu par une femme noble au IXe siècle: La perception du monde dans l'aristocratie carolingienne." *Le Moyen Age* 93 (1987): 162–184.

Dhuoda. E. Bondurand, ed. *Le Manuel de Dhuoda.* Paris, 1887.

———. Pierre Riché, ed. *Manuel pour mon fils.* Sources chrétiennes. Paris, 1975.

———. Carol Neel, trans. *Handbook for William: A Carolingian Woman's Counsel for Her Son. By Dhuoda.* Lincoln: U of Nebraska P, 1991.

Eleanor Shipley Duckett. "Dhuoda and Bernard of Septimania." In *Medieval Portraits from East and West,* pp. 197–218. Ann Arbor: U of Michigan P, 1972.

Margaret T. Gibson and Janet Nelson, eds. *Charles the Bald: Court and Kingdom,* 2nd ed. Aldershot, 1990.

Peter Godman and Roger Collins, eds. *Charlemagne's Heir: New Aspects of the Reign of Louis the Pious.* Oxford: Oxford UP, 1990.

M.M. Hildebrandt. *The External School in Carolingian Society*. E.J. Brill, 1991.

Rosamond McKitterick. *The Carolingians and the Written Word*. Cambridge: Cambridge UP, 1989.

CHAPTER 9

Hagiographer, Playwright, Epic Historian

Hrotswitha of Gandersheim (*ca*. 935–1001)

The tenth-century noblewoman Hrotswitha, canoness of the Benedictine monastery of Gandersheim in Saxony, was one of the most able and prolific writers of the Middle Ages. Her writing displays a significant awareness of female autonomy and is often marked by sprightliness and wit. Learned in the Latin classics, Hrotswitha was also deeply observant of the currents of her day, great and small. Notwithstanding her religious vocation, she was no mystic. She had a lively, extroverted flair for storytelling. She understood how sexual realities could dramatically punctuate a narrative, and was very knowing about the way people thought and talked of such matters.

Hrotswitha produced a body of literature in three genres. These are her eight saints' lives, celebrating the courageous faith of individuals in the unfolding struggle of Christianity; her dramas, which secure her place as the first Western nonliturgical playwright; and a pair of epics that identify the political and Christian purpose of her monastery and family. An example of each literary type is represented in this chapter.

Hrotswitha had connections and kin among the magnates at the court of Otto the Great. She would have spent time at court, sharing in its rich intellectual life and benefiting from the opportunity to converse with visitors to this cosmopolitan hub. Since Otto's reign enjoyed the prestige of strong church support, the court received ambassadors like those Russians sent by Olga of Kiev, looking for German missionaries to help convert the pagan Slavs. Under the influence of the cultured Bruno of

171

Cologne, the imperial court also welcomed scholars and authors both home-bred and foreign—Widukind and Ekkehard, Rather of Verona, and Liutprand of Cremona.

Bruno was Otto's learned and widely connected brother. He was chancellor and later archbishop of Cologne. Not only did he sponsor the cultural life at court, but he also kept in close touch with Gandersheim. Under the beneficial effects of the Ottonian cultural rebirth, and invested with complete autonomy by Otto, Gandersheim—with its wealth, courts, mints, and army—became its own small principality.[1]

Hrotswitha's earliest works, written in about 962 when she was not yet thirty (and incidentally, the year in which Otto imperially crowned himself), were her saints' lives, four men and four women. The lives are *Mary, The Ascension of Christ, Gongolf, Pelagius, Theophilus, Basilius, Dionysius,* and *Agnes. Pelagius* tells the martyrdom of a youth of Christian Galicia who refused a caliph's homosexual advances. The threatened rape of the adolescent Pelagius corresponds to Hrotswitha's usual model, in the plays and other saints' legends, of young women protecting their virginity as well as their religious faith.

The legend of Pelagius had a newsworthy savor, full of pathos and current interest, since the young man who was put to death was a recent contemporary. Hrotswitha says she based the story on the report of an eyewitness, a citizen of Córdoba. Pelagius's tormentor was not an ancient Roman but a Saracen pagan, flourishing in the same world as Otto the Great. The setting is the splendidly sophisticated caliphate of Andalusian Spain. Into the tale Hrotswitha weaves events from a century earlier, when a group of voluntary victims known as the Córdoba martyrs flung themselves on Arab swords. Although Pelagius was not one of their number, his plight tended to fuse with theirs, since all died at Moslem hands and many of their relics ultimately reposed at Oviedo in northern Spain.

Hrotswitha learned of Pelagius from a visitor to Otto's court. She reports (in the preface to her plays) that while she relied on old books for the sources of most of her saints' legends, she heard the story of Pelagius: "The sequence of events in his martyrdom was related to me by a certain man, a native of the city where Pelagius suffered. This person affirmed he had seen

Pelagius, the most beautiful of men, and that he truthfully knew how the matter had turned out."[2]

Otto's exchange with Moorish Córdoba has been documented. It grew from a minor crisis that kept threatening to explode as the two potentates, Abd ar-Rahman III and Otto the Great, sniffed at each other with wary curiosity, always through their envoys. However it was resolved, the encounter has left us illuminating reports about Islamic Spain.

The dialogue between Otto and Abd ar-Rahman III, emir and caliph of the Umayyad dynasty, began over a worrisome matter of maritime danger. The trading vessels of Umayyad Spain connected Al-Andalus and North Africa with Syria and Egypt. Arab fleets, together with Byzantine vessels, controlled the sea lanes along the shores of the Mediterranean. Navies based in Italy and Catalonia sailed there as well. Viking ships prowled the waters. The Umayyads allowed their *ghazi*—pirating and policing warrior fleets—to have free play.[3]

Whether Otto was trading with the Umayyads or the Christian kingdoms of Leon and Castile in northern Spain or with North Africa isn't clear. But he sent a message to Córdoba to complain to Abd ar-Rahman III about the piracy. The account of this embassy, preserved in the biography of John of Gorze, Otto's ambassador who was detained three years in Córdoba, is one of the few contemporary Latin descriptions of Umayyad Spain. It also provides glimpses into the lives of Mozarabs, the term applied to Christians who managed to practice their faith under Spanish Moslem rule.

The Germans and the Arabs communicated about the pirates between 951 and 955–56. Misunderstandings arose from the start over religious differences. When the caliph's initial reply sounded irreverent to the Christian clerical ears at Otto's court, the emperor refused to let the caliph's messenger depart. He sent his own envoy in 953, the monk John of Gorze, since churchmen still served ambassadorial roles that a secular administration would later fulfill. John leaped at the opportunity for possible martyrdom and had to be calmed by his superior abbot. When John of Gorze reached Córdoba, he was warned not to deliver his letters, which were feared to contain phrases insulting to the caliph. He might, in so doing, place the lives of his embassy in jeopardy, since a law of Islam demanded that no one speak against their religion on pain of death.

The caliph (called *rex* in John of Gorze's biography) decided to send a Mozarab bishop to visit John, who lingered outside Córdoba waiting for an audience. When John tells the bishop that Otto's letters were a just retort to the caliph's own so-called arrogant impieties, the bishop affords an insight into what life is like for Christians under this regime:

> "Consider under what conditions we labor. We are fallen into these things because of sin, that we are in the power of the Muslims (*paganorum*).[4] We are forbidden by the Apostle's word to resist power. Only one bit of comfort remains, that in the evil of such calamity they do not forbid us to follow our own religion; and when they see us diligently observing Christianity, they honour and understand us, the more so that they are drawn that way by their own conviction, since they are completely horrified by the Jews. For the time being, therefore, we should keep this counsel, that since nothing of our religion needs to be given up, we should obey them in all the other things, and observe their commands, so far as these do not conflict with faith."[5]

There is a good deal more of this dialogue between the Mozarab bishop and the Saxon monk. When at last John of Gorze gained an audience with Abd ar-Rahman III, monk and caliph had reached some kind of mutuality of respect and even, it appears, enjoyment in each other's company. But before this happened, further messengers had to travel to and fro for several years.

One of these was a man named Reccamund, who lived in Córdoba. A chancery official and a Christian fluent in Arabic, Reccamund was entrusted by the caliph to persuade Otto to write another set of letters, more respectful than the first. As he was leaving Córdoba, Reccamund paid a visit to John of Gorze, who still loitered outside the city. Reccamund wanted to get a sense of what Otto was like, whether he was a merciful or a temperamental monarch.

During his stay in Germany, Reccamund spent quite a bit of time at Gorze. At the court of Otto he made friends with the visiting Liutprand and gave him the idea of writing a history of contemporary Europe and its sovereigns. Liutprand followed the suggestion and produced his *Antapodosis*, which he dedicated to Reccamund. On Reccamund's return from this mission, the caliph rewarded him with the bishopric of Granada. Reccamund later performed another embassy for Abd ar-Rahman to Byzantium and Jerusalem. Once back in Spain, in 961, Reccamund dedicated a "calendar" to the new caliph, al-Hakam II, who had just ascended the throne.

This "calendar," written first in Arabic, then translated into Latin, dwells chiefly on astronomical and agronomical subjects. But it also contains a list of liturgical feasts celebrated by the Mozarabs (Reccamund calls them "Latins" or "Christians"). Reccamund names many more Spanish churches and monasteries than were noted in sources a century earlier. Most important, Reccamund mentions a number of the persons who died during the Córdoba martyr movement of the mid-ninth century. Appended to the list he names Pelagius under June 26, martyred in Córdoba in 925.[6] The well-traveled and well-apprised Reccamund is very likely to have been Hrotswitha's eyewitness and informant.

The emir and caliph Abd ar-Rahman III (912 to 961), viewed from the perspective of political and cultural history, enjoys the reputation of a gifted ruler. He centralized the government and built shipyards and navies. Having quelled disorders (which meant in part the Christian rioters to the north around Galicia), he stabilized the realm. His reign fostered growth in art and architecture and in the keeping of historical records. He patronized the sciences, botany and pharmacology, and had Greek treatises translated, such as that of Dioscorides. Libraries and schools of medicine flourished. Philosophy, poetry, and music prospered. Abd ar-Rahman III adorned Córdoba with palaces and bridges, baths and fountains, colonnaded gardens and mosques. He further embellished the Great Mosque, adding its first minaret. In 929, he built the magnificent palace complex, known as Madinat al-Zahra, outside Córdoba, which was called "the navel of al-Andalus."

In the same period, four years after Pelagius's death, he assumed both the political and religious titles of *emir* ("commander of the believers") and *al-Nasir* or *caliph* ("defender of the religion of God"). As a Mediterranean power, the caliphate of Córdoba extended from most of Spain to North Africa.[7]

The slave trade found a ready market in Umayyad Spain, since there was always a need, for instance, for the guards and soldiers called Mamelukes. Usually these were foreigners and Christians, relegated to guard service, the barracks, and the stabling of horses. Hrotswitha rather knowledgeably describes the plans to recruit the good-looking Christian hostage Pelagius into the palace guard.

Personal details about Abd ar-Rahman III are on record in the works of the seventeenth-century Arab historian al-Makkari, whose books preserve earlier Arab materials that do not otherwise survive. The Umayyads, while they defended Islam, generally "had mothers, wives, and slavegirls of indigenous Spanish origin," many of high rank, many of them former Christians. Some marriages were willingly negotiated by rulers in northern Spain, where tiny Christian kingdoms of Visigothic origins held out for three centuries until the Reconquest. Abd ar-Rahman, whose grandmother was a princess of Pamplona, is described as having blue eyes and light reddish hair, which he dyed black in order to look more typically Arab.[8]

Apparently, the caliph delighted in amazing his visitors by displaying mechanical wonders rather like those of the Byzantine emperors. In his palace audience chamber at Madinat al-Zahra, he "placed a large marble bowl filled with mercury, so contrived that a light touch could set it swaying in motion. Beams of light, aimed through the controlled access of windows placed high up in the chamber, were reflected off the rapidly moving mercury and sent flashing around the hall like thunderbolts." The apparatus was meant "to impress and intimidate, to overwhelm those received in audience, especially the envoys of less sophisticated peoples."[9]

Despite his accomplishments, Abd ar-Rahman III could have been nothing more in Hrotswitha's Saxon Christian eyes than a pagan thug who ranted like Attila, Pilate, and Herod. Whatever she learned of him she used to fuel her report of his depravities. Abd ar-Rahman III died in 961, and Hrotswitha began her legends of the saints after 962, so he was already out of the picture. Pelagius himself had been executed in 925. If Hrotswitha, who was born about 935, learned of Pelagius's fate in the 950s on one of the occasions when envoys visited Otto's court, she could have been anywhere between the ages of fifteen to eighteen, impressionable years to learn of the recent martyrdom of a beautiful young man close to one's own age. The martyr's remains were carried to Leon in 967, when Hrotswitha was perhaps thirty-two years old. By 985, when Hrotswitha would have been in her fifties, the relics were translated to Oviedo.[10]

To the martyrdom of Pelagius, Hrotswitha adds background details on the history and description of Córdoba that are quite accurate and must have come from her informant. What she has to say reflects the state of Christian-Moslem relations a century earlier.

Obviously there was strife between the Christians and Moslems that flared up in different forms. The demolition of churches and the bans placed on new church building would have grated. Hrotswitha's *Pelagius* shows her aware of how vulnerable the Spanish churches were, just as she seems confident about the inside of the Córdoba jail. The Great Mosque at Córdoba had formerly, it was said, been built on the site of the Christian church of the deacon St. Vincent. This most eminent of the Spanish martyrs had died at Valencia in 304 under Diocletian. Initially, his church was shared by both Christians and Moslems. Under Abd ar-Rahman I, the Moslems eventually purchased the building and converted it, while Christians obtained a new church across the Guadalquivir River and outside the city.[11]

Architecture played a role in the conflict between Christians and Moslems. The columns for the Great Mosque were constructed of *spolia*, reused stones from ruined churches, Roman baths, and civic buildings. There were Christians who could not approve of the influence of Moorish design on Christian churches, which, like the monasteries, began to imitate the arch and arcading seen in Umayyad Córdoba. Christians detested hearing the muezzins' call to prayer from their minarets, and Moslems uttered awful imprecations when they heard the ringing of bells from Christian towers. Church towers, seen as rival structures to minarets, were ordered torn down. Later in the century, when the shrine of Saint James of Compostela was sacked, torched, and looted of its bells, the bells were carried to Córdoba and converted into lamps for the Great Mosque.[12]

The episode of the Córdoba martyrs that Hrotswitha draws upon in *Pelagius* actually occurred between 850 and 859, under Abd ar-Rahman II and his successor Muhammed I. The main source of these events is Eulogius, a Córdoban priest and later a bishop-elect of Toledo, who ended by being beheaded like the other martyrs. It is not inconceivable that Hrotswitha had Eulogius's writings, or a part of them, in her hands, carried to Frankfurt by Reccamund.

Eulogius had wanted to go to Rome but was unable to leave his duties. Then he tried in 848 to travel north to cross the Pyrenees in an effort to locate a brother. He found his route impeded by bandits in league with a Carolingian warrior we have already encountered—none other than Dhuoda's son William![13]

Frustrated, Eulogius now journeyed to Christian Pamplona. In that small, formerly Visigothic kingdom he found at least four important monasteries, and had his choice of poetic and patristic works which he bore away with him, books to which the Christian community in the south had no access. Such texts as he unearthed may have come to Spain from Aquitaine. With a view to resuscitating Latin poetic meters in Córdoba, Eulogius brought back Augustine's *City of God*, Virgil's *Aeneid*, and Juvenal's and Horace's *Satires*. He also acquired a *Life* of Islam's founder. On the basis of this volume he began to make his assaults on Mohammed as a false prophet. Troubled by the decay of Latin Christian culture, he apparently longed to rekindle a popular awareness of the vanished glories of Christian Spain, "foremost in the blessed practice of the Christian faith, flourishing in the worthiness of most venerable bishops, and radiant in the most beautiful building of churches."[14]

Such nostalgia for a ravaged Germanic Christendom under Moslem rule must have spoken very directly to Hrotswitha. Moreover, many Spanish Christians had abandoned the faith in favor of Islam in order to elude taxation, which was not imposed on Moslems, and to gain admittance to other privileges—economic, political, and cultural, even the right to bear arms. So strong was the linguistic sway of the Moslems that there were translations of the Bible and of early Church councils into Arabic. Participation in Arab culture and language had its rewards, and the Islamic religion could not be disentangled from the culture. Christians, Moslems, and Jews grew dangerously friendly, in the view of many Christians. The whole problem "became a matter of deep concern to a small group of Christians in mid-ninth-century Córdoba. This band, many of whom were closely linked together by ties of family and friendship, deliberately sought martyrdom at the hands of the Moslem authorities by public denunciations of Mohammed and of Islam, offences known to be punishable by death."[15]

The first of the voluntary martyrs was a man by the name of Isaac, a public official turned monk. Of aristocratic background and well trained in Arabic, Isaac had prospered in political life before his retreat. One day he came back to Córdoba and began furiously to upbraid a local *qadi*, or judge. Shocked, the *qadi* struck him. When Isaac insisted that he was not drunk but inspired and that he was willing to die for his religious attack, one thing led to another and he was beheaded on June 3, 851; his body was crucified upside down, burned, then thrown into the Guadalquivir.[16] This custom of beheading and throwing bodies into the city's river occurs in Hrotswitha's story. Like Eulogius, she reports the fixing of a body to river rocks to keep it from floating to the surface. Eulogius's observations and record-keeping marked the start of the contagion, for one martyr caught the fervor from another. Paul Alvar, a fellow student and later Eulogius's close friend, eventually wrote his biography.[17]

Between 853 and 856, seventeen martyrs offered themselves, two of them the young girls Alodia and Nunila. Although most of the martyrs died in Córdoba, they were not necessarily citizens. Some had come as students, many hailing from monasteries beyond the city. Clandestine Christians and those who had converted from Islam found the rationale for voluntary martyrdom in the model of John the Baptist. They may have thought of founding a new martyr church like those dedicated to the victims of Diocletian's reign in 303–312. Perhaps they deemed it possible to arrest the Christian community's drift into Islam, and so they vehemently disputed Moslem law. When men and women in numbers willingly immolated themselves by defying Islam and had themselves brought up on charges of apostasy or blasphemy, such episodes began to add up to a campaign. It spread to other regions of Spain.[18]

But there was official Christian opposition to the enthusiasts. Bishop Reccafred of Seville denounced the self-willed martyrs, possibly at a Council of Córdoba in 852. When he had Eulogius imprisoned, both Eulogius and Alvar were moved to write in defense of the martyrs. Eulogius had given spiritual counsel to certain of them, heartening them, delivering them an "Exhortation to Martyrdom." He now felt particular anger against Reccafred as a heedless shepherd who deserted his flock to the slaughter. The biographies of the martyrs of Córdoba took shape. In his *Memorial of the Saints*, among the most prominent are Flora and Maria of Córdoba.

Maria's Christian father, upon the death of her Moslem mother, had placed her in a convent at Cuteclara. Her brother was in the monastery of St. Felix. When he died, Maria underwent a crisis that impelled her further actions, and it is possible, too, that Maria was influenced by her abbess, Artemia, whose sons had been executed years before. Maria met her sister-martyr Flora praying in a church, and formed a friendship that led to their deaths together.

Flora was born at Córdoba of a Mohammedan father and Christian mother. She was baptized and practiced the faith covertly with her mother's help. When she was orphaned, her brother denounced her to the *qadi*. She was arrested on charges of apostasy and sentenced to be beaten until she bled. The authorities returned her to the custody of her brother, who was told to make her give up the faith. Flora then escaped to her sister's house in Ossaria. Now the Córdoba authorities bore down on the Christians and any who harbored them. Flora's relatives feared reprisals and compelled Flora to leave their home.

Flora and Maria went together before the *qadi* to denounce Islam, and were imprisoned. Another secret Christian named Sabigotho visited the two women in their cell. She spent the night with them, not only to comfort them but also to reveal that she too intended to die.[19] Flora and Maria were threatened with prostitution if they did not recant, but instead, both were killed on November 24, 851. Sabigotho in a vision beheld them in their new glory and received their promise that she would die and join them, but her death would be in the company of a foreign monk. When Georgius, a stunningly unwashed monastic from outside Jerusalem, traveled first to Córdoba and then appeared in the monastery of Tabanos (from which Isaac, the first martyr, had come), the abbess there recognized his arrival as a sign. She sent him to Sabigotho (together with Sabigotho's husband Aurelius—born a Moslem but now a clandestine Christian) and the three sought martyrdom together. In this they were joined by a married couple, Felix and Liliosa, who had sold their belongings and were of like mind. The five died on July 27, 852. This trend continued until the number rose to some fifty martyrs.

Eulogius had been arrested back in November 851 along with other clerics, perhaps because the magistrates thought that in this way they could put a check to the escalating frenzy. All were let go in a short time. In the *Memorial of the Saints* Eulogius attributed his deliverance from prison to the intercession of the departed saints Flora and Maria. He recalls, deeply moved, how he had visited Flora after she had been whipped, and dared to touch her neck with his hands, "for I did not think I ought to caress the wound with kisses. I departed from you and for a long time I sighed thinking about it."[20]

The winter and spring of 852 were quiet. Then in September 852 the emir Abd ar-Rahman II fell suddenly sick, lost his power of speech, and died, even as more Christian bodies were being cremated. This seemed a happy portent. Eulogius ended his *Memorial of the Saints* with an invocation to Christ. However, with the deaths of five more martyrs (Fandila, Anastasius, Felix, Digna, and Benildus in June 853), he apologized for his disorganization and prolixity and had to start a third book. In it he gives particular attention to the death of a Spanish woman, Columba of Córdoba, who lived as a nun in a community her relatives had organized at Tabanos. When the Moslems broke up the community, Columba brazenly defied the judges at the Moorish tribunal. She was put to death by beheading (September 17, 853), and her body thrown into the Guadalquivir.

Before Eulogius died in 859, he had an opportunity to meet two relic hunters from Paris, Usuard and Odilard. They had come in the Spring of 858, originally hoping to find the body of St. Vincent of Saragossa, but this was too important a relic to let out of Spain. The questing monks were denied, although once the word was out that martyrs' bodies were in demand, there were always heathens offering to hawk Christian bodies. The story of the Moor Zacharias, who was willing to peddle information about Vincent's relics to a monk of Conques,[21] supports Hrotswitha's data about the non-Christian fishermen who were quick to calculate the money they could make selling a decapitated body.

News of the Córdoba martyrs had spread after the search of Usuard and Odilard. The two then went further south in Spain, their interest piqued by what they had read and by Eulogius's own stories of his first-hand acquaintances. The two monks located the bodies of Aurelius and Georgius, as well as the head of Sabigotho, which they were delighted to carry back with them to Paris.

Eulogius was finally arrested again in the winter of 859 when the authorities accused him of shielding and encouraging the apostate Leocritia, an Arab girl who converted to Christianity. Eulogius was given a chance to explain himself, avoid execution, and keep practicing his faith, but he must finally have felt that he could not keep running from what seemed inevitable. He chose death, and was beheaded in 859. Leocritia was beheaded four days later. Both bodies rested in Oviedo Cathedral.

Bulletins about the Córdoba martyrs, belatedly received at the court of Otto, clearly stirred the interest of the budding writer Hrotswitha. The martyrs' fates would form an appropriate background to the sexually resonant tragedy of Pelagius. Defiant young women defending their virginity were to become a staple of Hrotswitha's plays. The report that Pelagius had lashed out with his fist against the homosexual ogling of the caliph of Córdoba made a good story that complemented those that featured clever-talking women saints.

Attitudes toward homosexuality varied. Gays were accepted in the Arab world, according to John Boswell. The poetic language is rich with amatory terms for masculine love. "Erotic address by one male to another is the standard convention of Arabic love poetry. . . . Every variety of homosexual relationship was common, from prostitution to idealized love." While Hrotswitha's editorial voice objects to a ruler "debauched by the vice of sodomy," Boswell points to Pelagius's retort in the narrative's wooing scene as having more to do with repugnance against a Moslem-Christian union than with an indictment of gay love.[22]

Another view is that of Jewish Talmudic exegetes, who attempted to explain sodomy by proposing the notion that Adam and Eve had "allowed themselves to be penetrated by the serpent" in Eden.[23] Under Hrotswitha's monarch, Otto I, an edict promulgated at Rome in 966 was vehement against gays. It prescribed strangulation and burning for some homosexual act, possibly "the rape of one man by another."[24] And in Spain *The Visigothic Codes* contain this stricture:

> We shall attempt to abolish the horrible crime by which men do not fear to defile men by filthy debauchery, which is as contrary to Divine Precept as it is to chastity. . . . We establish by this law, that if any man whosoever, of any age, or race, whether he belongs to the clergy, or to the laity, should be convicted, by competent evidence, of the commission of the crime of sodomy, he shall, by order of the king, or of any judge, not only suffer emasculation, but also the penalty prescribed by ecclesiastical decree for such offences.[25]

Interestingly, in Hrotswitha's *Pelagius* there is no mention that the king even notices the boy when he initially drags him back to Córdoba as a hostage. It is only after the prison visitation that his procuring counselors, out of pity for the youth, recommend Pelagius's beauty to Abd ar-Rahman III.

A central image in the poem is that of the river on which Córdoba is built, although the Guadalquivir is not named. The poem opens with the poet's prayer for the refreshing dew of inspiration, which, though conventional, initiates the abundant flowing of liquid imagery throughout. The waters of baptism, the outpouring of blood, the tossing of the waves, the first pagan "burial" by water, the resurrection of the body from the river by fishermen form a pervasive network of suggestive imagery.

Throughout, the poet reminds us of the sprinkling of error, the flowing rivers of wisdom, the baptismal washing of an earlier king, and the martyrs cleansed in their blood. Pelagius is bathed before he is brought before the caliph. His first "burial" consigns him to the river's tossing waves, which fail, however, to wash away his blood. The fisherman recognizes him because he has been laved with baptism. In the fire test, the bathing waves of flames are said to replace the river's waters. The accumulating imagery, starting with the Guadalquivir, finds a final echo in the flowing rivers of the boy martyr's blood.

Hrotswitha also dwells on Christian heroes and martyrs in her dramas. These narratives, revealing some classical influence, mark the beginnings of nonliturgical theater in Europe. There is no reason to suppose they were not performed or read at court.

The plays are *Gallicanus; Drusiana and Calimachus; Mary the Niece of Abraham; The Conversion of Thais; The Martyrdom of the Holy Virgins Faith, Hope, and Charity;* and *The Martyrdom of the Holy Virgins Agape, Chionia, and Irene.*

The last-named play, in which the three virgins willingly die resisting the lascivious advances of a local governor, has a historical basis and points to the year 303 or 304 in the Roman province of Salonika under Diocletian. Their feast day is April 3. The documentary *Vita* amplifies the earliest records. Three sisters whose Greek names mean Love, Purity, and Peace were brought before Dulcitius, governor of Macedonia, for refusing to eat food offered in service to the gods. Their ideas, they said, had come from the Lord Jesus Christ. For their continued stubbornness Agape and Chionia were burned alive. Irene, who had some forbidden Christian books in her keeping, was seized, publicly stripped, and sent to a brothel, where she was not molested. Refusing again to obey, she was sentenced to death. The books and scriptures were burned publicly.

Hrotswitha's characterizations are lively; her central comic scene is liberally seasoned with "kitchen humor," a type of joke favored among earlier Latin writers, who saw the figure of the cook on a par with the vilest slave and therefore ripe for taunting. An example in Roman drama appears in *The Eunuch* of Terence, a playwright whom Hrotswitha emulates. In Hrotswitha's treatment, the governor is reduced to looking like a cook.[26]

The appeal of the three martyrs' legend was not limited to Hrotswitha's play. In the previous century, at a period that coincides with the deaths of the Córdoba martyrs, the legend of the three sisters appears in the *Old English Martyrology* under April 3.

On completing her eight saints' lives and the seven dramas, Hrotswitha turned in 965 to the composition of two Latin epics, which were intended to glorify the Ottonian dynasty and her monastery of Gandersheim. These works have considerable interest and appeal for their emphasis on women's roles. Both are historical family epics, connected in theme. *The Deeds of Otto (Gesta Ottonis, or Carmen de Gestis Odonis Imperatoris)* celebrates the feats of Emperor Otto the Great, under whose protection Hrotswitha's powerful monastery thrived and, indeed, a Christian humanist revival took place.

The reign of the Ottonian house from 919 to 1024 became a period of immense cultural and political ferment. Imperial prestige had weakened among Charlemagne's descendants. Now there was an imperial renaissance, its heart in the wild remoteness of Saxony. With the victories of the Saxon duke Henry "the Fowler" on the battlefield, who drove out the Huns, the *imperium* of divine election was revived and granted to Henry by his men. Henry's son Otto I reintroduced the Roman gala of the Carolingian coronation banquet when he had himself imperially crowned and anointed at Aachen in 962, with the dukes of Franconia, Swabia, Bavaria, and Lorraine waiting on him.

Otto's court developed thereafter as a cosmopolitan center of Roman Christian splendor and creativity devoted to the glory of God and empire. Otto built churches and libraries (though Widukind states that Otto himself didn't learn to read until after the death of Edith, his first queen). Otto fostered the collecting, production, and ornamentation of books, as well as painting and the decorative arts.

Hrotswitha's *Founding of Gandersheim Monastery (Primordia Coenobii Gandeshemensis)* commemorates the establishment of her house and traces its history. This was her last work, written between 963 and 973. Although *The Founding of Gandersheim* follows *The Deeds of Otto* in sequence, it actually records the ancestral doings of Otto's house, for the monastery had been established in 852, long before Otto's birth. *The Founding of Gandersheim* therefore gains a precedence, a primacy of divine authority.

After an invocation by Hrotswitha to Otto's niece, Gerberga II, as her abbess, mentor, and muse, two kinds of narrative are discernible in *The Deeds of Otto*. The work begins with Otto's family, his first marriage to Edith of England and her death, his own accession to the throne, and the troubles of his realm—the intrigues, rebellions, and the Italian campaigns, in which he successfully prevailed. Two-thirds of the way through, the narrative takes a different turn, shifting from Otto to the beautiful, accomplished Adelheid of Italy, formerly a Burgundian princess (whose later life was also written by Odilo of Cluny). Adelheid would be Otto's second wife.

Adelheid was living in Pavia in Lombardy with her small daughter Emma, who would eventually become a queen of the Franks. Adelheid was the widow of Lothar, and herself a capable claimant to the Italian crown. In this portion of the narrative Hrotswitha's epic gives us a most attractive and heroic tale. A powerful member of Adelheid's household, Berengar of Ivrea— previously a margrave at Otto's court—seized the throne and tried to consolidate his own claims to the crown by forcing Adelheid to marry his son. Meeting her resistance, Berengar held her confined in a mountain stronghold with only a serving woman and a priest, having himself seized the throne and its treasures. With her maid's help, as Hrotswitha tells it, Adelheid and her accomplices dug their way out of their prison, escaping by means of an earth tunnel.

Adelheid ran under cover of night; by day she hid in caves, woods, and ploughed furrows. Berengar followed her with his soldiers to a cornfield, where he slashed right and left with his spear, but Adelheid managed to elude him by hiding under the shelter of leaves of grain. On hearing of Adelheid's trials and her resourceful courage, Otto invaded Italy, determined to make her his wife and the worthy consort of his reign. With Adelheid's coronation as empress, Hrotswitha culminates her epic, simply sketching swiftly in the last thirty-four lines the subsequent warlike events about which she will refrain from writing, modestly kept back as she is by her womanly nature.

Effectively, the placement in the *Gesta* of Adelheid's heroic feats bestows a climactic importance on the empress. So the great deeds of Otto are framed by two significant female references: the invocation to Gerberga and Adelheid's coronation.

As a companion piece to *The Deeds of Otto*, Hrotswitha's *Founding of Gandersheim* also pays tribute to Otto's family in its creating the monastery and journeying to secure relics. But *The Founding of Gandersheim* especially honors Otto's female relatives and the women in charge of the convent thereafter. In this way Hrotswitha shifts much of the family glory to a female succession of patrons, visionaries, saints, and workers. Where Virgilian epic took as its theme the founding of a nation, Hrotswitha employs epic conventions to narrate the establishment of a female community whose right of power surpasses that of any earthly authority, even that of the imperial family who originated that power.

Instead of conquering alien peoples and territories, the founders chase the fauns and woodland creatures from the forests. They order the woods cut down and the rocks quarried. Hrotswitha emphasizes the women's involvement while glossing over the role of the bishops. In the course of events, husbands and overbearing suitors are conveniently struck down or simply die so that the women may freely employ their wealth and available time to the glory of Gandersheim convent. Aeda, Oda, and her three daughters who were the first three abbesses in succession—Hathumoda, Gerberga I, and Christine—are responsible for the inspiration, work, and financing of the monastery.[27]

Gerberga I, abbess from 874 to 896, though betrothed to a nobleman and forced to meet him in her courtly gown of rich gold, nonetheless secretly dedicated herself to Christ. The disappointed fiancé furiously swore by her white throat and his sword that he would return from his military campaigns and force her to break her sacred vow. He was, however, killed in battle, in heavenly retribution. Hrotswitha implies that divine power has allowed Oda to become a widow. Oda herself lived to a great age. "Perhaps," Hrotswitha writes of this first founder, "God took Liudulf from this world when he had hardly reached the fever of middle life, in order that the mind of the illustrious lady Oda, his wife, might remain concentrated on God."

1. The Passion of Saint Pelagius, Most Precious Martyr, Who in Our Own Times Was Crowned with Martyrdom at Córdoba

Glorious Pelagius, most valiant martyr of Christ and brave soldier of the King who reigns forever, look with gentle kindness on me—poor insignificant Hrotswitha—your handmaid who bows to you with devout intent and cherishes you in her thoughts. Graciously incline your heart to my song. Mercifully grant that the dim cave of my meager understanding may be refreshed with dew from heaven, so I can properly describe with my pen your wonderful excellence and renowned victory!

In the western regions of the world there shone a dazzling jewel, a majestic city extraordinarily proud of its ferocity in war. Spanish citizens had settled their homes in this city, whose illustrious name was Córdoba. The city was noted for its delights and all its riches. It flowed with the seven rivers of learning[28] and was famed for its continual victories. In former times the city had been faithfully obedient to the lawful Christ, and had sent forth its sons in white baptismal robes to the Lord. (lines 1–20)

Suddenly the forces of war changed the established laws of holy faith, spreading the error of sacrilegious teaching and damaging the people's faith. The perfidious race of untamed Saracens waged war against the stalwart settlers of this city. These Saracens violently seized for their own benefit the fate of the brilliant kingdom. They murdered the good king, who had been washed in baptism. For a long time he had meritoriously wielded the royal scepter, and had often tempered his people with the reins of justice. Now the enemy sword cut him down, and terrible slaughter left the people vanquished.

The military commander[29] of that barbarous race, the framer of the battle and a vicious man of lewd practices in his manner of living, finally claimed title to the destiny of the whole empire. He settled his criminal allies in the ravaged countryside.

He filled the mourning city with his hostile pack, and—a wretched thing to relate—he defiled with his barbarous rite that ancient mother of pure faith. He mingled his pagans among the lawful inhabitants so that the pagans could persuade them to discard the customs of their fathers. Once the Christian shrine was profaned, the pagans would corrupt the Christians by associating with them. (lines 21–41)

But the flock under the loving guidance of the shepherd Christ soon angrily spat out the command of the vile tyrant. They said they preferred to hold to their law and be put to death rather than live in folly, enslaved by the newfangled rites.

When the king found this out, he realized he could not impose the death penalty on everyone in this wealthy city without suffering loss himself, since he had taken the city with prolonged and bitter struggle. So he changed his earlier decree. He passed and promulgated a law allowing those who wished to serve the Eternal King and maintain the customs of their fathers to do so legally without fear of punishment. But one condition had to be carefully observed: no citizen of Córdoba could dare in addition to blaspheme the golden idols worshiped by that prince or any who held the scepter. A citizen who did this would have to yield his head to the sharpened sword and suffer the most grave sentence of shedding his blood. (lines 42–60)

Once this was done, the faithful city—subjected so often to a thousand evils—grew tranquil, of course, and enjoyed a semblance of peace. But there were those Christians who were inflamed by the fires of Christ's love and driven by the thirst for martyrdom. Outspokenly they defied the marble statues which the suppliant prince, prostrate and adorned in his crown, worshiped with Sabaean incense.[30] The king swiftly condemned these Christians to capital punishment. But their souls, washed in their blood, ascended to heaven.[31]

Many years elapsed and there were changes in Córdoba, but the city long remained subject to the rule of pagan kings. Then in our own times there was a prince of royal blood whose fortune it was to succeed to the throne of his fathers. But he was inferior to them, and sullied with the lusts of the flesh. He was proud in the splendor of his reign, and his name was Abd ar-Rahman. (lines 61–74)

This king claimed to treat the Christians as his fathers had, weighing the dispute already mentioned concerning their religion. Loyal to his father, he did not revoke the unjust decree which the perpetrator of that crime, that deceitful plunderer, had enacted when he overcame the Christian king in war. Instead, Abd ar-Rahman turned it over in his mind and carried it out with stern resolve. He often drenched the land with innocent blood, shattering the holy bodies of those good men who longed to compose sweet hymns to Christ and voice their rebukes against his foolish idols. In addition, this sacrilegious man behaved so arrogantly in his palace, garnering well-deserved punishments for himself, that he dared to believe he was the king of kings. All peoples would have to bow to his power. No nation would be so bursting with savagery that it would dare to make a military assault against his troops. (lines 75–90)

While Abd ar-Rahman was swelling with riotous pride, he heard of a people living in a remote spot in the land of Galicia. This was a country proud in war, worshiping Christ and resisting idolatry. These people would try to reject his laws, denying that they would obey such depraved masters. When the king found this out, he boiled with demonic anger. In his heart he bore the Serpent's ancient spleen, and with raging craftiness he pondered this dishonor for a long time, thinking over what he would do to such enemies.

Finally, it is true that this king disclosed his plan publicly, as it happened, and addressed the masterly leaders of the rich city, bawling his words from a poisonous maw:

"It is no secret that kings have submitted to our imperial power, and that all nations encircled by the deep ocean dwell under the control of our laws. But I do not know what boldness takes hold of the subordinate Galicians that makes them spit on our covenant and makes them ungrateful for our past affection. Does it not, therefore, remain for us to attack these Galicians with muscle and weaponry, to drive these rebel enemies hard until—prostrated forever by our missiles—they shall be forced, however unwillingly, to bend their necks to our bonds!" (lines 91–113)

He threw out these boasts and offered the justification for his tactics. He ordered his people to gather in war gear under their sundry heraldic banners so they could advance with him to wipe out the faithful Galicians. And Abd ar-Rahman showed his face in a jeweled helmet, and his wanton body sheathed in iron armor. When he reached the city with this pageantry, he attacked the people at once. It was his fortune to win such a victory that he seized twelve noblemen, together with the lord of the city. These captives he lashed securely in chains.

The vanquished Christians, having endured a fierce battle and having lost their princes, surrendered to their enemies and bowed to the pernicious yoke of the wicked king. The old pact was reinstated. The twelve princes, bound with leather thongs, were paraded together with their comrade, the ruler of the defeated Galicians. The princes were quickly freed from their bonds, since they were ransomed at the vast price of their own riches. But Abd ar-Rahman doubled his ransom demand for the Galician chief, which was more than the captive chief could pay from his treasury. When he tried to offer as ransom the costly belongings he had in his own home, he still happened to lack a small amount of the sum demanded. Abd ar-Rahman saw this and turned over a stratagem in his mind. He said he would not send the cherished ruler back to his people unless he paid the specified ransom in full. It was not the missing gold the king wanted, but to put the beaten ruler to death. (lines 114–142)

This ruler had an only son. Noble of birth, he was strikingly well-made in every aspect of his physical appearance. His name was Pelagius. He was handsome in the splendor of his body and intelligent in deliberation. He shone with decency. He had barely completed his boyhood years and now had reached the first bloom of young manhood. When Pelagius learned that the king was unrelenting toward his father, he pleaded with his afflicted parent in this way:

"My dear father, please hear my words. Take what I have to say with an open mind, since I know very well that your life is losing its vigor with stiffening age. Your muscles are wholly robbed of their former strength. You aren't able to endure toil, however light. But as for me, I can still exercise force with my strong arms. I'm capable of submitting to a harsh master for a period of time. So I urge you and beg you with sweet prayers to send me, your loved son, as hostage to the king until you're able to pay the full ransom. Don't let your white-haired old age waste away confined in chains." (lines 143–161)

But the old man checked him in a strict tone of voice: "Put aside such words, my sweetest son, put them aside! And don't let your sorrow drive my white head to the place of death. My life depends wholly on your being safe and sound. Without you, dear son, I could not live a single day. You are all my pride, and the great glory of your family. And you are, besides, the only hope of our conquered people. For that reason it is imperative for me to leave my dear country and make my way as a prisoner to proud Spain, rather than hand you over in shackles, you who are the hope of my old age!"

Pelagius would not permit his father to go on talking in this manner. With loving words he calmed the mind of his dear parent and softly compelled him to give in to his coaxing. The revered old man finally yielded to these prayers. In redeeming his own ransom, he handed over his unfortunate son. King Abd ar-Rahman then ordered Pelagius to be led away with him. He went back exultant to his own country, which he re-entered as a conquering hero.

No one should suppose that it was due to the king's merits that he prevailed in the midst of such gorgeous pomp. This was, rather, the equitable decree of the hidden Judge. Either it was done so that the Christian nation, properly scourged with so heavy a whip, might weep over sins for which all were charged, or it was so that Pelagius, about to be slain for Christ's law, might happen to seek the place where he could give himself to death and pour out the river of his blood for Christ. He would commend his soul, sanctified in death, to the Lord. (lines 162–187)

After the barbarous king had returned to the shelter of his rich city, he celebrated a dazzling triumph over the righteous Christians. He ordered Pelagius, glorious companion of Christ, shackled and thrown into the black darkness of a cell. Though the young man had been nourished on excellent food, he was now given meager provender.

Córdoba has a foul dungeon under a vaulted arch, bereft of light, a place consigned to oblivion and darkness. People report that the place is a cause of great misery to unfortunate captives. This is where Pelagius, glorious child of peace, was locked up on the imperious and evil order of the king. To this place hastened the leading courtiers, who were moved by pity to comfort the heart of the young man.

When they saw the prisoner's handsome face and savored the words of his sweet mouth, words gilded with the honey of rhetorical eloquence, they yearned to emancipate a young man of such beauty from his fetters. They advised the king who wielded the scepter. They knew that the lofty ruler of this rich city was debauched by the vice of sodomy. Passionately fond of boys who were lovely of face, the king desired to unite himself with them in friendship. (lines 188–207)

The courtiers, bearing these things in mind and sympathizing in their hearts with the fate of Pelagius, encouraged the king as follows: "It does not accord with your sovereignty, most powerful king, that you should pitilessly order an honorable young man to be punished, and that the tender virility of an innocent hostage should be bound in constricting irons. If you were even to see his exceptional good looks and to savor his honeyed speech—how you would want to bring such a young man into your retinue and engage him in the highest rank of your militia! Dazzling as he is in his person, he could serve in your palace!"

These words softened the king, and their plea roused him. He ordered that Pelagius should be released from his harshly knotted chains.[32] Once his body was completely cleansed in a purifying bath, his refreshed limbs were to be clothed in purple garments and his neck adorned with a gem-studded metal ornament. In this way he could fittingly become a Mameluke in that well-built hall. (lines 208–223)

When this lord's proud authority had enforced the order, the martyr was at once led out of his black cave. Arrayed in a toga, he was seated in the royal court. Now, placed among the palace attendants, his countenance outshone in splendor the palace guards and the courtiers wearing togas. All eyes turned to gaze at him, to marvel at both the young man's face and the sweet words he spoke. The king, too, drawn to him at that first glance, burned with desire for the good looks of that princely young man. Finally, kindled with immoderate longing, he ordered that Pelagius be seated with him on the royal throne so that he might touch him ardently. He bent his head and in his eagerness tried to kiss those adored lips, while putting his arms around his neck.

But the soldier of Christ would not suffer this kind of love from a pagan king who was polluted with the lust of the flesh. Laughing, he turned his ear against the royal lips, and making a great joke of it, he refused his mouth. He spoke and his excellent lips uttered these words: "It is not right for a man bathed in the baptism of Christ to bend his chaste neck to the embrace of a barbarian. A Christian who has been anointed with sacred oil should not seize a kiss from the slave of a filthy demon. You—with a free heart—embrace the witless men who worship senseless earthen gods with you! Let the men who grovel to images be your friends!" (lines 224–249)

However, the king was not stirred to anger. He tried to cajole the young man he desired with tender words: "O you petulant boy! You boast that you can boldly reject the sweet affection of our command, that you can brazenly go on ridiculing our gods! Doesn't the swift loss of your young life rouse you, and the possibility of leaving your sorrowing parents bereft? We must torture those who desecrate our religion and, afterwards, put them to death. We cut their throats with a sword unless they submit and thrust aside their blasphemous reasoning. And so I'm advising you, like a father, to be careful of words like those that arise from an unruly attitude. Come to me with a steadfast love in your heart, and don't try afterwards to violate our command. Obey my orders with great promptness. These must be followed. I adore you in my heart, and I'm choosing to esteem you over all the courtiers in my hall to the extent that—next to me—you shall be second in this proud kingdom."

He said this, and clamped his right hand around the martyr's face. With his left he tightly embraced that divine neck in order to fix at least one kiss. But Christ's witness thwarted the king's wily game. Swiftly he threw his brandished fist into the king's face and struck such a blow straight to that bent countenance that blood poured out of the wound he inflicted and sullied the king's beard and wet his clothing. (lines 250–275)

Then the king, savagely moved to a great fury, ordered Pelagius, child of Heaven's King, to be flung bodily over the walls from the spring-engine that usually catapulted stones onto the fighting enemy. This way the noble martyr would be smashed on the sands of the river whose huge waves flowed around the city. He would be splintered in every limb. Broken like this, he would quickly die. The king's henchmen followed these orders as he bellowed them, and rapidly devised a punishment unheard of before. They shot Pelagius to martyrdom like a missile from a sling, far over the high battlements of that notorious city. And yet, although the huge crags around him caught at him and drove into the martyr's sweet hurtling body, that companion of Christ remained untorn.

Of course, the news quickly reached the king's ears that the body of the martyr, which he had ordered to be crushed on the sharp rocks of the riverbank, could not be mutilated though smashed against them. The king, all the more outraged at being wholly defeated, directed at once that Pelagius should be decapitated with a sharpened sword so that the ultimate sentence could be carried out. At last the soldiers, quaking at the king's commands, beheaded the faithful witness of Christ with the sword and confided the dead body to the waters' keeping. (lines 276–298)

But Pelagius, soldier of the King, who is forever victorious over death laid low, soared through the constellations of the starry firmament and was sweetly led into heaven amid the hymns of angels. From the right hand of the true Judge, who presides above the stars, Pelagius accordingly received the shining palm for his martyred death, having earned it through his praiseworthy end. He was not denied the victory prize of burning love, for he had through his own bondage paid for his father's life. He had forsaken his own country and his conquered people. No tongue can describe in devout words that laurel wreath shimmering with celestial light with which Pelagius shines forth in splendor, since he kept his virginity well. He is joined to the throng allowed to enter the heavenly dwelling place to sing hymns in eternity to the Lamb. Amen. (lines 299–312)

After the king's soldiers had followed his orders and confided the precious mortal shell of the dead body to the lap of the river, they fixed the remains among the rocks so that the sacred relics could not have the sepulture they deserved. But Christ, who does not permit his own saints to lose by chance the slenderest hair of their glorious heads, did not allow his faithful martyr to lie in the river. Fittingly, he provided a worthy place for a tomb in which to preserve the saint's holy limbs.

It happened that fishermen, as they cleft the waters with their oars and caught in their many-colored nets the schools of fish that wander the waves, glimpsed on the river's farther shore the martyr's body pitching in the resounding billows. The fishermen made it out from a distance, with eyes warily trained on the sight. Swiftly they sailed toward the body and lifted it up. They did not recognize the beauty of the cherished person because the limbs were crimsoned with blood and the noble head floated at a distance where the waves had tossed it. But they understood and believed with unhesitating hearts that this man, whoever he was, had died for Christ's law. In this domain the only people condemned to capital punishment were those who, washed in the sacred waters of baptism, did not shrink from continually reviling the king's heathen worship. (lines 313–335)

Once the fishermen had recovered the head and replaced it on the shoulders, they recognized the glowing features of Pelagius. With pity in their hearts they burst into such lamentations as "Ah, he lies dead, the only hope of his people and the glory of his land. He's stained and bereft of the honor of a tomb. But don't we know how we can always sell—and for plenty of shekels—the tortured bodies of sainted men whose severed heads show they are the faithful? And who would doubt that this is the body of a praiseworthy martyr, since the trunk lies wretched without the ornament of the head?"

As they spoke, they loaded the holy limbs in their boat. Swiftly they turned sail and rowed back to the harbor of that city which is famous among all people. They hauled their boat on the land here, and proceeded clandestinely to seek out a sacred monastery dedicated to Christ within the city's venerable walls. They carried the dead body of that martyr, who is now venerated everywhere, in order to sell it at a high price.

The Christian congregation welcomed the relics with rejoicing and the singing of sweet hymns. They celebrated the holy funeral obsequies according to custom. Generously they paid the sailors a very elevated price, so excited were they about purchasing the body of the dear saint. After they had bought it at no small cost, they chose a fertile piece of earth to keep the body. There, once they had reassembled the limbs with great ceremony, they buried the holy relics in a grave-mound of earth. And the omnipotent Lord of the starry palace of heaven soon commanded that these relics should flash forth with radiant signs around the grave. Since the blessed soul now reigned with powerful sufficiency in heaven, the mortal members must reign with equal glory. (lines 336–365)

At length, the people of the city gathered here when they observed that those suffering from various long-term illnesses were healed and their sick bodies were cured of infection—free—without any payment for their treatment. They felt uncertain whether this new saint could be so holy that he might be the agent of such miracles. But finally the bishop of the monastery and the leader of the people, taking the excellent medicine of wholesome counsel, sensed that the highest Throne should be implored with a devout mind. Then might He, in his customary goodness, reveal the hidden cause of the healings to everyone and so allow all doubt to be removed. At once both men and women chose to do this, and of their own free will they fasted, eating only sparingly for three days. They applied themselves to the singing of sweet hymns and to holy prayers, which they uttered with a truly devout mind. They understood that their prayers, poured forth with fervent murmurs, had persuaded the gentle King of the skies, and that He was graciously disposed to a test of the relics they found dubious. Quickly they ordered a fierce furnace to be stoked, and all working together, they heaped up the fire. (lines 366–385)

When the fire was burning furiously in the huge lap of the furnace, the people took the severed head of Christ's companion, and in softly suppliant words they spoke with tongues of entreaty:

"Gracious King, noble lord of the starry throne, you who know how to discern all things with just judgment, allow the merits of this saint to be tested by fire. And if he is upheld in the honor of his virtue, and if his healing powers result from his merit, grant that the flame shall not touch the skin of his face and that the hairs of his head shall emerge uninjured. But if by chance he possesses a lower merit, command that as a sign at least the outer skin of his face shall be injured, since that is perishable according to the nature of frail flesh."

They spoke these words and entrusted the glorious head to a trial by fire in the deep-surging, flame-spewing waves. Finally, after a whole hour had passed, they at last pulled the same head from the scorching flames. They cast their eyes over it, surveying it to see whether the fiery heat had damaged it. But the head now shone more dazzlingly than refined gold, wholly immune from the heat and the flames.

The faithful throng gazed heavenward, their faces up-turned. With the singing of hymns they praised Christ on his high throne, for He so often caused the mortal relics of his steadfast martyrs to gleam forth with signs. The people now placed the relics close together in a mausoleum worthy of reverence. Humbly and most resolutely they venerated the relics with fitting respect. Forever after, they gave staunch credence to the saint's acclaimed merit, and rejoiced always in the protector Heaven had given them. (lines 386–413)

2. The Passion of the Holy Virgins Agape, Chionia, and Irene; or, Dulcitius

The Characters:

The Emperor Diocletian
Dulcitius, the provincial governor
Soldiers
Gatekeepers
Sisinnius
Agape
Chionia
Irene
Dulcitius's wife

The Story:

The Passion of the Holy Virgins Agape, Chionia, and Irene. In the silence of night the provincial governor Dulcitius came to them stealthily, lusting to gratify himself in their arms. But the moment he went in, his mind snapped. He embraced and kissed the cooking pots and skillets instead—he thought they were the virgins! His face and clothes grew repulsively filthy with black soot. Afterwards he sent the young women to the magistrate Sisinnius for punishment. Sisinnius himself was also remarkably deluded, but he at last ordered Agape and Chionia to be burned and Irene shot with an arrow.

Scene i:

Diocletian: Because of your illustrious rank and background, and your radiant loveliness, you are going to be joined in marriage to the leading officers of the palace. This is to take place at my command, if you willingly deny Christ and sacrifice to our gods.

Agape: Don't bother. And don't concern yourself about preparing us a wedding. Nothing can force us to deny our avowed faith in His holy name, or to soil our virginity.

Diocletian: What has got hold of you? What foolishness drives the three of you?

Agape: Do you see any sign of foolishness in us?

Diocletian: Most obviously.

Agape: In what way?

Diocletian: Mainly this. You abandon the worship of our established cult, and you chase after the futile novelty of Christian superstition.

Agape: You dare to malign the glory of the all powerful God! That is a danger —

Diocletian: Danger? To whom?

Agape: To you and the state you govern.

Diocletian: The girl is a lunatic. Take her away!

Chionia: My sister is not a lunatic. She's criticizing your stupidity.

Diocletian: That one's an even crazier maniac. Get her out of my sight as well. Let's question the third.

Irene: You'll find the third one rebellious and completely unyielding.

Diocletian: Irene. Even though you're younger in years, show that you're more mature, more honorable.

Irene: Show me how. I ask you, in what way?

Diocletian: Bend your neck to the gods. Be an example of good behavior to your sisters and set them free.

Irene: Let those cower before idols who want to provoke the wrath of God on High! My head is anointed with the unguent of a king. I will not dishonor it by groveling at the feet of statues.

Diocletian: To worship the gods brings no dishonor. In fact, it is the highest honor.

Irene: And what dishonor could be more shameful, and what could be a greater disgrace than to revere a slave as if he were a lord?

Diocletian: I'm not urging you to revere a slave, but the gods of lords and princes.

Irene: Isn't a person anybody's slave if he can be bought for a price from a craftsman? Like something up for sale?

Diocletian: The insolence of her jabbering will be crushed with torture!

Irene: This is what we want! It's what we welcome with open arms—to be mangled with tortures for Christ's love!

Diocletian: Tie them up in chains, these insubordinate girls. They're contesting our orders. They'll be brought to trial before the governor Dulcitius. They can serve their time in a dirty jail cell while they wait.

Scene ii:

Dulcitius: Soldiers, bring the prisoners forward!

Soldiers: Here they are, the girls you called for.

Dulcitius: Spectacular! Aren't they beautiful! Lovely. What gorgeous little girls!

Soldiers: They're perfectly dazzling.

Dulcitius: I'm seized by their looks.

Soldiers: We can see why.

Dulcitius: I have to make them want me. Love me.

Soldiers: We don't think you'll have any luck.

Dulcitius: Why not?

Soldiers: Because they're firm in their religion.

Dulcitius: What if I enticed them with sweet favors?

Soldiers: They look down on that.

Dulcitius: What if I frighten them with tortures?

Soldiers: They'll consider that insignificant.

Dulcitius: So what can I do?

Soldiers: Give it some thought.

Dulcitius: Put the girls in custody. In the pantry, the place inside the hallway where they store the household servants' pots.

Soldiers: Why there?

Dulcitius: So I can visit them as often as I want.

Soldiers: As you say.

Scene iii:

Dulcitius: What are our women prisoners doing at this time of night?

Soldiers: They're singing hymns.

Dulcitius: Let's get closer.

Soldiers: We can hear the sound of their bell-like voices from a long way off.

Dulcitius: Watch by the foyer with a torch. I'm going inside. I hope to taste my fill of those embraces I've been yearning for.

Soldiers: Go on in. We'll stand guard.

Scene iv:

Agape: What was that noise in the foyer?

Irene: That miserable Dulcitius is on his way.

Chionia: God preserve us!

Agape: Amen!

Chionia: Why is he crashing around with the cooking pots and casseroles and frying pans?

Irene: I'll see. Come, I tell you, look through this crack!

Agape: What's happening?

Irene: Look at the idiot! He's wholly out of his senses. He imagines he's got his arms around us!

Agape: What's he doing?

Irene: Now he's fondling the pot in his lap. Now he's hugging the skillet and the casserole, he's nibbling them with juicy kisses!

Chionia: It's ludicrous!

Irene: His face and hands and clothes are getting all grimy, they're growing filthy from the soot that's sticking to him. He looks like an Ethiopian.

Agape: It fits. His body should look the way his mind is, since the Devil has possessed him.

Irene: Look, he's getting ready to go. Let's see how his soldiers react when they see him outside the door.

Scene v:

Soldiers: Who's that coming out? Somebody possessed by fiends! Or it could be the Devil himself. Let's get out of here!

Dulcitius: Men! Why are you running away? Hold it! Wait for me. Bring the torch to light my way home.

Soldiers: It sounds like the chief's voice, but it's got the shape of the Devil! Let's not stick around, let's go. That phantom wants to do us in!

Dulcitius: I'm on my way to the palace. The bad treatment I've had to suffer! I'm going to reveal it to the authorities.

Scene vi:

Dulcitius: Guard, let me in the palace. I've got to have a private word with the emperor.

Guard: Who's that abominable worthless freak hanging around in those ripped-up filthy rags? Let's punch him out. Throw him down the steps. Keep him from getting free access here.

Dulcitius: Hey, hey! What's happened? I'm not dressed in the best clothes? It's not obvious from my sharp grooming who I am? Everybody's disgusted when they see me, I'm like some horrible monstrosity! I'm going back to my wife. Maybe I can find out from her what's going on. But here she is, coming out of the house with her hair all disheveled. And the whole household is following her, they're crying!

Scene vii:

Wife: Oh, no! my husband, Dulcitius! What have you been through? You're not in your right mind. The Christians have made a dunce out of you.

Dulcitius: Now I get it. Their magic has put an evil spell on me.

Wife: Oh, this is what upsets me so terribly, what especially
disheartens me—that you don't even know what you've
endured!

Dulcitius: I demand that those licentious girls be brought here
immediately. That they be publicly exposed and stripped of
their clothes. We'll turn the tables on them. Let them know
how it feels to be a butt of public ridicule.

Scene viii:

Soldiers: We're sweating for nothing. We're working with no
results. Look, their clothes stick to their virgin bodies like
skin. And him, the one who gave us the orders to strip them,
he's snoring in his chair. We can't even shake him out of his
sleep. Let's go report this to the emperor.

Scene ix:

Diocletian: It grieves me very much to hear about the abuse
Governor Dulcitius has been exposed to, that he's been so
insulted and reproached to such an extent. Those despicable
little females are not going to get away with bragging about
the way they've made a mockery of our gods—and those who
worship them. I'll direct Magistrate Sisinnius to carry our
revenge into effect.

Scene x:

Sisinnius: Soldiers, ho! Where are those lascivious girls? They've
got to be twisted on the rack. Yes, those girls.

Soldiers: They're pining in jail.

Sisinnius: Keep Irene there, and bring the others.

Soldiers: Why are you leaving her behind?

Sisinnius: I'm sparing her youth. She might be easier to convert if she's not coerced by her sisters' presence.

Soldiers: Very good.

Scene xi:

Soldiers: They're right here, these women you sent for.

Sisinnius: Agree to submit, Agape and Chionia, to what I recommend.

Agape: If we agree.

Sisinnius: Pour libations to the gods.

Agape: To the True and Eternal Father and to his Coeternal Son and also to the Holy Paraclete we do make a perpetual offering of the sacrifice of praise.

Sisinnius: That is not what I urge you to do. That is what I forbid, on pain of chastisement.

Agape: You shall not forbid it, nor will we ever sacrifice to demons.

Sisinnius: Put aside this hard-heartedness. Perform the sacrifice. Otherwise, I will have you put to death, in accordance with the rule of the Emperor Diocletian.

Chionia: It's fitting, then, that you bow to the emperor's orders—which you know we despise—and put us to death. If you delay and spare us, you might yourself be lawfully executed.

Sisinnius: Don't stand there, soldiers, don't just stand there. Grab these blaspheming women and fling them into the fire. Alive!

Soldiers: Right away. We'll build up the pyre and deliver them to the roaring flames. That will finally put an end to their tirade.

Agape: Nothing, O Lord, is impossible for your awful power! Even the fire forgets the force of its nature in obedience to you! But we are weary of waiting, Lord, and pray you to loosen the tether of our lives. Once our bodies have perished, our souls may clap hands with you in heaven.

Soldiers: Oh, this is weird! Oh, it's an astonishing miracle! Look, the life is gone from their bodies, but not a bit of disfigurement can be found! Their hair, their clothes! They haven't been burned in the fire, and their bodies aren't touched!

Sisinnius: Bring Irene.

Scene xii:

Soldiers: She's here.

Sisinnius: Tremble, Irene, at your sisters' death. And take care from their example that you do not perish.

Irene: I hope to follow their example by dying. I wish that I may deserve eternal rejoicing with them.

Sisinnius: Give in, give in to my advice.

Irene: I'll never give in to villainous advice.

Sisinnius: If you don't give in, I will not carry out a quick death for you. I'll prolong and multiply your torments every day.

Irene: The more cruelly I am tortured, the more gloriously I shall be exalted.

Sisinnius: You're not afraid of torture? I will command a thing that makes you shudder.

Irene: Whatever adversity you impose, I shall escape it with Christ's aid.

Sisinnius: I'll have you put in a brothel, where your body will be obscenely polluted.

Irene: It's better to soil the body with outrage than to pollute the soul with the worship of images.

Sisinnius: If you mingle with sluts and become debauched, you won't be numbered among the hosts of pure virgins.

Irene: Voluptuous pleasure carries a penalty. But submitting to force wins a crown. I shall not be accused of guilt unless the soul consents.

Sisinnius: It was pointless for me to spare her, pointless to pity her childish years.

Soldiers: We already knew that. There's no way she'll be driven to the worship of the gods. She's not going to be broken by any sort of terror.

Sisinnius: I won't spare her any longer.

Soldiers: You're right.

Sisinnius: Take her. Use no mercy. Manhandle her roughly, take her to the whorehouse. Don't give any consideration to propriety.

Irene: They will never take me there!

Sisinnius: Who's going to stop them?

Irene: The One whose providence rules the world.

Sisinnius: I'll see about that.

Irene: Sooner than you might want to.

Sisinnius: Don't let this blaspheming girl scare you, soldiers, with those fake predictions of hers!

Soldiers: We're not worried. We're eager to obey orders.

Scene xiii:

Sisinnius: Who are those men coming this way? They look exactly like the soldiers I handed Irene over to. They are, the same ones! Why are you back so fast? How come you're breathing so hard?

Soldiers: We came to get you.

Sisinnius: Where's that girl you took away?

Soldiers: On top of the mountain.

Sisinnius: What mountain?

Soldiers: The closest one.

Sisinnius: Dimwits! Numbskulls! You've gone completely haywire!

Soldiers: Why accuse us? Why that tone of voice? That threatening attitude?

Sisinnius: The gods blast you!

Soldiers: What did we do to you? How did we do anything wrong to you? How did we disobey your orders?

Sisinnius: Didn't I order you to take that religious renegade to a cathouse?

Soldiers: Yes, you did. And we raced to follow your orders. But these two male youths we never saw before stopped us and said you sent them to take Irene up to the mountaintop.

Sisinnius: I don't know a thing about it.

Soldiers: We realize that now.

Sisinnius: What did they look like?

Soldiers: Very richly decked out. Their looks were amazing.

Sisinnius: You went after them?

Soldiers: Yes, we did.

Sisinnius: And? What did they do?

Soldiers: One stood on her right, the other on her left. They told us to be frank and not conceal anything from you that occurred.

Sisinnius: There's only one thing to do, and that's to get on my horse and go up there. See who's trying to make fun of us.

Soldiers: Let's go in a hurry.

Scene xiv:

Sisinnius: Haagh! I don't know what's happening to me. I've been sunk low by the witchcraft of those Christians! Look, I'm circling the mountain and every time I find the trail I can't see how to climb it and I can't find the way down!

Soldiers: We've all been foxed by these miracles, we're completely drained with frustration. If you let this crazy individual live any longer, we're lost and you are too!

Sisinnius: Anyone of my men, bend your bow and shoot a bolt. Stick her through, this witch!

Soldiers: It's got to be!

Irene: Shame, you miserable wretch, blush for shame, Sisinnius, since you don't know how to conquer a tender little baby virgin without an arsenal of weapons!

Sisinnius: Whatever disgrace comes to me I can easily put up with it, since you—with hardly a doubt—are going to die!

Irene: For me this is high jubilation, for you it means anguish. Because of the harshness of your villainy, you shall be doomed to Tartarus below. But I shall receive the palm of the martyr, the virgin's crown! I shall enter the heavenly bridal chamber of the King Eternal. To Him are honor and glory forever!

3. Adelheid: From *The Deeds of Otto*

The Italian king Lothar[33] became afflicted with a serious illness and departed this world. Fittingly, he left the kingdom of Italy to be ruled by the most high queen to whom he had allied himself in love. She was the daughter of the illustrious king Rothulf, and descended from a long line of great kings. The high nobility of her distinguished parents left her rightly named Adelheid.

She was both splendid in the elegance of her royal beauty and diligent in causes that were worthy of her character. She clearly possessed a superior natural gift that well qualified her to rule the kingdom she inherited, if the nation itself had not given her cause for bitter grief. Upon the death of Lothar, whom I spoke of earlier, a certain faction of the people who had in the past been rebellious offered—with misguided and unfriendly purpose against their own rulers—to hand the kingdom back to the control of Berengar.[34] Their reason, they claimed, was that King Hugo had formerly seized it by force from Berengar when his own father died.

Now Berengar, elevated without a doubt by this hoped-for privilege, unleashed whatever hatred he had borne within his gloomy heart while mourning for the loss of his paternal realm. Inflamed with a bitter bile that was beyond justification, he poured out his fury on the guiltless, and carried out extreme violence against Queen Adelheid. She, during her reign, had not done the man any harm. (lines 467–493)

Berengar not only appropriated for himself the throne of the lofty palace, but after he had unlocked the gates of the public treasury, he also carried away in his greedy right hand everything he found: gold, several kinds of gems and riches, as well as the illustrious crown of her royal brow. He did not throw aside any small item of decoration, nor did he shrink from despoiling her of her own servants, and those whose allegiance was owed to royalty and—sorrowful to say!—her own queenly power. Finally, he wickedly denied her all her liberty, so that she was unable either to go freely or to remain where she wished. Instead he ordered her to leave with only one serving maid, and entrusted her to a certain official for the purpose of keeping her under surveillance. The official, who was obedient to Berengar, was so influenced by these unjust orders of the king that he did not scruple to keep her behind the prison gates of her own chamber with squadrons of guards posted all around.[35] In just such a manner are criminals customarily held!

But He who delivered Peter from the chains of Herod released this woman when He wished, with gentle love.

While she was unquestionably troubled at heart with many worries and had no hope of any sure relief for herself, the Bishop Adelhard,[36] lamenting the wretched deed and hardly willing to endure the grave injury done to his beloved lady queen, within a short time sent her a message in secret. With urgent admonitions he encouraged her to attempt an escape and to make her way to his city, built with very solid walls, where he had established his pontifical seat. He gave orders that a lodging should be readied for her that would offer the most secure protection, and that she should be provided with a servant fully worthy of her.

When these directives reached her royal ears, the excellent queen grew more cheerful because of the Bishop's benevolent arrangements. She wished earnestly to be freed of the chains that bound her fast. Yet she did not know what to do, since there was no gateway standing open that would permit her to escape in the hours of night while her wardens lay weighed down with heavy sleep. (lines 494–529)

There was no one in this prison vault who was subordinate to her or who might be assiduous in carrying out her commands, except for the one serving maid, mentioned earlier, and one priest of praiseworthy virtue. The queen, weeping continuously and despondent in spirit, told them of all that she was turning over in her grieving heart. Through prayer, they came to a common decision. It seemed that they could improve their situation by digging, zealously and in secret, an out-of-the-way tunnel in the earth through which they might escape from their cruel fetters.

And so these events were clearly accomplished more quickly through Christ's powerful aid. For when the three had prepared the tunnel, as they agreed, a night arrived that was suitable for their new freedom—a night during which slumber crept over the limbs of common folk. The most God-fearing queen, escaping with only her two companions, slipped past all the stratagems of the guards. By night she covered as much ground as she could on her delicate feet. (lines 530–549)

But before long, as soon as gloomy night had parted its shadows and flown, and the sky paled to yellow with the rays of the sun, the queen prudently hid herself in remote caves. Now she ranged through the woods, now she remained concealed in the furrows among the ripe ears of growing grain until night fell again, clad in its customary shadows, and covered the earth once more with shadowy darkness. The queen unflaggingly renewed the journey she had begun.

At length, when her guards did not find her, they reported with great trepidation to the official in charge of guarding the lady. He, terrified in his heart and smitten with deep fear, set out with a large number of comrades to track her down. When he failed and was unable to find where the glorious queen had directed her course, he anxiously reported everything to King Berengar. The king immediately flew into a great rage and sent out his followers right away to hunt all around in every direction. He enjoined them not to overlook the most obscure spot, but to examine every hiding place prudently in case the queen should be lurking in any of these.

Berengar himself set out with a host of strongly armed men as if he were bent on conquering a fierce army in battle. On this hasty trip he crossed through the same field of grain where the lady he hunted was hiding in the curving furrows under wings of the grain goddess Ceres. But while he moved quickly here and there, bypassing the very place where the queen cowered—troubled by no small terror—and while he attempted strenuously to part the tall stalks with his outstretched spear, yet he did not find this lady, who was shielded by God's grace.

When he fell back, perplexed and fatigued, the revered Bishop Adelhard arrived quickly and, rejoicing in his heart, conducted his lady within the securely fortified walls of his city. Here he attended her with great homage until she, through the merciful Christ, received the ornament of a realm greater than the one she had sorrowfully left behind. (lines 550–587)

4. Hrotswitha's Prologue: The Founding of Gandersheim Monastery

See! The devoted obedience of my modest aim bursts forth to tell of the founding of the blessed monastery of Gandersheim.

The chiefs of the Saxons, powerful in authority, built it with energetic care. The great illustrious Liudulf and his son Otto completed the work that was begun. The way these matters have turned out requires a suitable epic to be sung about the first founding of our renowned monastery Gandersheim. (lines 1–9)

I have said that Liudulf, the leader of the Saxons, is known to have constructed it with reverence. A child descended from the stock of a very distinguished family, his deeds matched the nobility of his lineage. Outstanding in his behavior and in the practice of his virtue, he grew in excellence among all the Saxons. For he was strong, very handsome in body, wise in his speech, and circumspect in all his actions. He alone was the hope and honor of his entire nation. Almost from his earliest years he served in the army of the great Louis, King of the Franks, who raised him to the highest honors. (lines 10–15)

5. Aeda's Vision of John the Baptist

The wife of Liudulf was the very celebrated Oda, illustrious offspring of the race of the powerful Franks. Her father was Billung, a benevolent prince; her mother was Aeda of good and noble reputation.

Aeda was many a time in the habit of delivering herself and her whole life over to praying to her Lord. Persisting very often in her pious acts, this diligent queen, who was well informed about the promises of heaven, earned the right to discover through the message of the blessed Baptist of Christ that her progeny would at some time in future centuries possess the glory of imperial authority.

On one occasion, therefore, when the dawn sheared through the night's shadows with the gleam of its red-glowing light, she lay at full length before the sacred altar that was consecrated in honor of the Baptist, beating with her ceaseless prayers against the inner shrines of heaven. And after she had unloosed her saintly thoughts in these devotions, she perceived—as she lay there face down—the feet of a man who was standing close to her. A little agitated, she greatly wondered in her mind who he might be that dared to disturb her solitude in this hour so fittingly associated with prayer. She turned a little with her forehead raised up from the ground, and gazed at a young man who glittered amazingly with light. He was clothed in a cloak of fleece so golden it seemed to be woven from the hair of a hump-backed camel. On his beautiful and shining face, he had a little fringe of beard, the same black as the hair of his head, which formed a crown of gleaming splendor.

The married lady, upon seeing him, did not believe he was mortal. She was stunned in her mind in the way of women, and constrained as she was by a great fear, she fell forward.

But he spoke to her sweetly to soothe her agitation, and said, "Do not tremble or be frightened or deeply disturbed, but—once you have driven away the terror of your strong fear—know who I am. I have come to bring you great solace. For I am John, who merited to touch Christ with the liquid water. Because you have often honored me, I bring you tidings that your illustrious descendant shall found a cloister for saintly virgins and a triumphant peace for the kingdom provided that his religious spirit stands firm. Your progeny will henceforth, at some time in future ages, attain to such a height of powerful sovereignty that no potentate among the kings of earth at that time will be able to rival it in authority."

He had spoken, and turning away suddenly, he entered the upper air, leaving the benevolent married lady a sweet consolation. The august promise of this lofty honor pointed specifically to the illustrous offspring of the lady Oda: her son, the noble ruler Otto became the father of Henry, so capable of reigning. (lines 21–70)

6. The Designation of the Site

According to the well-founded opinion of many knowledgeable people, there was near our monastery a little wood surrounded by shaded hills—the same that surround us today. In that wood there was a little farm where the men who herded Liudulf's pigs would take shelter in the paddock belonging to a certain man. There they would settle their weary bodies to rest in the quiet of the night, while the pigs in their charge ran to pasture.

Here, once upon a time, two days before the venerable feast of All Saints was to be celebrated, these same swineherds saw many luminous lamps burning in the forest in the dark of night. When they saw these, all the swineherds were dazed with stupefaction. They wondered what this could mean, this strange vision of brilliant light, shearing throught the night's shadow with astonishing brightness.

Shaken, they reported this to the householder of the farm, gesturing to show him the place that was bathed with light. He was avid to test with his own clear gaze what he had heard about, and left the protection of his house to remain outdoors in their company. He remained awake with them the following night, never closing his heavy-lidded eyes despite the inducements of sleep, until they could again see the enkindled lamps glowing redly. They saw the lamps, now increased in number, outdoing those of the previous night. They were indeed in the same place, but came at an earlier hour than before.

As soon as Phoebus scattered his first rays from the sky, this glad sign of a blessed omen became known when joyful tidings proclaimed it to all. Nor could it remain hidden from noble Liudulf, but it struck his ears more quickly than can be told. On the holy eve of the All Saints feast to come, Liudulf himself—observing carefully whether the vision would again reveal any heavenly sign—kept watch throughout the night with a throng of people in that same forest.

Before very long, when murky night had covered the earth with its cloud, everywhere within the circle of the wooded valley where the very celebrated temple was to be founded, a great many lights were seen arranged neatly in a row. And they sheared through the tree-shadows and the thick dark of night at the same time, with the bright dawn of their potent radiance. At once those who were present, giving praise to the Lord, affirmed that the place should be sanctified and dedicated to the divine service of him who had filled it with light.

Now the Duke Liudulf, joyful over heaven's beneficence and in harmonious agreement with his dear wife Oda, ordered that the trees and brambles should be cut and pruned, so that the valley should be completely cleared. He saw to it that this wooded place, filled with fauns and sprites, should be purified and made suitable for divine worship. As soon as he had first acquired for them the moneys that the work demanded, he immediately built there the walls of the beautiful church that the splendor of the redly glowing light had designated. And so in this circumstance the founding of our monastery was begun under the favorable auspices of God. (lines 185–237)

7. How a Supply of Building Stones Was Found

Meanwhile, appropriate stones for the structure could not be found in those areas. For this reason the completion of the temple suffered a delay. But the abbess Hathumoda, confident that those who believed in the Lord could prayerfully secure all things by faith, continually wore herself out with excessive toil, day and night ministering to God with sacred fervor. And with many of her subordinates acting in consort with her, she begged that the solace of heavenly aid might be conferred so that the work so well begun should not remain unfinished. Before very long, she sensed that the heavenly beneficence she was seeking would quickly take pity on her prayers.

For one day when she was fasting and allowing herself to be unoccupied, she lay prostrate before the altar. She was urged to go, through the counsels of a gentle voice, and follow a bird which she saw as she went forth. The bird had come to rest on the summit of a great rock. She embraced these summons with a prompt spirit and set forth, trusting in her heart the words of the One commanding her. She took experienced stonemasons with her, and went quickly in the direction where the Holy Spirit was guiding her, until she came to the place where the stately temple had been begun. There she beheld the white dove settle on the highest summit of the designated stone.

Then spreading its wings and soaring, it went ahead and moderated its flight—different from its usual way—so that the dear little maiden of Christ, together with her companions, might follow its airborne track in a direct route. And when the dove in its flight arrived at that place which we know now is not bereft of great rocks, it alighted and with its beak it struck against the earth, beneath which a great many stones lay hidden. Convinced by what she saw, the most meritorious virgin of Christ commanded her companions to clear the land, by delving to cut through the heap of earth. When they had done so, through the kindly beneficence of God, an immense quantity of great rocks was unearthed. From this quarry could be dragged all the raw material needed for the monastery walls and the church that had been begun. After this, the builders of the temple to be consecrated to the glory of the Lord labored more and more, both night and day devoting themselves to the new undertaking. (lines 238–279)

8. Gerberga

Gerberga was engaged to marry a distinguished and very powerful man named Bernard. But she had secretly devoted herself to Christ with a holy veil, filled as she was with a burning love for her heavenly Spouse and a total heartfelt contempt for any earthly lover. But she did not wish to create any disruption of a political sort, so she could not immediately put aside her gowns that were radiant with gold, and she continued to dress in expensive robes.

When Bernard, repudiated by this bride of Christ, came to see her in the hopes of freely taking his pleasure in her company, he learned of her vow to keep her virginal chastity unsullied. When Gerberga shrank back, unwilling to come out to meet Bernard, he grew very fearful that what he had heard about her might well be true. He impetuously appealed to her mother, the Lady Oda, and persuaded her by his pleading, so that she herself urged her daughter to meet Bernard beautifully gowned in rich apparel and jeweled ornaments such as brides usually wear.

Bernard, on seeing the darling object of his burning desire, is supposed to have reproached her with these words: "I have been hearing frequent evil rumors that you seek to violate our contract, that you intend to break utterly our promise of engagement. But this must be kept. Now by the command of the king our lord, I shall have to go off in haste to the war that threatens. There is not time to force you to revoke that vow of yours. But I swear that if I get back unharmed, with my health to sustain me, I will most certainly wed you and completely annihilate your futile vow!" This was how he spoke. With rage in his heart, he raised his right hand and swore by his sword and by her white throat that insofar as he could exert his powers to do so, he would carry out his words in action.

Gerberga, however, softly replied, "I entrust myself and my whole life to Christ. I pray that whatever happens to me will be according to the Lord's will." When they ended their conversation, Bernard left. Soon he realized by his own fate that no proud man can resist the Lord. He had committed an offense with the vanity of his talk, and because of this he fell in battle. The heavenly power triumphed over him. And the virgin Gerberga swiftly wedded herself to the love of Christ, who was her celestial Bridegroom, for she had always cherished Him with pure affection. (lines 319–360)

NOTES

1. Peter Dronke, *Women Writers of the Middle Ages* (Cambridge: Cambridge UP, 1984), pp. 55–58, gives an excellent picture of Gandersheim, Otto's court, and Hrotswitha's place there.

2. Helena Homeyer, ed., *Hrotsvithae Opera* (Paderborn: Ferdinand Schöningh, 1970), p. 227.

3. Archibald R. Lewis, *Nomads and Crusaders: A.D. 1000–1368* (Bloomington: Indiana UP, 1988), p. 85.

4. Pagan invasions and conquests were commonly explained as God's punishment against his faithful for their sins. Hrotswitha uses this argument in *Pelagius*. Boniface, the eighth-century British missionary to continental Germany, attributed the Moslem occupation in 711 to "the harlotry of Spain," and warned the English they would suffer such a fate if they failed to repent and reform. Similarly, Attila the rampaging Hun was called "the scourge of God."

5. Cited in Norman Daniel, *The Arabs and Medieval Europe* (London: Longman Librarie du Liban, 1975), p. 66. And see E.P. Colbert, *The Martyrs of Córdoba* (Washington: Catholic UP, 1962), pp. 382 ff.

6. Colbert, *The Martyrs of Córdoba*, p. 385. See also R.P.A. Dozy, ed., *Le calendrier de Courdoue de l'année 961: texte arabe et ancienne traduction latine* (Leiden, 1873; rev. ed. Leiden: Brill, 1961, annotated with French translation by C. Pellat), p. 102.

7. For the splendors of this high moment in the culture of the Umayyad dynasty, see Jerrilynn D. Dodds, ed., *Al-Andalus: The Art of Islamic Spain* (New York: Harry N. Abrams, dist. for the Metropolitan Museum of Art, 1992). The volume was published to coincide with the 1992 exhibit at the Metropolitan Museum of Art in New York.

8. From Ahmed ibn Mohammed al-Makkari, *The History of the Mohammedan Dynasties in Spain,* cited in Roger Collins, *Early Medieval Spain: Unity in Diversity, 400–1000* (New York: St. Martin's, 1983), pp. 174, 266.

9. Collins, *Early Medieval Spain*, p. 200, citing Al-Makkari.

10. For the Passion of Pelagius, see the *Acta Sanctorum*, June: 5.204–5. The liturgy for his feast is in *PL* 85, col. 1041. I am most grateful to John E. Halborg for providing me with a reference to the martyr Pelagius in *El Sacramentario de Vich*, ed. Dom Alejandro Olivar (Barcelona, 1953), pp. 56–57. This Sacramentary, one of the most important sources for the Mozarabic liturgy, is believed to have been written in about 1030 at the cathedral of Viche.

11. Dodds, *Al-Andalus*, pp. 13–14, suggests that this account by eighth-century Arab historians may be apocryphal. It would, however, have been the version available to Hrotswitha.

12. Dodds, *Al-Andalus*, pp. 17–18.

13. See chapter 8. William had at this point made a pact with Abd ar-Rahman II to rebel against his former overlord Charles the Bald, undoubtedly as vengeance for executing his father, Bernard of Septimania.

14. Collins, *Early Medieval Spain*, pp. 215–216. Collins quotes from Eulogius's *Memorial of the Saints*. The text, *Memorialis Sanctorum* (851 and 853), its sequel, the *Apologeticus Martyrum* (857), together with Eulogius's Life and letters, are in *PL* 115, cols. 703–870. See also Roger Collins, "Pippin I and the Kingdom of Aquitaine," in *Charlemagne's Heir*, eds. Peter Godman and Roger Collins, p. 369; Kenneth Baxter Wolf, *Christian Martyrs in Muslim Spain* (New York: Cambridge UP, 1988), pp. 53–54.

15. Collins, *Early Medieval Spain*, p. 213. Eulogius begins with a monk named Perfectus, killed in 850 for making accusations in public, but he had been provoked and badly frightened, and does not seem to have been an initiator of the movement.

16. Kenneth Baxter Wolf, *Christian Martyrs*, pp. 23–24.

17. Eulogius's *Memorialis* and its sequel tried to explain the martyrdoms, voicing personal support, while Alvar wrote the more general *Indiculus Luminosus* in 852 and 854.

18. Collins, *Early Medieval Spain*, p. 218.

19. On Flora, Maria, Sabigotho, Aurelius, Georgius, Felix, and Liliosa, see Wolf, *Christian Martyrs*, pp. 26–28, citing from the *Memorial of the Saints.*

20. Cited from Eulogius by Wolf, *Christian Martyrs*, p. 66.

21. The account is in the "Translation of the Relics of Saint Vincent." See Patrick Geary, *Furta Sacra* (Princeton: Princeton UP, rev. ed., 1990), pp. 61–62. Geary states that the Franks had long been interested in Spanish martyrs. "Ever since 527 when Childebert brought the stole of Saint Vincent to Saint Germain des Près [as Gregory of Tours points out, 2–29], the Spanish deacon had been venerated in the north. In the second half of the ninth century, Frankish interest again focused on Spain as a source of relics, since the despair of the Christian community of Córdoba had produced a number of men who had actively sought martyrdom at the hands of reluctant but ultimately cooperative Moslem officials." (Geary, p. 42). See also E.P. Colbert, *The Martyrs of Córdoba.*

22. John Boswell, *Christianity, Social Tolerance and Homosexuality* (Chicago: U of Chicago P, 1980), pp. 195–196, 199. And see Norman Roth, "'Fawn of My Delights': Boy–Love in Hebrew and Arabic Verse," pp. 157–172 in *Sex in the Middle Ages: A Book of Essays,* ed. Joyce E. Salisbury (New York: Garland, 1991).

Kathryn Gravdal discusses the attempted seduction of Pelagius in *Ravishing Maidens: Writing Rape in Medieval French Literature and Law* (Philadelphia: U of Pennsylvania P, 1991), pp. 30–31. As Gravdal perceptively notes, Hrotswitha's acknowledgement of men desiring men challenges "the Christian theological tendency to locate the cause of sexual transgression in the female."

23. Cited in Peter Brown, *The Body and Society* (New York: Columbia UP, 1988), p. 95.

24. Boswell, p. 176 n.25, citing Melchior Goldast, *Constitutiones imperiales* (Frankfurt, 1673), I.125, which is apparently an epitome of the edict of 390: "Qui tanto obscoenitatis furore et licentia abripitur, ut nec corporibus hominum ingenuorum parcendum putet, propter criminis foeditatem strangulatus flammis e medio populi Dei auferatur." (Whoever rapes with such fury and licentiousness that it is thought the bodies of young men cannot be spared shall according to criminal treaty be led strangled to the flames among God's people.)

25. Cited in Joyce N. Hillgarth, ed., *Christianity and Paganism, 350–750: The Conversion of Western Europe* (Philadelphia: U of Pennsylvania P, 1986), pp. 112–113.

26. E.R. Curtius, "Kitchen Humor and Other *Ridicula*," in *European Literature and the Latin Middle Ages*, trans. Willard R. Trask (New York: Bollingen, 1953), pp. 431–435. Gravdal (*Ravishing Maidens*, pp. 33–34) observes that the autoerotic scene with the governor and the pots leaves him dazed, soiled, and tattered, like a rape victim.

27. The saintly character attributed to the women of this family— Aeda, Oda, Hathumoda, Gerberga I, Christine, Edith and Adelheid, owes much to Hrotswitha's epic treatment of their worth, deeds, and reputations, as Patrick Corbet has amply demonstrated in *Les saints ottoniens: Sainteté dynastique, sainteté royale et sainteté féminine autour de l' an Mil* (Sigmaringen: Jan Thorbecke, 1986).

28. Hrotswitha does not identify the Guadalquivir River on which the city was built and which figures in the saint's martyrdom. The seven rivers of learning refer to the seven liberal arts: grammar, rhetoric, dialectic, geometry, arithmetic, astronomy, and music.

29. This is Abd ar-Rahman III, whom Hrotswitha names below in line 74.

30. Myrrh or frankincense were perfumes associated with the Sabaean people of Arabia, a land known for the production and export of myrrh and mentioned in Ovid's tale of Myrrha (*Metamorphoses* 10.480). Virgil describes the burning of Sabaean incense in Venus's temple (*Aeneid* I.416). In the fourth century the Christian author Prudentius in *Cathemerinon* (12.71), "The Daily Round," includes the sweet savor of Sabaean incense among the gifts to the infant Christ.

31. These are the Córdoba martyrdoms of the ninth century under Abd ar-Rahman II and Muhammed I.

32. *The Acta Sanctorum* (chap. 6) has Pelagius dragged to the palace in chains first, and then beautifully clothed.

33. Lothar, King of Lombardy and Marquess of Provence, died on November 22, 950. He was the son of Hugh of Arles. Hugh had married Adelheid's mother, Bertha, after the death of her first husband, Rudolph II of Upper Burgundy, Adelheid's father.

34. Berengar of Ivrea.

35. Adelheid was held prisoner in a mountain stronghold at Como on April 20, 951.

36. Bishop of Reggio. Hrotswitha gives him the title Praesul, "Prince" or "Protector." The city to which he directs Adelheid is presumably Reggio.

FURTHER READING

Edward P. Colbert. *The Martyrs of Córdoba*. Washington: Catholic UP, 1962.

Roger Collins. *Early Medieval Spain: Unity in Diversity, 400–1000*. New York: St. Martin's, 1983.

Norman Daniel. *The Arabs and Medieval Europe*. London and Beirut: Longman Librarie du Liban 1975.

Eulogius of Córdoba. *Vita; Memorialis Sanctorum; Apologeticus Martyrum*. *PL* 115, cols. 703–870.

Thomas F. Glick. *Islamic and Christian Spain in The Early Middle Ages*. Princeton: Princeton UP, 1979.

Anne L. Haight. *Hrotswitha of Gandersheim*. New York: The Hrotswitha Club, 1965.

Hrotswitha of Gandersheim. Mary Bernardine Bergman, trans. *Hrotsvithae Liber Tertius*. Covington, Kentucky: The Sisters of St. Benedict, 1943.

———. Helena Homeyer, ed. *Hrotsvithae Opera*. Paderborn: Ferdinand Schöningh, 1970.

———. M. Gonsalva Wiegand. *The Non-Dramatic Works of Hrotsvitha*. St. Louis: St. Louis UP, 1936.

———. Katharina M. Wilson, trans. *The Dramas of Hrotsvit of Gandersheim*. New York: Garland, 1989.

Edward Joseph James, ed. *Visigothic Spain: New Approaches*. Oxford: Oxford UP, 1980.

Evariste Lévi-Provençale. *Histoire de l'Espagne Musulmane*. 2 vols. Leiden, 1950.

——— and E. García Gomez, eds. and trans. *Crónica anónyma de Abderrahman III*. Granada, 1950.

Karl J. Leyser. *Rule and Conflict in an Early Medieval Society: Ottonian Saxony*. London, 1979.

Joseph F. O'Callaghan. *A History of Medieval Spain*. Ithaca: Cornell UP, 1975.

Katharina M. Wilson, ed. *Hrotsvit of Gandersheim: Rara Avis in Saxonia?* Ann Arbor: Marc Publishing Co., 1987.

Kenneth Baxter Wolf. *Christian Martyrs in Muslim Spain*. New York: Cambridge UP, 1988.

CHAPTER 10

A Byzantine Historian
of the First Crusade

Anna Comnena (December 2, 1083–1153)

At the age of fifty-five, Anna Comnena began writing the *Alexiad*, a prose epic which remains one of the foremost histories of the First Crusade, as well as of the Comnenus family and the Byzantine state, providing for us a mirror of Byzantine politics and society during her lifetime. For the previous twenty years Anna had been effectively retired, or exiled, from court, living in the monastery of Kecharitomene overlooking the Golden Horn. This religious house of retreat for imperial women and nuns had been founded by her mother, Irene Ducas, author of the *Typikon*, the charter and rule of the order.[1] Anna, known for her wit and learning, had gathered savants and philosophers around her at Kecharitomene, a coterie devoted to reviving Aristotelian studies. But this proud, strong woman had once believed herself cut out by birth and talent for a very different sort of life.

Born in the purple chamber—"porphyrogenite"—she was the daughter of Alexius Comnenus, ruler of the Eastern Empire at Constantinople when it stretched from Italy to Armenia. Anna had been given a crown as a child and had fully expected that at her father's death she would become the Basilissa of the Eastern Empire. The birth of her brother John—who would become John II—dashed these hopes. At the crucial age of nine, Anna heard her brother proclaimed Basileus. Her parents married Anna when she was fourteen to Nicephorus Bryennius, a court official and historian, to whom she bore four children.

Anna never gave up trying to persuade her father to accept her as his successor. When she was thirty-five, and Alexius lay dying, Anna and her mother strove fruitlessly to persuade him to leave the crown to Anna and her husband. With her mother's (though not her husband's) support, Anna then led a conspiracy to kill her brother.

About this fateful turning point in the Comnenus family's internal drama, a set of intriguing inferences may be drawn from certain works of pictorial art that ostentatiously adorned the palace walls. The art has vanished. But descriptions of it survive.

After his father's death, the new Emperor John ordered the creation of billboard-sized representations, in mosaics or painted murals, of his father's glory. Such an artistic rendering—either a panel or a portion of a mural—stirred the unbridled admiration of poet-physician Nicholas Kallikles, the court practitioner who tended the dying Emperor Alexius. Kallikles memorialized the picture in grandiloquent meters, indicating that it portrayed a son's anguish over his father's death. In a recent article, Paul Magdalino suggests that the pictured woe issued directly from the son's burden of guilt.

Anna's brother John, fearing that the family connived against him, "deserted his father on his deathbed in order to secure control of the Great Palace." The Byzantine historian Zonaras reports on the deathbed scene:

> Alexius was abandoned by almost all his servants, with the result that apparently there was none to bathe his corpse with the ritual ablutions, and no imperial attire was available to those round him, so that his body might be ceremonially arrayed, nor was his corpse borne out in a way appropriate to an emperor—and all this not with an outsider, but with his own son having succeeded to his imperial estate, a son whom he had appointed to rule.[2]

John evidently tried to make up for his filial neglect by commissioning the pictures. The scandalous situation that surrounded the expiring of their august parent also gave rise to Anna's protests of affection. These she accomplished in her own work of art. Anna's *Alexiad*, Magdalino proposes, fulfills an aim like her brother's but from the viewpoint of the disenfranchised imperial daughter. "[T]he author takes every opportunity to bring out her special relationship with Alexios; she describes his final illness and death in great detail, laying considerable emphasis on her own presence in distress, and concludes with a lament. . . . Anna's work breathes the spirit of family tension that hung over John II's accession to the throne; completed in scholarly seclusion thirty years after the event, it represents the loser's version of the official *Alexiad* that we glimpse in Kallikles' poem."[3]

The final chapter of Anna's *Alexiad* documents the emperor's dying and the daughter's emotion. The lost family pictures give a curious resonance to the event. Once Anna's plotting to do away with brother John was bared, the family sent her off to Kecharitomene where she might devote herself to authorship. The murderous accusation, the removal from court, and the pursuit of letters by the accused form a pattern that uncannily echoes the career of another Byzantine woman of rank, the Empress Eudocia (chapter 3), seven centuries earlier.

Ann's purpose was, as she writes, to glorify her father Alexius and his reign, so that future generations should not be deprived of a knowledge of him. History is a dam, she notes, erected against the moving river of time, which otherwise would carry everything to oblivion. The Comneni were a powerful, wealthy military family that had come to prominence in the middle of the eleventh century. Isaac Comnenus, Alexius's grandfather, had reigned as emperor; the succession shifted to the Ducas family when Isaac's brother refused the throne. Then in a coup d'état two years before Anna's birth, her father had himself crowned emperor.

An energetic warrior and gifted administrator, Alexius dealt ably with the pressing problems of the empire, consolidating it against three encroaching invaders in the main: the Scythians (also called Patzinaks) in the north, the Moslems from the east, and the European crusaders from the west. These last he kept at bay with the aid of the Venetians. He also had to deal with internal dissensions and pressures from the clergy, the bureaucratic nobility in his capital, and from the great feudal families from the provinces. Despite his mother's opposition, Alexius married a Ducas princess, for he hoped thus to neutralize the rivalry between the two families.

Anna's work is only nominally and partly about Alexius, however, for it is a monumental history in fifteen books, modeled on Homer with Christianized Byzantine variations. Her learning was considerable: she was thoroughly versed in classical literature (including Homer, Plato, and Aristotle) in Scripture and sacred writings, and in rhetoric, philosophy, and the sciences, notably medicine. She was acquainted with heresy. Her sources for the *Alexiad* were documents, treaties, letters, and an unfinished manuscript left by her husband at his death. The *Alexiad* contains Anna's personal memoirs and viewpoints. Interestingly, the *Alexiad* expresses only love and praise for Anna's father, despite any ambivalence she may have harbored toward him for denying her hopes of the throne. Her brother she passes over in silence.

Anna provides many eyewitness accounts, along with her own and other people's conversations, whether remembered or invented. Her chronology is sometimes confused, and yet she preserves material not available in other sources. There are details of court intrigues and military battles, stratagems and disguises, gougings, maimings, and public burnings. Stylistically flamboyant, Anna's writing is charged with the imagery of strife and disintegration: smashing, splintering, foundering. Events are in a state of dynamic change; things threaten continually to fall apart. A recurrent metaphor, a favorite with Byzantine writers and incidentally of Boethius, is that of the tempest. Whirlwinds and crashing waves buffet the ship of state. Against this sea of troubles, however, and in all weathers, emerges a heroic personality who manages to rise larger than life to quell the churning disorder.

Often this personality is Alexius himself, laboring tirelessly to stem the destructive tides, but there are others. Indeed Anna bases her view of history on a theory of personality, for at crucial junctures in the action strong figures decide the outcome. Anna's portraits—which include Saladin, Richard the Lion-hearted, and Godfrey of Bouillon—are vivid. The result is a theatrical effect, a spectacle in which historic personages, like the two whose portraits are given below, are the players engaged in dramatic exchanges and confrontations.

Passionate, self-willed, incandescent Anna stirred the imagination of writers long after her death. Sir Walter Scott mocked her learning in his medieval novel, *Count Robert of Paris,* and hinted at her secret infatuation for Bohemund the Norman, who figures so conspicuously throughout the *Alexiad*. In a sympathetic lyric, the modern Greek poet Constantine Cavafy attributes Anna's frequent tearful outbursts to her jealousy of her brother and her disappointed imperial hopes. A portrait of Anna was left by a contemporary, Georgios Tornikes, who wrote her funeral oration:

> Her large eyes . . . radiating a restrained joy . . . were endowed with a lively and easy movement when glancing around her, but most often were steady and calm. Her eyebrows were like a rainbow; her nose was slightly curved towards the lips edged like a rose blossom. The whiteness of her skin was tinged with a rosiness which gave color to her cheeks up to her old age. Her face was a perfectly chiseled circle. . . . Her shoulders, even . . . her limbs were agile and beautiful. . . . Her body was like a lyre or like a well-harmonized guitar, a fine instrument for a fine soul.[4]

Anna's own portraits of women in the *Alexiad* show them as strong and influential. Anna Dalassena (1025–1105), Anna's paternal grandmother, is the capable female ruler who appears in the epic's opening pages. Anna's description of her grandmother dwells on the matriarch's exemplary piety and habitual prayer in the beautiful Church of St. Thecla, which the emperor Isaac had built. But Anna goes beyond religious idealization. She gives an admiring account of a gifted administrator, a woman as desirous of reigning as Anna herself was.

Anna Dalassena had been fiercely disappointed when her husband, John Comnenus, had refused the crown from his abdicating brother Isaac. Resentful of the Ducases, who succeeded instead, Anna Dalassena intrigued, cultivated alliances, and nourished her sons' ambitions from 1059 to 1081, until at last with her constant urging Alexius mounted the throne. By then she was a widow with eight children. At seventy-five, after an energetic public life, Anna Dalassena entered the convent of Pantepoptes.

According to Anna Comnena, Alexius really wanted his mother to reign in his stead, having claimed that the survival of the empire depended entirely on her judgment. When he left to fight the Norman Robert Guiscard, Alexius issued his first chrysobull, a document inscribed in imperial purple ink and pressed with a gold seal that conferred authority upon his mother and any of her written decrees. Anna Comnena's lavish praise of her grandmother in her several lengthy tributes in the *Alexiad* serves as a reminder that her father had not at that time hesitated to entrust the state to a woman, and implies a protest against her being denied the same right.

The second portrait here is that of the Norman Bohemund of Taranto, prince of Antioch (*ca.* 1050–March 7, 1111). After the siege of Durazzo, in which Alexius defeats his lifelong enemy Bohemund, and which Anna also records, Bohemund stands at last before the emperor.

Hard-pressed by the Moslems to the east (Turkomen and Seljuks), Alexius appealed to Pope Urban II to recruit mercenaries to help him retake the Holy Land. Urban's somewhat delayed response, on seeing an opportunity to assert power in the East, was to preach his famous sermon at Clermont in November 1095. Its result was initially to draw independent adventurers from among the land-hungry French aristocracy. Then it unloosed in successive waves from Western Europe five great migrations toward Asia Minor.

The Normans, long eager to expand their holdings eastward from France and Italy, responded with alacrity to the call. Anna distinguishes two types of crusaders: those with pious motives and those intent upon conquest. To the latter class belonged the Hauteville men who, soon after other Normans had taken England, carved up Sicily and moved then into Italy. One of the Hauteville descendants was Marc, nicknamed Bohemund, who was called the most important leader of the First Crusade. Anna's description of this captivating "barbarian" (to Anna all of Europe was considered barbarian), marked by odium and admiration, accurately assesses his cunning, brutality, charm, and great military acumen.

Anna first saw Bohemund at court when she was a princess of thirteen. In May 1097, when Bohemund did homage to Alexius, emperor of Constantinople, Anna notes the mutual distrust of these two. Bohemund refused to eat the cooked food provided by the emperor, though he accepted his rich gifts.

Anna often writes of Bohemund's greed and treachery, while he continued to reassure Alexius of his friendly motives. Although many of the Normans—there were perhaps 30,000 of them—looted and raided for supplies, Bohemund restrained his own men.

From Constantinople, Bohemund proceeded to Antioch (Antakya in modern Turkey), where he was able to establish his kingdom and enlarge his territories. Imprisoned by the Turks and ransomed, he returned to Europe to raise money and was received as a conquering hero, even as "Christ himself." He married Constance of France, using the royal wedding at Chartres as an occasion for troop recruitment, climbing to the organ loft to address the crowds in the spring of 1106.

Now with papal approval, Bohemund organized a fresh crusade against Constantinople, envisioning for himself an entire eastern empire. He spent a year building a fleet at Brindisi and collecting the army that flocked to him. But at Durazzo, the modern city of Durres in Albania, a seaport city on the Adriatic coast considered the gateway to Constantinople, Bohemund met his defeat. Instead of doing hard battle with Bohemund, Alexius let the besieged city of Durazzo wait it out, tiring the Normans by starving them, blocking the mountain passes to prevent them from getting supplies. Soldiers deserted; famine and disease followed. By 1108 Bohemund finally had to sue for peace at Deabolis, an outlying district of Durazzo. Anna was twenty-five at the time; her husband, court official Nicephorus Bryennius, arranged the preliminaries of the surrender.

Anna has documented in full detail the treaty and terms of Bohemund's surrender, as well as Bohemund's arrogant outbursts, his insistence on standing at the head of the emperor's couch, and his refusal to bend his neck. The following passages describe the first part of the losing siege of Durazzo, giving a lively account of medieval warfare. The siege occupies a climactic place, near the close of the *Alexiad*, as a major victory of Alexius against the west. Following the battle is Anna's striking portrait of Bohemund, a powerful and satanic figure standing boldly in defeat. In Anna's dramatic vision of history, Bohemund symbolizes the terrible Norman power that the emperor was able to quell.

1. Anna Dalassena

It may cause some surprise that my father the emperor had raised his mother to such a position of honor, and that he had handed complete power over to her. Yielding up the reins of government, one might say, he ran alongside her as she drove the imperial chariot, and contented himself with the title only of Basileus. . . .

My father reserved for himself the waging of wars against the barbarians, and all the strains and hazards that these involved, while he entrusted to his mother the administration of state affairs, the choosing of civil servants, and the fiscal management of the empire's revenues and expenses. One might perhaps, in reading this, blame my father's decision to entrust the imperial government to the *gyneceum* (women's quarters).[5] But once you understood the capacity of this woman, her excellence, her good sense, and her remarkable capacity for hard work, you would turn from criticism to admiration.

For my grandmother really had the gift of conducting the affairs of state. She knew so well how to organize and administer that she was capable of governing not only the Roman Empire but also every other kingdom under the sun. Indeed she had a considerable experience: she understood the nature of all sorts of affairs of state; she knew how each affair began and how it would finish, and which things would destroy an enterprise and which, on the other hand, would strengthen it. She was very shrewd in seizing on whatever was called for, and clever in carrying it out with certitude. Not only did she have an outstanding intelligence, but also her powers of speech matched it. She was a truly persuasive orator, in no way wordy or long-winded. Nor did she run out of the breath of inspiration after a short time: she would begin speaking with purpose and she would end on a note of even greater resolution.

She was ripe in years when she ascended the imperial throne, at the moment when her mental powers were at their most vigorous and her understanding at its keenest, while her experience in affairs of state was also at its richest—all qualities that give strength to government.

Formerly, when Anna Dalassena was still a young woman, it was really wonderful to see her display the wisdom of old age in the flower of her youth. Her eyes alone revealed the Basilissa's courage and level-headedness to anyone who wished to take notice. . . .

The gyneceum of the imperial palace had been completely addicted to vice since the notorious Constantine Monomachos[6] had seized the imperial power and had been notorious—right up to my father's reign—for his foolish love affairs. But Anna Dalassena reformed the women's quarters and restored them to a wonderful propriety, while in the palace a marvelous orderliness prevailed. For she established specific hours for sacred hymns, she fixed the times for meals and for the choosing of civil servants; she herself became a model for others to emulate, so much so that the palace seemed instead to be a holy monastery as a result of this truly extraordinary and holy woman. For she surpassed the famous women of antiquity, who are so celebrated, as much as the sun outdazzles the stars.

As for her compassion toward the poor and the lavishness of her hand toward the destitute, how can words describe these things? Her house was a shelter for her needy relatives, and it was no less a haven for strangers. She venerated priests and monks in particular; she invited them to share her meals. One never saw her at the table without there being monks present. Her expression, which revealed her true character, demanded the worship of the angels but struck terror among demons. To licentious people—those carried away by their passions—her look alone was unendurable. Yet to those who were concerned about improving their ways, she seemed amiable and kind.

So well did she understand the right degree of control and seriousness that she herself betrayed neither a harsh, cruel restraint nor a lax, soft carelessness. And this, I think, is the definition of decorum: to balance bounty with moral seriousness.

Anna Dalassena's nature was conducive to reflectiveness. She was continually making fresh plans which, far from hurting the public good (as some people were whispering), were intended to restore the empire—which had already become corrupt—to its original vigor, and to raise up as much as possible the fallen condition of the people. Although she was involved in the ad-

ministration of the government, she did not neglect a single one
of the duties of the monastic life she embraced. She devoted the
better part of the night to sacred hymns, and fatigued herself
with continual prayers and vigils. And yet at dawn, at the second cockcrow, she set about attending to affairs of state.

2. The Siege of Durazzo

Bohemund, their leader, as we have said, had crossed over
from Italy into our territory with his formidable fleet, and had
unleashed the entire Frankish army to attack our province. Next
he marched in battle formation against Epidamnus[7] in the hopes
of taking it on the first onslaught. Failing in this, he decided to
level the city by using siege engines and catapults for hurling
rocks. This was his aim. He pitched his camp facing the eastern
gate, over which there is a bronze horseman, and after having
reconnoitered all the areas, he began to lay siege to the city.

Throughout the entire winter he made plans and marked
out all the places where Durazzo was vulnerable. When spring
began to smile and he had brought over all his troops, he set fire
to the ships that had transported his supplies, horses, and men.
This was a calculated move to prevent his army from looking
back toward the sea. He was moreover driven to this because of
the presence of the Roman[8] fleet. Bohemund now concerned
himself with the siege alone.

To begin with, he surrounded the city with his barbarian
forces and sent out detachments of the Frankish army to create
skirmishes. But the Roman archers responded by shooting at
them, both from the towers of Durazzo or from afar. In short,
there were attacks and counterattacks. Bohemund seized
Petroula and a place called Mylos, located on the farther side of
the Deabolis River. Other places like these that lay outside
Durazzo fell in his hands, through the luck of combat.

While his military ability in general brought about these
victories, his skill as an inventor impelled him at the same time
to build battle engines, and to prepare tortoise-like structures.
Some of these tortoises[9] bore towers and battering rams, while

others had covered roofs to protect the men who were miners and sappers digging under the city walls.

Bohemund worked throughout the whole winter and the summer, terrorizing the citizens both by his threats and his actions. But he did not manage to shake the might of the Romans. Food supplies, moreover, were causing him problems. Everything he had collected by pillaging the country around Durazzo had been consumed, and the places from which he had hoped to procure additional provisions were cut off by the Roman army, which from the first had occupied the valleys, occupied the defiles, and even guarded the sea. The result was a terrible famine which killed Bohemund's men and horses alike, the horses getting no fodder and the men no food. Dysentery also raged throughout the barbarian army, apparently because of the inadequate diet consisting of millet cereal. In reality, divine wrath struck down these innumerable and invincible forces, and slaughtered the men one after another.

However, these trials seemed slight to this man, Bohemund, who had the spirit of a commander and who was threatening to destroy an entire land. Despite his reverses, he continued to try all kinds of stratagems, and like a wounded wild animal he turned inward upon himself and fixed his gaze only on the siege. First he constructed a "tortoise" with a "ram," an indescribable monster, and had it brought up to the east wall of the city. You had only to look at it—it was a terrifying sight. It was built in the following way: A small rectangular "tortoise" was made under which wheels were placed. It was then covered on every surface, above and on the sides, by ox-hides stitched together, so that as Homer said, the roof and walls of this engine were made of "the hides of seven oxen."[10] Then the "rams" were hung on the inside.

Once this engine was finished, it was brought to the ramparts by a team of thousands of men armed with pikes, who pushed it forward from the inside and led it right up to the walls of Durazzo. When it was brought to within the desired distance, just close enough, they took away the wheels and fastened the engine solidly to the earth with wooden stakes, so that the violent jolting within would not cause the roof to collapse. After this, several very sturdy men positioned themselves to the right and left of the battering ram, which they drove violently against the bulwarks with a regular rhythmic pounding force. They thus drove the ram powerfully for the first time; this first time it struck the wall, bore into it, then rebounded. They thrust at it a second time, and continued to breach the wall.

This procedure was repeated many times, while the instrument came and went ceaselessly in a way that was intended to burst through the bulwark. Undoubtedly the inventors of antiquity who devised this engine near Gadeira [Cadiz] called it a "ram," borrowing a metaphor from actual rams which engage in butting against each other.

But the city's inhabitants, who were laughing at this goat-like attack and these futile attempts to besiege the city, actually threw open their gates and invited the soldiers to come in that way—making fun of the blows delivered by the ram. "This ram," they said, "with its thrusts against the ramparts, will never make a hole as big as the entrance the gate provides!"

[Anna goes on to describe other military weaponry deployed by Bohemund and his men. But while using sappers to mine under the great towers, the Normans met the Greeks, who tunneled toward them in the opposite direction and sprayed them with fire. Their final effort to construct immense towers overtopping the city walls, and equipped with drawbridges for running over the city roofs, also failed. The roofs of Durazzo had been provided with loose planks which would not support the invaders. Alexius's men threw "Greek fire"[11] down on Bohemund's towers, as they did upon the tortoise and battering ram described previously, reducing these to ashes, to the utter dismay of the Norman armies.]

3. Bohemund

In short, there had never been seen anywhere in the Roman world a man like him, whether Greek or barbarian. The sight of him inspired awe; his reputation caused terror. To give a detailed description of this barbarian: he was so great of stature that he was taller than other men by nearly a foot and a half. He was slim, without any excess of weight, broad-shouldered and big-chested, with muscular arms. His body overall was neither thin nor corpulent, but perfectly proportioned, in conformity one could say with the standards of Polycletus.[12] He had strong hands and stood firmly planted on his feet, stalwartly and well-built across the neck and shoulders. To a close observer he seemed slightly bent, though this was not due to any weakness of the spinal bones, since he apparently had this slight curvature from birth.

He had very white skin but, in his facial coloring, both fair and ruddy mingled. His hair was tawny and did not tumble over his shoulders as did the locks of the other barbarians; in fact, this man did not have a mania for long hair. Instead he kept it clipped short around the ears. Was his beard russet or some other color? I couldn't say, since the razor had shorn it and left the skin as smooth as marble; still, it seemed that it might have been russet. His blue eyes revealed both force and dignity. His nose and his nostrils breathed the air freely, his chest being proportioned to his nostrils and his nostrils to his chest. Through the nostrils, indeed, nature gives free passage to the breath that surges from the lungs.

A certain charm emanated from this warrior, but it was lessened a little by the terrifying quality that issued from his being. The man as a whole was tough and brutal, both in his stance and in his look, it seemed to me, and even his way of laughing—which in another person would have been a snorting shudder—made the court circle tremble. In body and soul he was so constituted that both violence and desire strove within him, and both of them drove him to combat. He had a spirit that was subtle, sly, and full of subterfuges for every occasion. His utterances were in fact calculated and his replies always double-edged. This man, so superior in all these ways, could be defeated by no other than my father the emperor, who surpassed him with respect to fortune, eloquence, and the gifts of nature.

NOTES

1. *Typikon, PG* 127, cols. 985–1120. See also Charles Diehl, *Byzantine Empresses*, trans. Harold Bell and Theresa de Kerpely (New York: Knopf, 1963), pp. 198–225.

2. Paul Magdalino, in collaboration with Robert Nelson, "The Emperor in Byzantine Art of the Twelfth Century," Article VI: 123–183, quoted on p. 128, in Paul Magdalino, *Tradition and Transformation in Medieval Byzantium. Collected Studies*. Brookfield, VT: Gower, 1991.

3. Magdalino, p. 129.

4. Cited in Rae Dalven, *Anna Comnena*, pp. 67–68.

5. Anna says elsewhere that the women's quarters, the gyneceum, were separated only by a curtain.

6. Constantine IX (1042–1054).

7. Epidamnus was the ancient name for Durazzo, which the Romans called Dyrrachium and which is today Durres in Albania.

8. By Roman, Anna means her father's men, since Alexius still considered himself to be reigning over the Roman Empire.

9. The military word (in Latin, *testudo*) used for shelters or sheds. Originally men held their overlapping shields above their heads to provide such a plated, tortoise-like carapace of shelter.

10. *Iliad* 7.545.

11. Greek fire was a flammable mixture, which might consist of pitch, sulfur, and burning charcoal. Tallow, saltpeter, quicklime, bitumen, and naptha were other possible ingredients. This incendiary technique was used in medieval warfare by the Byzantine Greeks especially.

12. A Greek sculptor of Argos, Polycletus was perhaps a younger contemporary of Phidias, living in the second half of the fifth century B.C. His great reputation, during his lifetime and afterwards, was based in part on his Olympic Victors.

FURTHER READING

Georgina Buckler. *Anna Comnena: A Study*. New York: Oxford UP, 1968.

Anna Comnena. Bernard Leib, ed. *Anne Comnène, l'Alexiade. Texte établi et traduit*. 3 vols. Paris: Les Belles Lettres, 1937–1945.

————. E.R.A. Sewter, trans. *The Alexiad of Anna Comnena*. Repr. New York: Penguin, 1979.

Rae Dalven. *Anna Comnena*. New York: Twayne, 1972.

Elizabeth A.S. Dawes, trans. *The Alexiad of the Princess Anna Comnena*. London: Routledge and Kegan Paul, 1967.

Joachim Herrmann, Helga Köpstein, and others, eds. *Griechenland— Byzanz—Europa*. Berlin: Akademie, 1985. Anna Comnena: "Anna Komnene—Kronprinzessin und Schriftstellerin," pp. 50–60, by O. Jurewicz.

Basile Skoulatos. *Les Personnages Byzantins de l'Alexiade*. Louvain: Nauwelaerts, 1980.

CHAPTER 11

The *Trobairitz* in Love and Strife

Tibors
Bieris de Romans
Lombarda
Almuc de Castelnou and Iseut de Capio
Alais, Iselda, and Carenza
Gormonda
Azalais de Porcairagues
The Countess of Dia
Anonymous

The voices of the *trobairitz* (female troubadors) are fresh, direct, intimate, and personal. They want love and don't mind asking for it. Underlying the lyric situation was a fictional plot that could be delineated as a narrative, and eventually was when it entered the genre of romance as "courtly love."

The lover falls in love. The lover wallows in an agony of desire. The beloved remains aloof. The lover and the beloved meet, make love. All is well. All is not well. Spies, slanderers, and gossips lurk. A jealous rival, a spouse or other relative, makes ominous threats to separate the pair. Misunderstandings arise; there are slurs, partings, betrayals. The lover continues to pine in a quandary of desire, and writes a letter in the form of a lyric, or a lyric in the form of a letter. This document revels in its own bliss, it utters passionate cries and recriminations. It posits an adversarial stance—lover against beloved. The writer hopes that this lyric epistle is polished and beautiful and elegant and conforms to the complex rules of poetic composition. Among the endless variations on this fictional situation is the gathering of two or three poets to debate the matter. What is especially strik-

241

ing is that this highflown yet ardent literary activity takes place in the local vernaculars.

Schools of rhetoric had flourished in southern Gaul since the early empire and now were causing this upsurge of interest in transferring schoolbook rules to the pleasantly risky game of love. A contemporary French scholar has called the literary endeavors of the troubadours "the greatest lyric/erotic adventure of the Middle Ages, and maybe of all time."[1]

With the social, economic, legal, and cultural renaissance of the twelfth century, the vernacular had begun to replace Latin as an expressive and eloquent medium. The south of France saw the emergence of a literary language that kept in touch with the stylistic formality of clerical neo-Latin, yet was also a hybrid of dialects containing common terms in daily use. Words about the weather, plants and birds, food and clothing, curtains and bedding, kissing and "doing it"—*faire-lo*, for making love—as well as a wittily employed vocabulary culled from grammar, religion, war, feudalism, law, and commerce with its wages, profits, and damages, entered the tightly intricate structures of the Provençal lyric (in a language now called Occitan).

Twenty-six lyrics, written in the twelfth and early thirteenth centuries, are ascribable to women authors, twenty-two bearing women's names. These women were said to be aristocratic and well-educated. They already had rank (*paratge*), or so it was claimed, and did not have to assume the gracefully groveling pose found among some of the humbler male poets. When women writers do adopt an air of anxious oppression, it is because of love not social difference.

Many of the women's poems are accompanied by *vidas* (biographies) and *razos* (commentaries). The *vidas* and *razos* are occasionally fanciful, as they are for the male troubadours, but from them and other sources we may gather that the women troubadours (*trobairitz*) were relatives, friends, colleagues, and lovers of the male poets.

Although there were at least 400 male troubadours, the names of some 20 women have survived, 18 of them attached to specific lyrics. The *trobairitz* had a choice of the following poetic genres: *canso* (love song), *tenso* (debate), *partimen* or *joc parti* (an intellectual dispute whose question was referred to an authority), *sirventes* (political, abusive, or satirical song), *alba* (exchange between lovers parting at dawn), *pastorela* (amorous exchange between poet-knight and shepherdess), and *planh* (lament, usually for the dead). Women's voices are always heard in the *alba* and the *pastorela*, even when written by men.

Yet the surviving songs of the *trobairitz* are *cansos* and *tensos*, except for the *sirventes* of Gormonda of Montpellier, with its excited reiteration of the word "Roma." For the rest, their lyric positions may be plaintive or accusatory, argumentative, and problem-oriented.

A distinction already existed in the writing of male troubadours between the lady, the *domna*, and the woman, or *femna*. If the *domna* is the aloof one, the ice queen, then the *femna* is the woman who needs and wants. The woman troubadour, however, can be viewed as playing all the accessible female roles: "The *trobairitz* is at once *femna*, *domna*, and poet through the kaleidoscope of her songs."[2] She is self-involved in these roles. In all but one case, that of Azalais de Porcairagues, she can dispense with the conventional business of describing Nature and plunge into her subject.

Precedents for a female lyric voice are found in Spain and Portugal, with the *cantigas de amigo*, in which a woman sings tearfully about an absent man. Women's love laments emerge in the Bible, with the voice of the spouse in the *Song of Songs*, and the conversations between the wise and foolish virgins in Matthew, chapter 25. In fact the virgins were dramatized in the eleventh-century play *Sponsus*, with the sisters addressing one another in an Occitan dialect. Saints directed love songs to God, as in the eleventh-century Occitan *Chanson de Sainte Foy*, in which St. Faith longs to laugh and rejoice with the Lord. Interestingly, the poem claims to be a good *canzon* for dancing, a reminder that women's dance songs, too, incorporated women's voices.

There is also a tradition of fictive letters, stemming from Ovid's *Heroides*, in which deserted heroines of antiquity such as Sappho and Dido address a beloved. Love letters in Latin verse survive, and of course, letter writing of every description had long been a genre available to women, affording a chance for rhetorical ornamentation. The lyrics of the troubadours themselves, both men and women, can be seen as a playful type of letter, with the salutation, special pleading, and closing envoy (or *tornada*) directed to a messenger.

In only one medieval text do we find the word *trobairitz*, or "trobaress." It does not appear in the lyrics, the *vidas*, or the *razos*, but it does in the thirteenth-century Occitan romance *Flamenca*. Flamenca and her women friends have been rearranging the words of a lyric by a colleague, Peire Rogier, in order to send a message to Flamenca's lover. Margarida strings together a stylized utterance of sentiments that are breathless, rhythmic, and musical in their mounting excitement:

> Alas! —Why do you sigh?—I'm dying—Of what?
> Of what? By God, my lady, that's good, isn't it? (4574–4575)

Flamenca exclaims:

> Margarida, that's very well done!
> You're already a good *trobairitz*. (4576–4577)

Margarida acknowledges the compliment:

> Yes, Madame, the best you've ever seen,
> after you and Alis, of course. (4578–4579)[3]

If the young women's utterances were gathered from the surrounding text and reconstituted in sequence, the result would build to a tight and driving narrative:

> "Alas!—Why do you sigh?—I'm dying!—Of what?—Of love —For whom?—For you—What can I do?—Heal me—How? —With a ruse—Think of one—I've got it—Which one?—You'll go—Where?—To the baths—When?—One happy day soon—That pleases me."[4]

Flamenca goes on to compliment Margarida by observing her mastery of *dialecta*, her capacity to unfold the opposing positions of the heart:

> Flamenca said to her, "Who has taught you,
> Margarida, who has shown you—
> by the faith you owe me—such dialectic?" (5441–5443)

This intriguing repartee suggests that women consciously absorbed and transformed male texts for their own use, and that there was an element of play, community, and competition in the endeavor. *Flamenca* shows women composing for each other's entertainment and approval, even though they may also have been writing for male friends and lovers. The following selections reveal the *trobairitz* in a variety of playful and languishing attitudes.

step up for women?

Tibors (b. ca. 1130)

This is one of the earliest of the troubadour women, and we have only a part of her lyric. Her *vida* tells us that "Lady Tibors was a lady of Provence from a chateau of Blacatz, a chateau called Séranon. She was courteous and well taught, gracious and extremely erudite, and knew how to compose poetry. She was in love, and very amorously loved in return. And by all worthy men of this country she was highly honored and by all noble women very deeply respected and obeyed. She wrote these verses and sent them to her lover."

The location of Tibors's chateau at Séranon was in the canton of Saint-Auban, arrondissment of Grasse (Alpes-Maritimes). She and the Comtessa de Proensa were the only two of the *trobairitz* known to be connected to Provence. Several contemporaries speak of her: She is supposed to have been the sister of Raimbaut d'Orange. Guiraut d'Espanha compares a beautiful lady of his acquaintance to her. And she was said to have been the judge of a *partimen*.

Unfortunately, her poem breaks off. Yet the fragment tells us enough, since this *trobairitz* has already stamped the lyric with her individual style. She declares her desire without ado. Avoiding the usual spring opening, she shows that the only "season" and "time" of importance are of the heart. Wittily she affirms her love in negatives and builds her emotional effect with the use of *anaphora*, the insistent reiteration of a word or phrase at the start of successive lines: "Nor was there ever—." Unfinished though it may be, it is self-contained and tells all it needs to.

Bieris de Romans (early thirteenth century)

Surely this is a most enigmatic poem, a *canso* or love song from one woman to another woman, pleading sweetly for "succor" (*socors*). Although several *tensos* feature women amicably debating some issue, this lyric is unique in the entire canon of troubadour poetry. There is a question as to whether this is a poem about lesbian love; two recent articles about the lyric are titled with queries.[5] Rieger's longer inquiry concludes that the poem is merely an expression of intense feminine tenderness. Bec's succinct judgment is to grant a range of possibilities—that the lyric is teasing, disruptive, seditious, earnest, and maybe even funny. But there is no reason to rule out a homosexual reading.

As a comment on the poem, we may cite a percipient remark on female sexuality in a treatise written close to this period:

> There is a certain category of women who surpass others in intelligence and subtlety. There is a great deal of the masculine in their nature, to such an extent that in their movements, and in the tone of their voice, they bear a certain resemblance to men. They also like being the active partners. A woman like this is capable of vanquishing the man who lets her. When her desire is aroused, she does not shrink from seduction. When she has no desire, then she is not ready for sexual intercourse. This places her in a delicate situation with regard to the desires of men and leads her to Sapphism. One has to look for the majority of those who possess these qualities amongst the elegant women, those capable of writing and reciting—amongst the cultivated women.[6]

Beatrice (Bieris) is in adept command of all the conventional praises and humble pleas for solace. She addresses her adoring poem to her friend Maria after cataloguing her graces, not failing to sing her own praises as well, both as a lover and a poet.

Lombarda (thirteenth century)

The feminine name Lombarda appears in many Toulousan documents, including a charter of June 1206. The woman mentioned in it may or may not be the poet represented here. There were several educated upper-class women in twelfth-century Toulouse, but they were not admitted to schools or to the university. Among the thirteen troubadors and "joculatores" of Toulouse, Lombarda is one of eight remembered in a *vida*:

> Na Lombarda was a lady of Toulouse, noble and beautiful, gracious of person, and learned. She knew very well how to write poetry, and composed beautiful stanzas on amatory subjects. Moreover, Bernart Arnaut, who was brother to the count of Armagnac, spoke of her goodness and merit. And he went to Toulouse to see her. He dwelled with her in great intimacy, he loved her, and was her very close friend. He composed the following stanzas on that subject, and sent them to her home. Then he mounted his horse without seeing her and rode off to his own estates.

Lombarda's only surviving lyric is contained in this exchange with Bernart. Bernart Arnaut of Armagnac of the *vida* was a brother of the Count of Armagnac, and succeeded to the countship in 1219.[7]

In the lyric translated below, Bernart addresses two stanzas, one to his beloved Lombarda, the second to his rival, Jordan. Bernart puns on Lombarda's name in two senses: money and real estate. The word *Lombard* had the meaning in Old French of a pawnbroker, money changer, merchant, or banker. As a sumptuous, erudite courtesan (the suggestion is John Mundy's), here is a female "lombarda" with commodities for sale or barter. Bernart's wordplay on his beloved's name, expressing a wish that he might be a "lombard" for her sake, implies that he would like to shower her with rich gifts to secure her affection. Preparing for the real estate metaphor in the next stanza, he claims to prefer a woman of this region over an Alamanda (German) or a Giscard. But while the enticing Lombarda dangles her love before his eyes, she nonetheless dawdles and keeps him waiting.

Perhaps she primps overlong before her mirror, whose hard passive surface alone enjoys the beauty she keeps unavailable to Bernart—the fine appearance, the beautiful smile that might give him pleasure if he could only reach her.

Continuing with the same commercial metaphor he began in the first stanza, Bernart addresses his rival, Jordan, offering him a deal in real estate. Now Lombarda's name refers to the region. Bernart scoops it into a job lot of lands and territories for possible exchange, together with the women of those lands. Bernart tells Jordan, "I'll trade you this batch of five valuable lands/ladies for a group of three as long as it includes Lombardy/Lombarda."

Turning again to Lombarda, Bernart calls her by the *senhal*, or code name, "Mirror of Excellence" (Miral-de-Pres). The complex, often conflicting, figure of the mirror in love lyric suggests ideal perfection, transcendence, transfiguration, deceptiveness, self-absorption, and remoteness. Elaborating the image of the mirror as a fragile object, Bernart urges his lady not to break up their love for the sake of this inferior rival.

Lombarda in true *tenson* fashion confronts the individual arguments of Bernart's poem point by point. If we paraphrase, Lombarda's reply might go like this:

"I can pun as well as you can, Bernart; I can turn both your names into women's names for myself if I choose. And, my thanks (ha!) for linking me to those two ladies whom I consider far less beautiful and gifted than I. Since you mention these two, confess that you must like one of them better than the other. Without any more of these tricky linguistic subtleties, tell me which you prefer.

"You address me as 'mirror,' but my mirror at least reveals my own image. The mirror you employ—the grammatical doubling of words (Lombard for Lombarda and so on)—is only a verbally clever feat that throws back no true image, no meaningful reflection. And this disturbs me.

"Now observe, I know how to play these word games too—see how fancifully I can pun on *descorda, acord, desacorda, record, acord, s'acorda!* But since you remind me of the significance of my name and its connection to wealth and treasure, I'm no longer ill at ease; in fact, I am quite in harmony with myself.

"What really counts is not all this witty posturing but the heart itself. Where is yours? You complain that I keep you waiting and you can't enjoy my beauty. Never mind vast territories; I can't see your heart in any dwelling place, large or small, house or hovel, because you won't let it speak."

Almuc de Castelnou and Iseut de Capio (late thirteenth century)

In this *tenso* between Lady Isolt (Iseut) and her friend Lady Almois (Almuc), the subject of debate is a third person, Gui de Tournon. Gui has been Almois's lover and has behaved badly. While one defends him the other accuses. Both are sizing up and judging this male culprit. The two ladies speak, really, as attorneys. The ambience resembles a court of law, but the language has a religious flair. Isolt pleads with Almois to pardon Gui de Tournon after Gui has been found guilty of wronging Almois. In this lyric—with its play on the language of prayer, sacrament, repentance, mercy, and conversion—Isolt acts as an intercessor before the wrathful, all-powerful, but ultimately merciful Almois. Almois's willingness to "convert" to a merciful verdict places her again on an earthly flesh-and-blood plane with her lover.[8]

Alais, Iselda, and Carenza

This three-way *tenso* among "sisters" doesn't deign to discuss any specific male lovers. Instead it upholds the advantages of the unmarried life, wedded only to Christ, or to an allegorical gentleman, "Crowned with Learning," or perhaps it advises wedlock with a real husband who will conveniently not insist on exerting his marital rights. Chaste matrimony, freedom from the cares of childrearing and the joys of having surviving spiritual offspring, may derive from the New Testament Apocrypha, for example, the Acts of Thomas 12. The earthy details about the female body in its subjection to motherhood and its terrible vexations find similar echoes in contemporary treatises on virginity, such the Middle English *Holy Maidenhead*. Ideas of knowledge, learning, and wisdom are scattered throughout. The spirit of the cloister seems to reign, whether Catholic or Cathar, or at least of an educated female community. Alais and Iselda seek the advice of their senior sister Carenza, who offers her protection and asks to be remembered when the other two get to a certain unnamed but desirable location. One reading of the poem proposes that there are only two speakers: "Alaisina Iselda" and "Carenza."

Gormonda of Montpellier (ca. 1225–1229)

Gormonda is the only woman known to have composed a *sirventes*, an extremely popular form of vernacular debate on a political topic rather than love. Her poem forms half of a double *sirventes*; that is, she writes stanzas to complement those of an opponent, thus creating matching pairs. Each of Gormonda's twenty-three stanzas retorts directly to the corresponding argument of her adversary, using an identical structure and rhyme scheme and picking up on his key words.

The poet she attacks was one of the most famed and outspoken Cathar troubadours of Toulouse, Guillems Figueira, "barfly, tailor, and the son of a tailor." His *vida* said that he nearly lost an eye in a fight and was not accepted among the nobility and polite society, since he associated with harlots and tavern keepers. It was customary for poets of the Midi to air their controversial political views in their vernacular work, and Figueira's notorious *sirventes* containing tirades against Rome was making the rounds in Toulouse.[9]

In the twelfth century, Toulouse was an affluent and independent county, whose growing economy thrived on clothmaking, viniculture, and mortgage lending and other usurious practices. It was "a kind of Italian city republic" of great towered houses with stone halls and private chapels, as well as attached and rented-out stores and workshops.[10] It was also a locale where the Cathars were favored and protected by Count Raymond VII.

In 1209 Pope Innocent III prompted the Albigensian Crusade against the Cathars of Albi and elsewhere in southern France, enlisting the eager support of the northern French nobility, who saw the opportunity to extend Capetian power throughout the country. Eventually these crusading wars led to the devastation of the whole area of Provence and Toulouse. Count Raymond VII of Toulouse held off the crusading armies until he was forced to yield up the city on April 11, 1229. In Toulouse, the crusade succeeded in crushing one of the most advanced and brilliant provincial cultures of Europe. The change, as John Hine Mundy summarizes it, brought a self-governing society that was "open and flexible," an economy that was "individualist," and an education system that was private with an emphasis on "scribal culture and lay poetry" to a rather more repressive and formalized system, with a renewal of monarchic and church control.[11]

By contrast, Gormonda's city of Montpellier was staunchly faithful to Roman Catholicism. A center of learning, it had a school known for the study of medicine. Montpellier had always maintained close relations with the Holy See. It became a Catholic outpost of operations against Catharism, and when the crusade was waged against the heretics of the south, the crusaders did not touch Montpellier.

Gormonda, as a conservative orthodox Catholic, lashes out vituperatively but indirectly against Figueira. Where Figueira denounces Rome head on, she addresses Rome with expressions of sympathy and support, obliquely heaping angry invective on him (without naming him) and on Toulouse as a hotbed of heresy, although Catharism was the only sect to thrive there. The double *sirventes* amounts to a battle of cities: Figueira against Rome, Gormonda against Toulouse.

Where Figueira opens his poem expressing pleasure at denouncing those rascals at Rome, Gormonda voices grief and says that she gets no pleasure from what Figueira says. In his fourth stanza Figueira complains that Rome gnaws the flesh and bones of the sinful; Gormonda's parallel verse points out that their flesh and bones are freighted with vice. In stanza 5, both find different reasons for the loss of Damietta to the Moslems. Both poets mention the king's death in stanza 6. Where Figueira complains in stanza 7 that Rome still hasn't defeated the Saracens, Gormonda claims that the heretics are worse than the Saracens. Figueira's stanza 10 rages against the pope's pilgrimage against Toulouse, while Gormonda alleges that Toulousans are tricksters. In stanza 11 each gives a view of Count Raymond. In stanza 20, Figueira wishes "the glorious one" to visit misfortune on Rome, while Gormonda wishes the same hard luck on the heretics.

Naturally, reading both lyrics together enables one to relish the debate more fully,[12] but the selected stanzas translated below serve as an introduction to this *trobairitz*. Since Gormonda notes the death of the French king Louis VIII in 1226 but still hopes for the fall of Toulouse, which did not capitulate until 1229, she clearly wrote between those two dates.

Azalais de Porcairagues

According to her *vida*, "Lady Azalais came from the region of Montpellier, a noble and educated lady. And she was in love with Gui Guerrejat, brother of Sir Guillem of Montpellier. And the lady knew how to compose poetry, and wrote many fine songs for him."

A single poem remains attributed to her; it appears in six song collections and is available on record and cassette. The little town she came from, which is probably modern Portiragnes, is about twelve miles southeast of Béziers, close to the seacoast.[13]

Azalais's lyric and *vida* mention contemporary people and places. Allusions can be pieced together about her personal acquaintances. Her *vida* states that she wrote many songs honoring Guy Guerrejat, "the warrior." Guy inherited two chateaux between Béziers and Montpellier, which placed him in the neighborhood of Porcairagues. He died in 1177 and was buried that year at the abbey of Valmagne, in the diocese of Agde, not far from Porcairagues.

The most conspicuous place reference in Azalais's poem is to the neighboring city of Orange, renowned for its poetic connections to the historic conqueror William of Orange. Azalais mentions the city's current *seignor*, widely taken to mean the troubadour Raimbaut d'Orange (b. ca. 1140). Raimbaut had rich land holdings in the region and was the cousin of Guy Guerrejat. Azalais in her lyric may even hint of a rivalry between the two for her affections.

Finally, Azalais addresses her *canso* in stanza 7 to the celebrated countess Ermengarda of Narbonne (1143–1192), to whom Andreas Capellanus in his *Art of Love* attributes three judgments of love.[14]

The only one of the *trobairitz* to open with a prelude to Nature, Azalais links winter's barrenness and the seasonal cold (stanzas 1 and 2) to her own grief, much as male troubadours liked to do. She introduces the city and the troubadour of Orange in stanza 2 and mentions them again in stanza 6. The hurt she suffers from the turmoil in Orange may mean Raimbaut's distress, because she loves not him but Guy, and this destroys her perfect happiness.[15] Stanzas 3 to 5 seem to be the core of the love lyric, while 6 is a leave-taking in the manner of the *planh*, a lament for the deceased or departed. It looks as though Azalais makes a last will and testament, disposing of all those aspects of the city of Orange that she loves and cherishes. Should we suppose that the poem is really a lament for the death of Raimbaut d'Orange?

The test or trial or assay (*assag*) of stanza 5 usually signifies in a love lyric some test of fidelity or affection that lovers put to each other. Often the meaning is sexual, and may even denote the power to resist sexuality if necessary. The same word applies to a battle, and so is translated here "test of battle." Azalais uses the word about her own personal relation to the man who is the love object of her song. By recollecting, in stanza 6, the past battles to which the city of Orange was subjected and the signs of the campaign recorded on its triumphal arch,[16] Azalais implies that the marks of love's tests and battles are inscribed on the poet's body.

The Countess of Dia

The four poems that have come to us from the Comtessa de Dia are polished and passionate compositions that seem to court emotional danger and then deftly evade it. There is no reason to call her "Beatriz." The countess was said in her *vida* to be married to a Guillaume of Poitou, not the troubadour count Guillaume IX. She might have been the daughter of Gigue V, dauphin of Viennois in the twelfth century. The *vida* also tells of her love for Raimbaut d'Orange, possibly the well-known twelfth-century troubadour, or his grand-nephew Raimbaut VI. If it was the younger Raimbaut, the countess would belong to a later generation of women writers, those affected by a wider access to poetic texts and whose writing might therefore be rooted more in theory and fantasy than in personal experience.

Whatever the conditions under which she wrote, the Comtessa's poetry is forthright and sensual, investigating a wide variety of moods while delighting in the play of language.

In the first lyric, *Ab joi et ab joven m'apais*, the singer revels narcissistically in her well-being. She is the *domna* whose own good points give her pleasure. Even while she praises her lover, she parallels his virtues with hers. The poem produces a key word in each line which is mirrored or punned upon in the next, repetitions that link the lovers or reinforce their qualities. In the *tornada* the woman asks the man's protection in feudal terms, as an overlord shields a vassal.

In contrast to the sanguine wittiness of this lyric, the second poem, *A chantar m'er de so q'ieu no volria*, explores an entirely different mood. Resentfully, the singer complains of her lover to a "jury" of hearers. Then, still defensive, she turns to accuse him directly. Her wounded anger gives way to pride, however, as she claims that she outdoes this valiant lover by being more valiant than he is—in the loving game. Now the poem views love in military terms, as a form of combat in which each vies to face down the other. In *Ab joi et ab joven m'apais*, the singer had invited her lover to be her protective feudal lord; here she chafes against his arrogant sovereignty.

The man's valor, she claims, consists in lording it over her, whereas hers lies in her steadfast loving. She's even better than Seguin, who was valorous in the world of *chanson de geste*, although he was killed in it. The confrontational eye-to-eye aspect of the poem becomes a triangle when the singer introduces the "other woman," thereby adding jealousy to her sufferings. But still undaunted, the singer claims to be stronger than *both* the man and *any* other woman. The music of this poem survives and is readily attainable.

The initial impression of the third lyric, *Estat ai en greu cossirier,* is one of vulnerable sensuality. Three time frames are evoked: a past in which the singer did not yield sexually to the man even though she says she had the opportunity; a present sense of loss; and a yearning toward future possession, oriented both to sexuality and to power. Sensuality is conveyed only through verbs of wishing, however. All is imagined; nothing physical occurs.

The poem deliberately creates rich, teasing doubts through images of the singer first in bed and, then, as a possible pillow for her lover. "Fully clad" is echoed by the contrasting word "naked" in the following stanza. The reference to Floris and Blancheflor is a reminder that these lovers from popular romance were discovered in bed together. The literary allusion opens the narrow confines of the lyric's highly cerebral space to the worldly hazards of romance, and keeps before the reader's mind the images of bed and naked lovers. At this point, however, the singer asserts her toughness, her readiness to give up everything, like Blancheflor, including her life.

But the third stanza contains a surprise. No more talk of sacrifice—the singer looks abruptly forward to a time when she can exert her power. Briefly she toys with the dangerous idea of putting the lover in a husband's place, which would make him the master. The ecstatic quality of their clandestine passion would end, and so would her reign as *domna,* powerful lady of the *canso.* Then she makes her final startling and outrageous demand: he must be her servant in everything, husband or no. Yet after all, he remains an *amour lointain,* a faraway, absent love.

In the fourth lyric, *Fin joi me don' alegranssa,* the singer flings a gleefully defiant challenge in the faces of malicious gossips.

The last selection under the Comtessa de Dia's name, *Amics en gran cossirer,* is a *tenso* sometimes attributed in part to her. In it a woman and a man compete once again on the battlefield of love, each speaking a part. Which should win the prize for greater suffering? Perhaps it is the lady, since her lover finally promises not to think about another woman *again*.

Anonymous Dance Song

One of the earliest troubadour lyrics, anonymous but attributable to a woman writer, is the following *balada*, or dance song. Basically it is a "chanson de mal mariée," a complaint about a husband, comparing him unfavorably to a lover. Its refrain is meant to be sung by a chorus of dancers, but in its closing verse it contains a wider appeal in to the community of learned women everywhere to perpetuate the song.

1. Tibors

Bels dous amics, ben vos puosc en ver dir

> Fair sweet friend, I can truthfully tell you
> I've never stopped wanting you
> since you allowed me to cherish you as my gentle
>   lover.
> Nor was there ever a time that I didn't yearn—
> fair sweet friend—to gaze at you.
> Nor was there ever a season that I repented.
> Nor did it ever happen, if you went away angry,
> that I felt any joy before you returned.
> Nor—

2. Bieris de Romans

Na Maria, pretz e fina valors

Lady Maria, your worth and excellence,
joy, understanding, and exquisite beauty,
the warmth of your welcome, your excellence and
   honor,
your elegant conversation and charming company,
your gentle face and amiable gaiety,
your gentle gaze and amorous mien—
all these things are yours, without deviousness.
And these things have drawn my truant heart to
   you.

For this reason I plead with you—if true love pleases
   you—
and my joyfulness and sweet submission
could elicit from you the succor that I need,
then give me, lovely woman, if it's pleasing to you,
the gift in which I have most joy and hope.
For in you I have fixed my heart and desire,
and from you I have derived all my happiness,
and from you—so many times—my painful yearning.

And since your beauty and worth enhance you
above all women, so that no other is superior,
I plead with you—please! It would bring you honor,
too, not to love some suitor who'd betray you.

Glorious lady, woman, enhanced by worth, joy,
and gracious speech, my verses go to you.
For in you are gaiety and happiness,
and every good that one demands of a lady.

3. Lombarda

Lombards volgr'eu eser per na Lonbarda

Bernart writes:

> I'd like to be a Lombard for Lady Lombarda,
> for Alamanda doesn't please me as well—nor does
>   Giscarda.
> Her lovely eyes regard me so sweetly,
> she appears to grant me her love. But she puts me off
>   too long!
>> And her fine looks,
>> and my pleasure,
>> And so gracious a smile—she keeps
>>   them so well guarded
>> that a man can't get at them.
>
> My lord Jordan, if I leave you Germany,
> France and Poitiers, Normandy and Brittany,
> you must leave me—without counterclaim—
> Lombardy, Livorno, and Lomagna.
>> If you help me,
>> I'll help you tenfold
>> to a lady who is stranger to
>> anything mean.
>
>> Mirror-of-Excellence,
>> you can console yourself
>> that for some shoddy devil
>> you aren't smashing the love you bear me!

Lombarda replies:

> I'd like to have for Bernart the name of Lady
>   Bernarda
> and for Arnaut the name of Lady Arnauda.
> And many thanks, my lord, since it pleases you
> to name me along with two ladies like those.
>> I wish you to tell me

which of them you like better—
without covert deceit—
and in what mirror are you gazing.

For the mirror that shows no image brings such
  discord
to my inner concord that it jars discordantly.
Yet when I record what my name records,
all my thoughts fall in accord with sweet accord.

But concerning your heart—
Where you have put it?
Neither in house nor hovel
do I see it, for you keep it mute.

4. Almuc de Castelnou and Iseut de Capio

Dompna n'Almucs, si'us plages

Lady Almois, if it pleases you,
I would very much like to pray to you in this
  manner:
put aside your wrath and ill will,
and show mercy
toward him who sighs and groans,
and dies as he languishes. He laments
and most humbly seeks your pardon.
Perform the sacrament for him
if you want everything completed with him,
so that he'll be guarded against further failings.

Lady Isolt, if I knew
that he repented truly of the very great deception
  that he committed against me,
it would be right for me

to show him tender mercy. But it doesn't suit me—
since he doesn't refrain from his wrongdoing,
nor does he repent of his fault—
to show indulgence toward him.
Yet, if you can make him repent,
you might convert me to his favor.

5. Alais, Iselda, and Carenza

Na Carenza al bel cors avinen

Alais:

> Lady Carenza, you of the graceful and lovely body,
> give counsel to us two sisters.
> And since you know best how to sift over the best,
> counsel me according to your own wisdom.
> Shall I take a husband from among our
>   acquaintance?
> or remain a virgin? That would please me,
> since I don't think much of having babies,
> and being married seems too depressing to me.

Iselda:

> Lady Carenza, having a husband would agree with
>   me,
> but I think having babies is a great penance.
> Your breasts hang right down to the ground
> and your belly is burdensome and annoying.

Carenza:

> Lady Alais and Lady Iselda, you have a good
>   education,
> reputation and beauty, youth and fresh color,
> you have understanding, courtesy, and merit—
> above all the other ladies of my acquaintance.
> For this reason I counsel you, in order to get good
>   seed,

take Coronat de Scienza for your husband.
From him you'll have the fruit of glorious children.
Those who marry him remain virgins.

Lady Alais and Lady Iselda, your remembrance of
     me
is a guarantee that you'll be protected.
When you arrive, pray to the Glorious One,
that on my departure, he may keep a place for me
          beside you.

6. Gormonda of Montpellier

Greu m'es a durar

It grieves me to endure it when I hear such faithlessness uttered
and spread around. It neither pleases nor satisfies me. For no one
should love a person who denies the source from which all
goodness comes and is born—and which is salvation and faith.
Therefore I shall make plain and clear what weighs upon me.
(stanza 1)

None should marvel if I wage war against a false, ill-taught
person who exerts his power to drive all good, courteous acts
underground, to harry them and lock them up. He behaves too
boldly in speaking ill of Rome, the head and guide of all those on
earth whose souls are virtuous. (stanza 2)

In Rome all good things are perfected. Whoever denies this is out
of his senses and deceives himself. He shall be wrapped in his
shroud and stripped of his pride. May God hear my prayers that
those who wag their evil tongues, young and old, against the
Roman faith may fall from the balancing scales [of justice.]
(stanza 3)

Rome, I think they are fools, all those coarse folk, blind and
shrunken, whose flesh and bones are freighted with base vices
that drag them into the pit. There a fire, stinking and malevolent,

is readied for them. They'll never be unbound from the pack of their sins. (stanza 4)

Rome, it does not please me that a vile man should lash out at you. You are at peace with the virtuous, and each one praises you. As for these fools—their folly made them lose Damietta.[17] But your wisdom makes anyone incontestably wretched and grief-stricken who rises up against you and governs himself badly. (stanza 5)

Rome, truly I know and believe without doubt that you will direct all France to true salvation—yes—as well as the other folk who are willing to aid us. But since Merlin said in his prophecy that the good king Louis would die in Monpensier of a malady of the paunch,[18] these things have become clear. (stanza 6)

They are worse than the Saracens and more false-hearted, these miserable heretics. Whoever favors their estate enters the savage fire of damnation. As for those from Avignon you have put down, it does me good, Rome. Their abusive toll laws[19] have reaped great gains. (stanza 7)

Rome, with reason you have unstintingly redressed many wrongs and opened the gates of justice, though its key had been counterfeit. For with a firm authority you have thrown down foolish scorn. May the angel Michael guide whoever follows your path, and guard him from the inferno. (stanza 8)

Summer and winter, a man should—without contradicting Rome—read the Book, veering from nothing in it. And when he sees the scorn with which Jesus was martyred, let him meditate upon the case if he is a good Christian. And if he has no concern for this, he is completely foolish and vain. (stanza 9)

Rome, the perfidious man with his suspect laws and coarse foolish words seems to be from Toulouse, where trickery has certainly never been put to shame. But within two years the noble Count, rejecting the trickery and the dubious faith, must make restitution for the damage. (stanza 10)

Rome, may the great king, lord of justice, bring great misadventure to the false Toulousans. For they commit such great outrage against his commandments—actions that each one conceals—

and the world is in turmoil. If the Count Raimon relied on them further, I would not think it good. (stanza 11)

Rome, he is overcome, and his strength is worth little who grumbles against you and builds up castle and fortress. For he can't thrust himself up nor climb so high a peak that God will not remember his pride and iniquity. This way he will have to lose his hide and suffer death twice over. (stanza 12)

Rome, I hope that your supremacy and that of France, who truly take no pleasure in evil ways, will force the downfall of pride and heresy. These false, furtive heretics do not fear interdictions, and they do not believe the mysteries—so plentiful are their felonies and wicked thoughts! (stanza 14)

Rome, may the glorious one who pardoned the Magdalene and from whom we hope for a great boon, bring death to the rabid fool who disseminates so much false talk, death to him and his treasures and his wicked heart—in the same way and with pain equal to a heretic's death! (stanza 20)

7. Azalais de Porcairagues

Ar em al freg temps vengut

> Here we've come to the frigid weather
> with ice and snow and mud,
> and the little birds are mute
> for not a single one yearns to sing.
> Dry are the branches of the hedgerows,
> bereft of flower and leaf.
> No nightingale cries there—
> whose song once wakened me in the Maytime of the
>   year.
>
> So unruly is my heart
> that I'm estranged from everyone,
> and I know that my losses

are greater than my gains.
And if my true words falter
the strife from Orange torments me.
That is why I stand distraught—
I've lost my share of serenity.

A lady loves unwisely
if she tries to plead with a powerful man
who ranks higher than a vassal.
If she does so, she's a fool.
They say in Velay
that money doesn't help things along,
and the lady who is chosen by a man of wealth
will in time be gossiped about.

I have a friend of great mettle —
he is superior to any man.
He doesn't treat me with a treacherous heart
for he grants me his love.
And I say to you that I love him in return.
And anyone who says I don't—
may God send him misfortune!
I feel safeguarded from that!

Dear friend, most willingly
I'm bound to you
with courtesy and mannerliness
so long as you demand no scandal of me.
Soon we'll come to the test of battle,
and I'll place myself at your mercy.
You've solemnly vowed
you wouldn't ask me to go astray.

To God's care I entrust Beauregard Castle
and the city of Orange besides—
and Glorieta Palace and the old fortress,
and the lord of Provence,
and all those who wish me well,
and the triumphal arch that bears the marks of
    battle.

I have lost the one for whom all my life
I must forever mourn.

Messenger joyful of heart—
over there in Narbonne, carry
my song, with its ending,
to the Lady who is guided by joy and youth.

8. The Countess of Dia

a. *Ab joi et ab joven m'apais*

By joy and youth I'm made content;
Joy and youth nourish me.
My friend is the most gallant of men,
and so I'm gallant and charming.
And since I'm true to him,
he must be true to me.
I've never strayed from loving him,
nor have I a heart that leads me astray.

It pleases me greatly to know he's most worthy—
    the man I want most to have me.
And to the one who brought us first together,
I pray God may bring great joy.
If anyone should bear him an evil tale,
let him believe nothing but what I bear to him.
People often gather broom twigs
only to be swept with the same broom.

A lady who delights in true worth
should place her delight
in a worthy, valiant cavalier.
Once she understands his valor,
let her dare to love him openly.
And when a lady loves openly,

worthy and gracious people
will say only that she is gracious.

I've chosen a daring and noble man
in whom daring itself is enhanced and ennobled.
Generous, skillful, and knowing,
he possesses wit and knowledge;
I beg him to believe in me;
let no one make him believe
I'd ever fail him
unless I found some failing in him.

Floris, your valor
is known to the valiant and brave.
That is why I ask you now—
if it pleases you—to enfeoff me with your love.

b. *A chantar m'er de so q'ieu no volria*

I must sing of things I would rather not sing.
So much rancor have I against the man whose sweet
    friend I am.
For I love him more than anything.
Pity and courtesy are worth nothing to him.
Neither are my beauty or my merit or my good
    sense.
I'm as trapped and betrayed
as I might have deserved to be, if I hadn't the least
    charm.

But this consoles me—that I have committed no
    injury against you, dear friend, through any fault
    of mine.
I love you more than Seguin loved valor.
It gives me pleasure to vanquish you in loving—
since you, dearest friend, are the most valiant of
    men.
You treat me proudly in words and looks,
while showing gentleness to all the others.

I marvel at your arrogant presence
confronting me; for I have good reason to grieve.
It's unjust that another love tears you from me.
Whatever she may say—however she may welcome
    you—
remember the beginning
of our love. Please God that I'm not at fault
for this parting of ours!

Both the great prowess that lodges in your heart,
and your striking pride make me unhappy.
For I don't know of any woman, near or far,
who wouldn't be drawn to you—if she were ready
    for love.
But you, dear friend, are so knowing, that you ought
    to recognize the truest woman.
Remember the verses we exhanged at our parting.

My merit, my high rank, should count for
    something,
and my beauty, and my faithful heart above all.
And so I'm sending you—there to your great
    house—
this song that serves as my messenger.
I want to know, best and dearest of noble friends,
why you show yourself so fierce, so savage to me.
I don't know if it's arrogance or ill will.

Messenger, I wish you to tell him this besides:
that lofty pride damages many a man!

c. *Estat ai en greu cossirier*

I've been in great anguish
over a noble knight I once had,
and I want everyone to know, for all time,
that I loved him—too much!
Now I see I'm betrayed
because I didn't yield my love to him.

For that I've suffered greatly,
both in my bed and when I'm fully clad.

How I'd yearn to have my knight
in my naked arms for one night!
He would feel a frenzy of delight
only to have me for his pillow.
I'm more in love with him
than Blancheflor ever was with Floris.
To him I'd give my heart, my love,
my mind, my eyes, my life.

Beautiful, gracious, sweet friend,
when shall I hold you in my power?
If I could lie with you for one night,
and give you a kiss of love,
you can be sure I would desire greatly
to grant you a husband's place,
as long as you promised
to do everything I wished!

d. *Fin joi me don' alegranssa*

Perfect joy brings me delight!
This is why I sing the more gaily,
and neither harbor heavy thoughts
nor give a thought
to base and lying slanderers.
For I know they're trying to damage me.—
Their spiteful speech doesn't frighten me—
it makes me live twice as gaily!

I have no faith
in wicked-tongued gossips,
for you can't keep your honor
if you deal with them.
They're in every sense
a cloud that spreads
until the sun loses its rays.
That's why I don't like false people.

And you, jealous people with your barbed tongues,
 don't imagine that I falter,
or that joy and youth don't give me pleasure:
let your grief over that destroy you!

e. *Amics en gran cossirer*

Friend, I'm in great torment
because of you, and in great pain.
Of the ill I'm suffering
I believe that you scarcely feel any.
Why, then, do you play the role of lover,
since you leave all the wretchedness to me?
For the two of us do not play an equal part.

Lady, Love's ministry is such
that when he enchains two lovers,
both of them feel suffering and joy
in their own fashion.
I think—and I'm not a braggart—
that the heart's bitter anguish
has been altogether mine.

Friend, if you had felt a quarter
of the pain that harrows me,
you would well appreciate my burden.
But you scarcely care for the damages I suffer,
and when I can't avoid them,
it's a matter of indifference to you
that I endure both well-being and woe.

Lady, since there are slanderers
who have reft me of my sense and breath
and who are warring bitterly against us,
I am leaving you—not out of true desire—
but because I'm not beside you. Their braying
deals us such a mortal blow
that we cannot taste a day of joy together.

Friend, I feel don't feel grateful to you
that these evils prevent

you from seeing me—when I long for you.
If you set about guarding my good name
more than I myself wish,
I'll consider you more zealously loyal
than a knight of St. John the Hospitaler.

Lady, I strongly fear that
I'll lose my gold and you'll lose the arena,
and that through the gossip of these slanderers
our love will be spoiled.
That's why I must be more guarded
than you by St. Martial,
for you are the thing of greatest value to me.

Friend, you are so careless
in matters of love
that I think you have changed
from the cavalier you once were.
I feel I must say this,
for you seem to be thinking of someone else,
since my sorrow means nothing to you.

Lady, may I never again carry a sparrow hawk,
or hunt with falcon,
if—since you first gave me complete joy—
I have ever desired another woman.
I'm not such a liar,
but envious and disloyal people
have made me seem that way and have maligned
    me.

Friend, should I have such trust in you
that I can believe you'll always be faithful?

Lady, from now on I will be faithful to you,
and I'll never again think of another woman.

9. Anonymous Dance Song

Coindeta sui, si cum n'ai greu cossire

I'm lovely but miserable
because of a husband I don't want or desire.

I'll tell you why I'm someone else's lover:
     (I'm lovely but miserable)
I'm fresh and young, I've a dainty body,
     (I'm lovely but miserable)
and I ought to have a husband who can make me
    glad,
someone I can play and laugh with.
     (I'm lovely but miserable
      because of a husband I don't want or desire).

God knows I'm not the least in love with him.
     (I'm lovely but miserable)
I've little wish to make love with him.
     (I'm lovely but miserable)
I'm filled with shame to look at him.
I wish that death would do him in.
     (I'm lovely but miserable
      because of a husband I don't want or desire).

But let me say one thing:
     (I'm lovely but miserable)
this friend of mine makes it up to me in love,
     (I'm lovely but miserable)
I indulge in fondest, sweetest hopes;
I cry and sigh when I don't see or gaze at him.
     (I'm lovely but miserable
      because of a husband I don't want or desire).

And let me say another thing:
     (I'm lovely but miserable)
since my friend has loved me a long time,
     (I'm lovely but miserable)
I'll indulge in love

and fondest hopes for the one I crave.
    (I'm lovely but miserable
    because of a husband I don't want or desire)
I've made a pretty dance song to this tune,
    (I'm lovely but miserable)
and I ask everyone to sing it, far and wide,
    (I'm lovely but miserable)
And let all learned ladies sing it too,
about my friend whom I love and long for.
    (I'm lovely but miserable
    because of a husband I don't want or desire).

NOTES

1. Pierre Bec, *Burlesque et Obscénité chez les Troubadours* (Paris: Stock, 1984), p. 7.

2. Matilda Tomaryn Bruckner, p. 875, "Fictions of the Female Voice: The Women Troubadours," *Speculum* 67 (October, 1992): 865–891.

3. René Lavaud and René Nelli, eds., *Les Troubadours* (Bruges: Desclée de Brouwer, 1960), vol. I: 881, lines 4574–4579.

4. As Jean-Charles Huchet points out, in "Les Femmes Troubadours ou La Voix Critique," *Littérature* 51 (1983): 65:

> Ailas!—Que plans?—Mor mi—De que?—D'amor—
> Per cui?—Per vos—Qu'en puesc?—Guarir!—
> Conssi?—Per engin—Pren li—Pres l'ai—Es cal?—
> Iretz!—Es on?—Als banz—Cora?—Jorn breu e gent—
> Plas mi.

5. Angelica Rieger, "Was Bieris de Romans Lesbian? Women's Relations with Each Other in the World of the Troubadours," in William Paden, *The Voice of the Trobairitz: Perspectives on the Women Troubadours* (Philadelphia: U of Pennsylvania P, 1989), pp. 73–94; Pierre Bec, "Un poème homosexuel? Bieris de Romans," in *Burlesque et Obscénité*, pp. 197–200.

6. Danielle Jacquart and Claude Thomasset, *Sexuality and Medicine in the Middle Ages*, trans. Matthew Adamson (Princeton UP,

1988), p. 124, citing from the *Book of Conversation with Friends on the Intimate Relations Between Lovers in the Domain of the Science of Sexuality.* The author is a Jew converted to Islam, as-Samau'al ibn Yahâ (d. 1180).

7. Information on Lombarda and Bernart is drawn from John Hine Mundy, "Urban Society and Culture: Toulouse and Its Region," in Robert L. Benson and Giles Constable, with Carol D. Lanham, eds., *Renaissance and Renewal in the Twelfth Century* (Harvard UP, 1982), p. 245. Mundy points out that the title of "lady" is no indication of rank; in written records at the time, the title *domina* or *na* would apply to women of every social level.

8. The legalistic basis of troubadour lyric is discussed in R. Howard Bloch, "The Text as Inquest," Chapter 4 in *Medieval French Literature and the Law* (Berkeley and Los Angeles: U of California P, 1977), pp. 162–189.

9. John Hine Mundy, *Men and Women at Toulouse in the Age of the Cathars* (Toronto: Pontifical Institute of Medieval Studies, 1990), p. 64; also John Hine Mundy, "Urban Society and Culture: Toulouse and Its Region." Both works provide the information about Toulouse in this section. On Figueira, see also Karen Wilk Klein, *The Partisan Voice: A Study of the Political Lyric in France and Germany, 1180–1230* (The Hague: Mouton, 1971). For a recent edition and discussion of Gormonda's poem, see Katharina Städtler, "The *Sirventes* by Gormonda de Monpeslier," in William Paden, *The Voice of the Trobairitz,* pp. 129–155.

10. Mundy, "Urban Society and Culture," pp. 230, 232–233.

11. Mundy, *Men and Women at Toulouse,* p. 2.

12. Städtler ("The *Sirventes* by Gormonda") prints Figueira's and Gormonda's lyrics side by side, and translates Gormonda's.

13. On a full study of Azalais, see Aimo Sakari, "Azalais de Porcairagues, le Joglar de Raimbaut d'Orange," in *Neuphilologische Mitteilungen* 50 (1949): 23–43; 56–87; 174–197. Information about Azalais and her acquaintance comes chiefly from this study. The poem is also edited and translated, pp. 184–187.

14. "Milady of Narbona" was reputed to be prudent, powerful, and energetic. The troubadour Guiraut de Borneil, a friend of Raimbaut's, referred a question to her about an impetuous lover.

15. This is Aimo Sakari's reading, "Azalais de Porcairagues," p. 181.

16. There is an excellent modern photograph of the Roman triumphal arch of Orange in James J. Wilhelm, *Lyrics of the Middle Ages*

(New York: Garland, 1990), p. 44, accompanying the chapter "Provençal Lyrics" (pp. 45–118).

17. Damietta, at the Nile Delta, was the object of the Fifth Crusade (1218–1221). After the crusaders had besieged Damietta for seventeen months, they had to give it up to the Moslems. Figueira imputes the loss of Damietta to the Pope. Gormonda blames Rome's enemies, perhaps because she didn't want to accuse the dawdling Frederic II.

18. Did Merlin make such a prophecy? Louis died in Montpensier in Auvergne of a dysentery that beset the whole army while they laid siege to Avignon. There seems to be a pun on *pansa* (paunch, or belly) and the *pensier* element of Montpensier.

19. There is a reference in Städtler, "The *Sirventes* by Gormonda," p. 144, explaining the papal reprimand against a count of Toulouse for raising road tolls and tariffs.

FURTHER READING

Alais, Iselda, and Carenza. Pierre Bec, ed. and trans. *Burlesque et Obscénité chez les Troubadours: Pour une approche du contre-texte médiéval*, pp. 201–205. Paris: Stock, 1984.

Anonymous song. "Coindeta sui, si cum n'ai greu cossir." In Kàrl Appel, *Provenzalische Chrestomathie*. Leipzig, 1895; 6th ed. 1932, repr. Geneva, 1974.

Azalais de Porcairagues. Martín de Riquer, ed. and trans. *Los Trovadores: Historia Literaria y Textos*. 3 vols. I: 460–462. Barcelona: Planeta, 1975.

Pierre Bec. "'Trobairitz' et chansons de femme. Contribution à la connaissance du lyrisme féminin au moyen âge." *Cahiers de civilisation médiévale* 22 (1979): 235–262.

Bieris de Romans. Pierre Bec, ed. and trans. *Burlesque et Obscénité chez les Troubadours*. Paris: Editions Stock, 1984, pp. 197–200.

Meg Bogin, trans. *The Women Troubadours*. New York: Paddington P, 1976.

J. Boutiére and A.H. Schultz. *Biographie des troubadours*. 2nd ed. Paris, 1973.

William E. Burgwinkle, trans. *"Razos" and Troubadour Songs.* New York: Garland, 1990.

Comtessa de Dia. Gabrielle Kussler-Ratyé, ed. "Les chansons de la comtesse Béatrix de Dia," *Archivum Romanicum* 1 (1917): 161–182.

———. Martín de Riquer, ed. *Los Trovadores: Historia Literaria y Textos.* 3 vols. I:452–454; II:794–802. Barcelona: Planeta, 1975.

Glynnis M. Cropp. *Le vocabulaire courtois des troubadours de l'époque classique.* Geneva: Droz, 1975.

Doris Earnshaw. *The Female Voice in Medieval Romance Lyric.* New York: Peter Lang, 1988.

Margarita Egan, trans. *The Vidas of the Troubadours.* New York: Garland, 1984.

Frederick Goldin. "The Mirror in the Provençal Lyric." In *The Mirror of Narcissus in the Courtly Love Lyric,* pp. 69–106. Ithaca: Cornell UP, 1967.

Gormonda de Montpellier. Katharina Städtler, ed. and trans. In William Paden, ed., *The Voice of the Trobairitz:* Perspectives on the Women Troubadours, pp. 130–137. Philadelphia: U of Pennsylvania P, 1989.

Laura Kendrick. *The Game of Love: Troubadour Word Play.* Berkeley: U of California P, 1988.

Lombarda. Tilde Sankovitch, ed. and trans. In William Paden, ed., *The Voice of the Trobairitz,* pp. 187–188.

Christine Mouratoff. "Les Femmes troubadours: femmes et musique." *Action Musicale* (1983): 18–19, 22–30.

Linda Paterson. *Troubadours and Eloquence.* Oxford: Clarendon P, 1975.

Angelica Rieger, ed. *Trobairitz: Der Beitrag der Frau in der altokzitanischen höfischen Lyrik.* Tübingen: Niemeyer, 1991.

Oskar Schultz-Gora, ed. *Die provenzalischen Dichterinnen.* Leipzig: G. Fock, 1888. Rpt. Geneva: Slatkine, 1975.

Marianne Shapiro. "The Provençal *Trobairitz* and the Limits of Courtly Love." *Signs* 3 (Spring 1978): 560–571.

Robert A. Taylor. *La littérature occitane du moyen âge. Bibliographie sélective et critique.* Toronto: U of Toronto P, 1977.

Tibors. Schultz-Gora, ed. *Die provenzalischen Dichterinnen,* p. 25. Leipzig: G. Fock, 1888. Rpt. Geneva: Slatkine, 1975.

Jules Véran, ed and trans. *Les poétesses provençales.* Paris: Librarie Aristide Quillet, 1946.

Stephen Weinberger. "The Status of Women in Medieval Provence." *Medieval Perspectives* 3 (1988): 133–147.

James J. Wilhelm. *Seven Troubadours: The Creators of Modern Verse*. University Park: Pennsylvania State UP, 1978.

CHAPTER 12

"Marie Is My Name: I Am of France"

Marie de France (twelfth century)

Marie was the first of the great and well-educated French women writers, a nobly born woman who lived and wrote in England during the latter part of the twelfth century, when Anglo-Norman was still the language in dominant use. The period is now recognized as a renaissance of learning and literary ferment, along with a growing sense of the individual. Marie had connections with the Anglo-Norman court, where her work was evidently commissioned. She dedicated one book to King Henry II of England, and another to a Count William, perhaps William Marshal, Earl of Pembroke, called the "flower of chivalry."

The author's precise identity eludes us. She is alleged to have been Marie de Champagne, a daughter of Eleanor of Aquitaine. Or she may have been Marie of Boulogne, King Stephen's daughter, who was first an abbess of Ramsey and eventually married to Matieu of Flanders. Another suggestion makes her the wife of Henry I of Champagne, or perhaps she was an abbess of Shaftesbury, half-sister to King Henry II, hence an illegitimate daughter of Geoffrey Plantagenet. Or a daughter of Waleran II, Count of Meulan? These and other Maries have been proposed.

Instead of remaining conventionally anonymous, Marie signs her first name in her three books to assure her authorship—in the opening *lai* of *Guigemar*, at the close of her translation of *St. Patrick's Purgatory*, and in the epilogue to her *Fables*: "Listen, lords, to what Marie says," "I, Marie, have included the Book of Purgatory in a romance," and "I will name myself in order to be remembered: Marie is my name, I am of France. Perhaps several clerks will declare my work is theirs. I do not

277

want them to take credit for it!" Each of the three works belongs
to a different literary genre: the *Lais* consist of a dozen brief tren-
chant narratives of love; *Isopet*, 102 fables based on Aesop, are
short exemplary tales about animals, things, or people; and the
Espurgatoire Seint Patriz is a translation from a Latin work by the
English Cistercian Henry of Saltrey of an underworld and paradisal journey, earlier than Dante's *Commedia*, describing the
perilous moral adventures of a knight named Owein, who
follows the example of St. Patrick's visits.

Although much of the literature of the twelfth century
dwelled on love in all its heavenly and earthly manifestations,
Marie writes of love from a secular, aristocratic, and chiefly female viewpoint, showing herself influenced by the amatory cult
abstracted from the lyrics of Provence and northern France. But
where some of the male troubadours might depict women as
august and unattainable figures, Marie, like the *trobairitz*, explores the emotional tenderness and susceptibility of women
under the stresses of love. The voices of her female protagonists,
though less polished, resemble those of the troubadour women.

Love for Marie's women comes as a sudden, unquestioned
emotion to which they surrender with no reluctance. It may be
adulterous love, its outcome may be unpredictable. These heroines are impassioned and impenitent, heedless of nagging moral-
ists. Excess does not worry them. They embrace the men they
desire without coyness, without demanding the time-consuming
chivalric services of courtly love. The well-brought-up young
woman who falls in love with the handsome Milun sends for
him and lets him know what she wants. He is glad to provide it.
Over and over the two meet secretly in an orchard outside her
room. "Milun came so often and made love to her so often that
the girl became pregnant."

Love's simplicity and power are allowed to guide Marie's
women, who follow their hearts and bodies unhesitatingly.
 Individuals and relationships are what count, not conventional
behavior. Marie rejects any corpus of rules where love is
concerned. Her lovers are individuals caught in straits peculiar
to them.

Marie also reacts in her writing against the currently fashionable genre of *chanson de geste*, epic celebrations of battle, the

play of weaponry and male valor, the brawling of barons, and devotion to (or rebellion against) a warlord in the interests of history and glory. Instead of male characters who are heroes, or heroic villains, Marie's protagonists tend to be luckless, landless soldiers of fortune, struggling against the actual hazards and miseries of the profession of arms, dragging through lives of restless raiding and tourneying. Marie repudiates the mentality of the aggressive male military world, finding in it the sources of feminine unhappiness. Instead of praising boisterous heroic action, she attunes her talents to probe the psychological nuances of men and women who are subject to the demands of epic and romance.

Marie enjoyed wide fame as a writer, not only in her immediate circle but abroad, where her *lais* were translated into Latin, Italian, German, Old Norse, and English. She knew her powers and she was well aware of her detractors. In the opening of her first *lai*, just after giving her name, Marie comments shrewdly about those who sneer at her success:

> When there is a man or woman of distinguished reputation living in an area, people who envy their gifts often spread hateful gossip about them in order to demean them. They start behaving like malicious dogs, base cowards who nip spitefully at others.

> I don't ever plan to give up because of that. If chatterboxes and slanderers want to do me an evil turn, it's their right. Let them carp! (*Guigemar*, lines 7–17)

One such disgruntled rival, annoyed by Marie's popular appeal, pays her a wonderful backhanded compliment. The author, Denis Piramus, a specialist in miracles and hagiography and a regular at the court of Eleanor of Aquitaine and Henry II, complains that audiences—women especially—admire the *lais* of "dame Marie." The *lais* are, the critic maintains, "patently untrue in content, though artfully composed. Court audiences love them." Noble folk enjoy delightful stories, continues Denis, because such stories "dismiss and thrust aside sadness, tedium, and weariness of heart. They make people forget their anger and banish irksome thoughts."

"*lais*" *writer*

The *lais* do entertain. They are full of marvels and surreal elements like magic potions, humans who change into animals, visitors from another world, and a curiously decked ship that conveys a young man to his destined mistress. But the *lais* offer more; they are also remarkable for their psychological interest: Marie introduces characters whom she identifies as admirable and then allows them to fall into problem situations that force them to reveal their deeper, crasser natures. She realistically explores the initiation into adulthood as well as the dilemmas and hardships created by different kinds of love. Adolescent sexuality, tenderness, lust, jealousy, married love, adultery, and sacrifice are matters that she reports with her characteristically understated simplicity and economy, leaving the reader to make a final judgment.

The *lais* often center on a symbolic object, such as the nightingale in the poem translated below. The enamored wife has invented the nightingale as a pretext for her nocturnal absences from her husband's bed. Above all, the nightingale is her lover himself, as she conceives him. *He* is her reason for leaving her husband's side.

Birds figure often in Marie's narratives. The nightingale develops as a figure full of meaning. Not unsurprisingly, a real nightingale does materialize in the moonlight. Its song, pathetic death, and costly embalming offer a rich, concentrated comment on the fantastic and doomed eroticism that is being celebrated. At the same time the nightingale functions realistically to reveal the husband's brutality, both when he kills the bird and when he throws its bloody body at his wife. From the viewpoint of love as a religious devotion, the man and woman are love's martyrs, with the blood of the innocent bird staining the woman's gown. In a romance context, however, the sullying of a woman's skirts is both a potent visual image and a deadly insult, as in Chrétien's *Perceval* and Robert Biket's *Lay of the Horn*, in which a clumsy courtier spills or throws wine on a lady's dress. In *Laüstic* the bloodstained gown adds up to a spectacle that is sexually charged.

During the sorrowing calm after the husband's fury and displaced sexual outburst by hurling the phallic bird, the lovers' quelled emotions are laid together with the bird's little embalmed corpse, enfolded in a silk that is embroidered and inscribed. The lover honors the bird by placing it in a richly gemmed coffer, the whole constituting a sacred artifact like a saint's body in a reliquary.

The *lai* of *Chevrefoil*, literally "goatleaf," represents the lovers' plight in the poignant central image of the honeysuckle vine that twines itself around a hazel branch for their mutual sustenance. Marie is particularly succinct in this *lai*, for she can count on her audience's familiarity with the tale of Tristan and Isolt, the narrative's adulterous tragic lovers.

In the several versions of this celebrated romance triangle, the noble harper Tristan has recommended the Irish princess Isolt the Blond, as a bride for his uncle, King Mark of Cornwall. Tristan escorts Isolt as they sail back to Cornwall. But on shipboard Tristan and Isolt inadvertently drink a fateful love potion that Isolt's mother has prepared for the bride and groom. Surprised by passion, Tristan and Isolt become lovers at sea, understanding that they must now be forever bound to each other.

Still, Isolt must marry Mark, and she enlists the help of her maid Brangane to deceive the new husband. Loyal to Isolt, Brangane sleeps with Mark on the wedding night, offering her own virginity in order to shield Isolt. The lovers continue their clandestine meetings, while hostile courtiers gossip and try to entrap them. At last Mark banishes the two. For a time Tristan and Isolt live in the wilderness before they are allowed to return to court. As their trials multiply, Tristan leaves the court alone in an attempt to start his life anew elsewhere. However, their love compels them to find each other again, as they do in the brief design of Marie's *lai*.

Marie names Tristan, but calls his mistress simply "the Queen." Exiled from the court, Tristan hopes for a meeting with her when he learns that the court will be passing by. Glancing references are made to the king's invidious barons and to the fidelity of Brangane, but none to the love potion. Perhaps Marie felt that to attribute desire to an aphrodisiac would depersonalize the relationship. Although Marie and her audience knew that Tristan and Isolt were doomed to die in each other's arms, unable to live apart, Marie allows Isolt to voice the false but bolstering hope of a reconciliation at court. The focus in this *lai* is on a brief, intense encounter in which delight and sorrow mingle. As in *Laüstic*, fleeting emotions find permanence in the form of an artifact, here the humble one of a wood fragment, carved and incised.

In various romances, Tristan enjoyed the reputation of being a poet, harper, linguist, and storyteller. Even his aptitude for the hunt in Gottfried von Strassburg's *Tristan* shows him a master of a complex terminology. His knightly investiture in that same romance consists of raiment suggestive of poetry and the literary arts. While he is also a noble fighter, as a hero he represents a departure from the purely fighting knight of epic. He is the epitome of the *miles literatus*, the poet knight.

In Marie's *lai*, Tristan finds himself alone, deprived of the civilized resources of pen and parchment. Tristan the poet then uses materials at hand to create an object that will symbolize mutual love. First he writes his name. Then laboriously he scrapes on a piece of wood with a knife point—apt emblem of the poet's toil—to say in a great many words how he has loitered and hoped. Finally he hits upon a beautifully balanced, compressed inscription: "Neither you without me, nor me without you."

To be literate often meant writing skillfully of love and its lore. Tristan proves even more economical a poet when he transmutes the enlaced flora, objects found in nature, into a speaking artifact. In order to speak, however, the plants must be torn from their favorable habitat and allowed to lament their bereft state.

Marie shows a strong affection for the written word, which she often weaves in as a motif in the narrative. Like women throughout the Middle Ages, Marie's heroines send and receive letters, as they do in *Chevrefoil*, *Milun*, and *Les Deus Amanz*. Writing as she did for an Anglo-Norman audience, Marie likes to explain titles and words by giving both the English and the French. Conspicuous in both the *lais* translated below is the sense that a story's vitality is in the verbalizing. Words embroidered on silk wrap the nightingale's body and the lovers' dead hopes. In "The Honeysuckle" Marie reminds her hearers often of the story's telling (*dire*), recounting (*cunter*), and writing (*écrire*). At the close Tristan eventually renders the incident and the artifact in the

form of a new *lai*, while Marie at a further remove composes the
lai before us, achieving the ultimate distillation of the lovers'
turmoil. In many ways Marie's *Chevrefoil* addresses the poet's
loving to write about love.

Oral delivery was traditionally built into the *lai*. Marie
frames *Laüstic* with two allusions to Breton singers, harpers, and
storytellers. She credits these itinerant performers, as do others,
with having brought their short, sung narratives from the French
province of Brittany to England. The word *lai*, like *lied*, indicates
a musical composition meant to be sung to an accompaniment.
Because the Bretons are thought to have migrated from England
to France many centuries earlier during the Saxon invasions,
these narrative *lais* seem to preserve ancient British and Celtic
legends that over a long period acquired French traits and settings. No "Breton *lais*" exist today, inasmuch as they always depended on oral performance. But there some thirty-six poems
that call themselves *lais* and possess their features. Marie tells us
in several of her *lais* that she has heard these sung, and that hers
are written versions.

Marie's writing disp*lais* none of the rambling chattiness so
common in medieval narrative. She goes straight to the heart of a
situation, making of the *lai* a genre comparable to the short story
rather than to the novel, which medieval romance resembles.
Her poetry is taut and bare, even strenuously so, and marked by
a certain brusque cynicism that saves it from sentimentality.
Despite their brevity the *lais* are richly detailed as to foreground;
events seem to float in an unspecified space that is left vague and
mysterious.

While the *lais* leave the reader to reflect upon possible
meanings, the even shorter fables from *Isopet* provide a moral
conclusion that is often allegorical. Many show Marie's preoccu-
pation with feudalism, chivalry, and the quest for honor and
power—in short, aristocratic concerns. Certain of them deplore
human imperfection. The fables translated at the end of this
chapter give a harsher, earthier view of love than is found in the
lais.

Although the first fable is about a knight and a worthy
woman and the next two about peasant couples, both demon-
strate the fleeting nature of fidelity, and the realities of adult

sexuality. The first, an old Milesian tale that has an analogue in the *Satyricon* of Petronius and becomes known as "the Widow of Ephesus,"[1] claims to illustrate the way of the world generally, but like the second it really singles out the lustfulness of women. The second and third fables contain a commonplace found in other narratives, notably Chaucer's *Merchant's Tale*, that a woman caught in adultery will usually extricate herself with a canny, farfetched answer. There is even a resemblance between these shrewd wives and the well-bred wife in *Laüstic*: challenged, she quickly produces the alibi of the nightingale. An examination of the full range of Marie's works will reveal her linking motifs and themes in works that seem on the surface to be dissimilar.

1. The Nightingale: Laüstic

I am going to tell you an adventure about which the Breton singers have composed a lay. It's called "Laüstic"; I believe that is what they call it in their country. It's "Rossignol" in French, and in plain English "Nightingale."

In the Breton country of Saint-Malo there was a famous city. Two knights were living there in two strongly fortified houses. It was the excellence of these two barons that gave the city its good name. One had married a wife who was well-behaved, courteous, and elegant. It was wonderful to see how she arrayed herself to advantage in decorous keeping with the custom and style. The other young man was a bachelor knight, unmarried, well-known among his peers for his bold exploits, his worthiness, and his readiness to conduct himself honorably toward people. He took part in tournaments and spent money lavishly. He was generous with what he had.

He fell in love with his neighbor's wife. He begged so hard and pleaded with her, and he was so excellent a man, that she came to love him more than anything in the world. It was because of the good things she heard about him and because he lived close to her. They loved each other prudently and discreetly. They took care to conceal their behavior and to guard against being perceived, disturbed, or suspected.

They succeeded in this since they lived near each other. Their houses, with all the chambers and dungeons, were in close proximity. There was no barrier, nothing to separate them except a high wall of darkened stone. From the chambers where the lady slept she was able, when she stood at the window, to converse with her friend on the other side, and he with her. They were able to exchange their love tokens by tossing or throwing them. There was nothing to mar their pleasure; the two of them savored their happiness even though they could not come together to fulfill their desires. For the lady was closely guarded when her husband traveled throughout the country. Day and night their sole recourse was to talk together. No one could prevent them from going to the window to gaze at each other.

For a long time they were in love, until summer came, when woods and fields grow green again and orchards bloom. Small birds sing sweetly from the flowering treetops. It's not surprising that whoever longs for love can think of this and nothing else. I will speak to you candidly about this knight: he yielded entirely to his feelings, and the lady did, too, both in words and looks.

At night when the moon shone and her husband lay sleeping, she would often steal from his side; with her cloak wrapped about her she would go to the window, for she knew her friend would be at his. This is how they lived, gazing at each other for most of the night. They derived pleasure from seeing each other, denied as they were a greater bliss. She stayed so often at the window and would get up out of bed so often at night, that her husband lost his temper, and more than once demanded to know the reason why she rose this way and where she went. "My husband," replied the lady, "anyone who hasn't heard the nightingale sing has not experienced joy in the world. That is why I go to stand at the window. I hear its sweet voice in the night, and it seems a very great pleasure to me. So much delight does it give me, and so intensely do I long to hear it, that I cannot close my eyes to sleep."

When her husband heard what she said, he laughed with angry contempt. An idea occurred to him to trap the nightingale. He ordered the household servants to work on traps, nets, and snares and to set them in the orchard. There wasn't a hazel or a chestnut tree anywhere that was not hung with nets or smeared with lime. Eventually they captured the nightingale. They took it alive to the lord, who was overjoyed when he saw it. He went to the lady's chambers. "Madam, where are you? Come now, let us talk. I've used birdlime to catch this nightingale, the cause of your nightlong vigils. Now you'll be able to slumber in peace, as it will never bother you again."

In hearing her husband speak this way, she grew anxious and distressed. She asked him to give her the nightingale, but in a fit of perversity he killed it. He villainously broke its neck with his two hands. He threw the dead bird at his wife so that the front of her gown was bloodied over her breast. Then he went out of the room.

The lady took the little corpse and softly wept over it. She cursed those who had treacherously caught the nightingale and set the traps and snares, for they had killed a great joy. "Alas," she murmured, "how miserable it is for me! I'll not be able to get up at night and stand by the window where I've been accustomed to see my friend. I know one thing—he will think that I've swerved from my love. I must do something. I will have the nightingale sent to him and he will know what has happened."

In a length of satin embroidered and inscribed in letters of gold thread she wrapped the body of the tiny bird. She called one of her servants and entrusted him with a message to her friend. He arrived at the knight's house on his lady's behalf, saluted him, delivered the message, and offered him the nightingale. When the messenger had said and shown everything, and the knight had listened carefully, the adventure filled him with sadness. But what he decided was neither hesitant nor vengeful. He had a little coffer made, fashioned not of iron or steel but of pure gold ornamented with precious stones. It had a closely fitting lid. In it he placed the nightingale. Then he had the chest sealed. He carried it with him always.

This adventure became the subject of a story, for it couldn't remain concealed very long. The Bretons have made a lay about it which they call *Laüstic*.

2. The Honeysuckle: Chevrefoil

It pleases me very much, and I really wish to recount to you the true story of the "lai" they call *Chevrefoil*, and why it was written and how it came about. Many people have told me the story and recounted it to me, and I have also found it written down. It's about Tristan and the Queen and their love which was so strong that they suffered greatly, and they both died on the same day because of it.

King Mark was embittered, outraged against his nephew, Tristan, and drove him from the land because of his love for the Queen. Tristan went back to his own country, to his birthplace in South Wales. He spent a year there, unable to return without risking death and ruin.

Don't be surprised. Anyone who loves most faithfully will grieve and grow pensive if he cannot have what he desires. Tristan grieved, he grew melancholy, and so he left his own country and went straight to Cornwall, where the Queen lived. He hid alone in the forest, for he did not want anyone to see him. At evening he emerged when it was time to seek lodging, and he stayed with peasants and poor people. He asked them for news of the King's doings. They told him they'd heard that the barons had been summoned to Tintagel where the King wished to hold court. Everyone would be in attendance for Pentecost. There would be rejoicing and festivity, and the Queen would also be there.

Tristan heard this news with great joy. The Queen would not be able to journey to Tintagel without his seeing her pass by. The day the King set forth, Tristan returned to the wood by the road that he knew the royal company would have to take.

He split a hazel branch in half, and whittled it on four sides to make it square. Having prepared the wood, he inscribed his name on it with his knife. If the Queen saw it (for this had happened once before and she had perceived it then), she would know that the hazel wand came from her beloved.

The sum of what he wrote and said was to tell her that he had been there a long time, he had waited and tarried in the hope of learning how he might see her, since he could not live without her.

For the two of them it was like the honeysuckle spiraling itself around the hazelwood, the two enlaced and grown completely together. Together they can live, but if anyone tries to tear them apart, the hazel swiftly dies and the honeysuckle too. "Sweet friend, so it is with us: neither you without me, nor me without you." *Bele amie, si est de nus—ne vus sanz mei, ne mei sanz vus!*

The Queen rode on horseback along the road. She glanced at a hill slope and noticed the little branch and saw what it was. She recognized all the letters. She ordered the knights who escorted her, those who rode alongside with her, to stop. She wished to dismount and rest. They obeyed her command and she moved far away from her attendants. To her side she summoned her maidservant, Brenguein, who was very faithful.

At a short distance from the road she found in the forest the man she loved more than any living person, and they shared great joy. He felt at ease as he spoke, and she told him her desires. She let him know how he might become reconciled to the King, and how unhappy the King was that he had banished Tristan because of the accusations against him. Then she had to leave, and she parted from her beloved. But when it was time to go, they both wept. Tristan returned to Wales to await his uncle's orders.

Because of the joy he had shared with his beloved when he saw her, and because of what he had written (for the Queen had said he should) and his desire to remember the words, Tristan —who was an excellent musician on the harp—composed a new "lai." Briefly I'll name it for you: The English call it *Goteleaf* and the French name it *Chevrefoil*. I have told you the truth of the "lai" I've recited for you.

3. The Widow and the Knight

There's a story written about a man who had died and was buried. His wife mourned bitterly over his grave both night and day. Now in the vicinity a robber had been hanged for his crime. A knight who was a kinsman of his cut down the body and buried it. But a proclamation had been issued throughout the land that anyone who took down the robber's body would be given the same sentence. If discovered, he would be hanged.

The knight didn't know what to do to save himself, for it was widely known that he was a relative of the hanged man. He went directly to the cemetery where that worthy woman was weeping copiously for her lord. The knight spoke to her very sweetly, urging her to be consoled; in fact, he would be very happy if she would love him. This worthy woman regarded him with immense joy, and said that she would do as he wished.

Then the knight explained the plight he was in because of the robber he had taken down from the scaffold. If she couldn't give him some assistance, he would be forced to leave the country. The worthy woman responded, "Let us unbury my lord here, and if he is suspended there where the other one was, it will never be noticed. The living man must be rescued by the dead, for it is to the living that we look for solace."

The moral of this story makes it clear to us how much the dead can expect from the living. So false is this world and bent on pleasure.

4. The Peasant Who Saw Another Man with His Wife

There's a story about a peasant who lurked inside his hut and spied on another man whom he saw in his bed taking his pleasure with his own wife.

"Ah!" he said, "what have I seen?"

Then the wife replied to him. "What *did* you see, fair sir, sweet friend?"

"Another man, that's what I think! He had you in bed and was embracing you!"

The wife retorted, very angrily, "I know very well, and haven't any doubt that this is your old folly. You stick to a lie as if it was the truth!"

"I saw it," he said, "I have to believe it."

She said, "You're mad if you believe that everything you see is true."

She took him by the hand and led him to a basin full of water. She made him look inside it. Then she started to ask him what he saw there. He said to her that he saw his own image.

"All the same," she said, "you're not inside that basin with all your clothes on. What you see is an illusion. You ought not to believe your eyes, which often tell lies!"

The peasant said, "I repent! Each person had better believe and know what his wife tells him to see, instead of what false eyes see. These things can deceive him and lead him astray."

By this exemplum we understand that common sense and cleverness are more helpful to many a person than having riches and relatives.

5. The Peasant Who Saw His Wife with Her Lover

I want to tell you about a peasant who saw his wife heading for the woods with her lover. He went after them, but they escaped and were hidden in the bushes. The peasant went back home, furious. Later he began to harass and abuse his wife. She asked him why he spoke to her that way. Her husband replied that he had seen her lecherous friend accompany her to the woods to shame and dishonor her.

"Husband," she said, "please, for the love of God, tell me the truth. Did you see a man go with me? Don't hide anything!"

"I saw him," he said, "go into the woods."

"Heavens," said she, "I'm done for! I'm going to die tomorrow, or even today. Such a thing happened to my grandmother and my mother too just before they died—I saw it myself. Other people saw it plainly. Two young men were seen leading them away, and no one else was with them. Now I know I'm close to my death. Husband, send for all my relatives, for we'll have to divide up our belongings. I mustn't remain here in the world. I'll have to take my share of the property and retire to a convent."

The peasant heard this and cried out, begging her forgiveness: "Let it be, my dear friend! Don't leave me this way! I was lying about what I saw."

"Wait," she said, "I have to think of the welfare of my soul,
especially with this great disgrace you've done me by inventing
such a tall story. You'll be bringing it up constantly, saying I've
viciously strayed. You'll have to swear absolutely, in such a way
that our relatives will be convinced, that you did not see any
man with me. Then you must swear on your faith that you will
never utter another word on the subject or reproach me with it."

"Gladly, lady," he acquiesced. Together they went to a
chapel, and he swore to everything she wanted and more
besides.

Because of this tale, men accuse women of deviousness.
You can see how false they are—they're craftier than the Devil!

NOTES

1. The versions of this literary motif, including Marie's, are discussed by Heather M. Arden, "Grief, Widowhood, and Women's Sexuality in Medieval French Literature," pp. 305–319, in Louise Mirrer, ed.,
*Upon My Husband's Death: Widows in the Literature and Histories of
Medieval Europe* (Ann Arbor: U of Michigan P, 1992).

FURTHER READING

Glyn S. Burgess. *Marie de France: An Analytical Bibliography.* London:
     Grant and Cutler, 1977.

————. *Marie de France: An Analytical Biography.* Supplement. London:
     Grant and Cutler, 1986.

————. *The "Lais" of Marie de France: Text and Context.* Athens, Georgia:
     U of Georgia P, 1987.

Paula Clifford. *Marie de France: Lais.* London: Grant and Cutler, 1982.

Marie de France. Glyn S. Burgess and Keith Busby, trans. *The Lais of Marie de France*. New York: Penguin, 1986.

———. Alfred Ewart, ed. *Lais*. Oxford, 1947. Repr. 1965.

———. Michael Curley, ed. and trans. with introduction. *St. Patrick's Purgatory: A Poem by Marie de France*. Binghamton: State University of New York P, 1993.

———. Robert Hanning and Joan Ferrante. *The Lais of Marie de France*. Trans., with an introduction and notes. New York: Dutton, 1978.

———. Jeanne Lods, ed. *Les Lais de Marie de France*. Paris: Champion, 1959.

———. Mary Lou Martin. *The Fables of Marie de France*. Trans., with text. Birmingham: Summa, 1984.

———. Jean Rychner, ed. *Les Lais de Marie de France*. Paris, 1966; 2nd ed. 1981.

———. Harriet Spiegel, ed. and trans. *Marie de France: Fables*. Toronto: U of Toronto P, 1987.

———. Karl Warnke, ed. *Die Lais der Marie de France*. Halle, 1885; 2nd ed., 1900; 3rd ed. 1925. Repr. Geneva, 1974.

———. Karl Warnke, ed. *Die Fablen der Marie de France*. Halle, 1898. Repr. Geneva, 1974.

———. Karl Warnke. *Das Buch vom Espurgatoire S. Patrice der Marie de France und seine Quelle*. Halle, 1938. Repr. Geneva, 1976.

Chantal Marechal, ed. *In Quest of Marie de France, a Twelfth-Century Poet*. Lewiston, NY: Edwin Mellen P, 1992.

Philippe Ménard. *Les Lais de Marie de France*. Paris: Presses Universitaires de France, 1979.

Emanuel J. Mickel, Jr. *Marie de France*. New York: Twayne, 1974.

Wendy Pfeffer. *The Change of Philomel: The Nightingale in Medieval Literature*. New York: Peter Lang, 1985.

Eva Martin Sartori and Dorothy Wynne Zimmerman. *French Women Writers: A Bio-Bibliographical Source Book*. New York: Greenwood, 1991.

T.A. Shippey. "Breton Lais and Modern Fantasies." In Derek Brewer, ed. *Studies in Medieval English Romances: Some New Approaches*, pp. 69–91. Cambridge, England: Brewer, 1988.

CHAPTER 13

Good Queen Maud

Matilda, Queen of the English People (1080–1118)

> When I was quite a young girl and went in fear of the rod
> of my Aunt Christina, whom you knew quite well, she to
> preserve me from the lust of the Normans which was
> rampant and at that time ready to assault any woman's
> honour, used to put a little black hood on my head and,
> when I threw it off, she would often make me smart with a
> good slapping and most horrible scolding, as well as
> treating me as being in disgrace. That hood I did indeed
> wear in her presence, chafing at it and fearful; but, as soon
> as I was able to escape out of her sight, I tore it off and
> threw it on the ground, trampled on it and in that way,
> although foolishly, I used to vent my rage and hatred of it
> which boiled up in me. In that way, and only in that way, I
> was veiled. . . . My father, when by chance he saw me
> veiled, snatched the veil off and tearing it in pieces in-
> voked the hatred of God upon the person who had put it
> on me.[1]

So did Princess Edith chafe at the bit when she feared she would
not be allowed out of Wilton Monastery to marry the new King
Henry I.

Orphaned at thirteen, the girl who first was called Edith
and later renamed Matilda upon her marriage and coronation
came of English, Scottish, and Hungarian forebears rich in
saintly and royal blood. Her mother was the Hungarian-born St.
Margaret of Scotland, canonized on April 21, 1245.[2] Matilda's
father was Malcolm Canmore that same King of Scotland who
regained his crown when Macbeth the usurper was slain. Her
great granduncle, Edward the Confessor, was the object of a de-

veloping hagiographical cult. Later, when she became queen, she would collaborate with the Westminster monks, helping to further the cult when his tomb was opened for inspection in 1102. Her uncle was Edgar Atheling, descended from Alfred the Great, and heir to the English throne when the Norman conquerers destroyed his hopes. He had been named to lead the Anglo-Saxon revolt against the Normans after the Battle of Hastings but was compelled to yield to William the Conquerer.

By marrying Henry I, the only one of the Conquerer's sons born on English soil and after his father's royal coronation, Matilda would significantly strengthen Henry's otherwise shaky hold on the scepter and restore her own family's hereditary claim to England.

Henry's older brother, Robert Curthose, Duke of Normandy, was alive and on crusade. Robert naturally considered himself the next king. But when William Rufus died in a hunting accident on August 2, 1100, Henry galloped to Westminster to seize the treasury and the throne. He was crowned on August 5, 1100. Henry's plan to wed the Scottish princess probably had a strong political motive. Initially hostile to the English, he might not have found the marriage so attractive. But in facing the Norman barons, the alliance with a daughter of Scotland's king would give him needed protection.[3]

Henry lost no time in demanding this twenty-year-old Scottish princess as his wife, which meant prying her free from Wilton Monastery, where she had lived for seven years under the tutelage of her aunt Christina, abbess of Romsey and Wilton. It was at Wilton that Matilda received her outstanding education. Wilton was a refuge for well-born English girls during the Conquest, as it had been earlier. A house that boasted a long, prestigious history, Wilton was known for its fostering of literary study. The poet Muriel, whose works have not survived, had been a nun of Wilton. Eve, another Wilton nun who later became a recluse at Angers, was the recipient of a *Liber confortatorius* written for her by the hagiographer Goscelin. Chaplain for a time to the Wilton nuns, Goscelin provides a good source of information on the history of the house, describing, for instance, St. Dunstan's dedication of the monastery's new church. Under Wilton's abbess Brihtgyva, Goscelin wrote a *Life of St. Edith*,[4] who was Matilda's great grandaunt. Edith is also praised by the anonymous author of the *Life of St. Edward the Confessor*, who tells how she generously endowed Wilton because (as the author says) women are likely to be more helpless in the face of poverty than men. This biographer of Edward addresses Wilton in an epithalamium as a bride about to become a mother, "loved by your spouse for your fecundity." Matilda, therefore, was a daughter of Wilton, descended from a succession of learned women connected with Wilton.[5]

Matilda showed a talent for letters, but no taste for monastic life. (This may be why she later chose not to send her daughter to the nuns to be educated.) Matilda appealed for her release from Wilton to the aged Anselm, whom Henry recalled from exile on September 23, 1100. Matilda hotly insisted that the veil had been forced on her, as Eadmer reports in the passage above.

Anselm, fearing that the Devil had goaded the tempestuous Matilda to throw aside the habit in favor of the world, avoided responding directly to her plea. He had already weathered a comparable struggle with another young woman, also placed in Wilton Monastery and similarly veiled to elude the Normans' soldierly savagery. This was Gunhilda, the daughter of Harold Godwinson, the last of the Anglo-Saxon kings. Gunhilda was his last known descendant, and her story remains elusive and tantalizing.

Gunhilda had stirred the matrimonial hopes of a nobleman whom Matilda's father had originally chosen for *her*. This was Count Alan Rufus, "lord of Richmond, founder of St. Mary's York, for twenty-five years one of the most constant witnesses of royal charters, the greatest man in the north of England." He was some forty years older than the adolescent Matilda, but such unions were designed for political reasons, not for marital compatibility. Perhaps the wicked Norman her Aunt Christina really wanted to protect her against was Count Rufus.[6] Rufus, however, had caught sight of the thirty-year-old Gunhilda, perhaps on a visit to Matilda. He fell in love with Gunhilda and selected her instead of the Scottish princess, who would have been a more expedient choice.[7] Rufus had Gunhilda removed from the abbey for the purpose of matrimony. But before the wedding could take place, the would-be bridegroom died, possibly on August 4, 1093.

Anselm, having bitterly opposed Gunhilda's departure from Wilton, wrote her a harshly gloating letter, which he rhetorically punctuated with the classic *ubi sunt* trope—"Where are they now?"

> You loved Count Alan Rufus, and he you. Where is he now? What has become of the lover whom you loved? Go now and lie with him in the bed where he now lies; gather his worms into your bosom; embrace his corpse; kiss his bare teeth from which the flesh has fallen. He does not care for your love in which he delighted while he lived; and the flesh which you desired now rots.[8]

When the thorny issue of marriage and cloister arose with Matilda seven years later, Anselm reacted at first with the same outrage, but then retreated to a more circumspect position. Reluctantly he handed the question over to the bishops, allowing the views of Lanfranc, Archbishop of Canterbury, to prevail: If a woman could prove that she had taken monastic refuge to avoid the invaders and not for reasons of vocation, she was free to leave the cloister. Perhaps Anselm did not wish to enter into fresh disputes with King Henry.

Anselm assembled a synod at Lambeth, the Bishop of Rochester's manor, and allowed the matter to be decided by archdeacons and others learned in church and civil law. Permission was granted for the marriage. Anselm was not overwhelmingly happy. Matilda eventually secured his blessing, nevertheless, and was both married and crowned queen at Westminster on November 11, 1100. The crowds at the church door roared their approval.

The contemporary chronicler William of Malmesbury reports: "Henry was crowned king at London, on the nones of August. . . . Soon after, his friends, and particularly the bishops, persuading him to give up meretricious pleasures and adopt legitimate wedlock, he married, on St. Martin's day, Matilda, daughter of Malcolm, king of Scotland, to whom he had long been greatly attached."

Now Matilda—her new Norman name, together with Maud and "Mold the gode Quene"—transformed herself from the impetuous girl of Eadmer's report into a ruler with a reputation for saintliness and authority. In 1117 Matilda founded the Hospital of St. Giles for the care of forty lepers, a house that thrived until Henry VIII's dissolution of the monasteries in 1537. Once a year she bestowed sixty shillings for each leper. Whether she personally undertook to nurse them is not clear, but William of Malmesbury leaves this record of her mortifications:

> Clad in hair cloth beneath her royal habit, in Lent, she trod the thresholds of the churches barefoot. Nor was she disgusted at washing the feet of the diseased; handling their ulcers dripping with corruption, and, finally, pressing their hands, for a long time together to her lips, and decking their table.[9]

Better documented is Matilda's role as the king's representative in his absence. While she sometimes traveled with her husband, making her one and only visit to Normandy with him in 1106–1107, Henry was more often in Normandy independently and left her in charge of the realm. Matilda issued two writs in her hand from the king's bench in the *curia regis* in favor of Faritius, abbot of Abingdon, who was a royal physician. One writ was witnessed by Grimbald, another royal physician. Both involved the tenure of lands and manors. Matilda witnessed charters at Exeter, Canterbury, Norwich, Aylesbury, Rockingham, Cannock, and Cirencester, as well as Windsor and Westminster, where great courts were regularly held. *The Metrical Chronicle* of Robert of Gloucester, filled with her praises, remarks:

> Monie were the gode lawes . imad in engelonde .
> thoru Mold this gode quene.[10]

Matilda is credited with defusing the anger of the king's brother, Robert Curthose, who planned to march on Westminster to contest Henry's succession. Learning that Matilda was in childbed, he changed his mind and approached London by a different route. She later used her influence to persuade Robert to give up his annual pension of 3,000 silver marks. A woman who took after her mother in devotion, determination, and strength, Matilda may have wielded a powerful influence over her young brother David at the Norman court while he was growing up, encouraging his eventual dedication to good works.[11]

Of Matilda's three children, the first died in infancy in 1101. Her son William (b. 1103) died at seventeen in the wreck of the White Ship. Her daughter (b. 1102) would become the empress Matilda when she married Henry V of the Holy Roman Empire; widowed, she became through a second, English marriage the mother of Henry II. And so good Queen Edith/Matilda, "la bone Mahalt," receives praise in a twelfth-century *Life of Edward the Confessor*, by an anonymous nun of Barking Abbey, for having regrafted the now flowering and fruitful tree of English succession.[12]

Matilda's affinity for books and learning made her a generous patron of literature. She commissioned writings in French and Latin. "Crowds of scholars, equally famed for verse and for singing, came over; and happy did he account himself who could soothe the ears of the queen by the novelty of his song." So wrote William of Malmesbury, grumbling furthermore that she especially favored foreigners. Among the books she ordered were the poetic version of the *Voyage of St. Brendan* by one Benedeit. Significantly, she asked, too, for a biography of her mother, St. Margaret, presumably by the scholar Turgot, a prior of Durham from 1087 and 1109 and later the bishop of St. Andrews.

The author claims to have known Margaret very well and, in the preface to *The Life of Saint Margaret*, acknowledges the learned Matilda's commissioning the work, since she wished not only to hear about her mother but to read about her. The dedication reads: "To the honourable and excellent Matilda, Queen of the English, forasmuch as you have requested, you have also commanded me, to present to you in writing the story of the life of your mother." In addition to praising Margaret's holy devotions and charitable works, her biographer draws attention to her fondness for books, whereas her kingly and soldierly husband didn't know how to read. He would caress her books, as if they were surrogates for the woman herself:

> Also the books which she used either in her devotions or
> for reading, he, though unable to read, used often to
> handle and examine, and when he heard from her that one

of them was dearer to her than the others, this he also regarded with kindlier affection, and would kiss and often fondle it. Sometimes also he would send for the goldsmith, and instruct him to adorn the volume with gold and precious stones, and when he finished he would carry it to the Queen as proof of his devotion.

This gospel book was "beautifully adorned with jewels and gold, and ornamented with the figures of the four Evangelists, painted and gilt. The capital letters throughout the volume were also resplendent with gold. For this volume she had always a greater affection than she had for any others that she was in the habit of reading. It happened that while the person who was carrying it was crossing a ford, he let the volume, which had been carelessly folded in a wrapper, fall into the middle of the stream, and, ignorant of what had occurred, he quietly continued his journey. But when he afterwards wished to produce the book, he, for the first time, became aware that he had lost it. It was sought for a long time, but was not found. At length it was found at the bottom of the river, lying open, so that its leaves were kept in constant motion by the action of the water, and the little coverings of silk, which protected the letters of gold from being injured by the contact of the leaves, were carried away by the force of the current."[13]

Matilda's lifelong friendliness toward Anselm, and her concern for the realm, involved her in the controversy over investiture, which Anselm had already waged with the previous king, Henry's brother William Rufus. In and out of exile, Anselm continued to clash, though less dramatically, with Henry. The issue was whether those churchmen should be excommunicated who had been invested with their offices by secular princes. Anselm refused to countenance lay investiture. During Anselm's exile from 1103 to 1106, Matilda pleaded with him repeatedly to return, and attempted to reconcile his differences with Henry. Matilda's affection for Anselm is evident from her letters, and is also noted by his biographer Eadmer. There was general rejoicing when Anselm came back to England, but as for the Queen,

no earthly concerns, no pageantry of this world's glory could keep her from going on before to the different places to which Anselm was coming; and, as the monks and

canons went out as usual to meet the Archbishop, she
went on ahead and by her careful forethought saw to it
that his various lodgings were richly supplied with suitable furnishings.[14]

The dispute that preoccupied Henry and Anselm from
1101 to 1106 was resolved in a compromise when Henry relinquished his rights of ring and crozier but insisted on receiving
homage before bishops and abbots were consecrated. He also
controlled the right to nominate candidates for ecclesiastical ap-
pointments. Matilda's letters show her personal and official involvement in the matter, as well as her concern for Anselm's
well-being.

Matilda's letters exude her apparent devotion. Another
view of them, however, is that her sentiments are carefully polished and conventional, and that a politic shrewdness actually
underlies her protestations. The first letter translated below
shows Matilda's addressing Anselm (in the first year or two after
her marriage and queenship) in acknowledgment of his claims in
England, Ireland, and the Orkneys, but significantly omitting the
province of York and the kingdom of Scotland.[15]

Anselm's responses to Matilda's warm expressions of concern and support appear rather cautiously temperate. He had
written in a more personal and unleashed manner to the enigmatic Gunhilda. Perhaps the archbishop had felt more secure
with Gunhilda, more confident toward her in his towering
young authority than he would seven years later with Matilda,
Queen of the English.

Six daughterly letters have come to us from Queen
Matilda, letters written to Anselm as Archbishop of Canterbury.
She wrote chiefly in an effort to calm the storms over lay in-
vestiture that raged between Anselm and her husband, King
Henry I of England. She addressed a seventh letter to Pope
Pascal II on Anselm's behalf in the same dispute.

These letters speak out over the centuries with emotional
energy, together with a flamboyant rhetorical facility founded in
Matilda's solid Latin training. They display a realistic political
awareness and the writer's determination to affect the course of
events.

1. To the lord and reverend father, Anselm, Archbishop of the foremost see [of Canterbury], and primate of all the Irish islands of the Northern hemisphere, which are called the Orkneys:

From Matilda, by God's grace, Queen of the English people, his most humble handmaid. May she, once the course of this present life is happily over, arrive at its goal, which is Christ.

There is almost no doubt that you thwart nature in your daily fasting; this is not unknown to me. What I marvel at all the more is that after long fasting you take your customary food, not because nature demands it but because someone or another of your domestic staff persuades you. I have learned this from the frequent reports of many reliable witnesses. I am also aware that you take this food so sparingly that you seem to have assaulted nature by weakening its claims rather than by breaking its law.

For this reason many people—and I especially—fear that the body of so great a priest may waste away. For he is a priest to whose kindness I have been obliged, a priest who is a strong athlete of God and a victor over human nature. The peace of the realm and the dignity of the priesthood have been strengthened and defended through the unfailing energy of this priest, of this steward of God, who is as faithful as he is wise. By his blessing I was consecrated in lawful marriage; through his anointing I was raised to the dignity of earthly rule; through his prayers I shall be crowned in heavenly glory, by God's grace.

It is to be feared that his body may wither, that the windows of his eyesight and hearing and other senses will grow dull, that his spiritually edifying voice will grow hoarse, and that this voice—which formerly used to impart with quiet and gentle discourse those things of song and speech that are sweet to God—may grow much quieter from now on. Then those persons who are at the time farther away from you may be deprived of hearing that voice and may be bereft of its benefit.

Do not, therefore, good and sainted father, give up your bodily strength by such inopportune fasting as this, for fear that you may cease to be an orator. For as Cicero says in the book he has written *On Old Age*: "The orator's gift is not only talent, but also lung power." Once this is gone, your great spiritual renown would quickly be lost, and so would your great memory of the past and your ability to foresee the future. So much art, so much learning, so much invention, so much understanding of human affairs, along with the clear wisdom of the divine, would swiftly be lost.

Consider the abundance of talents that your rich Lord has given you. Consider what he has entrusted to you and what he may require. Reap the profit for the common use, for once this profit has been reaped, it will shine forth more beautifully and may be yielded up to the Lord with manifold interest.[16]

Do not deprive yourself of these two things in turn. Just as spiritual drink and food are necessary to the soul, so are bodily drink and food necessary to the soul. You must, therefore, eat and drink, since by God's grace, the great path of this life remains to you. A great harvest is to be planted, hoed, weighed, and gathered to God's granary, so that no thief can carry it off. You see that there are extremely few day-laborers in this greatest of harvests. You have embarked on this labor on behalf of many people, so that you may bring back wealth to many.

Remember, in truth, that you hold the place of John, the apostle and beloved of the Lord, whom the Lord wanted to survive him so that this virgin, cherished and chosen above the others, might take care of [the Lord's] virgin mother. You have undertaken the care that must be assumed of Mother Church, out of whose womb are your brothers and sisters in Christ. They are in daily peril, unless you hasten to their aid with great devotion. Christ himself, who redeemed them with his own blood, entrusted them to you.

O shepherd of so great a God, feed his flock so that it does not fall by the wayside untended. Let the holy priest Martin be an example to you—an indescribable man who, although he foresaw that his heavenly repose was prepared for him, nevertheless said that he would not refuse to labor for the people's needs.

Indeed, I know that you are encouraged and strengthened in your fasting by the examples of many men, and by the many testimonies of Scripture. And yet diligent reading has often shown you how, after fasting, the ravens fed Elijah, the widow fed Elisha, the angel fed Daniel according to Habakkuk, or how Moses, once he had fasted, merited to read the tablets written by the finger of God, and recovered them in the same way when they were broken. Several examples incite you to the frugality of the pagans; for there is no one who does not know that you have read of the sobriety of Pythagoras, Socrates, Antisthenes, and the other philosophers. It would be too long to enumerate them, and so it is not necessary to do so for this little treatise at hand.

We must, accordingly, come to the grace of the New Law. Christ Jesus, who consecrated fasting, also consecrated feasting when he went to the wedding feast where he changed water to wine, and when he attended the banquet of Simon. There, after he drove the seven demons from Mary, he fed her for the first time with spiritual dishes. He did not refuse the meal of Zacchaeus, whom he pulled back from the power of the earthly army and called to the army of heaven.

Heed, father, heed Paul's urging to Timothy to drink wine on account of the pain in his stomach, when he said, "Do not drink water now." Clearly he indicates that he had previously drunk nothing but water. Imitate Gregory, who relieved the weakness and fatigue of his stomach with the comfort of food and drink, while he continued without interruption and in a manly way with his teaching and preaching. Do, therefore, as he did, so that like him you may arrive at Jesus Christ, the fountain of life and the lofty mountain, with whom in immortal glory he has now long rejoiced, and does rejoice, and will rejoice forever and ever.

Let your holiness flourish in the Lord, and with your prayers do not cease to help me, your faithful servant who cherishes you with all the affection of her heart. Deign to receive, read, heed, and obey this letter, which is not framed with art but sent with strong and faithful love, from me to you.

2. Matilda Queen of the English to Anselm:

To her most beloved lord and father, Anselm Archbishop of Canterbury, Matilda Queen of the English sends wishes for his continuing good health, with her love and faithful service.

Let the Divine Comforter—the love of God—not fail to
recognize that my heart is sorely troubled because of the excessively long and wearisome absence of Your Holiness. The more I
am assured by many people of the swift and imminent date of
your wished-for return, the more eager I am, in the hope of
enjoying your desired presence and conversation.

My soul will in no way rejoice with perfect joy, most
reverend Lord, and in no true pleasure will it be gladdened until
I am happily able to see you before me again, a thing that I desire
with all the strength of my mind.

Indeed, I pray the sweet love of Your Benevolence that
during the time I am deprived of the pleasant comfort of your
rebuke, you deign to console and gladden me with the sweetness
of your letters.

May the almighty and loving God keep you in all things,
and may he cheer me soon with your return and your presence.
Amen.

3. To her lord and dearest father Archbishop Anselm, Matilda, Queen of the English, sends greetings for good health:

How much joy and solace was to be given to me in the
delight of anticipated elation at your Holiness's promised arrival! And how much more misfortune befalls me, forsaken and
sorrowing, now that your illness prevents you!

I come, therefore, weeping and wretched, to prevail upon
your fatherly affection, which I know I can count on. If my
solicitude is not wholly despicable to you, soothe the anguish of
my concern for your health by whatever messenger you wish—
as quickly as possible.

For either I will rejoice without delay over your well-
being, and indeed my own, or—may God's mercy avert it—I
shall endure the blow that strikes indiscriminately against our
common fate.

May the most loving omnipotence of God make you completely well. Amen.

4. Matilda, Queen of the English, noble in her queenly heart and filled with pious emotions, to Anselm:

Turn my lamentations to rejoicing, blessed lord, merciful father, and encircle me with happiness. See, lord, your humble handmaiden has fallen to her knees before your mercy. Stretching her suppliant hand to you, she pleads for the favor of your accustomed generosity.

Come, lord, come and visit your servant. Come, I say, father, and relieve my sighs, wipe away my tears, soften my sorrows, banish my mourning. Fulfill my longing with a favorable answer to my prayers. But—you will say—"I am forbidden by the law, held by the chains of these certain constraints imposed by my lords, whose decrees I dare not transgress."

What then of the instance, father, of that learned Apostle of the people, the vessel of election, when he was laboring to overturn the Old Law? Did he not offer sacrifice in the temple so as not to offend those among the circumcised who were believers? Can it be said that he himself, although he condemned circumcision, yet circumcised Timothy, so that he might become all men? How then should his disciple—the son of mercy—do amiss, he who offers himself in the face of death to redeem his servants?

See your brothers, your fellow servants, the people of your God, already enduring shipwreck, already slipping down into death. But you do not help, nor do you extend your right hand, nor do you interpose yourself between us and the danger. Was not the Apostle willing to be cursed by Christ on his brother's behalf? Therefore, good lord, pious father, blunt this severity and—pardon what I say—soften the steeliness of your heart! Come and visit your people, your handmaiden among them, who thirsts for you with all the vitality of her being. Find a road on which you can travel ahead of us as our shepherd, without giving offense and without breaking the laws of kingly majesty.

But if both these things should not be possible at the same time, let the father come at all events, let him come to his daughter, to the handmaiden of the Lord, and teach her how she ought to act. Let him come to her before she departs from the world. For if it happens that I should die before I see you, I fear—and I will speak shockingly—that even in that land of the living and the joyful, I may be cut off from the opportunity of all exultation.

You indeed are my joy, my hope, my refuge. Without you my soul is like the earth without water, and it is for this reason that I have opened my hands wide to you so that you may flow through its parched deserts with the oil of exultation, and nourish them with the dew of your inborn sweetness.

If, however, neither my weeping nor my public prayers should move you, I will disregard my queenly dignity, relinquish the insignia of my reign, I will put aside the scepter, despise the diadem, I will trample the purple linen underfoot, and I will come to you consumed with my grief. I will embrace the ground you have walked on, I will kiss your feet, nor will anything move me from this, even if Giezi should come,[17] unless the sum of my desires is fulfilled. May the peace of God, which passes all understanding, keep your heart and mind, and cause your innermost feelings to abound with mercy.

5. Matilda, by God's grace Queen of the English, and the lowest handmaid of his Holiness [Anselm], sends perpetual greetings in Christ to the affectionately remembered father and lord worthy of reverence, Archbishop Anselm:

I send innumerable thanks to your unceasing Goodness. I am not unmindful that you have deigned to offer me the favor of the letter at hand during your absence. Indeed, now that the clouds in which I was enwrapped have been driven away, the rivulet of your words has purified me like the ray of a new dawn. I hug the little scrap of writing sent from you in your fatherly stead. I cherish it in my bosom; I have carried it as close as I can to my heart. I reread with my lips the words flowing from the sweet fountain of your goodness. I go over them in my mind; I reflect upon them in my heart, and after I have done this, I put them away in the heart's own secret hiding place.

Now that all these things have been properly praised, I marvel at this one thing alone, which the excellence of your discretion has introduced concerning your nephew. For in my judgment I cannot deal differently with your people than with my own—differently, that is, from my own who are my very own. Certainly, your people are yours by nature, and they are mine by adoption and affection.[18]

Truly, the comfort of your writing strengthens me in all my suffering; it lifts up my hope and sustains it; it raises me when I fall, supports me when I falter, gladdens me when I am sorrowful, lessens my anger, and pacifies my weeping. These things offer me frequent and secret counsels that promise the return of the father to the daughter, the lord to the handmaid, the shepherd to the sheep. Similar promises come to me from the trust that I have in the prayers of good people, and from the kindness that arises in the heart of my lord [King Henry]—as I infer, after having sagaciously made inquiries. For his spirit is better disposed toward you than many people think. With my favorable influence and my prompting him insofar as I can, he will grow more accommodating and more friendly toward you.

Concerning your return—what he allows to happen in the present, he will allow in a better way and more fully to come about in the future, once you have made your request as to the circumstances and the time. Yet, even though he may be more tenacious than the just judge, I beg you nonetheless, out of the abundance of your affection, to shut out the rancor of human bitterness—which is not usual in you. Do not turn the sweetness of your love away from him, but rather prove yourself a pious intercessor with God on behalf of him, and me, and our common offspring, and the state of our kingdom. May Your Holiness flourish always.

6. To her lord and father, Anselm Archbishop
of Canterbury, both revered and cherished, Matilda,
devout handmaiden of his Holiness,
sends her greetings in Christ:

As often as you have shared the citadel of holiness with me through the kindness of your letters, just so often have you brightened the clouded darkness of my spirit with the light of renewed joy. For even when you are absent, there is a certain revisiting with you, as it were, the repeated touching of your bits of writing, and the thoroughly joyful and frequent rereading of your letters, which have been committed to memory.

Now, my lord, what is more elegant in style, more bursting with significance than your letters? The seriousness of Fronto, of Cicero, of Fabius, the subtlety of Quintilian are not lacking in them. The wisdom of Paul wells up in them, the diligence of Jerome, the midnight labor of Gregory, the exegesis of Augustine—and what is even greater than these—the sweetness of evangelical eloquence that distils from your writing. Because of this grace that pours from your lips, therefore, my heart and my body have exulted with deep affection in your love, and in carrying out your fatherly teaching.

Relying on the support of Your Holiness, therefore, I have entrusted the abbacy of Malmesbury to Eudolph, monk of Winton—formerly known to you, I believe, as the sexton. To you is entirely reserved anew whatever pertains to the investiture and the decree, of course, so that the mandate of the staff as well as of the pastoral care shall be bestowed through the process of your own judgment.[19]

May the power of heavenly grace grant a worthy recompense to the favor of your goodwill, which has not grown cool toward me. Concerning the rest, may Christ safeguard your office, and may he who blesses you on earth gladden me with your swift return. Amen.

7. To the highest pontiff and universal father,
Pope Pascal, Matilda, Queen of the English
by the grace of God. May he so administer
the authority of the apostolic high office on earth
that he shall deserve to be enrolled—together
with the hosts of the just—among the apostolic
senate in the joys of perpetual peace.

I bring the greatest thanks and praises that I can to Your Sublime Holiness, O apostolic man, for those things that your fatherly kindness has deigned to bestow upon the king, my lord, and me, by way of religious instruction. These dispatches you have both entrusted to the living voices of legates and included with your own writings.

I do not desist and I will not desist from what is proper and what I am able to do with my whole heart, soul, and mind: I will frequent the threshold of the most holy Roman apostolic see, embrace the ground on which my holy Father and apostolic pope has walked, and while prostrating myself at their paternal knees, pray with fitting urgency. I will steadfastly remain until I feel I am being heard by you, either because of my submissive humility or rather because of the persistent importuning of my entreaties.

Let Your Excellency not be angered by this boldness of mine and because I dare to speak this way. And let the wisdom of the Roman clergy, the people, and the Senate not be astounded. For under your apostolic high office, Anselm, our Archbishop, was indeed once a protégé of the Holy Spirit. He *was*, I say, for us and for the people of the English—so blessed as we were then—our preacher, the most prudent comforter of the people, and their most devoted father.

What he took in abundance from his Lord's most opulent treasury—whose key-bearer we acknowledged him to be—he distributed among us even more lavishly. As his Lord's loyal minister and wise steward he seasoned each morsel he paid out to us with a generous serving of the condiment of wisdom, softened it with the sweetness of eloquence, and flavored it with the marvelous charm of his speech. And so it happened that the tender lambs did not lack the Lord's abundance of milk, nor did the sheep lack pasturage of the richest fertility, nor did the shepherds lack the most plentiful abundance of provisions. Now that all these things have ceased to be, however, there is nothing left but the shepherd who—hungry for food—weeps with many a groan, the sheep that hungers for its grazing, and the lamb that longs for its udder.

As long as the greatest shepherd, namely Anselm, is absent, not only is each one deprived of each of these things, but rather all of them are deprived of everything.

In such sorrowful weeping, in such shameful grief, in such disgrace to our realm, in the outrage arising from so great a loss, nothing remains to me—dazed and suffering as I am—but to fly for help to the blessed Peter's apostle and vicar, the apostolic man.

And so I appeal to your generosity, lord, lest we and the people of the English realm should, because of so great an eclipse, sink into an equally great decline. For what use are our life and our lineage, as long as we are descending into error?

Therefore, let your fatherhood think well of it, insofar as it touches us, to deign to open your paternal heart to us within the time period that my lord the king asks of your goodness. Allow us to rejoice in the return of our most beloved father, the Archbishop Anselm, and to preserve our dutiful subjection to the Holy Apostolic See.[20] Certainly, I have been instructed by your most wholesome and beloved reminders. To the extent that my woman's strength is available to me and the help of good men is provided me, I will strive to the utmost, so that my humility discharges as far as possible what Your Highness advises. May Your Fatherhood blessedly thrive.

NOTES

1. Eadmer's *History of Recent Events in England (Historia Novorum in Anglia)*, Geoffrey Bosanquet, trans., with a foreword by R.W.

Southern (London, 1964), pp. 127–128. Eadmer was a monk of Christ Church, Canterbury. He first knew Anselm, Archbishop of Canterbury, in 1071, and became his close friend and biographer.

2. Margaret herself was the daughter of Edmund Atheling and granddaughter of King Edmund Ironside. She was also a granddaughter or grandniece of St. Stephen (or Istvan), Hungary's first Christian king and patron saint (975–1038). Margaret's father, Edmund Atheling, had been sent as a young boy into exile, along with his brother Edward, by the conquering Cnut of Denmark when their own father, Edmund Ironsides, was murdered. The two brothers were hostages first at the court of Sweden, then in Kiev, and finally in Hungary. Young Edward died, and Edmund married Agatha (or Agota), a relative of the King St. Stephen. Margaret, one of their three children, was born about 1045 and was taken to Scotland at about the age of seven. See Kazmer Nagy, *Saint Margaret of Scotland and Hungary* (Glasgow: John S. Burns, 1973). A contemporary chronicler Nagy cites is Geoffrey Gaimar, *L'Estoire des Engles*, vv. 4584–4649. Gábor Klaniczay also discusses this ancestry in *The Uses of Supernatural Power: The Transformation of Popular Religion in Medieval and Early-Modern Europe*, translated by Susan Singerman, edited by Karen Margolis (Cambridge: Polity Press in Association with Basil Blackwell, 1990), citing Sándor Fest, *The Hungarian Origin of St. Margaret of Scotland* (Debrecen, 1940), pp. 89 and 212.

3. R.W. Southern, *St. Anselm and His Biographer: A Study of Monastic Life and Thought 1059–c. 1130* (Cambridge: Cambridge UP, 1963), p. 188: "In his early policy he was markedly hostile to the English and an alliance with a princess of the old stock would not in itself have appealed to him. The English could not harm him, but the Norman baronage presented difficulties of alarming proportions."

4. "La légende de Saint Edith en prose et vers par le moine Goscelin," *Analecta Bollandiana* 56 (1938): 5–101, 265–307.

5. Antonia Gransden, *Historical Writing in England c550–c1307* (Ithaca: Cornell UP, 1974), pp. 64–65, 108–109. *The Life of Edward the Confessor* is edited and translated by Frank Barlow (Nelson's Medieval Texts, 1962). Gransden dates both the Life of Edith and the *Liber confortatorius* at about 1080.

6. As Marjorie Chibnall suggests in *Empress Matilda: Queen Consort, Mother and Lady of the English* (Cambridge, Mass.: Basil Blackwell, 1991), p. 8.

7. R.W. Southern speculates that Malcolm, Matilda's father, had plucked the veil from her head in a rage after Count Alan Rufus had rejected her on the original pretext that she was a nun.

8. Cited in R.W. Southern (*St. Anselm and His Biographer*), pp. 184–188, which gives a well-documented account of the matter. The motivations for Rufus's actions have not been explained. Anselm's two letters to Gunhilda are undated, but Southern believes they were "among his earliest letters as archbishop."

9. *Chronicle of the Kings of England*, trans. J.A. Giles, p. 453.

10. Ed. and trans. William Aldis Wright, repr. (New York, 1965), lines 8750–8751. And see Marjorie Chibnall, *Empress Matilda*, p. 10.

11. See the views of Derek Baker, "A Nursery of Saints," pp. 140–41.

12. *La Vie d'Edouard le Confesseur: Poème Anglo-Normand du XIIe Siècle*, ed. Östen Södergard (Uppsala, 1948), lines 4977–4990.

13. *The Golden Age of Anglo-Saxon Art: 966–1066*, ed. Janet Backhouse, D.H. Turner, Leslie Webster, and others (Bloomington: Indiana UP, 1984), p. 83 (plates, pp. 84, 85), gives a brief account of the book's miraculous survival. This work of "extracts from the Gospels, with miniatures of the four Evangelists . . . had a binding of gold and precious stones, which was probably a case rather than an actual binding." The first and last leaves still show water damage, according to D.H. Turner.

14. Eadmer, *History of Recent Events in England*, p. 196.

15. The view of a calculating Matilda is Southern's, *St. Anselm*, p. 191. Derek Baker, on the other hand, considers her emotional attachment to Anselm convincing. As a "high-spirited girl" who did not have parents close to her, Matilda could not have found that her aunt Christina and Wilton Abbey satisfactorily supplied the lack. (Baker, "A Nursery of Saints," p. 124.)

16. The parable of the talents is in Matthew 25.14–28.

17. Gehazi, an official who tried to push away the Shunammite who approached to embrace the feet of Elisha (II Kings 4.27).

18. Matilda claims she refuses to give preferment to Anselm's nephew, for fear of showing favoritism.

19. Matilda's appointment is important in view of the investiture controversy. In this only letter of hers from which she omits mention of her queenly rank, Matilda bestows an abbacy and seeks Anselm's approval after the fact.

20. There is a veiled suggestion of disobedience, together with a plea not to excommunicate Henry, whose precarious claim to the throne needed the prestige of papal support.

FURTHER READING

Derek Baker. "'A Nursery of Saints': St. Margaret of Scotland Reconsidered," pp. 119–141. In *Medieval Women*. Derek Baker, ed. Oxford: Basil Blackwell, 1978.

Melville Madison Bigelow. *Placita Anglo-Normannica: Law Cases from William I to Richard I*, pp. 137, 100. London, 1879.

Marjorie Chibnall. *Empress Matilda: Queen Consort, Mother and Lady of the English*. Cambridge, Mass.: Basil Blackwell, 1991.

Eadmer, *History of Recent Events in England (Historia Novorum in Anglia)*. Translated from the Latin by Geoffrey Bosanquet, with a foreward by R.W. Southern. London, 1964.

Matilda, Queen of England. Letters. *Patrologia Latina*, vol. 159, cols. 88–90, 131–32, 134–36, 156, 239, 240; vol. 163, cols. 466–67.

Kazmer Nagy. *St. Margaret of Scotland and Hungary*. Translation of Skocia pannoniai kiralyneja. Glasgow: John S. Burns, 1973.

R.W. Southern. *St. Anselm and His Biographer: A Study of Monastic Life and Thought: 1059–c. 1130*. Cambridge: Cambridge UP, 1963.

Turgot. *Life of St. Margaret* in *Ancient Lives of Scottish Saints*. Trans. W.M. Metcalfe, Paisley, 1895. pp. 297–321.

William of Malmesbury's Chronicle of the Kings of England. Trans. J.A. Giles. London: Bohn's Antiquarian Library, 1847, 1866; repr. New York: AMS, 1968.

CHAPTER 14

A Benedictine Visionary in the Rhineland

Hildegard of Bingen (1098–1179)

Abbess, preacher, prophet, poet—Hildegard revealed in her writings an extraordinary genius and personal energy. The power and variety of her works are unparalleled among medieval women writers: she produced works of drama and lyric, music, mysticism, and cosmology. She made forays into scientific fields: the lore of animals and gems, and medicine (some of it admittedly folkloric). To accompany her three books of dazzling and encyclopedic allegorical visions, she left directions for the artistic illuminations that would elucidate her meaning.

Much of what Hildegard wrote contains autobiographical information. She dispatched hortatory letters, carrying on a voluminous, sometimes vehement correspondence with notable people of her day, among them Eleanor of Aquitaine and Henry II of England; Bernard of Clairvaux; popes Eugenius III, Anastasius IV, Adrian IV, and Alexander III; and the emperors Conrad III and Frederick Barbarossa.

After German emperors had appropriated vast powers in the previous century, and princes of state became guardians of the papacy, there followed a new period of unrest. During Hildegard's lifetime, the Church now wanted more control. Hildegard's contemporary, Pope Gregory VII, won supporters to his cause, and a schism developed. When Emperor Frederick Barbarossa endorsed one pope and Hildegard another, Hildegard unleashed a letter of rage against Frederick. "Listen to this, O King, if you wish to live," she threatened, "or else my sword will strike you!" Another of her scathing letters to the archbishop of Mainz proved astoundingly oracular, for soon after she foretold his doom the archbishop was deposed and banished.

Other gentler letters passed between Hildegard and the neighboring Benedictine mystic, Elisabeth of Schönau. An important letter to Guibert of Gembloux, who served as her secretary, vividly describes the workings of Hildegard's visions, and the appearance in them of a mirroring "shadow of the Living Light." Further sources on her life emerge from two contemporary biographies by the monks Godefrid and Theodoric, for which Hildegard herself wrote a dozen passages. A later inquiry into her life and miracles, conducted in the thirteenth century for Pope Gregory IX, adds to her *Vita*.

The woman who would be known as the "Sybil of the Rhine" was born into a noble family at Bermersheim near Alzey. Hildegard recalls that her visions of great light began when she was five. From the age of eight, she lived at Disibodenberg, founded by the 7th-century Irish bishop, St. Disibod. The convent had stood for four centuries, but the admitting of women was recent. There her parents, Hildebert and Mechthild, had placed her, their tenth and last child, under the tutelage of the anchoress Jutta of Sponheim. The monk Volmar was another teacher, later to be her friend and secretary. The Benedictine house of Disibodenberg emphasized prayer and study, the reading of scripture and psalms, together with physical labor. For women this meant nursing, spinning, and weaving, but Hildegard's spiritual daughters also attained high skill in copying and illuminating manuscripts. Despite Hildegard's protestations of ignorance, she certainly studied Latin, although she may not have had the same kind of classical education in Ovid, Horace, Terence, and Virgil as Hrotswitha had in the Ottonian renaissance of the tenth century.

Hildegard reluctantly succeeded her beloved Jutta as *magistra* of the community in 1136. She was thirty-eight. Five years later, when she was nearly forty-three, she experienced a vision of stunning radiance in which a heavenly voice commanded her to write what she saw. She resisted, however, until sickness compelled her to record the succession of visions she experienced over the next ten years.

Sickness was for many mystics a fruitful source and accompaniment of their visionary life, as it would be for Elisabeth
of Schönau and, in fifteenth-century England, for Julian of Norwich. Hildegard describes her bodily pains "in all her veins and
flesh to the marrow," declaring that from her birth she was
"entangled as it were in a net of suffering."[1] Debility would prevent the mystic from performing her usual tasks and serve to
separate her from others. If sickness befell the woman who was
unwilling to write or dictate her visions, relief came only when
she finally consented to record them. Hildegard's visions formed
the beginning of her first book, *Scivias (Know the Ways)*, short for
Scito vias domini, "Know the ways of the Lord." Pope Eugenius
read parts of the *Scivias* before the Synod of Trier in 1147. He also
examined Hildegard, ascertaining the authenticity of her visions.
She answered his interrogations with truth and simplicity. Once
she gained papal approval, she began to be famous.

The next year, 1148, Hildegard wished to found her own
convent, a move that would give her greater independence. She
was refused permission by Kuno, abbot of Disibodenberg, who
probably intended to retain control over a community that was
gaining renown. Hildegard's temper flared. She was adamant, "a
rock of stone." She bitterly upbraided Kuno, calling him an
"Amalekite," a member of the bedouin tribe named in Exodus
17.8 as enemies of the Israelites in the desert. Her further enfeebling sickness persuaded Kuno that divinity had a hand in
Hildegard's affairs, and she was allowed to begin building the
independent convent of Rupertsberg near Bingen on the Rhine.
She moved with fifty nuns, all noblewomen, to the new site in
1150.

During this same period Hildegard was completing the
Scivias with the aid of Volmar. She also had the help of her
secretary-companion Richardis von Stade, to whom she was
intensely devoted. When a transfer for Richardis was proposed
to a position of authority in another convent, Hildegard wrote
letters denouncing Richardis's brother, the archbishop Hartwig,
who had sought the promotion for his sister. Hildegard wrote to
Pope Eugenius as well, but did not succeed in stopping
Richardis's departure. She suffered. When Richardis died within

a few years, Hildegard, now submissive to God's will, wrote a sympathetic letter to Hartwig.

She began her second book of visions, the *Liber vitae merito-rum (The Book of Life's Rewards)* (1158–1163), while traveling and preaching throughout towns and cities in Germany. Though chronically ill she made four preaching journeys from the ages of sixty to seventy-two, not shrinking from contact with large numbers of people. She visited Cologne on three occasions and was very taken with the St. Ursula legend, then at its height with the discovery of what appeared to be bones belonging to the saint and her companions. Hildegard composed thirteen lyrics honoring the saint. Her admirer and correspondent Elisabeth of Schönau, recorded her own visions of Ursula's band (see chapter 15), refashioning the legend in what would be its most influential form.

Hildegard wrote her third and final book of visions, the *Liber divinorum operum (The Book of Divine Works)* between 1163 and 1173. In it she suggests a human microcosm, mapping the interconnections between humanity and the cosmos; between the human and divine Christ; between the physical body, with its humors, and the soul, with its emotions and capacity for salvation. An in-dwelling fiery force, the *ignea vis*, unites all aspects of the universe in a way that is tranquil, rational, and harmonious. The composing unity of this work contrasts with the swirling commotion of the *Scivias*.

In the last year of her life when she was over eighty, Hildegard became embroiled in a controversy when she agreed to the burial of a nobleman, said to be excommunicated, at Rupertsberg. She insisted that the dead man had been sanctified at the end. All the same, her convent was placed under episcopal interdict. Hildegard refused to yield, she appealed to a powerful ally, and the interdict was lifted. On September 17, 1179, according to her biographer, she went to meet her Celestial Bridegroom in a blessed death. The sky was said to be illuminated with circles of light and shining red crosses, as if to reveal to her sisters the visions she had received.

Hildegard's visions, converted into marvelous, even hallucinating poetry and prose, are characterized by lights, fires, smokes, and stenches. Her universe abounds in geometric forms—circle, square, and oval. Cosmic elements of earth, air, fire, and water are manifest through suns and stars, skies and winds, lights and shadows, mountains and grottoes. Society is represented by kings and soldiers and hunters. Edifices rear up with their stone columns and balustrades, towers and temples, altars and crosses. Birds, fish, and animals appear that are naturalistic or monstrous. Speaking or trumpeting through clouds, fogs, and winds are vivid human forms: men and women with massive body, feet, hands, head, and hair. Hildegard's womanly presences are august and potent, with intensely feminine bodies, breasts, and wombs. A pregnant Ecclesia continually teems with offspring. The Cosmic Egg, filled with stars, similarly imparts a sense of female fertility. For Hildegard, the feminine divinity in her writing is represented with maternal fecundity and procreative force, not—as among later German mystics like Mechthild of Magdeburg—with the bridal and erotic imagery of the celestial marriage.

In a characteristic vision, a light will pour over some central scene (such as a mountain, a river, or an abyss) while an apocalyptic human presence, a beast, or an architectural structure materializes. Following the revelation will be an explanation of its meaning. Colors are conspicuous. Christianity and holy scripture are associated with the redness of the Savior's blood. White is the color of martyrs, and the dove of the holy spirit. Greenness and greening—*viriditas*—have a peculiar meaning for Hildegard, associated with the divinely energetic life-force that pulses through all being. "The soul is the body's green life-force," states *The Book of Divine Works*.[2]

Hildegard's visions—startling, even hallucinating, in their brilliance—have attracted the notice of modern pathologists, who trace their source in her lifelong illnesses.[3] And yet, the effective power of her visions, like those of seers from Elisabeth of Schönau to Joan of Arc, remains undiminished by scientific diagnosis. The mystic's gift was in some way dependent upon her physical suffering.

Passages 1–4, translated here from Hildegard's works, include her "Solemn Declaration" (*Protestificatio*) and selections from the first three visions in book I of the *Scivias*. The *Scivias* comprises twenty-six visions. The six visions of Book I trace the

history of God, humankind, and the world from the Creation
and Fall to the promise of a Savior. In seven visions, Book II
describes the redemption through Christ, as the Sun, and his
mystic marriage with the Church at the foot of the Cross. Book
III, in thirteen visions, represents through architectural imagery
the rebuilding of salvation by divine powers, or virtues; the last
days of the world; the last struggle against Satan; and the
Church's entrance into the apocalypse of Eternity.

Passages 5–7 are taken from the *Liber Vitae Meritorum*. The
Book of Life's Rewards is a vast cosmic psychomachia of verbal
battles. Vices and Virtues, represented as universal forces, confront one another, using words as weapons. These verbal battles
culminate in the triumphs of human goodness, with the
Church's entrance into eternal glory. The book opens with a
central figure of God. Hildegard's dazzled eyes behold him as a
powerful, perfect, and transcendant Man, who reaches from the
clouds to the depths of the abyss. He is the principle of all being,
who guides human salvation on its course. Hildegard observes
his cloud-shaped trumpet that blasts forth three winds. Above
these hover three clouds: one fiery, one turbulent, and one
luminous. These trumpeted winds of God's blowing invite comparison with Chaucer's windy, smoky trumpets in *The House of
Fame*. Now Hildegard's verbal psychomachia unfolds. The book
also dramatizes eternity's punishments and rewards. The last
selection tells of the heavenly virgins, ecstatic companions of the
Lamb. The scene is reminiscent of the biblical Book of Revelations, and anticipates the procession of 144,000 maidens in the
fourteenth-century English *Pearl*.

A sample of Hildegard's gem lore appears in passages 8
and 9, from the book commonly known as *Physica*, or *Liber
Simplicis Medicinae (The Book of Simple Medicine)*. This work, together with her *Causae et Curae*, or *Liber compositae medicinae (The
Book of Advanced and Applied Medicine)*, belongs to Hildegard's
great work on the natural sciences, the *Liber subtilitatum diver-
sarum naturarum creaturarum*. The *Physica* lists in nine sections the
basic and curative properties of plants, the elements, trees,
stones, fish, birds, animals, reptiles, and metals. In the fourth
book of the *Physica*, called *De lapidibus*, Hildegard composed
twenty-six short chapters on precious stones: emerald, jacinth,

onyx, beryl, sardonyx, sapphire, sard, topaz, chrysolite, jasper, prasius, chalcedony, chrysophrase, carbuncle, amethyst, agate, diamond, magnet, ligurius, crystal, pearl—both true and false—carnelian, alabaster, chalk, and a category of "other gems."

Section 10 includes seven lyrics from the *Symphonia harmoniae caelestium revelationum (Symphony of the Harmony of Celestial Revelations)*. The first two honor the Blessed Virgin Mary, the third celebrates St. Maximinus, and the fourth consists of an antiphon and responsory to St. Ursula, to whom Hildegard was especially devoted. There is a love song chanted to Christ by his virgin brides, written for the spiritual daughters of her convent. On ceremonial occasions, the nuns were permitted to wear bridal white, veils, and coronets, a custom that brought a rebuke from one of Hildegard's male critics. The last two lyrics are hymns to the green life-force, that *viriditas* which is one of Hildegard's pervasive presences.

In addition to these works, the letters, and the three visionary books mentioned above, Hildegard's opus includes her drama (the *Ordo Virtutum*), two books on her secret language (the *Lingua ignota* and the *Litterae ignotae*), a book of exegesis on the Psalms, the *Expositio Evangeliorum*, and two works of hagiography, honoring St. Rupert and St. Disibod.

1. A Solemn Declaration Concerning the True Vision Flowing from God: *Scivias*. Protestificatio

Lo! In the forty-third year of my temporal course, when I clung to a celestial vision with great fear and tremulous effort, I saw a great splendor. In it came a voice from heaven, saying:

"O frail mortal, both ash of ashes, and rottenness of rottenness, speak and write down what you see and hear. But because you are fearful of speaking, simple at expounding, and unlearned in writing—speak and write, not according to the speech of man or according to the intelligence of human invention, or following the aim of human composition, but according to what you see and hear from the heavens above in the wonders of God! Offer explanations of them, just as one who hears and understands the words of an instructor willingly makes them public, revealing and teaching them according to the sense of the instructor's discourse. You, therefore, O mortal, speak also the things you see and hear. Write them, not according to yourself or to some other person, but according to the will of the Knower, Seer, and Ordainer of all things in the secrets of their mysteries."

And again I heard the voice from heaven saying to me: "Speak these wonders and write the things taught in this manner—and speak!"

It happened in the year 1141 of the Incarnation of the Son of God, Jesus Christ, when I was forty-two years and seven months old, that a fiery light of the greatest radiance coming from the open heavens flooded through my entire brain. It kindled my whole breast like a flame that does not scorch but warms in the same way the sun warms anything on which it sheds its rays.

Suddenly I understood the meaning of books, that is, the Psalms and the Gospels; and I knew other catholic books of the Old as well as the New Testaments—not the significance of the words of the text, or the division of the syllables, nor did I consider an examination of the cases and tenses.

Indeed, from the age of girlhood, from the time that I was fifteen until the present, I had perceived in myself, just as until this moment, a power of mysterious, secret, and marvelous visions of a miraculous sort. However, I revealed these things to no one, except to a few religious persons who were living under the same vows as I was. But meanwhile, until this time when God in his grace has willed these things to be revealed, I have repressed them in quiet silence.

But I have not perceived these visions in dreams, or asleep, or in a delirium, or with my bodily eyes, or with my external mortal ears, or in secreted places, but I received them awake and looking attentively about me with an unclouded mind, in open places, according to God's will. However this may be, it is difficult for carnal man to fathom.

Once the term of my girlhood was completed, and I had arrived at the age of perfect strength which I mentioned, I heard a voice from heaven saying:

"I am the Living Light who illuminates the darkness. I have, according to my pleasure, wondrously shaken with great marvels this mortal whom I desired, and I have placed her beyond the limit reached by men of ancient times who saw in me many secret things. But I have leveled her to the ground, so that she may not raise herself up with any pride in her own mind. The world, moreover, has not had any joy of her, or sport, or practice in those things belonging to the world. I have freed her from obstinate boldness; she is fearful and anxious in her endeavors. She has suffered pain in her very marrow and in all the veins of her body; her spirit has been fettered; she has felt and endured many bodily illnesses. No pervading freedom from care has dwelt within her, but she considers herself culpable in all her undertakings.

"I have hedged round the clefts of her heart, so that her mind will not elevate itself through pride or praise, but so that she will feel more fear and pain in these things than joy or wantonness.

"For the sake of my love, therefore, she has searched in her own mind as to where she might find someone who would run in the path of salvation. And when she found one and loved him,[4] she recognized that he was a faithful man, one similar to herself in some part of that work which pertains to me. Keeping him with her, she strove at the same time with him in all these divine studies, so that my hidden wonders might be revealed. And the same man did not place himself above her. But in an ascent to humility, and with the exertion of goodwill when he came to her, he yielded to her with many sighs.

"You, therefore, O mortal, who receive these things—not in the turmoil of deception but in the clarity of simplicity for the purpose of making hidden things plain—write what you see and hear!"

But although I was seeing and hearing these things, I nevertheless refused to write for such a long time because of doubt and wrong thinking—on account of the various judgments of men—not out of boldness but out of the duty of my humility.

Finally, I fell to my sickbed, quelled by the whip of God. Racked by many infirmities, and with a young girl[5] of noble blood and good character as witness—as well as a man I had secretly sought out and discovered, as I have already said—I put my hand to writing.

While I was doing this, I sensed the profound depth of the narration of these books, as I have said. And despite the strength I experienced when I was raised up from my sickness, I carried out that work with difficulty to the end, completing it after ten years. These visions and these words took place during the days of Heinrich, Archbishop of Mainz;[6] Conrad, Emperor of the Romans;[7] and Kuno,[8] abbot of Mount St. Disibodenburg under Pope Eugenius.[9]

I have spoken and written this, not according to the invention of my heart, or of any man, but as I saw these things in the heavens and heard and perceived them through God's sacred mysteries. And again I heard a voice from the sky saying to me, "Shout, therefore, and write this way!"

2. The Iron-Colored Mountain and the Radiant One: *Scivias*. Book I, Vision 1

I saw what seemed to be a huge mountain having the color of iron. On its height was sitting One[10] of such great radiance that it stunned my vision. On both sides of him extended a gentle shadow like a wing of marvelous width and length.[11] And in front of him at the foot of the same mountain stood a figure full of eyes everywhere.[12] Because of those eyes, I was not able to distinguish any human form.

In front of this figure there was another figure, whose age was that of a boy, and he was clothed in a pale tunic and white shoes.[13] I was not able to look at his face, because above his head so much radiance descended from the One sitting on the mountain.[14] From the One sitting on the mountain a great many living sparks cascaded, which flew around those figures with great sweetness.[15] In this same mountain, moreover, there seemed to be a number of little windows, in which men's heads appeared, some pale and some white.[16]

And see! The One sitting on the mountain shouted in an extremely loud, strong voice, saying: "O frail mortal, you who are of the dust of the earth's dust, and ash of ash, cry out and speak of the way into incorruptible salvation! Do this in order that those people may be taught who see the innermost meaning of Scripture, but who do not wish to tell it or preach it because they are lukewarm and dull in preserving God's justice. Unlock for them the mystical barriers. For they, being timid, are hiding themselves in a remote and barren field. You, therefore, pour yourself forth in a fountain of abundance! Flow with mystical learning, so that those who want you to be scorned because of the guilt of Eve may be inundated by the flood of your refreshment!

"For you do not receive this keenness of insight from man, but from that supernal and awesome judge on high. There amidst brilliant light, this radiance will brightly shine forth among the luminous ones. Arise, therefore, and shout and speak! These things are revealed to you through the strongest power of divine aid. For he who potently and benignly rules his creatures imbues with the radiance of heavenly enlightenment all those who fear him and serve him with sweet love in a spirit of humility. And he leads those who persevere in the path of justice to the joys of everlasting vision!"

3. The Fall of Lucifer, the Formation of Hell, and the Fall of Adam and Eve: *Scivias*. Book I, Vision 2

Then I saw what seemed to be a great number of living torches, full of brilliance. Catching a fiery gleam, they received a most radiant splendor from it. And see! A lake appeared here, of great length and depth, with a mouth like a well, breathing forth a stinking fiery smoke. From the mouth of the lake a loathsome fog also arose until it touched a thing like a blood vessel that had a deceptive appearance.

And in a certain region of brightness, the fog blew through the blood vessel to a pure white cloud, which had emerged from the beautiful form of a man, and the cloud contained within itself many, many stars. Then the loathsome fog blew and drove the cloud and the man's form out of the region of brightness.

Satan's fall

Once this had happened, the most luminous splendor encircled that region. The elements of the world, which previously had held firmly together in great tranquillity, now, turning into great turmoil, displayed fearful terrors.

[Hildegard hears a voice explaining the meaning of what she has seen:]

The "great number of living torches, full of brilliance" refers to the numerous army of heavenly spirits blazing forth in their life of blessedness. They dwell with much honor and adornment, for they have been created by God. These did not grasp at proudly exalting themselves, but persisted steadfastly in divine love.

"Catching a fiery gleam, they received a most radiant splendor from it" means that when Lucifer and his followers tried to rebel against the heavenly Creator and fell, those others who kept a zealous love of God came to a common agreement, and clothed themselves in the vigilance of divine love.

But Lucifer and his followers had embraced the sluggardly ignorance of those who do not wish to know God. What happened? When the Devil fell, a great praise arose from those angelic spirits who had persisted in righteousness with God. For they recognized with the keenest vision that God remained unshaken, without any mutable change in his power, and that he will not be overthrown by any warrior. And so they burned fiercely in their love for him, and persevering in righteousness, they scorned all the dust of injustice.

Now "that lake of great length and depth" which appeared to you is Hell. In its length are contained vices, and in its deep abyss is damnation, as you see. Also, "it has a mouth like a well, breathing forth a stinking, fiery smoke" means that drowning souls are swallowed in its voracious greed. For although the lake shows them sweetness and delights, it leads them, through perverse deceit, to a perdition of torments. There the heat of the fire breathes forth with an outpouring of the most loathsome smoke, and with a boiling, death-dealing stench. For these abominable torments were prepared for the Devil and his followers, who turned away from the highest good, which they wanted neither to know nor to understand. For this reason they

certainly Biblical in the use of metaphor

were cast down from every good thing, not because they did not know them but because they were contemptuous of them in their lofty pride.

"From that same lake a most loathsome fog arose, until it touched a thing like a blood vessel that had a deceptive appearance." This means that the diabolical deceit emanating from deepest perdition entered the poisonous serpent. The serpent contained within itself the crime of a fraudulent intention to deceive man. How? When the Devil saw man in Paradise, he cried out in great agitation, saying, "O who is this that approaches me in the mansion of true blessedness!" He knew himself that the malice he had within him had not yet filled other creatures. But seeing Adam and Eve walking in childlike innocence in the garden of delights, he—in his great stupefaction—set out to deceive them through the serpent.

Why? Because he perceived that the serpent was more like him than was any other animal, and that by striving craftily he could bring about covertly what he could not openly accomplish in his own shape. When, therefore, he saw Adam and Eve turn away, both in body in mind, from the tree that was forbidden to them, he realized that they had had a divine command. He realized that through the first act they attempted, he could overthrow them very easily.

The line "in this same region of brightness he blew on a white cloud, which had emerged from the beautiful form of a man, and the cloud contained within itself many, many stars" means this: In this place of delight, the Devil, by means of the serpent's seductions, attacked Eve and brought about her downfall. Eve had an innocent soul. She had been taken from the side of innocent Adam, bearing within her body the luminous multitude of the human race, as God had preordained it.

Why did the Devil attack her? Because he knew that the woman's softness would be more easily conquered than the man's strength, seeing, indeed, that Adam burned so fiercely with love for Eve that if the Devil himself could conquer Eve, Adam would do anything she told him. Therefore the Devil "cast her and that same form of a man out of the region." This means that the ancient seducer, by driving Eve and Adam from the abode of blessedness through his deceit, sent them into darkness and ruin.

4. The Cosmic Egg: *Scivias*. Book I, Vision 3

After this I saw a huge creation, rounded and shaded and shaped like an egg.[17] It was narrow at the top, wide in the middle, and compact below. At the circumference was a blazing fire[18] that had a kind of shadowy membrane beneath it. Within that fire was an orb of glittering red flame,[19] of such great size that the whole creation was illuminated by it. Above it were aligned in a row three little torches[20] that steadied the orb with their fires so that it would not fall. Sometimes the orb reared itself upwards, and many fires rushed to meet it, so that it then further lengthened its own flames.[21] At other times it sank downwards and a great cold obstructed it, and the glittering red orb quickly retracted its own flames.[22]

But from the fire around the circumference of that creation, a wind gusted forth with its tornadoes.[23] And from the membrane that was under the fire another blast boiled up with its whirlwinds, and they spread here and there throughout the creation. In that same membrane there was a dark fire so horrifying that I was not able to look at it.[24] This fire tore through the entire membrane with its force, full of thundering, storms, and the sharpest stones, both large and small. As long as it raised up its thunder, the brilliant fire and the winds and air were thrown into a turmoil,[25] and lightning flashes outdid the thunder. For that brilliant fire was the first to feel the thunder's commotion.[26] Below that membrane was the purest ether, which had no membrane under it. In the ether I saw an orb of dazzling white fire,[27] very great in size. Two little torches[28] were set brightly above it, steadying the white orb so that it would not swerve from its course. And in that ether, many bright spheres[29] were placed everywhere. Into these spheres the dazzling white orb emptied some portion of itself from time to time, sending out its radiance. And so, the white orb, hastening back toward the glittering red orb and renewing its own flames there, breathed forth those flames among the spheres. And from that ether, a wind blasted forth with its tornadoes, and it whirled everywhere through that creation I spoke of.[30]

Below that same ether I saw a watery air that had a white membrane under it. This air, blowing here and there, provided moisture to the entire creation. Now and then it would suddenly gather itself together, and with a great spattering spew forth a sudden torrent. Then it would softly spread itself and drop a caressing, gently falling rain. But from this place too, a wind gusted forth[31] with its whirling force, and blew everywhere throughout that creation I spoke of.

In the midst of these elements was a sandy globe[32] of great size, and the elements enveloped it in such a way that it could slip neither here nor there. But occasionally, when the elements clashed together in alternation with the winds I mentioned, they caused the sandy globe to be moved to some degree by their force.[33]

And I saw between the North and the East what seemed to be a huge mountain. Toward the North it had much darkness, and toward the East it had much light, so that the light was unable to extend to the shadows, nor could the shadows extend to the light.[34]

5. The Three Trumpeted Winds of God: *Liber Vitae Meritorum*. Vision I, Part 1

I saw a man of such height that he touched everything from the summit of heaven's clouds down to the abyss. From his shoulders upward he was above the clouds in the clearest ether. From his shoulders down to his thighs, he was below the clouds, and in the midst of another white cloud. From his thighs to his knees he was in terrestrial air, and from the knees to his calves, in the earth. From his calves downward to the soles of his feet he was in the waters of the abyss, so that he was standing above the abyss. And he turned toward the East so that he was gazing both East and South. His face flashed forth with such brightness that I could not look at him completely.

At his mouth he had a white cloud shaped like a trumpet, which was full of a rapidly ringing din. When he blew the trumpet it blasted three winds. Each wind had a cloud above it: a fiery cloud, a turbulent cloud, and a luminous cloud. The winds were holding those clouds up. But the wind that had the fiery cloud above it remained in front of the man's face. The other two winds, with their clouds, descended to his chest, and there they spread their blasts. The wind before his face stayed there, and blew from the East to the South.

In the fiery cloud was a living fiery multitude, who were all together in one will and one conjoined life. And before them was spread a tablet full of wings everywhere, which flew with God's commands. When God's commands lifted that tablet on which the Wisdom of God had written its secrets, this multitude zealously examined it together. When they had examined these writings, the power of God rewarded them, so that they resonated together in a single chord of music like that of a mighty trumpet.

The wind that had the turbulent cloud above it blew with the cloud from the South to the East, so that the length and breadth of the cloud were like an open city square. Because of its extent, it could not be grasped by the human intellect. On that cloud was an enormous crowd of the blessed, who all possessed the spirit of life, and who were too numerous to count. Their voices were like the rushing of many waters, and they said: "We have our dwelling places according to the pleasure of the One who has brought forth these winds. And when shall we receive them? For if we were to have our clouds, we would rejoice more than we do now."

But the crowd that was in the fiery cloud responded to them in voices full of psalms: "When the Divinity takes hold of his trumpet he will breathe forth lightning and thunder and burning fire toward the earth. And he will touch the fire that is in the sun, so that all the earth will be moved; and it will come about that God will make manifest his great sign. And then in that trumpet all the tribes of earth and all the families of tongues will shout, as well as all who are inscribed in that trumpet, and here you will have your dwelling place.

very detailed could she had made fun up

The wind over which the luminous cloud was hovering, together with that same luminous cloud, spread itself from the East to the North. But very great shadows, thick and horrible, were coming from the West, and spreading themselves toward the luminous cloud. But the shadows were unable to proceed beyond the luminous cloud.

Within that luminous cloud a Sun [Christ] and a Moon [the Church] appeared. In the Sun there was a lion, and in the Moon a horned goat. The Sun shone above the heavens and through the heavens, and on the earth and beneath the earth, and so it proceeded in its rising and returned to its setting. But as the Sun was moving, the lion advanced with it and in it, plundering and despoiling as they went. When the Sun returned, the lion went back with it and in it, and roared greatly for joy. The Moon, too, in which there was a horned goat, gradually followed the rising and setting of the sun. Then the wind blew and said, "A woman will bear a child, and the horned goat will fight against the North."

In the shadows there was a crowd of lost souls beyond number. When they heard the sound of those singing from the South, they turned away, since they did not wish their society. The leader of these lost souls was called the "Deceiver," for they all follow his works and have been smitten by Christ, so that they are powerless. And all of these were crying in sorrowful voices, saying, "Woe, woe to the injurious and dreadful deeds that flee from life and travel with us toward death."

Then I saw a cloud coming from the North, which extended itself toward these shadows. This cloud was barren of all joy and happiness, for even the Sun did not touch it or extend to it. It was full of evil spirits, who were drifting here and there on it, and contriving to set traps for me. These spirits began to blush with shame on account of the Man. And I heard the old serpent saying among them, "I will make my strong men ready for the bulwarks, and I will fight with all my strength against my enemies."

Then among the men he spat out of his mouth a foamy froth, full of filth with all the vices, and puffed them up with mockery and said, "Ha! Those who are named suns because of their luminous deeds, I will drive them to the baleful, horrible shadows of night." And he blew out a loathsome fog which covered all the earth like the blackest smoke, and from it I heard a great roaring that thundered forth. It roared, "No man will worship another God unless he sees and knows him. What is this, that man cherishes what he does not recognize?" In that same cloud I saw different kinds of vices, each in its own image.

6. Worldly Love and Celestial Love: *Liber Vitae Meritorum*. Vision I, Part 1

The Words of Worldly Love:
    The first figure had the form of a man and the blackness of an Ethiopian. Standing naked, he wound his arms and legs around a tree below the branches. From the tree all kinds of flowers were growing. With his hands he was gathering those flowers, and he said:
    "I possess all the kingdoms of the world with their flowers and ornaments. How should I wither when I have all the greenness? Why should I live in the condition of old age, since I am blossoming in youth? Why should I lead my beautiful eyes into blindness? Because if I did this I should be ashamed. As long as I am able to possess the beauty of this world, I will gladly hold on to it. I have no knowledge of any other life, although I hear all sorts of stories about it."
    When he had spoken, that tree I mentioned withered from the root, and sank into the darkness of which I spoke. And the figure died along with it.

The Reply of Celestial Love:
    Then from that turbulent cloud of which I spoke I heard a voice replying to this figure:
    "You exist in great folly, because you want to lead a life in the cinders of ashes. You do not seek that life which will never wither in the beauty of youth, and which will never die in old age. Besides, you lack all light and exist in a black fog. You are enveloped in human willfulness as if enwrapped with worms. You are also living as if for the single moment, and afterward you will wither like a worthless thing. You will fall into the lake

of perdition, and there you will be surrounded by all its embracing arms, which you with your nature call flowers.

"But I am the column of celestial harmony, and I am attendant upon all the joys of life. I do not scorn life, but trample underfoot all harmful things, just as I despise you. I am indeed a mirror of all the virtues, in which all faithfulness may clearly contemplate itself. You, however, pursue a nocturnal course, and your hands will wreak death."

7. The Celestial Joys of the Virgins: *Liber Vitae Meritorum.* Book VI, Part 6

In that same brightness I looked, as if through a mirror, upon air having the purity upon purity of the most transparent water, and radiating from itself the splendor upon splendor of the sun. The air held a wind which contained all the green life-force of the plants and flowers of paradise and earth, and which was full of all the scent of this greenness, just as summer has the sweetest scent of plants and flowers.

In that air, which I regarded as if through a mirror, were those beings arrayed in the most gleaming robes, seemingly interwoven with gold; they had long sashes encrusted with the most precious stones, that hung from the breast to the foot. From them, moreover, breathed forth the intensest fragrance like that of spices. And they were girded round with belts ornamented with what seemed to be gold, gems, and pearls beyond human understanding.

Encircling their heads they wore crowns of gold intertwined with roses and lilies and stems studded with the most precious stones. When the Lamb of God called to them, the sweetest breath of wind, coming from the mysteries of Divinity, touched those stems so that every kind of lyre song, and lyre and organ music, rang out from them, together with the voice of the Lamb. No one else sang except for those wearing the crowns. Indeed the others were listening to it and rejoicing in it, just as one rejoices in beholding the splendor of a sun not seen before.

And their slippers were so transparent, so bathed in light that they seemed to be shod with a living fountain. Sometimes they stepped forth as if walking on wheels of gold, and then they were carrying their lyres in their hands and playing the lyres. Then they understood and knew and spoke a strange tongue that no one else knew or could speak. I was not able to see the rest of their ornaments, of which there were more.

For while they had lived in the world in their bodies, they had acknowledged their faith in the Creator, and had performed good works. They now, therefore, existed in this blessed tranquillity of bright joy. And since, in the purity of their minds, they had eschewed the fleeting vanities of fleshly delights and had ascended by the Law's commands into the love of the true, burning sun above, they possessed the air having the purity upon purity of the most limpid water, and the splendor upon splendor of the sun radiating forth.

Because of their most sweet desires, which they had proven to God and mortals through the green life-force of their virginity, and the flower-bloom of their minds and bodies when they poured forth the good savor of many virtues—for they had been kindled with ardor by the Holy Spirit—they felt that breath which contained all the green life-force of the plants and flowers of paradise and earth, and which was full of the scent of all greenness, just as summer has the sweetest scent of plants and flowers.

8. Preface on Precious Gems: *Physica*

All stones contain fire and moisture. But the Devil abhors precious stones. He hates and despises them, because he remembers that their beauty shone within him before he fell from the glory that God had given him, and also because precious stones are born of fire, and fire is where he receives his punishment. For he was defeated by God's will and plummeted into the fire. Just so, he was conquered by the fire of the Holy Spirit, when humanity was snatched from his jaws by the Holy Spirit's first breath.

Precious stones and gems arise in the East and in those regions where the sun is especially hot. For the mountains that are in those zones contain a very high temperature like that of fire because of the sun's heat. The rivers in those regions flow and boil continuously because of the sun's excessive heat. Occasionally, a flood gushes forth from those rivers and, swelling, flows upward toward those burning mountains. When the same mountains, burning because of the sun's heat, are touched by those rivers, they hiss wherever the water touches fire or the rivers splash their foam, like a fiery iron or fiery stone when water is poured on it. In that place the foam sticks like a burdock. In three or four days it hardens into stone.

But after the flood of these waters subsides so that the waters return again to their streambed, the foam which had clung in several places to the mountains becomes thoroughly dry, depending on the various hours of the day and the temperature of those hours. And, depending on the temperature of those hours, they acquire their colors and their virtues. As they dry they harden into precious stones. Then from various places they loosen like fish scales and fall into the sand.

When the flood of those running streams rises again, the rivers carry off many stones and conduct them to other countries, where they are found by men. The mountains I mentioned—on which gems of such quality and number are born in this manner—glitter like the light of day.

So precious stones are engendered by fire and by water, and therefore they contain fire and moisture within themselves. They possess many virtues and great efficacy so that many benefits can be brought about by their means. These are good and worthy effects and useful to mankind—not effects of corruption, fornication, adultery, hatred, murder, and similar things that lead to sin and are inimical to man. For the nature of precious stones procures the worthy and the useful, and wards off the perverse and evil, just as virtues cast down vices and just as the vices cannot operate against the virtues.

There are, however, other gems that are not born of those mountains or in the manner described. They arise from certain other, harmful things. From these, according to their natures, good or evil can be brought about with God's permission. For

God beautified the foremost angel as if with precious stones. He, Lucifer, seeing them glitter in the mirror of divinity, gained knowledge from this. He recognized that God wished to create many wonderful things. Then his spirit grew proud because the beauty of the gems in him shone forth against God. He thought his power was equal to God's, even greater than God's. For that reason his splendor was extinguished.

But just as God saved Adam for a better destiny, so God did not abandon the beauty and virtue of those precious stones, but desired them to remain on earth with honor and praise, and for medical use.

9. The Emerald: *Physica*

The emerald is formed in the morning of the day and in the sunrise, when the sun is powerfully situated in its sphere and about to set forth on its journey. Then the greenness of the earth and the grasses thrives with the greatest vigor. For the air is still cold and the sun is already warm. The plants suck the green life-force as strongly as a lamb sucks its milk. The heat of the day is just beginning to be adequate for this—to cook and ripen the day's green life-force and nourish the plants so that they will be fertile and able to produce fruit.

It is for this reason that the emerald is powerful against all human weaknesses and infirmities; because the sun engenders it and because all of its matter springs from the green life-force of the air.

Therefore, whoever suffers a malady of the heart, the stomach, or the side, let that person carry an emerald so that the body's flesh may be warmed by it, and the sick one will be healed. But if diseases so overwhelm the patient that their tempest cannot be resisted, then let the patient place an emerald in the mouth so that it may be wetted by the saliva. Let the body frequently absorb the saliva, warmed by the stone, and then spit it out. The sudden attack of those diseases will then in all likelihood cease.

If a person falls down, stricken by epilepsy, place an emerald in the patient's mouth while he is still lying down, and presently the spirit will revive. After the patient is raised up and the emerald is removed from the mouth, let the patient look attentively and say, "Just as the spirit of the Lord fills up the earthly sphere, so let his mercy fill the house of my body so that it may never again be shaken." Let the patient do this for nine consecutive days, in the morning, and the cure will follow. But the patient should always keep the same emerald and gaze at it daily in the morning, all the while saying these words. And the sick person will be made well.

Anyone who suffers especially from headache should hold the emerald before the mouth and warm it with his breath, so that the breath moistens it. The sufferer should then rub the temples and forehead with the moisture. Let it be placed in the mouth and held there for a little while, and the patient will feel better.

Whoever has much phlegm and saliva should heat up a good wine, and then place a linen cloth over a small vessel and the emerald upon the cloth. Pour the warm wine so that it flows through the cloth. This should be done again and again, as if one were preparing lye. Then consume at frequent intervals a mixture of that wine with bean flour, and drink the same wine prepared this way. It purges the brain so that the phlegm and saliva will be lessened.

And if one is gnawed by worms, place a linen cloth on the sore, and on this the emerald, and tie another strip of cloth over it like a poultice. Do this so that the stone may thus grow warm. Keep it there for three days, and the worms will die.

10. Lyrics: *Symphonia Harmoniae Caelestium Revelationum*

O tu, suavissima virga

> O you, most delightful branch,
> putting forth leaves from the rod of Jesse,
> O what a great splendor it is
> that Divinity gazed at a most beautiful girl

—just as the eagle fixes his eye on the sun—
when the heavenly Father strove toward
the Virgin's brightness
and he wanted his word to be made flesh in her.

Now when the Virgin's mind was illuminated
by God's mystical mystery,
miraculously a bright flower sprang forth
from that Virgin—
with the celestial!

Glory to the Father and the Son
and to the Holy Spirit,
as it was in the beginning—
with the celestial!

O splendidissima gemma

O brightest jewel,
and serene splendor of the sun,
the fountain springing from the Father's heart
has poured into you.
His unique Word,
by which he created the primal matter of the world
     —thrown into confusion by Eve—
the Father has forged this Word, as humanity,
for you.

Because of this, you are that lucent matter, through
     which that same Word
breathed all the virtues—
just as it drew forth all creatures
from primal matter.

Columba aspexit per cancellos

The dove gazed through the latticed window screen:
before her eyes, the balsam's fragrant moisture
flowed from the luminous Maximinus.

The sun's heat flamed forth
and glittered among the shadows;
from them arose the jewel
of which the purest temple was built
in the virtuous heart.

He stands, a lofty tower made of
the tree of Lebanon, of cypress,
and ornamented with carnelian and jacinth;
he is a city surpassing the arts of all artificers.

He runs, the swift stag, to the fountain
of purest water, flowing
from the most potent stone,
which has refreshed with sweet perfumes.

O makers of unguents and colors, who dwell
in the sweetest greenness
of the gardens of the king,
you rise up to perfect the holy sacrifice
among the rams.

Among you shines this artificer,
this rampart of the temple,
he who desired the wings of an eagle
so that he might kiss Wisdom, his nurse,
in the glorious fecundity of Ecclesia.

O Maximinus, you are the mountain and the valley:
In both you appear, a high edifice,
where the horned goat sprang forth
with the elephant,
and Wisdom dwelled in delight.

You are strong and sweet in sacred ceremonies:
in radiance you ascend the altars
as a smoke of spices
to the pillar's summit of praise.

There you intercede for the people,
who reach to the mirror of light—
to whom there is praise on high.

Antiphon: *O rubor sanguinis*

O crimson blush of blood,
you who have streamed from that eminence
bordering on divinity,
you are a flower
which the wintry serpent's blast
has never withered.

Responsory: *Favus distillans*

A trickling honeycomb
was the virgin Ursula;
she yearned to clasp the Lamb of God.
Honey and milk are beneath her tongue—
for she gathered to herself
a garden yielding fruit, and the flower of flowers
in a throng of virgins.

And so, in the most noble morning light,
be glad, Daughter Zion,
that she gathered to herself
a garden yielding fruit, and the flower of flowers
in a throng of virgins.

Glory be to the Father and the Son
and the Holy Spirit,

for she gathered to herself
a garden yielding fruit, and the flower of flowers
in a throng of virgins.

O dulcissime amator

O sweetest lover,
O sweetest embracing love,
help us to guard our virginity.

We have been born out of the dust, ah! ah!
and in the sin of Adam:
most harsh is it to deny
one's longing for a taste of the apple.
Raise us up, Savior Christ.

Ardently we desire to follow you.
O how difficult it is for us, miserable as we are,
to imitate you, spotless and innocent
king of angels!

Yet we trust you,
for you desire to recover a jewel
from what is rotten.

Now we call on you, our husband and comforter,
who redeemed us on the cross.
We are bound to you through your blood
as the pledge of betrothal.
We have renounced earthly men
and chosen you, the Son of God.

O most beautiful form,
O sweetest fragrance of desirable delights,
we sigh for you always in our sorrowful
    banishment!
When may we see you and remain with you?

But we dwell in the world,
and you dwell in our mind;
we embrace you in our heart
as if we had you here with us.
You, bravest lion, have burst through the heavens
and are descending to the house of the virgins.
You have destroyed death, and are building life
in the golden city.

Grant us society in that city,
and let us dwell in you,
O sweetest husband,
who has rescued us from the jaws of the Devil,
seducer of our first mother!

O viriditas digiti Dei

O green life-force of the finger of God,
through which God sets his planting,
you gleam with sublime radiance
like an upright column.
You are full of glory
in the completion of God's work.

O mountain's height,
you will never be overthrown
because of God's indifference.

Solitary you stand
from ancient times as our defense.
Yet there is no armed might
that can drag you down.
You are full of glory.

Glory be to the Father and the Son
and the Holy Spirit.
You are full of glory!

O nobilissima viriditas

> O noblest green life-force,
> you are rooted in the sun
> and in pure white serenity.
> You illuminate in a wheel
> what no excellence on earth can encompass.
> You are encircled in the embrace
> of the divine retinue.
>
> You redden like the morning
> and burn like the flame of the sun.

NOTES

1. Richard Kieckhefer, *Unquiet Souls: Fourteenth-Century Saints and Their Religious Milieu* (Chicago: U of Chicago P, 1984), p. 57, remarks on the mystic's "heaven-sent affliction" of illness and its role in achieving ecstasy.

2. See Marie-Hélène Moya, "Le Symbolisme sacré des couleurs chez deux mystiques médiévales: Hildegarde de Bingen; Julienne de Norwich," *Les Couleurs au Moyen Age*, Sénéfiance No. 24 (Aix-en-Provence: Université de Provence, 1988): 255–272; Peter Dronke, "Tradition and Innovation in Medieval Western Colour-Imagery," *Eranos Jahrbuch*, 1972.

3. Oliver Sacks, *Migraine: Understanding a Common Disorder,* (Berkeley, 1985); John F. Benton, "Consciousness of Self and Perceptions of Individuality," in *Renaissance and Renewal in the Twelfth Century*, ed. Robert L. Benton and Giles Constable (Cambridge: Mass., Harvard UP, 1982), pp. 267–268. Sabina Flanagan discusses Hildegard's migraines in her chapter "Potent Infirmities," in *Hildegard of Bingen: A Visionary Life* (London: Routledge, 1989), pp. 200–206.

4. The monk Volmar of Disibodenberg, Hildegard's secretary.

5. This was Richardis von Stade, toward whom Hildegard felt deep affection.

6. Heinrich I of Wartburg, archbishop between 1142 and 1153.

7. Conrad III (1138–1152), who died on crusade in the Holy Land.

8. It was Kuno (fl. c. 1136–1155) who had attempted to bar Hildegard's move to Rupertsberg.

9. Eugenius III (1145–1153). After examining Hildegard, Eugenius gave her permission and encouragement to continue writing her books. This authorization proved a stroke of inspiration or good fortune during a time when it was possible for popes and councils to condemn and burn such books.

10. Notes 10 through 16 represent in abbreviated form the explanations Hildegard receives from the One sitting on the mountain. The iron-colored mountain signifies the strength and immutability of God's eternal realm. The One who has stunned Hildegard's vision is the same One who, reigning over all the spheres of earth and heavenly divinity in unwavering brightness, is incomprehensible to the human mind.

11. The shadow is the sweet, gentle protection of the blessed Defense. It both admonishes and chastises, justly and affectionately, showing the way to righteousness with true equity.

12. This figure is Fear of the Lord *(Timor Domini)*. Armored by the keen sight of good and just intentions, he inspires in human beings his own zeal and steadfastness. His acute vigilance drives away that forgetfulness of God's justice that often afflicts mortals.

13. The boylike figure in white shoes is the poor in spirit. In pale submission to God, it puts on a white tunic and faithfully follows the gleaming white footsteps of the Son of God.

14. The radiance descending from the One on the mountain is the shining visitation from that One who governs all creatures, pouring down the power and strength of his blessedness.

15. The living sparks cascading down from the One on the mountain are the many potent virtues that emanate from him. These virtues ardently embrace and soothe those who truly fear God and love poverty of spirit, enfolding them with their aid and protection.

16. The men's heads, some pale and some white, appearing in the little windows, show that human actions cannot be hidden. The pale, dull-colored ones indicate those who are lukewarm and sluggish in their deeds, and therefore dishonorable. The white and shining ones are those who are vigilant.

17. Notes 17 through 34 represent in abbreviated form Hildegard's allegorizations of what she sees. The firmament is Almighty God, in-

comprehensible in his majesty and unfathomable in his mysteries, the hope of all the faithful.

18. In this fiery circumference, God consumes those who are outside the true faith with the fire of his vengeance, but those remaining within the Catholic faith he purifies with the fire of his consolation.

19. The sun, explained allegorically as the solar Christ, or the Sun of Justice, whose fiery love illumines all things.

20. Mars, Jupiter, and Saturn represent the Trinity, their descending order showing the earthward descent of Christ.

21. The Sun's lengthened rays signify the fecundating power of the Father, at the time of Christ's incarnation, by which the heavenly mystery was effected in the Virgin Mary.

22. This sinking indicates Christ's descent to earth to put on wretched human form and physical suffering, after which he ascended again to the Father, as the Scriptures record.

23. Each of the four speaking winds carries a specific report. The first wind, coming from the South and located in the fiery circumference, is God's word. God the Father reveals his power through the just words of his truth.

24. The North wind, boiling up from the dark region of fire, is the Devil's insane and futile speech.

25. Cosmic storms are provoked by the sin of murder, which brings on heavenly retribution. These storms pelt creation with thunder, lightning, and hail.

26. Divine majesty foresees the crime of murder and punishes it.

27. The Moon, to be understood also as the unconquered Church.

28. Venus and Mercury, to be understood also as the Old and New Testaments guarding the Church.

29. The stars in the ether signify the many splendid works of piety appearing everywhere in the purity of the faith.

30. The West wind, emanating from the purest ether, spreads the strong and glorious teachings of the faith.

31. The East wind, blowing from the humid, airy region, brings salvation through true speech and sermons, with the inundation of baptism.

32. The globe is earth, surrounded by the elements in commotion. Human beings on earth, though connected to the elements, are meant to rule over them.

33. These are divine miracles that shake the bodies and minds of mortals.

34. The mountain is the great fall of man. It stands between diabolical wickedness and divine goodness, between the Devil's deceit—which leads toward damnation—and the light of redemption. The peak of the mountain points downward into the earth's green-growing particles, or grains; its base is rooted in the white membrane of air.

FURTHER READING

Anton Brück, ed. *Hildegard von Bingen 1179–1979: Festschrift zum 800. Todestag der Heiligen.* Mainz, 1979.

Peter Dronke. "Hildegard of Bingen as Poetess and Dramatist: The Text of *The Ordo Virtutum,*" in *Poetic Individuality in the Middle Ages.* Oxford: Clarendon P, 1970.

———. "Problemata Hildegardiana." *Mittellateinisches Jahrbuch: Internationale Zeitschrift für Mediävistik/International. Journal of Medieval Studies* 16 (1981): 97–131.

Sabina Flanagan. *Hildegard of Bingen: A Visionary Life.* London: Routledge, 1989.

Mary Ford-Grabowsky. "Angels and Archetypes: A Jungian Approach to Saint Hildegard." *American Benedictine Review* 41 (1990): 1–19.

Hildegard of Bingen. *Hildigardis abbatissae opera omnia. Patrologiae cursus completus: series latina.* Ed. Jacques-Paul Migne, 221 vols. (Paris, 1841–1868), Vol. 197.

———. Lyrics. Pudentiana Barth, Maria-Immaculata Ritscher, and Joseph Schmidt-Görg, eds. *Lieder: Nach den Handschriften herausgegeben.* Salzburg: Otto Müller, 1969.

———. Audrey Ekdahl Davidson, ed. *The Ordo Virtutum of Hildegard of Bingen: Critical Studies.* Kalamazoo: Medieval Institute Publications, 1984.

———. Letters. Adelgundis Führkotter, ed. and trans. *Briefwechsel: Nach den ältesten Handschriften übersezt und nach den Quellen erläutert.* Salzburg, 1965.

————. Adelgundis Führkötter and Angela Carlevaris, eds. *Scivias*. Corpus Christianorum, Continuatio Mediaevalis 43–43a. 2 vols. Turnhout: Brepols, 1978.

————. Adelgundis Führkötter, ed. *The Miniatures from the Book Scivias of Hildegard of Bingen from the Rupertsberg Codex*. Trans. Fr. Hockey. Turnhout: Brepols, 1978.

————. Columba Hart and Jane Bishop, trans. *Scivias*. With an introduction by Barbara Newman. New York: Paulist Press, 1990.

————. Bruce W. Hozeski, trans. *Book of the Rewards of Life (Liber Vitae Meritorum)*. New York: Garland, 1993.

————. Bruce Hozeski, trans. "'Ordo Virtutum': Hildegard of Bingen's Liturgical Morality Play." *Annuale Medievale* 13 (1972): 45–69.

————. Paul Kaiser, ed. *Hildigardis Causae et Curae*. Leipzig, 1903.

————. Lyrics. Barbara Newman, ed. and trans. *Symphonia: A Critical Edition of the Symphonia Armonie Celestium Revelationum [Symphony of the Harmony of Celestial Revelations]*. Ithaca: Cornell UP, 1988.

————. J.B. Pitra, ed. *Sanctae Hildigardis Opera. Liber vitae meritorum*. Analecta Sacra, 8. Monte Cassino, 1882. Repr. Farnborough: Gregg Press, 1966.

Barbara Lachman. *The Journal of Hildegard of Bingen: Inspired by a Year in the Life of the Twelfth-Century Mystic*. New York: Bell Tower, 1993.

Werner Lauter. *Hildegard-Bibliographie*. Alzey, 1970.

Barbara Newman. *Sister of Wisdom: St. Hildegard's Theology of the Feminine*. Berkeley: U of California P, 1987.

Miriam Schmitt. "Blessed Jutta of Disibodenberg: Hildegard of Bingen's Magistra and Abbess." *American Benedictine Review* 40 (June 1989): 170–189.

Bernhard W. Scholz. "Hildegard von Bingen on the Nature of Woman." *American Benedictine Review* 31 (1980): 361–383.

Charles J. Singer. *From Magic to Science: Essays on the Scientific Twilight*. Repr. New York: Dover, 1958.

Carolyn Wörman Sur. *The Feminine Images of God in the Visions of Saint Hildegard of Bingen's Scivias*. Lewiston, N.Y.: Edwin Mellen, 1993.

Ingeborg Ulrich. *Hildegard of Bingen: Mystic, Healer, Companion of the Angels*. Trans. by Linda M. Maloney. Collegeville, MN: Liturgical Press, 1993.

Ulrike Wiethaus. "Cathar Influences in Hildegard of Bingen's Play 'Ordo Virtutum.'" *American Benedictine Review* 38 (1987): 192–203.

Emilie Zum Brunn and Georgette Epiney-Burgard. "Hildegard of
   Bingen." In *Women Mystics in Medieval Europe*. Trans. Sheila
   Hughes, pp. 3–38. New York: Paragon House, 1989.

CHAPTER 15

Handmaid of God

Elisabeth of Schönau (1128/9–1164/5)

Hildegard of Bingen received at least one visit and three letters from her younger contemporary, Elisabeth of Schönau, a gifted and tormented Benedictine mystic who also lived in the Rhineland. Both women were visionaries who had been ordered to spread the word about their divine revelations. Their names were linked in their lifetimes as two women whom God had endowed with the spirit of prophecy. But Elisabeth had suffered mockery, and she defends herself to Hildegard against those who expressed doubt about her extraordinary and debilitating visions. She also explains her method of keeping a little book at her bedside in which to record them.

As a young girl of twelve Elisabeth had entered the Benedictine double monastery of Schönau in the diocese of Trier, not far from Cologne and the Rhine. The monastery was a recent foundation (in 1114) of the count of Laurenberg, with whose house Elisabeth's family had some connections. No medieval *vita* was written about her, it appears, though inferences can be made about Elisabeth's noble background and kinfolk in the church. One great-uncle was the Bishop of Munster, and she had relatives among the nuns of the Augustinian monastery of St. Andernach. What we know of her is assembled from the autobiographical portions of her visions and her letters, and from her brother Ekbert's testimony, both in his introduction to her works and his letter about her death (*de Obitu*) to their cousins.

Six years after her parents dedicated her to the monastery of Schönau, Elisabeth took the veil. Given to acute depressions and nervous crises, even a wish for death, Elisabeth spoke of her mind being clouded with shadows, sadness, and depression. She was often ill. In the letter to Hildegard translated below, Elisabeth describes how her personal angel lashed her with a whip, so that she had to keep to her bed for three days, a punishment for not revealing her visions.

She began in 1152 to experience a series of ecstatic visions that continued until her death at age thirty-six. Despite her wide recognition late in her life and afterward, the canonization process on her behalf was never completed.[1] The first of these visions occurred in her eleventh year at the convent. During a trance she could not speak; she felt sensations of stifling and paralysis, or she lost consciousness. It was Elisabeth's brother Ekbert (d. 1184), who became a monk of Schönau at Elisabeth's pleading and afterwards an abbot, who wrote down Elisabeth's experiences, disseminated them, and put an end to the jeering. Ekbert's relinquishment of a potentially illustrious career to serve as his sister's amanuensis and spokesman can only mean that he strikingly believed in Elisabeth as a conduit to heaven's grace.[2] His prologue to his sister's visions declares his reverence for her as a handmaid of God (*ancilla Dei*). Concerning their collaboration he is explicit about the languages the angel spoke. Ekbert writes:

> Let all those who are about to read the words of this book know this without a doubt. Some of the discourses of God's Angel—which he is said to have delivered to the handmaid of God, Elisabeth—he revealed wholly in the Latin language; some, on the other hand, wholly in the German language. Some, however, he used to utter partly in Latin and partly in the words of the German tongue.

This is how Ekbert dealt with the language problem:

> When the Angel's words were Latin I left them unchanged, but when they were German I translated them into Latin, as clearly as I was able to do. I did not presume to add anything of my own. I sought neither human approval nor earthly gain. God, to whom all things are naked and revealed, is my witness.

Ekbert describes his sister's trances, which would customarily come on Sundays or other feast days.

A certain malady in the region of the heart came over her and she grew violently agitated. At last she lay as if lifeless, so that at times no breath or vital motion could be felt in her. But after a long period of unconsciousness, after her spirit had gradually revived, suddenly she would utter some exceedingly divine words in the Latin language, which she had not at any time learned from another person, nor could she have devised them all by herself, since she was not learned and had no skill—or very little—in spoken Latin.

Elisabeth experienced her first vision during the Feast of Pentecost in 1152, and the visions continued until September 23, 1157. It is worth noting that Hildegard's *Scivias* had been completed in 1151. In 1156 Elisabeth visited Hildegard, whose influence over the younger woman is evident, even though Elisabeth's scope is more modest. Elisabeth's *Book of the Ways of God* (*Liber Viarum Dei*) resembles the title of Hildegard's first work, and there is some similarity in visual content, for example, the sight of a high mountain at whose summit stands a divine figure bathed in light.

Elisabeth's imagery derives chiefly from popular theology, however, as well as from the liturgy and the Bible, and differs from the powerful cosmologies, grandiose allegories, and august "Blakean" presences of Hildegard. Certain of Elisabeth's trances carry her, accompanied by her angel, to a mountaintop or pleasant meadow where she may encounter young women, youths, or venerable men. From book II of the *Visions*, it is recorded that the angel carries Elisabeth to a green meadow where she meets three young girls, one with a name close to Elisabeth's own— "Libista." They plead for the prayers of Elisabeth and her congregation. Here is saintly intercession in reverse: dead souls in purgatory require earthly penance to free them. Elisabeth's visionary meeting with the three young women in the next world is translated below. There is a resemblance between these heavenly friends and intercessors and the three young saints who appear to Elisabeth from among the considerably more numerous heavenly troop of saintly maidens accompanying St. Ursula.

Elisabeth experienced visions of saints, conversed with the Blessed Virgin, and suffered the taunts of devils, animal shapes, and small boys in the garb of clerics. Elisabeth's devotion to

Jesus led to her vision of Jesus in his feminine aspect, a concept that contributed significantly to the image of the feminized Jesus in later medieval piety. She also beheld a special angel who visited and befriended her. But even this caused her trouble, at least initially. Goaded by her monastic brothers to challenge the angel as to his trustworthiness, Elisabeth fearfully did so. The angel became angered, according to her reports, and told her to direct the brothers and sisters of her monastery to offer up masses for him and his brothers. This done, the angel was mollified and agreed to continue to visit Elisabeth.

The visions seized the imagination of people in Elisabeth's neighborhood, making her a local celebrity. Her exhortations and apocalyptic warnings drew crowds. Bishops and divines consulted her on various matters, which she was asked to refer to her angel and to the other beings with whom she conversed. As the extraordinary number of manuscripts shows, her popularity spread to the western part of the country, and to France and England.

When she was twenty-seven, the fifteenth year after she became a nun, Elisabeth entered in conversation with the Blessed Virgin concerning the Virgin's Assumption. From these visions, lasting for three years, Elisabeth established the date of the Virgin's Assumption as forty days after her death. This portion of her visions was translated into Anglo-Norman and Old French as separate poems which named her "Ysabeau."[3]

Among her other writings, Elisabeth left twenty-two letters. Two of these identify further relics of the martyrs of Cologne; the rest are counsels to bishops, abbesses, and abbots. Three are addressed to Hildegard, one of which is translated here. It reveals Elisabeth's deep anxiety about her visions.

By far the most popular work of Elisabeth's, and the one that guaranteed her renown, was the *Revelations of the Sacred Band of Virgins of Cologne*. When the walls of Cologne were being extended to fortify the city in 1106 on orders of Emperor Henry IV, the excavators reached the suburbs and the ring of churches of Saints Gereon, Cunibert, Severin, and Ursula. The discovery of large numbers of bones in a Roman necropolis outside the walls gave, it seemed, corroboration to the legend of St. Ursula and the 11,000 Virgins.

This appealing tale had been in circulation since the tenth century in the form of a Birthday Sermon (*Sermo in Natali*), dated 922, and two Latin Lives, usually called Passio I (*Fuit tempore pervetusto*) and Passio II (*Regnante domino*). Earlier there had been a stone inscription that credited a man named Clematius with rebuilding the basilica dedicated to the virgins. Martyrologies and liturgical notices had listed a handful of holy virgins, marking the celebration of their feast on October 21.

The legend of the seafaring virgins is this: The beautiful and devout British princess Ursula has received an angelic vision foretelling God's plan for her life and her martyrdom. Shunning marriage with a pagan prince, Ursula persuades her father, the British king Deonotus, to build her a fleet of eleven ships in which she and her 11,000 selected maidens may sail for three years to honor their virginity. The Sermon, dated earlier than the two legends, indicates that the women left England to escape the persecutions raging against Christians at the time. In the full-blown legend Ursula follows her angel's directions and pretends to agree to the marriage as her father wishes.

With the fleet made ready, Ursula and her women gird themselves as if for naval exercises. They execute intricate maneuvers with their ships to delight the spectators on shore, before contriving to drift gradually to sea. Sped by a strong wind which the Lord sends, they sail to the market city of Tiel, where they purchase utensils.[4] The young women arrive at Cologne. Again Ursula receives a visitation from her angel. He foretells the women's martyrdom on their return visit to this city.

The women rejoice in their coming martyrdom and set sail for Basel. Disembarking, they complete their pilgrimage to Rome where they visit the holy places. They then board their ships and sail down the Rhine for Cologne. Met by the barbarian tribe of the Huns, all the women except Ursula are slain like lambs before wolves. Ursula spurns marriage with the Prince of the Huns as a way of saving herself. The barbarian orders his archers to shoot.

> And so Ursula, the queen of the most radiant army, pierced through by the shot of an arrow, sank upon the noble heap of her followers like a heavenly pearl. She was purified by the royal purple of her own blood as if she had

been baptised again. With all her victorious troops she ascended, crowned with laurels, to the celestial palace.[5]

One young woman named Cordula, who feels a cowardly reluctance to die, creeps to hide in the hull of an empty ship while her companions fall. Smitten with remorse, however, Cordula changes her mind and the next day offers herself to be slaughtered like the rest.

Terrifed by a God-sent delusion that the dead virgins are rising up in battle lines to pursue them, the fierce Huns break rank and run for their lives. The townspeople of Cologne flock from the city gates. Rejoicing, they bury the virgins, whose holy bodies will guard their city from then on.

Elisabeth's contemporaries who discovered the bodies out-side Cologne (notably the Abbot Gerlach of Deutz) were eager to prove these to be the 11,000 virgins of the legend. A worrisome fact, of course, was that many of the bodies were male. Because of Elisabeth's reputation as a visionary, three bodies, as well as some stones inscribed with names, were brought to her as a way of inspiring one of her trances.

In a series of prayed-for visions, Elisabeth ascertained names for the three: Albina, her sister Emerentiana, and their ten-year-old companion Adrianus, a king's son. Another of the virgin martyrs, St. Verena, showed herself frequently to Elisabeth, informing her that St. Ursula and her companions had singled Elisabeth out for special favor and promising her a place among their blessed number in the next life. The imaginative *Revelations* that grew out of this experience call to mind literary dreams of the other world, from the earliest Christian vision of Perpetua to the *Comedy* of Dante, *The Romance of the Rose*, Chaucer's *Parlement of Foules*, and the Middle English *Pearl*.

Elisabeth's revelations were written down between 1156 and 1157, the first occurring on October 28, the Feast of the Apostles Simon and Jude.

Elisabeth doesn't trouble to retell the legend. It was well known. Instead she engages in conversations with Verena that are dramatic and intimate and lively on both sides. Elisabeth does more than only listen; she has information about the older legends, and she has the inscriptions.[6] What she learns is how men happened to join the women's pilgrimage: Bishop Pantalus of Basel, Bishop Simplicius of Ravenna, and Pope Cyriac of Rome.

The *Revelations*, moreover, introduce the notion of kinship. The martyrs and their masculine escorts turn out to be part of an extended family network, whose relationships emerge in a series of miniature narratives. A young soldier confides to Elisabeth that he received strength from his aunt, Gerasma, a former queen in Sicily. This Germanic concept of kinship, or *Sippe* (compare the English "sib"), welds privileged individuals into a vast and holy clan. Ursula and her maidens have joined in an overarching mystical community from East to West. Sisterhood now draws male relatives into its fold, with the sisters leading nephews, brothers, sons, and at least one fiancé, as well as soldiers, lay-men, pre-lates, and a pope.[7]

The amiable saints prove approachable. They are touch-ingly eager to clear up doubts. They are friendly schoolmis-tresses who designate the visionary, an apt and humble pupil, to carry their teachings to the world.

Elisabeth's contributions to the Ursula legend are of incal-culable importance in validating the legend and guaranteeing its wide circulation. The expanded legend became the accepted one, the basis of *The Golden Legend* version of Jacob de Voragine. The males in the company, including Pope Cyriac, become perma-nent participants in the pilgrimage to martyrdom.

In England in 1136, twenty years before Elisabeth dictated the revelations, Geoffrey of Monmouth had given a brusque account of the British princess's shipwreck without naming her. In about 1200 Layamon's *Brut* described the rape, enslavement, and slaughter at sea of the Princess Ursula and her women. Layamon's is a tale infused with the grimness of his Anglo-Saxon models. Neither Geoffrey nor Layamon mentions Ursula's saintly status, but they report the women's fate as a pitiful chapter in the harrying of England by pagan Vikings. *The South English Legendary*, late in the thirteenth century, transforms the life and death of the martyrs into a tale that verges on the courtly. Instead of executing nautical maneuvers in their ships, the virgins try out new dance steps, the fashionable French *tresca*, on shipboard. At the climactic moment of martyrdom,

Ursula's fiancé willingly dies with her so that the two may marry in heaven.[8]

Elisabeth's legacy in the reshaping of the Life of Ursula continued throughout the English versions of the Ursula legend, for several of the names she assigned remain in *The South English Legendary* and in Bokenham's *Legendys of Hooly Wummen* in the fifteenth century. The visions proved enormously popular. Sixty-nine medieval manuscripts survive, and the *Revelations of the Sacred Band of the Virgins of Cologne* inspired cycles in pictorial art of the life of St. Ursula. The legend and the art spread from Germany to Italy to France. If, however, as Elisabeth points out in the opening of her *Revelations*, the cult had been in danger of falling into neglect before the discovery of the bones, a similar complaint was recorded by the fourteenth century. A recollection of Sister Ida von Sulz by Elsbet Stagel in the Book of Töss notes that Ida

> had much love for the Eleven Thousand Virgins. The provincial had ordered them not to sing the Virgins' office as had been the custom. And when it was the Virgins' feast, Ida was serving at mass with the others, and she saw Saint Ursula with all her virgins in the choir, all of them beautiful and finely dressed. And when the mass began and no one sang of them, the Virgins turned away contemptuously and went out. And after that we never omitted their office again.[9]

1. Elisabeth's Letter to Hildegard of Bingen

To the Lady Hildegard, revered Superior of the Brides of Christ who are in Bingen, Elisabeth, a lowly nun, sends devout prayers with all love.

May the grace and solace of the Most High fill you with joy! For you have been kind and compassionate to me in my distress, as I have understood from the words of my Comforter—whom you have earnestly reminded to console me.

For you have said that things have been disclosed to you about me. I confess that I have recently conceived in my mind a certain cloud of uneasiness because of the absurd talk of people saying many things about me—things that are not true. But I would easily endure the talk of the common people, if it were not for the fact that those who walk about wearing the garb of the religious also deride the grace of God in me, and do not fear to pronounce judgment rashly on those things of which they are ignorant. I hear that some letters, inspired by them, are even being circulated in my name. They have spread the rumor that I have prophesied about the Day of Judgment, a thing that I have certainly never presumed, since its coming eludes the understanding of all mortals.

But I shall reveal to you the circumstance of this rumor, so that you may judge whether I have done or said anything presumptuous in this matter. As you have heard from others, the Lord has magnified his mercy in me beyond what I have deserved or might in any way be capable of deserving—to such an extent that he even has often deigned to reveal certain heavenly mysteries to me. He has also indicated to me many times, through his Angel, what kinds of things would befall his people in these times unless they were to do penance for their sins. He commanded me to make this known openly. However, in order to avoid arrogance, and so as not to seem to be the proposer of novelties, I have been zealous to conceal all these things, as much as I have been able.

Therefore, when in my accustomed manner I was in a trance one Sunday, the Angel of the Lord appeared by my side, saying, "Why do you hide gold in the mud? This is the word of God which has been sent to earth through your lips, not so that it should be hidden but so that it may be made known to the praise and glory of our Lord and for his people's salvation." And when he had said this, he raised a whip above me, which he lashed most harshly against me five times as if in great anger, so that for three days I was weary in my whole body from that beating. After this, he laid a finger on my lips saying, "You shall be silent until the ninth hour; then you shall reveal these things which God has accomplished in you!"

Accordingly, I remained silent until the ninth hour. Then I signaled to the superior that she should bring me a little book which I had hidden in my bed. It contained a part of these things which the Lord had revealed to me. When I offered it into the hands of the lord abbot who had come to visit me, my tongue was loosened to say these words: "Not to us, Lord, not to us, but to Your Name give the glory!"

After this, when I had also revealed to him certain other things that I had not wished to be committed to writing, namely concerning God's great vengeance which—as I had learned from the Angel—would befall the world within a short time, I pleaded with him most earnestly to keep that message hidden within himself. However, he ordered me to exert myself to pray and to ask the Lord that he allow me to understand whether or not he wanted those things that I had said to be veiled in silence.

When I had prostrated myself for some time, persevering in prayer on that account, it was in the season of our Lord's Advent, on the feast of St. Barbara [December 4] during the first vigil of the night, that I fell into a trance. And the Angel of the Lord stood by my side, saying, "Cry loudly and say 'Woe!' to all nations, because the whole world has been returned to darkness. And you shall say, 'Depart! He has called you, he who has created you out of earth. And he says, "Repent, because the Kingdom of God is at hand!"'" (Matthew 3.2; Luke 21.31).

Stirred by this message, the lord abbot began to spread the word before the magistrates of the church and religious men. Several of them received the message with respect. But some did not; they spoke perversely of the Angel who was friendly toward me, saying that he was a deceitful spirit who had been transformed into the shape of an Angel of light. Hence, the abbot bound me in obedience, commanding me that if the Angel should ever appear to me, I should entreat him to swear in God's name to disclose to me whether or not he was a true Angel of God. But I thought this was presumptuous, and accepted this command with great fear.

One day, therefore, when I was in my trance, he appeared to me as he was accustomed to do and stood in my sight. Trembling, I said to him, "I entreat you to swear by God the Father, and the Son, and the Holy Spirit, that you tell me accurately if you are the true Angel of God, and if these visions that I have seen in my trance and the words I have heard from your lips are true!" He replied and said, "Know certainly that I am the true Angel of God, and that the visions you have seen are true, and what you have heard from my lips is true, and will truly come to pass if God is not reunited in harmony with men. And I am that very one who has labored long within you."

After this, on the eve of the Epiphany while I was praying, my lord again appeared to me. But he stood at a distance and had his face turned away from me. I, therefore, understanding his displeasure, spoke to him with fear: "My lord, if I offended you because I entreated you to swear, do not attribute it to me, I beg you. Turn your face toward me, I beseech you, and be forgiving toward me. For I acted bound by obedience, and I have not dared to violate the order of my superior."

When I had shed abundant tears amid words of this sort, he turned toward me saying, "You have shown disdain for me and my brothers because you harbored a lack of faith concerning me. Hence you will know with certainty that you will see my face no more, nor will you hear my voice, unless the Lord is placated, as well as we ourselves." And I said, "My lord! How will it be possible for you to be placated?" And he said, "You shall tell your abbot that he must solemnly celebrate a divine office in remembrance of me and my brothers."

When the solemnities of the masses had been celebrated in honor of the holy Angels, not once but several times, both by the lord abbot and by the rest of the brothers, and when at the same time the sisters had honored them with readings from the Psalms, my lord appeared to me again with a tranquil mien, and he said to me, "I know that inasmuch as what you have done has been performed in love and obedience, you have therefore won forgiveness, and from now on I shall visit you more often than I previously have."

After this, when the lord abbot arranged to go to a certain place—at the request of the clergy residing there—in order to preach the Lord's word of warning among the people (if perhaps they might repent so that God's anger might be turned away from them), he went first to pray to the Lord together with all of us, in order that God might deign to reveal to his handmaid whether the message, already partly revealed, should be spread more widely.

And so, when he was celebrating the divine mysteries, and we were praying most fervently, suddenly the joints of my limbs slackened and I grew faint and went into a trance. And lo and behold! the Angel of the Lord stood before my eyes, and I said to him, "My lord, remember what you told me, your handmaid, that the word of God has been sent to earth through my lips, not in order to be hidden but to be revealed for the glory of God and the salvation of his people. And now show me what ought to be done about that word of warning which you have spoken to me. Has it already been sufficiently revealed, or must it still be preached?"

And he, gazing at me with a stern look, said, "Do not tempt God, for those who tempt him will perish. You shall say to the abbot, 'Do not be afraid, but carry through to the end what you have begun.' Those who hear the words of your admonition and preserve them are truly blessed, and will not be scandalized at you. You shall advise him, moreover, that he must not change the form of preaching he has used until now. For in this I have been his counselor. Tell him that he must in no way heed the words of those who spitefully express doubt about these things which have been accomplished within you. But let him heed what has been written: 'For nothing is impossible with God'" (Luke 1.37).

Heartened by this message, therefore, the abbot went to the place where he had arranged to go and exhorted to repentance the people awaiting his arrival. He announced that God's wrath would befall all of them unless they strove to prevent it through fruitful penance. He did not, however, recount in any of his preachings, for he had been maligned, what plagues were threatening the world. So it turned out that many of those among whom that sermon was spread very fearfully prostrated themselves in penance throughout the whole season of Lent, and diligently persisted in almsgiving and prayer.

At that time, someone—driven by what zeal I do not know—sent a letter to the city of Cologne in the name of the lord abbot, who himself was unaware of it—God knows! In it certain terrible threats were read within the hearing of all the people. Therefore, although we have been ridiculed by some foolish people, the wise ones nevertheless (as we have heard) reverently paid attention to the sermon, and did not disdain to worship God with the fruits of penance.

It happened, in addition, on the fourth holy day before Easter, when I had fallen into a trance after great bodily turmoil, the Angel of the Lord appeared to me. I said to him, "Lord, what will become of the message that you uttered to me?" And he answered, "Do not be downcast or troubled if those things that I foretold do not happen on the day I designated to you. For the Lord has been appeased by the atonement of the throng."

After this, on the sixth holy day around the third hour, amid severe suffering, I went into a trance. And again he stood by my side saying to me, "The Lord has seen his people's distress and has turned the wrath of his outrage away from them." I said to him, "My lord, shall I not be the laughingstock of all those among whom this message was proclaimed?" He said, "You shall patiently and willingly endure all that has befallen you because of this. Earnestly turn to him, who—although he was Creator of the whole world—has endured men's mockery. Now for the first time, the Lord is testing your patience!"

See, my Lady, I have explained the whole sequence of the affair to you, so that you too may be aware both of my innocence and that of our abbot, and so that you may make it clear to others. I beseech you, moreover, that you both include me in your prayers, and that—insofar as the spirit of the Lord advises you—you requite me with some comforting words.

2. On the Feminine Aspect of Jesus

During the celebration on the eve of our Lord's Nativity, around the hour of the divine sacrifice, I entered a trance and saw something like a sun of marvelous brightness in the heaven, and in the middle of the sun the likeness of a virgin whose appearance was exceedingly beautiful in form and desirable to see. She was seated on a throne. Her hair was loosened over her shoulders, and on her head was a crown of the most splendid gold. In her right hand was a golden chalice. She was emerging from the sun, which surrounded her on all sides. From the virgin herself emanated a splendor of great brilliance, which seemed at first to fill the place of our dwelling. Then gradually expanding itself after some period of time, it seemed to fill the whole earth.

Now next to that same sun there appeared a great cloud, extremely dark and horrible to see. When I gazed at the cloud, it suddenly began to race and I saw it shade the sun. Repeatedly I saw it happen that the world was alternately darkened by the cloud and again illuminated by the sun. Whenever it occurred that the cloud approached the sun and obstructed its light from the earth, the virgin, who was enthroned within the sun, seemed to weep copiously, as if grieving greatly because of the darkening of the world. I beheld this vision throughout that day without interruption, and all the following night, for I remained ever wakeful in prayer.

On the holy day of Christmas, now, when the solemnities of the masses were being celebrated, I asked the holy Angel of God who appeared to me what sort of vision that was and what significance it had. He replied to me concerning that virgin, for I especially desired to know who she was. He said: "That virgin whom you see is the sacred humanity of the Lord Jesus. The sun in which the virgin is enthroned is the godhead, which wholly contains and illuminates the humanity of the Savior. The dark cloud which by turns keeps the brightness away from the earth is the iniquity that reigns in the world. It is this cloud that obstructs the benevolence of the omnipotent God, which ought to watch over the sons of men through the mediating humanity of the lord Jesus. The cloud brings the darkness of his anger upon the world.

"Now the fact that you see the virgin weeping is similar to what you read, namely, that before the destruction of the first generation, God was inwardly touched by a pain of the heart because of the abundance of human iniquity, and said, 'I regret that I created man.'

"For just as it was at that time, so it is also in these days, that the sins of men have disproportionately grown to the highest magnitude. Men do not realize what great things God has done for them through the Incarnation of his only Son— whom they dishonor with the worst acts, and they basely trample underfoot the benefits of his redemption. Nor do they give fitting thanks to him for all his toils, by which he was worn down on account of all their sins. This is the reason for the bitter accusation against them before the eyes of the terrible God. And now the Son of Man has no joy in this generation of men who provoke him, but he has more regret over those who do not show thanks for his kindness.

"This is the lamentation of the virgin who cries out against the cloud. Now the fact that you see the earth at times illuminated by the sun while the cloud departs means this: that God, because of the abundance of his mercy, does not altogether cease to watch over earth from heaven, because of his blessed seed, which is still preserved for him on earth.

"The golden crown which is on the virgin's head is the celestial glory that has been won through Christ's humanity for all those believing in him. The chalice in her right hand is the fountain of living water, which God has offered to the world, teaching and refreshing the hearts of those who turn to him, saying, 'If anyone is thirsty let him come to me, and let him drink, and from his womb shall flow the living waters'" (cf. John 7.37–38).

But on the third day after this, God's chosen one, St. John the Evangelist, appeared to me, when the office of the mass was being celebrated according to the custom, and together with him appeared the glorious Queen of Heaven. And I questioned him, as I had been advised, and said, "Why, my lord, was the humanity of the Lord the Savior shown to me in the form of a virgin and not in the form of a man?"

And he responded to my questioning, saying, "The Lord wished this to be done for this reason—so that the vision could be all the more aptly fitted to signify his blessed mother as well. For she, too, is truly a virgin enthroned within the sun, since the majesty of the highest God glorified her wholly, above all who preceded her on earth, and because Divinity descended through her to visit the darkness of the world.

"The golden crown which you have seen on the virgin's head signifies that this illustrious virgin was begotten of the seed of kings in the fleshly sense, and reigns over heaven and earth by her royal power. The drink of the golden chalice is the sweetest and most generous grace of the Holy Spirit, which has come down upon her more abundantly than upon any of God's saints.

She herself offers this drink to others, when through her intervention God grants a share of that same grace in his holy church to his faithful.

"Now the virgin's weeping is the constant intercession of that same most compassionate mother, by which she always intercedes with her son for the sins of God's people. These words which I tell you are true, because if she were not to restrain God's anger by her unceasing prayer, all the world would already have fallen into damnation because of its abounding iniquity."

3. Three Lovely Girls in Purgatory Who Need Elisabeth's Help

At once the Angel of the Lord carried me aloft, and we came to a verdant and beautiful meadow. And there appeared three lovely girls, wandering by a stream. They wore dresses that were somewhat soiled. They were barefooted, and their feet were extremely red. While I wondered inwardly who they could be and what they were doing there alone, they spoke to me:

"Do not be astonished. We are souls who were subjected to monastic discipline—one of us from the age of childhood, one from adolescence, and the third at a somewhat later age. And because people believed we had lived quite meritoriously, after we died we were not given so much help from the prayers of the faithful as we needed. And so, although we might have been released within the space of one year—if the help we were due had been rendered to us—see now, we have been kept here for thirty years! To be sure, we do not undergo any punishments other than the terrible fear we feel at the three grisly dogs that threaten continually to bite us. But if you would willingly request your abbot to offer up the divine sacrifice for the salvation of our souls and the souls of all the other faithful dead, we hope that we will be saved more swiftly and be able to ascend to the joys that have been prepared for us."

And when I had informed our sisters of these matters, they assembled themselves with devout mind, and undertook all together to suffer physical mortifications for those departed souls. They also distributed the psalter among themselves and prayed to the Lord with diligence for the salvation of those souls.

I also urged our lord abbot to come on the next day when the office of the vigil was recited, and he fervently celebrated the divine office for the faithful deceased. Once more, at the same moment of the mass, I was carried to that meadow I mentioned and again those same young girls appeared. They were hastening in the direction against the flowing course of the stream. I went over to them. I wanted to get to know where they had come from and what their names were. One responded for the three of them:

"It would take a long time to tell you our story, but I shall say it briefly. We are from Saxony. I am called Adelheid, beside me is my sister Mechthild—in the flesh as well as in spirit—and this is Libista, who is our spiritual sister."

I saw that they didn't wish to linger, and so I didn't want to hold them longer. But I earnestly sought their favor on behalf of myself and our entire congregation. I asked them to be mindful of us when they were received in the company of the saints. As soon as they had generously promised to do so, they began to make their way in greater haste. And as they made their way, an Angel of the Lord appeared in their presence in the form of a handsome young man. He led them, going rapidly before them.

As they approached a great hall where frequently I see the souls of the blessed being welcomed, three reverend men came from that hall. Each held a gold thurible in his hand, and they proffered incense to each of the three young girls. And soon the faces of the young girls and their gowns were made whiter than snow on account of the incense. And so they were led in bliss into that hall.

At the end of this vision, I was left depleted and ill.

4. The Book of Revelations of the Sacred Band
of Virgins of Cologne

To you who entertain pious sentiments toward those
things that are sacred, I, Elisabeth, maidservant of the hand-
maidens of the Lord who are at Schönau, disclose these things
which were revealed to me by the grace of God, concerning the
virginal band of St. Ursula, Queen of Britain. In ancient days this
band suffered martyrdom in Christ's name, in the suburbs of the
city of Cologne.

There are certain men of good repute who do not permit
me to be silent about these things. Although I resisted greatly,
they compelled me by their prolonged demands to investigate
this matter. To be sure, I know that those who are opposed to the
grace of God in me are therefore going to take the opportunity to
flog me with their tongues. But I shall endure it willingly. For I
hope that I shall receive some reward, if the honor of so many
martyrs may be increased—as a result of these words that the
Lord deigns to reveal about them—through my efforts.

When it was pleasing to the Lord to pity his precious martyrs, who had lain for many ages without honor under the feet of
men and beasts of burden alongside the walls of Cologne, it
happened that certain men dwelling in the same place approached the location of their martyrdom and opened up the
many tombs of the saintly bodies. Once these were removed
from there, the men transferred them to sacred grounds in the
vicinity, as it had been ordained by God. Now that was the year
1156 of the Lord's Incarnation when these things began to be
done. The emperor Frederick held the principate of the Roman
Empire, and Arnold II presided in the pontifical cathedral in
Cologne.

It was then that one precious martyr was found in that
same place among the others. On her tomb was the following
inscription: "St. Verena, virgin and martyr." This virgin martyr
was brought from there to our residence by the hand of our
reverend abbot Hildelin, after she had been given to him by
Gerlach, the lord abbot of Deutz, who was greatly inflamed with

pious devotion to gather and to honor the bodies of that sainted company.

While she was being awaited by the convent of our brothers, who were about to receive her near the entrance of the church, I, who was living in our chapter house—before I had heard anything of her arrival—received from the Lord the following evidence of her holiness: I entered a trance, and I saw on the road along which the sacred bones were being carried something like a flame of the most radiant whiteness, in the shape of a sphere. An angel of extraordinary beauty preceded it. In one hand he carried a smoking censer, while in the other he had a burning candle. Together they moved through the air in a gentle course as far as the interior of the church.

When on the next day, as the solemnities of the mass were being celebrated in her honor, I was in a trance. The same virgin appeared to me, standing in heavenly radiance, wondrously crowned and gloriously adorned with a palm of victory. I addressed her, therefore, and asked whether her name was exactly as it had been reported to us. In the same way, I inquired about the name of a certain martyr whose body had been brought together with hers, but without a definite name. And she responded saying, "My name is such as you have heard. However, through an error it was almost bound to be written differently, but I myself restrained the writer. Caesarius came with me, and when we entered this place, peace entered with us."

Again, on another day when the divine service was being celebrated for that martyr, he himself appeared to me in great glory. When I asked him what his rank had been in his earthly life, and for what reason he had undergone martyrdom with those virgins, he said, "I was a soldier in my earthly life, the son of the aunt of this holy virgin to whom I am now attached. She was very dear to me, so that when she left the country I followed her. Indeed, she gave me the strength to suffer my martyrdom, and when I saw how self-possessed she was in suffering pain, I suffered together with her. For a long time our bones were separated from one another, and now we have had our request granted by the Lord that they may be united."

I was led into considerable doubt over this speech, for I supposed, as everyone believes who reads the story of the British virgins, that the blessed sisterhood had journeyed on their pilgrimage without a retinue of men. Above all, I discovered something else to the contrary that further disproved this view strongly.

At the same time that the two above-mentioned martyrs were found, many bodies of holy bishops and of other great men were found among the tombs of the virgins. In the tombs of some individuals, stones were deposited with their titles inscribed upon them. From these it was recognized who they had been and where they had come from. The abbot I mentioned from the city of Deutz sent me the most distinguished, the most striking of these, hoping that something about them might be revealed to me by God's grace. He wanted to ascertain through me whether they should be believed. He had, to be sure, a suspicion about those men who had found the sacred bodies, for fear that they had perhaps fraudulently had those inscriptions written for the sake of profit.

I have taken care, however, throughout various passages in the present discourse, to set before the readers' eyes what sort of inscriptions these were, and what has been revealed to me about them. From this it may be perceived how that sisterhood—which the divine Fatherhood has deigned to honor with the escort of such high-ranking persons—ought to be worthily attended with all honor by Christ's faithful.

I was pondering to myself for some time these things which I have recounted, and I was longing to receive the revelations from the Lord which were being demanded of me. And it happened that the feast of the Blessed Apostles Simon and Jude [October 28, 1156] came up. While the office of the mass was being celebrated for them, a certain affliction of the heart came over me which I was accustomed to suffer when God's mysteries began to be revealed to me for the first time. After being plagued for a considerable period, I went into an ecstasy and so I grew calm. When I gazed in spirit upon heaven, as was my custom, I saw the martyrs I have mentioned. They were proceeding from the place of radiance, in which I am used to seeing visions of the saints, a long way down into the lower air. My faithful guardian angel of the Lord went before them. As I was in a trance I spoke to them, saying, "My lords, it is very kind of you that you deign to visit me now in this way, although I have offered you no service."

To this the blessed Verena responded, "We have sensed that your heart's desire has generously invited us, and for this reason we have come to visit you." So I said, questioning, "My lady, what does it mean that in the grave-plot of your martyrdom the bodies of bishops are also found buried? And should we believe in the inscriptions of the titles that are discovered there on some gems? And who was the inscriber of the stones?"

And she said to me, "God has singled you out a long time ago for this very thing: that he may cause these things to be revealed through you, which until now were unknown about us. For this reason do not bear it ill that you are being harassed by some people's requests to inquire into these matters. Let it be enjoined upon you, moreover, that through all the span of your life you fast upon bread and water on the eve of our passion each year. Or, if you are unable to carry this out, redeem yourself by the celebration of one mass, so that the Lord may deign to reveal to you what he has arranged to make known about us, and so that you may deserve to be joined one day to our company."

After this she began to speak the following words, saying with great joyfulness of countenance: "When we first began to congregate in our native country, our holy fame became widespread, and many people flocked together from everywhere to see us. It happened through God's ordinance that certain of the bishops of Britain also joined with us. Crossing the sea in our company, they arrived with us as far as Rome. On that journey the blessed Pantalus, Bishop of Basel, also joined us and led us as far as Rome, and became a companion in our suffering. His inscription was as follows: 'St. Pantalus, Bishop of Basel, who led the sacred virgins to Rome, where they were joyfully received. From there he turned back and came to Cologne, where he endured martyrdom with them.'"

After this, I interposed an objection to her words: "In their story we read specifically that when the blessed Ursula was playing at sea with her virgin companions according to her custom, and when the ships that the virgins were steering were driven farther out to sea than usual, a sudden gust of wind swept all the ships away from those seas and they did not return there any more. According to this account, it is indeed likely that they went on without a retinue of men."

To this she replied as follows: "The blessed Ursula's father, the King of Scottish Britain, a faithful man by the name of Maurus, was aware of his daughter's wishes, and he knew, just as she herself knew, what God had ordained for her. This he disclosed to some men whom he regarded as close friends. Upon their advice, he made cautious arrangements beforehand that his daughter, whom he loved most tenderly, should have on her departure men in her retinue whose comfort she herself needed as much as did her troop."

One of the noble inscriptions that was the most remarkable went like this: "St. Cyriac, the Pope of Rome, who received the holy virgins with joy and, upon his return with them to Cologne, endured martyrdom." Another was found beside it with the following: "St. Vincent, priestly cardinal." When I questioned the blessed Verena about these things, she said, "At the time when we entered the city of Rome, a holy man by the name of Cyriac presided over the apostolic see. He had left our borders, and since he was a wise and noble man and agreeable to all, he had been elevated to apostolic rank, and had already reigned over the Roman church for an entire year and eleven weeks. He was the nineteenth in number among the Roman pontiffs.

"When he heard that we had arrived, he was delighted, as were all his clergy, and he received us with great honors. To be sure, he had a great many blood relatives among us. But the next night after our arrival it was revealed to him by the Lord that if he relinquished the apostolic throne and set out with us, he would receive the palm of martyrdom together with us. Now he was keeping this revelation to himself, and he gave the benediction of holy baptism to many of our sisters who had not yet been reborn in Christ. When he found the opportune moment he made his wishes known.

"In the presence of the entire church he resigned the rank of his office amid the protestations of all, especially of the cardinals, who judged it to be madness, so to speak, that he was going astray, as if following the foolishness of mere women. The cardinals did not know the divine admonition that was impelling him. He, however, remained firm in his resolution, out of love for our virginity, for he himself had also—since his infancy—guarded a spotless virginity within himself. Consequently, from that time we lost all favor that we had previously enjoyed in the sight of the Roman church, and those who formerly had applauded us became strangers as far as we were concerned. However, our same venerable father, the blessed Cyriac himself, did not leave the city until on his advice another bishop of Rome named Anterus took his place as Pope."

After this, when I had examined the roll of the Roman popes and nowhere had found there the name of St. Cyriac, I questioned the blessed Verena again when she presented herself to me on a certain day. I asked why he had not been recorded among the other Roman prelates. And she said that this was the result of the clergy's outrage, since he had not been willing to complete his term in the rank of his high office.

Again on another day, when I had asked her about a certain Jacob, whose name was found written in his tomb without any addition, she seemed to me pleased to a certain extent about my question, and she joyfully responded to me, saying, "There was at that time a certain noble father of revered life, the archbishop Jacob, who had set out from our country to go abroad to Antioch. There he rose to the rank of prelate and reigned over that church for seven years. When he heard that the blessed Cyriac, a countryman of his, was elevated at Rome to the apostolic office, he went to visit him. He had already left the city before our arrival. When this was pointed out to us, a messenger was speedily dispatched to summon him back. He was found in a certain castle, which was about a two-day march away from Rome. When he heard of our coming, he immediately returned to us and became a companion of our journey and shared our martyrdom at Cologne. He himself, moreover, had some nieces among our religious order. At the exhortation of the blessed Pope Cyriac, since he was a wise man, he applied great diligence to learn the names of our sisters. These he inscribed to a large degree on the stones after we had been murdered, and he put them over our bodies. But before he was able to finish this, he was caught at this work by wicked men, and was slaughtered in our midst. Hence it is that certain of us are found with inscriptions, but others are not. Moreover, in the very hour of his martyrdom, when he was already about to be struck down, he requested this alone of his murderers—that his martyrdom might be deferred just long enough for him to be able to inscribe his own name on the stone. And this was granted him."

I asked also about the day of his martyrdom, because it was not believable from this account that he himself had also been killed on the same day that the virgins suffered. To this, too, she replied this way, "On the third day after our martyrdom, he suffered his martyrdom at the hands of the same tyrant who slew the blessed Cordula."

She also went on to add the account of a certain martyr whose inscription was "St. Maurisus, Bishop," and said, "The blessed Bishop Maurisus was also associated with us when we were still in Rome. This man had been a bishop for two years in Lavicana, though his place of origin was also our country. He was the son of a certain count from a line of great princes. He was the uncle of two virgins, Babila and Juliana, with whom he was found buried. He was, moreover, a man of the holiest life, and his preaching had great power. His greatest desire was that, whatever person outside the faith—whether Jew or Gentile—came to him, that person should not depart from him until he had laved him with the water of holy baptism. And so his name 'of Lavicana' correctly agreed with his office. To us he brought with him the blessed Claudius, a Spoletan whom he himself had ordained as a deacon, and his brother Focatus, a young layman who had not yet been advanced to military service. These two remained constant to our bishops; they served them diligently and underwent martyrdom with them."

She said this because I had also questioned her about these men, having seen their inscriptions. She also added of her own accord, "All the bishops who were on the voyage with us had their quarters apart from us, but on Sundays they usually came into our midst, strengthening us with divine discourse and with the communion of the Lord's sacrament."

At one point I longed to inquire about the two bishops whose inscriptions I had received, which were as follows: "St. Foilanus, Bishop of Lucca, sent from the apostolic see, was struck down in this place and slain by the sword, and was buried with these virgins." And: "St. Simplicius, Bishop of Ravenna." It happened that on a certain day we were celebrating the memory of the blessed Virgin, Our Lady St. Mary, and St. Verena revealed her face to me as was her benevolent custom. When she had addressed several words to me, I asked her about these bishops, and she said, "These two had at that time set out for Cologne; on their return from Cologne they met the sacred band and so joined with the pope and clergy who were there. Returning again with them, they won the palm of martyrdom together with them."

I had been asked to investigate the inscription of a certain venerable tomb which had been inscribed in this manner: "Here in the earth lies Etherius, who lived twenty-five faithful years. He departed in peace." Beneath it was written in capital letters: REX. The letter R was large, and so arranged that within it two letters could be distinguished, namely, *P* and *R*. The two letters *E* and *X* were on the left side of the same figure, while on the right side a capital *A* had been inscribed.[10] On a certain stone found next to it this inscription was read: "Demetria the Queen." I therefore asked the blessed Verena about these things, and at the same time about a certain little girl who was found next to it, with the inscription "The maiden Florentina." And she replied with respect to all these things, saying, "King Etherius was the betrothed spouse of the queen St. Ursula. Now, Demetria was the mother of Etherius, while Florentina was the same man's sister."

Of her own accord she added, saying, "I will explain to you also the meaning of the letter *A* which has been written on the king's inscription. Take the same letter *A* three times in succession and add to it the three letters *X* and *P* and *R* and you will have AXPARA. This is the name of a certain duchess who was discovered to have lived in a place in the vicinity. Now, she was the daughter of an aunt of Etherius, and she was closely tied to him by the bond of love. This is what the inscriber wished to signify when he entwined her name with the king's name. It was not necessary to explain this more clearly, since it would eventually happen that all these things would be made clear through you."

While I was marveling to myself about these things, therefore, and supposing it to be altogether unbelievable according to the sense of history that the betrothed of St. Ursula had also undergone this martyrdom, one day the angel of the Lord, who customarily visited me, presented his appearance. And I questioned him, saying, "Lord, how did it happen that the youth who, as we read, had betrothed St. Ursula was joined with her in martyrdom although it has been written that she avoided marriage to him by fleeing?" And he said, "When the band of holy virgins was coming back from Rome on the very night on which their six-day journey was completed, King Etherius, who was remaining in English Britain, was advised by the Lord in a vision to encourage his mother Demetria to become a Christian. Because his father, whose name was Agrippinus, had departed from life in the first year in which he himself had received the grace of baptism. At the same time it was revealed to him that he was about to leave his country and meet his betrothed, who was already returning from Rome, and that he was going to suffer martyrdom with her and would receive an unwithering crown from God.

"He assented immediately to the divine admonition and caused his mother, who agreed to his urging, to be reborn in Christ. Taking her with his little sister, Florentina, also a Christian, he hastened to meet his most blessed betrothed. And he became her companion in martyrdom and in celestial glory."

I moreover questioned the angel, saying, "Why is it, lord, that this inscription says that he lived twenty-five faithful years? For we learn from history that he had not yet accepted the Christian faith when he began to negotiate his marriage to the blessed Ursula, and that three years before the marriage he was obliged to be instructed in the Catholic faith." And the angel replied, "Although this was so, nonetheless, before he had accepted the Christian faith, he had lived so temperately and so blamelessly, in keeping with the circumstance of that life he led at that time, that it seemed to the writer of his inscription that all those years of his could properly be called faithful."

After this, I was instructed, through our blessed Lady when she spoke with me one day, about a certain holy man whose inscription was "St. Clemens, bishop and martyr." She told me that the king I spoke of had brought Clemens with him when he had left his country.

Similarly, when I asked about a certain man whose inscription was "St. Marculus, Bishop in Greece," I received this response from the angel: "There was in the city that is called Constantinople a certain king by the name of Dorotheus, who had originally come from Sicily. His wife's name was Firmindina, and they had an only daughter called Constantia. It happened that both parents died while the daughter was still a virgin and without the solace of a husband. Her nearest relatives had betrothed her, therefore, to a certain youth, the son of another king. But he too was hindered by death before the time of the wedding. Constantia was happy at her reprieve and dedicated the inviolacy of her virginity to God, praying and beseeching that he would never permit her to be fettered to another man.

"Approaching the man of God, St. Marculus, the bishop of the aforementioned city about whom you have inquired, and who was according to the flesh an uncle of hers, Constantia begged his advice as to the protection of her virginity, and most earnestly entreated him to be her helper in this matter. While he was disturbed about this, it was revealed to him one night, through a vision from the Lord that St. Ursula and her virgins were about to come to Rome very soon. He was told that he should take Queen Constantia and together with her speedily make his way to that place. And he trusted the Lord's revelation. Taking the queen, who for the sake of the Lord spurned her kingdom and all the things of this world, he came to Rome, although the virgins about whom he had received the revelation had not yet arrived there. When they did arrive not long afterwards, the bishop and the queen joined their company. Upon their arrival with them at Cologne, they endured martyrdom for Christ. Moreover, Constantia herself is that woman whom your brother very recently brought to this place."

I asked, "Lord, she who was brought to this place, as they say, had the name 'Firmindina' in her inscription. How can you say that she was named Constantia?" And he said, "Many people in ancient times were accustomed to be called by their parents' names, so that they were designated by even two or three names. So she was given her mother's name of Firmindina. As a result of this it may have turned out that when her inscription was about to be written it was engraved under this name of Firmindina, while her own name, which was Constantia, was disregarded because the thing was done hastily. This very same thing happened to many others as well—that on that same occasion their names were disregarded, and other names were inscribed for them that were not their proper names."

An inscription also of the following sort was sent to me: "St. Gerasma, who led the holy virgins." Many requests were made of me to inquire about her for this reason: that she seemed to have been distinguished and worthy of being the leader of so great a company. But although I often had the opportunity and the will to ask the question, it was not granted to me, for the question slipped away from my memory so that I marveled over it to myself why it should happen this way.

But at length it turned out that the very person who had wanted me to ask questions about her sent to us three dear holy bodies which were from the company of virgins I have spoken of. And after three days of novena, there was the feast of the blessed apostle Andrew, and he himself appeared to me in the silent parts of the mass. With him were one exceedingly glorious martyr and two virgins. And I understood that they were the ones whose bodies had come to us. I therefore questioned the blessed Andrew about their names because they were completely unknown. And he said to me, "Ask them themselves, and they will tell you." When I had done this, one virgin replied and said, "I have been called Albina, and she who is with me was called Emerentiana. We were sisters in the flesh, the daughters of a certain count whose name was Aurelianus. This martyr, who came with us, was called Adrianus, and he was a king's son. When he was ten years old, he suffered martyrdom for Christ's sake."

And I said, "Lady, how shall we distinguish among your bodies? Which one belongs to which name?" She declared, "Mine is the tallest, while my sister's is the smallest; that of Adrianus, however, is of middle height." And I did not venture to question her further. But God placed in the mouth of the two witnesses this word about the name of the aforesaid martyr: how it was, and what his name was, and that he had been a king's son. This was revealed through a vision during the preceding night to the same brother who had brought the bodies.

After this, as I was pondering over that same martyr and longing to know something more definite about him, it seemed to me one night, in a vision of sleep, as if I were given a book written in golden letters. I read in it a lengthy account about him and his parentage, and how he had left his country with his four sisters, and how he had endured martyrdom with them. The names of those sisters, which I read there, were Babila, Juliana, Aurea, and Victoria. But although it seemed to me that I read all things in that same vision many times over and carefully, I was nevertheless unable to retain in my memory the sequence of the matter exactly as it was.

After a few days, however, the feast of the blessed Nicholas [December 6] approached, and while the office of the mass was being celebrated for him, he appeared to me in a manner consistent with his usual kindness. With him again were the three martyrs I have mentioned. I asked him, therefore, to reveal to me something more definite about St. Adrianus, and at the same time it occurred to me that I might inquire about St. Gerasma, about whom I have spoken. He replied to me with great kindness and said, "St. Gerasma, about whom you ask, was a queen of Sicily. She was truly of Aaron's faithful stock, and abundantly possessed the spirit of the Lord. She converted her husband King Quintianus. Although he was at first an extremely cruel ruler, she made of this wolf, as it were, the tamest lamb. This man had taken her from Britain, where she was the sister of the bishop St. Maurisus and of Daria,[11] the mother of the holy queen Ursula. She had three sons and six daughters. The smallest among them was the martyr St. Adrianus, this one of whom you have inquired. Adrianus's older brother was Dorotheus, King of Greece, who was the father of St. Constantia, who has been brought to you.

"At the same time, however, when the blessed Ursula was secretly discussing her sacred intention with her father, her father was feeling great uneasiness about the matter. He sent a letter to the blessed Gerasma, and revealed to her his daughter's wish, and disclosed to her the revelations that they had received from heaven. He desired to hear her advice, for he knew she was a woman of considerable wisdom. Now that woman, inspired with divine power, and knowing that the word had issued from God, set forth on the journey with her four daughters, Babila, Juliana, Victoria, and Aurea and with her little son Adrianus. Out of his love for his sisters he voluntarily flung himself into the pilgrimage. She left the realm in the hands of one of her sons and two daughters, and sailed as far as Britain. And so that entire sacred band of virgins was assembled and organized by her counsels. She was the leader of all of them on all the routes of their pilgrimage, through the guidance of her counsels. At the end she suffered martyrdom with them."

When St. Nicholas had recounted this, he perceived that I was marveling greatly to myself about this arrangement, and he said, "You have good cause to be surprised, for all this business was miraculously arranged by divine disposition." He added still further, "The martyrs whom God has sent you are very precious. For that reason, show your devotion in rendering them honor and service, for their coming is the beginning of great grace."

One time when she presented herself to my sight, I asked St. Verena (as it was suggested to me by a certain brother) who was responsible for the martyrdom of that blessed band. For bearing in mind the story which has been told in the preceding pages about Pope Cyriac, I noted that it was certainly not Attila, King of the Huns, who was, as some think, responsible for their persecution. The persecution carried out by Attila followed afterward at an interval of many years. To that query she answered as follows:

"When we were at Rome there were at the time in that very place two unjust princes whose names were Maximus and Affricanus. When they saw that we had a great throng and that many people were flocking to us and allying themselves with us, they became violently opposed to us. They feared that through us the Christian religion would gain many converts and become strengthened. Therefore, when they had reconnoitered the route along which we were to travel, they speedily sent envoys to a certain relative of theirs named Julius, who was a prince of the nation of the Huns. They incited him to lead out his army and to inflict persecution upon us and to destroy us. He swiftly obeyed their desire, and setting forth with an armed mob, rushed upon us when we reached Cologne, and there shed our blood."

But neither is this to be passed over in silence—what she said when I questioned her about the body of the blessed Ursula: "Her body has never been removed from its original burial place except in these days; truly she is there where her inscription is preserved." And she added to this, saying, "Our prayers have procured this from the Lord; that our bodies have been thus revealed in these days. He no longer desires our groans, which we uttered because we had been put away with such disregard and because no worthy praise was being accorded to God on our behalf. It will come about, however, before the last day, that our whole troop will be made known."

I received these words of God's revelations, not as acts of justice toward me, but through the merits of the holy virgins and the martyrs of Christ, who obtained them on the various feast days of the saints, as it has pleased God. These writings have been completed within the space of a little more than one year. And it happened that when nearly all these discourses had been completed, the feast day arrived of the martyrdom of those same 11,000 holy virgins [October 21].

While I was participating in the divine service, I went into a trance after the reading of the gospel lesson, as I was accustomed to do. I saw in a region of light a sight that is continually before my mind's eye, a numerous throng of virgins, remarkable in appearance and crowned as if with the purest gold. In their hands were the likenesses of palms, greatly gleaming. Their garments appeared a radiant white, sparkling in the likeness of snow when it is illuminated by the sun's splendors. And on their foreheads was the redness of blood, in testimony of the fresh blood they had shed in their holy confession. With them, moreover, there also appeared a great many illustrious men with these same tokens.

Now I had a desire still to ask something of them. But because there was such a large number of them, I did not know which one of them I could address. Immediately two of them, strikingly distinguished in appearance, stepped forth from the company of the others. They stood apart in front of the rest and gazed directly at me. And I understood that this had been done because of me, and I addressed them saying, "I pray, my ladies, that you may deign to tell me who you are and what your names are."

One of them said, "I am Ursula, and she who stands with me is my sister Verena, the daughter of one of my uncles, the great prince." I spoke to her who was conversing with me, saying, "I beseech you, most holy lady, that you now deign to finish the history, and that you may be willing to clear up for me the manner of your burial. For so many things about you have been revealed to me, an unworthy sinner, through God's grace. Who were those men who at the time of such great persecution so attentively laid your sainted bones to rest and provided you with such honorable burials?"

To that she replied to me in this way: "There was at that time in Cologne a certain sacred bishop filled with the holy spirit named Aquilinus, who was the fourth after the blessed Maternus to guide the church there. When we were about to return from Rome, and were already preparing ourselves for that return, this man saw our entire throng (since it was revealed to him by God), and he became aware of the whole course of the martyrdom that we were about to endure. He also heard a voice saying to him that he should be prepared to bury our bodies, and that he should procure with haste all the things that would be necessary for our interment. Now while he was distressed about these things, two bishops came to him, of whom you have already heard something, that is to say, from Lucca and Ravenna. They recounted to him how it had been revealed to them by God through a vision that they were as yet uncertain as to the manner and under what circumstances this would come about. However, he about whom it was said on his inscription that he had been sent by the apostolic see received instruction about his journey from the leader of the apostolic see before we arrived. When, moreover, they themselves also had heard from the aforementioned bishop of Cologne about the vision that he had seen concerning us, they returned again upon the route by which they had come, and met us, and so remained constantly in our company until the end."

When she had said these things, I interposed a remark of this sort, saying, "I would like to know, my lady, what specific charge your adversaries made against you to put you to death." In particular I desire to know about you yourself. By what manner of death did you end your life?"

And she replied, saying, "The unjust tyrant who was responsible for our death demanded this of us, both with threats and cajolery that we renounce our spouse in heaven, the Lord Jesus Christ, and that we submit to his embraces and those of his men. But we had not come there for such a purpose, and we steadfastly refused to comply with his injurious desire. We chose rather to die than to be separated from our spouse. For this reason they vented their rage upon us. I myself was struck down by the shot of an arrow to my heart.

"When, therefore, all of us were lying in our blood, that venerable prelate carried out the deed of great piety towards us as he had been instructed, and fulfilled the duty of our burial with great attentiveness and dignity. The majesty of the Lord was present with him and those who labored with him, and God's angels directed them, and the work of our burial was swiftly completed. We, however, did not delay asking the Lord that he might grant him a reward for his toil. And it happened that soon after this he was removed from this life, and God gave him a unique reward for those honors that he paid us. Now, not many days afterwards, when our burial had been completed, there came a respectable man, Clematius, and he conveyed certain bodies which until that time had remained in a certain place. He buried them with great honor, just as he himself had been advised beforehand by the majesty of the Lord."

I immediately submitted a question, saying, "Was it Clematius, lady, who is said to have built your church?" And she answered, "Not at all; the truth is, that man came a long time afterwards." And when she had finished these explanations she added at the end, "May God grant a reward of his handiwork to that person who has revived the memory of our martyrdom!"

And now, may God reveal those hidden things to the one who is the witness of hidden things, and to those to whom he desires to reveal them, neither favoring the position of the great nor despising the humility of the small. To the benevolent and merciful God, let there be honor and glory and thanksgiving forever and ever. Amen.

NOTES

1. The standard text of Elisabeth's visions is F.W.E. Roth, ed., *Die Visionen von der hl. Elisabeth und die Schriften der Aebte Ekbert und Emecho von Schönau* (Brünn, 1884). Corrections to the text have been made by Kurt Köster in *Archiv für mittelrheinische Kirchengeschichte* 3 (1951): 243–315 and 4 (1952): 79–19. Of Elisabeth's popularity, Anne L. Clark notes "there are 145 known medieval manuscripts, forty-five of which transmit collections of these texts [of the visionary experiences] while the remainder transmit individual works or fragments thereof. By the end of the fifteenth century, Elisabeth's visions had been translated into Provençal, German, and Icelandic." *Elisabeth of Schönau: A Twelfth Century Visionary* (Philadelphia: U of Pennsylvania P, 1992), p. 2.

2. Clark (*Elisabeth of Schönau*, p. 19) quotes and translates from Ekbert's *de Obitu*, written after his sister's death: "Through you heaven was opened to earth and the secrets of God hidden from the ages flowed forth to us through the instrument of your mouth, and your eloquence was more precious than gold, sweeter than honey [cf. Psalm 18.11]. You made the glory of the citizens of heaven known to us and placed it as if before the eyes of our mind, and your blessed stories greatly inflamed our hearts with the desire for the homeland which we await." The nature and extent of Ekbert's influence on Elisabeth is fraught with interest, even mystery. "The fact that Ekbert took Elisabeth's experience seriously is demonstrated by his repeated recourse to her as a source of truth." (Clark, *Elisabeth of Schönau*, p. 18).

3. J.P. Strachey, *Poem on the Assumption* (Cambridge: Cambridge UP, 1924).

4. Why did the author of Passio II drop in this charmingly mundane detail? Was Tiel his or her native home? Tiel, a Frisian city at the mouth of the Rhine, had already been a crucial center in the development of Frankish trade and coinage. The Rhine was a major trade route in Dark Ages Europe, and by the ninth century weekly markets were held at Tiel. See Peter Spufford, *Money and Its Use in Medieval Europe* (Cambridge: Cambridge UP, 1988, repr. 1989), pp. 12, 28.

5. *The Passion of Saint Ursula [Regnante Domino]*, trans. with notes and introduction by Pamela Sheingorn and Marcelle Thiébaux (Toronto: Peregrina Publishing Co., 1991, 2nd printing), chapter 3, part 16. Thiébaux and Sheingorn, "Sermon on the Birthday of the 11,000 Holy Virgins," *Vox Benedictina* 10 (Summer 1993): 39–55.

6. Older versions of the legend had mentioned, or repeated in its entirety, the inscription in stone which told of the martyring of virgins in Christ's name. Clematius named on the stone now gets short shrift. Significantly, Elisabeth minimizes Clematius and *his* stone inscription, replacing these with the current, more telling inscriptions found in the tombs themselves.

7. The importance of *Sippe* emerges in the next century in the German grail romance, *Parzival*, by Wolfram von Eschenbach. At the close, the inheritors of the Grail castle are members of an extended family. My thanks to Pamela Sheingorn for suggesting a parallel to the Holy Kinship. And see Pamela Sheingorn, "Appropriating the Holy Kinship: Gender and Family History," pp. 169–198, in K. Ashley and P. Sheingorn, *Interpreting Cultural Symbols: Saint Anne in Late Medieval Society* (Athens: U of Georgia P, 1990). The concept of the Holy Kinship "created familial relationships among various named figures in the New Testament and apocryphal Gospels" with an emphasis on female genealogy (p. 169). We may further note that Elisabeth of Schönau uses the name of Emerentiana (originally the grandmother of the Virgin Mary) for one of Ursula's companions.

8. For an account of the English versions, see Marcelle Thiébaux, "'Dameisele' Ursula: Traditions of Hagiography and History in the *South English Legendary* and Layamon's *Brut*," in Klaus P. Jankofsky, ed., *The South English Legendary: A Critical Assessment* (Tübingen: Francke Verlag, 1992), pp. 29–48.

9. I am indebted to Jo Ann McNamara for this reference from *Das Leben der Schwestern zu Töss*, ed. F. Vetter (Berlin: Weidmannsche Buchhandlung, 1906).

10. Tervarent provides an explanation of the actual inscription Elisabeth was attempting to read. A Chi/Rho representing Christus Rex would appear as *X* over an *R*. Flanking this configuration would appear Alpha and Omega, appearing as *A* and *W*. Elisabeth would have had to read the *W* tipped to give her an *E*. Some ingenious rearranging yielded the words Rex and Axpara. *La légende de Sainte Ursule dans la littérature et l'art du moyen age*, I, p. 27.

11. The twelfth-century British chronicler William of Malmesbury writes that relics of Daria, Ursula, and two other virgin companions re-

pose at Glastonbury. *The Early History of Glastonbury: An Edition, Translation, and Study of William of Malmesbury's De Antiquitate Glastonie Ecclesie,* ed. John Scott (Woodbridge, Suffolk: Boydell Press, 1981), pp. 70–71.

FURTHER READING

Anne L. Clark. *Elisabeth of Schönau: A Twelfth Century Visionary.* Philadelphia: U of Pennsylvania P, 1992.

Ruth J. Dean. "Manuscripts of St. Elisabeth of Schönau in England." *Modern Language Review* 32 (1937): 62–67.

———. "Elisabeth, abbess of Schönau, and Roger of Ford." *Modern Philology* 41 (1944): 209–220.

Elisabeth of Schönau. F.W.E. Roth, ed. *Die Visionen von der hl. Elisabeth und die Schriften der Aebte Ekbert und Emecho von Schönau.* Brunn: Verlag der "Studien aus dem Benedictiner- und Cistercienser-Orden," 1884.

———. Adelgundis Führkotter, trans. *Briefwechsel: Hildegard von Bingen.* Salzburg: Muller, 1965.

Gertrud Jaron Lewis. "Christus als Frau: Eine Vision Elisabeths von Schönau." *Jahrbuch für Internationale Germanistik* 15 (1983): 70–80.

Schönauer Elisabeth Jubiläum 1965. Festschrift anlässlich des achthundert jährigen Todestages der heiligen Elisabeth von Schönau. Schönau, 1965.

Guy de Tervarent. *La légende de Sainte Ursule dans la littérature et l'art du moyen age.* 2 vols. Paris, 1931.

Marcelle Thiébaux and Pamela Sheingorn. *The Passion of Saint Ursula [Regnante Domino].* Trans. with notes and introduction. Toronto: Peregrina Publishing Co., 1991. 2nd printing.

CHAPTER 16

Brides of the Celestial Bedchamber

Mechthild of Magdeburg (*ca.* 1212–*ca.* 1282)
Beatrijs of Nazareth (1200–1268)

From the early thirteenth century, German and Dutch mysticism flowered among women visionaries who expressed their piety in the erotic imagery of divine love and marriage. Notable among these ecstatic authors are Mechthild, a native of Lower Saxony, and Beatrijs, a woman who spent her life in the duchy of Brabant.

Glimpses of Mechthild's life may be had from the autobiographical segments of her writing as well as the recollections of her younger companions, the nuns of Helfta. She was born in the diocese of Magdeburg, in a family that was apparently noble and well-to-do. She received her first "greeting"—the courtly *gruss* of an amorous glance—from the Holy Spirit when she was twelve. At twenty-three Mechthild left her family to be nearer to God, and took up a life of relative obscurity as a beguine in Magdeburg.

The urban sisterhood of the beguines that spread throughout France, Germany, the Netherlands, Belgium, and to some extent Italy took no religious vows, embraced no order or specific rule, and initially sought no authority from the church. Jacques de Vitry, Bishop of Acre (d. 1240), designates the beguines as the religious women of Flanders and Brabant. He wrote of them: "They melted altogether in wondrous love for God until it seemed that they bowed under the burden of desire and for many years they did not leave their beds except on rare occasions. . . . Resting in tranquility and with the Lord, they became deformed in body but comforted and made strong in spirit."[1]

Their name presumably derives from their patroness St. Begga, the older sister of Gertrude of Nivelles; both were women of the Carolingian dynasty. The mother of Pepin the Short, the widowed Begga founded an abbey at Andennes near Namur in Belgium, where her remains are laid.[2]

This movement of religious women (*mulieres sanctae*) received papal protection and recognition in 1216 and again in 1233. Beguines did not precisely renounce the world. They did not always live in groups, though some resided in houses in small walled communities. They might keep their own homes and carry on trades. They were pious women who dedicated their energies to prayer and charitable works at a time when there were no institutionalized hospitals or homes for the elderly. The *mulieres sanctae*—comprising nuns, recluses, virgins, and beguines—were active from about 1180 to 1270. However, their conspicuousness and their lack of formal affiliation were to make them vulnerable to accusations of mendicancy and vagabondage, even heresy. In 1273 Gilbert Bishop of Tournai sent a report to Pope Gregory X:

> There were among us women called beguines, some of whom blossom forth in subtleties and rejoice in novelties. They have interpreted in vernacular French idiom the mysteries of Scripture which are scarcely accessible to experts in divine writings. They read aloud in common irreverently and boldly, in conventicles, convents and public squares.[3]

The women certainly attracted disagreeable attention. The thirteenth-century French satirist Rutebeuf writes on a surly note in his *Dit des Béguines* that one couldn't trust a beguine: "If she sleeps, she's ravished away; if she dreams she's having a vision." The eventual condemnation of the beguines led to their being lumped together with so-called undesirables, as a sixteenth-century English source does: "young wanton wenches, and beguines, nuns and naughty packs." Actually they were women who chose a contemplative life in modest poverty and self-support through labor, following an apostolic ideal. Roger De Ganck has singled out three main principles by which they abided: frugality, virginity, and self-knowledge.[4]

Whether Mechthild lived independently or in a community is not known. She did, however, attract hostile attention by her outspoken warnings and denunciations of the clergy as "goats" and "wolves." In danger of persecution, she took refuge twelve years before her death with the nuns of Helfta monastery, near Eisleben in Saxony. Helfta was an outstanding center of female piety and learning. The best known of the Helfta women were Gertrude of Hackeborn, Mechthild of Hackeborn, and Gertrude the Great of Helfta, of whom the last two also left a significant corpus of mystical writing. Never formally Cistercian, since they were kept from being part of the order, the gray-clad nuns however followed the rule laid down in eleventh-century Cîteaux. The rule stressed work, prayer, study, and a balance between an individual inner life and the group's well-being.

Beatrijs van Tienen is better known as Beatrijs of Nazareth for the religious house where she spent the last half of her life and served as abbess, the Cistercian abbey of Our Lady of Nazareth. The convent was near Lierre, just south of Antwerp.

The chief facts of Beatrijs's life can be assembled from her mystical treatise *The Seven Manners of Minne,* from recollections of nuns with whom she lived, and from the *Vita Beatricis,* which her Latin biographer based on her own vernacular diary. This personal diary has since disappeared.[5] Born in Tienen in about 1200, Beatrijs was the youngest of six children. At age five she could recite the psalter by memory. Her mother, who was her first teacher, died when Beatrijs was seven. Her father, Bartholomew, sent her to a house of beguines at Zoutleeuw, or Léau, to be educated in the virtues, but she continued her liberal arts education at a school for girls and boys in the town. Eventually Bartholomew sent her to Bloemendaal (or Florival), a Cistercian abbey for which he acted as a manager, perhaps as a collector of revenues.

Beatrijs made her profession when she was about sixteen, and was sent by her abbess to La Ramée (Rameya), a Cistercian house where she was trained to write manuscripts, especially liturgical choir books. At La Ramée she formed a friendship with Ida of Nivelles, who was close to her age and who had been trained in the mystical life with the beguines of Nivelles. Beatrijs's own spirituality developed.

The rest of her family meanwhile followed the religious life. Her father and her brother Wikbert became lay brothers at Bloemendaal, and her sisters Christine and Sybille also entered that community. Eventually all of the family were sent to Maagdendaal, a foundation created by Bloemendaal near Beatrijs's birthplace of Tienen, a town not far from Leuven. It was at Maagdendaal that Beatrijs, at the age of twenty-five, received her consecration as a virgin. While Maagdendaal was setting up another foundation at Nazareth, Beatrijs had the task of copying the choir books for the new community's use. Beatrijs, Christine, and Sybille moved to Nazareth in May 1236. Beatrijs's early assignment was to care for the novices. The following year she became prioress, an office she held until her death in August 1268 after a severe illness of eight or nine months. Her *Seven Manners of Minne* was composed late in her life. In it "she gathered everything under one dynamic concept: *Minne*."[6]

The writings of both Mechthild and Beatrijs creatively synthesize two major traditions of amatory literature. These are the imagery of holy nuptials from the *Song of Songs*, and the secular *Minnesang*, or *Minnelied*, the body of courtly love lyric that thrived for 300 years in Germany. A brief look at both these traditions will illuminate the borrowings and the individual departures of Beatrijs and Mechthild.

The Old Testament *Song of Songs* (also called the *Song of Solomon*, or the *Canticles*) is an epithalamium, a marriage song, made up of lyric, dramatic, and narrative elements. The text, with its voluptuous imagery, gave rise to an extensive Christian exegesis. In the third century, the Alexandrian churchman Origen composed a commentary which proved influential thereafter. The *Song of Songs*, he wrote, is sung "after the fashion of a bride to her bridegroom, who is the word of God, burning with celestial love. Indeed, he loves her deeply, whether she is the soul, made in his own image, or the Church."[7]

Bernard of Clairvaux and William of St. Thierry further developed the allegorical reading of this rich and sensual text. Eventually, the Bridegroom (*Sponsus*) was both Christ and God the Father; the figure of the Bride (*Sponsa*) might signify the Self, the Soul, the Church, the Virgin Mary, the nurturing Mother, or Woman as prophet.[8]

Along with this current in theological writing, the secular and courtly literature of Minnesang flourished. The literary conceit of "courtly love" migrated from the troubadours in the south of France to Germany in the twelfth century, to give shape to *Minne*. Sometimes the concept is personified as Lady Minne (Frau Minne), a powerful feminine figure as coercive and adamant a force as the goddess Venus. Lady Minne demands compliance, service, and feudal allegiance. She plants her triumphant banners in the human heart, and there she reigns, causing much suffering and elation.

The word *Minne* is thought to have arisen from Latin *mens* (mind) or the Greek *memini* (remember). The Middle English word *minnen* meant to ponder or to remember. In present-day Oslo the "memorial park" preserving the ruins of a medieval church and monastery is called the *Minne-park* in Norwegian.

As lover-protagonist, the poet is devoted to the praise of a lady. In the development of the love lyric, the man entreats a lady, pledging her his love service (*Frauendienst*, "the service of women"). She may seem remote, but possession is part of the courtly bargain: solace in return for service. The reward of mercy the lover hopes for in his lyric stance is sexual union and rapture. Often the language of religion is adopted to express erotic longing: the lover's agony is that of a "martyr," his beloved is an "angel," she is "heaven." Winning her sexual favor leads her lover to "redemption"; their union is described in terms of a divine ascent.

Even while he loves her, the poet is intent on recording his deep absorption in the yearning, sorrowing mental states that Minne goads him into. The contemplation of Minne leads to an intensely interior concentration on desire; a private, intimate exaltation; a spiritual and physical soaring. Built into the lyrics of love are concepts of grief and inadequacy, the lover's fear that his efforts may prove insufficient, and his anxiety over abandonment.

Minnesang embodied an elaborate system of wildly oscillating contraries of mood, but the object was the fulfillment of desire through union with the beloved. The persona of the sorrowing Minne servant presents himself as agonized and submissive, ravished, wounded, mournful, groveling, and grateful for the slightest favor. He languishes in pain for love that either is or is not granted. The lady is both kind and cruel, she is despotic and adorable, she kills and gives life. Parting from her is a form of exile, reaching her is a quest or pilgrimage. The poet swings between abject misery and sheer bliss. He begs for mercy and favor; the joy he strives for is *hôher muot*—the pure joy, the exaltation, the "high mood" that comes with mutuality and union. The poet-lover claims he is steadfast and faithful.

Theorizing about "what is Minne" arose in the romances, such as Gottfried von Strassburg's *Tristan* and Wolfram von Eschenbach's *Parzival* and *Titurel*, and from the lyrics themselves. At the height of the tradition, a well-known poet opens his lyric with these words: "Saget mir ieman, waz ist minne?" ("Let anybody tell me—what is Minne?") The question is playful, since hundreds of poems already dealt with the question. This thirteenth-century poet, Walther von der Vogelweide, gives a simple answer of "joy shared by two hearts," in his disarmingly simple lyric, knowing that other, fiercely complicated definitions might also be advanced. It is a question that lies seriously at the core of mystical writing as well. Hadewijch of Brabant, a thirteenth-century beguine, writes in her book of visions (vision 3): "What and who is Minne?" a query that is answered rather solemnly by God, who declares his identity.

The German mystic Mechthild and the Dutch mystic Beatrijs adopt the language and imagery of Minnesang to sing of the soul's ecstatic and erotic pleading with God. Interestingly, among male theologians, the concept of the love between God and the soul was worded as *amor, dilectio,* and *caritas,* sometimes interchangeably and sometimes with specific shades of meaning.[9] By using the vernacular, however, and depending on the popular noun *minne* and the verb *minnen,* women mystics unlettered in Latin gain access to a whole system of immediate meanings and images in the erotic vocabulary. Nor do they appropriate only the most polished Minnesang conventions. Their lyric stance also harks back to the genre of the earliest women's songs. The lonely woman plays the actively petitioning role and begs her lover to come to her. The genre was often called *trûtliet* ("sweetheart song") from *mîn trût* ("my dear").[10] As we have seen, the songs of barbarian women (chapter 7) and of the more sophisticated *trobairitz* (chapter 11) belong to this type. Women's songs were often anonymous, but men liked to write them in a female voice. "The man from Kürenberg" (Der von Kürenberc) adopts a female persona in his "Falcon Song": a woman trains a falcon and tries to secure it to her with gold fetters, but it takes flight. The lyric is a succinct statement about the restless male who is hard to subdue to love.

In the writings of the beguines and other consecrated women, the conventions of the *Song of Songs* and Minnesang appear side by side, often entwined. The fusion is perfectly exemplified by Mechthild's "For I am sick with love for him!" The line is translated from the *Song of Songs* (2:5), in which the loving soul portrays herself as "minne-sick" ("und das ich minnesiech nach ime bin").[11] Both Mechthild and Beatrijs borrow freely from the erotic conventions and vocabulary of Minnesang and the *Song of Songs*. There is a wonderful boldness, an unleashed vigor in their demands for joyous union with their heavenly beloved.

Mechthild began *The Flowing Light of Godhead* when she was forty-three. Its seven books represent stages of her experience. She had written the first six parts of her visions, meditations, dialogues, lyrics, and allegories outside the cloister; these were gathered and rearranged by the Dominican Heinrich of Halle, who may have been her confessor. At Helfta, elderly, sick, and blind, she dictated the seventh part to her companion nuns.

Claiming to know no Latin (book II.iii), Mechthild used the Low German vernacular. Heinrich of Halle later made a "smoother" Latin version of the first six books. In the fourteenth century Heinrich of Nördlingen turned the work into High German verse, helping to spread Mechthild's cult among the mystics who were his followers in Basel. The Latin and High German versions are extant, but Mechthild's original is lost.

In addition to the poetic imagery of the celestial erotic embrace, Mechthild draws upon medieval cosmic elements. Air, fire, and water inform her visions of divinity, as in the merging of the soul's breath with heaven's purifying fire, or in "flowing light." Liquidity especially becomes a godlike quality, with the parched soul's thirsting for the Spouse's divine moisture—dew, rain, blood, honey, milk, and wine.

Chief among the personages in Mechthild's dramatic dialogues are God, his messenger Love (the courtly Minne), and Mechthild's own Soul. The Soul is feminine, a poor and lonely courting maiden, not passive but brazen in her frank desire. Through Soul, the mystic's rapture burdened with spiritual torment finds voice in the language of Minne's dialectic—love's sweetness shot through with anguish—which began with the lyrics of the troubadours. God's messenger can be Frau Minne, a noble lady ranking high in heaven's court who is empowered to woo the Soul as a queenly bride for the Lord. At another time Minne appears as a beautiful young man in a garden or orchard, a jousting knight, a dancer, or a drinking companion.

In the first selection, after an exchange of greetings and bargainings, Lady Minne woos the Soul for God, not gently but fiercely, stalking her prey as would a huntress. In this guise Minne also appears in secular lyrics and romances. A daring set of erotic figures is drawn from the love chase, in which her soul joins in an ecstatic union with divine Minne. Liberated from actual sexual love, the poet can use the body's terminology, openly uttering a transcendent joy in being clubbed into submission. The hunt of love, an image from Greek and Latin antiquity, was fully developed in Ovid's *Art of Love* and enjoyed a long and rich tradition in medieval literature. Mechthild's secular German contemporaries, Burkart von Hohenvels, Wolfram von Eschenbach, Gottfried von Strassburg, and others wrote of the *Minnejagd*, the "hunt of Minne."[12]

For Mechthild nothing less than the capture, clubbing, binding, and slaying of herself as quarry will ensure her union with the heavenly Bridegroom on an Easter day of joyous resurrection. The dialogue varies the hunt imagery with that of the letter and seal, images of enfeoffment seen in the troubadour lyric.

The second selection tells of the Soul's arrival at court and the trade of amorous conversation between her and God. The third selection, in the tradition of the *Song of Songs*, describes Mary's spousal reception of God's love, the Soul's preparation as a bride, and her divine wedding dance of love.

In the fourth selection Minne is a seductive young man inflamed with longing for Mechthild's soul. The poet boasts of her thirst for divinity in the heavenly wine cellar. As the dialogue opens, Mechthild's Soul is already drunk with God. The wine cellar of celestial love became a commonplace of mystical writing, following the more restrained notions of Augustine and Bernard of Clairvaux of "sober inebriation" (which Bernard says is *not* like a wine-induced madness). Of Ida of Nivelles, who was Beatrijs of Nazareth's young teacher, her biographer wrote: "She was frequently brought by the Beloved into the wine cellar. There she received the goblet filled with the seasoned wine of his divine love. She became inebriated and carried away."[13]

The metaphor of an alcoholic carouse in the heavenly tavern anticipates by six centuries Emily Dickinson's paradisal drunkenness on the bounties of summer ("I taste a liquor never brewed/From tankards scooped in pearl") that ends with seraphs and saints staring in amazement from heaven's windows "to see the little tippler/Leaning against the sun!"

Mechthild's erotically oriented imagery, however, features a male companion, Minne, who invites the Soul to drink further and who reveals his own desire for her. The besotted feminine Soul, eager and unrepentant, acknowledges her degraded condition. Minne's delicious promises must be paid for. The dramatic situation of the tavern prodigals gives way to that of the *Song of Songs*, in which the inebriated Bride first enjoys the Bridegroom's caresses but later wanders destitute and scorned through the streets looking for him. Lost though she may be, she continues to hear the Bridegroom's whispers of solace to her.

The imagery of deep drinking occurs in Beatrijs of Nazareth as well, though with a slightly different emphasis. Beatrijs's Christmas meditation in her *Vita*, as Caroline Bynum has pointed out, employs the metaphor of "drinking Christ, as rivulets, as streams, or as a mighty river."[14]

Beatrijs writes:

> She looked and behold, the all-powerful and eternal Father was emitting from himself a great river from which many brooks and brooklets here and there branched off and offered a drink of water springing up to eternal life to those who willed to approach them. Some drank from the

river, some drank from the brooks, and some drank from
the brooklets. Beatrice, to whom it was granted to see
these things, was allowed to drink from all of them.[15]

In her Sixth Minne, Beatrijs expresses a joy that is orgasmic, like
a vessel filled to overflowing that spills at a touch.

The concept of *minne dienst*, service to Minne, pervades
Beatrijs's writing. The *Seven Manners of Minne*—its title nicely
assonanced and alliterating—builds a stepwise ascent to bliss in
clearly defined stages: (1) the beginning of desire and the ridding
of wayward impulses; (2) the image of the soul as a young
serving girl who waits on her lord, not for wages, but because
she adores him; (3) the feeling of anxious despair that the soul's
efforts may be fruitless; (4) a first sense of ecstasy, of sinking and
melting, when the soul is like a vessel filled to the brim and in
danger of overflowing; (5) the vehemence of heat and fever
mounting so strongly that the overwrought body sickens and the
mind is driven to lunacy; (6) the attainment of clear joyful serenity, in which the soul orders herself like a prudent housewife,
swims deeply like a fish in the flood, and soars like a bird; (7) the
sweet immersion in Minne, a holy force that toys with the soul,
both pleasurably and cruelly, while the soul—exiled in this
world—thirsts for the celestial marriage with her Bridegroom.

Mechthild of Magdeburg: *The Flowing Light*
of the Godhead

1. *Minne's Greeting to the Queen, Mechthild's Soul,*
and the Hunt of Love

How Minne and the Soul spoke together:

Mechthild's Soul came to Minne and greeted her with
deep meaning, saying, "God greet you Lady Minne."

Minne: God reward you, dear lady Queen.
Soul: Lady Minne, you are very welcome to me.
Minne: Lady Queen, I'm honored by your greeting.

Soul: Lady Minne, you struggled a long time with the high holy ghost, and you conquered him so that he gushed all at once into Mary's humble maidenhead.

Minne: Lady Queen, it was for your honor and delight.

Soul: Lady Minne, you have taken from me everything I ever won on earth.

Minne: Lady Queen, you've made a blissful exchange.

Soul: Lady Minne, you've taken my childhood from me.

Minne: Lady Queen, I've given you heavenly freedom for it.

Soul: Lady Minne, you've taken my whole youth.

Minne: Lady Queen, I've given you many holy virtues for it.

Soul: Lady Minne, you've taken my friends and kin.

Minne: Ah, Lady Queen, that's a worthless lament!

Soul: Lady Minne, you've taken the world from me, worldly honor, and all worldly riches.

Minne: Lady Queen, in an hour I'll recompense you on earth with all you desire of the Holy Ghost.

Soul: Lady Minne, you have so harassed me that my body is seized by sundry ills.

Minne: Lady Queen, I've given you much high wisdom.

Soul: Lady Minne, you have squandered my flesh and my blood.

Minne: Lady Queen, by that you've been enlightened and raised up with God.

Soul: Lady Minne, you are a robber woman. Pay me back for that!

Minne: Lady Queen, then take my very self!

Soul: Lady Minne, now you have repaid me a hundredfold here on earth.

Minne: Lady Queen, now have you claimed God and his whole kingdom! (Book I.i)

The Soul's handmaids and Minne's beatings:

The holy Christian virtues are the Soul's handmaids. The Soul in sweet sorrow cries out her anguish to Minne.

Mechthild's Soul speaks:

      Ah, dearest Lady,
      you've been my lady-in-waiting, lurking so long,
      now tell me what's to become of me?

You have hunted, seized, and tied me so fast
and wounded me so deeply
that I shall never be healed.
You have beaten me with a club.
Tell me whether I shall ever finally recover!
Shall I not be slain by your hand?
It would have been better for me if I had never
    known you.

Lady Minne's reply:

I hunted you for my delight;
I seized you for my desire;
I bound you tightly for my joy;
When I wounded you, you became one with me.
When I beat you with a club, I became your strong
    ravisher.
It was I who drove out the Almighty from
    heaven's kingdom
and deprived him of his human life,
then gave him gloriously back to his father.
How could you, vile worm, think you could
    recover from me?

Mechthild's Soul:

Tell me, my Queen, I thought a small medicine
    from heaven
that God had often given me
might help me to escape you.

Lady Minne:

If a captive wants to escape death,
let her reach for water and bread.
The medicines that God has given you
are nothing more than days of grace in this life.
But when your Easter Day dawns
and your body then meets its death blow,
I shall be there, encircling you, piercing you,
and I shall steal your body
and give it to Love.

Mechthild's Soul:

> Ah, Lady Minne,
> I have written this letter dictated from your lips.
> Now give me your great seal to affix to it.

Lady Minne:

> She whom God has captured for himself
> knows where the seal must be pressed.
> It lies between the two of us.

Mechthild's Soul:

> Be quiet, Minne, give me no more advice; I and all
>   earthly creatures bow to you.
> Oh my dearest lady,
> tell my friend his couch is ready,
> and I am lovesick for him.
> If this letter is too long, I have plucked a few
>   blossoms from its meadow.
> This is its sweet lament:
> Whoever dies of love shall be entombed in God.
>   (Book I.iii)

2. *The Soul Comes to Court*

The courtly journey of the Soul to whom God shows himself:

When the poor soul comes to court, she is prudent and well-behaved. She joyfully gazes at her God. Ah, how lovingly she is welcomed there! She keeps quiet, but is extravagantly eager for his praise. And he shows her with great yearning his sacred heart. It is like red gold burning in a great coal fire. And God lays her in his glowing heart so that the high prince and the little maidservant embrace and are made one like water and wine. Then she is annihilated and takes leave of her senses so that she can do no more, and he is sick with love for her as he always was, for he neither grows nor diminishes. She says, "Lord, you are my solace, my desire, my flowing stream, my sun, and I am your mirror!" This is the journey to court for the enamored Soul, who cannot live without God. (Book I.iv)

How God comes to the Soul:

> I come to my love
> as a dew upon the blossom. (Book I.xiii)

How the Soul welcomes and praises God:

Ah joyful sight! Ah loving greeting! Ah minne-like embrace! Lord, the wonder of you has wounded me! Your favor has quelled me! O you lofty rock, you are so nobly cleft; none may nest in you but your dove and nightingale. (Book I.xiv)

How God receives the Soul:

Be welcome, darling dove; you have flown so fervently over earth's kingdom that your feathers rise strong to the kingdom of heaven. (Book I.xv)

How God compares the Soul to four things:

You taste of the grape, you smell of balsam, you glitter like the sun, you are the increase of my highest love. (Book I.xvi)

The soul praises God in five things:

> O you God, gushing forth with your gifts!
> O you God, flowing in your love!
> O you burning God in your desire!
> O you melting God in the union of your love!
> O you God resting on my breast, I cannot be without
>   you! (Book I.xvii)

God compares the soul to five things:

> O you fair rose in the thornbriar!
> O you fluttering bee in the honey!
> O you pure dove in your being!
> O you lovely sun in your shining!
> O you full moon in your sphere!
> I can never turn away from you. (Book I.xviii)

God caresses the soul in six things:

> You are my pillow, my minne-bed, my secret resting place, my deepest desire, my highest honor. You are a delight of my godhood, a solace of my manhood, a brook for my burning heat. (Book I.xix)

The Soul responds to God in six things:

> You are my mirror—mountain peak of perfection—a feast for my eyes, a losing of myself, a storm of my heart, a ruin and scattering of my forces, and my highest safety! (Book I.xx)

3. *The Celestial Wedding of Mary and of the Soul*

The tidings to Mary; how the virtues follow one another and how the soul is a jubilus—a shout of joy—in the Trinity:

> The sweet dew of the Trinity that has no beginning sprang from the eternal Godhead in the flower of the chosen Virgin, and the fruit of the flower is an immortal god, a mortal man and a living consolation of everlasting love.
>
> Our Redeemer has become our Bridegroom! The Bride has become drunk with the sight of his noble face. In her greatest strength she takes leave of her senses; in her greatest blindness she sees most clearly; in her greatest clarity she is both dead and living. The longer she is dead, the more joyously she lives. The more joyously she lives, the more she journeys. The more she tastes Minne, the more she is flowing. The richer she grows, the poorer she becomes. The deeper she dwells, the wider she ranges. The more she offers herself, the deeper are her wounds. The more she storms, the more minne-like is God toward her. The higher she floats, the more beautifully she shines from the glance of the Godhead as she comes nearer to him. The more she labors, the more softly she rests. The more she grasps, the more quietly she falls silent. The more loudly she cries out, the greater wonder she works with his power and her might. The more her desire grows, the greater the wedding feast, the more enclosed the minne-bed. The tighter the embrace, the sweeter the kisses of their mouths. The more lovingly they gaze at each other, the

harder it is to part. The more he gives her, the more she squanders, the more she has. The more humbly she takes her leave, the sooner she comes back. The more ardent she is, the more she glows again. The more she burns, the more gloriously she shines. The more enveloping God's praise of her, the more avid is her longing for him.

This is how our sweet Bridegroom went in the shout of joy of the holy Trinity. Since God wished to be alone no longer, he made the soul and gave his own great love to her.

Therefore, O Soul, what are you made of that you soar so high above other creatures and, though you mingle with the Holy Trinity, yet you remain yourself?

Soul: You spoke about my origins, and now I will tell you the truth—I was created in the same state of Minne, and so nothing can solace or arise from my nobility except Minne alone. (Book I.xxii)

The Bridegroom's beauty, and how the Bride shall follow him:

Vide, mea sponsa! See, my Bride! How beautiful my eyes are, how fair is my mouth, how fiery is my heart, how gentle are my hands, how swift my feet—and follow me!

You shall be martyred with me, betrayed through envy, tracked to an ambush, seized in hatred, bound through hearsay, your eyes bandaged so that you won't recognize truth, beaten by the world's rage, dragged to judgment through confession, beaten with sticks, sent to Herod with mockery, stripped with banishment, scourged with poverty, crowned with temptation, spat upon with abuse. You shall carry your cross in the hatred of sin, be crucified in the denial of all things by your own will, nailed on the cross with the holy virtues, wounded with minne, die on the cross in holy steadfastness, your heart pierced with indwelling oneness, released from the cross in true victory over all your enemies, buried in paltriness, raised up from death to a blessed end, carried to heaven on a draught of God's breath. (Book I.xxix)

You shall be a lamb in your pain, a turtledove, a bride:

> You are my lamb in your pain—
> You are my turtledove in your moaning—
> You are my bride in your abiding. (Book I.xxxiv)

God asks the Soul what she brings:

> You hunt sorely for your love.
> Tell me—what do you bring me, my Queen? (Book
> I.xxxix)

The Soul answers that it is better than four things:

> Lord, I bring you my treasure:
> It is greater than the mountains,
> Wider than the world,
> Deeper than the sea, higher than the sky,
> More beautiful than the sun, more manifold than
> the stars,
> And more weighty than earth's whole kingdom.
> (Book I.xl)

The seven ways to Minne, the bride's three gowns, and the dance:

God speaks: Ah, Soul filled with minne, do you wish to know where your path lies?

The Soul: Yes, dear Holy Ghost, teach it to me.

[God Speaks:] You must overcome the sorrow of contrition, the pain of confession, and the labor of repentance, the love of the world, the temptation of the Devil, the luxuriance of the flesh, the destruction of your own will which so fiercely drags down many souls that they never can come back to true love. Then when you have beaten down most of your enemies, you are so tired that you cry out, "Beautiful youth, I'm longing for you—where shall I find you?" The young man will say:

> "I hear a voice
> that speaks a little of minne.
> I have courted her many days

> but her voice has never come to me.
> Now I am stirred,
> I must go to her.
> She is the one who bears pain and minne together.
> In the morning, in the dew, there is the sheltered
>   rapture that first enters the soul."

Her chambermaids, the five senses, speak: Lady, you must gown
    yourself in many colors.
Soul: Love, where shall I go?
The senses:

> We have heard it rumored
> that the Prince is coming to you
> in the dew and in the lovely song of birds.
> Ah, lady, do not delay!

So the Soul dresses herself in a shift of gentle humility, so
lowly that she can endure nothing under it. Over it goes a white
gown of clear chastity, so pure that she can endure neither
thoughts nor words nor sentiments that might sully it. Then she
covers it with a mantel of holy reputation, which she has gilded
with all the virtues.

Then she goes into the wood, which is the company of
blessed folk. There the sweetest nightingales sing in harmonious
union with God, both day and night, and she hears many sweet
voices there of the birds of holy understanding. But the young
man still does not come. He sends her messengers, for she wants
to dance. He sends her Abraham's faith, the Prophets' yearnings,
and the chaste humility of our lady St. Mary, all the holy virtues
of Jesus Christ, and all the goodness of his chosen ones.

And so a lovely dance of praise will take place. Now the
young man comes and speaks to her:

"Maiden, as gallantly as you follow the dance, now, my
chosen partner, you will lead the dance!" But she says:

> I cannot dance, lord, unless you lead me.
> If you want me to leap ardently,
> you must yourself first dance and sing.
> Then I will leap into minne,
> from minne into understanding,
> from understanding to enjoyment,

from enjoyment to far beyond all human sense.
There shall I stay and whirl still dancing in a ring.
(Book I.xliv)

4. *The Heavenly Wine Cellar*

Minne speaks:

If you'll come with me to the wine cellar
it will cost you a great deal.
Even if you buy a thousand marks worth of wine,
your money will be squandered in an hour.

If you want to drink wine straight, without water, you'll keep spending more than you have, and the tavernkeeper won't pour you the full amount. You'll be poor and naked, despised by all those people who'd rather seek pleasure in a pool of muddy water than waste their wealth in the lofty wine cellar.

You'll also have to suffer
when those people who go with you to the wine
cellar envy you.
How scornful they'll be of you
because they dare not risk the huge expense,
preferring to drink their wine diluted with water!
Darling lady bride, I'll go to the tavern,
and eagerly spend all that I have,
and let myself be dragged through hot coals of
love,
and submit to being beaten with the fiery brands
of love's slanderers,
so that I can go often to that blessed wine cellar!

Mechthild's Soul answers:

I choose eagerly to go there, since I can't do without Minne. While he torments and insults me—this one who pours out the tavernkeeper's wine for me—still, he has been drinking it too.

I've become so drunk with wine
that I am truly thrall to all creatures,

and it seems to me in my human disgrace
and my newfound wantonness
that no man ever treated me so badly before—
he can do any kind of sin with me, unblessed
    woman that I am.

And so I would not take vengeance on my enemies for my
sorrow, even though I know they might break God's law.

Minne comforts the Soul:
    Dearest playmate, when it happens that the wine cellar is
locked, you must take to the street, hungry, poor and stripped
bare, and so despised that nothing is left for you of the banquet
of Christian living except your own faith; then you can still have
Minne, for that is never spoiled.

Lady Bride, I have such hunger for the heavenly
    father
that I forget all sorrow.
And I have such thirst for his son
that it takes all earthly yearning from me.
And I have for both of them such a ghostly need
that it goes higher than all I can grasp
of the father's wisdom.
But I can endure all the work of the son,
and all the solace of the Holy Ghost
that befalls me.

Whoever is seized by this torment must always—however
unworthy—hold fast to God's holiness. (Book III.iii)

Beatrice of Nazareth: *The Seven Manners of Holy Minne*

Seven manners of loving come down from the highest place, and
work their way back again to the uppermost place.

The Soul's First Yearning

First is the yearning that comes and arises out of Minne. It must reign a long time in the heart before it can drive out its adversary, and work its might and understanding and valiantly grow in us. This manner is a desire that surely comes out of Minne. The good soul truly wants to serve and to follow Minne. (from "The First Minne")

The Soul Is Like a Young Girl Eager to Serve for Nothing

Sometimes the soul has another way of loving. She undertakes to give her Minne-service freely out of love alone, without any reason and without any reward of grace or glory. The soul is like a young girl who serves her lord only because she loves him greatly, and not for any wages. She is content to be able to serve him and content that he lets her serve him lovingly. So the soul yearns to perform her Minne-service—above measure and beyond measure and beyond human sense and reason—fulfilling all her service with constancy.

When the soul has reached here, she is so burning with desire, so ready with her service, so lighthearted in her labors, so sage in the face of sorrow, so blithe despite annoyance! With all that she is and has, she desires so much to love and serve him that it is enough for her to act and endure for the sake of honor and Minne-service. ("The Second Minne")

The Soul Suffers Many Griefs

Another Minne has many griefs locked into it. This is when the soul yearns to fulfill Minne and yield to it in all obedience and honor and service. Once in a while this yearning will so shake the soul that she strives with strong desire to try everything, to pursue every virtue, to suffer and undergo everything, to accomplish all the works of Minne, to hold nothing back, to spare nothing. In this condition she is ready to fulfill every service and is eager to toil and suffer.

Yet she remains unfulfilled and unsatisfied in all her works. And her greatest sorrow is being unable to satisfy her great yearning for Minne and so she must fall short of Minne. (from "The Third Minne")

In Her First Rapture the Soul Is Like a Brimming Vessel

Then she feels all her senses made holy with Minne, and her will becomes Minne, and she is so deeply sunken and swallowed in the chasm of Minne that all her self is turned to Minne. The loveliness of Minne has enclosed her, the force of Minne has devoured her, the sweetness of Minne has sunk her, the greatness of Minne has swallowed her, the nobility of Minne has held her high, the purity of Minne has sustained her, and the loftiness of Minne has hefted and drawn her above herself, so that she can do nothing else but become Minne and yield to Minne's playing.

And then the soul feels herself so laden with bliss and the great fullness of heart that her spirit sinks into Minne, and her body is sinking and her heart is melting and all her might is dwindling, and sorely she becomes so won over by Minne that she can barely lift herself, and she loses the force in her limbs and senses. And like a vessel that is filled to the brim and will hastily overflow if it is touched, so it happens that the soul will be so won over with fullness of heart that often she must—no thanks to herself—spill over. (from "The Fourth Minne")

She Grows Demented and Sick with the Violence of Minne

At times Minne grows so violent and so overabundant in the soul, and it flames so powerfully and strongly in the heart that the soul thinks the heart has been wounded in manifold ways and these wounds daily worsen; they sorely and woefully smart, raging anew. And so she thinks that her veins split open and the blood wells up, the marrow shrivels, and her bones crack and her breast burns and her throat dries—so that her face and body in every part feel this heat within that is the very madness of Minne.

She feels that her whole body is shot through much of the time, pierced to the heart and throat and farther, even to the brain; it is as if she would lose her senses. And it is also like a squandering fire that drags everything to itself, consuming all it can. Then the soul feels Minne driving her to a frenzied madness, working unsparingly in her soul, unchecked, dragging everything into itself and devouring it.

And this is a malady in the soul. It sickens her sorely, and her strength languishes. (from "The Fifth Minne")

The Soul's Serene Joy

When the Bride of our Lord has come further and climbed higher in strength, she feels still another manner of Minne which is even nearer in being and higher in knowing. She feels that Minne has won over all her foes within, and bettered her faults and adorned her nature. She has mastered her senses and heightened and raised herself and grown powerful without strife, and she can with all certainty take pleasure in her rest and use it with freedom.

Here, now in this condition, she thinks that all that needs to be done is light and clean and pure. Everything is easy to do or to leave undone—for it is sweet to busy herself in all that pertains to the great worthiness of Minne. And so she finds in herself a loftiness in Minne. She feels now in herself a divine strength in Minne, a clear purity, a ghostly sweetness, a delicious freedom, a knowing wisdom, an intimacy and symmetry with God.

And now she is like a housewife who has ruled her household well, and wisely arranged it, and beautifully ordered it. She acts with foresight, she hovers prudently, she works with understanding. And she brings in and she takes out, she does and she lets go, as it suits her will. So that's how it goes with this soul. It is Minne, and Minne reigns in her with a victorious and all-powerful force. She works and she rests, she takes hold and she lets go; outside and inside, she follows Minne's will.

And like a fish that swims in the wide flood, resting in the deeps, and like a bird that boldly soars in the space and immensity of the air—so the soul feels her spirit move freely in the space and depth and the extent and height of Minne.

The prowess of Minne has caught the soul and led it; Minne has hovered and protected her, has given her wisdom and intelligence, sweetness, and the force of Minne. But Minne has hidden its violence from the soul until she has climbed to a greater height and become altogether free from herself and until Minne holds potent sway within her.

Then Minne makes the soul so keen and free—in all her taking hold and letting go, in working and resting—that she fears neither men nor the fiend nor angels nor saints, nor even God! And she feels stongly that love is wakened and working in her, in the whole of her body and in all its work. She strongly knows and feels that Minne doesn't engage those in whom it reigns in toil or pain.

But all those who want to come to Minne must seek it with dread and follow it with trust, and use it with yearning. And they mustn't spare themselves arduous toil and great pain and hardship and mockery. They must take all little things for great things until they come to where Minne reigns potently within them—and then Minne works its mighty works in them and lightens every drudgery and sweetens every pain and quits every debt.

There is freedom of conscience and sweetness of heart, goodness of sense, nobility of soul, the soaring of spirit, and the beginning of life everlasting.

Here below there is already an angelic life, and what follows it is everlasting life. May God in his all his goodness give it to us all! ("The Sixth Minne")

She Is Wholly Immersed in Love

The blessed soul has still one more manner of high Minne that gives her no little inward trouble. She is enticed into a Minne that is above the human and above human sense and counsel, above the heart's travail. She is lured by everlasting Minne alone into the ungraspable wisdom and the unreachable height into the deep vault of the godhead, which is *all in all things* and remains ungraspable above all things and which is unchanging in all its being—all-mighty, all-embracing, all-wielding in its working.

And here is she so sweetly immersed in Minne and so strongly seized by yearning that her heart is sorely frenzied and restless within. The soul melts and flows with Minne, her spirit is crazed, it rises up in its strong desire, all its senses drag it upward until it can revel in Minne. This is what she earnestly demands of God; she seeks it ardently from God; she needs to sorely yearn for it. For Minne will not let her dawdle or find rest or peace. Minne takes her up and casts her down, comforts her sweetly, then quells her, then quickens her to life again, then heals her and hurts her, makes her a lunatic, and makes her sane again. So in this way Minne draws her aloft. So in this way she climbs with her spirit high above time and in everlasting Minne which is beyond time, and she is lifted high above the human manner of Minne and above her own nature in her yearning to rise above.

That is her being and her will, her yearning and her Minne. All are there in sure truth and in pure clarity and noble loftiness and in supreme loveliness—and in the sweet company of celestial spirits who flood over with overflowing Minne and who dwell in the clear knowing and having and reveling in Minne.

She longs to be there with those celestial spirits, especially with the burning seraphim. And in the great godhead, the most high Trinity, she hopes to dwell in dear rest and delight.

She seeks her beloved Majesty, she follows him and looks at him with heart and mind. She knows him, she loves him, she yearns for him so sorely that she can't heed the saints or the angels, men, or creatures unless with that same Minne that she shares in common toward him and toward them. She has chosen him alone in Minne—above and beneath and within all things. With all her yearning and heart and mind, she desires to look at him, to have him, to take pleasure in him.

This is why earth is a harsh banishment, a stark dungeon, and a severe torment. She scorns the world, earth wearies her, all that is here has no sweetness for her.

[For this reason, the soul is eager to travel to its home with God.]

There will the soul become one with her Bridegroom and become one spirit with him in a troth that can never be parted, in everlasting Minne. She honored him in the time of grace; she shall delight in him in everlasting glory where there will be no other play than praise and Minne. May God bring us all there. Amen. (from "The Seventh Minne")

NOTES

1. Cited in Shulamith Shahar, *The Fourth Estate: A History of Women in the Middle Ages*, trans. Chaya Galai (New York: Methuen, 1983), p. 59.

2. On Begga (d. 693), see Jo Ann McNamara, John E. Halborg, E. Gordon Whatley, eds. and trans., *Sainted Women of the Dark Ages* (Duke UP, 1992), p. 220 and *passim*. The beguines' name has more tenuously been linked to Lambert le Bègue ("the stammerer"), a twelfth-century priest of Liège who protected an early female community, or possibly, to the gray cloth the women wore.

3. Cited by Roger De Ganck, from the *Collectio de scandalis ecclesiae*, in *The Life of Beatrice of Nazareth: Part One*, pp. xxx-xxxi. On the beguines, see Roger De Ganck, *Beatrice of Nazareth in Her Context: Part Two* (Kalamazoo, Michigan, Cistercian Publications 1991); Brenda Bolton, "Mulieres Sanctae," in *Women in Medieval Society*, ed. Susan Mosher Stuard (Philadelphia, 1976); Caroline Walker Bynum, *Jesus as Mother: Studies in the Spirituality of the High Middle Ages* (Berkeley, 1982); Ernest W. McDonnell, *The Beguines and Beghards in Medieval Culture* (New York, repr. 1969).

4. De Ganck, *Beatrice of Nazareth in Her Context*, chapter 1.

5. Roger De Ganck, *The Life of Beatrice of Nazareth, 1200–1268*, pp. xiii-xxxii, speculates that the disappearance of Beatrijs's original diary was not accidental. Inquisitions into beguine writings (and the execution of one beguine for heresy) in the diocese of Cambrai, where Nazareth was located, may have motivated someone to destroy the vernacular diary as a prudent act (pp. xxviii ff.).

6. De Ganck, *Life of Beatrice*, p. xix.

7. Cited in E. Ann Matter, *The Voice of My Beloved: The Song of Songs in Western Medieval Christianity* (Philadelphia: U of Pennsylvania P, 1990), p. 28.

8. Ann W. Astell, *The Song of Songs in the Middle Ages* (Ithaca and London: Cornell UP, 1990), p. 13.

9. "Minne," chap. 15 in Roger De Ganck, *Towards Unification with God: Beatrice of Nazareth in Her Context: Part Three* (Kalamazoo, Michigan: Cistercian Publications, 1991).

10. See James J. Wilhelm, *Lyrics of the Middle Ages* (Garland, 1990), pp. 201–224. Included is a poem by Mechthild, pp. 220–221.

11. Cited in Matter, *Voice of My Beloved*, who points out Mechthild's frequent reliance on *The Song of Songs* (pp. 182, 195n.).

12. See Marcelle Thiébaux, *The Stag of Love: The Chase in Medieval Literature* (Ithaca: Cornell UP, 1974), pp. 167–238, on the love chase in German literature.

13. Cited in De Ganck, *Towards Unification with God*, pp. 479–80.

14. Caroline Walker Bynum, *Holy Feast and Holy Fast* (Berkeley: U of California P, 1987), p. 164.

15. *The Life of Beatrice of Nazareth, 1200–1268*, trans. De Ganck, III.vii.215 (p. 249).

FURTHER READING

Jeanne Ancelet-Hustache. *Mechthilde de Magdebourg: Etude de psychologie religieuse*. Paris, 1926.

Beatrijs. Translated and annotated by Roger De Ganck, assisted by John Baptist Hasbrouck. *The Life of Beatrice of Nazareth, 1200–1268: Part One*. Kalamazoo, Michigan: Cistercian Publications, 1991.

———. Marc Eemans. *Béatrice de Nazareth. Les sept manières d'amour divin*. Hermès, 1938.

———. H.W.J. Vekeman and J.J.T.M. Tersteeg. *Beatrijs Van Nazareth. Van Seuen Manieren Van Heileger Minnen*. Zutphen: Thieme, 1970.

Odo Egres. "Mechthilde von Magdeburg: Exile in a Foreign Land," pp. 133–147. In Rozanne Elder, ed., *Goad and Nail*. Kalamazoo, Michigan: Cistercian Publications, 1985.

James C. Franklin. *Mystical Transformations: The Imagery of Liquids in the Work of Mechthild von Magdeburg.* Madison, N.J., 1978.

Roger De Ganck. *Beatice of Nazareth in Her Context: Part Two.* Kalamazoo, Michigan: Cistercian Publications, 1991.

————. *Towards Unification with God. Beatrice of Nazareth in Her Context: Part Three.* Kalamazoo, Michigan: Cistercian Publications, 1991.

Gertrud Jaron Lewis, with Frank Willaert and Marie-José Govers. *Bibliographie zur deutschen Frauenmystik des Mittlealters mit einem Anhang zu Beatrijs van Nazareth und Hadewijch.* Berlin: Erich Schmidt, 1989.

Mechthild. Lucy Menzies, trans. *The Revelations of Mechthild of Magdeburg, or The Flowing Light of the Godhead.* London: Longmans, 1953.

————. Christine Mesch Galvani, trans. Susan L. Clark, introduction. *Mechthild von Magdeburg: Flowing Light of the Divinity.* New York: Garland, 1991.

————. P.G. Morel, ed. *Offenbarungen der Schwester Mechthild von Magdeburg oder Das fliessende Licht der Gottheit.* Darmstadt, repr. 1963.

————. Hans Neumann and Gisela Vollmann-Profe, ed. *Mechthild von Magdeburg, "Das Fliessende Licht der Gottheit": Nach der Einsiedler Handschrift in kritischen Vergleich mit der gesamten Uberlieferung. I: Text. II: Untersuchungen.* Munich: Artemis, 1990.

————. *Revelationes Gertrudianae ac Mechtildianae.* Vol. II. Ed. the Monks of Solesmes. Paris, 1878.

CHAPTER 17

A Woman of Letters at the French Court

Christine de Pizan (*ca.* 1365–*ca.* 1430)

It may seem strange that much of the work of such a prolific, versatile, and authoritative woman of letters as Christine de Pizan should have remained for centuries neglected, often omitted from literary histories and anthologies. Certain of her writings were untranslated or had not been republished in modern editions since the fifteenth century. A few scholars, notably Charity Cannon Willard, have devoted their talents to keeping Christine's reputation alive. Now that the women's movement has inspired important discoveries among women writers of early periods, each year's crop of bibliographies bears witness to new editions, translations, and fresh research about Christine's life and work. The slighting of Christine is symptomatic of that very disregard meted to women of ability that Christine herself censured in her day.

As a child, Christine was taken from her native Venice to Paris. Her father was Tommaso di Benvenuto, whose family hailed from Pizzano; he had studied medicine and astrology at nearby Bologna. Invited to France, he came to enjoy a respected post as astrologer and physician at the court of Charles V. Although Christine felt she was denied a formal education because of her sex, she had access in these royal surroundings to a considerable library which the enlightened king had amassed. In fact, her reading program in mythology, philosophy, and history shaped her encyclopedic literary output. As Christine grew successful and gained renown, she received offers of employment from both Henry IV of England and Gian Galeazzo Visconti, Duke of Milan. Prudently she chose to remain in France, where she had powerful protectors in the royal house as well as in Jean,

Duke de Berry, a keen patron of hers, and among the Dukes of Burgundy.

Married at fifteen to a Picard nobleman named Etienne du Castel, a notary and secretary to the king, Christine enjoyed a period of happiness with her beloved husband. They had three children, two of whom survived. But by 1390, Etienne died of a contagion while traveling with the king, leaving the widowed Christine at twenty-five to support her children, her aged mother, and a niece.

Three years earlier, at the death of the French king, Christine's father lost his position at court as well as his resources. He died in near poverty. Stunned at this sudden turn of Fortune's wheel (a favorite theme of Christine's) and burdened with financial hardships, Christine turned in this dark phase of her life to writing as a means of solace and income. The resulting lyric poems that are among her earliest work form an autobiographical document of her own love. Within an artistically controlled structure, the pure accents of grief pierce through in a lyric such as "Alone Am I" ("Seulete sui"), translated below as selection 7, with its compulsive *anaphora*—the repeating of a phrase at the opening of successive lines for an emotional buildup. In other love lyrics, Christine explores imaginary situations for the pleasure of her royal and noble patrons. Among these are her sprightly "games of barter" (*jeux à vendre*) of which several verses are translated here.

Between 1393 and 1402 Christine composed about 20 virelais, 70 rondeaux, and 300 ballades, her favorite lyric genre, with which she experimented continually. These poetic forms, evolving from early dances, used variously the refrains that were once assigned to a chorus. An example of one of these dance songs is seen in chapter 11, on troubadour women.

As a beneficiary of the corpus of courtly love literature that had been developing since the troubadours, Christine explored, in her elegant lyrics and lyric dialogues, every possible angle of the man and woman in and out of love: the advances and retreats, the pleas and rejections, praises, joys, sufferings, recriminations, partings, reunions, and inconsolable losses. Love's ending is her poignant specialty. Deeply personal are her poems of her widowhood, to which she brings the language of *amour lointain*—the faraway or unattainable love made popular in the lyrics of a troubadour like Jaufre Rudel. Another early genre in which Christine composes some pleasantly raucous complaints is the song of the *mal-mariée*, the wretchedly married wife, exemplified in poems 8 and 9 below.

Love outside of marriage appears in the lyrics, as in the *The Tale of the Shepherdess* (*Dit de la Pastoure*; 1403), about a shepherd girl who yearns for a knight, and in the *Book of the Duke of True Lovers* (*Livre du duc des vrais amants*, 1403–1405). This work, combining poetry and prose, includes many letters and centers on the agonized devotion of a princess and a duke, told chiefly from the male viewpoint. In its concern with the life of the emotions under the stress of formal constraints, *The Duke of True Lovers* with its epistolary insertions anticipates a novel enthralled with feminine conduct like Lafayette's *La Princesse de Clèves* and, ultimately, the novel-in-letters of the eighteenth century, from Laclos' *Les Liaisons Dangereuses* to Richardson's *Pamela* and *Clarissa*. A portion of one of the letters, from Lady Sybille de la Tour, is given below, in which she counsels the princess on her conduct. Lady Sybille as a personage transcends the voice of the conventional advice-giving genre and, in her bubbling loquacity, begins to emerge as a rounded novelistic character.

Christine also uses epistolary forms for the sake of addressing humanist and feminist issues in a public voice that proffers advice and consolation.[1] Examples are her *Epistle to the Queen, Epistle on the Prison of Human Life,* and *Epistle to the God of Love.* This last-mentioned though early letter involved her in the dispute over the *Romance of the Rose.* Mindful of women's vulnerability to slander, Christine turned her epistolary arsenal to protest against the misogyny she found in this popular longwinded poem.

The *Romance* was a thirteenth-century love allegory. Guillaume de Lorris had composed the shorter first part, in which a dreaming youth discovers a rose garden, and is stalked there and pierced with arrows by the god of Love. The Rose that he seeks to pluck represents the desired woman. Jean de Meung, the continuator of the *Romance*, wrote an encyclopedic work that hurled tireless invectives against women, whose suitable role he regarded as serving Nature through the propagation of the species. At the end of this extravagantly lengthy poem the Lover plucks the Rose.

The quarrel over the *Romance of the Rose* involved a number of learned people in Christine's day. Jean Gerson, chancellor of the University of Paris, was one of those who agreed with Christine's view, and he fueled the debate in 1402 with his sermons.

In her moral poem of advice to her son Jean du Castel (for whom she may also have written Othea's letter of advice to young Hector), Christine urged him never to read either Ovid's *Art of Love* or the *Romance of the Rose*. Two of her lyrics, translated as selections 10 and 11, address the famous quarrel, which Christine's *Letter to the God of Love* (*L'Epistre au dieu d'amour*) may have launched in 1399. A portion of the *Letter* follows the two lyrics. In it Christine takes men, especially clerics, to task for their contemptuous attitudes.[2]

Christine's defenses of women are pervasive.[3] *The Book of the City of Ladies* (1404–1405) aims to counteract evil reports and rehabilitate women's good name by gathering heroines from history and from Christine's own time. In the book Christine presents Raison, Justice, and Droiture as three female figures who seek her help in building a city with the lives of illustrious women in order to shelter others. It might be a symbolic convent of Poissy (discussed below), where Christine's daughter was a nun.

Many of Christine's heroines are those praised by earlier women writers. Like Eudocia in the fourth century, she recounts the story of Justine and Cyprian, but completely downplays the hallowing of the evil magus. Like Hrotswitha she singles out the Christian martyrs Agape, Chionia, and Irene. The popular harlot-saint, Mary Magdalene, receives attention in several places. Among her heroes, Christine praises Judith and the warriors Camilla, Semiramis, and Penthesilea. She gives particular attention to her own patron saint, Christina of Tyre. And among the historic women, Christine pays tribute to the proselytizing achievements of St. Clothilda, the mother-in-law of Radegund of Poitiers. Succinct though they are, these biographical exempla often serve to reinforce Christine's outspokenness on burning issues. Citing the case of the rape of

Lucretia and the death penalty consequently meted to rapists (of which sentence she approves), Christine declares that she is angered by men who claim that many women want to be raped, or that women are not in the least distressed by being raped—even when they cry out against it.[4]

If many of the biographies are summary sketches, building blocks with which to fortify the city of ladies, Christine showed herself capable of composing a telling first-hand biography when asked. In 1404, she received a commission from Philip the Bold, Duke of Burgundy, to write the life of the dead monarch Charles V, under whom Christine's father had served. Her panegyric launches into the wisdom, nobility, and generosity of this *vray chevalereux*, but also puts together a curious array of his personal habits and utterances. She also has gracious words to say of his queen, Jeanne de Bourbon.[5]

In other areas Christine had an encyclopedist's aptitude for ranging through earlier authorities and producing a compilation. One such work on a subject very much in demand was *The Book of Feats of Arms and of Chivalry*.[6] Apologizing for her boldness in writing such a treatise, Christine states that her aim is to help noblemen who follow the profession of arms. She deals with the qualities of leaders and of good soldiers. She goes into the business of how a leader should choose campsites and draw up troops for battle. This leads her to supplies: bedding, food, and wine (vinegar to drink in summer). Weaponry, both for assault and defense, includes powder, stones, guns, timber, and cords—using women's hair if the supply should be short. Christine also handles questions of how civilians and the military should behave in wartime. Prisoners of war should not be killed or made to labor; laborers and shepherds should never be taken prisoner, since they never want war and shouldn't be made to suffer for it.

There is a section on heraldry, the wearing of coats of arms in battle as well as the painting of blazons on banners and pennants. Who has the right to bear arms and how did the customs begin? Finally, Christine lists the six colors of chivalry: gold is the most noble; red or purple signify fire and can only be worn by princes; azure is the color for air; the others are white, black, and green. The work drew the attention of the first Tudor king,

Henry VII, who requested that Caxton print it in 1488 as *The Book of Fayttes of Armes and of Chyvalrye.*

Christine addressed women in *The Book of the Three Virtues* (also called *The Treasury of Ladies*), setting down their obligations. This book is fascinating for what it tells of daily domestic life in Christine's France. A woman, she writes, was expected to replace her husband during his absence "because that knights, esquires and gentlemen go upon journeys and follow wars, it beseemeth their wives to be wise and of great governance, and to see clearly in all that they do, for that most often they dwell at home without their husbands, who are at court or in divers lands."

> The lady must therefore be skilled in all the niceties of tenure and feudal law, in case her lord's right should be invaded; she must know all about the management of an estate, so as to supervise the work of the bailiff, and she must understand her own métier as housewife. The budget of a great lady, Christine suggests, should be divided into five parts, of which one should be devoted to almsgiving, one to household expenses, one to the payment of officials and women, one to gifts, and one should be set apart to be drawn upon for jewels, dresses, and miscellaneous expenses as required.[7]

As she states, women effectively replaced men at war. Christine lived in a time of heady perils, abroad and at home. There were the drawn-out campaigns against the English, the Hundred Years War, with the English ferociously intent on hanging on to what they perceived as their rights in France. Besides the foreign wars, there were rival factions in Paris for the throne that kindled uprisings and massacres. The Armagnacs and the Burgundians (who sided with the English) were at each other's throats. Christine's fears for the plight of France moved her to compose several works of history, patriotism, and moral allegory.

Her political works include the *Livre de la Paix* and the *Epistre de la prison de la Vie Humaine*, offering solace to women of France. In her partly autobiographical *Livre du chemin de longue estude*, Christine follows the guidance of the Cumaean Sybil. The convention of an author following a literary escort occurred throughout medieval literature: Lady Philosophy led Boethius,

Virgil led Dante, the windy Eagle led Chaucer. The purpose of Christine's journey is to secure wisdom for France and Europe.

When Paris became too dangerous in 1418, Christine and her son Jehan left the city. Jehan, a royal secretary, finally died in exile. Christine took refuge in the abbey of Saint-Louis in Poissy, where her daughter had taken orders in 1396. Poissy was a royal abbey of Dominicans. The Dauphin's young sister, Marie of France, was a nun there, and the prioress was another relative, which probably meant that the women of Poissy were kept well informed of what went on outside the walls.

Years before, in 1400, Christine had celebrated a visit to her daughter there in the *Livre du dit de Poissy*.[8] In "the gracious month of gay April" their party sets out on horseback from Paris. They ride along the banks of the Seine, where shepherds tend their flocks; they traverse the forest of Saint-Germain-en-Laye laughing, talking, singing, devising games to pass the time. The grass is fresh and green, the air sweet, nightingales flutter here and there, and the songbirds expertly carry on with their pleasures. In the densest part of the forest the oaks grow so close together and rise to such massive height that the sun cannot pierce through the dimness. Eventually Christine and her companions cover the journey of six leagues from Paris to Poissy:

> We found that everything at Poissy was ready for us. We dismounted and saw that everyone was attired in the finest possible clothing. We proceeded together into the abbey through doors that were stout and hasped with metal.
>
> We went to meet the ladies in the parlor. There we found ladies of noble character. None in that place were dissembling or mischievous, but were most honorable. They wore simple coifs and robes, but not habits. They were modest and prudent and ready to serve God. Our friends made us greatly welcome, they made us a holiday with expressions of cheer. Then she whom I hold dear came to my side, and in a very humble manner she knelt and I kissed her sweet and tender face. Hand in hand, without delay, we went to Church to render service to God. We heard mass. Then we thought it was time to be leaving. But the ladies very earnestly begged us to drink a cup and be seated. Then and there they led us to a lovely

spot, bright and cool, for lunch, since it was not yet time to
dine. But we did not have time to linger or take up our
horses' reins. For the very worthy noble nun, that gracious
lady, Marie de Bourbon, who is prioress of this place and
aunt to the King of France, commanded us with her
benevolent grace to go to her side. We were glad, since we
would not have wished to go away from this convent
without seeing her. So we were taken by the hand and led
to this esteemed lady. By steps of stone we mounted to a
fine royal apartment which we found very well adorned,
and we entered her chamber and knelt before her. And
there the very modest lady summoned us to come closer
to her.

Christine and her company also meet the eight-year-old
princess Marie of France, daughter of Charles VI. Rules of the
convent are explained: the ladies sleep fully clothed on their
austere mattresses and usually converse with visitors only
through grilles of iron. But the lunch is quite splendid, with wine
and food served in gold and silver dishes. The ladies sleep in
charming rooms that open out on a cloister in which a tall pine
tree grows. Orchards shade the convent grounds, and there is a
park where deer and hare run. Christine's daughter, still holding
her hand, begs her not to leave, and so the company plan to
spend the night. They take supper in the trellised garden and
talk of holy matters. With their dessert of apples, pears, and tarts,
they taste the wine which the prioress sends them in gilded
vessels.

After supper they walk to the Seine to watch the fishermen
cast their nets and to listen to the singing of the nightingales. The
next morning, after hearing mass in the abbey church, they
mount and set off for the forest again. On the homeward journey
the travelers entertain one another with a full-scale love debate.
This charming 2,075–line poem is reminiscent of other storytelling journeys and pilgrimages like Boccaccio's *Decameron*,
Sercambi's *Novelle*, and *The Canterbury Tales* of Chaucer. It's
worth noting, by the way, that Christine's pure admiration for
aristocratic convent life in all its elegance contrasts with
Chaucer's ambiguous view of that representative character of
his, the ladylike Prioress.

For Christine the visit to Poissy had occurred in an earlier, happier time. Much was changed. Now the war with the English brought France humiliating defeats. Even though the English king Henry V had died in 1422 at the relatively young age of thirty-five, the English nobility were determined to go on claiming their chunk of France. In October 1428 they laid siege to the city of Orléans. They battered the walls with stones heaved by bombards—huge cast-bronze, muzzle-loading cannons set in wooden troughs. They cut off supplies. The siege went on for months.

Then came the strange news of a girl who had gone to the king of France, saying that the King of Heaven had sent her to help him regain his realm. By the eighth of May of the next year, the dauphin finally allowed the Maid of Orléans to lead the French armies. They stormed one of the English garrisons that prevented access to Orléans. They broke through the lines, scattering English troops and forced the raising of the siege. The jubilant French entered the city. Eventually they were inspired to crown the dauphin, King Charles VII at Rheims Cathedral on July 17, 1429. The occasion gave Christine a fresh impulse to take up her pen, and she wrote a glowing tribute to the still living warrior-saint, Joan of Arc:

> In the year 1429
> The sun shone once again.
> It brings back a good new season
> such as we have not seen for a very long time.
> Many people lived in mourning because of this—
> I am one who did.
> But I no longer mourn for anything,
> since I now see what I desire!

Joan had done, Christine points out, what men were unable to do: recover a lost kingdom. Like the handful of women who had donned armor during the crusades to accompany their husbands to the Holy Land, Joan had worn male garb. Like other military leaders, Joan offered up her armor on the altar of St. Denis, as William of Toulouse, Dhuoda's father-in-law, had offered his war gear to St. Julien de Brioude after fighting the Saracens. The growing custom meant that by the fifteenth century, swords and sword mounts, coats of armor, lances, banners, and other martial accoutrements decorated the interiors of cathedrals. Indeed, Joan had found the rust-covered sword she herself fought with behind the altar of the church of Saint Catherine of Fierbois.

In the style of the hagiographers, Christine ecstatically compares the sixteen-year-old Maid to Judith, Esther, and Deborah, biblical heroines and saviors of their people. Joan, too, declared Christine, would lead the French to fight the Saracens. Eustache Deshamps, whom Christine much admired, devised a list of nine female worthies to which he attempted, not with great success, to add Joan of Arc as a tenth. Christine may not have lived to learn of Joan's being sold to the English and of her martyrdom. Presumably, Christine died within the sheltering walls of the convent at Poissy. The *Ditié de Jehanne d'Arc* of 1429 seems to be her last work.

1. *Je vous vens la passerose: Jeux à vendre.*

She: "I'll sell you a hollyhock."

He: "Lovely one, I don't dare tell you
how much Love draws me to you.
You can see it all without my saying it!
I'll sell you a trembling leaf."

She: "Many false lovers put up a front
to make their huge lies seem true.
One shouldn't believe everything they say.
I'll sell you the paternoster."

He: "You know very well I'm yours;
I never belonged to anyone else,
so don't refuse me,
beautiful girl that I love, but without delay
grant me your love!
I'll sell you a parrot."

She: "You're fine and good and gallant,
sir, and well-bred in every way.
But I've never learned to love,

and I still wouldn't want to learn
how to fall in love or to be made love to!"

He: "I'll sell you a turtle dove."

She: "Left all alone and by herself—
led astray by a man who's fled—
That's how I'd live.
I'd never feel any joy in that,
no matter what I had."

He: "I'll sell you a pair of wool gloves."

She: "It would be too vile of me
to refuse your love;
since my love would willingly—if I dared—
be given to you;
I'd be loved by you,
for you're worthy of having
Helen, and even her lovely person.
I'll sell you the dream of love
that brings either joy or sorrow
to those who've dreamed it."

He: "My lady, the dream I've dreamed
at night would come true
if I could win your love.
I'll sell you the soaring lark."

She: "Your charming speech
and your fine and gentle manner,
gentle friend, make my heart joyful,
and so I can't refuse you—
I'll be yours without a quarrel!"

2. *Doulce chose est que mariage: Aultres Balades*

A sweet thing is marriage;
I can prove it from my own experience:
it's true for a woman who has a husband
as wise and good as the one God found for me.
Let him be praised who has willingly
protected me, for I feel

the great worth of his conduct.
And surely my sweet one loves me very much.

The first night of our marriage
I could straightaway appreciate
his great worth, for he never treated me
    presumptuously,
or did anything to make me unhappy.
But as soon as it was time to rise,
he kissed me a hundred times, giving me pleasure,
demanding nothing rude of me.
And surely my sweet one loves me very much.

And he said in such gentle words,
"God permitted me to come to you,
sweet friend, and in order to serve you
I think he allowed me to prosper."
That is how he ended his reverie
throughout the night, and that is how he
    comported himself
steadfastly, never changing his mind.
And surely my sweet one loves me very much.

Prince, loving makes me lose my senses
when he tells me he is wholly mine;
and I'm bursting with sweetness—
and surely my sweet one loves me very much.

3. *Ce moys de May tout se resjoye:*
Cent Balades d'Amant et de Dame

In this month of May everything rejoices,
it seems to me—except for poor, wretched me! —
who doesn't have the one she used to have.
For this reason I sigh in a small stifled voice.
He was my fair love, my sweeting,
who now is so far away from me.
Ah, come back quickly, my dear friend!

In this sweet month of May when everything's
    greening,
let us seek our joy on the tender grass

where we'll hear the joyful singing
of the nightingale and many a lark.
You know the place! In a small clear voice
I beg you, saying,
"Ah, come back quickly, my dear friend!"

For in this month when Love often captures
his prey, I think it's the duty
of every lover to take his pleasure
with his lady, his sweet little darling.
He shouldn't leave her all, all alone,
it seems to me, even for a day and a half.
Ah, come back quickly, my dear friend!

My heart's breaking in half for love of you;
Ah, come back quickly, my dear friend!

4. *Pour quoi m'avez vous ce fait: Rondeaux*

Why have you done this to me,
handsome one—you've only to reply.
You know the martyrdom I'm suffering,
and I never did you any harm.

And indeed you went away
not deigning to say goodbye to me;
why have you done this to me?

I took my complaint to the God of Love,
concerning this wrong, saying, "Lord God,
you made me choose my sweet friend,
who's rewarded me so cruelly.
Why have you done this to me?"

5. *Source de plour, riviere de tristesce: Rondeaux*

A fount of tears, a river of grief,
a flood of sorrow, a sea full of bitterness:
these engulf me and drown my poor heart in great
    pain—
my heart that feels overwhelming loss.

They drench me, plunge me violently,
for around me swirls
more forcefully than the Seine
a fount of tears, a river of grief.

And their great tides break over me in a great
    deluge,
as Fortune's wind drives them
upon me, dashing me so low
that I can scarcely rise again, so harshly do they
    stifle me—
a fount of tears, a river of grief.

6. *Quant je voy ces amoureux: Aultres Balades*

Whenever I see these lovers
casting such tender looks
between them—looks of sweetness—
and trading such tender glances,
laughing with joy, and drifting off
together, apart from the rest, with their special
    games,
it would take little to melt my heart!

For when, because of them, I remember
the one from whom I can never be parted,
my heart hungers
to bring him back to me.
But my sweet love, my kind friend,
is far away. For him I mourn so deeply
it would take little to melt my heart!

So my heart languishes
in heavy sorrow.
It brims with aching sighs
until he comes back to me—
whom Love caused to please me so much.
But with the grief that harries me
it would take little to melt my heart.

Prince, I cannot keep silent
when I see lovers two by two

giving each other solace—
it would take little to melt my heart.

7. *Seulete sui et seulete vueil estre: Cent Balades*

Alone am I, willing to be alone,
alone, my sweet love has abandoned me;
alone am I, I have no friend or lord.
Alone am I, in sorrowful distress;
alone am I, languid, ill at ease;
alone am I, more adrift than anyone;
alone am I, I live without my love.

Alone am I, in the doorway, by the window;
alone am I, hidden in a corner;
alone am I, nourished by my tears;
alone am I, whether sorrowing or calm.
Alone am I, nothing can delight me.
Alone am I, locked fast within my chamber;
alone am I, I live without my love.

Alone am I, everywhere, every place;
alone am I, whether I walk or rest;
alone am I, more than any earthly thing.
Alone am I, abandoned by everyone.
Alone am I, harshly bowed down,
alone am I, suffused with frequent tears.
Alone am I, I live without my love.

Prince, now my sorrow is beginning:
alone am I, appalled by my mourning.
Alone am I, in colors duller than dun.
Alone am I, I live without my love.

8. *Que ferons nous de ce mary jaloux?:*
Cent Balades

What shall we do with this jealous husband?
I pray to God he gets skinned alive!

He goes around keeping such a close watch on us
that we can't get near each other.
We could hoist him in a tough noose,
the filthy, ugly churl—all twisted with gout—
who gives us so much trouble, so much grief!

Let his wolfish body strangle.
It's of no use to him—it's only a hindrance.
What good is this old man, full of coughs,
apart from scolding, scowling, spitting?
The devil can love him and cherish him.
I hate him too much, the twisted old hunchback,
who gives us so much trouble, so much grief!

Hey, he deserves to be cuckolded by us,
the baboon who does nothing but search
through his house. Hey, what's to be done? Shake
his pelt a little to make him crouch.
Or let him—not walk—
but quickly fall down the stairs, the suspicious
    churl,
who gives us so much trouble, so much grief!

9. *Dieulx! on se plaint trop durement:*
Aultres Balades

God! Everyone complains too bitterly
about these husbands. I've heard too many
    slanders
about them, and how they're ordinarily
jealous, snarling, full of wrath.
But I could never say such a thing,
because I've a husband exactly to my liking—
fine and good; he's never against me.
He wants absolutely whatever I want!

He wants nothing but enjoyment,
and scolds me when I sigh.
And he's pleased—unless he's lying—
to have me amuse myself with my lover,
if I happen to choose someone besides him!

Nothing I do makes him doleful.
Everything pleases him; he's never against me.
He wants absolutely whatever I want!

So I must live merrily,
for such a husband is enough for me,
who—in all my behavior—
never finds fault with anything.
And when I'm drawn to my lover,
and welcome him sweetly,
my husband laughs about it—the gentle lord—
he wants absolutely whatever I want!

God help me! Don't let this husband
change for the worse. He has no peer,
for whether I want to sing, dance, or laugh,
he absolutely wants whatever I want!

10. *Jadis avoit en la cité d'Athènes: Aultres Balades*

Once long ago in the city of Athens
dwelt the flower of zeal for sovereign learning.
But despite certain noble sentiments
arising from their great philosophy, an excessively
    ugly error
misled them, so that they wished to have
several different gods. For their own good
someone should have preached to them what they
    should have known:
that there is only one God, who wasn't well
    received by them.
One is often scourged for saying what is true!

The very wise Aristotle, versed in
esoteric learning, was a fugitive from this same
    city
full of such error; he suffered many griefs
because of it. Socrates, who was the fount
of reason, was driven from the place.
Many others were slain by invidious men
for telling the truth; and everyone can plainly see

that everywhere under heaven
one is often scourged for saying what is true!

So that is the way the world's wisdom goes.
For this reason I say that many people are angered
    with me.
Because with vain words,
with dishonor and dubious ill-fame,
I dared to find fault in young and old,
and with the *Romance*—pleasant and quaint—
of the Rose—a book that should be burned!
Yet for that opinion, many would leap at my eyes.
One is often scourged for saying what is true!

11. *Mon chier seigneur, soiez de ma partie: Rondeaux*[9]

My cherished lord, be partisan of mine!
They have openly attacked me in all-out war—
the allies of the *Romance of the Rose*—
because I've not converted to their ranks.

Against me they have waged such cruel battle
that surely they think they have me under siege;
my cherished lord, be partisan of mine!

Despite their onslaught, I will not retreat
from my position. But it's a common fact
that people will fall upon one who dares defend
    what's right.
Still, if my understanding is too weak,
my cherished lord, be partisan of mine!

12. Letter to the God of Love

There are people who say that women are deceitful, un-
derhanded, false, and worthless. Others say too that many
women are liars—fickle, flighty, and frivolous. Several others accuse them of terrible vices. They blame them excessively, they

forgive them nothing. This is what the clerics do, night and day. First they put it into French verse, then into Latin. I don't know what kind of books they base this on, books that tell more lies than drunkards do.

Ovid wrote a book called *The Remedy of Love*, in which he recounts women's numerous faults, but I maintain that he was wrong. He insists they have many vile traits—filth, ugliness, vulgarity. That women have such vices I deny. I'll wage a fight to defend them against all those who'll take the challenge. Really, though, I mean honorable women. Those who are not upright have no place in my argument.

All that clerics learn from their boyhood in little books and grammar school primers, and then teach to others, is intended to prevent them from ever loving a woman. But they are fools and are wasting their time. Trying to prevent that is useless. Between me and Lady Nature—so long as the world lasts—we won't allow women to go uncherished and unloved, no matter who wants to malign them. And don't let those who malign women the most then take their hearts and ravish them and make off with them.

Without any fraud and extortion, let men be influenced by us alone and never again by subtle clerics and all their little verdicts. And it doesn't matter what the books say to besmirch those who don't deserve it. If anyone says we have to believe what's in those books that men of great repute are writing, men of great intellect (who wouldn't hesitate to lie to try to prove feminine malice), my response to them (writing such things in their books) is that they're spending their lives in the effort simply to deceive women. . . .

And speaking of deception I can't imagine or conceive how a woman could mislead a man. She's not the one who looks for him and seeks him out, or pleads and lowers herself, or entreats him. She doesn't think about him or even remember him. When it comes to deception, it's the man who comes to tempt and deceive her. How could she tempt him? Only in such a way as to make it easy for him to endure and bear his burdens.

[Christine enumerates women in antiquity whom men betrayed, such as Medea, Dido, and Penelope.]

And so are women defamed by numerous people and wrongfully blamed both in speech and in writing. Whether or not it is true, the reproach is always the same.

But whatever slanderers have said or written, I don't find any in a book or text that speaks of Jesus' life and death (hunted as he was by invidious people). The Acts of the Apostles, who suffered many harsh blows for the faith, do not bear witness to women's evils nor do the evangelists. Instead, women are said openly to display great prudence, intelligence and constancy, perfect love, and firm strength of heart in serving God. Jesus, living or dead, was never deserted by women—sweet Jesus, pierced, dying, and wounded was abandoned by all except for women!

Since all fidelity lives in one woman, it is folly to keep defaming women. For in commemoration of the goodness of this glorious Queen, there has only been reverence, for she was virtuous and noble, virtuous enough to bear the son of God. The Father paid her great honor, for he wished to make woman his spouse and his mother, the temple of God conjoined to the Trinity. Women should really be joyful and cognizant that they have the same body that she did. God has never created anything as upright as she or as good—apart from Jesus—so it is pure folly to chide women for nothing. Inasmuch as a woman is seated on the high throne beside her son, at the right hand of the Father, this is a great honor for a woman who is a mother. We never find that the good Jesus dispraises women. Rather he loves and esteems them.

Really, God created woman in his own worthy likeness. He gave her knowledge and intelligence, and for her salvation he bestowed understanding upon her. The form he gave her was very noble. She was not at all created from clay of the earth—but from the rib alone of the man who already existed as the sum of all things and the noblest on earth. . . . And on the basis of these just and reliable arguments, I conclude that all reasonable men ought to appreciate, cherish, and love women. They shouldn't have the heart to dispraise those from whom all men are born. Women shouldn't receive harsh treatment for the good they do. For there is no creature in the world a man should love more than her, both in the cause of justice and lawful nature. It's ugly and shameful to find fault with the one who should be most loved, the one who does the most to give men joy.

By nature man without woman can feel no joy. She is his mother, his sister, his loving friend. She is seldom his enemy.

13. Two Saintly Lives from *The Book of the City of Ladies*

Justine

Born in Antioch, Justine was a holy virgin. She was extremely young and beautiful, and she conquered the fiend. When a necromancer summoned the Devil forth, the Devil bragged that he could force Justine to comply with the will of a man who was completely infatuated with her love and who would not leave her alone. That man believed the Devil would assist him, since his pleading and promises were of no use. But nothing availed. The glorious Justine continued to drive the Devil away, even though he appeared to her in a variety of forms to tempt her. All the same, she defeated and overthrew him. Then with her sermons she converted the stupid man who lusted for her. The necromancer, a man named Cyprian, was also converted. He had led a heinous life and she transformed him into a good man. Many other people were converted by the signs that our Lord caused to shine forth in Justine. She left this world at the last as a martyr.

Clothilda

Since we were talking of the great good brought about by women where the spirit is concerned, wasn't Clothilda, daughter of the king of Burgundy and spouse of the great Clovis, king of France, the first who converted the kings and princes of France to the faith of Jesus Christ? How could anyone have accomplished more than she did? Once she herself had received the illumination of the faith, like the virtuous Christian and sainted lady she was, she did not desist from urging and pleading with her lord to receive the holy faith and baptism.

But he did not wish to submit. This lady, therefore, never ceased to pray to God with weeping, fasts, and devotions to open the king's heart. She prayed so constantly that our Lord pitied her in her distress. He inspired King Clovis so that when he waged war against the king of the Germans and saw the outcome of the battle turn against him, he lifted his gaze to Heaven and made this vow (as God intended) with great devotion:

"Almighty God, you in whom my spouse and queen trusts and worships, bring me aid in this battle. I promise I will receive your holy law." As soon as he said this, the tide of the battle turned and he gained a total victory. He therefore thanked God. Upon his return—to his and the queen's great joy and solace—he received baptism, and so did all the barons and all the people. From then on, thanks to the prayers of this virtuous and saintly Queen Clothilda, God has so abundantly bestowed his grace on France that here the faith has never been conquered. And, may God be thanked, there has never been a heretic among our kings. This has not been true with other kings and many emperors. This is a reason for greatly lauding the kings of France, and explains why they are therefore called "most Christian."

14. The Letter of Lady Sybille de la Tour, to the Beloved Lady of the Duke of True Lovers

My very revered lady:

Once I have presented my humble respects to you, may it please you to know that I've received your very kind and friendly letter, for which I thank you with all my simple heart. You do me so much honor by recalling the slight services that I have rendered you in the past—services not at all worthy of what your excellent and noble person merits. I am more grateful than I can ever deserve in all my life.

My dear lady, as for visiting you at present, please excuse me, I humbly beg you. Upon my faith my daughter is very seriously sick, so that I can in no way leave her. God knows how distressed I am over this particular illness.

My very revered lady, since I cannot talk with you as soon as I would like, and I'm bound to advise you as one who has been in my charge from childhood until now—though I haven't been worthy of this—it seems to me I would be wrong to keep silent on a subject that I know might bring harm to you if I didn't mention it to you. And so, dear lady, I'm writing upon the following matters. I humbly beg you that no ill will can impel you to hold it against me, for you can be sure that very great love and the desire for your increasing noble reputation and honor move me to do this.

My lady, I've heard certain news of your behavior, about which I'm pained with all my heart, for fear of the loss of your good name, since it seems to me that the news concerns this. For it is correct and reasonable that every princess and high-born lady—since she is exalted in honor and rank above all others—should surpass them in goodness, wisdom, mores, position, and manners. And she should excel in these in order to serve as a model for other ladies and even for all women to pattern their behavior on her.

And so it's fitting for her to be devout toward God. She should have an air of assurance, calm, and self-containment. She should be temperate and not extreme in her pleasures. Her laughter should be low and not pointless. She should have a dignified bearing, a modest look, a noble expression, a gentle rejoinder, and a friendly word for everyone. Her clothing and attire should be rich but not excessively ornate. She should welcome strangers with formality and self-possession, without too much familiarity.

She should be deliberate in her judgment and not flighty, never appearing severe, wicked or spiteful, or overly proud when served, but humane and kindly to her waiting-women and servants, not too arrogant but reasonably generous with her gifts. She should know how to recognize which people are the worthiest as to goodness and prudence, and which are her best servants. These she should draw to her, both maids and menservants, and reward them as they deserve.

She shouldn't put credence or faith in flatterers, men or women, but if she spots them, she should drive them away from her. Let her not believe lightly carried stories, or be in the habit of whispering with strangers or close friends, secretly or in seclusion—even to one of her servants or women—so that none of them think they know her secrets more than anyone else does. She should never laughingly say anything to anyone at all in front of other people that isn't comprehensible to all, so that those who hear it may not suppose there to be any silly secret between them.

She shouldn't keep herself locked in her chamber and too isolated, nor should she be too commonly seen by people, but should sometimes be withdrawn and other times in company.

Now, while these conditions and all other kinds of behavior proper to a high-born princess used to be observed by you, it's been said that you have changed. You've become more pleasure-loving, more animated in your conversation, even lovelier than before. When outward behavior changes, people commonly judge that the heart, too, has changed. Now you want to be alone and away from people, except for one or two of your women and some of your servants with whom you confer and laugh even in the presence of others, and talk covertly as if you understood one another quite well. And only their company pleases you. No one else can serve you to your liking. These things and mannerisms stir envy among your other servants, and they judge that your heart is enamored or something.

Ha! my very gentle lady—for the love of God, take care of who you are, and the high rank to which God has exalted you. Don't forget your soul and your honor for any foolish pleasure, and don't indulge in vain notions that several young women have who allow themselves to believe that there's nothing wrong in being passionately in love as long as there's no coarseness involved—for I'm certain you would prefer death to this!—and that it makes life more delightful and that it makes a man valiant and renowned for good. Ha! my cherished lady, it's quite otherwise, and for God's sake don't deceive yourself about it.

Take the example of such great mistresses that you have known in your time, who, simply because they were suspected of such love—even though the truth was never known about it—

lost both their honor and their lives. And yet, I am convinced, upon my soul, that they were guilty of no sin or vulgar wrong-doing. And yet their children saw them reproached and maligned. And as dishonorable as such foolish love is in every woman, rich or poor, how much more unseemly and injurious it is in a princess and a lady of rank—the more highly born she is, the worse it is.

There is good reason for this. A princess's fame is carried everywhere throughout the world; and so if there is any stain on her good name, it becomes more widely known in foreign countries than that of ordinary women, and also because of her children, who will rule over lands and become princes of other people. It's a great misfortune when there is any suspicion that they may not be the rightful heirs, and great misfortune can come of it. For even if there hasn't been any physical wrong-doing, nobody will believe it who has heard it said, "This lady is in love." And because of a little foolish glance, cast perhaps in one's youth and without naughty intent, wicked tongues will judge and will add things that were never done or thought of. So the tale that goes from mouth to mouth is never lessened but keeps on growing.

NOTES

1. Earl Jeffrey Richards analyzes Christine's letters in "'*Seulette a part*'—The 'Little Woman on the Sidelines' Takes Up Her Pen: The Letters of Christine de Pizan," pp. 139–170, in *Dear Sister: Medieval Women and The Epistolary Genre*, ed. Karen Cherewatuk and Ulrike Wiethaus (Philadelphia: U of Pennsylvania P, 1933).

2. The English poet Thomas Hoccleve (ca. 1368–ca. 1450) translated this poem of Christine's. *Hoccleve's Minor Poems* (London, 1932), pp. 72–91.

3. Discussions of how to evaluate Christine's "feminism" are in Beatrice Gottlieb, "The Problem of Feminism in the Fifteenth Century," in *Women of the Medieval World*, ed. Julius Kirshner and Suzanne F. Wemple (New York: Basil Blackwell, 1985), pp. 337–364; and Sheila Delany, "'Mothers to Think Back Through': Who Are They? The Am-

biguous Example of Christine de Pizan," in *Medieval Texts and Contemporary Readers*, ed. Laurie A. Finke and Martin B. Schichtman (Ithaca: Cornell UP, 1987), pp. 177–197. Delany finds that Christine's allegiance to her aristocratic class values overrides her feminist considerations and that her function as a feminist has been overestimated.

4. Kathryn Gravdal points this out in *Ravishing Maidens: Writing Rape in Medieval French Literature and Law* (Philadelphia: U of Pennsylvania P, 1991), pp. 142–143.

5. See Claire Richter Sherman, "Taking a Second Look: Observations on the Iconography of a French Queen, Jeanne de Bourbon (1338–1378)," in Norma Broude and Mary D. Garrard, eds., *Feminism and Art History* (New York: Harper & Row, 1982), pp. 101–117; *Le Livre des fais et bonnes meurs du sage roy Charles V*, ed. Solange Solente, 2 vols. (Paris: Champion, 1936, 1941).

6. Ed. A.T.P. Byles, 2nd ed. (London, 1937). Christine's main model was Vegetius, *De Re Militari*, which Jean de Meun had translated as *l'Art de Chevalerie*; another source was the work of Giles of Rome, or Aegidius Colonna. Honoré Bonet, Christine's contemporary, had written *l'Arbre des Batailles*. Ancient military treatises of this type included Frontinus, *Stratagemata*, and Valerius Maximus, *Facta Dictaque Memorabilia*. For a full discussion, see Philip Contamine, *War in the Middle Ages*, trans. Michael Jones (New York: Basil Blackwell, 1984).

7. G.C. Crump and E.F. Jacob, eds., *The Legacy of the Middle Ages* (Oxford: Clarendon P, 1927), pp. 418–19. The entire work is translated with an introduction by Sarah Lawson (New York: Penguin, 1985, repr. 1986).

8. Among those who have written about this captivating poem are Enid McLeod, *The Order of the Rose* (Totowa: Rowman and Littlefield, 1976), pp. 54–57; Barbara K. Altmann, "Diversity and Coherence in Christine de Pizan's *Dit de Poissy*," in *French Forum* 12 (September 1987): 261–271; Kathleen E. Kells, "Christine de Pizan's *Le Dit de Poissy*: An Explanation of an Alternate Life-Style for Aristocratic Women in Fifteenth-Century France," in *New Images of Medieval Women*, ed. Edelgard E. DuBruck (Lewiston, N.Y.: Edwin Mellen, 1989), pp. 103–119; Kittye Delle Robbins-Herring, "Springtime, Solitude, and Society in the *Dit de Poissy*," *Romance Languages Annual* 2 (1990): 153–160. Philip IV had founded the abbey of St. Louis de Poissy a century earlier and dedicated it to Louis IX, the sainted king of France.

9. Christine may be addressing Louis duc d'Orléans, father of the poet, Charles d'Orléans.

FURTHER READING

Diane Bornstein, ed. *Ideals for Women in the Works of Christine de Pizan*. Detroit, Mich.: Consortium for Medieval and Early Modern Studies, 1981.

Kevin Brownlee. "Martyrdom and the Female Voice: Saint Christine in the *Cité des Dames*." In *Images of Sainthood in Medieval Europe*, pp. 115–135. Timea Szell and Renate Blumenfeld-Kosinski, eds. Ithaca: Cornell UP, 1991.

————. "Structures of Authority in Christine de Pizan's *Ditié de Jehanne d'Arc*." In *Discourse of Authority in Medieval and Renaissance Literature*, Kevin Brownlee and Walter Stephens, eds. Hanover: UP of New England for Dartmouth College, 1989.

Christine de Pizan. Maurice Roy, ed. *Oeuvres poétiques de Christine de Pisan*, 3 vols. Paris, 1886. Repr. Johnson Reprint, 1965.

————. Jacqueline Cerquiglini, ed. *Cent Ballades d'Amant et de Dame*. Paris: Union générale d'Editions, 1982.

————. *Christine de Pizan: Ballades, Rondeaux, Virelais: An Anthology*. Kenneth Varty, ed. Leicester: Leicester UP, 1965.

————. *The Book of the Duke of True Lovers*. Trans. with an introduction by Thelma S. Fenster, poetry trans. by Nadia Margolis. New York: Persea, 1992.

————. *Poems of Cupid, God of Love: Christine de Pizan's "Epistre au Dieu d'Amours" and "Dit de La Rose," Thomas Hoccleve's "The Letter of Cupid."* Ed. and trans. Thelma S. Fenster and Mary Carpenter Erler. Leiden: E.J. Brill, 1990.

————. *The Treasure of the City of Ladies, or, The Book of the Three Virtues*. Sarah Lawson, trans. New York: Penguin, 1985.

————. *The Book of the City of Ladies*. Earl J. Richards, trans. New York: Persea, 1982.

————. *L'Avision Christine*. Mary-Louise Towner, ed. Washington, D.C.: Catholic University of America, 1932.

————. *Ditié de Jehanne d'Arc*. Angus J. Kennedy and Kenneth Varty, eds. Oxford: Society for the Study of Medieval Languages and Literature, 1977.

————. *A Medieval Woman's Mirror of Honor: The Treasury of the City of Ladies [Le livre des trois virtues]*. Charity Cannon Willard, trans.; edited, with an introduction by Madeleine Pelner Cosman. New York: Persea, 1989.

————. "The Epistle of the Prison of the Human Life," with "An Epistle to the Queen of France" and "Lament on the Evils of the Civil War." Josette A. Wisman, ed. and trans. New York: Garland, 1985.

Eric Hicks, ed. *Le débat sur le Roman de la Rose.* Paris: H. Champion, 1977.

Angus J. Kennedy. *Christine de Pizan: A Bibliographical Guide.* London: Grant and Cutler, 1984.

Nadia Margolis. *Joan of Arc in History, Literature, and Film: A Select, Annotated Bibliography.* New York: Garland, 1990.

Enid McLeod. *The Order of the Rose: The Life and Ideas of Christine de Pizan.* Totowa: Rowman and Littlefield, 1976.

Glenda K. McLeod, ed. *The Reception of Christine de Pizan from the Fifteenth Through the Nineteenth Century: Visitors to the City.* Lewiston, N.J.: Edwin Mellen, 1991.

Régine Pernoud. *Christine de Pisan.* Paris: Calmann–Levy, 1982.

Maureen Quilligan. *The Allegory of Female Authority: Christine de Pizan's Cité des Dames.* Ithaca: Cornell UP, 1991.

Revue des Langues Romanes 92 (1988). Special issue on Christine de Pizan.

Earl Jeffrey Richards, ed., with Joan Williamson, Nadia Margolis, and Christine Reno. *Reinterpreting Christine de Pizan.* Athens: U of Georgia P, 1992.

————. *Gender, Genre and Politics, Essays on Christine de Pizan.* Boulder: Westview Press, 1992.

Charity Cannon Willard. *Christine de Pizan: Her Life and Works.* New York: Persea Books, 1984.

————. "Christine de Pizan." In *French Women Writers: A Bio-Bibliographical Source Book,* pp. 56–65. Eva Martin Sartori and Dorothy Wynne Zimmerman, eds. New York: Greenwood, 1991.

Edith Yenal. *Christine de Pizan. A Bibliography of Writings by Her and about Her.* 2nd ed. Metuchen, N.J., 1989.

CHAPTER 18

An Anchoress of England

Julian of Norwich (1343–1416/19)

On the morning of Friday, May 13, 1373, three days after being struck down with the illness she had prayed for, a woman of thirty who was called Julian of Norwich experienced sixteen visions or "shewings" in rapid succession. These lasted twelve hours, from four o'clock in the morning until four o'clock in the afternoon, in the presence of her mother and close friends. Her priest held the crucifix before her eyes, for she fully expected to die. Nearly twenty years later, in February 1393, Julian received inner teachings that enabled her, as she wrote, to understand these showings more fully. Her revelations have been left to us in two versions: The short text records the original experience, and remains in a single manuscript. The long text, set down much later, represents not only the experience of the visions themselves but also her thoughts about them, illuminated and amplified after prayer and meditation. This long text is extant in a printed version and five manuscripts.[1]

Julian was born in about 1343. This was approximately Chaucer's birth year, and so the two were contemporaries in very different worlds—though Chaucer's work was not unknown in convents. Julian's place of birth may have been in the East Riding of Yorkshire between Beverley and the sea. She lived as a recluse, an anchoress with a female servant. Her cell was attached to the church wall of St. Julian in Conisford at Norwich. She took the saint's name for her own. At what age she became enclosed is not known, but she may have lived as a nun throughout a good part of her life, not seeking to be immured until after she wrote her long text.[2] In 1413 she is mentioned as still being alive: the "recluse atte Norwyche as yitt ys on lyfe."

Evidence of her living as late as 1416 comes from the wills of
money made to the anchoress of St. Julian's Church. For instance, a priest bequeaths a shilling to "Juliane anchorite apud St.
Juliane in Norwice."

The anchorite movement was widespread in England from
the eleventh to the fifteenth centuries. Both men and women
chose this extreme form of asceticism, which was favored and
encouraged by the crown, the church, and the laity. Anchorholds
were small, narrow houses or cells attached to churches or fri-
aries. After the complicated application procedure to be allowed
to be immured, an anchorite was sealed up, never to re-emerge
into the world. Penance, meditation, reading, and in some cases
writing were the anchorite's sole activities. The practice began in
the English countryside in the eleventh and twelfth centuries
under the protection of the Anglo-Saxon gentry. It spread, gaining royal and noble support, as well as that of the society generally. Richard Rolle, the poet and mystic (who was not wholly
immured), had his cell on the estate of Sir John and Lady Dalton,
and addressed one of his books to the mystic Margaret de
Kirkeby.

Women in numbers were drawn to this reclusive form of
life. Three young women of aristocratic background are remembered not by name but because of the Rule written for them in
about 1200 by a cleric, a family friend. *The Ancrene Riwle*, one of
the gems of medieval English, leaves an intriguing picture of the
daily life of the anchoress—she is urged not to hang from her
window, gazing at the passing scene; she must not speak to men,
must not engage in trade and barter, and is allowed to keep no
animal but a cat. She may read and bathe as often as she likes,
but must keep in mind that "an anchoress is not a housewife."

Anchorites had to be funded materially to thrive, and they
were. Henry V endowed the anchoress Matilda Newton, formerly a nun of Barking abbey and an abbess of Syon monastery,
with a pension of twenty marks. His son, Henry VI, known for
his extreme piety (and, at intervals, his mental breakdowns) continued the royal support of anchorites. Merchants and men of
law left bequests to the poor—to prisoners and lepers and anchorites. Gradually anchoritism became well organized and en-

tered the urban centers. By the fifteenth century what had begun as a rural movement was now established in the cities.[3]

Norwich was a large, important English city in the fourteenth century. It had a flourishing religious and intellectual life, supported numerous convents, and possessed an excellent library. Facing Julian's anchorhold across the lane was a house of Augustinian friars. There was ample opportunity for learning. Julian could have received her education in her convent, if she was a nun, or further training from a tutor or a community of sisters, such as the nuns at the Benedictine priory of Carrow. In 1377 Carrow consisted of eleven nuns, and Julian's anchorhold came under its patronage. Her disclaimer in the long text that she was a "symple creature unlettred" belies Julian's achievement. Adopting this humility formula even betokens a certain literary sophistication, placing her in the company of such accomplished rhetoricians as Chaucer. Or, it may be a device intended to point to Christ as the ultimate teacher. In either case, it should not be accepted at face value.

Julian's language is wonderfully crisp and plain. Although her affective piety emerges in simple images and homely exempla, yet she is a theologian whose interpretations of her visions after she received them continued to evolve for twenty years. She was well read in Scripture, dwelling especially on the Psalms, the gospels, and the epistles of Paul and John. She knew William of St. Thierry, *The Cloud of Unknowing*, *The Scale of Perfection*, and the *Ancrene Riwle*. Quite possibly she read Chaucer's *Boece*, his translation of Boethius's *Consolation of Philosophy*, which he finished in 1380.[4]

Julian's *Revelation* displays visual and tactile qualities that evoke the arts in her time. As she writes, the "payntyngs of crucifexes" have made her familiar with the appearance of Christ's sufferings.

During her life Julian gained a reputation for sanctity and wisdom and became the object of deep reverence. At the age of seventy-one, she received a visit from the younger English mystic Margery Kempe, who was seeking advice, for Margery feared that the Devil rather than God might be acting upon her soul. Margery's testimony of Julian's prudent counsels is given in chapter 19.

very well & knowledgable

Although far fewer manuscripts of Julian's *Revelation* have survived than those of contemporary mystics such as Richard Rolle and Walter Hilton—and, indeed, her work was nearly forgotten until the seventeenth century—there is today a remarkable upsurge of interest in her on three fronts: feminist, religious, and literary. She emerges as an inspiring supporter of women, and develops a pervasive imagery of the motherhood of God, notably through her observations on the maternal roles of Christ, the second person of the Trinity. Moreover, contemporary theologians have turned to her for guidance, for she offers living lessons in spirituality. Such a collection as *Julian, Woman of Our Day*[5] confirms this interest.

As the first English woman to write a book, Julian is both a rhetorically adept author and a literary figure of intense appeal. British novelist Iris Murdoch, in *Nuns and Soldiers*, created a modern Julian character whose visitation from Christ is modeled on the visions of the medieval mystic. And T.S. Eliot's *Four Quartets*, his cycle of religious and philosophical meditations, reveals in the closing poem "Little Gidding" (the name of an Anglican religious community) the poet's dependence on Julian's *A Revelation of Love*:

> Sin is Behovely, but
> All shall be well, and
> All manner of thing shall be well.

and again—

> And all shall be well and
> All manner of being shall be well
> By the purification of the motive
> In the ground of our beseeching.[6]

The first group of passages from Julian's work given below tells of her wish for sickness, often regarded as a softening and purification that enables the soul to receive, waxlike, the experience of God's love and to embark on the contemplative life. She desired to experience what Christ experienced, and to suffer along with others who were present at the crucifixion. The next section focuses on Julian's startlingly physical contemplation of the suffering Christ, "discolored, dry, shriveled, deathly, and pitiful." Her chapters provide a moving example of affective devotion to Christ's human body with its plenteous flow of blood. The vision is rendered with a hallucinating realism: the body actively dies, it deteriorates as she beholds it.

In the third group of selections, Julian voices her optimism in the face of sin, with the refrain "All shall be well." While sin has no substance, Julian writes, it has a purpose. We may be reminded of Boethius's justification of Fortune's evils, which teach, exercise, and correct the tormented one. Julian is remarkable in speaking of the purpose of sin as self-knowledge. Knowledge of self is a theme that appears elsewhere in Julian's writing. Meditation on the Virgin's qualities, even death, are ways to "oure self clerely knowyng."

What follows is Julian's theological affirmation of the motherhood of God, and the knitting up of the soul in the knot of God's being. Illustrated by a selection of passages in this fourth group, Julian's idea of God's mothering is not unique, as recent scholarship has abundantly shown. But God's maternity appears far more deliberate and enveloping here than it does among Julian's predecessors or contemporaries. Motherhood's functions form "a complete connected cycle of life from before birth through after death" as Jennifer Heimmel has demonstrated in her study of Julian. Christ's motherhood involves "enclosure and growth within the womb; the trauma of labor and birth; the suckling of the infant and feeding of the child; the care and education of the older child; the setting of examples and disciplining of the child; the washing, healing, forgiving, and comforting of the child as it matures; and the continual loving, touching, and guiding of the child even to the point of its own death."[7] After death the maternal God restores the child to rebirth and return to the divine womb.

Caroline Walker Bynum stresses the implications of these mothering functions in Julian's theology as they specifically touch on the female body:

> To Julian mothering means not only loving and feeding; it also means creating and saving. The physiological role of the mother, whose uterine lining provides the stuff of the fetus (according to medieval medical theory) and whose blood becomes breast milk, clearly underlies Julian's sense that, if gender is to be used of God at all, Christ is mother

feminist

more than father when it is a matter of talking of the
Incarnation.[8]

Group five unfolds Julian's temptations when she is
visited and harassed by the Devil. This assault occurs after her
feelings of sickness, barrenness, and delirium have cast her
down. Despite his return, the Devil is rendered ultimately
powerless. Julian is given to understand by God that she will
never be overcome.

The sixth set of passages below concerns Julian's image of
the soul as a city in which God sits enthroned. Although he reveals himself as reigning both on heaven and earth, God's only
real dwelling place is in the "wurschypfulle cytte" of the human
soul. When the city is seen to be uninhabitable by God because
of sin, the Lord willingly sits on the ground to wait until the soul
is fittingly ready for him to occupy it. The city radiates different
degrees of light. God never removes himself from the city; in
fact, the Trinity itself in its three persons permanently dwells in
the city of the human heart. One of Julian's favorite concepts is
"ground" and "grounding," alluding to a building's foundation.
The grounding of God in the virgin's womb provides another
such architectural image. The city and the womb of the maternal
God are reciprocal figures: as humanity is enclosed in God's
womb, so is God enclosed in the city of the heart.

The final selection is taken from Julian's closing chapter of
A Revelation of Love. It explains the visions' meaning, which is the
simple, powerful message of love.

Preface by a Scribe

Here is a vision shown by the goodness of God to a devout
woman, and her name is Julian, a recluse at Norwich, and still
alive in the year of our Lord 1413. In this vision are very many
comfortable words, greatly stirring to all those who desire to be
Christ's lovers. (from chapter 1 of the short text)

1. Julian Tells of Her Longing for God's Gift

I desired three graces by the gift of God. The first was to be mindful of Christ's passion. The second was bodily sickness, and the third was to have, through Christ's gift, three wounds. Now the first came to my mind with devotion; I thought I had great feeling for Christ's passion, but yet I desired to have more by the grace of God. I thought I wanted to be, that time, with Mary Magdalene and with others who were Christ's lovers, so that I might have seen bodily the passion of our Lord that he suffered for me, and so that I might have suffered with him as others did who loved him. To be sure, I believed solemnly—to the extent that human understanding can reach—all the pains of Christ as Holy Church shows and teaches, and as do the paintings of crucifixes that are made, by the grace of God, according to the teaching of Holy Church, in the likeness of Christ's passion. Yet notwithstanding this true belief I desired a bodily sight, wherein I might have more knowledge of the bodily pains of our Lord, our Savior, and of the compassion of our Lady, and of all his true lovers who believed his pains at that time and since that time. For I wanted to be one of them and to suffer with them. (from chapter 1 of the short text)

Julian's First Gift of Bodily Sickness

And when I was thirty and a half winters old, God sent me a bodily weakness in which I lay three days and three nights; and on the fourth night I received all my rites of Holy Church, and believed I would not live until day. And after this I languished further two days and two nights, and on the third day I believed oftentimes that I would not live until day. And after this I languished further two days and two nights, and on the third day I believed oftentimes that I was about to pass away. And those who were around me thought so too.

But in this I was really sorry, and thought it was loathsome to die. It was not for anything on earth that it seemed pleasant to live, nor was it for anything that I feared, for I trusted God. But it was because I wanted to have lived so as to have loved God better, and for a longer time, in order that I might, by the grace of that living, have a greater knowledge and love of God in the bliss of heaven. For I thought all the time that I had lived here was so little and so short from the viewpoint of endless bliss. I thought this way: Good Lord, does my being alive no longer honor you? And I was answered in my reason, and through the feelings of my pains, that I must die; and I assented fully with all the will of my heart to conform to God's will.

So I endured until day, and by then my body was dead from the middle downward, as to any feeling I might have. Then I was stirred to ask to be set upright, leaning, with clothes behind my head, so as to have more freedom of heart to conform to God's will and think about him while my life should last. And those who were with me sent for the parson, my curate, to be present at my life's ending. He came, and a child with him, and brought a cross. And by then I had fixed my eyes, and was not able to speak. The parson set the cross before my face and said, "Daughter, I have brought you the image of your Savior. Look upon it and be comforted by it, in reverence of him who died for you and me."

I thought then that I was well, for my eyes were cast upward toward heaven, where I trusted that I was to come. But nevertheless I agreed to fix my eyes on the face of the crucifix if I could, so as to endure the longer until the time of my ending. For I thought I might endure longer by gazing directly forward rather than upward. After this my sight began to fail and it was all dark about me in the chamber, and murky as if it had been night, save that in the image of the cross there remained a common light, and I never knew how. Everything but the cross was ugly to me, as if it had been thickly occupied by fiends.

After this the upper part of my body began to die, as far as I could feel. My hands fell down on either side, and also because of my weakness my head sank down to one side. The greatest pain I felt was short-windedness and the failing of life. Then I truly thought I was at the point of death.

In a sudden instant all pain left me, and I was completely hale, and especially in the upper part of my body, as much as I ever was before or after. I marveled at this change, for I thought it was a secret working of God and not of Nature. And yet because of this feeling of ease, I trusted I should live no more. Nor was this feeling of ease fully easy to me, for I thought I would as lief be delivered of this world, for my heart was willing. (from chapter 2 of the short text)

Julian's First Showing

And in this sudden instant I saw the red blood trickle down from under the garland, all hotly, freshly, plentifully, and vitally, just as it seemed to me it was at that time that the garland of thorns was thrust upon his blessed head. Just so, as both God and man, did he suffer for me. I grasped truly and mightily that it was he himself that showed it to me without any go-between; and then I said, "Thanks to the Lord!" This I said with reverent meaning and in a strong voice, and I was greatly astounded with the wonder and marvel I felt that he would be so humble with a sinful creature living in this wretched flesh. (from chapter 3 of the short text)

Julian's Understanding of God's Kindly Love

And at this same time that I saw this bodily sight, our Lord showed me a spiritual sight of his homelike loving. I saw that he is all things good and comfortable to us for our help. He is our clothing, for love wraps us and winds around us, hugs us and teaches us everything, hangs about us—for tender love—so that he may never leave us. And so in this sight I saw truly that he is everything good, as I understand it.

And in this he showed me a little thing, the quantity of a hazelnut, lying in the palm of my hand, and to my understanding it was round as any ball. I looked upon it and thought: What may this be? And I was answered generally this way: It is all that is made. I marveled how it might last, for I thought it might fall into nothing because of its littleness. And I was answered in my understanding: It lasts and always shall, for God loves it; and so all things have being through the love of God. (from chapter 4 of the short text)

2. Julian Beholds the Dying Christ

After this Christ showed me a part of his passion near the time of his dying. I saw the sweet face as it was—dry and bloodless with pale dying and deadly pale, and languishing. And then it turned more deathlike to blue, and afterwards to a brown blue as the flesh deadened more deeply. For his passion appeared most fully to me in his blessed face, and especially in his lips, which turned these four colors. Where at first they had been fresh and ruddy, lifelike and pleasing to my sight, now there was a painful change. I saw his deep dying, and also his nostrils pinched together and dried before my eyes, and the sweet body turned, all changed as it turned from his own fresh and lifelike color to this dry dying.

For at the same time as our blessed Savior died upon the cross there was a dry, sharp wind, wondrously cold to my eyes. And during the time that the precious blood was bled out of the sweet body that it poured from, yet there was some moisture in the sweet flesh of Christ as it was shown to me. Bloodshed and pain dried within and the blowing of the wind and the cold outside him met together in the sweet body of Christ, and these four dried the flesh of Christ as time was passing. And though this pain was bitter and sharp, yet it lasted very long in my eyes.

This long pain seemed to me as if he were dying for seven nights, dying as life passed from him, always suffering great pain. (from chapter 16 of the long text)

Christ's Words: "I Thirst"

And throughout this dying, there came to my mind the words Christ said: "I thirst." For I saw in Christ a double thirst, one bodily and the other spiritual. I shall speak of this spiritual thirst afterwards.[9]

I understood by his bodily thirst that the body had a lack of moisture, for the blessed flesh and bones were left drained of blood and moisture. The blessed body had dried for a long time, with the twisting of the nails and the weight of his body. For I understood that the great grievous harshness of the nails had caused the wounds to gape open on account of the tenderness of the sweet hands and sweet feet. The body sagged because of its weight, because of the length of time it hung there, because of the piercing and scraping of his head and the binding of the crown all baked with dry blood, with the sweet hair and the dry flesh clinging to the thorns, and the thorns drying and sticking to the flesh.

At the beginning when the flesh was fresh and bleeding, the continual pressure of the thorns widened the wounds. And furthermore, I saw that the sweet skin and tender flesh, the hair, and the blood were all scraped and loosened because of the thorns. Torn into shreds, they hung as if they would drop while retaining their natural moisture. How it happened I could not see, but I understood it was because of the sharp thorns and the ruffianly, grievous placing of the garland—unsparing and pitiless—that had torn the skin from the bone. Where it was torn into pieces, like a piece of cloth, it sagged downward. It seemed that it might have dropped for heaviness and looseness. And this was a great sorrow and horror to me, for I would not for my life have wanted to see it fall.

This continued a while, and then it began to change and I marveled at how it looked. I saw what it was. It began to dry and a part of its weight fell around the garland. So a garland of flesh formed a garland around a garland. The garland of thorns was dyed with the blood, and that other garland of flesh and the head was all one color, that of clotted blood when it dried. The skin and flesh of his face and body that showed were rumpled with a tawny color, like a dried board when it is aged, and the face was browner than the body.

This showing of Christ's pain filled me full of pains, for I knew well that he suffered only once, but it seemed he was willing to show it to me and fill my mind as I had desired before. And in all this time in Christ's presence, I felt no pain but Christ's pains. Then I thought I knew very little what pain it was that I had asked for. Like a wretch I repented, thinking that if I had known what it would be like, I would have been reluctant to ask for it. For I thought my pains surpassed any bodily death. I thought, "Is any pain in hell like this?" And my own reason answered, "Hell is a different pain, for there is despair." But of

human pain isn't important anymore

all the pains that lead to salvation, this is the greatest, to see your
Lover suffer. (from chapter 17 of the long text)

3. Sin Is Examined: "All Shall Be Well"

After this our Lord brought to my mind the longing that I
had for him before; and I saw that nothing had prevented me but
sin. And so I beheld sin generally in us all, and I thought to
myself, "If sin had not been, we would all have been clean and
like our Lord, as he made us." And thus in my folly before this
time I often wondered why, through the great foreseeing wisdom of God, the beginning of sin had not been prevented. For
then, I thought, all would have been well.

Steering my thoughts this way was a course I should have
forsaken. Nevertheless, I mourned and sorrowed without reason
or discretion. But Jesus, who in this vision informed me of all
that was needful to me, answered in these words, and said: "Sin
is behooveful, but all shall be well, and all manner of things shall
be well."

In this naked word "sin" our Lord brought to my mind
generally all that is not good, and the shameful scorn and the
utmost tribulation that he bore for us in this life, and his dying
and all his pains, and the passion of all his creatures, spiritual
and bodily. For we have all a part in trouble, and we shall be
troubled, following our master Jesus, until we are fully purged
of our mortal flesh, and of all our inward affections that are not
very good.

And beholding this, and all the pains that ever were or
ever shall be, I understood the passion of Christ in its greatest
and surpassing pain. And yet, all this was shown in a moment's
touch, and was readily passed over, replaced by comfort. For our
good Lord did not want the soul to be afraid of this ugly sight.
But I saw not sin, for I believe it had no kind of substance, or any
part of being, nor might it be known except by the pain that is
caused by it. And this pain in my view is something for a time,
for it purges us and enables us to know ourselves and ask for
mercy. For the passion of our Lord is a comfort to us against all
this, and so is his blessed will, and through the tender love that

our good Lord has for all who shall be saved, he comforts readily and sweetly, meaning this: "It is true that sin is the cause of all this pain, but all shall be well, and all manner of things shall be well."

These words were shown very tenderly, showing no manner of blame to me or to any who shall be safe. So it would be a great unkindness on my part to blame or wonder at God because of my sin, since he does not blame me for it. (from chapter 27 of the long text)

4. The Motherhood of God

And so I saw that God enjoys being our father, and God enjoys being our mother, and God enjoys being our true spouse and our soul, his beloved wife. And Christ enjoys being our brother, and Jesus enjoys being our Savior. (from chapter 52 of the long text) *(rem. of Abelard & Heloise letters)*

Our Souls Are Preciously Knitted in a Knot with God

I saw that he wants us to know that he takes no more seriously the fall of any creature that shall be saved than he took the fall of Adam. We know that Adam was endlessly loved and securely preserved in the time of all his need, and now is blissfully restored on high with surpassing joy. For our Lord God is so good, so gentle, and so courteous that he will never find fault with anyone who is going to bless and praise him forever.

In what I have said, my desire was partly fulfilled and my great fear somewhat assuaged, by the lovely gracious revelation of our Lord God. By means of this revelation I understood most certainly that in each soul to be saved is a godly willingness that has never assented to sin and never will assent. This willingness is so good that it never wants evil but constantly and forever wants good and accomplishes good in the sight of God. Therefore, our Lord wishes us to know this through the Faith and the Creed, and especially and truly he wants us to know that we

have all this blessed will, whole and safe in our Lord Jesus
Christ.

Therefore all human beings who are to fill heaven must
necessarily—through God's righteousness—be knitted and
"oned"[10] with him so that they may partake of a substance which
may never and should never be parted from him. It is through
his own goodwill and eternal, provident purpose that this is so.

And yet despite this rightful knitting and this endless
"oneing," it is still imperative that humanity must urgently be
redeemed and bought back. This is why Holy Church teaches us
in our Faith.

He wishes us to know that the noblest thing he ever made
is humankind, and the fullest substance and the highest virtue is
the blessed soul of Christ. And furthermore he wishes us to
know this dear, worthy soul was preciously knitted to him when
it was created, with a knot so subtle and so strong that it is
"oned" with God. In this "oneing" it is made endlessly holy.
Furthermore he wants us to know that all the souls that are to be
saved in heaven, without end, are knitted in this knot and
"oned" in this "oneing," and made holy in this holiness. (from
chapter 53 of the long text)

God Dwells in Us and We Dwell in God

We ought nobly to enjoy that God dwells in our soul, and
more ought we to enjoy that our soul dwells in God. Our soul is
made to be God's dwelling place, and the dwelling of our soul is
God, who is uncreated. It is a noble concept to grasp inwardly
and to know that God, who is our maker, dwells in our soul, and
it is a noble understanding and more to see inwardly and know
that our soul that is created dwells in God in substance. In this
substance, through God, we are what we are. (from chapter 54 of
the long text)

We Are One with God

And in our making God knit us and "oned" us to himself,
by which "oneing" we are kept as clean and noble as when we

were made. By virtue of each precious "oneing" we love our maker and like him, praise him and thank him, and endlessly have joy in him, and this is the working that is continually wrought in each soul that shall be saved, and this is the godly will we have spoken of earlier.

And so in our making, God Almighty is our kindly father and God All-Wisdom is our kindly mother, with the love and the goodness of the Holy Ghost, which is all one God, one Lord. And in the knitting and in the "oneing" he is our very true spouse and we his beloved wife, and his fair maiden, and he was never displeased with this wife, for he says, "I love you and you love me and our love shall never part in two." (from chapter 58 of the long text)

God's Motherly Bearing, Feeding, and Tending

Our natural, kindly mother, our gracious mother—for he wished to be wholly our mother in all things—laid his groundwork most low within the maiden's womb, and gently. And he showed this from the first when he brought that meek maiden before the eye of my understanding, in the simple stature she had when she conceived. That is to say, our high God, the sovereign wisdom of all, arrayed himself in this lowly place, and decked himself very readily in our poor flesh, in order to do the service and office of motherhood himself in all things.

The mother's service is nearest, readiest, and surest: nearest for it is the most natural, readiest because it is the most loving, and most sure since it is the most faithful. This office might never and could never be done to the full by anyone but by him alone. We know that all our mothers bear us to pain and to dying. Ah, what is that? But our true mother Jesus, he alone bears us to joy and to endless living—blessed may he be! Thus he sustains us within him in love and labor, up to the full term when he would suffer the sharpest thorns and most grievous pains that ever were or shall be, and he died at the last. And when he had finished, and had borne us to bliss, yet none of this could sate his marvelous love.

He showed this in these high, surpassing words of love: "If I were able to suffer more, I would suffer more." He could not die again, but he would not stint of his working.

Therefore, it behooves him to find us, for the precious love of motherhood has made him our debtor. The mother may give milk to her child to suck, but our precious mother Jesus may feed us with himself, and does so most courteously and most tenderly with the blessed sacrament that is the precious food of true life. And with all the sweet sacraments he sustains us most mercifully and graciously, and this is what he meant in these blessed words where he said: "I am what Holy Church preaches to you and teaches you. That is to say: all the health and the life of the sacraments, all the virtue and the grace of my words, all the goodness that is ordained for you in Holy Church—I am these things."

The mother may lay her child tenderly to her breast, but our tender mother Jesus may lead us, in a homelike way, into his blessed breast through his sweet open side, and show us there a part of the godhead and the joys of heaven with the spiritual surety of endless bliss. (from chapter 60 of the long text)

The Word "Mother"

This fair, lovely word "mother" is so sweet and so natural and kind in itself that it cannot truly be said about anyone or to anyone but about and to him who is the true mother of life and of all. To the property of motherhood belongs nature, love, wisdom, and knowing—and this is God. For although it is true that our bodily bringing forth is only a little thing, low and simple, compared to our spiritual bringing forth, yet it is he who does it in the creatures by whom it is done. The kind, loving mother who knows and understands the need of her child cares for it most tenderly, according to the nature and condition of motherhood. And always, as it grows in age and in stature, she changes her way of working but not her love. And when it has grown older, she allows it to be chastised in order to break down its vices, so that the child may acquire virtues and grace. All that is fair and good in this work, our Lord does in those by whom it is done. Thus he is our mother in nature by means of the working of grace in the lower part, out of his love of the higher. And he wills that we know it, for he wishes to have all our love fastened to him.

And in this I saw that all the debt that we owe to God's bidding to fatherhood and motherhood is fulfilled in truly loving God, a blessed love that Christ works in us. And this was shown in all, and namely in the high, plentiful words where he says: "I am this that you love." (from chapter 60 of the long text)

We Are Sometimes Allowed to Fall

The mother may allow her child to fall sometimes and be hurt in various ways for its own benefit, but she may never allow any kind of peril to come to her child because of her love. And though our earthly mother may allow her child to perish, our heavenly mother Jesus may never allow his children to perish. For he is mighty, all wisdom, and all love, and so there is none but he, blessed may he be!

But oftentimes when our falling and our wretchedness are shown us, we are so sorely worried and so greatly ashamed of ourselves that we scarcely know where we can hide ourselves. But then our courteous mother does not wish us to flee away, for nothing would be more hateful to him. But he wishes us to assume the condition of a child. For when the child is hurt and afraid, it runs hastily to the mother, and if it can do no more, it cries to the mother for help with all its might. So does he will us to act like a meek child, who says: "My kind mother, my gracious mother, my precious mother, have mercy on me. I have made myself foul and unlike you, and I may not and cannot amend it, except with your help and grace." (from chapter 61 of the long text)

He Is Our Nurse

The sweet, gracious hands of our mother are ready and diligent about us, for in all these workings our mother assumes the true office of a kind nurse, who has nothing else to do but to

tend to the salvation of her child. (from chapter 61 of the long
text)

5. The Devil Assails Julian

And in my sleep at the beginning I thought the Fiend set
himself at my throat, putting forth a visage very near my face
that was like a young man's, and it was long and wonderfully
lean. I never saw anything like it. The color was red, like a tile
stone when it is newly baked, with black spots on it like freckles
which are filthier than the tile stone. His hair was red as rust, not
sheared in front, and with sidelocks hanging over his temples.
He grinned at me with a shrewd expression, showed me white
teeth, and looked so much the uglier, it seemed to me. His body
and hands were not in any way shapely, but with his paws he
held me by the throat and would have stopped my breath and
killed me, but he was not able.

This ugly showing came to me while I was asleep. No
other came like this. But all this time I trusted I would be saved
and preserved by the mercy of God. And our courteous Lord
gave me the grace to wake up, and there was scarcely any life in
me.

The people who were with me saw me and bathed my
temples, and my heart began to take comfort. And soon a thin
curl of smoke came through the door creating a great heat and a
foul stench. And then I said, "*Benedicite Dominus!* Is everything
on fire here?" And I thought it was an actual fire that would
burn us all to death. I asked the people who were with me if they
noticed any stench. They said no, they noticed none. I said,
"Blessed be God!" for then I knew that it was the Fiend that had
come only to tempt me. And then I remembered what our Lord
had showed me that very day, together with all the Faith of Holy
Church. I perceived it all as a single thing, and I fled to it for
comfort. And at once then it all vanished away, and I felt great
rest and peace, without any more bodily sickness or fear in my
conscience. (from chapter 67 of the long text)

Another Visitation of the Devil

The Fiend came again with his heat and with his stench, and made me very agitated. The stench was so vile and so painful, and the bodily heat so dreadful and heavy to bear. Also I heard a bodily voice as if it came from two bodies, and both— to my thinking—talked at one time, as if they were holding a parliament full of busy affairs and they were doing it all in soft whispers. I didn't understand what they said, and all this was to drive me to despair. This is what I thought: It seemed they heaped scorn on the habit of telling one's prayer beads by simply mouthing the prayers, without the devout meaning and serious diligence which we owe to God when we say our prayers.

And our Lord God strongly gave me grace to trust him with all my strength, and to comfort my soul with bodily speech, just as I should have done to another person who was burdened in the same way. It seemed to me that this business wasn't like any other bodily business. (from chapter 69 of the long text)

"My Bodily Eye I Set on the Same Cross"

My bodily eye I set on the same cross I had seen comforting me before. And my tongue spoke of Christ's passion, and repeated the creed of Holy Church. I fastened my heart on God with all my trust and strength, and this is what I believed it signified: "You have busied yourself in keeping yourself in the Faith so that you would not be seized by your enemies. If you were from this time forth and for evermore this busy keeping yourself from sin, it would be a good and a sovereign occupation." For I thought, faithfully: If I were wholly safe from sin, I would be safe also from all the fiends of hell and the enemies of my soul.

And in this way did the Fiend occupy me all that night and the next day until mid-morning. Then suddenly all the fiends were gone; they disappeared and left nothing behind but stink which lasted a while. And I scorned him. So in this way I was delivered from him by the virtue of Christ's passion, for this is how the Fiend is overcome, as our Lord Jesus Christ said before. (from chapter 70 of the long text)

6. The City of the Soul

He made man's soul to be his own city and his dwelling place, which is the most pleasing to him of all his works. (from chapter 51 of the long text)

Julian Perceives the City of Her Soul

And then our good Lord opened my spirit's eye and showed me my soul in the midst of my heart. I saw the soul as broad as if it were a vast stronghold, and also as if it were a blessed kingdom. In the midst of that city sits our Lord Jesus, a true God and true man, a person fair and tall of stature, highest bishop, most solemn king, and lord most worthy of worship.

And I saw him solemnly clothed in honor. He sits within the soul righteously in peace and rest, and he rules and guards heaven and earth and all that is. His humanity together with his godhead sits in rest; the godhead rules and guards without any instrument or exertion. And the soul is all occupied with the blessed godhead that is sovereign might, sovereign wisdom, and sovereign goodness.

The place that Jesus takes in our soul, he shall never move away from, without end, in my view. In us is his most homelike home, and his everlasting dwelling. (from chapter 68 of the long text)

The Light of That City

And the highest light and the brightest shining of that city is—in my view—the glorious love of the Lord. (from chapter 68 of the long text)

"This Light Is Charity"

This light is charity and the light is beneficially measured for us by God's wisdom. The light is not so abundant that we can behold it as clearly as we will on our most blessed day. Nor is the light barred from us. It is just such a light in which we may live and reap our great reward and in which we may labor so we may deserve the worshipful thanks of God.

This was seen in the sixth revelation where he said to me: "I thank you for your service and your labor." So charity keeps us in faith and in hope. And faith and hope lead us in charity, and at the end all shall be charity.

I understood this light of charity in three ways: The first is uncreated charity, the second is created charity, the third is charity given. Charity uncreated is God. Charity created is our soul in God. Charity given is virtue. And that is a gracious gift which works within us, so that we love God for himself, and ourself in God, and we love all that God loves, for the sake of good. (chapter 84 of the long text)

7. "Love Is His Meaning"

This book was begun by God's gift and his grace, but it is not yet completed in my view. Let us all pray together to God for charity—working, thanking, trusting, enjoying him—for this is how our Good Lord wishes us to pray to him. This was my understanding of all his own meaning when he most merrily said those sweet words: "I am the ground of your beseeching."

For truly I saw and understood this from our Lord's meaning when he revealed it, for he wants it to be better known than it is. In our knowledge of his meaning he will give us grace to love him and cleave to him. For he beholds us, his heavenly treasure on earth, with such great love that he will give us more light, more solace in heavenly joy. He draws our hearts away from the sorrow and darkness we are in.

And from the time that this was shown to me, I desired to know what was our Lord's meaning. And fifteen years after and more, I was answered in spiritual understanding, with these words:

"What, would you know your Lord's meaning in this thing? Know it well, love was his meaning. Who shows you this? Love. What did he show you? Love. Why does he show it to you? For love. Hold yourself to this, and you shall know more of the same. But you shall never know anything else from this— without end."

So it was that I learned that love is our Lord's meaning. And I saw very surely in this and in all, that before God made us he loved us. This love was never slackened nor ever shall be. And in this love he has done all his works, and in this love he has made all things profitable for us, and in this love our life is everlasting. In our making we had beginning, but the love in which he made us was in him from time without beginning. In this love we have our beginning, and all this we shall see in God, without end.

Thanks be to God.

Here ends the book of the revelations of Julian, anchoress of Norwich. May god have mercy on her soul. (chapter 86 of the long text)

NOTES

1. Edmund Colledge and James Walsh, eds., *A Book of Showings to the Anchoress Julian of Norwich*, 2 vols., Studies and Texts No. 35, (Toronto: Pontifical Institute of Medieval Studies, 1978), I, pp. 1–18. Nicholas Watson, "The Composition of Julian of Norwich's *A Revelation of Love*," *Speculum* 68 (1993): 637–683. Argues for a date after 1382 for the short text and after 1393 for the long text.

2. This surmise is put forth by Colledge and Walsh, I, p. 43.

3. The anchorite movement is authoritatively explored in Ann K. Warren, *Anchorites and their Patrons in Medieval England* (Berkeley: U of California P, 1985).

4. The fact that Chaucer was known to monastic readers is confirmed by a piquant marginal jotting in a nun's book. It comments on a warning against the "sweet poison" (of illicit love) that forms an impediment to the contemplation of God:

Of which poison, if ye lust more to rede
Seeth the storie of Troilus, Creseide and Diomede.

Cited in Colledge and Walsh, ed., I, p. 40.

5. Ed. Robert Llewelyn (Mystic, Conn.: Twenty-Third Publications, 1987). And, there is in the American Episcopal Church an order of Julian of Norwich.

6. Brant Pelphrey, *Christ Our Mother* (Wilmington, Del.: Michael Glazier, 1989), pp. 59–60, reads Eliot's poem as "an extended meditation" on Julian, "perhaps prompted by a visit which Eliot paid to the site of Julian's cell in Norwich." Eliot's closing lines address "the ascetical life and the end of time—two themes which are important to Julian." The passage, referring to Julian's vision of the crown of thorns on Jesus' head, is taken from the opening passages of *A Revelation*, then from chapter 27 and elsewhere in the book, where Julian develops the meaning of the Incarnation for humanity. Using the traditional English metaphor of the rose for the Incarnation and suffering of Christ, Eliot introduces to modern English literature the phrase for which Julian is now most famous:

Quick now, here, now, always—
A condition of complete simplicity
(Costing not less than everything)
And all shall be well and
All manner of things shall be well
When the tongues of flame are in-folded
Into the crowned knot of fire
And the fire and the rose are one.

7. Jennifer Heimmel, *"God Is Our Mother": Julian of Norwich and the Medieval Image of Christian Feminine Divinity* (Salzburg, 1982), pp. 54–55.

8. *Fragmentation and Redemption* (New York: Zone Books, 1991), p. 97. See also Bynum, *Holy Feast and Holy Fast* (U of California P, 1987), pp. 266–267: "What is new in Julian is . . . [Christ's] taking on of our physical humanity in the Incarnation, a kind of creation of us as a mother gives herself to the foetus she bears" (p. 266).

9. Christ's spiritual thirst (*the goostly thyrst of Cryst*), his love-longing for us, will not be quenched until after the day of Judgment. Julian explains this in chapter 31.

10. I have chosen to avoid the Latinate "to unite," and kept Julian's English verb "to one," by which she means "to make one."

FURTHER READING

Ritamary Bradley. "Julian of Norwich: Writer and Mystic." In *An Introduction to the Medieval Mystics of Europe*, pp. 195–216. Paul E. Szarmach, ed. Albany: State University of New York P, 1984.

Caroline Walker Bynum. *Jesus as Mother: Studies in Spirituality of the High Middle Ages*. Berkeley: U of California P, 1982.

Jennifer P. Heimmel. *"God Is Our Mother": Julian of Norwich and the Medieval Image of Christian Feminine Divinity*. Salzburg: Institut für Anglistik und Amerikanistik Universität Salzburg, 1982.

Grace M. Jantzen. *Julian of Norwich: Mystic and Theologian*. New York: Paulist Press, 1988.

Julian of Norwich. *A Book of Showings to the Anchoress Julian of Norwich*. Edmund Colledge and James Walsh, eds. 2 vols. Studies and Texts No. 35. Toronto: Pontifical Institute of Medieval Studies, 1978.

———. Clifton Wolters, trans. *Revelations of Divine Love*. Baltimore: Penguin, 1982.

Richard Kieckhefer. *Unquiet Souls: Fourteenth-Century Saints and Their Religious Milieu*. Chicago: U of Chicago P, 1984.

May McKisack. *The Fourteenth Century: 1307–1399. Oxford History of England*. Oxford: Oxford UP, 1959.

Joan Nuth. *Wisdom's Daughter: The Theology of Julian of Norwich*. New York: Crossroad, 1991.

Margaret Ann Palliser. *Christ, Our Mother of Mercy: Divine Mercy and Compassion in the Theology of the "Shewings" of Julian of Norwich*. Berlin and New York: Walter de Gruyter, 1992.

Brant Pelphrey. *Christ Our Mother*. Wilmington, Del.: Michael Glazier, 1989.

Wolfgang Riehle. *The Middle English Mystics*. Trans. David Standring. London: Routledge and Kegan Paul, 1981.

Elizabeth Robertson. "Medieval Views of Women and Female Spirituality in the *Ancrene Wisse* and Julian of Norwich's *Showings*." In *Feminist Approaches to the Body in Medieval Literature*, pp. 142–167. Linda Lomperis and Sarah Stanbury, eds. Philadelphia: U of Pennsylvania P, 1993.

Norman P. Tanner. *The Church in Late Medieval Norwich: 1370–1532*. Toronto: Pontifical Institute of Medieval Studies, 1984.

Patricia Mary Vinje. *An Understanding of Love According to the Anchoress Julian of Norwich.* Salzburg: Institut für Anglistik und Amerikanistik, Universität Salzburg, 1983.

Ann K. Warren. *Anchorites and Their Patrons in Medieval England.* Berkeley: U of California P, 1985.

Nicholas Watson. "The Composition of Julian of Norwich's *A Revelation of Love.*" *Speculum* 68 (1993): 637–683.

CHAPTER 19

Four English Women
of the Fifteenth Century

Margery Kempe (*ca.* 1373–*ca.* 1440)
Julians Barnes (*ca.* 1486)
Queen Margaret of Anjou (March 23, 1439–April 25, 1482)
Margery Brews Paston (*d.* 1495)

Fifteenth-century England fostered the writing activity of at least four women, none of whom moved in the literary mainstream. Aristocratic culture was preoccupied with courtly and chivalric romance, summed up in *Le Morte D'Arthur*, which Malory finished in 1469. University thinkers like Grosseteste and Ockham produced theology and philosophy. Townsfolk enjoyed fables and the great dramatic cycles: plays of morality, saints, and the Bible.

Yet the writings of Margery Kempe, Julians Barnes, Margaret of Anjou, and Margery Brews Paston open perspectives on the age's popular piety, practical country life, royal pastimes, and domestic letters. All four contribute to a nuanced view of female language and experience in their century. This was a time when English in its diversity, both as a written and a spoken language, was replacing French and Latin. Royal wills, parliamentary records, statutes, and guild records were appearing in English, and so was other writing, popular and elite.

An awareness of literary models pervades the writing of these women authors, and they in turn herald developments in later English narrative. Margery Kempe, the most fluent, was a religious pilgrim who traveled through northern Europe, Rome, and the Holy Land, a visionary whose emotionally shattering episodes made her conspicuous and vulnerable. She shows her acquaintance with continental and English religious works, which she had a priest read to her for nearly seven years. She grew familiar with leading mystics: the *Stimulus Amoris (The Prick of Love)*; Walter Hilton's *Scale of Perfection*; the *Incendium Amoris (The Fire of Love)* by Richard Rolle of Hampole, dead in 1349 and the object of an effort to make him a saint; and the *Revelations* of St. Brigitta of Sweden ("Bride's" book), who died the year in which Margery was born.

Margery Kempe had a strong affinity for Brigitta, the founding saint of the well-known English convent of Syon, and she visited Syon to obtain her "Pardon of Syon" in the 1430s. Henry V had royally endowed this strict Carthusian house of Augustinian canonesses in 1415. Syon was one of the few convents restored during the reign of Mary, and it remained in England until Elizabeth I ascended the throne. When the house was dissolved the nuns went to the continent. They later returned, and today have a house in Devon.[1]

Julians was a countrywoman with a brisk, affectionate schoolmarm's approach to her topic, which was what any rural gentleperson wanted to learn to do—hunt. Her *Boke of Huntyng* relies on the catechising structure of the teacher-pupil dialogue that was used in earlier Latin didactic works and in Aelfric's tenth-century English Colloquies on the occupations of the ploughman and the hunter. Julians's verse primer of the chase bookishly illuminates a corner of English country life.

Women letter-writers imprinted their voices in their texts, voices that would eventually be heard in the earliest novels. Margaret of Anjou, as Queen of England for sixteen trouble-torn years, leaves letters giving evidence of pleasure-seeking earlier days.

Margery Brews emerges as a romantic, lovelorn girl, later as a wife busy with children and household. Her single recorded pilgrimage took her no further from her Norfolk house than London. Her Valentine letters incorporate popular poetry and the formal features of letter-writing. Suffused with her feelings, the letters reflect the verse love epistle of her time and look forward to epistolary fiction.

The period was marked by wars and religious strife. The church reform movement disparagingly called Lollardy, perhaps from *lollen*, to sing softly or mumble, was entrenched at Oxford University. Followers of the Oxford don and royal chaplain John Wycliffe (ca. 1320–1384), the Lollards denounced what they saw as a rapacious clergy snapping up property for themselves, needlessly demanding tithes, and robbing the miserable poor of their goods for prayer, shrift, baptisms, and burials. Lollards preached in random groups and urged a return to apostolic poverty. The "poor preachers" went through England disseminating the gospel in the late fourteenth and early fifteenth centuries, winning popular and middle-class support. They encouraged the laity to read and interpret Scripture for themselves. Chaucer's Parson, with his simple stern teachings of the good shepherd who exemplifies biblical virtue, stirs the Host's suspicion: "I smelle a Lollere in the wynd," he mutters facetiously.

The Lollards' manifesto in 1395 declared that the church's worldliness was undoing faith, hope, and charity. They assailed the celibacy enforced on clerics and nuns, an unnatural requirement that led to fornication and infanticide. They denied the doctrine of transubstantiation, whereby bread and wine became flesh and blood. They censured the Church's obsession with crosses and statuary, with prelates' mitres and costly vestments. The use of images and gold and silver chalices they declared idolatrous and wasteful.

There are hints of Lollard sympathy in *Piers Ploughman*, with its resentment of the Roman clergy and its commiseration with landless commoners duped by canny monks, friars, and pardoners. The work recalls the clergy to the care of souls. Langland, the priest in minor orders credited with this monumental poem, shows himself well versed in sermons and Scripture. He is unimpressed by pilgrims who take their wenches on holiday to foreign and local shrines. There are plowing and preaching to be done at home in the fair field of folk. While English rulers fulfilled their medieval kingly ideal of raising troops and revenues for glorious foreign conquests, Langland's poem urges the king to be guided by Conscience to bring the country back to good government.

Lollard doctrines, a menace to those in power, provoked strong reactions from the monarchy. By 1401 an Act, *De Heretico Comburendo*, provided for the burning of heretics. Some Lollards recanted, others were intransigeant. The first two Lollards were put to death at Smithfield early in the century. William Sawtre, a priest of St. Margaret's Church of Lynn, was burned on March 2, 1401, and John Badby on March 4, 1410. Richard II had ordered Lollards arrested; Henry IV harried them, somewhat reluctant to execute high-ranking Lollard clergy. But young King Henry V—known to readers of Shakespeare as the madcap Prince Hal, who turned into a calculating ruler and rejected his old tavern friends—determined to crush the sect. On his accession in 1413, and armed with his new severe piety, he hounded the Lollards relentlessly. Before sailing on his campaign to France in August 1415 to claim the French crown as an English right, Henry authorized the renegades to be seized and burned. Among those arrested was Sir John Oldcastle, on whom Shakespeare's fat knight Falstaff was modeled.

The persecution, which would continue to the time of Henry VIII, caught up with Margery Kempe, who was several times arrested, cross-examined, and threatened for her bizarre conduct—weeping, preaching, wearing white. Somehow she defended herself and escaped burning.

England was wracked by the wars, abroad and at home. The English kept trying to subdue the French and, under Henry V, won a major victory at Agincourt. But Henry's death of dysentery at thirty-five checked English hopes. In 1431 the English burned Joan of Arc at Rouen, a barbarous act that gave them a certain advantage. At Paris, they crowned their own Henry VI (still a child) as king of France. But there was no clear-cut victory. Greatly enriched by the wars, the nobility at home raised their own liveried private armies, challenged the succession of the crown, feuded among themselves, and terrorized the countryside. These civil wars, the so-called Wars of the Roses between the Lancastrian and Yorkist factions, continued for most of the latter part of the century. The loss of France, the periods of insanity of the Lancastrian King Henry VI, and the wrangling of the barons helped to keep the country in turmoil.

Margery Kempe

Margery Kempe journeyed and wrote during the first four decades of the century. She may have known of the burning of Joan of Arc for witchcraft, a punishment that was an ever-present danger for strong-willed women who were troublesome to the authorities. Margery Kempe had no political agenda, but as a mystic she already shows a dissenting sensibility.

Her dictated life story, moreover, bristles with individuality and a spirit of contentiousness. It records the memoirs of a determined, exuberant, and controversial woman. A work of mysticism—the private communion with God—it tangles nonetheless with social structures, marriage, sex, clothing, travel, and property with enough day-to-day realism for a work of fiction. The earliest autobiography in English, it is told in the third person, calling its subject "this creature." The persona of Margery gives pith and pungency to her narration. It surges forward with a novelistic drive as the protagonist collides with husband, employees, neighbors, the public, an unsympathetic clergy, the law, her son, her scribes and the very act of writing, the Devil, and herself. She speaks in an English voice that rises off the page, a voice that might have been heeded by Chaucer when he dreamed up the wife of Bath, or consulted by Defoe when he inscribed the adventures of the unquenchable Moll Flanders. While Margery Kempe earns a significant place among the pious women of the late Middle Ages,[2] her *Book* is also a landmark of literary magnitude that points out the route to the English autobiographical novel. Long lost to public view, the *Book of Margery Kempe* was begun on St. Brigitta's day, July 23, 1432.[3]

Margery Kempe was born in about 1373. This was the year of St. Brigitta's death and the year of Julian of Norwich's first revelation. Margery's father was John Burnham, several times a mayor of King's Lynn in the north of England. She married John Kempe in 1393, saying later that she felt prouder of her father's family than of her husband's. A wife and mother of fourteen, she rarely speaks of her children except for her grown son, with whom she quarrels over his dissolute ways before he mends them. She was an entrepreneur, a brewer, and then a miller, failing at both trades before she was seized by God.

She opens her story on the cusp of a conflict, with the account of her breakdown after the birth of her first child. Thinking she was near death, she sent for her confessor to whom she could not, however, acknowledge a sin so heinous that it remained unconfessed and would always trouble her. A period of frenzy possessed her until a visit from Christ brought her back to sane health. Still, she was unable to give up her worldly ways, her flamboyant costumes, and her business ventures to further the family fortunes.

Punished with the failure of these enterprises, Margery one day sees her life alter when she feels the divine pull of God—"the *drawt* [draft] of owyr Lord" (chap. 1). The usage occurs again, as in "Euer after this drawt, sche had in hir mende the myrth & the melodye that was in Heuen" ("Ever after this divine pull she was mindful of the mirth and melody that was in Heaven," chap. 11). Later (book II, chap. 2), she uses "this meruelyows drawte of owr Lord" to compel her son to virtuous living. The word becomes the Modern English "draft," in its military sense. Immediately after the first use of the word Margery describes her brewing venture, which fizzles, then her hapless efforts with her horse mill. The animals will "drawe no drawt," or pull a load in harness. The balky animal is like Margery herself, resisting the superior pull of her lord, persisting in her own mulish stubbornness and her outrageous foolhardiness, as long as she stays mired in the world. Like the beast she goes backward instead of forward. She finally yields to the lesson, gives up her inordinate love of finery and engages in penances and prayer. She discovers a strong distaste for her husband's sexuality, submitting to him only out of obedience.

A turning point came on a Friday before Christmas when God spoke to her while she knelt in the chapel of St. John in St. Margaret's church and "ravished her spirit." He gave her directives about her clothing and food. He foretold that she would be maligned by the people of the world but that she would not suffer Purgatory. He ordered her to visit a certain anchorite, a recluse at the Dominican house at Lynn. This man greeted Margery with respect, declaring amid tears, "Daughter, you suck even at Christ's breast—and you have an earnest-penny for Heaven!" (chap. 5). The first of these images echoes the motherhood of Jesus that Julian of Norwich had made known, but which already had a long tradition. And the second refers to "earnest money" received as an installment, with payment in full to follow.

Hers is a striking document of late medieval religious ardor in which the author converses with God and relives scenes of Christ's life and the Virgin's—scenes resembling pictorial and literary art. She takes her perceptions of bright flying particles to be angels. Besides the *Revelations* of Brigitta, Margery emulated other mystics whom the Carthusians and Brigittines appreciated. The Carthusians evidently found her writings congenial, since the surviving manuscript, written by the scribe Salthows, or Salthouse, was owned by a Charterhouse monastery. Some of her visionary experiences seem familiar, perhaps influenced by her reading. Her mystical sensations, for example, of flame, melody, and fragrance are very reminiscent of Rolle's *calor, canor, dulcor*—heat, song, and sweetness.

All the same, the voice that seems most to be Margery's own has a homely vigor. She finds fault with a priest who "blabbers" the divine service. Christ speaks to her in plain accents (chap. 5): "You shall be eaten and gnawed by people of the world as any rat gnaws at stockfish" (that is, dried codfish). Christ praises her for cleaving as sorely to him as the skin of a boiled stockfish sticks to a man's hands (chap. 37). When she rejects her husband, it is because she finds sex worse than drinking muck and ooze from a sewer. She tells an archbishop a parable about an ugly bear (signifying the bad cleric), who devours pear blossoms, after which he turns his tail end and voids them out again at the hinder part.

After the age of forty, Margery began to visit prelates: the Bishop of Lincoln (chap. 15) and the Archbishop of Canterbury (chap. 16). In 1413 she departed on pilgrimage for the Holy Land, now in the control of the Moslems, who charged fees for visiting the holy places. She progressed to Assisi and Rome. It was in the Church of the Apostles in Rome that she experienced a divine communication in which God beckoned her to her celestial wedding with him (chaps. 35–37). This invitation to embrace the godhead in intimacy is an unusual feature of Margery's life, since the mystical marriage was generally bestowed upon virgins and not married women, especially one so aware of her sexuality as Margery.

She made further pilgrimages, some with her husband, to the shrine of St. Thomas à Becket in Canterbury, to St. James of Compostela, and to Aachen, where she saw four holy relics: Mary's smock during the virgin birth, Jesus' swaddling clothes, the cloth that held the head of John the Baptist, and Christ's loincloth that covered him on the cross. She visited Rome in 1415 to honor Brigitta of Sweden's canonization. She went to Norway and Danzig, possibly to visit the mystic Dorothea of Montau.[4] Again she returned to Rome after Brigitta's death, conversing with the saint's former maidservant in Brigitta's house.

Margery suffered many trials, as God told her she would. Unsure about the validity of her visions, she believed that God sent her to Norwich—barely forty miles from King's Lynn—to consult the now aging and eminent Julian. The two mystics had several things in common: both had suffered a crisis of illness before experiencing their visions, though Margery's ailment was mental. Margery's autobiographical writing is far more intimately detailed than is Julian's. Julian is better educated, her theology is more rigorous, and she speaks in none of the erotic imagery of the mystical marriage. From Julian, however, Margery received encouraging counsels.

But Margery's contemporaries and traveling companions usually disliked her and refused to associate with her. When she garbed herself all in white, people grew angry and suspicious. Did she think she was a virgin? Most dramatic are her bitter bouts of weeping and loud public lamentations during sermons and at holy places. Her piety, gusty and lachrymose, offended others and involved her in violent altercations. People wanted to know what was wrong with her. They said she howled like an epileptic, a madwoman, a drunk, a dog. Preachers resented her interrupting their sermons. The feeling about public weeping and displays had changed over the centuries. An array of early authorities who lauded the cleansing, prayerful, repentant, or compassionate "gift of tears" can be found in Scripture and among Western patristic writers and the fathers of the Eastern Church.[5]

St. Jerome had admired Paula's emotion in the Church of the Holy Sepulchre, but Margery's compatriots shied away. If tears had once been universally regarded as a gift of grace, by the fifteenth century wild wailing was something of an embarrassment, or worse. It could be the dangerous mark of a heretic. Constantly, Margery is subjected to odium and threats.

On her return from a Holy Land pilgrimage, she is apprehended for Lollardy. Two Preaching Friars identify her, and as she is about to board a boat to cross the River Humber, they order her arrested by a pair of yeoman in the service of the Duke of Bedford, a son of Henry IV. At the time that Margery was in Yorkshire, he was Lieutenant of the kingdom while Henry V was absent in France. She is told that the duke has sent for her: "You are considered the greatest Lollard in this region of the country, and around London too. We have been searching for you in a good many places, and shall be getting a hundred pounds for bringing you in before our lord." At her arrest people denounce her. Women run out of their houses with their distaffs, crying, "Burn this false heretic!" Others commiserate: "Damsel, give up this life of yours, and go and spin and card, as other women do, and stop suffering so much shame and so much wretchedness!" (chap. 53).

A monk declines to hear her confession; a preaching friar denies her entry into his church, although during a fire in Lynn, Margery is vindicated as people believe that her prayers have saved them.

Stoutly she refuses to be discouraged, but inwardly she harbors fears about her spiritual condition and doubts about her "holy dalliance" with God, her divine Spouse. Can it be that the Devil wields control over her, dallying with her and proffering cursed thoughts as our Lord had seemed to dally with holy thoughts? She imagines "horrible and abominable sights," such as visions of men's private parts. She feels sexually tempted by men.

Once, walking with her husband on a hot Midsummer's Eve (she with a bottle of beer in her hands, he carrying bread), Margery tells him that she has no wish to continue their marital intimacy. In 1413 the two separate after taking vows of chastity. A married couple can expect no privacy: she feels that the neighbors gossip about her, refusing to believe in her abstention from intercourse. Despite her vow, ambivalence is never far from surfacing. When she cares for her dying husband, Margery remembers her youthful passion for his body and their former love for each other.

Margery Kempe was an independent, footloose visionary. Unattached, belonging to no order, she had "none of the institutional and psychological support that the cloister would have provided."[6] Far from having a personal charisma that would have attracted a following, she proved in her eccentricity to be an irritant to others. She had no one to promote a cult for her. This determination drove her to get her own story told, and it is her outspokenness, her excesses, her articulate challenge to the patriarchal monopoly, her provocative voice, and her visions that make her book a treasure.[7]

In turning her life into a book, Margery met further difficulties. Attempting as an unlettered woman to commit her experiences to writing, she dictated them unsuccessfully to one scribe at first, and then to another amanuensis, who was able to make sense of them. Her first scribe was a man who had spent part of his life in England, but most of it in Germany. After his death, she showed his manuscript to a priest, who couldn't make it out. Was it the handwriting? The syntax? Was it a mixture of German and English? The priest's attempts to read it failed at first, but he persisted and found that he could decipher and recopy it. Margery dwells on this troubling transformation of raw female experience to authoritative script.

Women who relied on scribes to mediate between their visions and the written word (and this was true of Amalasuintha, Dhuoda, Hildegard, Elisabeth, and Julian) knew of the dangers of another's language and the stylistic whims that could creep in and distort the author's intent. The "mediated female text" and the altered text have recently been perceptively discussed.[8] Worthy clerics whom Margery sought as amanuenses feared to write for her in case they should imperil their souls. The scribe who did write was converted to believing in her. Writing, Margery averred, was a sanctifying act that, for this literary period of her career, necessarily replaced prayer. Lynn Staley Johnson suggests the possibility that Margery's amanuenses might have even been a necessary fiction on her part, a metaphor for the inscribing act, since the male scribe's acquiescence would lend authority to a woman's written text.

The manuscript that survives is not the one Margery Kempe dictated, but one signed by the East Anglian scribe named Salthows, or Salthouse. The fate of the manuscript version is curious, for public taste and the printing press gave it a second life in a distinctive form. Caxton seems to have shown little interest in printing mystical books, at least not until late in his career. Margery Kempe's first printer was Wynkyn de Worde.

Through ingenious editing, the manuscript became the greatly shortened seven-page version that Wynkyn de Worde printed in 1501, *A shorte treatyse of contemplacyon . . . taken out of the boke of Margerie kempe of lynn*. Whether excerpted by de Worde himself or another person (perhaps Margery's confessor, Master Robert Springhold), the new version selects and arranges the original to create a different meaning, one that is less idiosyncratic, a guidebook to mysticism that is sanitized and acceptable. Sue Ellen Holbrook[9] closely analyzes the excerpted version, showing how food, sexuality, and Margery's public displays of tears are removed, as are individualizing allusions to persons, places, holidays, books, sensory visions—in short, all extravagant and controversial matter, all that is "radical, enthusiastic, feminist." What remains is a more inward dialogue between the Lord and Margery, in which she seeks and obediently receives guidance on self-control and patient submissiveness. Evidently, this type of treatise found a wide and receptive reading public, in private chambers and parlors and in religious houses. It was printed as a quarto, a form Wynkyn de Worde found salable, for as Holbrook points out, "Quartos fit the hand well."

Caxton's press was at Westminster, where his assistant Wynkyn de Worde continued the business. In 1479, a schoolmaster set up another press at St. Albans, north of London, with the chief aim of printing schoolbooks and learned Latin texts. Two significant exceptions, both in English, issued from the school

master's press: *The Chronicles of England* and, in 1486, Julians
Barnes's *Boke of Huntyng.*

Julians Barnes

As Dame Julians's hunting book shows, the time and taste
for diversion were never lacking. Her address to "gentill men"
and "gentill persons" indicates the status of the sport, which had
always been a distraction reserved for kings and nobles. And
now the barriers were dissolving, and the pleasures of the English forests beckoned to every class. Julians's little treatise might
have engaged the interests of upwardly striving families like the
Pastons. Men on business carried their falcons along the route
and sent them after game. "Merchants as well as gentry were
securing licenses in ever increasing numbers to enclose parks
and build warrens." They "secured warrants from well-placed
friends to shoot, or have killed for them, deer in the royal forests
or a nobleman's preserve." English hunting dogs—"greyhounds
and mastiffs—and English and Irish horses were highly regarded on the continent." Kings and nobles sent large sums "to
buy hunting animals in England because they were 'of rare
excellence.'"
   Hunting in the grand style continued to be claimed as the
prerogative of kings and magnates. A hunting party was thrown
in Waltham Forest in 1481, to which King Edward IV invited the
Mayor of London and other eminent citizens. In the greenwood
a shelter of boughs had been constructed beneath tall trees for
the forest banquet. The guests were served with splendidly
prepared meats and wines, both white and red. "After dinner the
Londoners mounted their horses to hunt with the King and
killed many deer." Edward sent the wives of the Mayor and the
aldermen "two harts and six butts and a tun of wine 'to make
them merry with.'"[10]
   Julians's book borrows mainly from the *Craft of Venery* by
William Twiti, of which there was also a French version. Twiti
was similarly a source for the ambitious *Master of Game* of
Edward, Second Duke of York (ca. 1406). Later printings display
the popularity of the subject by amplifying the scope of Julians's

book with treatises on hawking, fishing, and heraldry, although only the hunting portion is attributable to her. It closes with the line "Here ends Dame Julyans Barnes in her Book of Huntyng" (Explicit Dam Julyans Barnes in her boke of huntyng). The second edition of 1496 calls her Julyans Bernes.

Who was Julians (or in modern English, Gillians) Barnes? Was she a daughter of Sir James Berners, dead in 1390? Or a prioress of Sopwell nunnery in Hartfordshire? These are the only hints put forth at locating her, but neither has been confirmed, and as yet her identity has not been discovered.

The treatise has thirty-three parts. Parts 1–22 are in a woman's voice, that of a charming teacherlike "dame" addressing her apparently juvenile pupils as *my son* and *my dere chylde*. From 23 to 31 a man's voice enters, that of a master forester who calls his pupil "man" or "brother," and once lapses into *my deere sonnys* (line 383), perhaps under the influence of the earlier section. With the male voice, the treatise breaks into dialogue, the impetuous pupil even once interrupting the master. The woman's voice takes over again with parts 32–33 and the breaking of the deer, an intricately detailed sequence that ends the poem.

Earlier, more ostentatious handbooks included allegorical interpretations of the animals of the chase (identifying the boar with the Devil, for example, or the stag with Christ), especially when such handbooks were commissioned by aristocratic patrons. Connections to "hunting" saints such as Eustace, Hubert, and Giles might be included, as well as anecdotes about Godfrey of Bouillon, Perceval, and Charlemagne. Descriptions of the lavish "gathering" in the woods, when hunters feasted in a landscape of sunlit trees, tuneful birds, and fresh streams to cool the wine, also embellished these treatises.[11] Julians is not so fanciful, but shows herself a woman with a practical turn of mind, intending her instructions presumably for the landed gentry and middle classes whose fortunes were rising and who were inheriting the tastes of the nobles as they were acquiring their castles and titles. A correct and precise terminology is at the heart of Julians's work, which ranks with other fifteenth-century instructional books that cover manners, chess, husbandry, weapons, and military strategy.

Even so, Julians does manage a few modest literary and individual flourishes. She writes in verse, creating very simple rhymes. As in medieval romance, in which feasts of the liturgical calendar mark the activities of the court, seasons of the chase conform to holy days. Her opening stanza mentions Tristram, known to romance not only as a lover but also as as a knowledgeable hunter who taught the royal huntsman how to prepare the quarry and march in procession to the castle. Conspicuous in French and German romance, this hero appears in Middle English only in the late thirteenth-century *Sir Tristrem* and in Malory's treatment of the *Prose Tristan.*

At the poem's close Julians urges her pupils to perform the ceremony of the "play" of the hunt outside the lord's gate. Boldly the company must sound the horn in notes that announce "the price," a word that conflates two Old French terms, *pris,* for "prize" and *prise,* for "capture."

> At the lord's gate, then,
> Boldly blow the "Price" out front
> To show off your hunting
> Before you come in.

Margaret of Anjou

The skills that Julians was eager to teach the upwardly aspiring middle classes of England were bred in the bone of royals and nobles. As Margaret of Anjou's letters show, she was an ardent practitioner of the hunt. Many of her collected letters reveal her in quest of this pleasure, or more likely, seeking vigorous release from her queenly cares—for hunting manuals claim that the rigors of the hunt afforded sovereigns just such a reprieve from the anxieties of the realm. We read of Margaret commanding that the royal parks be stocked with game and asking peremptorily that these preserves be kept for her use alone. A different kind of letter shows her providing for a young leper, while another furthers the charitable works of her twelfth century predecessor, Queen Matilda of England.

In later life, Margaret's career and military struggles would flare up with the most desperate élan. Despite her political importance as an embattled queen and her failure to save her son, none of her letters illuminate her in this role.

A French princess, Margaret of Anjou arrived in England at fifteen as a bride for the mentally unfit Henry VI. Not only was the match doomed, but Margaret caused controversy from the start. The times were economically precarious. Just bringing her to England cost a fortune. "The estimates . . . included provision for fifty-six ships to transport her and her household, and her escort was to include five barons and baronesses, thirteen knights, forty-seven esquires (each with his own valet), eighty-two valets, twenty sumpterers [pack-horse drivers], and others." Seven trumpeters needed to be paid. Someone presented Margaret with a lion when she landed, and money had to be laid out to transport the animal to the Tower of London.[12]

After a rough boat crossing, the bride rested for several days. The marriage was negotiated for King Henry by William de la Pole, Duke of Suffolk, who—three times Margaret's age—was apparently smitten with her from the time he first saw her. The royal marriage was solemnized at Titchfield, the Benedictine abbey near Southampton, with Suffolk standing proxy for the absent bridegroom. Till the end of his life (when, accused of having "sold himself to France," he was banished and murdered at sea, his head hacked off with a half dozen strokes of a rusty sword), Suffolk supported Margaret loyally, though his steadfastness gave rise to wicked gossip and wagging tongues. The poet Drayton gave credence to the rumors in his *Heroicall Epistles*, and Shakespeare played up the alleged intimacy with a dramatist's license. Suffolk himself wrote several conventionally courtly lyrics to Queen Margaret, one of which opens with this stanza:

> Myn hert ys set, and all myn hole entent
> To serue this flour in my most humble wyse
> As faithfully as can be thought or ment
> Wyth-out feynyng or slouthe in my seruise[13]

In the same poem, Suffolk—whose wife was Alice Chaucer, granddaughter of the poet—complains that Chaucer is dead and cannot help him to praise his sovereign lady.

Although the kingdom's finances were shaky, no money was spared for Margaret's personal luxury. It is possible to peruse her detailed account books and treasury books, rarities among the surviving records of fifteenth-century queens. These documents disclose Margaret's prodigal ways and her largesse of jewels and gold to friends and servants, notably at the New Year's festivities of 1453.[14] Perhaps she was feeling the need to buy supporters. Her bounty grew inflationary, especially as her lavish style set the tone at court: "In the garter ceremony of 1453 she wore a fine new robe of blood-red color. The queen's example was followed by other Lancastrian ladies, including the Duchesses of Somerset and Suffolk and the Countess of Shrewsbury."

When her son was born on October 13, 1453, Margaret had to contend with the fact that her husband, who suffered one of his breakdowns at the time, refused to acknowledge the baby as his heir. The Yorkist factions joined in, leveling their opprobrium against her and her son. To make a christening feast that was splendid and public, Margaret invited ten duchesses and eight countesses to the event and ordered a sumptuously embroidered christening mantle that was crusted with jewels.[15]

A later glimpse of Margaret's private life shows her attending a play in Yorkshire in 1457:

> On Corpus Christi Eve, at night, the Queen came privily to see the plays, and on the morrow she saw all the pageants played save Doomsday, which might not be played for lack of day. The wagons halted first at the dwelling of Richard Wood, grocer, where the Queen lodged. For refreshments, the Mayor sent her three hundred loaves of fine bread, a pipe of red wine, a dozen fat capons, and a dozen fat pikes, panniers of peascods and pippins and oranges, two "coffins" of comfits and a pot of green ginger.[16]

Margaret's royal revels were ultimately cut short. Her husband, impaired as a ruler, swung between periods of lucidity and insanity. Fearing the boy was being accused of illegitimacy (rumors began to fly in about 1455), Margaret took her son to show him to the people. "In the summer of 1459 she organized a progress through Cheshire to display the five-year-old prince of Wales and to distribute his livery badge of the white swan."[17]

All the same, the house of York claimed a superior hereditary right to the throne. Margaret garnered supporters among
the Scots and the French to build up the Lancastrian party. In a
time of hardship, one of her old allies who befriended her was
Chaucer's granddaughter Alice, Duchess of Suffolk. Though
Margaret fought against the Yorkists with energy, struggling to
defend the rights of her husband and her disinherited son,
Edward Prince of Wales, she warred against the odds. In the
end, her fortunes turned at the Battle of Tewkesbury in the
spring of 1471. Margaret's eighteen-year-old son was slain.
Henry VI was seized, led to the Tower, and killed there on
orders of the new king, Edward IV.

Margaret herself was captured in her place of refuge in
Little Malvern Priory. She remained a prisoner in England for
five years until the French king, Louis XI, offered a ransom of
50,000 crowns to bring her back to France. In return for this
favor, for his aid in her fruitless bid to regain the English throne
for her husband and son, and for a meager pension of 6,000
livres, Margaret handed over to Louis her entire inheritance in
Lorraine, Anjou, Bar, and Provence. She died at age fifty-two in
obscurity and poverty on her father's estates in Anjou, leaving
only her hunting dogs.

A contemporary of Margaret described her as a "grete and
stronge labourid woman, for she spareth no peyne to sue hire
things to an intent and conclusion to hir power." Among her
achievements, Margaret founded Queens College, Cambridge, in
1448. In this, she was persuaded by Andrew Doket, the principal
of St. Bernard's hostel, and she "readily adopted the new
foundation, conscious of the efforts of the women foundresses of
Clare and Pembroke.[18]

Margery Brews Paston

The lives of the Paston family, affluent Norfolk landown-
ers, were played out against this background of political upheaval. Their papers, a vast collection of carefully kept letters,
deeds, and documents from 1422 to 1509, known as *The Paston
Letters*, betray constant worry about the violence of the times and

the precariousness of the family's goods and estates. Even when Margery Brews was being courted by John Paston III, the question of assets was uppermost. The families couldn't come to an agreement on the properties that should be joined together with the marriage. Margery's father, Sir Thomas Brews of Sall and Topcroft in Norfolk, demanded more than John could offer.

By the fifteenth century in England, people were sending many more private letters than ever before—and these are among the first to be written in English. *The Paston Letters* record the family's financial ups and downs, the management of their properties, their enemies' threats, and the lawsuits that bedeviled them. Their domestic life is fascinating: weddings and pregnancies, the struggles between parents and children, the runaway match of a daughter. John III's sister fell in love with a bailiff, Richard Calle, and eloped. The family tried to separate them. Richard's letter to her ("My lady and my mistress"), all that survives of their affair, is eloquent in its yearning sadness. Very often throughout the letters thoughts and strong feelings surface.

The earliest known member of the Paston family was allegedly the good, plain husbandman Clement de Paston, who ploughed his acres, married a bondwoman, and took his surname from a nearby village about twenty miles north of Norwich.[19] Clement died in 1419, having scrimped to give his son William an excellent education. William became a lawyer and prospered, especially after his marriage to the heiress Agnes Berry. Their eldest son John inherited a substantial fortune and bought up lands in Norfolk and Suffolk.

Many of the Paston letters were written during the lifetime of this John Paston (1421–1466) and his eldest son. John, like his father William, was a lawyer and often stayed in London on business. His wife, Margaret Mauteby Paston (d. 1484), continued a voluminous dictated correspondence on county affairs. Margaret would advise her husband of dangers, for example, when it was needful to stockpile crossbows, bolts, and poleaxes in anticipation of trouble.

Neighborly rancor against the parvenu Pastons put the family on the alert. Three times armed gangs attacked them in their houses. The Pastons found themselves caught up in property disputes with powerful nobles—John de la Pole, Duke of Suffolk, for one, and John Mowbray, Third Duke of Norfolk, who seized Caister Castle from the Pastons in 1461. The family had inherited this "rich jewel," Caister, from old Sir John Fastolf, a wealthy veteran of Agincourt who built it in 1454. John Paston spent much of his life in litigations, bribes, and bargainings. Then, for a time, at least, he enjoyed favor at the court of Edward IV.

When John Paston died in 1466, he willed forty pence for Julian of Norwich; fifteen years later his wife bequeathed money to Julian and to three other anchorites. John Paston's body was buried in Bromholm Priory, where a fragment of the True Cross had been brought from Constantinople a little over two centuries before. The Pastons had made donations to the priory. At the holy site miracles were reported and pilgrims came, as they had in Chaucer's time. "Help! hooly croys of Bromholm!" cries out the good wife in Chaucer's *Reeve's Tale*, wild with confusion when she leaps up out of sleep to see her husband brawling and to discover that she has just made love with one of the Cambridge students. The priory and the Cross were about seventy-five miles from where she lived in Trumpington.

John Paston's two eldest sons were both, oddly enough, named John. John II had a taste for books and luxurious living, it was said. He behaved with impudence to his parents and was, his father said, "a drone among bees," but when he died, he left his younger brother a considerable inheritance. It was the younger John Paston, John III, who negotiated for the hand of Margery Brews.

On Valentine's Day 1477, Margery Brews sent her fiancé a letter enclosing two love poems. She beseeches him not to desert her for the sake of mere money. Her anxiety is genuine as she protests her fidelity. Her forthright letter follows the graceful pleading form of a courtly love epistle, sprinkled with verses, demonstrating the writer's familiarity with poetic styles of the day. Margery's mother, Elizabeth Brews, has her say in a letter of her own: "And cousin, Friday is St. Valentine's Day, when every bird chooses its mate." Chaucer's *Parlement of Foules* had made the notion familiar.[20]

Obstacles to the marriage were planted. Margery's father objected to the extent of John's estates and could not be induced to provide a larger dowry, which would have beggared his other daughters. In the marriage negotiations John II was not inclined to help his brother. And there was another lady in the running for John III's affections, a lady reputed to sing very well to the harp, a lady who might offer a better portion. Finally, John's mother gave him one of her estates, and the marriage business progressed more brightly.

Margery and John III did marry after all, late in 1477. On January 21, 1478, John wrote his brother that Margery was pregnant: "And syr, as for my huswyff, I am fayne to cary hyr to se hyr fadyr and hyr frendys now thys wynter, for I trow she wyll be ought of facyon in somer."[21] Their oldest son, Christopher, who was born in August 1478, died in 1482 at the age of three or four. They had a second son, William, born in about 1479. Margery and John lived in Norwich until 1481. In 1486 they were back in Caister. Margery's husband was a Member of Parliament for Norwich, and sheriff of Norfolk and Suffolk. Throughout the vicissitudes of the Wars of the Roses, the Pastons had their worries. John III had to plead for a pardon for having supported the ill-fated Lancastrian Henry VI.

The Battle of Bosworth Field in 1485 put an end to the thirty-year struggle for the English crown when Henry Tudor, soon to be Henry VII, secured the throne. The next year, a company decked out in green and white livery greeted the new king at York with alliterating verses to the "Most prepotent prince of power Imperiall," and handed him a sword of victory. The Pastons were now loyal to the new king. Margery Paston's letter as a married woman is dated five months after the coup at Bosworth, and mentions the new King Harry. At the Battle of Stoke in 1487, in which Henry VII put down a rebel pretending to be an earl, John III was knighted.

Margery Brews Paston left six letters. It seems evident that like many of the Paston women, she dictated her letters and could do no more than sign her name. The first two letters to John, pleading her love, were written in the hand of her father's clerk, Thomas Kela. Her signature appears laboriously inscribed, that of someone just learning how to write.

And yet she was able to read, and reveals her acquaintance with contemporary popular love poetry. The Pastons owned books. Several of Chaucer's works were in Paston libraries, including one about Troilus. There was a book about King Arthur, another concerning the Green Knight. They owned Christine de Pizan's book of Othea, Cicero's *On Old Age* and *On Friendship*, and treatises dealing with chess, heraldry, and jousting. "The Pastons were all avid readers, and the booklist of their library confirms their acquaintance with literary aristocratic society, via romances and courtesy books."[22]

This was a time when more people read in private, and when printing presses made more books available. In 1477, the year of Margery's marriage, William Caxton had set up his press and his sign "At the Red Pale" over a shop in Westminster, where he would devote himself to bringing out literary works in English—not Latin. That year he printed Chaucer's translation of Boethius's *Consolation of Philosophy* and his *Parlement of Foules*, retitled *The Temple of Brass*. In 1478, the year after Margery's marriage, Caxton printed Christine de Pizan's *Moral Proverbs* and the first edition of Chaucer's *Canterbury Tales*.

After Margery's two earliest valentine letters to her fiancé, she settles into the comfortable life of a wife and mother. Her letters as a married woman are about their children, the neighbors, and household concerns, and yet she gives an occasional glimmering of her feelings and inner life. Closing her letter of November 1, 1481, she adds a postscript: "Sir, I pray you, if you are going to tarry long at London, that it will please you to send for me, for I think it long since I lay in your arms."

As for the Valentine letters, they are engaging for their emotional and their poetic content. The first in particular displays the perfect fusion of Margery's human emotion and pathos with literary convention. Margery fears losing her sweetheart; she is the imploring courtly lover who also follows the norm for letter-writing. Her complaint, her insistence on her own loving constancy, is reminiscent of the pleading of the three eagles who woo the formel eagle in Chaucer's *Parlement of Foules*.[23]

Margery's valentine letter is important testimony to the widespread consciousness of the letter as a special form of the love lyric and even of its connection with occasions such as St.

Valentine's Day. If the poetic fragments tie the letter to the love epistle tradition, the structure of the letter observes a conventional epistolary model.

"To my right well-beloved Valentine" forms the *superscription*. "Right reverend and worshipful" begins the *commendation*: the writer's recommending herself to the recipient is a greeting formula that means "I present myself to you in the hopes of enjoying your favor." A *salutation* follows: the inquiry into or concern for the health and emotional well-being ("your heart's desire") of the recipient, paralleled by news about the bad health of the writer. The *narration* conveys the substance of the letter about her mother's efforts on the lovers' behalf and her own sorrow. A *petition* follows, a plea that he not desert her as well as an entreaty for secrecy, which is a long-standing convention of epistolary love lyrics.[24] In the closing she quaintly likens herself to John's "beadswoman," a woman of prayer endowed to pray for the souls of others. But the term may be simply a convention for "your petitioner" or, as in more modern times, "your humble servant."

Margery was in London on her pilgrimage in 1489, while her husband was ordered to meet the Earl of Oxford at Cambridge with a body of men to do the king service. Margery Brews Paston died in 1495, three years after Columbus discovered the West Indies. She was buried at White Friars Church in Norwich. Her husband remarried, and died in 1503. Her son William married Bridget, daughter of Sir Henry Heydon. He was a knight by 1520, when he was present at the Field of Cloth of Gold, and became a magnate at the court of Henry VIII.

The Boke of Margery Kempe

1. Preface

A short treatise about a creature set in great pomp and pride of the world, who then was drawn to Our Lord by great poverty, sickness, shame, and great rebukes in many different countries and places. Some of these tribulations will be described later on, not in the order they happened but as the creature was able to remember them while this was being written. For it was twenty years and more from the time this creature had forsaken the world and busily cleaved to Our Lord before this book was written, even though this creature had been strongly advised to have her hardships and her feelings written down. A White Friar[25] offered to write freely if she was willing, but she was warned in her spirit that she should not write so soon. And many years later she was bidden in her spirit to write. And yet the book was then written first by a man who could write neither English nor Dutch[26] so it couldn't be read except by special grace, for there was so much obloquy and slander about this creature that few men would believe her.

And so at last a priest was seriously moved to write this treatise, and he could not read it clearly for four years. And afterward at the request of this creature and the urging of his own conscience, he tried again to read it, and it was much easier than before. And so he began to write in the year of Our Lord 1436 on the next day after Mary Magdelene [July 23], according to the information of this creature.

2. Her Marriage, Her Mental Illness after the Birth of a Child, and How She Was Healed

When this creature was twenty years of age or a little more, she was married to a respectable burger and was with child in a short time, as nature willed. And after she had conceived, she was afflicted with harsh attacks of sickness till the child was born, and then, with the labor she went through in childbirth on top of the sickness she had suffered earlier, she despaired of her life—thinking she might not live. And then she sent for her spiritual father, for she had a thing on her conscience which she had never divulged before in all her life. For she was always prevented by her enemy, the Devil, continually saying to her while she was in good health that she had no need of confession but could do penance alone, by herself, and all should be forgiven because God is merciful enough. And therefore this creature often did great penance, fasting on bread and water, and performed other deeds of almsgiving with devout prayers, except that she would not reveal her sin in confession. And when she was at any time sick or diseased, the Devil said in her mind that she should be damned, for she was not absolved of that fault.

Therefore after her child was born, she was not sure she would live, and she sent for her spiritual father, as I said before, fully willing to be absolved of her entire lifetime as nearly as she could. And when she came to the point of saying that thing which she had so long concealed, her confessor was a little too hasty and sharply scolded her before she had fully said what she intended. And so she would say no more, no matter what he did. And soon—for the fear she had of damnation on the one side and his sharp scolding on the other—this creature went out of her mind and was tremendously vexed and tormented by spirits for half a year and eight weeks and several days.

And at this time she saw, as she thought, devils opening their mouths all ablaze with burning flames of fire as though they would swallow her in, sometimes rearing up against her, sometimes threatening her, sometimes pulling her and hauling her both night and day during all that time. And also the devils yelled at her with great threats, and told her she ought to forsake her Christian faith, and deny her God, His Mother, and all the saints in heaven, her good works and all good virtues, her father, her mother, and all her friends. And so she did.

She slandered her husband, her friends, and herself. She spoke many a reproachful word and many a sharp word. She knew no virtue or goodness. She desired all wickedness. Just as the spirits tempted her to say and do, so she said and did. She would have destroyed herself many a time at their goading and have been damned with them in hell. For example, she bit her own hand so violently that the mark was seen afterward for the rest of her life. And also she tore her skin on her body against her heart with her nails so pitilessly—for she had no other instruments—and she would have done worse except that she was tied down and held by force both day and night so that she couldn't do as she pleased.

And when she had been long harassed by these and many other temptations so that men thought she never would have escaped or lived, then one time, as she lay alone and her custodians were away from her, our merciful Lord Christ Jesu, ever to be trusted—may his name be worshiped!—never forsaking his servant in time of need, appeared to his creature (who had forsaken him) in the likeness of a man. He was the most handsome, most beautiful, and most amiable man that ever might be seen with human eye. He was clothed in a mantle of purple silk, sitting on her bedside and looking at her with so blessed a mien that she was strengthened in all her spirits. He said these words to her: "Daughter, why have you forsaken me, and I never forsook you?"

And as soon as he said these words, she saw truly how the air opened as bright as any lightning, and he rose up into the air, not very hastily and quickly, but sweetly and easily so that she was able to see him in the air till it was closed again. And at once the creature was made as sound in her wits and her reason as she had been before, and she begged her husband as soon as he came to her to let her have the keys of the buttery to get her food and drink as she had done before. Her maids and her custodians advised him not to hand the keys over to her. They said she would only give away such provisions as there were, since they thought she didn't know what she was saying.

Nevertheless, her husband, who always had tenderness and compassion for her, ordered them to hand over the keys to her. And she took her food and drink as her bodily strength would permit. And she recognized her friends and her household servants and all the others who came to see how Our Lord Jesus Christ had accomplished his grace in her—so blessed may he be who is ever near in tribulation! When men think he is far from them, he is very near, through his grace. Afterward this creature did her other duties that she was required to do, wisely and soberly enough, except that she did not fully recognize Our Lord's power to draft her to his service. (chapter 1)

3. *Her Fanciful Clothing, Her Brewing and Horse Mill Ventures*

And when this creature had through grace recovered her senses again, she believed she was bound to God and that she would be his servant. Still, she would not abandon her pride or

the ostentatious style of dress that she was always used to before. She wouldn't follow her husband's advice or anyone else's.
And yet she knew very well that people gossiped viciously
about her, for she wore gold pipes on her head and her hoods
with the tippets were dagged.[27] Her cloaks also were dagged and
lined with many colors between the dags so that her outfit
would draw people's stares and she would be more admired.

And when her husband told her to give up her pride, she
answered sharply and shortly and said that she had come from
an excellent family—he seemed an unlikely man to have married
her, since her father had formerly been mayor of the town of N-
and afterwards had been alderman of the prestigious Guild of
the Trinity in N-.[28] And therefore she maintained the lofty status
of her kin, no matter what anyone said. She was very envious of
her neighbors lest they dress as well as she did. Her whole desire
was to have people admire her. She would not put up with
criticism, or be content with the goods God had sent her, as her
husband was, but always desired more and more.

And then out of pure greed and the wish to keep up her
pride, she began to brew and was one of the greatest brewers in
the town of N- for three or four years till she had lost a good deal
of money, for she had never had any experience in brewing. For
no matter how good her servants were and clever at brewing, yet
things never went well with them. For even when the ale looked
as splendid—standing under its head of froth—as anyone might
see, suddenly the froth would sink down so that the ale was ruined, one brewing after another, and her servants were mortified
and would not stay with her.

Then this creature thought how God had punished her
already, and she refused to be warned, and now again she was
punished with the loss of her goods, and then she gave up
brewing and did it no more. Then she asked her husband's
forgiveness for she had not followed his advice, and she said that
her pride and sin had brought about her punishment and she
would willingly make amends for her faults.

Yet she would not leave the world entirely, for now she
thought of a new kind of housewifely venture. She had a horse
mill. She got herself two good horses and a man to grind people's corn, and in this way she felt sure she could make her

living. This enterprise did not last long, for a short time after the
Eve of Corpus Christi, the following marvel occurred. This man
was in good health of body, with two horses that were lusty and
in good condition, and up till now had drawn well in the mill.
Now when the man took one of these horses and put him in the
mill as he had done all along, this horse would not drag a load in
the mill no matter what the man did. Sometimes he led him by
the head, sometimes he beat him, and sometimes he cajoled him,
but it was all useless because the horse would rather go backward than forward. Then this man set a pair of sharp spurs on
his heels and rode on the horse's back to make him pull but it
was never any better.

When this man saw it was useless, then he put up the
horse in the stable and fed him, and he ate well and freshly. Then
he took the other horse and put him in the mill. And just as his
fellow horse had done, so this one did, for he wouldn't pull
despite anything the man did. And then this man quit his service
and would no longer stay with this creature we have mentioned.
As soon as the word got around the town of N- that no man or
beast would work for that creature, then some people said she
was cursed. Some said God took open vengeance on her. Some
said one thing and some said another. And some wise men
whose mind was more grounded in the love of our Lord said it
was the high mercy of our Lord Jesus Christ that commanded
and called her from the pride and vanity of the wretched world.
(from chapter 2)

4. *"It Is Full Merry in Heaven."*
Her Disgust with the Acts of Marriage

One night as this creature lay in her bed with her husband,
she heard a sound of melody so sweet and delectable she
thought she was in Paradise. And with that she started out of her
bed and said, "Alas that ever I did sin, it is full merry in heaven!"
This melody was so sweet that it surpassed all the melody that
ever might be heard in this world, without any comparison. And
it caused this creature—when she heard any mirth or melody
afterward—to shed very plentiful and abundant tears of high

devotion, with great sobbings and sighings for the bliss of heaven, with no fear of the disgrace or malice of this wretched world. And ever after God drafted her to his service in this way, she kept in mind the joy and the melody that there was in heaven, so much so that she could not fully restrain herself from speaking of it. For wherever she was in any company with people she would often say, "It is full merry in heaven!"

And those who knew about her previous conduct and now heard her speak so much of the bliss of heaven said to her, "Why do you speak so of the mirth that is in heaven? You don't know it, and you haven't been there any more than we have." And they were angry with her because she would not hear or speak of worldly things as they did and as she had formerly.

And after this time she never had any desire to commune in the flesh with her husband, for the marriage debt[29] was so abominable to her that she would rather, she thought, eat or drink the ooze, the muck in the gutter than consent to any fleshly communing, except out of obedience. (from chapter 3)

5. *God Speaks to Margery and Guides Her*

Then on a Friday before Christmas Day as this creature knelt in a chapel of Saint John within a church of Saint Margaret in N-, weeping very sorrowfully, she asked mercy and forgiveness for her sins and her trespasses. Our merciful Lord Christ Jesus—blessed may he be!—ravished her spirit and said to her, "Daughter, why do you weep so sorrowfully? I have come to you, Jesus Christ who died on the Cross, suffering bitter pains and passions for you. I, the same God, forgive your sins to the utmost point. And now you shall never go to Hell or Purgatory, but when you shall pass out of this world, within the twinkling of an eye you shall have the bliss of heaven, for I am the same God that have brought your sins to your mind and absolved you of them. And I grant you contrition until the end of your life.

"Therefore, I bid and command you, boldly call me Jesus, your love, for I am your love and shall be your love without end. And daughter, you have a hair shirt on your back, I want you to take it off and I will give you a hair shirt in your heart that will please me much better than all the hair shirts in the world. Also, my dear daughter, you must forsake what you love best in the world; that is, eating meat. And instead of that flesh you shall eat my flesh and my blood,[30] which is the true body of Christ in the sacrament of the altar. This is my will, daughter, that you receive my body every Sunday, and I shall flow so much grace into you that all the world shall marvel at it. You shall be eaten and gnawed by the people of the world as any rat gnaws a stockfish. Have no fear, daughter, for you shall have the victory over all your enemies. I shall give you sufficient grace to answer every clerk in the love of God. I swear to you by my majesty that I shall never forsake you in well or woe. I shall help you and protect you, so that there shall be never a devil in hell that shall ever part you from me, nor angel in heaven, nor man on earth—for devils in hell may not, and angels in heaven will not, and man on earth shall not. (from chapter 5)

6. *She Is Threatened by a Woman*
in the Archbishop's Hall

Then this creature went to London with her husband, to Lambeth where the Archbishop was at that time. And as they entered the hall in the afternoon, many of the Archbishop's clerics were there, and other careless men, both squires and yeomen who swore many violent oaths and spoke many rash words. And this creature boldly confronted them and said they should be damned if they didn't stop their swearing and the other sins they committed.

And with that a woman from the same town came up in a pilch[31] and abused this creature, cursed her, and spoke very hatefully to her in this manner: "I wish you were in Smithfield, and I could bring faggots to burn you with. It's a pity you are still alive!"

This creature stood still and answered nothing, and her husband suffered with great anguish and was full of sorrow to hear his wife so threatened. (from chapter 16)

7. Her Visit to Norwich with the Vicar of Saint Stephen's. Her Acquaintance with Books

One day long before this time, while this creature was in her childbearing years and had just given birth to an infant, our Lord Christ Jesus said to her that she should not bear any more children, and therefore he ordered her to go to Norwich. And she said, "Ah, dear Lord, how shall I go? I am both faint and feeble!"

"Do not be afraid, I shall make you strong enough. I command you to go to the Vicar of Saint Stephen's there,[32] and say that I greet him well and that he is a high-chosen soul of mine, and tell him that he pleases me very much with his preaching. Show him your secrets and my counsels such as I reveal to you."

Then she made her way toward Norwich and entered his church on a Thursday a little before noon. And the Vicar was walking up and down with another priest, his father confessor, who was alive when this book was written. And this creature was wearing black clothing at that time. She greeted the Vicar, begging that she might speak with him an hour or else two in the afternoon—after he had eaten—of the love of God.

She told him how sometimes the Father of Heaven dallied with her soul as plainly and as truly as one friend speaks to another with bodily speech. Sometimes the Second Person in Trinity, sometimes all Three Persons in Trinity and one substance in Godhead, dallied with her soul, and informed her in her faith and in his love how she should love him, worship him, and dread him. So excellent was it that she never heard any book, whether Hilton's book, or Bride's book, or *Stimulus Amoris*, or *Incendium Amoris*, or any other book she ever heard read, that spoke so gloriously of the love of God, which she felt gloriously working in her soul—if only she could have expressed what she felt! (from chapter 17)

8. Margery Visits Dame Julian of Norwich

And then she was commanded by our Lord to go to an anchoress in the same city whose name was Dame Jelyan, and so she did. She showed her the grace that God put in her soul of compunction, contrition, sweetness and devotion, compassion with holy meditation and high contemplation and a great many holy speeches and dalliances that our Lord offered to her soul. She showed the anchoress many wonderful revelations, to learn if there were any deceit in them, for the anchoress was expert in such things and could give good counsel. The anchoress, hearing such marvelous goodness of our Lord, exaltedly thanked God with all her heart for his visitation, counseling this creature to be obedient to the will of our Lord God, and fulfill with all her might whatever he put in her soul, as long as it was not against the worship of God and the good interest of her fellow Christians. For if it were, than it was not the urging of a good spirit but rather of an evil one. The Holy Ghost never urges anything against charity, and if it did it would be contradictory to its own essential nature, for it is all charity. (from chapter 18)

9. She Weeps at the Church of the Holy Sepulchre in Jerusalem

Then they went to the Church of the Holy Sepulchre in Jerusalem, and they were let in on the one day at evensong time, and remained until the hour of evensong on the next day.[33] Then the friars lifted up a cross and led the pilgrims about from one place to another where our Lord had suffered his pains and his Passion, every man and woman carrying a wax candle in one hand. And as the friars went about, they continually told them what our Lord suffered in every place. And this creature wept and sobbed as copiously as though she had seen our Lord with her bodily eyes suffering his Passion at that time. Before her in her soul she saw him in truth through contemplation, and that moved her to compassion. And when they came up on to the Mount of Calvary, she fell down because she could not stand or kneel, but writhed and wrestled with her body, spreading her arms out wide, and cried with a loud voice as though her heart would have burst apart. For in the city of her soul she saw truly and freshly how our Lord was crucified. Before her face she heard and saw in her spiritual sight the mourning of our Lady, of St. John and Mary Magdalene, and of many others that loved our Lord.

She had such great compassion and such great pain to see our Lord's pain that she could not keep herself from crying and roaring even though she should have died for it. And this was the first crying that she ever cried in any contemplation. And this kind of crying lasted for many years after this time, despite anything that anyone might do, and she suffered much scorn and much reproach for it. The crying was so loud and so amazing that it astounded people, unless they had heard it before or else knew the reason for the lamentations. And she had them so often that they made her very weak in her bodily strength and especially if she heard of our Lord's Passion.

And sometimes when she saw the crucifix, or if she saw a man who was wounded, or an animal, whichever it was, or if a man beat a child in her presence, or hit a horse or another animal with a whip, if she saw or heard it, she thought she saw our Lord being beaten or wounded, just as she saw it in the man or in the beast, either in the fields or in the town, and alone by herself as well as among people. (from chapter 28)

10. Her Sensations and Visions and Her Burning Love

When this creature was in the Apostles' Church at Rome on St. Lateran's Day [Saturday before Easter], the Father of Heaven said to her, "Daughter, I am well pleased with you, since you believe in all the Sacraments of Holy Church and in all the faith that pertains to these, and especially since you believe in the manhood of my Son and because of the great compassion that you have for his bitter Passion." The Father also said to this creature, "Daughter, I will have you wedded to my Godhead, because I shall show you my secrets and my counsels, for you shall dwell with me without end."

Then the creature kept silence in her soul and did not answer, for she was very afraid of the Godhead, and she had no skill in the dalliance of the Godhead, for all her love and affection was set on the manhood of Christ and she had skill in this and would not be parted from it for anything.

She was so affected by the manhood of Christ that when she saw women in Rome carrying children in their arms, if she might find out if any were male children, she would cry, roar, and weep as though she had seen Christ in his childhood. And if she could have had her way, often she would have taken the children out of their mothers' arms and kissed them instead of Christ. And if she saw a handsome man, it caused her great pain to look at him, lest she might see him that was both God and man. And therefore she cried many times and often when she met a handsome man, and wept and sobbed most sorrowfully for the manhood of Christ as she walked in the streets of Rome, so that those who saw her were greatly astonished at her, for they didn't know the cause.

Therefore it was no wonder that she remained still and did not answer the Father of Heaven when he told her that she should be wedded to his Godhead.

Then the Second Person, Christ Jesus, whose manhood she loved so much, said to her, "What do you say, Margery, daughter, to my Father about these words that he speaks to you? Are you well pleased that it may be so?" And then she would not answer the Second Person, but wept terribly sorrowfully, still desiring to have him, and in no way to be parted from him. Then the Second Person of the Trinity answered his Father for her, and said, "Father, let her be excused, for she is still young and has not fully learned how she should answer."

And then the Father took her by the hand in her soul, before the Son and the Holy Ghost, and the Mother of Jesus, and all the twelve apostles, and St. Katherine and St. Margaret[34] and many other saints and holy virgins, with a great multitude of angels, saying to her soul, "I take you, Margery, for my wedded wife, for fairer, for fouler, for richer, for poorer, provided that you are obedient and gentle in doing what I command you. For, daughter, there was never a child so obedient to the mother as I shall be to you, both in joy and sorrow, to help you and comfort you. And of that I make you a pledge."

And then the Mother of God and all the saints who were there present in her soul prayed that they might have much joy together. Then this creature with high devotion, with great effusion of tears, thanked God for this spiritual comfort. She considered herself in her own feeling very unworthy of any such grace as she felt, for she felt many great comforts, both spiritual comforts and bodily comforts. Sometimes she sensed sweet smells in her nose; they were sweeter, she thought, than any earthly sweet thing ever was that she smelled before, nor could she ever tell how sweet they were, for she thought she might have lived on them if they had lasted.

Sometimes she heard with her bodily ears such sounds and melodies that she couldn't clearly hear what a man said to her at that time unless he spoke louder. These sounds and melodies she had heard nearly every day for twenty-five years when this book was written, and especially when she was in devout prayer, also many times while she was at Rome and in England both.

She saw with her bodily eyes many white things flying all about her on all sides, as thickly in a way as motes in a sunbeam. They were very subtle and comforting, and the brighter the sun shone, the better she could see them. She saw them many different times and in many different places, both in church and in her chamber, at her food and at her prayers, in field and in town, both walking and sitting. And many times she was afraid what they might be, for she saw them at night in darkness as in daylight.

Then when she was afraid of them, our Lord said to her: "By this token, daughter, believe it is God who speaks in you, for wherever God is, heaven is, and where God is, there are many angels, and God is in you and you are in him. Therefore, be unafraid, daughter, for these mean that you have many angels around you, to keep you both day and night so that no Devil shall have power over you and no evil man will hurt you." Then from that time forward she used to say when she saw them coming: *"Benedictus qui venit in nomine Domini."*[35]

Our Lord also gave her another token which lasted about sixteen years, and always increased more and more, and that was a flame of fire—wondrously hot and delectable and very comforting, never wasting but ever increasing. For no matter how cold the weather was, she felt the heat burning in her breast and at her heart, as truly as a man would feel the material fire if he put his hand or his finger into it.

When she first felt the fire of love burning in her breast, she was afraid of it, and then our Lord answered to her mind and said, "Daughter, be unafraid, for this heat is the heat of the Holy Ghost, which will burn away all your sins, for the fire of love quenches all sins." (from chapter 35)

11. In the Same Scene in the Church of the Apostles, the Lord Invites Her to the Celestial Marriage Bed

"And if I were on earth as bodily as I was before I died on the cross, I would not be ashamed of you, as many other people are, for I would take you by the hand among the people and greet you warmly, so that they would certainly know that I loved you very much.

"For it is fitting for the wife to be on intimate terms with her husband. However great a lord he is, and however poor a woman she is when he weds her, yet must they lie together and rest together in joy and peace. Just so must it be between you and me, for I take no heed of what you have been but what you would be, and I have often told you that I have clean forgiven you all your sins.

"Therefore I need to be intimate with you, and lie in your bed with you. Daughter, you greatly desire to see me, and you may boldly, when you are in bed, take me to you as your wedded husband, as your dear-worthy darling, and for your sweet son. For I want to be loved as a son should be loved by the mother, and I want you to love me, daughter, as a good wife ought to love her husband. Therefore you may boldly take me in the arms of your soul and kiss my mouth, my head, and my feet as sweetly as you will. And as often as you think of me or would do any good deed to me, you shall have the same reward in heaven as if you did it to my own precious body, which is in heaven. For I ask no more of you than that your heart should love me—who loves you—for my love is always ready for you." (from chapter 36)

"Daughter, you are obedient to my will, and cleave as sorely to me as the skin of stockfish sticks to a man's hands when it is boiled, and you will not forsake me for any shame that any

man can do to you. And you say also that—even though I stood
before you in my own person and said to you that you should
never have my love, never come to heaven, nor ever see my
face—yet you say, daughter, that you would never forsake me
on earth. You would never love me the less, never be less diligent to please me, even though you should lie in hell without
end, since you cannot give up my love on earth nor can you have
any other comfort but me alone, who am I, your God, and am all
joy and all bliss to you. Therefore I say to you, dear-worthy
daughter, it is impossible that any such soul should be damned
or separated from me that has such great meekness and charity
toward me." (from chapter 37)

12. She Cares for Her Husband in His Old Age

It happened one time that this creature's husband—a man
of advanced age, over sixty years old—wanted to come down
from his chamber bare-footed and bare-legged, and he slithered
or else missed his footing. He fell to the ground from the steps,
with his head under him, dangerously shattered and bruised, so
much so that he had five bandages[36] on his head wounds for a
number of days while his head was healing. And as God willed,
it was known to some of his neighbors how he had fallen down
the stairs, perhaps because of the noise and lurching of his fall.
And so they came to him and found him lying with his head
bent under him, half alive, all smeared with blood and likely
never to be able to speak with priest or clerk, except through
heavenly grace and miracle.

Then the said creature, his wife, was sent for, and so she
came to him. Then he was taken up and his head was sutured,
and he was sick for a long time afterward, so that people thought
he would die. And then people said, if he died, his wife deserved
to be hanged for his death, inasmuch as she could have looked
after him and did not. They did not live together, nor did they
sleep together, for—as it has been written earlier—they both
made a vow to live chastely. And therefore, to avoid all danger,
they dwelled and sojourned in different places, where no suspicion could be had of their wantonness. For at first, they lived
together after they had made their vow, and then people slan-

dered them, and said they enjoyed their lust and their pleasure as they did before they had made their vow. And when they went out on pilgrimage, or to see and speak with other devout creatures, many evil folk whose tongues were their own hurt, and failing in the fear and love of our Lord Jesus Christ, believed and said that they went instead to woods, groves, or valleys, to enjoy the lust of their bodies so that people wouldn't spy on them or know about it.

These two knew how prone people were to judge evil of them, and they desired to avoid all occasion as far as they rightly could. By mutual good-will and consent, they parted from each other where their board and chambers were concerned, and went to board in different places. And this was the reason she was not with him, and also because she would not be prevented from her contemplation.

[Margery prays for guidance, and Our Lord tells her to care for her husband.]

Then she took her husband home with her and looked after him for years afterwards, as long as he lived. She had a great deal of trouble with him, for in his last days he turned childish again and lacked reason, so that he could not relieve himself on his own by going to the stool, but like a child he voided his natural bowels into his linen clothes as he sat there by the fire or at the table; wherever it was, he would spare no place. And therefore she had so much more labor in washing and wringing, and the cost of keeping a fire going, and these kept her very much from her contemplation. Many times this labor would have irked her, except that she remembered how in her young age she had enjoyed a great many delectable thoughts, fleshly pleasures, and an inordinate love of his body. And therefore she was glad to be punished through this same body, and took it much more easily, and served him and helped him, so it seemed to her, as she would have done for Christ himself. (from chapter 76)

Julians Barnes, *The Boke of Huntyng*

Prologue

Just as these books about hawking are written to explain
the terms of pleasure that concern gentlemen who delight in fal-
conry, so, similarly, this book shows gentle persons how to hunt
all sorts of beasts, whether they are beasts of venery or the chase,
or "rascal." And it also explains all the terms used of the hounds,
besides the animals we mentioned. And there is certainly a great
variety of these terms, as this book will show.[37]

1. Beasts of Venery

Wherever you ride through wood or dell,
My dear child, take heed to what Tristram can tell
Of the beasts of venery you will find;
Attend to your mistress, and she'll teach you the
    kinds.
There are four kinds of beasts of venery:
The first is the hart, the second the hare,
    The boar is another
    And the wolf—there is no more.

2. Beasts of the Chase

And when you come to a plain or some place
I'll tell you which are the beasts of the chase:
One is the buck, another the doe,
The fox and the martron and the wild roe.
And you shall, my dear child, other beasts call—
Wherever you find them—"*rascals*" all.
    In wood or in dell
    Or in forest, as I tell.

3. The Age of a Hart

To speak of the hart—if you would hear—
Call him a calf in his first year,

The second year a "broket" you shall him call,
The third year a "spayad." Learn this all!
The fourth year, a "stag" call him always,
The fifth year, "a great stag," your mistress says,
In the sixth year, "a hart" he's named.
Do so, my child, while you have strength.[38]

4. The Different Heads of the Hart

He's not a hart until his sixth year,
And if you'd like to speak further about this same
deer
And of the horns he carries on his head—
A hart of the "first head" cannot be judged.
In this we see
Such diversity:
From his sixth year on, at the very least
You can judge the "perch" of this same beast.
When his antlers freely grow
"Royal" and "Surroyal," I call them so.
With two points on top, when you recognize them,
You may call him a "forked hart of ten."
And when there are three points on top of the
same,
A "trochid hart of twelve" is his name.[39]
When there are four points on the top of his head
He's termed "a summit hart of fourteen."
And beyond that, whatever happens,
However many his points—"summit" still is the
term.

5. A Herd, a Bevy, a Sounder, a Rout

My child, "herds" mean gatherings of hart and
hind
And buck and doe, wherever they're found.
A "bevy" means roes, whatever place they're in,
And a "sounder" is for wild swine.
A "rout" is for wolves, where they may run.
That's what you call them, whatever the sum.

These beasts all
You shall them call.

6. *A Little Herd, a Middle Herd, a Great Herd*

Twenty is a little herd, though it may be of
   females,
And forty is a middle herd, to call them by their
   nature,
And eighty is a great herd, be sure to call them
   so—
Whether of hart, or hind or buck or doe.

13. *The Rewards for the Hounds*

When your hounds run in force, and do a hare to
   death,
The hunters shall reward them with the head,
The shoulders and sides, and the bowels, all
That is found in the belly, except the gall,
         And the paunch—
         Give them none of that.
The reward is dealt out on the ground.
All good hunters call this the *halow*.
But the loins of the hare, be sure not to forget—
These you bring to the kitchen for the lord's meat.
         And of this same hare
         Let's speak no more.[40]

20. *The Crying of These Beasts*

A hart bellows and a buck groans, I say,
And each roebuck certainly bells, it's his way.
The noises of these beasts by these names you
   must call,
It's pride in their mates that inspires them all.
         Say, child, wherever you go
         It was your dame who taught you so.

21. *Mark Well the Following Seasons*

The time of grease begins Midsummer Day
And lasts until Holyrood Day, as I say.
The season of the fox goes from the Nativity
Until the Annunciation of Our Blessed Lady.
The roebuck's season shall begin at Easter
And lasts until Michaelmas before it's over.
The roe's season opens at Michaelmas
And shall last and endure up to Candlemas.
At Michaelmas opens the hunt of the hare
Which lasts until Midsummer, no man will it
   spare.
The season of the wolf in each country
Is the same as the fox, evermore shall this be.
The season of the boar goes from the Nativity
Till the Purification of Our Blessed Lady.
For at the Nativity of Our Lady sweet,
The boar finds where he treads, under his feet,
Both in woods and fields, corn and other fruit,
When he seeks his food, and there he can rootle,
For crabapples, acorns, and nuts where they grow,
Haws and hips and enough other food,
As long as the Purification lasts, you'll find,
And this makes the boar good to hunt all this time,
     For while these fruits may last
     His time is never past.[41]

24. *Two Reasons Why the Hart Desires the River*

"One reason why the hart is 'descendant' to the
   river,
Or any water he passes on his way—"
"Why do you call him 'descendant,' Master, I
   pray?"
"Because he's impaired in strength, it is true.
Another reason he takes to the water a while,
He hopes that the hounds in pursuit are beguiled."
"But about this hart," said his man, "Master, I ask
   you,
When he leaps in the water, then what does he do?"

"He 'profers,' or wavers," said the master, "you'll
  see,
For he doesn't yet know how he'll get away—
Whether he'll manage to swim across the water
Or return back the same way he first came,
Or whether to dive back into the water
And try to drown the hounds by pushing them
  under.
That is why hunters call this 'profer.'
If he turns back again, we call it 're-profer.'
If he makes it to the opposite bank
Then you shall call it the 'soiling of the hart.'
Now because of the water, his legs are wet.
Water streams from his feet and soaks his tracks.
If he jumps back into the river or pool,
Be sure to use the term refoule.
When he's in the water, making his attempt,
He breaks it and beats it, be observant.
If he drifts down with the stream, you shall
Say he's defouling the water, for so it's called."[42]

28. What Three Things Keep the Hounds Going?

"I'd like to know, Master, if it's your will,
Why is it when hounds run after a hart,
The farther they go, the gladder they grow?"
"For three reasons," he said, "as often is seen.
One is, when the hart runs fast in a race,
He sweats so hard it runs down through his claws.
Then when the hounds catch wind of his sweat,
They're more eager to run, more unwilling to quit.
Another reason—when the hart is worn down,
He throws off a white froth as he runs on.
When the hounds get wind of it they are glad,
Hoping to have him, their chase is more rapid.
The third reason is that when the hart is near dead,
He throws off from his mouth a froth and red blood,
Then the hounds know he'll be taken soon,
And the farther they go, the gladder they run.
        These are the causes three
        That cause them glad to be."

29. Which Beast Does a Slow Hound Catch as Fast as a Swift?

"Which beast is it, Master, I ask without spite,
That most hounds will chase in hot pursuit,
So that the slowest overtakes him as fast
As the swiftest, whatever the beast's path?"
"That beast is a badger, a brock, or a gray,
He has these three names, the truth to say.
And this is the reason: it is the beast's nature
To run through thorns, the thickest he finds.
There the swiftest hounds can't chase any further
Than the slowest of foot, though they ardently
    try."[43]

32. To Undo the Wild Boar

"My child, to speak of the boar once more,
When he shall be undone, as I told you before,
Thirty-two breadths you shall make of him.
Now, my son, you shall learn what to do with
    them:
The first is the head, whatever befalls,
The next is the collar, neck, so it is called.
The shields of the shoulders, these are two,
Both sides of the swine are divided in three;
The forelegs and hams, cut them in two
And the filets he has, don't forget those.
Take his legs and feet and display your craft,
For among his portions they're counted as eight.
Cut the backbone in four pieces and no more,
And take your pieces, thirty plus two.
Neatly place the fat—once it's taken out—
In the boar's bladder, my child, I pray you,
      For it is medicine
      For many kinds of pain."

Letters of Margaret, Queen of Anjou

1. *To the Keeper of a Park*

Dated 1445–1455

By the Queen
Well-beloved,

We know truly that our cousin the Earl of Salisbury will be extremely content and pleased that upon our visit to the castle of Hertford, we shall be taking sport and recreation in his Park at Ware. And so we embolden ourselves to desire and pray to you that the game there shall be spared, kept, and cherished for the same purpose—without allowing any other person to hunt there or shoot, course, or engage in other sport which would destroy or diminish the game we mentioned, until you receive different orders from our cousin in the matter.

As we trust you, etc.
To the Parker of Ware.[44]

2. *To the Master of a Hospital for Lepers in London*

Dated after 1445

By the Queen
Trusty [and Well-beloved],

We have been informed that one Robert Uphome, seventeen years of age and recently chorister to the most reverend father in God, our noble uncle the Cardinal (may God absolve him) at his college at Winchester, is now by God's visitation become a leper.

We desire, therefore, and pray you, since he has no other support or livelihood to live on—apart from the alms of Christian people, as it is said—that in reverence of our blessed Creator and in contemplation of this our prayer, you will accept and receive him into your hospital of Saint Giles. Please allow him such maintenance and livelihood as other persons in his situation are accustomed to have, as we trust you. In this you would do not only a most meritorious deed to please God, but also would deserve from us our very especial thanks.

To the Master of Saint Giles in the Field beside the City of London.[45]

3. To the Keeper of a Park

August 28, 1449

By the Queen
Well-beloved,

We wish, and expressly command you—for certain considerations moving us—that you with all diligence cherish, favor, and keep our game within our park of Apchild, since their protection and safekeeping are in your care. Do not allow any person, whatever rank, estate, or condition he may be, to hunt there or ride, shoot or engage in any other sport that would diminish our game until it is our pleasure to resort there. Your true acquittal may be found in the good keeping and replenishment of the game when you accomplish our intention in this matter.

Do not in any way obey or serve any other warrant, unless it be under our signet and signed with our own hand.

And if any person presume to attempt anything contrary on the premises, you are to certify us of their names. If you would avoid displeasing us, you will not fail to do this, at your peril, and upon forfeiture of the keeping of this park.

Given, etc., at Pleshy, the 28th day of August, the 27th year [of the reign of Henry VI].

To the Keeper of the Park of Apchild or his Deputy there.[46]

4. To the Keeper of Henry VI's Park at Shene Palace

Undated

By the Queen
Trusty and Well-beloved,

Since within a short time we suppose that we shall be arriving at my lord's manor of Shene, we desire and pray you heartily that you will keep for our visit there, for our sport and recreation, two or three of the greatest bucks in my lord's park there, unless my lord commands otherwise when he is present.

As we trust, etc.

To my lord's squire and ours, J.B., keeper of Shene Park, or his deputy there.[47]

5. *To a Trainer of Bloodhounds*

August 16, 14—

By the Queen
Trusty and Well-beloved,
     We are informed that you have the art and knowledge to train bloodhounds in the best manner. We desire and pray you that you will, out of reverence for us, take such diligence and care upon yourself to train us two bloodhounds for our use. Keep them safely and properly under your discipline, rule, and management, until we send for them. Do not fail to do this if you wish to do us pleasure, and to stand in the favor of good grace, therefore, in future time.
     At Windsor, the 16th day of August.
     To Robert Hiberdon.

Three Letters from Margery Brews Paston

1. *To my right well-beloved Valentine, John Paston, Squire, let this bill be delivered, etc.*[48]

February 1477

     Most revered and worshipful and my right well-beloved Valentine, I recommend myself to you, for I most heartily desire to hear of your welfare, and I beseech Almighty God that he will long preserve it for his own pleasure and for your heart's desire. And if you would like to hear of my own welfare, I am not in good health of body or of heart, nor shall I be till I hear from you.

> For no creature knows the pain I feel—
> Though it may cause my death, I dare it not reveal.

And my lady, my mother, has very diligently tried to persuade my father in this matter, but she is unable to get any further with him than you have already heard. And for this reason God knows I am full of sorrow. But if you love me, as I truly trust that you do, you will not leave me on account of it. Because even if you didn't have half the income that you have, I would perform the greatest tasks of any woman alive so that I would not forsake you.

> And if you command me to keep true wherever I go,
> Surely I will do all my might to love you and never another.
> And if my friends say that I do wrong,
> They shall never hinder me from doing so.
> My heart urges me forever to love you
> Truly over all earthly things,
> And even if my friends grow angry with me,
> I trust that all shall be better in the times to come.

I write no more to you at this time, but may the Holy Trinity keep you safe, and I beseech you that this bill shall not be seen by any earthly creature except yourself alone, etc. And this letter was written at Topcroft, with full heavy heart, etc.

By your own,
M. B.

2. *To my right well-beloved cousin, John Paston, Squire, let this letter be delivered, etc.*

February 1477

Right worshipful and well-beloved Valentine, in my most humble manner I recommend myself to you, etc. And heartily I thank you for the letter which you sent me by John Becurton, by which I understand and know that you plan to come to Topcroft soon, without any errand or purpose but to bring to conclusion the business between my father and you.

I would be the happiest of any creature if the matter were settled. And you say that if you come and find that the matter proves no more favorable to you now than it was before, you wouldn't put my father and my lady, my mother, to any further trouble or expense for a long time. This makes me very heavy-hearted! And if you come and the matter doesn't reach any good conclusion, I would be much more sorrowful and full of grief.

And as for me, I have done and endeavored all I could in this matter, as God knows. And I let you plainly understand that besides all this my father won't part with any more money than a hundred pounds and fifty marks, which is very far from satisfying your desire. So, if you could be content with that amount and my poor person, I would be the merriest maiden on earth. And if you think you would not be pleased with that and that you might get a richer dowry from someone else, as I have already understood you to suggest—good, true, and loving Valentine!—don't take the trouble on yourself to come here any more on this account. Let it pass, and never be spoken of again, as I may be your true lover and beadswoman during my life.

No more to you at this time, but may almighty Jesus preserve you both in body and soul, etc.

By your Valentine,
Margery Brews

3. *To be delivered to my master John Paston*

Jan. 21, 1486

Right reverent and worshipful sir, in my most humble manner I recommend myself to you, desiring to hear of your welfare. I beseech God to preserve it, to his pleasure and to your heart's desire.

Sir, I thank you for the venison that you sent me. And your ship has sailed out of the haven as of today.

Sir, I send you by my brother William your damask waistcoat. As for your short cloak of velvet, it is not here. Ann says that you put it in your chest at London.

Sir, your children are in good health, may God be blessed.

Sir, I pray you to send me the gold that I spoke about to you, by the next man who comes to Norwich.

Sir, your mast that lay at Yarmouth is hired out to a ship from Hull for thirteen shillings and four pence. And if any damage is done to it you shall have a new mast in its place.

No more to you at this time, but may Almighty God have you in his keeping.

Written at Caister Hall the twenty-first day of January in the first year of King Harry the VII.

By your servant Margery Paston.

I pray to God that no ladies continue to captivate you so you can have no leisure for your concerns.

Margery Paston

NOTES

1. Brigitta (1303–July 23, 1373), daughter of a governor and judge of Uppland in Sweden, married the nobleman Ulf Godmarsson and bore eight children. A lady-in-waiting at the royal court, Brigitta earnestly preached to Queen Blanche and King Magnus II. She made pilgrimages to Compostela and Rome. After her husband's death in 1344, she founded the Brigittines, the Order of the Holy Savior, mainly for women. Brigitta's dictated *Revelations*, often controversial, dwelt on the sufferings of Christ, the reform of the world, and prognostications for the future. She spent her last years in Rome, caring for the sick and poor and offering advice to the popes about church and state. She died in Rome on returning from a pilgrimage to the Holy Land. She was canonized in 1391. Her cult spread rapidly in Scandinavia and northern Europe. Her *Revelations* were translated into Middle English.

On Brigitta, see Julia Bolton Holloway, "Bride, Margery, Julian, and Alice: Bridget of Sweden's Textual Community in Medieval England," in Sandra J. McEntire, ed., *Margery Kempe: A Book of Essays* (New York: Garland, 1992), pp. 203–222; Aron Andersson, *St. Birgitta and the Holy Land* (Stockholm, 1973); Johannes Jörgensen, *St. Bridget of Sweden*, trans. Ingeborg Lund, 2 vols. (1954); J.R. Fletcher, *The Story of the English Brigittines of Syon Abbey* (Bristol, 1933); William P. Cumming, ed., *Revelations of St. Birgitta, EETS o.s.*, vol. 178 (1929); John Audelay's poem "A Salutation to Saint Brigitte," in the 1420s in the *EETS* ed.

My thanks to Jo Ann McNamara for information about the contemporary Syon House.

2. Susan Dickman surveys women on the continent, many of them married, who lacked the money or connections to join a community but pursued lives of devotion while continuing their housewifely tasks. See "Margery Kempe and the Continental Tradition of the Pious Woman," in Marion Glasscoe, ed., *The Medieval Mystical Tradition in*

England: Papers Read at Dartington Hall, July 1984 (Cambridge: D.S. Brewer, 1984); pp. 150–168.

3. The book came to light in 1934 in the possession of the Butler-Bowdon family in England, who had owned it since the eighteenth century. Before that it had reposed in the archives of the Carthusian monastery of Mount Grace Priory near Northallerton in Yorkshire. The British Museum acquired *The Book of Margery Kempe* in 1980.

4. On Dorothea of Montau, "Housewife and Anchoress," see Richard Kieckhefer, *Unquiet Souls: Fourteenth-Century Saints and Their Religious Milieu* (Chicago: U of Chicago P, 1984), p. 22–33.

5. For analyses of the pious overflow of tears, viewed favorably, see the entries under "Larmes," in both *Dictionnaire de Spiritualité* and *Dictionnaire d'Archéologie chrétienne et de liturgie*. Sandra McEntire, "The Doctrine of Compunction from Bede to Margery Kempe," in Marion Glasscoe, ed., *The Medieval Mystical Tradition in England: Exeter Symposium IV. Papers Read at Dartington Hall, July 1987* (Wolfeboro, N.H.: D.S. Brewer, 1987), pp. 77–90, also provides a cross-section of approving attitudes toward weeping on the part of earlier English writers. The *Ancren Riwle*, for instance, sees tears as weapons to scald Satan with.

6. Richard Kieckhefer, *Unquiet Souls*, p. 190.

7. Two significant recent studies that reevaluate Margery Kempe's importance are Karma Lochrie, *Margery Kempe and Translations of the Flesh* (Philadelphia: U of Pennsylvania P, 1991); and Sandra J. McEntire, ed., *Margery Kempe: A Book of Essays* (New York: Garland, 1992).

8. Lynn Staley Johnson, "The Trope of the Scribe and the Question of Literary Authority in the Works of Julian of Norwich and Margery Kempe," *Speculum* 66 (October 1991): 820–838. Both Julian and Margery recognized "the constraints on female devotional writers." Both "sought to create texts that were not simply annals of spiritual experience but narratives intended to give a particular form or meaning to experience." (pp. 828–829).

9. "Margery Kempe and Wynkyn de Worde," in Marion Glasscoe, ed., *The Medieval Mystical Tradition in England: Exeter Symposium IV. Papers Read at Dartington Hall, July 1987* (Wolfeboro, N.H.: D.S. Brewer, 1987).

10. Cited from Paul Murray Kendall, *The Yorkist Age: Daily Life During the Wars of the Roses* (New York: W.W. Norton, 1962), pp. 234, 355, 156.

11. On the hunt and its literary connections, see Marcelle Thiébaux, *The Stag of Love: The Chase in Medieval Literature* (Ithaca:

Cornell UP, 1974), and "The Medieval Chase," *Speculum* 42 (April 1967): 260–274.

12. Alec Reginald Myers, "The Household of Queen Margaret of Anjou," pp. 135–208, quote pp. 142–43, in *Crown, Household, and Parliament in Fifteenth Century England*, ed. Cecil H. Clough, introduction by R. B. Dobson. London: Hambledon P, 1985; Gordon Kipling, "The London Pageants for Margaret of Anjou: A Medieval Script Restored," *Medieval English Theatre* 4 (1982): 5–27.

13. My heart is set, and all my whole intent
   To serve this flower in my most humble wise
   As faithfully as can be thought or meant
   Without feigning or sloth in my service.

In Praise of Margaret the Queen: How the lover is sette to serve the flower. The "flower" was the French *marguerite*, or daisy. Chaucer's *Legend of Good Women* in the previous century also paid homage to the daisy. Suffolk's are printed in Rossell Hope Robbins, *Secular Lyrics of the XIVth and XVth Centuries*, 2nd ed. (Oxford: Clarendon P, 1952), Nos. 187–189, pp. 185–90.

14. "The Household of Queen Margaret of Anjou"; also "The Jewels of Queen Margaret of Anjou," pp. 211–229, *Crown, Household, and Parliament*.

15. Michael K. Jones and Malcolm G. Underwood, *The King's Mother: Lady Margaret Beaufort, Countess of Richmond and Derby* (Cambridge: Cambridge UP, 1992), pp. 39, 254.

16. Cited in Kendall, *The Yorkist Age*, p. 66.

17. Jones and Underwood, *The King's Mother*, p. 254.

18. John Twigg, *A History of Queens College, Cambridge, 1448–1986*. Wolfeboro, N.H.: The Boydell P, 1987, pp. 1–3, also citing John Boking's contemporary view of Margaret. The women who had previously established colleges were Elizabeth Lady Clare and Marie de Valence, Countess of Pembroke.

Queens College would later become the short-term residence in Cambridge of the Dutch priest and satirist, Desiderius Erasmus.

19. Colin Richmond, *The Paston Family in the Fifteenth Century: The First Phase* (Cambridge UP, 1990), cites this "Remembraunce" of Clement (p. 13), though the family claimed they were never unfree. Another tradition states they were "gentlemen discended lineally of worshipfull blood sithen the Conquest" (p. 6).

20. Jack B. Oruch explores the convention in "St. Valentine, Chaucer, and Spring in February," *Speculum* 56 (1981): 534–65.

21. "And sir, as for my housewife, I am glad to be taking her now to see her father and friends this winter, for I believe she will be out of fashion by summer."

22. Ann Haskell, "The Paston Women on Marriage in Fifteenth-Century England," *Viator* 4 (1973): 461. And see Lisa Kiser, "The Books of a Fifteenth Century Gentleman," *Neuphilologische Mitteilungen* 88 (1987): 200–217.

23. Martin Camargo wittily points this out: *The Middle English Verse Love Epistle* (Tubingen: Max Niemeyer, 1991), pp. 17ff.

24. This analysis of Margery Brews's letter is in Martin Camargo, *The Middle English Verse Love Epistle*, p. 12.

25. The Carmelite Alan of Lynn.

26. Margery uses Dewtch and Dewtchland for German and Germany.

27. Tippets in this case were bands, ribbons, or tails of cloth that flowed from a garment. The hood was "dagged," that is, decorated with open slashes.

28. N- means *nomen* for "name."

29. I Corinthians 7.3. "Let the husband render his duty to the wife and also she to him."

30. Caroline Walker Bynum makes a point that is germane to this directive Margery experiences: "Women's mysticism was more histori-cal and incarnational—more fleshly and bodily, if you will—than ordi-nary Christian piety. The eucharist as body, flesh, meat, was a central focus of female religiosity." *Fragmentation and Redemption: Essays on Gender and the Human Body in Medieval Religion* (New York: Zone Books, 1991), p. 66.

31. A pilch, or pelisse, was a fur garment, or one of coarse cloth or leather.

32. The name of the Vicar of St. Stephen's appears later in chapter 43 as Richard of Caister, who died on March 29, 1420. He was the author or reviser of a metrical prayer, the popular lyric, "Jesu, Lorde, that madest me."

33. Under the Moslems' regulation of the holy sites, the pilgrims were required to stay overnight in the church.

34. St. Katherine of Alexandria and St. Margaret of Antioch.

35. Blessed is he that comes in the name of the Lord.

36. Soft rolls of cloth were inserted to distend the wounds and allow them to drain.

37. "Rascal" meant the inferior animals of the herd, too young or undergrown to hunt, as distinct from full-grown antlered game.

38. The designations of the hart correspond to the points or tines of its antlers. *Broket* is the animal in its second year when its first horns are simply spikes, from the French *broche*, the tines of the antlers. A *spayad* (sometimes seen as *spittard*), the animal in its third year, comes from Anglo-Norman *espayard*, probably formed from *épée*, or sword.

39. *Perch*: the beam or main stem of a deer's horns which bears the branches or antlers.

   Royal: the second branch or tine of a deer's horn, lying immediately above the brow-antler.

   Surroyal: the third branch or tine of a deer's horn, above the "Royal."

   Forchid ("forked"): having two tines or prongs at the top of the beam.

   Trochid: having three or more tines, or prongs, at the top of the beam.

40. The *hallow* is both the cry that urges the dogs to the pursuit, as well as the portions of the hare (sides, shoulders, neck, head) fed to them. The portions fed the stag are called the *quarry*.

41. The "time of grease" refers to the deer at its fattest.

   Holyrood Day: September 14.

   Nativity of the Virgin Mary: September 8.

   Annunciation of the Virgin Mary: March 25.

   Feast of St. Michael: September 29.

   Candlemas: February 2.

   Haws and hips: the fruits of the hawthorn and the wild rose, respectively.

42. *Profer*: to make a series or variety of efforts.

   Soiling: rolling or wallowing in water or mud.

   Refoule, from *fouler*: to beat or paw (the water) with the hooves.

43. The Celtic word *broc*, or brock, turns up in Irish, Welsh, and Cornish usage.

44. A park was an enclosed tract of land (as distinct from a forest or chase) held by royal grant for beasts of the chase. The Parker was the keeper of the preserve.

   The Queen's "cousin," the Earl of Salisbury, was Richard Neville. He acquired the title through his marriage to the daughter of Thomas de Montacute, Earl of Salisbury, upon the elder Salisbury's death at the siege of Orléans in 1428.

This Neville (whose son was dubbed Warwick the King-maker) remained loyal to Henry VI and the House of Lancaster for thirty-three years, until 1455, when he joined the Yorkists. At the Battle of Wakefield, 1460, he was captured and beheaded.

45. The Hospital of Saint Giles had been founded in 1117 by Queen Edith/Matilda (see above chapter 13). The afflicted youth was a church choirboy.

46. Apchild or Abfield was an estate in the parish of Great Waltham, Essex, and was a few miles from Pleshy. It was probably part of Queen Margaret's dower lands.

47. Shene was a royal palace that Edward III had built. It was a favorite of Richard II's queen, Anne of Bohemia, and when she died there in 1394, Richard had it torn down. This action is reflected in Chaucer's *Legend of Good Women*, for in the later version of the poem Chaucer removes the reference to Shene. It was again rebuilt by Henry V. Margaret's letter shows that she and the king went there to hunt.

48. "Bill" meant any sealed document, letter, or charter, from the word "bull" (as in a Papal Bull). The meaning came from "bubble" (*bulla*), the lump of wax that officially sealed the letter. Margery sealed her letters with red wax.

FURTHER READING

David Aers. *Community, Gender, and Individual Identity: English Writing 1360–1430.* London: Routledge, 1988.

David G. Allen and Robert White. *Traditions and Innovations: Essays on British Literature of the Middle Ages and Renaissance.* Newark, Del.: U of Delaware P, 1990.

Margaret Aston. *Lollards and Reformers: Images and Literacy in Late Medieval Religion.* London: Hambledon P, 1984.

Clarissa W. Atkinson. *Mystic and Pilgrim: The Book and the World of Margery Kempe.* Ithaca: Cornell UP, 1983.

Richard Barber, ed. *The Pastons: A Family in the Wars of the Roses.* Rochester, NY: Boydell and Brewer, 1993.

Julians Barnes. *Boke of Huntyng.* Edited and translated into French by Gunnar Tilander. Cynegetica 11. Karlshamn, 1961.

Henry Stanley Bennett. *The Pastons and Their England.* Cambridge: Cambridge UP, 1968.

Martin Camargo. *The Middle English Verse Love Epistle.* Tubingen: Max Niemeyer, 1991.

Louise Collis. *Memoirs of a Medieval Woman: The Life and Times of Margery Kempe.* New York: Crowell, 1964; repr. 1983.

Claire Cross. "'Great Reasoners in Scripture': The Activities of Women Lollards 1380–1530." In *Medieval Women,* pp. 359–380. Derek Baker, ed. Oxford: Basil Blackwell, 1978.

Norman Davis. "The Language of the Pastons." In *Middle English Literature: British Academy Gollancz Lectures.* J.A. Burrow, ed. Oxford: Oxford UP, for the British Academy, 1989.

Susan Dickman. "Margery Kempe and the Continental Tradition of the Pious Woman." In *The Medieval Mystical Tradition in England,* pp. 150–168. M. Glasscoe, ed. Cambridge, 1984.

Philippe Erlanger. *Margaret of Anjou: Queen of England.* Trans. Edward Hyams. London: Elek, 1970.

Nona Fienberg. "Thematics of Value in Margery Kempe." *Modern Philology* 87 (1989): 132–141.

James Gairdner, ed. *The Paston Letters.* 3 vols. London: Public Record Office, 1872–1875.

Anthony Goodman. "The Piety of John Brunham's Daughter, of Lynn." In *Medieval Women,* pp. 347–358. Derek Baker, ed. Oxford: Basil Blackwell, 1978.

John C. Hirsh. *The Revelations of Margery Kempe: Paramystical Practices in Late Medieval England.* Leyden: Brill, 1989.

Sue Ellen Holbrook. "Order and Coherence in the Book of Margery Kempe." In *The Worlds of Medieval Women: Creativity, Influence and Imagination.* Constance H. Berman, Judith Rice Rothschild, and Charles W. Connell, eds. Morgantown, W.Va.: West Virginia UP, 1985.

E.F. Jacob. *The Fifteenth Century 1399–1485. The Oxford History of England.* Oxford: Clarendon P, 1961.

Leyvoy Joensen. "The Flesh Made Word: Allegory in the Book of Margery Kempe." *A/B: Autobiography Studies* 6 (1991): 169–182.

Barbara Kanner, ed. *The Women of England from Anglo-Saxon Times to the Present.* London, 1980.

Margery Kempe. *The Book of Margery Kempe, Fourteen Thirty-Six: A Modern Version by W. Butler-Bowdon.* Introduction by R.W. Chambers. New York: Devin-Adair, 1944.

————. Sanford Brown Meech and Hope Emily Allen, eds. *The Book of Margery Kempe. EETS* o.s. 212. Oxford: Oxford UP, 1940; repr. 1961.

————. Barry A. Windeatt, trans. *The Book of Margery Kempe.* New York: Viking Penguin, 1985.

Richard Kieckhefer. *Unquiet Souls: Fourteenth-Century Saints and Their Religious Milieu.* Chicago: U of Chicago P, 1984.

Lisa Kiser. "The Books of a Fifteenth Century Gentleman." *Neuphilologische Mitteilungen* 88 (1987): 200–217.

Karma Lochrie. *Margery Kempe and the Translations of the Flesh.* Philadelphia: U of Pennsylvania P, 1989.

Margaret of Anjou. *Letters of Queen Margaret of Anjou and Bishop Beckington and Others,* Cecil Munro, ed. Camden Society: 1863. Repr. London and New York: Johnson Reprint, 1968. Letters nos. 61 (pp. 90–91); 64 (p. 95); 69 (pp. 100–101); 105 (p. 137); 110 (p. 141).

Kenneth Bruce McFarlane. *England in the Fifteenth Century.* London, 1981.

Nancy F. Partner. "Reading the Book of Margery Kempe." *Exemplaria* 3 (1991): 29–66.

Margery Brews Paston. Norman Davis, ed. *Paston Letters and Papers of the Fifteenth Century.* Vol. I, nos. 415–420, pp. 662–669. Oxford: Clarendon P, 2 vols. 1971, 1976.

Lee Patterson, ed. *Literary Practice and Social Change in Britain, 1380–1530.* Berkeley: U of California P, 1990.

Colin Richmond. *The Paston Family in the Fifteenth Century: The First Phase.* Cambridge: Cambridge UP, 1990.

Wolfgang Riehle. *The Middle English Mystics.* Trans. David Standring. London: Routledge and Kegan Paul, 1981.

Ann Rooney. *Hunting in Middle English Literature.* Rochester, N.Y.: Boydell and Brewer, 1993.

R.N. Swanson. *Church and Society in Late Medieval England.* Oxford: Basil Blackwell, 1989.

Paul Szarmach, ed. *An Introduction to the Medieval Mystics of Europe.* Albany: State U of New York P, 1988.

Marcelle Thiébaux. *The Stag of Love: The Chase in Medieval Literature.* Ithaca: Cornell UP, 1974.

William Twiti. *The Art of Hunting* (1327). Ed. Bror Danielsson. Almqvist and Wiksell, 1977.

Diane Watt. "'No Writing for Writing's Sake': The Language of Service and Household Rhetoric in the Letters of the Paston Women," pp. 122–138. In *Dear Sister: Medieval Women and the Epistolary Genre*, ed. Karen Cherewatuk and Ulrike Wiethaus. Philadelphia: U of Pennsylvania P, 1993.

Hope Weissman. "Margery Kempe in Jerusalem: *Hysterica Compassio* in the Late Middle Ages." In *Acts of Interpretation: The Text and Its Contexts 700–1600. Essays in Medieval and Renaissance Literature in Honor of E.T. Donaldson*, pp. 201–217. M.J. Carruthers, ed. Norman, Oklahoma: Pilgrim Books, 1982.

Daniel Williams. *England in the Fifteenth Century: Proceedings of the 1986 Harlaxton Symposium*. Woodbridge, Suffolk: Boydell, 1987.

Virginia Woolf. "The Pastons and Chaucer." In *The Common Reader*, pp. 3–23. London: Hogarth, 1925.

Index